The **Rough Guide** to

Sri Lanka

written and researched by

Gavin Thomas

with additional contributions by

Edward Aves

www.roughguides.com

ෂක්වා
කොමියුනිකේෂන්
ෆොටෝ කොපි
උසාවි ලිපි ද්‍රව්‍ය
ලේන්බාන්
හරස් වීදිය

Contents

Sri Lankan Buddhism colour section following p.184

Ceylon tea colour section following p.408

◄◄ Countryside near Hunas Falls ◄ Street sign, Galle

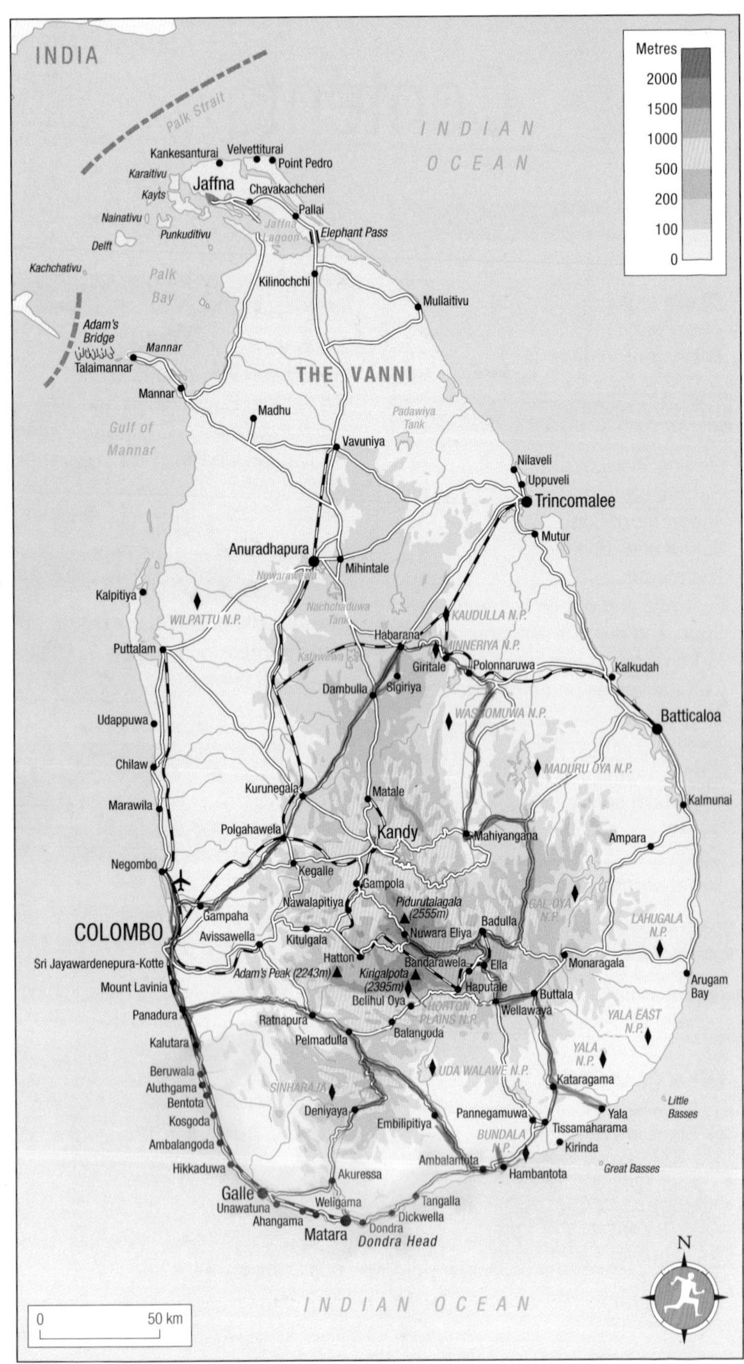
INDIA
Palk Strait
INDIAN OCEAN
Metres
2000
1500
1000
500
200
100
0
Kankesanturai
Velvettiturai
Point Pedro
Karaitivu
Kayts
Jaffna
Chavakachcheri
Pallai
Nainativu
Punkuditivu
Delft
Jaffna Lagoon
Elephant Pass
Kachchativu
Palk Bay
Kilinochchi
Mullaitivu
Adam's Bridge
Mannar
Talaimannar
THE VANNI
Madhu
Padawiya Tank
Gulf of Mannar
Vavuniya
Nilaveli
Uppuveli
Trincomalee
Mutur
Anuradhapura
Nuwarawewa
Mihintale
Kalpitiya
WILPATTU N.P.
Nachchaduwa Tank
KAUDULLA N.P.
Habarana
MINNERIYA N.P.
Puttalam
Kalawewa
Giritale
Polonnaruwa
Kalkudah
Dambulla
Sigiriya
WASGOMUWA N.P.
Batticaloa
Udappuwa
Chilaw
MADURU OYA N.P.
Kurunegala
Matale
Marawila
Kalmunai
Polgahawela
Kandy
Mahiyangana
Ampara
Negombo
Kegalle
Gampola
GAL OYA N.P.
Gampaha
Nawalapitiya
Pidurutalagala (2555m)
LAHUGALA N.P.
COLOMBO
Avissawella
Kitulgala
Nuwara Eliya
Badulla
Sri Jayawardenepura-Kotte
Hatton
Bandarawela
Monaragala
Adam's Peak (2243m)
Kirigalpota (2395m)
Ella
Arugam Bay
Mount Lavinia
Haputale
Belihul Oya
Buttala
Panadura
HORTON PLAINS N.P.
Wellawaya
Ratnapura
YALA EAST N.P.
Kalutara
Pelmadulla
Balangoda
YALA N.P.
Beruwala
UDA WALAWE N.P.
Aluthgama
SINHARAJA
Kataragama
Bentota
Little Basses
Deniyaya
Pannegamuwa
Yala
Kosgoda
Embilipitiya
Tissamaharama
BUNDALA N.P.
Ambalangoda
Kirinda
Ambalantota
Hikkaduwa
Hambantota
Great Basses
Akuressa
Galle
Tangalla
Unawatuna
Weligama
Dickwella
Ahangama
Dondra
Matara
Dondra Head
N
INDIAN OCEAN
0
50 km

Introduction to Sri Lanka

Sri Lanka has seduced travellers for centuries. Marco Polo described it as the finest island of its size in the world, while successive waves of Indian, Arab and European traders and adventurers flocked to its palm-fringed shores, attracted by reports of rare spices, precious stones and magnificent elephants. Poised just above the equator amidst the balmy waters of the Indian Ocean, the island's legendary reputation for natural beauty and plenty has inspired an almost magical regard even in those who have never visited the place. Romantically inclined geographers, poring over maps of the island, have compared its outline to a teardrop falling from the tip of India or to the shape of a pearl (the less impressionable Dutch likened it to a leg of ham), while even the name given to the island by early Arab traders – Serendib – became, through the English word "serendipity", a synonym for the making of happy accidents by chance.

Marco Polo's bold claim still rings true. Sri Lanka packs an extraordinary variety of attractions within its modest physical dimensions, and few islands of comparable size can boast a natural environment of such beauty and diversity. Lapped by the Indian Ocean, the coast is fringed with idyllic – and often refreshingly undeveloped – **beaches**, while the interior boasts a compelling variety of landscapes ranging from wildlife-rich lowland **jungles**, home to extensive populations of elephants, leopards and rare

Fact file

- Sri Lanka lies just seven degrees north of the equator. In area, it's slightly smaller than Ireland and a little larger than the US state of West Virginia.
- Sri Lanka achieved independence from Britain in 1948, and did away with its colonial name, Ceylon, in 1972. The country has had a functioning democracy since independence, and in 1960 elected the world's first ever female prime minister.
- Sri Lanka's population of 21 million is a mosaic of different ethnic and religious groups, the two largest being the mainly Buddhist Sinhalese (69 percent), and the predominantly Hindu Tamils (17 percent); there are also considerable numbers of Christians and Muslims. Sinhala, Tamil and English are all officially recognized languages.
- Sri Lankans enjoy a healthy life expectancy of 75 years and a literacy rate of 91 percent, although in recent years they've also set some less enviable records, including one of the world's highest female suicide rates and one of the highest incidences of death from snakebite – while in 2008 the island was ranked 165 out of 173 countries in terms of press freedom, below Saudi Arabia, Somalia and Zimbabwe.
- The country's main export is clothing, followed by tea; rubber, coconuts and precious gems are also important. Revenues from tourism are vital to the national economy, while remittances from the hundreds of thousands of Sri Lankans working overseas (mainly in the Gulf) are also significant.

▲ Sea Street, the Pettah, Colombo

endemic bird species, to the misty heights of the **hill country**, swathed in immaculately manicured tea plantations. Nor does the island lack in man-made attractions. Sri Lanka boasts over two thousand years of recorded history, and the remarkable achievements of the early Sinhalese civilization can still be seen in the sequence of ruined cities and great religious monuments that litter the northern plains.

Sri Lanka packs an extraordinary variety of attractions within its modest physical dimensions

The glories of this early Buddhist civilization continue to provide a benchmark of national identity for the island's Sinhalese population, while Sri Lanka's historic role as the world's oldest stronghold of

Theravada **Buddhism** lends it a unique cultural unity and character which permeate life at every level. There's more to Sri Lanka than just Buddhists, however. The island's geographical position at one of the most important staging posts of Indian Ocean trade laid it open to a uniquely wide range of influences, as generations of Arab, Malay, Portuguese, Dutch and British **settlers** subtly transformed its culture, architecture and cuisine, while the long-established Tamil population in the north has established a vibrant Hindu culture which owes more to India than to the Sinhalese south.

It is, however, this very diversity which has continually threatened to tear the country apart. For much of the past three decades the island has been the scene of one of Asia's most pernicious **civil wars**, as Sri Lankan government forces and the LTTE, or Tamil Tigers, have battled it out in the island's north and east. As of early 2009, government forces had succeeded in wresting back control of northern Sri Lanka from the LTTE for the first time in a generation, though whether this spectacular military success signals a new era of long-overdue peace, or simply a change in the nature of the conflict, remains to be seen. Away from these areas, though, life goes on as normal. The tourist industry continues to develop apace, and, with much of the damage caused by the 2004 tsunami now repaired and hostilities in the north apparently coming to an end, most Sri Lankans are once again looking to the future with guarded optimism.

▼ Hunas Falls

Where to go

All visits to Sri Lanka begin at the international airport just outside **Colombo**, the island's capital and far and away its largest city – a sprawling and chaotic metropolis whose contrasting districts offer an absorbing introduction to Sri Lanka's myriad cultures. Many visitors head straight for one of the west coast's beaches, whose innumerable resort hotels still power the country's tourist industry. Destinations include the package-holiday resorts of **Negombo** and **Beruwala**, the more stylish **Bentota** and the old hippy hangout of **Hikkaduwa**.

Beyond Hikkaduwa, the south coast presents a more laid-back and budget-oriented face. Gateway to the region is the marvellous old Dutch city of **Galle**, Sri Lanka's finest colonial townscape, beyond which lies a string of outstanding beaches, still largely the preserve of independent travellers. Foremost of these is the personable village of **Unawatuna**, currently the island's most popular backpacker hangout, while further along the coast is a number of quieter spots including **Thalpe**, **Weligama**, **Mirissa** and **Tangalla**, as well as the lively provincial capital of **Matara**, boasting further Dutch remains. East of here, the amenable town of **Tissamaharama** serves as a convenient base for the outstanding **Yala** and **Bundala national parks** and for the fascinating temple town of **Kataragama**, one of Sri Lanka's most important pilgrimage destinations.

▲ Mosque monkey near the summit of Sigiriya

Once more unto the beach . . .

Sri Lanka has beaches for all persuasions, from the mainstream resorts of Negombo, Hikkaduwa and Beruwala to the more upmarket Bentota and Kalutara and remote backpacker hideaways like Arugam Bay. The west-coast beaches are the most developed, awash with package tourists during the winter season; by contrast, much of the east coast remains completely untouched, with only a few places boasting any kind of tourist facilities, and many others waiting to be discovered – security situation permitting. Many of the island's finest beaches are found along the south coast: much more somnolent than the west, but with plenty of unpretentious and inexpensive amenities. Wherever you go, though, the basic formula is the same: fine golden sand backed by dense swathes of toppling palm trees, often with a few colourful wooden fishing boats and palm-thatch villages thrown in for good measure. The following (in no particular order) are our five favourites.

Arugam Bay First discovered by the surfing crowd, but now firmly on the backpacker circuit thanks to its fine arc of golden sand, lively surf and beach scenes and wealth of nearby attractions.

Bentota and Induruwa The top west-coast beaches offer a superb spread of luxury accommodation (plus a few cheaper options) and a huge swathe of deserted golden sand.

Mirissa Intimate little hideaway, with a low-key atmosphere and a mainly backpacker crowd.

Unawatuna The most popular beach in Sri Lanka, picturesquely spread around a superb crescent of sand, and with excellent swimming, a lively atmosphere and heaps of appealing guest houses and restaurants.

Uppuveli The ultimate east-coast escape, with a picture-postcard beach, fine golden-white sands and calm water. And, best of all, you'll probably have the place virtually to yourself.

Inland from Colombo rise the verdant highlands of the **hill country**, enveloped in the tea plantations (first introduced by the British) which still play a vital role in the island's economy. The symbolic heart of the region is **Kandy**, Sri Lanka's second city and the cultural capital of the Sinhalese, its colourful traditions embodied by the famous Temple of the Tooth and the magnificent

Esala Perahera, Sri Lanka's most colourful **festival**. South of here, close to the highest point of the island, lies the old British town of **Nuwara Eliya**, centre of the country's tea industry and a convenient base for visits to the spectacular **Horton Plains National Park**. A string of characterful towns and villages – **Ella**, **Haputale** and **Bandarawela** – along the southern edge of the hill country offer an appealing mixture of magnificent views, wonderful walks and olde-worlde British colonial charm. Close to the hill country's southwestern edge, the soaring summit of **Adam's Peak** is another of the island's major pilgrimage sites, while the gem-mining centre of **Ratnapura** to the south serves as the best starting point for visits to the elephant-rich **Uda Walawe National Park** and the rare tropical rainforest of **Sinharaja**.

Elephants

No animal is as closely identified with Sri Lanka as the elephant. The kings of Anuradhapura used them to pound down the foundations of their city's huge religious monuments, while the rulers of Kandy employed them to execute prisoners by trampling them to death. During the Dutch era they helped tow barges and move heavy artillery, and under the British they were set to clearing land for tea plantations. Even today, trained elephants are used to move heavy objects in places inaccessible to machinery. Elephants also play an integral role in many of the island's religious festivals, and remain revered creatures – killing an elephant was formerly a capital offence, while the death of the great Maligawa Tusker Raja in 1998 prompted the government to declare a national day of mourning. And given Sri Lanka's world-famous Pinnewala Elephant Orphanage as well as its numerous national parks, few other countries offer such a wide range of opportunities to see them both in captivity and in the wild.

▲ Kusta Raja, Weligama

North of Kandy, the hill country tumbles down into the arid plains of the northern dry zone. This area, known as the **Cultural Triangle**, was the location of Sri Lanka's first great civilization, and its extraordinary scatter of ruined palaces, temples and dagobas still gives a compelling sense of this glorious past. Foremost amongst these are the fascinating ruined cities of **Anuradhapura** and **Polonnaruwa**, the marvellous cave temples of **Dambulla**, the hilltop shrines and dagobas of **Mihintale** and the extraordinary rock citadel of **Sigiriya**.

▲ Tuktuks, Kandy

For most visitors, the east coast's main (indeed perhaps only) draw is the crashed-out backpacker village and surfing centre of **Arugam Bay**. The rest of the east coast is impoverished and largely undeveloped. The main landmarks are the interesting but war-torn cities of **Batticaloa** and **Trincomalee**, while a few foreigners still make it as far as the remote and extremely low-key beach enclaves at **Nilaveli** and **Uppuveli**, just north of Trincomalee The **north** is still currently out of bounds to foreign travellers, although with the end of fighting now in sight it may become accessible again in the next year or two.

When to go

Sri Lanka's **climate** is rather complicated for such a small country, due to the fact that opposite sides of the island are affected by two separate monsoons – though this also means that there is always good weather somewhere on the island, whatever the time of year. It's worth bearing in mind, however, that the basic pattern described below can vary from year to year, and that global warming has disrupted these already complex weather patterns and caused severe periods of drought.

The **southwest monsoon** brings rain to west and southwest coasts from late April or May to September/October (wettest from May–June). The less severe **northeast monsoon** hits the east coast from October to March (wettest from Nov–Dec). The **best time to visit** Sri Lanka as a whole is from around January to April; January and February are particularly good, with dry and pleasantly cool (at least by Sri Lankan standards) weather in most parts of the island. The **west coast** is best from November to mid-April; from May to October the southwest monsoon hits, bringing daily deluges and overcast skies. It's still feasible to visit during the monsoon months, since rain is usually confined to a couple of hours in the afternoon, although many guest houses and restaurants shut up shop for the duration. The situation on the **east coast** is more or less the reverse of that on the west, with the best time to visit being from around April to September. The **hill country** sees significant rainfall all year and is particularly affected by the southwest monsoon – the southwestern corner of the hill country around Ratnapura and Sinharaja is especially wet. As such, the best time to visit is during the early months of the year, from January to April. The **southeast** and **north** are the driest parts of the island and see little rain for most of the year, although the Cultural Triangle receives sporadic (and sometimes severe) inundations from November to January. For more information on individual regions, see the weather notes in the introductions to each of the guide chapters.

Sri Lanka's legendary reputation for natural beauty and plenty has inspired an almost magical regard even in those who have never visited the place.

Sri Lanka's position close to the equator means that **temperatures** remain virtually constant year-round. Coastal and lowland areas enjoy a high temperature of 27 to 29°C. Temperatures decrease with altitude, reducing to the temperate average of around 20°C in Kandy, and a pleasantly mild 16°C in Nuwara Eliya and the highest parts of the island – nights in the hills can be quite chilly, with temperatures sometimes falling close to freezing. **Humidity** is high everywhere, rising to a sweltering ninety percent at times in the southwest, and averaging sixty to eighty percent across the rest of the island.

Average monthly temperatures and rainfall

	Jan	Feb	Mar	Apr	May	Jun	Jul	Aug	Sep	Oct	Nov	Dec
Colombo												
Max/min (°C)	31/22	31/23	32/24	32/25	31/25	30/25	30/25	30/25	30/25	30/24	30/23	30/23
Max/min (°F)	88/72	88/73	89/75	89/76	88/78	87/78	86/77	86/77	86/77	86/75	86/74	87/73
Rainfall (mm)	62	69	130	253	382	186	125	114	236	369	310	168
Nuwara Eliya												
Max/min (°C)	20/9	21/9	22/10	23/11	21/13	19/13	18/13	19/13	19/12	20/12	20/11	19/11
Max/min (°F)	68/49	70/49	72/50	73/52	70/55	66/56	65/55	66/55	67/54	68/53	68/53	67/52
Rainfall (mm)	107	75	71	151	178	176	174	159	176	228	215	194
Trincomalee												
Max/min (°C)	28/24	29/24	31/25	33/26	34/26	35/26	34/26	34/25	34/25	32/25	29/24	28/24
Max/min (°F)	82/76	85/76	88/77	91/78	94/79	95/79	94/78	94/78	93/77	89/76	85/76	83/76
Rainfall (mm)	132	100	54	50	52	26	70	89	104	217	334	341

25 things not to miss

It's not possible to see everything that Sri Lanka has to offer in a single trip – and we don't suggest you try. What follows is a selective taste of the island's highlights: outstanding religious and cultural sites, memorable scenery and wildlife, spectacular festivals. They're arranged in five colour-coded categories with a page reference to take you straight into the Guide, where you can find out more.

01 **Yala National Park** Page **213** • The country's most popular and rewarding national park, home to birds, monkeys, crocodiles and elephants, as well as the island's largest population of leopards.

02 Cricket Page **51** • Take part in a knock-around on the beach, or join the crowds of cricket-crazy spectators for a Test, or one-day international in Colombo, Kandy, Dambulla or Galle.

03 Adam's Peak Page **294** • One of the island's foremost pilgrimage sites, this soaring summit bears the revered impression of what is said to be the Buddha's own footprint, and offers the island's most magical – and enigmatic – views.

04 Big Buddhas Page **444** • The Buddha's superhuman attributes are captured in a sequence of massive statues which dot the island, from the majestic ancient figures of the Gal Vihara, Aukana and Sasseruwa to the contemporary colossi at Dambulla, Wewurukannala and elsewhere.

05 World's End Page **276** • Marking the point at which the hill country's southern escarpment plunges sheer for almost a kilometre to the plains below, these dramatic cliffs offer one of the finest of the hill country's many unforgettable views.

06 Rice and curry Page **41** • Eat your way through this classic Sri Lankan feast, with its mouthwatering selection of contrasting dishes and flavours.

07 Ayurveda Page **138** • Sri Lanka's ancient system of healthcare uses herbal medicines and a range of traditional techniques to rejuvenate the body and promote holistic well-being.

08 Anuradhapura Page **356** • From immense dagobas to mysterious forest monasteries, this vast ruined city bears witness to the great Sinhalese civilization which flourished here for almost 1500 years.

09 Bawa hotels Pages **39** & **146** • With their memorable blend of modern chic and superb natural settings, the hotels of architect Geoffrey Bawa exemplify contemporary Sri Lankan style at its most seductive.

10 Birds Pages **18** & **452** • Sri Lanka is one of Asia's classic birdwatching destinations, with species ranging from delicate bee eaters and colourful kingfishers to majestic hornbills.

11 Galle Page **165** • Sri Lanka's most perfectly preserved colonial townscape, with sedate streets of personable Dutch-era villas enclosed by a chain of imposing ramparts.

12 **Kandy Esala Perahera** Page **232** • One of Asia's most spectacular festivals, with huge processions of magnificently caparisoned elephants accompanied by ear-splitting troupes of Kandyan drummers, plus assorted dancers and acrobats.

13 **Ella** Page **282** • Sri Lanka's most beautiful village, offering verdant walks amongst the surrounding tea plantations and a marvellous view through Ella Gap to the plains below.

14 **Katarágama** Page **215** • Join the crowds thronging to the colourful nightly temple ceremonies at this remote pilgrimage town, held sacred by Buddhists, Hindus and Muslims alike.

15 **Bentota** Page **142** • The pleasantly unspoilt southern end of Bentota beach is home to the island's finest selection of luxury beachside hotels.

16 **Arugam Bay** Page **393** • Crashed-out little east-coast beach retreat, with a sociable atmosphere, world-class surfing and a wide range of absorbing attractions in the surrounding countryside.

17 **Polonnaruwa** Page **336** • Home to the island's finest collection of ancient Sinhalese art and architecture, from the giant Buddha statues of the Gal Vihara to the remarkable religious buildings of the Quadrangle.

18 **Whale-watching, Mirissa** Page **192** • Head out to sea in search of majestic blue and sperm whales, which migrate to and fro around southern Sri Lanka, and can regularly be seen within a few miles of the coast.

19 **Sigiriya** Page **329** • Climb the towering rock outcrop of Sigiriya, home to the fascinating remains of one of the island's former capitals, complete with ancient graffiti, elaborate water gardens and perfectly preserved frescoes of voluptuous heavenly nymphs.

20 **Pinnewala Elephant Orphanage** Page **227** • One of the island's most popular attractions, Pinnewala is home to the world's largest troupe of captive elephants, best seen during their twice daily river-bathing sessions.

21 The Pettah Page **99** • Colombo's colourful and chaotic bazaar district offers an exhilarating slice of Asian life, crammed with shoppers, traders, tuktuks and a bewildering assortment of merchandise.

22 Kandyan dancing and drumming Page **253** • Traditional Sinhalese culture at its most exuberant, with brilliantly costumed dancers performing carefully stylized dances to an accompaniment of explosively energetic drumming.

23 Kandy Page **230** • Beautifully situated amidst the central highlands, this historic city remains the island's most important repository of traditional Sinhalese culture, exemplified by the great Esala Perahera festival and the Temple of the Tooth.

24 Unawatuna Page **178** • The island's most popular backpacker beach boasts a sheltered swathe of sand tucked into a picturesque bay, and a lively cluster of beachfront cafés and guesthouses.

25 Dambulla Page **322** • These five magical cave temples are a treasure box of Sri Lankan Buddhist art, sumptuously decorated with a fascinating array of statues and shrines and the country's finest collection of murals.

Basics

Basics

Getting there

At present, the only way to get to Sri Lanka is to fly into the island's international airport at Katunayake, just north of Colombo. Sri Lanka is reasonably well served by international airlines, although you'll probably have to change planes somewhere en route. The island is also well connected to Asian air networks, as well as numerous points in the Gulf.

Air fares remain fairly constant year-round – in general, the further ahead you book your flight, the better chance you have of getting a good deal. Another possibility is to pick up a **package deal** from a high-street travel agent – even if you don't use the accommodation provided (or only use it for a few days), packages can work out to be reasonable value thanks to the cheap flight.

Flights from the UK and Ireland

The only nonstop scheduled flights **from the UK** to Sri Lanka are with SriLankan Airlines from London Heathrow; flying time to Colombo is around eleven hours. Emirates, Qatar Airways, Kuwait Airways and Etihad all offer one-stop flights from Heathrow via the Gulf, while Jet Airways and Kingfisher have recently begun operating one-stop routes via India. There are also more circuitous routings via various points in Southeast Asia, including Singapore, Kuala Lumpur, Bangkok and Hong Kong. Travelling **from Ireland**, you can either make your way to Heathrow and pick up an onward connection there, or fly via one of the various European cities which have direct connections with Colombo – these include Paris, Rome and Frankfurt (served by SriLankan Airlines).

Scheduled **fares** from London to Colombo start at around £400 return year-round. The cheapest tickets are usually offered by Qatar Airways, SriLankan Airlines and Etihad. Fares for more circuitous routings with Thai Air (via Bangkok), Malaysia Airlines (via Kuala Lumpur), Singapore Airlines (via Singapore) and Cathay Pacific (via Hong Kong), are usually significantly more expensive, starting at around £900.

Flights from the US and Canada

It's a long journey from North America to Sri Lanka, and chances are you'll want to break your flight somewhere or include the island as part of a longer visit to the region. The journey from North America to Sri Lanka takes at least 24 hours, and necessitates at least one change of plane, and probably more like two or three. **From the east coast**, there are various routes via Europe. One possibility is to fly to London and then pick up one of the onward connections described above. Alternatively, you could fly to Paris, Frankfurt or Rome, all of which have nonstop connections to Colombo with various airlines. There are also various routes via Europe and the Middle East with Gulf Air, Emirates, Etihad, Qatar Airways and Kuwait Airways. Travelling **from the west coast**, the most direct routes go via east and Southeast Asia, flying via Hong Kong, Kuala Lumpur, Singapore, Bangkok or Tokyo, all of which have nonstop connections on to Colombo.

Fares to Colombo start from around US$1200 from New York; from around US$1500 from Los Angeles and Toronto; or about Can$1800 from Vancouver.

Flights from Australia and New Zealand

Flying **from Australia** to Sri Lanka is straightforward, although you'll have to change planes at least once; the most direct routings to Colombo are via Singapore, Kuala Lumpur and Bangkok. There are also a few one-stop options **from New Zealand** via Singapore, Bangkok and Kuala Lumpur. Fares from Sydney to Colombo start at around A$1750, and from Auckland at around NZ$2200.

Getting there from the rest of Asia

Sri Lanka isn't normally considered part of the overland Asian trail, although the island is well connected with other countries in **South and Southeast Asia**. There are regular nonstop flights with SriLankan Airlines to various places in India, including Delhi, Mumbai (Bombay), Chennai (Madras), Bangalore, Thiruvananthapuram (Trivandrum) and Tiruchirappali; to Bangkok with SriLankan and Thai Airways; Kuala Lumpur with SriLankan and Malaysia Airlines; Singapore with SriLankan and Singapore Airlines; Tokyo with SriLankan; and Hong Kong with SriLankan and Cathay Pacific. There are also direct connections to many places in **the Gulf**, including frequent services to Dubai (Emirates), Abu Dhabi (Etihad), Qatar (Qatar Airways) and Kuwait (Kuwait Airways).

Airlines, agents and operators

Airlines

Air Canada Ⓦwww.aircanada.com. Flights from Vancouver to London, Hong Kong and Tokyo, and from Toronto to London, Paris, Zurich and Frankfurt.

American Airlines Ⓦwww.aa.com. Flights from many US cities to London, Frankfurt, Paris, Zurich and Tokyo, from where there are connections to Colombo.

Cathay Pacific Ⓦwww.cathaypacific.com. Flights from numerous US cities, plus Vancouver, Toronto and London Heathrow, to Hong Kong, from where there are daily services to Colombo via Bangkok or Singapore.

Continental Airlines Ⓦwww.continental.com. Direct flights from New York to Hong Kong and from New York and Houston to Tokyo, with connections from numerous other cities in the US and Canada.

Delta Ⓦwww.delta.com. Connections from numerous US and Canadian cities to London, Paris, Zurich, Frankfurt, Tokyo, Hong Kong, Singapore, and Mumbai (Bombay).

Emirates Ⓦwww.emirates.com. Direct flights from London, Birmingham, Manchester, Newcastle, Glasgow, New York, Houston, Los Angeles, San Francisco and Toronto to Dubai, from where there are direct flights on to Colombo. Also flies from Melbourne and Brisbane to Colombo via Singapore.

Etihad Ⓦwww.etihadairways.com. London, Manchester, Dublin, New York and Toronto to Colombo via Abu Dhabi.

Jet Airways Ⓦwww.jetairways.com. London to Colombo via Mumbai.

Kingfisher Airlines Ⓦwww.flykingfisher.com. London to Colombo via Bangalore.

Kuwait Airways Ⓦwww.kuwait-airways.com. London Heathrow to Colombo via Kuwait City, plus connections from London to New York.

Malaysia Airlines Ⓦwww.malaysia-airlines.com. Flights to Colombo via Kuala Lumpur from London, Sydney, Melbourne, Perth, Brisbane, Adelaide and Auckland.

Qantas Ⓦwww.qantas.com. Flights to Singapore (from Sydney, Melbourne, Adelaide, Perth and Brisbane), and to Bangkok and Mumbai (from Sydney). SriLankan has connections to Colombo from all three of these cities.

Qatar Airways Ⓦwww.qatarairways.com. London Heathrow and Manchester to Colombo via Doha. Usually has some of the cheapest fares from the UK.

Singapore Airlines Ⓦwww.singaporeair.com. Flights to Colombo via Singapore from London, Manchester, New York, Los Angeles, Sydney, Melbourne, Perth, Adelaide, Brisbane, Auckland and Christchurch.

SriLankan Airlines Ⓦwww.srilankan.lk. Nonstop flights from London Heathrow to Colombo, and also

The ferry from India

The **ferry service** which formerly connected Rameswaram in India and Talaimannar in Sri Lanka was suspended in 1983 at the outbreak of civil war. Following the original ceasefire in 2002, the reintroduction of ferry services was repeatedly promised but has so far failed to materialize. The entire subject has become something of a running joke, to the point where it now seems unlikely that services will ever recommence – and certainly not until the current round of fighting has concluded. Until ferries do resume, the shortest way of crossing from India to Sri Lanka is to fly to Colombo from Tiruchirappali in Tamil Nadu with SriLankan Airlines.

Six steps to a better kind of travel

At Rough Guides we are passionately committed to travel. We feel strongly that only through travelling do we truly come to understand the world we live in and the people we share it with – plus tourism has brought a great deal of benefit to developing economies around the world over the last few decades. But the extraordinary growth in tourism has also damaged some places irreparably, and of course climate change is exacerbated by most forms of transport, especially flying. This means that now, more than ever, it's important, to travel thoughtfully and responsibly, with respect for the cultures you're visiting – not only to derive the most benefit from your trip but also in order to preserve the best bits of the planet for everyone to enjoy. At Rough Guides we feel there are six main areas in which you can make a difference:

- Consider what you're contributing to the local economy, and indeed how much the services you use do the same, whether it's through employing local workers and guides or sourcing locally grown produce and local services.
- Consider the environment on holiday as well as at home. Water is scarce in many developing destinations, and the biodiversity of local flora and fauna can be adversely affected by tourism. Patronize businesses that take account of this rather than those that trash the local environment for short-term gain.
- Give thought to how often you fly and what you can do to redress any harm that your trips create. Reduce the amount you travel by air; avoid short hops and more harmful night flights.
- Consider alternatives to flying, travelling instead by bus, train, boat and even by bike or on foot where possible. Take time to enjoy the journey itself as well as your final destination.
- Think about making all the trips you take "climate neutral" via a reputable carbon offset scheme. All Rough Guide flights are offset, and every year we donate money to a variety of charities devoted to combating the effects of climate change.
- Travel with a purpose, not just to tick off experiences. Consider spending longer in a place, and really getting to know it and its people – you'll find it much more rewarding than dashing from place to place.

via the Maldives. Also nonstop flights to Colombo from Paris, Frankfurt, Rome, Tokyo, Bangkok, Kuala Lumpur, Singapore, Hong Kong and most major Indian cities.

Thai Airways ⓦwww.thaiair.com. Flights to Colombo via Bangkok from London, Los Angeles, Sydney, Melbourne, Perth, Brisbane and Auckland.

United Airlines ⓦwww.united.com. Connections from the US and Canada to London, Paris, Frankfurt, Tokyo, Hong Kong, Singapore and Bangkok, all of which have nonstop connections with Colombo.

Booking flights online

ⓦ**www.expedia.ca** (Canada), ⓦ**www.expedia.co.uk** (UK), ⓦ**www.expedia.com** (US)
ⓦ**www.lastminute.com** (UK)
ⓦ**www.opodo.co.uk** (UK)
ⓦ**www.orbitz.com** (US)
ⓦ**www.travelocity.ca** (Canada), ⓦ**www.travelocity.com** (US), ⓦ**www.travelocity.co.uk** (UK)
ⓦ**www.zuji.com.au** (Australia)

Agents and operators

Organized guided tours of the island – either with your own car and driver, or as part of a larger tour group – can be arranged through numerous companies both in Sri Lanka and abroad. Tours obviously take virtually all the hassle out of travelling, and some can offer good value in terms of transport and accommodation. The downside is that those offered by foreign companies tend to be much of a muchness – if you want something a bit more unusual you might be better off contacting one of the Colombo-based operators we've listed.

Tours offered by **foreign operators** usually feature a mix of wildlife and culture followed by a few days on the beach, although some are oriented more towards a particular interest, while others offer more adventurous possibilities such as trekking, cycling and whitewater rafting. Many of the operators below can also arrange honeymoon, wedding and cricketing packages, and virtually all of them will customize tours on request. Some tours are by private car, with your own personal chauffeur; others are in larger groups of up to sixteen people travelling by minibus. Note that almost all the leading foreign Sri Lankan tour operators are based in the UK; travellers from north America and Australasia shouldn't have any problems booking tours through these companies, although you might have to organize your own flights.

Setting up a tour with one of the **Colombo-based operators** listed below is a very viable alternative to arranging one at home. They probably won't work out any cheaper than their overseas rivals, but insider knowledge gives several of the following companies a distinct edge over foreign firms, with unusual tours and expert local guides.

Tour operators abroad

Ampersand Travel UK ⓣ020/7289 6100, ⓦwww.ampersandtravel.com. Luxury island tours (10–19 days) focusing on nature or culture, with accommodation in top-end hotels or luxury villas. Also does twin-centre holidays combining Sri Lanka with the Maldives.

Boutique Sri Lanka UK ⓣ0845/123 8380, ⓦwww.boutiquesrilanka.com. Offers possibly the best portfolio of mid- and top-range properties of any Sri Lankan tour operator. Itineraries are customized to suit your interests, from beaches or Ayurveda to nature, surfing and adventure.

Carolanka UK ⓣ01822/810230, ⓦwww.carolanka.co.uk. Small Sri Lankan specialist offering two general island tours (15 nights), plus customized itineraries and special-interest trips – anything from military tours and golf to birdwatching and meditation.

Equinox Travel UK ⓣ020/7831 4888, ⓦwww.equinoxtravel.co.uk. Unusual adventure, cultural and wildlife tours visiting a mix of mainstream attractions along with an interesting selection of off-the-beaten-track sites.

Explore! UK ⓣ0845/013 1539, ⓦwww.explore.co.uk. Twelve- to sixteen-day islandwide trips. One includes a four-day placement on a community project.

Imaginative Traveller UK ⓣ0845/077 8802, ⓦwww.imaginative-traveller.com. Offer a ten-day "Adventure and Honeymoon" package plus a very inexpensive fifteen-day general island tour, including cycling and walking.

Insider Tours UK ⓣ01233/811771, ⓦwww.insider-tours.com. Sri Lanka specialist offering a range of innovative and ethical customized tours – see the website for prices and possibilities. Run in conjunction with Sri Lankan guides and organizations to create unusual itineraries, tours give a real first-hand taste of the island and provide stimulating encounters with locals.

North South Travel UK ⓣ01245/608 291, ⓦwww.northsouthtravel.co.uk. Friendly, competitive travel agency, offering discounted fares worldwide. Profits are used to support projects in the developing world, especially the promotion of sustainable tourism.

On the Go Tours UK ⓣ020/7371 1113, ⓦwww.onthegotours.com. Standard nine-day island itinerary plus a more extended and interesting fifteen-day tour covering some refreshingly unusual attractions.

Passport Travel Australia ⓣ03/9867 3888, ⓦwww.travelcentre.com.au. Offers an interesting sixteen-day cycling tour, covering up to 80km per day, and with a spot of hiking, canoeing and camping en route.

Red Dot Tours UK ⓣ0870/231 7892, ⓦwww.reddottours.com. Leading Sri Lankan specialists offering holidays based around wildlife, adventure, culture, cricket, golf and more, along with wedding and honeymoon packages. They also offer cheap flights and have an outstanding selection of properties around the island in most price ranges.

Taprobane Travel UK ⓣ020/7434 3921, ⓦwww.srilankatours.co.uk. A good source of discount airfares to Sri Lanka.

Trans Indus UK ⓣ020/8566 2729, ⓦwww.transindus.co.uk. Reputable South Asia specialist offering a standard fourteen-day islandwide tour of Sri Lanka plus customized trips.

Wildlife Worldwide UK ⓣ0845/130 6982, ⓦwww.wildlifeworldwide.com. Wildlife-oriented trips (10–16 days), including elephant- and leopard-spotting tours.

Worldwide Holidays UK ⓣ01202/606160, ⓦwww.worldwideholidays.co.uk. Various tours (8–14 nights) including special elephant-spotting, soft adventure and golfing holidays.

Tour operators in Sri Lanka

Adventure Asia ⓣ011-536 8468, ⓦwww.ad-asia.com. One of Sri Lanka's leading outdoor adventure specialists; running biking, climbing, hiking and rafting trips, plus spectacular balloon flights (see p.54).

Aitken Spence Travels ⓣ011-230 8021, ⓦwww.aitkenspencetravels.com. Well-organized travel wing of one of Sri Lanka's top hotel chains, offering general

island tours, tea country tours, activity holidays (hiking, cycling, rafting and canoeing) and eco-tours.

Eco Team ⓣ011-583 0833, ⓦ**www.srilankaecotourism.com.** Specialist eco-tourism and activity holiday operator, offering a vast range of water- and land-based activities at locations islandwide – anything from surfing and caving to study tours and "nature weddings". Also runs camping trips in national parks through its Mahoora wing (ⓦwww.mahoora.lk).

Jetwing Eco Holidays ⓣ011-238 1201, ⓦ**www.jetwingeco.com.** Far and away Sri Lanka's best eco-tourism operator, offering an vast range of wildlife and adventure activities including birdwatching, leopard-spotting, whale-watching, trekking, cycling, whitewater rafting and much more. Nature activities are led by an expert team of guides, including some of Sri Lanka's top naturalists.

Jetwing Travels ⓣ011-471 4830, ⓦ**www.jetwingtravels.com.** Travel division of Sri Lanka's largest hotel group, with a range of islandwide tours (7–10 days), including golfing and Ayurveda trips, plus a special Geoffrey Bawa tour.

Journey Lanka Tours ⓣ011-251 9233, ⓦ**www.journeylankatours.com.** Personable and well-organized small operation running standard or tailor-made islandwide tours at excellent rates.

The Kulu Safari Company ⓣ011-259 9450, ⓦ**www.kulusafaris.com.** Luxury tented safaris in or around various national parks. Tents come complete with hot showers, queen-size beds and gourmet cuisine, offering a very civilized way of getting completely off the beaten track. Rates from around US$290 per person per night.

Malkey ⓣ011-236 5365, ⓦ**www.malkey.lk.** Inexpensive islandwide tours, customized to suit, in private a/c cars with trained chauffeur-guides. Also has a good range of self-drive cars for hire.

Rail Tours **Railway Tourist Information Service office, Fort Railway Station, Pettah** ⓣ**011-244 0048.** Reputable agents organizing very inexpensive islandwide tours (from around US$65 per day per couple) using train and a/c car (the only travel agents to offer this combination), with accommodation in simple but comfortable guesthouses.

Sri Lanka in Style ⓣ011-239 6666, ⓦ**www.srilankainstyle.com.** Luxury tours with unusual and insightful itineraries (either customized or off the peg) and accommodation in some of Sri Lanka's most magical villas and boutique hotels.

Walkers Tours ⓣ011-230 6719, ⓦ**www.walkerstours.com.** Large operator offering a good range of islandwide itineraries including specialist birding, wildlife, trekking, golfing and cycling tours. They also arrange fancy weddings – if you want to ride into your marriage service on an elephant whilst dressed as an eighteenth-century Kandyan princeling, these are the people to talk to.

Wild Holidays ⓣ011-272 1663, ⓦ**www.wildernesslanka.com.** Eco-oriented and adrenalin-charged holidays based around Ella, Kitulgala and Bolgoda (near Colombo), including mainstream pursuits like rafting, trekking and jeep safaris through to parasailing, caving and canyoning.

Getting around

Given Sri Lanka's fairly modest size, getting around can be a frustratingly time-consuming process. The island's narrow roads, congested with pedestrians, cyclists and tuktuks make bus travel laborious, while in many cases travel by rail is even slower. Even with your own vehicle you shouldn't expect to make rapid progress. Getting from Colombo to either Galle or Kandy, for instance (a distance of not much over 100km), takes around three hours by bus or train, while the bus trip across the island from Colombo to Arugam Bay takes at least ten hours by public transport for a distance of 320km.

Buses are the standard means of transport. Services reach even the remotest corners of the island, though they are often a nerve-shredding and uncomfortable way of travelling. **Trains** offer a more characterful, if generally slower, means of getting about, and will get you to many parts of the country – eventually. If you don't want to put up with the vagaries of public transport, hiring a **car and driver** can prove a reasonably affordable and extremely convenient way of seeing the island in relative comfort.

Buses

Buses are the staple mode of transport in Sri Lanka. Any town of even the remotest consequence will be served by fairly regular connections, whilst buses screech past on the island's major highways every few seconds. That's the good news. The bad news is that bus travel in Sri Lanka is almost uniformly uncomfortable and is often nerve-racking as well, given that most drivers are willing to try anything to gain an extra metre. The average Sri Lankan bus journey is a stop-start affair: stomach-tightening bursts of speed alternate with periods of creeping slowness, all played out to an accompaniment of constantly parping horns, blaring Sinhala pop music and the awful noises of mechanical protest as the long-suffering bus careers around yet another corner with every panel rattling – before the inevitable slamming-on of brakes sends everyone lurching forward in their seats. And if you haven't got a seat, so much the worse. If you do, you'll probably find yourself serving as an impromptu armrest to one of the countless unfortunates standing packed in the aisle. The rear seats in large buses are the best place to sit, both because there's usually enough legroom to stow luggage comfortably under the seat in front, and because you won't have a very clear view of whatever craziness the driver is attempting.

Buses come in assorted forms. The basic distinction is between government or CTB (Ceylon Transport Board) buses and private services. Almost all **CTB buses** are rattling old TATA vehicles, painted yellow or (less commonly) red. These tend to be the slowest and cheapest on the road.

Private buses come in various different forms. At their most basic, they're essentially the same as CTB buses, consisting of large, arthritic old rustbuckets which stop everywhere; the only difference is that private buses will usually be painted white and emblazoned with the stickers of whichever company runs it. Some private companies operate slightly faster services, again in large

buses known variously as "semi-express", "express", or "inter-city", which (in theory at least) make fewer stops en route.

At the top end of the scale, **private minibuses**, often described as "express" and/or "luxury" services (although the description should be taken with a large pinch of salt) offer the fastest way of getting around. These are smaller vehicles with air-conditioning and tinted, curtained windows, though the tiny seats and lack of luggage space (your rucksack will often end up on your lap or between your legs) can make them more uncomfortable than CTB services, especially if you're tall. (If the vehicle isn't packed to capacity you could try paying for an extra seat on which to put your luggage – the conductor might insist you do this anyway.) In theory, express minibuses only make limited stops at major bus stations en route, although in practice it's up to the whim of the driver and/or conductor as to where they stop and for how long, and how many people they're willing to cram in.

Bus **fares** are extremely cheap. For journeys on non-express buses, count on around Rs.20 per hour's travel, rising to

Rs.40–50 on express minibuses. Note that on the latter you'll usually have to pay the full fare for the entire route served by the bus, irrespective of where you get off. If you do want to get off before the end of the journey, let the driver/conductor know when you board.

Services on longer routes and less frequently served routes run to fixed **timetables**. Services on shorter on particularly popular routes tend to leave as soon as the vehicle is full. Seat **reservations** are almost unheard of.

Another problem with Sri Lankan buses is the difficulty of finding the relevant service. Most timetables and signs are in Sinhala only, as are many of the destination boards displayed by buses – it's useful to get an idea of the characters you're looking for (see the list of place names on p.471). The larger terminals often have some kind of information booth – usually little wire-mesh enclosures in the middle of the station – whose staff will usually be able to point you in the right direction. If arriving at a larger terminal by tuktuk, it's a good idea to enlist the help of your driver in locating the right bus.

Express services generally only halt at bus terminals or other recognized stops. Other types of services will usually stop wherever there's a passenger to be picked up – just stand by the roadside and stick an arm out. If you're flagging down a bus by the roadside, one final hazard is in getting on. Drivers often don't stop completely, instead slowing down just enough to allow you to jump aboard. Keep your wits about you, especially if you're weighed down with a heavy rucksack, and be prepared to move fast when the bus pulls in – or risk seeing it simply pull off again without you.

Trains

Sri Lanka's **train** network, constructed by the British during the nineteenth century and little changed since, offers a characterful way of getting around the island, and for many visitors a trip aboard one of these chuntering old relics (especially on the marvellously scenic hill country line) is a highlight of a trip to Sri Lanka. Travel by rail is, however, generally slower than by bus, and the charm of the experience is often leavened with a fair dose of frustration – delays are the norm and progress can be incredibly laborious, and can seem even more tedious if you end up standing up in an overcrowded carriage. Nonetheless, Sri Lankan trains are worth experiencing, if only once.

The network comprises three principal lines: the **coast line**, which runs along the west coast starting from Puttalam in the north and heading south via Negombo, Colombo, Kalutara, Bentota, Beruwala, Aluthgama, Ambalangoda, Hikkaduwa and Galle to Weligama and Matara. The **hill country line** runs from Colombo to Kandy then on to Hatton (for Adam's Peak), Nanu Oya (for Nuwara Eliya), Haputale, Bandarawela, Ella and Badulla. The **northern line** runs from Colombo through Kurunegala to Anuradhapura and Vavuniya. Two additional branches run off this line: the first to Polonnaruwa and Batticaloa, the second to Trincomalee.

Trains comprise three classes. Most services consist exclusively of **second-** and **third-class** carriages. There's not actually a huge amount of difference between the two: second-class seats are slightly more padded and comfortable, and there are fans in the carriages, but the main bonus is that the carriages tend to be (very slightly) less overcrowded. **First class** covers three different types of seating, which are only available in selected trains. These are seats on inter-city trains and in the observation carriage on hill country trains; seats in the air-conditioned carriage on trains to Anuradhapura and Batticaloa; and sleeping berths on overnight services. The smallness of the island means that, unlike in neighbouring India, there are only a few **overnight trains**. These comprise first-class sleeping berths and second- and third-class "sleeperettes" (fold-down seats), plus ordinary seats.

Despite recent price increases, **fares** are still extremely cheap. A ticket from Colombo to Kandy in second class, for instance, is currently Rs.190, while even an overnight first-class air-conditioned sleeping berth from Colombo to Batticaloa costs just Rs.900. **Advance bookings** are only available for first-class seats and sleeper berths, and for second-class sleeperettes and seats on inter-city express services between Colombo

Observation cars

All inter-city services on the hill country route from Colombo to Kandy and Badulla carry a special carriage, the so-called **"observation car"**, with large windows and what passes on Sri Lankan railways for plush seating. All seats are reservable in advance, and tend to get snapped up quickly – you'll be lucky to get seats anything less than a week in advance, especially on the popular Colombo to Kandy run. Booking observation car seats is slightly complicated. They are available from ten days in advance of the date of travel. There are 24 seats in the whole observation car; twenty of these are sold in Colombo and the other four in Kandy. You can buy tickets over the counter at Kandy or Colombo (it's possible to buy tickets in Colombo to travel from Kandy, and vice versa). If you want to reserve an observation car seat from other stations along the line, they'll have to be ordered through either Kandy or Colombo, which obviously requires time and a degree of pre-planning. Fares in observation class are currently Rs.360 from Colombo to Kandy, and Rs.750 from Colombo to Badulla.

and Kandy. Reservations can be made up to ten days in advance at the Berths Booking Office (Mon–Sat 8.30am–3.30pm, Sun 8.30am–noon) at Fort Railway Station in Colombo. You can also make reservations at other stations, though they'll have to contact Colombo, so try to reserve as far ahead of the date of travel as possible. Tickets for all other types of seat can only be bought on the day of travel.

Flying

The domestic flights which used to operate from Colombo's Ratmalana Airport (near Mount Lavinia) to Trincomalee and Jaffna are currently suspended due to the civil war, though may resume once (if) peace is finally re-established. Check with the Colombo tourist office for the latest news.

If money's no object and you're really in a hurry, you can charter a **helicopter** or **private plane** through Deccan Aviation (Ⓦwww.simplifly.com).

Driving

As Sri Lankans say, in order to **drive** around the island you'll need three things: "good horn, good brakes, good luck". Although roads are generally in quite good condition, the myriad hazards they present – crowds of pedestrians, erratic cyclists, crazed bus drivers and suicidal dogs, to name just a few – plus the very idiosyncratic set of road rules followed by Sri Lankan drivers, makes driving a challenge in parts of the island – although, equally, in areas the roads can be pleasantly empty and peaceful.

If you want to drive yourself, note that foreign driving licences on their own aren't valid in Sri Lanka, so you'll need to obtain additional documentation before you can get behind the wheel. To get a **temporary driving permit** you need to go to the Department of Motor Traffic (Mon–Fri 9am–3pm) at Werahera, in Boralesgamuwa (on the southeastern edge of the city, 2km from Boralesgamuwa Junction and around 12km from the city centre – a 30min drive). Bring one passport photo, your passport, driving licence, plus photocopies of your licence and the ID and visa pages of your passport. It's a confusing operation, and time-consuming unless you have a Sinhala-speaking friend smoothing the path for you. One month's validity costs Rs.600. Note that if your licence isn't in English, you'll have to get your embassy to produce a translation.

Alternatively, to save yourself the tedious trip out to Boralesgamuwa, get hold of an **International Driving Licence** before you leave home, then take it to the AAC (Automobile Association of Ceylon) office (Mon–Fri 9am–4pm), next to the *Holiday Inn* at 40 Sir Mohamed Macan Markar Mawatha in Colombo. They will endorse it for use in Sri Lanka for a fee of Rs.500.

It's also worth equipping yourself with a good **map or atlas** (such as the Arjuna's Road Atlas). In terms of driving rules, it's worth remembering that, in Sri Lanka, might is right: drivers of larger vehicles (buses especially), will expect you to get out of the way if they're travelling faster than you. In addition, many drivers overtake freely on blind corners or in other dangerous places. Expect to confront other vehicles driving at speed on the wrong side of the road on a fairly regular basis.

Car and driver

Given the hassle of getting around by public transport, a large proportion of visitors opt to tour Sri Lanka by hiring a **car and driver**, which offers unlimited flexibility and can be less expensive than you might think. The main caveat is that drivers (and the travel companies they represent) work on **commission**, which they receive from some, but not all, hotels, plus assorted restaurants, shops, spice gardens and jewellers. This means that you and your driver's opinions might not always coincide as to where you want to stay and what you want to do – some drivers will always want to head for wherever they get the best kickbacks (and you'll also pay over the odds at these places, since the hoteliers, restaurateurs or shopkeepers have to recoup the commission they're paying the driver). Unfortunately, despite the fact that you're the customer, it's often not as easy to get your own way as you would imagine – stories of manipulative and dishonest drivers abound. If you find you're spending more time stressing out about dealing with your driver than enjoying your holiday, find another one – it's not worth messing up your trip for.

It's best, of course, to find a decent driver in the first place – it pays to go with a reputable company which employs only properly qualified CTB chauffeur-guides. Make sure your driver speaks at least some English and emphasize from the outset where you do and don't want to go. Some drivers impose on their clients' good nature to the point of having meals with them and insisting on acting as guides and interpreters throughout the tour. If this is what you want, fine; if not, don't be afraid to make it clear that you expect to be left alone when not in the car.

Cars and drivers can be hired through any of the **Colombo tour operators** listed on pp.30–32, or from many other tour companies and travel agents around the island – we've listed the most reliable outfits in the relevant places in the Guide. Alternatively, most hotels and guesthouses can fix you up with a vehicle, or you could come to some arrangement with a taxi driver. One of the island's largest and most reliable **car-hire companies** is Malkey (Ⓦwww.malkey.lk), based in Colombo, which has a large fleet of modern and well-maintained vehicles which can be hired with or without driver. All their drivers speak at least basic English and operate according to a code of conduct, while some have also been trained in defensive driving techniques. Rates are extremely competitive, and are published on their website. Another possibility is Quickshaws (Ⓦwww.quickshaws.com), which also has a good range of cars for hire with or without driver.

Prices depend more on quality than size of transport – a posh air-conditioned car will cost more than a non-air-conditioned minivan. Rates start from around US$30 per day for the smallest cars, plus drivers' fees and living allowances. All top-end hotels provide meals and accommodation for drivers either for free or for a small additional charge. If you're staying in budget or mid-range places, you'll have to pay for your driver's room and food – as ever, it's best to try to establish a daily allowance for this at the outset of your trip to avoid misunderstandings and arguments later. Your driver will also expect a tip of US$5–10 per day, depending on how highly trained they are. You'll also probably have to pay for **fuel** – now very expensive in Sri Lanka – which can add significantly to the overall cost. In addition, most companies only offer a decidedly mean 100km per day **free mileage**, which doesn't go far on the island's twisty roads, so you may well have to stump up for some excess mileage as well.

Finally, if this all sounds too stressful (and it can be, unfortunately), you could always just hire vehicles by the day as you go round the island. This is likely to be a bit more expensive, but you won't have to worry about having to house and feed your driver, and they're less likely to insist on supplementing their income by forcing you to visit their favourite shops, restaurants and spice gardens.

Rickshaws

The lines of motorized **rickshaws** which ply the streets of every city, town and village are one of Sri Lanka's most characteristic sights. Known by various names – tuktuks, three-wheelers, trishaws or (rather more optimistically) "taxis" – they are the staple means of travelling short distances in Sri Lanka, principally short hops within towns, although they can also be useful for excursions and can even, at a pinch, be handy for long journeys if you get stranded or can't be bothered to wait around for a bus. The vehicles themselves are mainly Indian-made Bajaj rickshaws, often decorated by their drivers with whimsical fluorescent stickers, statuettes, plastic flowers or other items both decorative or talismanic.

It's impossible to walk far in Sri Lanka without being solicited for custom by the owner of one of these vehicles. If you do need a ride, tuktuks are extremely convenient and can even be fun, in a slightly nerve-racking way, as they weave through the traffic, often at surprising speeds. In addition, the sheer number around means that you always have the upper hand in bargaining – if you can't agree a decent fare, there'll always be another driver keen to take your custom.

Tuktuks do have their drawbacks, however. They're not particularly comfortable for long journeys, and you can't see much. In addition, tuktuks' diminutive size compared with the buses and lorries they share the road with (and the often gung-ho attitudes of their drivers) can put you at a certain risk, and you're likely to experience at least a couple of near misses with speeding traffic if you use them consistently for longer journeys.

Sri Lankan tuktuks are never metered; the **fare** will be whatever you can negotiate with the driver. *Never* set off without agreeing the fare beforehand, or you run the risk of laying yourself open to all sorts of trickery. The majority of Sri Lanka's tuktuk drivers are more or less honest, and you'll often be offered a decent fare without even having to bargain; a small minority, however, are complete crooks who will (at best) simply try to overcharge you or, at worst, set you up for some kind of scam (for more on which, see p.62). Given the wildly varying degrees of probity you'll encounter, it's often difficult to know exactly where you stand. A basic fare of Rs.50 per kilometre serves as a slightly useful general rule of thumb, though you might find yourself paying more than this in Colombo, Kandy, Negombo and other heavily touristed areas, and less in more rural areas which see fewer visitors – and, obviously, it also depends on how ruthlessly you're prepared to bargain. Also bear in mind that the longer the journey, the lower the per-kilometre rate should be.

Finally, beware of tuktuk drivers who claim to have **no change** – this can even apply when trying to pay, say, for a Rs.70 fare with a Rs.100 note, with the driver claiming (perhaps truthfully) to have only Rs.10 or Rs.20 change, and hoping that you'll settle for a few rupees less. If you don't have change, check that the driver does before you set off. If you make the position clear from the outset, you're guaranteed that your driver will go through the hassle of getting change for you rather than risk losing your fare.

Bicycle

Bikes are available for **hire** in most tourist towns (alternatively, just ask at your guesthouse – they'll probably have or know someone who has a spare bike knocking around, or who will be prepared to surrender their own to you for a small price). In some places it's also possible to hire good-quality mountain bikes. **Costs** vary wildly, but will rarely be more than a few dollars a day, often much less.

Cycling can make for an extremely enjoyable way of getting around and exploring the island's backroads, although as a cyclist you are extremely vulnerable – bus and truck drivers consider cyclists a waste of valuable tarmac, and as far as they're concerned you don't really have any right to be on the road at all. Be prepared not only to get out of the way quickly, but even to get off the road completely. You are at risk not only from traffic coming from behind, but also from oncoming vehicles overtaking another vehicle, who will think nothing of forcing you into the ditch, even though they're on what is technically your side of the road.

An increasing number of tour operators are offering specialist cycle tours of the island – see p.53 for details.

Accommodation

Sri Lanka has an excellent range of accommodation in all price brackets, from basic beachside shacks to elegant colonial mansions and sumptuous five-star resorts – indeed staying in one of the country's burgeoning number of luxury hotels and villas can be one of the principal pleasures of a visit to the island, if you can afford it.

Types of accommodation

Travellers on a budget will spend most of their time in **guesthouses**, usually family-run places either in or attached to the home of the owners. Some of the nicer guesthouses can be real homes from home, with good cooking and sociable hosts. Rooms at most places cost between US$10 and US$15, although you'll sometimes find cheaper deals, especially around the coast. Note that there are no youth hostels in Sri Lanka.

Hotels come in all shapes, sizes and prices, from functional concrete boxes to luxurious establishments which are virtual tourist attractions in their own right. Some of the finest hotels (particularly in the hill country) are located in old colonial buildings, offering a wonderful taste of the lifestyle and ambience of yesteryear, while the island also boasts a number of stunning modern hotels, including many designed by Sri Lanka's great twentieth-century architect **Geoffrey Bawa** (see opposite, and box on p.146). The coastal areas are also home to innumerable **resort hotels**, the majority of which – with a few honourable exceptions – are fairly bland places, populated largely by European package tourists on full-board programmes and offering a diet of horrible buffet food and plenty of organized fun.

Sri Lanka is gradually waking up to its massive **eco-tourism** potential, and now boasts a few good eco-oriented hotels and lodges (see box, p.40). You can also stay in bungalows or camp within most of the island's national parks, although this can be difficult to arrange – see p.55 for details. The national parks are the only places in Sri Lanka with official **campsites**, and elsewhere camping is not a recognized activity. Pitching your tent unofficially in rural areas or on the beach is likely to lead to problems with local landowners and villagers – and given the cheapness of accommodation, is not worth the hassle.

Sri Lanka also boasts a huge (and continually increasing) number of **villas** and **boutique hotels**, many set in old colonial villas (including a number of old tea estate bungalows in the hill country – see p.268) and offering stylish and luxurious accommodation.

Hotels are **classified** using the usual one- to five-star system. In addition, some smaller

Sri Lankan accommodation online

Although not all hotels have their own websites, pretty much all the island's larger establishments feature on myriad websites run by overseas tour operators – typing the hotel name into a search engine will usually turn up a fair number of photos and reviews. Some good **internet resources** include the websites of Sri Lankan specialists Eden Villas (Ⓦwww.villasinsrilanka.com), Boutique Sri Lanka (Ⓦwww.boutiquesrilanka.com), Red Dot Tours (Ⓦwww.reddottours.com) and Sri Lanka in Style (Ⓦwww.srilankainstyle.com). Between them, these outfits cover pretty much all the best mid-range and top-end places in the island, including numerous gorgeous little villas and tea estate bungalows which you might not hear about otherwise, as well as more mainstream hotels.

Thirteen top places to stay

Amangalla, Galle (p.168)
Amanwella, Tangalla (p.201)
Club Villa, Bentota (p.143)
The Fortress, near Galle (p.186)
Galle Fort Hotel, Galle (p.169)
Helga's Folly, Kandy (p.239)
Heritance Kandalama, Dambulla (p.324)
Jetwing St Andrew's, Nuwara Eliya (p.272)
Jetwing Vil Uyana, Sigiriya (p.331)
The Kandy House, Kandy (p.239)
The Sun House, Galle (p.171)
The Tea Factory, Nuwara Eliya (p.272)
Tintagel, Colombo (p.95)

hotels and guesthouses are officially approved by the Sri Lanka Tourist Board, though it must be said that such approval means absolutely nothing – indeed, if anything, approved places often tend to be worst than their non-approved rivals.

Finding a room

Sri Lanka has its fair share of accommodation **touts**. One way of avoiding hassle is to ring ahead; most guesthouses will pick you up for free from the local bus or train station if given advance warning.

What you'll need from your room depends on where you are in the island; basic necessities change as you move up into the hill country and things become progressively colder. Virtually all accommodation in Sri Lanka comes with **private bathroom** (we've mentioned any exceptions in the relevant listings). In **lowland areas**, you should also always get a **fan** (usually a ceiling fan; floor-standing fans are much less common, and much less effective) – don't stay anywhere without one, unless you're happy to sleep in a puddle of sweat. It's also worth checking that the fan works properly (both that it runs at a decent speed and doesn't make a horrible noise). In lowland areas, room size and ceiling height are both important in determining how hot somewhere will be – rooms with low ceilings can become unbearably stuffy. In some areas (notably Arugam Bay) many places are built with their roofs raised slightly above the top of the walls, so that cool air can circulate freely through the gap (although, equally, it provides free access to insects). Smarter places (roughly categories ❸ or ❹ and upwards) will also usually have air-conditioning and/or hot water; category ❶ and ❷ places in the lowlands are extremely unlikely to have either – we've mentioned any exceptions in the listings (though given how humid it is, cold-water showers are no particular hardship). Most lowland places in all categories also have **mosquito nets**.

In the cooler climes of the **hill country**, most places in all categories have hot water (again, we've mentioned any exceptions). As a general rule, you'll need a fan in all places up to and including Kandy, and hot water in Kandy and anywhere higher. In the highest parts of the island, particularly Nuwara Eliya, you'll usually need some form of **heating** and/or a good supply of **blankets**. Few hill country establishments provide mosquito nets, which isn't generally a problem – these irritating little creatures shouldn't (in theory at least) be able to

Geoffrey Bawa hotels

For more on Geoffrey Bawa, see p.146.

Bentota Beach Hotel (p.143)
Blue Water, Kalutara (p.135)
Club Villa, Bentota (p.143)
Heritance Ahungalla, Ahungalla (p.149)
Heritance Kandalama, Dambulla (p.324)
Jetwing Beach, Negombo (p.124)
Jetwing Lighthouse, Galle (p.169)
Kani Lanka, Kalutara (p.135)
Lunuganga, Bentota (p.143)
Neptune, Beruwala (p.139)
Serendib, Bentota (p.144)
Villa Mohotti, Bentota (p.144)

Ten top eco-lodges and hotels

Boulder Garden, Sinharaja (p.307)
Ella Adventure Park, Ella (p.283)
Galapita, near Buttala (p.393)
Jetwing Hunas Falls, Kandy (p.239)
KumbukRiver, near Buttala (p.393)
Rainforest Edge, Sinharaja (p.307)
Ranweli Holiday Village, Waikkal (p.130)
Samakanda, near Galle (p.178)
Tree Tops Jungle Lodge, Buttala (p.393)
Jetwing Vil Uyana, Sigiriya (p.331)

survive at these altitudes, though in practice you might be unlucky enough to have an unusually hardy specimen buzzing in your ear anywhere in the island.

There are few other things worth bearing in mind when choosing a room. Check how many lights there are and whether they work: Sri Lankan hoteliers have a penchant for twenty-watt bulbs, and rooms can be very dingy. And if you're staying in a family guesthouse, keep an eye out for noisy children, dogs or television sets in the vicinity of your room; and make sure you get a room away from any noisy nearby roads.

Other recurrent problems include **power cuts** (particularly common during periods of low rainfall, when the country's hydroelectric system runs dry). Many mid- and top-end places have their own generators; in budget places it pays to keep a torch handy. Finally, remember that most Sri Lankans go to bed very early. If you're staying at a small guesthouse and you go out for dinner and a few beers, it's not uncommon to find yourself locked out on your return – any time after 9pm. Let them know when to expect you back.

Room rates

Room rates in lower-end places reflect Sri Lanka's **bargaining culture** – exact rates are often somewhat notional, as owners will vary prices to reflect the season, levels of demand and how rich they think you look. It's always worth bargaining (but also see the section on ethical bargaining on p.71), even in top-end places, especially if you're planning to stay a few nights, or if business is slow. If you're travelling on your own, you'll have to work harder to get a decent price since many establishments don't have **single rooms or rates** (where they exist, they're usually two-thirds to three-quarters of the price of a double). Try to establish what the price of a double would be, and bargain from there.

In many places, your hotel or guesthouse will also be the place you're most likely to eat, and **half- and full-board rates** are common. These can often work out to be extremely good value, though the food can be bland; obviously, the attractiveness of these all-inclusive options depends on the presence or absence of other places to eat in the vicinity.

Prices in most coastal areas are also subject to **seasonal variations**. The most pronounced seasonal variation is along the west coast, where rates at almost all places rise (usually by between 25 and 50 percent) from November 1 through to mid- or late April. Some places along the south coast also put up their prices during this period. East coast places tend to raise rates from around April through to September. Rates in particular towns also rise if there's a big procession or festival going on locally – as

Accommodation price codes

All the accommodation in this book has been categorized according to the following **price codes**. These are for the price of a **double room in high season**, inclusive of any taxes (in some places these prices also include breakfast, and in all-inclusive resorts they also cover other meals and drinks for two people in a double room).

❶ US$10 and under
❷ US$11–15
❸ US$16–25
❹ US$26–40
❺ US$41–65
❻ US$66–100
❼ US$101–150
❽ US$151–200
❾ US$201 and over

during the Esala Perahera at Kandy – or during important holidays, as during the Sinhalese New Year in Nuwara Eliya, when accommodation prices everywhere treble or quadruple.

Room rates at mid- and top-end places are often quoted in **dollars** for convenience, but are payable in rupees only. Make sure you clarify whether any **additional taxes** will be added to the bill – the more upmarket the place you're staying in, the more likely this is. Many places levy a service charge of ten percent, while some also charge a government service tax of fifteen percent and a "development" tax of one percent – taken together, these can add a nasty twist to a bill, especially since they are also added to food and drink.

Finally, note that many hotels operate a **dual-pricing system** whereby foreigners pay more (sometimes significantly more) than locals. There's nothing you can do about this unless you have a resident's visa, in which case you may be able to wangle local rates.

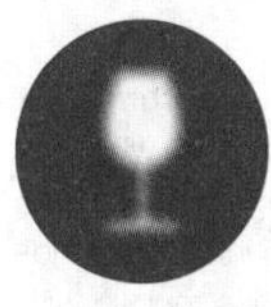

Eating and drinking

Sri Lanka boasts a fascinatingly idiosyncratic culinary heritage, the result of a unique fusion of local produce with recipes and spices brought to the island over the centuries by Indians, Arabs, Malays, Portuguese, Dutch and English.

The staple dish is **rice and curry**, at its finest a miniature banquet whose contrasting flavours – cinnamon, chillies, curry leaves, garlic, coconut milk, pandanus leaves and "Maldive fish" (an intensely flavoured pinch of sun-dried tuna) – bear witness to Sri Lanka's status as one of the original spice islands. There are plenty of other unique **specialities** to explore and enjoy – hoppers, string hoppers, *kottu rotty*, *lamprais* and *pittu* – as well as plentiful **seafood**.

Sri Lankan cuisine can be incredibly fiery – sometimes on a par with Thai, and far hotter than most Indian cooking. Many of the island's less gifted chefs compensate for a lack of culinary subtlety with liberal use of **chilli** powder; conversely as a tourist you'll often be seen as a weak-kneed individual who is liable to faint at the merest suspicion of spiciness. You'll often be asked how hot you want your food; "medium" usually gets you something that's neither bland nor requires the use of a fire extinguisher. If you do overheat during a meal, remember that water only adds to the pain of a burnt palate; a mouthful of plain rice, bread or beer is much more effective.

Sri Lankans say that you can't properly enjoy the flavours and textures of food unless you **eat with your fingers**, although tourists will always be provided with cutlery on request. As elsewhere in Asia, you're meant to eat with your right hand, although this taboo isn't really strictly observed – if you'd really prefer to eat with your left hand, you're unlikely to turn heads.

Costs are generally low. You can get a filling rice and curry meal for a couple of dollars at a local café, while main courses at most guesthouse restaurants usually cost less than US$5, and even at the island's poshest restaurants it's usually possible to find main courses for under US$10. Note that many places add a ten percent service charge to the bill, while more upmarket restaurants usually add an additional government service tax of fifteen percent on top of that.

Be aware that the typical vagaries of Sri Lankan **spelling** mean that popular dishes can appear on menus in a bewildering number of forms: *idlis* can become *ittlys*, *vadais* turn into *wadais*, *kottu rotty* transforms into *kotturoti* and *lamprais* changes to *lumprice*. You'll also be regaled with plenty of unintentionally humorous offerings such as "cattle fish", "sweat and sour" or Adolf Hitler's favourite dish, "nazi goreng".

Where to eat

Although Sri Lankan cooking can be very good, few **restaurants** really do justice to the island's cuisine. There's no particular tradition of eating out and, except in Colombo, few independent restaurants of note. Locals either eat at home or patronize the island's innumerable scruffy little cafés, often confusingly signed as "hotels", which serve up filling meals for a dollar or two: rough-and-ready portions of rice and curry, plus maybe hoppers or *kottu rotty*. However as the food is usually pretty ordinary, eating in local cafés is more of a social than a culinary experience.

Given the lack of independent tourist restaurants, most visitors end up taking the majority of their meals in their **hotel** or **guesthouse**. The sort of food and setting you'll encounter varies wildly, from the big bland restaurants at the coastal resorts to the cosy guesthouses of Ella and Galle, where you can experience the sort of home-cooking which rarely makes its way onto menus at larger hotels. In general, however, choice is limited, with most places offering a standard assortment of fried noodles or rice, a small range of seafood and meat dishes (usually including a couple of devilled options) and maybe a few kinds of curry.

Most of the island's **independent restaurants** can be found in Colombo and, to a lesser extent, Kandy and Negombo, where tourism has inspired the growth of a modest local eating scene. The most common independent restaurants are aimed at tourists, with a mix of Sri Lankan, seafood and Western dishes; Chinese restaurants are popular too (though these often double as local drinking holes), and you'll also find a few South Indian places, especially in Colombo.

In terms of **opening hours**, the vast majority of restaurants and cafés open daily from early or mid-morning until reasonably late in the evening (around 9/10pm), although some places (especially in Colombo) close from around 3pm to 6 or 7pm. Unless otherwise stated, all the places listed in the Guide are open daily for both lunch and dinner.

If you want to eat like the locals, you'll find **lunch packets** on sale at local cafés and street stalls all over the country between around 11am and 2pm. These usually include a big portion of steamed rice along with a piece of curried chicken, fish or beef (vegetarians can get an egg), some vegetables and *sambol* (see below). At a dollar or under, they're the cheapest way to fill up in Sri Lanka, although they're probably best avoided until you're properly acclimatized to the local cooking.

What to eat

The island's staple is **rice and curry** (not "curry and rice" – it's the rice which is considered the principal ingredient). Basic rice and curry, as served up in cafés island-wide, consists of a plate of rice topped with a few dollops of veg curry, a hunk of chicken or fish and a spoonful of *sambol*. More sophisticated versions comprise the inevitable mound of rice accompanied by as many as fifteen side dishes. These generally include a serving of meat or fish curry plus accompaniments such as curried pineapple, potato, aubergine (*brinjal*), sweet potatoes, okra (lady's fingers) and dhal. You'll probably also encounter some more unusual **local vegetables**. Curried jackfruit is fairly common, as are so-called "drumsticks" (*murunga* – a bit like okra). Other ingredients you might encounter include ash plantain (*alu kesel*), snake gourd (*patolah*), bitter gourd (*karawila*) and breadfruit (*del*), along with many more outlandish and unpronounceable types of regional produce. Another common accompaniment is **mallung**: shredded green vegetables, lightly stir-fried with spices and grated coconut.

Rice and curry is usually served with a helping of **sambol**, designed to be mixed into your food to give it a bit of extra kick. *Sambols* come in various forms, the most common being *pol sambol* (coconut *sambol*), an often eye-watering combination of chilli powder, chopped onions, salt, grated coconut and "Maldive fish" (salty, intensely flavoured shreds of sun-dried tuna). Treat it with caution. You might also come across the slightly less overpowering *lunu miris*, consisting of chilli powder, onions, Maldive fish and salt; and the more gentle, sweet-and-sour *seeni sambol* ("sugar sambol").

Funnily enough, the **rice** itself is often fairly uninspiring – don't expect to find the delicately spiced pilaus and biryanis of North India. Sri Lanka produces many types of rice, but it's usually fairly low-grade stuff, with a greyish colour and a tendency to clump, although you may occasionally come across the nutritious and distinctively flavoured red and yellow rices (a bit like brown rice in taste and texture) that are grown in certain parts of the island.

Other Sri Lankan specialities

Sri Lanka's tastiest snack, the engagingly named **hopper** (*appa*) is a small, bowl-shaped pancake traditionally made from a batter containing coconut milk and palm toddy, and is usually eaten either at breakfast or, most commonly, dinner. Hoppers are cooked in a small wok-like dish, meaning that most of the mix sinks to the bottom, making hoppers soft and doughy at the base, and thin and crisp around the edges. Various ingredients can be poured into the hopper. An egg fried in the middle produces an egg hopper, whilst sweet ingredients like yoghurt or honey are also sometimes added. Alternatively, plain hoppers can be eaten as an accompaniment to curry. Not to be confused with the hopper are **string hoppers** (*indiappa*), tangled little balls of steamed rice noodles, often eaten with a dash of dhal or curry for breakfast.

Another rice substitute is **pittu**, a mixture of flour and grated coconut, steamed in a cylindrical bamboo mould – it looks a bit like coarse couscous. Derived from the Dutch *lomprijst*, **lamprais** is another speciality: a serving of rice baked in a plantain leaf along with accompaniments such as a lump of chicken or a boiled egg, plus some veg and pickle.

Muslim restaurants are the place to go for **rotty** (or *roti*), a fine, doughy pancake – watching these being made is half the fun, as the chef teases small balls of dough into huge sheets of almost transparent thinness. A dollop of curried meat, veg or potato is then plonked in the middle and the *rotty* is folded up around it; the final shape depends on the whim of the chef – some prefer crepe-like squares, others opt for samosa-style triangles, some a spring roll. *Rottys* can also be chopped up and stir-fried with meat and vegetables, a dish known as **kottu rotty**. You'll know when *kottu rotty* is being made because of the noise – the ingredients are usually simultaneously fried and chopped on a hotplate using a large pair of meat cleavers, producing a noisy drumming sound – part musical performance, part advertisement.

Devilled dishes are also popular, and can be delicious. These are usually prepared with a thick, spicy sauce plus big chunks of onion and chilli, though the end-product often isn't as hot as you might fear. Devilled chicken, pork, fish and beef are all common – the last is generally considered the classic devilled dish and is traditionally eaten during drinking binges. Another local staple is the **buriani**. This has little in common with the traditional, saffron-scented North Indian biryani, being nothing more than a mound of rice with a hunk of chicken, a bowl of curry sauce and a boiled egg, but it makes a good lunchtime filler and is usually less fiery than a basic plate of rice and curry.

South Indian food

Colombo is home to numerous "pure vegetarian" **South Indian restaurants** (vegetarian here meaning no meat, fish, eggs or alcohol). These cheerfully no-nonsense places cater to a local clientele and serve up a delicious range of Tamil-style dishes at giveaway prices. The standard dish is the **dosa**, a crispy rice pancake served in various forms: either plain, with ghee (clarified butter), onion or, most commonly, as a masala dosa, folded up around a filling of curried potato. You'll also find **uttapam**, another (thicker) type of rice pancake that's usually eaten with some kind of curry, and **idlis**, steamed rice cakes served with curry sauces or chutneys. Another classic Tamil savoury which has entered the Sri Lanka mainstream is the **vadai** (or *wadai*), a spicy doughnut made of deep-fried lentils – no train journey is complete without the sound of hawkers marching up and down compartments shouting "Vadai-vadai-vadai!". Platefuls of *vadais*, *rottys* and bread rolls are

Vegetarian food in Sri Lanka

Surprisingly for such a Buddhist country, **vegetarian** food as a concept hasn't really caught on in Sri Lanka. Having said that, a large proportion of the nation's cooking is meat-free: vegetable curries, vegetable *rottys*, hoppers and string hoppers – not to mention the bewildering variety of fruit on offer. Colombo's numerous pure veg South Indian restaurants are a delight, while if you eat fish and seafood, you'll have no problems finding a meal, especially around the coast.

often served up in cafés under the name of **short eats** – you help yourself and are charged for what you eat, though be aware that these plates are passed around and their contents indiscriminately prodded by all and sundry, so they're not particularly hygienic. Some South Indian places (again, particularly in Colombo) serve a fascinating array of **sweets**, luridly coloured and heavily spiced.

Other cuisines

There are plenty of **Chinese restaurants** around the island, though many are just glorified local drinking holes serving up plates of fried rice and noodles. Genuine places, as listed in the Guide, are often good, with predominantly Cantonese-style menus which are often spiced up for Sri Lankan tastes. As usual, Colombo has easily the best range of such places.

Indonesian dishes introduced by the Dutch are also sometimes served in tourist restaurants – most commonly *nasi goreng* (fried rice with meat or seafood, topped with a fried egg) and *gado gado* (salad and cold boiled eggs in a peanut sauce), although these rarely taste much like their Indonesian originals.

Other cuisines are restricted to Colombo. **Thai** food has made some limited inroads, while **Japanese** cuisine is also modestly popular. Colombo is also where you'll find Sri Lanka's surprisingly small number of decent **North Indian** restaurants, along with a few excellent European places. Smarter hotels all over the island make some attempt to produce **European** cuisine, though with wildly varying results.

Seafood

Not surprisingly, **seafood** plays a major part in the Sri Lankan diet, with fish often taking the place of meat. Common fish include tuna, seer (a firm-bodied white fish), mullet and the delicious melt-in-the-mouth butter-fish, as well as pomfret, bonito and shark. You'll also find lobster, plentiful crab, prawns and cuttlefish (calamari). The Negombo lagoon, just north of Colombo, is a particularly prized source of crab and prawns.

Seafood is usually a good bet if you're trying to avoid highly spiced food. Fish is generally prepared in a fairly simple manner, usually fried (sometimes in breadcrumbs) or grilled and served with a twist of lemon or in a mild garlic sauce. You will, however, find some fiery fish curries, while chillied seafood dishes are also fairly common – chilli crab is particularly popular.

Sri Lankan desserts and sweets

The classic Sri Lankan dessert is **curd** (yoghurt made from buffalo milk) served with honey or **kitul** (a sweet syrup from the kitul palm). When boiled and left to set hard, kitul becomes **jaggery**, an all-purpose Sri Lanka sweet or sweetener. Other characteristic desserts are **wattalappam**, an egg pudding of Malay origins which tastes faintly like crème caramel, but with a sweeter and less slippery texture. **Kiribath** is a dessert of rice cakes cooked in milk and served with jaggery – it's also traditionally made for weddings, and is often the first solid food fed to babies. A South Indian dessert you might come across is **faluda**, a colourful cocktail of milk, syrup, jelly, ice cream and ice served in a tall glass like an Indian knickerbocker glory. **Ice cream** is usually factory made, and safe to eat; the most widely available brand is Elephant House. You'll also find a wide selection of **cakes**, often in fluorescent colours and in a bizarre variety of curried flavours.

Fruits

Sri Lanka has a bewildering variety of fruits, from the familiar to the bizarre, including several classic Southeast Asian fruits introduced from Indonesia by the Dutch. The months given in brackets below refer to the periods when each is in season (where no months are specified, the fruit is available year-round). Familiar fruits include pineapple, mangoes (April–June & Nov–Dec), avocados (April–June) and coconuts, as well as a wide variety of **bananas**, from small sweet yellow specimens to enormous red monsters. **Papaya** (pawpaw), a distinctively sweet and pulpy fruit, crops up regularly in fruit salads, but the king of Sri Lankan fruits is undoubtedly the **jackfruit** (April–June & Sept–Oct), the world's largest fruit, a huge, elongated dark-green monster, rather like an enormous marrow in shape, whose fibrous flesh can either be eaten raw or used as an ingredient in curries. **Durian** (May–July) is another outsized specimen: a large green beast with a spiky outer shell. It's very much an acquired taste: though the flesh smells rather like blocked drains, it's widely considered a great delicacy, and many also believe it to have aphrodisiac qualities. Its distinctive aroma wafts across the island from July to September, when it's in season. The strangest-looking fruit, however, is the **rambutan** (July–Sept), a delicious, lychee-like fruit enclosed in a bright-red skin that's covered in tentacles. Again, it's in season from July to September. Another prized Sri Lankan delicacy is the **mangosteen** (July–Sept), which looks a little like a purple tomato, with a rather hard shell-like skin which softens as the fruit ripens. The delicate and delicious flesh tastes a bit like a grape with a slight citrus tang. Equally distinctive is the **wood apple** (or *beli* fruit), a round, apple-sized fruit covered in an indestructible greyish bark, inside which is a red pulpy flesh, rather bitter-tasting and full of seeds. It's sometimes served with honey poured over it. You might also come across **custard apples**: greenish, apple-sized fruits with knobbly exteriors (they look a bit like artichokes) and smooth, sweet white flesh; **guavas**, smooth, round yellow-green fruits, usually smaller than an apple and with slightly sour-tasting flesh around a central core of seeds; as well as rarities such as soursop, *lovi-lovi* and *sapodilla*. Finally, look out for the tiny **gulsambilla** (Aug–Oct), Sri Lanka's strangest fruit – like a large, furry green seed enclosing a tiny, tartly flavoured kernel.

What to drink

It's best to avoid tap water in Sri Lanka (see p.65). **Bottled water** is available absolutely everywhere, sourced from various places in the hill country and retailed under a baffling range of names – every town seems to have its own brand. Bottles come in half-litre, litre and 1.5 litre sizes. Check that the seal hasn't been broken – but note that they're all usually pretty grubby.

International brands of **soft drinks** – Pepsi, Coca-Cola, Sprite – are widely available and cheap, but it's much more fun (and better for the Sri Lankan economy) to explore the glorious range of outlandish soft drinks produced locally by Olé, Lion and Elephant. These include old-fashioned favourites like cream soda and ginger beer, and unique local brands like Portello (which tastes a bit like Vimto) and the ultra-sweet, lollipop-flavoured Necta. Ginger beer is particularly common, and very refreshing – the Elephant brand uses natural ginger, which is meant to be good for the stomach and digestion.

The slightly sour-tasting **coconut water** (*thambili*) isn't to everyone's taste, although it's guaranteed safe, having been locked up in the heart of the coconut. It's also claimed to be an excellent hangover cure thanks to its mix of glucose and potassium, which also makes it good to drink if you're suffering from diarrhoea.

Tea and coffee

Despite the fame of Sri Lanka's **tea**, most of the best stuff is exported and you have little chance of getting a top-class cuppa unless you buy your own and make it yourself. Tea is usually made weak and milky, and you won't find the marvellous masala teas of India. Normal tea is often called "milk tea"; "bed tea" is just ordinary tea brought to your room for breakfast. **Coffee** is often a better bet. This is generally either Nescafé or locally produced coffee – the latter is usually perfectly drinkable, although you're normally left with a big layer of silt at the bottom of the cup.

Alcoholic drinks

Sri Lanka has a strong drinking culture – beer was introduced by foreign captives during the Kandyan period, and the islanders have never looked back. The island's two staple forms of alcohol are lager and arrack. **Lager** is usually sold in large (625ml) bottles; draught lager is rare. There's not a great choice of brands; all clock in with an alcohol content of just under five percent. The staple national tipple, the ubiquitous Lion Lager, is uninspiring but perfectly drinkable. More palatable beers include Carlsberg (brewed under licence in Sri Lanka), and the delicately malty, but relatively difficult to find Three Coins (which also does a good white beer, Three Coins Riva). Lion also brew a very dense stout, Lion Stout, which is virtually a meal in itself. As you'd expect, lager is relatively expensive in Sri Lankan terms, ranging from around Rs.100 in a liquor shop or supermarket to Rs.200–250 in most bars and restaurants. Imported beers, on the rare occasions you can find them, come with a hefty mark-up.

Two more distinctively local types of booze come from the versatile coconut. **Toddy**, tapped from the flower of the coconut, is non-alcoholic when fresh but ferments into a beverage faintly reminiscent of cider – it's sold informally in villages around the country, though unless you're travelling with a Sinhala-speaker it's difficult to track down. When fermented and refined, toddy produces **arrack** (33 percent proof), Sri Lanka's national beverage for the strong-livered – you won't go far before finding a group of voluble Sri Lankan men clustered around a bottle. Arrack is either drunk neat, mixed with coke or lemonade or used in tourist-oriented bars and restaurants as a base for cocktails. It's available in various grades and is usually a darkish brown, though there are also clear brands like White Diamond and White Label; the smoother, double-distilled arrack tastes faintly like rum. Imported **spirits** are widely available, but are predictably expensive. There are also locally produced versions of most spirits, including rather rough whisky, brandy, rum and vodka, as well as lots of brands of quite palatable lemon gin.

Most people drink in their hotel bar or guesthouse. There are a few decent **bars** and English-style **pubs** in Colombo, Kandy and a few tourist resorts, but most local bars are gloomy and rather seedy places, and very much a male preserve – potentially fun for blokes on a bender, although women will feel less comfortable. Alcohol is available from supermarkets in larger towns. In smaller places, there are usually a few rather disreputable-looking **liquor shops** – usually a small kiosk, piled high with bottles of beer and arrack and protected by stout security bars. You're technically not allowed to buy alcohol on full-moon (poya) days, although tourist hotels and bars will often discreetly serve visitors.

The media

Sri Lanka has an extensive English-language media, including numerous newspapers and radio stations, though journalistic standards are not especially high, thanks at least partly to the state control exercised over large sections of the media.

There are also several good **online** resources for Sri Lankan news. The BBC's ⓦwww.bbc.co.uk/news has a huge searchable archive of news stories dating back to around the turn of the millennium, while ⓦwww.bbc.co.uk/sinhala offers a dedicated portal for breaking Sri Lankan stories. In addition, ⓦwww.theacademic.org has

Tamilnet

An important alternative perspective on the civil war is provided by the pioneering **Tamilnet**, Ⓦwww.tamilnet.com, which reports on the conflict from a pro-Tamil, and generally pro-LTTE, point of view, offering a valuable corrective to the Sinhalese-dominated national media. The site is widely perceived as being the official propaganda mouthpiece for the LTTE, although contrary to popular belief, it's not directly affiliated to the Tigers, and has apparently run into conflict with the LTTE on occasion. Not surprisingly, Tamilnet staff have been repeatedly threatened by Sinhalese nationalists, most obviously in 2005, when its then editor, Taraki Sivaram, was abducted and murdered in Colombo.

comprehensive links to Sri Lanka-related news stories across the web, including to local stories not found on the BBC sites.

Newspapers and magazines

Sri Lanka has a good spread of **English-language newspapers**, including three dailies – *The Island* (Ⓦwww.island.lk), the *Daily News* (Ⓦwww.dailynews.lk) and the *Daily Mirror* (Ⓦwww.dailymirror.lk) – and two Sunday papers, The *Sunday Observer* (Ⓦwww.sundayobserver.lk) and the *Sunday Times* (Ⓦwww.sundaytimes.lk). The *Daily News* and *Sunday Observer* are both owned by the government, and therefore tend to reflect the opinions of whichever political party has control of the Information Ministry – the *Daily News*, in particular, is one of the worst newspapers in Asia, though it provides an interesting insight into the degree of control the state wields over sections of the media. Standards are higher in the independent papers, though all devote the majority of their coverage to domestic politics and cricket. English-language newspapers are generally sold by hawkers at the roadside or at small stalls and tend to sell out by midday – and you'll usually only find one or two available in any one place; the *Daily News* is perhaps the most widely distributed. All these papers are also available online.

There are also a fair number of English-language **magazines** available. The best and longest-established of the island's various monthly titles are the widely available *Travel Sri Lanka* (Ⓦwww.travelsrilanka.com) and *Explore Sri Lanka*, both of which have decent, tourist-oriented articles about all aspects of the island. The business-oriented *Lanka Monthly Digest* (Ⓦwww.lmd.lk) also sometimes runs interesting general features on the island. True seekers after socialite tittle-tattle should look no further than *Hi!!* Magazine (Ⓦwww.hi.lk), Sri Lanka's answer to *Hello!* – essential reading for anyone seeking an insight into the Colombo cocktail-party circuit.

Radio

There are a surprising number of **English-language radio stations** in Sri Lanka, although reception can be hit and miss outside Colombo and most stations broadcast on a confusing variety of frequencies in different parts of the island. Most stations churn out a predictable diet of mainstream Western pop, presented by hillariously inept DJs. The main broadcasters include TNL Rocks (101.7 FM; Ⓦwww.tnlrocks.com), Yes FM (101.0 FM; Ⓦwww.yesfmmusic.com), Lite FM (89.2 FM in Colombo, 90 FM islandwide; Ⓦwww.lite892.com), E FM (100.4 FM in Colombo; Ⓦwww.efm.lk), plus Gold FM (99.9 FM in Colombo, 93 FM and 104.2 FM islandwide), which dishes up retro-pop and easy listening. One **Sinhala-language station** which you might end up hearing a lot of (especially if you do much bus travel) is Shree FM (99.0), beloved of bus drivers all over the island and offering a toe-curling diet of Sinhala pop interspersed by terrible adverts. For a more interesting selection of local music, try Sirasa FM (88.8FM, 106.5 FM and other frequencies; Ⓦwww.sirasa.com).

Television

You're not likely to spend much time watching **Sri Lankan television**. There are three state-run channels (Rupavahini, Channel Eye and ITN), which broadcast almost entirely in Sinhala and Tamil, plus various local satellite TV channels which offer a small selection of English-language programming, though this is a fairly deadly mixture of shopping programmes, children's shows, pop music, soaps and the occasional duff film. Rooms in most top-end hotels have **satellite TV**, usually offering international news programmes from the BBC and/or CNN along with various channels from the India-based Star TV, including movies and sports.

Cinema

Sri Lankan **cinema** has a long history, although it continues to struggle to escape the huge shadow cast by the film industry in neighbouring India; the increasingly wide availability of television poses another challenge. The first Sinhala-language Sri Lankan film was *Kadawunu Poronduwa* (Broken Promise), premiered in 1947, although the first truly Sinhalese film is generally considered to be Lester James Peries' *Rekawa* (Line of Destiny), of 1956, which broke with the Indian all-singing all-dancing model and attempted a realistic portrayal of Sri Lankan life. Peries went on to score further triumphs with films like *Gamperaliya* (Changing Village), based on a novel by Martin Wickramasinghe (see p.186), and served as a role model for a new generation of Sri Lankan directors. Modern Sri Lankan film-makers have tended to focus on themes connected with the country's civil war, most famously in Prasanna Vithanage's *Death on a Full Moon Day* (1997), which portrays a blind and naive father who refuses to accept the death of his soldier son. At present, about a hundred films are released each year in Sri Lankan cinemas, with offerings in English, Tamil, Sinhala and Hindi. Sri Lankan-made films are almost exclusively in Sinhala, apart from a few in Tamil.

There are only a very modest number of **cinemas** on the island, concentrated largely in Colombo. A couple show recent Hollywood blockbusters in English; others specialize in Tamil, Hindi and Sinhala releases, and are easily spotted by their huge advertising hoardings showing rakish, moustachioed heroes clutching nubile heroines. Tickets for all movies cost around a dollar. You might also catch screenings of more highbrow Sri Lankan movies at the various cultural centres in Colombo and Kandy.

Festivals and public holidays

It's sometimes claimed that Sri Lanka has more festivals than any other country in the world, and with four major religions on the island and no fewer than 25 public holidays, things can seem to grind to a halt with disconcerting frequency. Public holidays in the listings below are marked "(P)".

Virtually all the festivals are religious in nature and follow the **lunar calendar**, with every full moon signalling the start of a new month (an extra month is added every two or three years to keep the solar and lunar calendars in alignment). As a result, most festival **dates** vary somewhat from year to year, apart from a couple (such as Thai Pongol and Sinhalese New Year). Muslim festivals also follow a lunar calendar but without the corrective months which are inserted into the Buddhist lunar calendar, meaning that the dates of these festivals gradually move backwards at the rate of about eleven days per year, completing one annual cycle roughly every 32 years. Exact dates of forthcoming events are posted at Ⓦwww.srilanka.travel.

Buddhist festivals revolve around the days of the full moon – or **poya days** – which are official public holidays as well as having special religious significance (the Buddha urged his disciples to undertake special spiritual practices on each poya day, and according to traditional belief he himself was born, attained enlightenment and died on the poya day in the lunar month of Vesak). On poya days, Sri Lankan Buddhists traditionally make offerings at their local temple and perform other religious observances, while the less pious section of the population marks the occasion with riotous behaviour and widespread drunkenness. The island's most important Buddhist festivals are traditionally celebrated with enormous **peraheras**, or parades, with scores of fabulously accoutred elephants accompanied by drummers and dancers. People often travel on poya days, so transport and accommodation tend to be busy; there's also (in theory) a ban on the sale of alcohol, although tourist hotels and guesthouses will usually serve you.

Sri Lanka's main **Hindu festivals** rival the island's Buddhist celebrations in colour – in addition to the ones listed below, there are numerous other local temple festivals across the Jaffna peninsula. Sri Lanka's **Muslim festivals** are more modest affairs, generally involving only the Muslim community itself, with special prayers at the mosque. The three main celebrations are the Milad un-Nabi (Feb 26, 2010), celebrating the Prophet's birthday; Id ul-Fitr (Sept 10, 2010), marking the end of Ramadan; and Id ul-Allah (Nov 16, 2010), marking the beginning of pilgrimages to Mecca.

Festival calendar

January

Duruthu Poya (P) Marks the first of the Buddha's three legendary visits to Sri Lanka, and celebrated with a spectacular perahera (parade) at the Raja Maha Vihara in the Colombo suburb of Kelaniya. The Duruthu poya also marks the beginning of the three-month pilgrimage season to Adam's Peak.

Thai Pongol (Jan 14/15) (P) Hindu festival, honouring the sun god Surya, Indra (the bringer of rains) and the cow, in no particular order. It's marked by ceremonies at Hindu temples, after which the first grains of the new paddy harvest are ceremonially cooked in milk in a special pot – the direction in which the liquid spills when it boils over is thought to indicate good or bad luck in the coming year.

Galle Literary Festival (late Jan/early Feb). Eminent local and international wordsmiths and culture vultures descend on Galle. See p.167.

February

Navam Poya (P) Commemorates the Buddha's announcement, at the age of 80, of his own impending death, celebrated with a major perahera at the Gangaramaya temple in Colombo. Although this dates only from 1979, it has become one of the island's biggest festivals, featuring a procession of some fifty elephants.

Independence Day (Feb 4) (P) Celebrates Sri Lanka's independence on February 4, 1948, with parades, dances and games.

Maha Sivarathri (Feb/March) (P) Hindu festival dedicated to Shiva, during which devotees perform a one-day fast and an all-night vigil.

March

Medin Poya (P) Marks the Buddha's first visit to his father's palace following his enlightenment.

Good Friday (March/April) (P) An Easter Passion play is performed on the island of Duwa, near Negombo.

April

Bak Poya (P) Celebrates the Buddha's second visit to Sri Lanka.

New Year (April 13–14) (P) Coinciding with the start of the southwest monsoon and the end of the harvest season, the Buddhist and Hindu New Year is a family festival during which presents are exchanged and the traditional *kiribath* (rice cooked with milk and cut into diamond shapes) is prepared. Businesses close, rituals are performed, new clothes are worn and horoscopes are cast. April 13 is New Year's Eve; April 14 is New Year's Day.

May

Labour Day (May 1) (P) The traditional May Day bank holiday.

Vesak Poya (P) The most important of the Buddhist poyas, this is a three-fold celebration commemorating the Buddha's birth, enlightenment and death, all of which are traditionally thought to have happened on the day of the Vesak Poya. In addition, the last of the Buddha's three alleged visits to Sri Lanka is claimed to have been on a Vesak poya day. Lamps are lit in front of houses, and pandals (platforms decorated with scenes from the life of the Buddha) are erected throughout the country. Buses and cars are decorated with streamers, and free food (from rice and curry to Vesak sweetmeats) is distributed in roadside booths (dansal). Meanwhile, devout Buddhists visit temples, meditate and fast. The day after the Vesak Poya is also a public holiday. Vesak also marks the end of the Adam's Peak pilgrimage season. Note that laws introduced in 2006 forbid the consumption of alcohol, meat and fish in public restaurants for a six-day period around the poya day, though hotels and guesthouses may be able to circumvent this when serving their own guests.

National Heroes' Day (May 22) Honours soldiers who have died in the civil war.

June

Poson Poya (P) Second only in importance to Vesak, Poson Poya commemorates the introduction of Buddhism to Sri Lanka by Mahinda, marked by mass pilgrimages to Anuradhapura, while thousands of white-robed pilgrims climb to the summit of Mihintale.

July

Esala Poya (P) Celebrates the Buddha's first sermon and the arrival of the Tooth Relic in Sri Lanka. The lunar month of Esala is the season of festivals, most notably the great Esala Perahera in Kandy (see p.232), Sri Lanka's most extravagant festival. There are also festivals at Kataragama (see below), Dondra and Bellanwila (a southern Colombo suburb) and a big seven-day celebration at Unawatuna, during which thousands descend on the village and beach.

Kataragama Festival at Kataragama during which devotees fire-walk and indulge in various forms of ritual self-mutilation, piercing their skin with hooks and weights, and driving skewers through their cheeks and tongues.

Hikkaduwa Beach Festival (July/Aug) Five-day beach bash with international DJs.

Vel (July/Aug) Colombo's most important Hindu festival, dedicated to Skanda/Kataragama (see p.216) and featuring two exuberant processions during which the god's chariot and *vel* (spear) are carried across the city from the Pettah to temples in Wellawatta and Bambalapitiya.

August

Nikini Poya (P) Marks the retreat of the Bhikkhus following the Buddha's death, commemorated by a period of fasting and of retreat for the monastic communities.

September

Binara Poya (P) Commemorates the Buddha's journey to heaven to preach to his mother and other deities.

Dussehra (Sept/Oct) Also known as Durga Puja, this Hindu festival honours Durga and also commemorates the day of Rama's victory over Ravana.

October

Vap Poya (P) Marks the Buddha's return to earth and the end of the Buddhist period of fasting.

Deepavali (late Oct/early Nov) (P) The Hindu Festival of Lights (equivalent to North India's Diwali), commemorating the return from exile of Rama, hero of the *Ramayana*, with the lighting of lamps in Tamil households, symbolic of the triumph of good over evil, and the wearing of new clothes.

Galle Art Trail (late Oct/early Nov) Impromptu art festival, with dozens of temporary art galleries opening all over Galle.

November

Il Poya (P) Commemorates the Buddha's ordination of sixty disciples.

December

Unduvap Poya (P) Celebrates the arrival of the Bo tree sapling in Anuradhapura, brought by Ashoka's daughter, Sangamitta.

Christmas (25 Dec) (P)

Christian New Year's Eve (31 Dec)

Sport and outdoor activities

Sri Lanka's vast potential for outdoor and activity holidays is only just starting to be tapped. Water-based activities like diving and surfing are reasonably well covered, but other pursuits such as mountain biking and trekking remain the preserve of a few pioneering operators. The island's eco-tourism potential is huge, but although its reputation amongst birdwatchers is well established, other wildlife attractions – from turtle-spotting to whale-watching – remain almost completely unexploited. Finally, if you fancy something a bit livelier and you're lucky enough to coincide with a match, a trip to watch Sri Lanka's cricket team in action – always an occasion of huge national excitement – is an absolute must.

Cricket

Of all the legacies of the British colonial period, the game of cricket is probably held dearest by the average Sri Lankan. As in India and Pakistan, cricket is undoubtedly king in the Sri Lankan sporting pantheon. Kids play it on any patch of spare ground, improvising balls, bats and wickets out of rolled-up bits of cloth and discarded sticks, whilst the country virtually grinds to a halt during international matches, with excitable crowds clustered around every available radio or television set.

Although the national team is a relative newcomer to international cricket – they were only accorded full Test status in 1982 – they've more than held their own since then. It's in the one-day game, however, that Sri Lanka has really taken the world by storm, capped by their triumph in the 1996 World Cup, when their fearsomely talented batting line-up – led by elegant left-hander Aravinda da Silva and the explosive Sanath Jayasuriya – blasted their way to the title (a feat they almost repeated during the 2007 World Cup, when they reached the final, only to lose to Australia in controversial circumstances).

Not surprisingly, the success of the Sri Lankan team has proved an important source of national pride and cohesion. Although Sinhalese players have traditionally dominated the squad, the Tamil population has provided present-day Sri Lanka's finest player, Muttiah Muralitharan (or Muralidaran, as it's sometimes transliterated, although the nickname "Murali" usually suffices for linguistically challenged commentators the world over). One of the world's most lethal spin bowlers, Muralitharan became the leading wicket taker in the history of Test cricket in December 2007, and currently holds the world record with an astonishing 766 wickets, a feat which is unlikely to be broken for many years. Other star players include world-class batsmen Mahela Jayawardene and Kumar Sangakkara, both of whom currently average over fifty in test matches, and new spin sensation Ajantha Mendis.

If you get the chance, it's well worth taking in a cricket match – the vociferous crowds and carnival atmosphere are a world away from the rather staid ambience of most English cricket grounds. The island's principal Test-match venues are the Sinhalese Sports Club in Colombo (see p.118), the Asigiriya Stadium in Kandy and the cricket ground in Galle. One-day internationals are mainly held at the Premadasa Stadium in Colombo, the Asigiriya Stadium in Kandy and the cricket stadium in Dambulla. Tickets for matches are available from the relevant venues. Note also that many of the tour operators listed on p.30, Red Dot Tours in particular, offer cricketing tours to Sri Lanka. For more on Sri Lankan cricket, check out Ⓦwww.srilankacricket.lk.

Diving and snorkelling

Sri Lanka isn't usually thought of as one of Asia's premier diving destinations, and although you probably wouldn't come here specifically to dive, there are enough underwater attractions to make a couple of days' diving a worthwhile part of a visit. Sri Lanka is also a good and cheap place to learn to dive, with schools in Bentota, Beruwala, Hikkaduwa, Unawatuna, Weligama and Uppaveli – see the relevant Guide accounts for details.

Unfortunately, however, Sri Lanka's marine environment, and a significant proportion of its coral, has been adversely affected by a host of factors: dynamite fishing; the collection of coral for souvenirs and limestone production; damage caused to reefs by boats; and the El Niño effect of 1998 – although the tsunami itself caused mercifully little underwater destruction. The west coast has relatively little living coral but, in compensation, boasts plenty of marine life, including big fish such as barracuda, whale shark, tuna and seer plus various smaller pelagic species such as angel, lion, Koran, scorpion, parrot and butterfly fish (to name just a few). In addition, the diving here is three-dimensional and technically challenging, with deep dives, swim-through cave complexes, drop-offs and various wreck dives. Popular targets include the wreck of an old steam-driven oil tanker from 1860s known as the *Conch*, near Hikkaduwa, which is a favourite amongst less experienced divers. The most impressive wreck currently diveable in Sri Lanka lies 9km offshore from Colombo, and comprises the remains of a car ferry, sunk by the Japanese in World War II and lying at a depth of around 40m, with cars and trucks scattered all over the seabed around.

By contrast, the east coast offers better coral but a relative paucity of marine life. Diving here is more two-dimensional, with shallow, flat coral beds. No wrecks have yet been opened up for divers along the east coast, and although there are some excellent possibilities near Batticaloa (including the wreck of the *Hermes*, a 270m-long aircraft carrier sunk during World War II and lying at a depth of 60m), ongoing unrest in the east means that these are likely to remain off limits for the foreseeable future.

The diving season on the west coast runs roughly from November to April, and on the east coast from May to October; pretty much all the island's diving schools shut up out of season, although if you're really keen and don't mind diving in rough seas with poor visibility you might be able to find someone willing to take you out off-season. Diving packages and courses are good value compared to most other places in the world. A three-day Open-Water PADI course goes for around US$380, a PADI Advanced Open-Water course for around US$260 and single dives for US$32.

There's not a lot of really good snorkelling around Sri Lanka: little coral survives close to the shore, although this lack is compensated by the abundant shoals of tropical fish which frequent the coast. The island's better snorkelling spots include the beach at Polhena and, if you don't mind the boats whizzing around your ears, the Coral Sanctuary at Hikkaduwa.

Surfing

Many of the waves which crash against the Sri Lankan coast have travelled all the way from Antarctica, and not surprisingly there are several excellent surfing spots. The outstanding destination is Arugam Bay on the east coast, the one place in Sri Lanka with an international reputation amongst surfheads. The low-key south coast village of Midigama is another good spot, while Hikkaduwa is also popular. Boards are available to rent at all three places. Various places in Arugam Bay and Hikkaduwa arrange surfing trips around the coast, sometimes combined with visits to other attractions. The surfing season runs from April to October at Arugam Bay, and from November to April at Midigama and Hikkaduwa.

Whitewater rafting and other watersports

The island's premier spot for whitewater rafting is around Kitulgala, where the Kelani Ganga river comes tumbling out of the hill country, creating boulder-strewn grade 3–4 rapids. You can either arrange trips locally or plan something in advance – reputable operators include Adventure Asia (Ⓦwww.ad-asia.com), who also arrange kayaking trips, while Jetwing Eco Holidays (Ⓦwww.jetwingeco.com) also arrange comprehensive fourteen-day trips combining whitewater rafting with kayaking and canoeing.

Sri Lanka's watersports capital is **Bentota**, whose lagoon provides the perfect venue for all sorts of activities, including jet-skiing, windsurfing, speed-boating, waterskiing, inner-tubing and banana-boating. You can also arrange watersports in **Negombo** through the *Jetwing Beach* hotel and various other ad hoc operators. Kitesurfing (in **Kalpitiya**) and wakeboarding (in **Hikkaduwa**) have also both begun to take off over the past couple of years.

Trekking

Sri Lanka's huge trekking potential remains largely unexploited. The hill country, in particular, offers the perfect hiking terrain – spectacular scenery, marvellous views and a pleasantly temperate climate – while trekking through the wildlife-rich lowland jungles can also be a deeply rewarding experience. A few of the tour operators listed on pp.30–32 offer walking tours. Alternatively, contact Sumane Bandara Illangantilake (see p.254), who can arrange walking tours pretty much anywhere in the island, including spectacular treks through the Knuckles range; or Neil Rajanayake ("Raja") at Nuwara Eliya (see p.275), who leads walks throughout the southern hill country. In addition, shorter walks can be made from all the eco-lodges and eco-oriented hotels listed on p.40, most of which have resident guides to lead guests on walks.

Cycling

So long as you avoid the hazardous main highways (see p.37 for more on these), cycling around Sri Lanka can be a real pleasure, and a welcome change from sitting in a stuffy car or braving the anarchic bus system. The island's modest dimensions and scenic diversity make it great for cycling, especially the hill country, with its cooler climate, relative lack of traffic and exhilarating switchback roads. Although the main highways are busy, smelly and dangerous, Sri Lanka has myriad byways on which vehicles are relatively infrequent. A number of the operators listed on pp.30–32 offer cycling or mountain-biking tours, usually including a mixture of on- and off-roading and with a backup vehicle in support. Good options include Jetwing Eco Holidays (see p.32) and Adventure Asia (Ⓦwww.ad-asia.com).

Eco-tourism

Sri Lanka's vast eco-tourism potential is slowly being tapped into by local companies who are belatedly beginning to realize the economic and environmental benefits of encouraging tourists to explore the island's remarkable natural biodiversity, rather than simply building yet another beach hotel. The island's best eco-lodges and eco-oriented hotels are listed on p.40; the best general eco-tourism tour operator is Jetwing Eco Holidays (Ⓣ011-238 1201, Ⓦwww.jetwingeco.com).

Birdwatching is well established, and even if you've never previously looked at a feathered creature in your life, the island's outstanding range of colourful birdlife can prove surprisingly fascinating. A number of companies run specialist tours (see pp.30–32), while bird-spotting usually forms a significant part of trips to the island's national parks – although you'll see birds pretty much everywhere you go, even in the middle of Colombo. See p.452 for more on the island's avifauna.

Elephants can be seen in virtually every national park in the country, at the famous Pinnewala Elephant Orphanage and in temples and at work on roads around the country. For **leopards**, the place to head for is Yala National Park, while **whale-watching** trips start from Mirissa, just down the coast. Sri Lanka is also an important nesting site for **sea turtles**; turtle watches are run nightly at the villages of Kosgoda and Rekawa.

Yoga and meditation

Yoga isn't nearly as established in Sri Lanka as in India, although many of the island's numerous Ayurvedic centres now offer classes as part of their treatment plans, and it's sometimes possible to enrol for them without taking an Ayurveda course. Otherwise, your options are pretty limited. Serious students of yoga might consider signing up for a stay at Ulpotha (Ⓦwww.ulpotha.com), a wonderful rural retreat in the Cultural Triangle near Embogama (not far from the Sasseruwa and Aukana Buddhas), attracting leading international yoga teachers; prices start at around US$955 per person per week inclusive of accommodation, meals and tuition.

Meditation courses are mainly concentrated around Kandy – see p.238 for further details.

Other activities

Adventure Asia (Ⓦwww.ad-asia.com) offer spectacular one-hour **balloon trips** from October to April (weather permitting) around Kandalama, Dambulla, Sigiriya and Galle for US$225.

Horse-riding day-trips and longer tours can be arranged through Sri Lanka Horse Safaris (Ⓦwww.horsesafarissrilanka.com) at various locations around the island, including Bentota, Yala, Kandy, Ella, Dambulla and Sigiriya. Prices are around US$200 per person per day.

Sri Lanka has three gorgeous **golf courses**, at Colombo (see p.118), Kandy (p.254) and Nuwara Eliya (p.274); a number of the operators listed on pp.30–32 offer special golfing tours.

National parks and reserves

Nature conservation has a long and illustrious history in Sri Lanka – the island's first wildlife reserve is said to have been established by King Devanampiya Tissa in the third century BC, while many of the national parks and reserves that make up today's well-developed network date back to colonial times and earlier. Administered by the Department of Wildlife Conservation (Ⓦwww.dwlc.lk), these protected areas cover over thirteen percent of the island's land area and encompass a wide variety of terrains, from the high-altitude grasslands of Horton Plains National Park to the coastal wetlands of Bundala. Almost all harbour a rich selection of wildlife and birds, and several are also of outstanding scenic beauty. The only fly in the ointment is the absurdly discriminatory entrance fees imposed on foreign tourists.

Sri Lanka has twenty **national parks**, of which the most touristed are Yala, Uda Walawe, Horton Plains, Bundala, Minneriya and Kaudulla. A number of parks lie in areas affected by the civil war, and several were closed for long periods during the fighting, including Maduru Oya, Gal Oya (both reopened) and Yala East (currently closed), Lahugala, which remains technically closed (although a lot of people visit it unofficially) and Wilpattu (which is currently closed).

There are numerous other protected areas dotted across the island which are run under government supervision. These are categorized variously as **nature reserves**, **strict nature reserves** (entry prohibited) and **sanctuaries**. In general these places possess important botanical significance but lack the wildlife found in the national parks, as at (to name just one example) the unique, World Heritage-listed Sinharaja Forest Reserve, Sri Lanka's last undisturbed pocket of tropical rainforest.

Visiting national parks

All national parks are open daily from 6.30am to 6.30pm. Other than in Horton Plains, where you're allowed to walk, you'll have to hire a jeep to take you around. There are usually jeeps (plus drivers) for hire at park entrances, although it's generally easier to hire one at the place you're staying to take you to and from the park, as well as driving you around it. Count on around US$30–40 for half a day's jeep (and driver) hire, or US$60–70 for a full day.

All vehicles are allocated an obligatory "tracker", who rides with you and acts as a

guide. Some are very good, but standards do vary considerably and unfortunately many trackers speak only rudimentary English, which can seriously impair their effectiveness as a guide – it's entirely a matter of chance whether you get a good tracker or one who only speaks three words of English, has a bad hangover and wouldn't recognize an elephant at three paces. One way of insuring yourself against the chance of getting a dud tracker is to go with a good **driver** – the best are expert wildlife trackers and spotters in their own right, and also carry binoculars and wildlife identification books or cards. Note that except at designated spots, you're supposed to stay in your vehicle at all times; in Yala, you're also obliged to keep the hood on your jeep up.

The basic **entrance charge** per person ranges from between US$10 at the less popular parks up to US$15–16 at places like Yala and Uda Walawe (locals, by contrast, pay entrance fees of around US$0.25). This basic charge is significantly inflated by the various **additional charges** which are levied, including a "service charge" (US$8 per vehicle), which covers the services of your tracker (the fact that you still have to pay this at Horton Plains, even though no tracker is supplied, is typical of the rip-off ethos which permeates the Wildlife and Conservation Department); a "vehicle charge" (US$2.50 per vehicle); plus tax on everything at fifteen percent (the exact entrance cost per person thus becomes slightly cheaper the more people you share a vehicle with). Children aged 6–12 pay half price; under 6s get in free. The bottom line is that, once you've factored in the cost of transport as well, you're looking at something like US$75–100 for two people for a half-day visit to a national park.

It's also possible **to stay** in many national parks, most of which are equipped with simple but adequate bungalows for visitors. Unfortunately these are difficult to book – they have to be reserved in person at the Department of Wildlife Conservation, which is inconveniently located on the outskirts of Colombo at 382 New Kandy Rd, Malabe (Ⓣ011-256 0380, Ⓦwww.dwlc.lk) – the best ones tend to get snapped up very quickly. The ludicrous charges levied on foreigners are a further disincentive. As well as paying the basic bungalow fee (around US$25–30 per person), you'll have to pay two days' park entrance fees, plus a ridiculous raft of other massively inflated add-ons (including "service charge" and "linen charge"), and tax on everything at fifteen percent. It typically costs around US$150 per night for two people to stay in a park bungalow – significantly more expensive than the price of a room in one of Colombo's cheaper five-star hotels – and this is before you've even begun to cover your transport costs to, from and around the park.

You can also **camp** in any of the national parks: again you'll have to pay two days' entrance charges, plus around US$15 in camping fees (plus, of course, your transport costs). You'll also have to pre-book a camping space through the Department of Wildlife Conservation in Colombo. Alternatively, Eco Team and Kulu Safari (see p.32) run (expensive) camping trips to various national parks.

Cultural values and etiquette

Sri Lanka is the most Westernized country in South Asia – superficially at least – and this, combined with the widespread use of English and the huge tourist industry, can often lure visitors into mistaking the island for something more familiar than it actually is. Scratch the surface, however, and examples of cultural difference can be found everywhere.

Behaving yourself

They are all very rich, and for a thing that costs one shilling they willingly give five. Also they are never quiet, going here and there very quickly, and doing nothing. Very many are afraid of them, for suddenly they grow very angry, their faces become red, and they strike any one who is near with the closed hand.

From *The Village in the Jungle*, by Leonard Woolf

Sri Lankans place great emphasis on politeness and manners, as exemplified by the fabulously courteous staff at top-end hotels – raising your voice in a dispute is usually counterproductive and makes you look foolish and ill-bred.

Sri Lankans are very proud of their country – "Sri Lanka good?" is one of the questions most commonly asked of visitors – and they tend to take a simple and unquestioning pride in their island, its national achievements and (especially) their cricket team. Criticisms of Sri Lanka are not usually appreciated; remember that because something about the country seems archaic, hopelessly bureaucratic or just plain stupid to you, it doesn't mean that Sri Lankans will agree – or appreciate hearing your views.

A few Western concepts have yet to make their way to the island. Nudity and toplessness are not permitted on any Sri Lankan beaches. Overt physical displays of affection in public are also frowned upon – Sri Lankan couples hide behind enormous umbrellas in the quiet corners of parks and botanical gardens. You should eat and shake hands with people using your right hand. For more on money and ethical bargaining, see p.71.

Temple etiquette

All visitors to Buddhist and Hindu temples should be appropriately dressed. In **Buddhist temples** this means taking off shoes and headgear and covering your shoulders and legs. Beachwear is not appropriate and can cause offence. In large temples, the exact point at which you should take off shoes and hats is sometimes ambiguous; if in doubt, follow the locals. Finally, note that walking barefoot around temples can sometimes be more of a challenge that you might imagine when the tropical sun has heated the stone underfoot to oven-like temperatures. Wimps wear socks.

Never have yourself photographed posing with a Buddha image (i.e. with your back to the image). Two traditional Buddhist observances are only loosely followed in Sri Lanka: the rule about not pointing your feet at a Buddha image is not as widely followed as in, say, Thailand, though you occasionally see people sitting in front of Buddhas with their legs neatly tucked under them. Equally, the traditional Buddhist rule that you should only walk around dagobas in a clockwise direction is not widely observed.

The same shoe and dress rules apply in **Hindu temples** (with a couple of twists). In some, non-Hindus aren't permitted to enter the inner shrine; in others, men are required to take off their shirt before entering, and women are sometimes barred entirely. In some temples you will be shown around by one of the resident monks and expected to make a donation. At other places, unofficial "guides" will sometimes materialize and insist on showing you round – for a consideration. Try not to feel pressured into accepting the services of unofficial guides unless you want them.

Begging, bon-bons and schoolpens

Whether or not you decide to give to beggars is of course a personal decision, though there's nothing wrong with handing out a few coins to the obviously old and infirm, who often congregate outside temples, churches and mosques. What is important, however, is that you do not contribute to a cycle of excessive dependence or create unrealistic expectations of foreign beneficence. For this reason, be sparing in the amounts you distribute (it's always better to give small amounts to lots of people rather than a big sum to a single unfortunate who catches your fancy) and never give handouts to children. In addition, avoid giving to beggars who specifically target tourists.

What is unfortunately widespread is a kind of pseudo-begging practised by perfectly well-to-do schoolchildren (and sometimes teenagers and even adults). This generally takes the form of requests for bon-bons (sweets), schoolpens or money (often in the form of "one foreign coin?"). Sadly, this behaviour is the result of the misguided munificence of previous visitors, who have handed out all of the above in the mistaken belief that they are helping the local population, but who have instead created a culture of begging that both demeans Sri Lankans themselves and creates hassles for all the visitors who follow in their wake. If you really want to help local communities, make your donation to a local school or contribute to a recognized charitable agency working in the area.

"Where are you going?"

Western concepts of privacy and solitude are little understood or valued in Sri Lanka, whose culture is based on extended family groupings and closely knit village societies in which everyone knows everyone else's business. Natural curiosity usually expresses itself in the form of endless repeated questions, most often "Where are you going?", closely followed by "What is your country?" and "What is your name?". These may drive you crazy if you're spending a long time in Sri Lanka, but it's important to stay polite and remember how potentially negative an impact any rudeness or impatience on your part will have on perceptions of foreigners, and on the treatment of those who follow in your wake. A smile (even through gritted teeth) and a short answer ("Just walking. England. John.") should suffice. If you really can't bear it any more, a little surreal humour usually helps relieve the tension ("To Australia. Mars. Lord Mountbatten.") without offending local sensibilities – Sri Lankans usually take great pleasure in being given first-hand proof of the generally recognized fact that all foreigners are completely mad.

Shopping

Sri Lankan craftsmanship has a long and vibrant history. A visit to any museum will turn up objects testifying to the skill of the island's earlier artisans, who have for centuries been producing exquisitely manufactured objects in a wide variety of media, ranging from lacework and ola-leaf manuscripts to carvings in ivory and wood and elaborate metalwork and batiks.

Unfortunately, despite these fine traditions, much modern Sri Lankan craftsmanship has largely degenerated into the mindless mass production of a few stereotypical items, and shopping is generally a disappointment compared to nearby countries such as India or Thailand. The decline in creativity is exemplified by the nationwide chain of government-run **Laksala** shops, whose outlets are stuffed to the gills with a predictable assortment of clumsily painted wooden elephants, kolam masks, ugly batiks and other tourist tat. It's not all bad news, however, and there are still a few worthwhile exceptions, especially in **Colombo**, which is also the best place to buy everything else Sri Lanka has to offer, from books to tea and discount clothing.

All larger shops have fixed, marked **prices**, although if you're making a major purchase or buying several items, a polite request for a "special price" or "small discount" might knock a few rupees off, especially for gems or jewellery. The smaller and more informal the outlet, the more scope for bargaining there's likely to be – if you're, say, buying a sarong from an itinerant hawker on the beach, you can haggle to your heart's content.

Finally, there are a couple of things you shouldn't buy. Remember that buying **coral** or **shells** (or any other marine product) contributes directly to the destruction of the island's fragile ocean environment; it's also illegal, and you're likely to end up paying a heavy fine if you try to take coral out of the country. Note that it's also illegal to export **antiques** (classified as anything over fifty years old) without a licence (see p.73).

The superb **website**, ⓦwww.craftrevival.org (follow the Sri Lanka link under "Crafts"), has copious information on all the island's traditional arts and crafts.

Handicrafts

The most characteristic – and clichéd – Sri Lankan souvenirs are brightly painted **masks**, originally designed to be worn during kolam dances or exorcism ceremonies (see p.151) and now found for sale wherever there are tourists (though the sheer quantity churned out means that many are of indifferent quality and sloppily painted). Masks vary in size from the tiny to the huge; the vast majority depict either the pop-eyed Gara Yaka or the bird demon Gurulu Raksha, though if you hunt around you may find other designs. Some masks are artificially but attractively aged to resemble antiques – a lot easier on the eye than the lurid colours in which most are painted. The centre of mask production is at Ambalangoda, where there are a number of large shops selling a big range of designs, some of heirloom quality.

Second in popularity are **elephant carvings**. These range from small wooden creatures painted with bright polka-dot patterns to the elegant stone carvings sold at places like *The Gallery Café* and Paradise Road in Colombo. **Batiks** (an art introduced by the Dutch from Indonesia) are also widespread. Designs are often stereotypical (the Sigiriya Damsels and naff beach scenes are ubiquitous), though a few places produce more unusual and interesting work. More entertaining are the **puzzle boxes** offered for sale around Sigiriya (and sometimes elsewhere in the Cultural Triangle) – delicately carved little wooden boxes which can only be opened by a series of Rubik-cube-like manoeuvres. Also fun are the **wooden models** of tuktuks and other vehicles – wonderful souvenirs or children's toys. They're most commonly found in Negombo, but are also increasingly available in Colombo and elsewhere on the island.

A number of other traditional crafts struggle on with a little help from the tourist trade. **Metalwork** has long been produced in the Kandy area, and intricately embossed metal objects such as dishes, trays, candlesticks and other objects can be found in all the island's handicraft emporia, though they're rather fussy for most foreign tastes. **Leatherwork** can also be good, and you'll find a range of hats, bags, boots and footrests (the shops at Pinnewala Elephant Orphanage have a particularly good selection). **Lacquerware**, a speciality of the Matale area, can also sometimes be found, along with Kandyan-style **drums** and, occasionally, **carrom boards** (see p.180).

Finally, if you've a day in Colombo, it's well worth seeking out the **modern handicrafts** found at a few Colombo boutiques, such as Paradise Road, *The Gallery Café* or, especially, Barefoot, whose range of vibrantly coloured fabrics have become synonymous with modern Sri Lankan style.

Religious items

Wood or stone **Buddha carvings** of varying standards are common, while Kandyan Antiques in Colombo has a wide and interesting range of real and fake antiques of Buddhist and Hindu deities. For something a bit more unusual, the brightly coloured **posters** or strip-pictures of Buddhist and Hindu deities which adorn tuktuks and buses across the island are sold by pavement hawkers and stationers' shops across the island and make a cheap and characterful souvenir, while a visit to Kataragama or a trawl along St Anthony's Mawatha in Colombo (see p.101) will uncover an entertaining assortment of other **religious kitsch**, from bleeding Catholic saints to illuminated Ganesh clocks.

Tea and spices

Most top-quality **Ceylon tea** is exported, although there's still plenty on sale which is likely to satisfy all but the most dedicated tea-fancier. The main local brand is the reputable Dilmah (ⓦwww.dilmahtea.com), though look out too for the Tea Tang range (ⓦwww.teatang.com), comprising a first-rate selection of speciality teas, ranging from standard Sri Lankan blends through to some rare connoisseur varieties, all retailed in cute old-fashioned metal tins. Alternatively, for a real taste of Sri Lanka, look for unblended ("single estate") high-grown teas – a far cry from the heavily blended and homogenized teabags which pass muster in Europe and the US. You'll also find a wide range of flavoured teas made with a huge range of ingredients, including standard offerings like lemon, orange, mint and vanilla, as well as the more outlandish banana, rum, kiwi fruit or pineapple.

Teas can be bought at outlets of the specialist Mlesna chain, which has branches in Colombo, Kandy and at the airport, and you'll also find good selections in Cargills supermarkets islandwide. In addition, a few factories around the hill country sell their tea directly to the public.

Sri Lanka's **spice gardens**, mostly concentrated around Kandy and Matale, pull in loads of visitors on organized tours and sell packets of spices, often at outrageously inflated prices. You'll get much better deals in local shops and markets.

Gems and jewellery

Sri Lanka has been famous for its **precious stones** since antiquity, and gems and jewellery remain important to the national economy even today. This is nowhere more obvious than at the gem-mining centre of **Ratnapura**, where locally excavated uncut gems are traded daily on the streets. All foreign visitors to the town will be offered stones to buy, but unless you're an expert gemologist there's a strong chance that you'll end up with an expensive piece of coloured glass. Another variant on this scam is that you will be persuaded to buy gems at a special "cheap" price, with assurances that you will be able to resell them back home for several times the price you paid for them. Again, unless you're an expert, steer well clear of these deals.

Ratnapura apart, you'll find **gem and jewellery shops** all over the island – the major concentrations are in Negombo, Galle and Colombo. These include large chains, such as Zam Gems or Sifani, and smaller local outfits. If you are going to buy, it's worth doing some homework before you arrive so you can compare prices with those back home. You can get gems tested for authenticity in Colombo. See p.115 for details.

For silver and, especially, **gold** jewellery, try Sea Street in Colombo's Pettah district, which is lined with shops. These see few tourists, so prices are reasonable, although the flouncy designs on offer aren't to everyone's taste.

Clothes and books

Sri Lanka is a bit of a disappointment when it comes to **clothes**, and doesn't boast the gorgeous fabrics and nimble-fingered tailors of, say, India and Thailand. Having said that, the island is a major garment-manufacturing centre for overseas companies, and there are lots of good-quality Western-style clothes knocking around at bargain prices. In Colombo, places to try include the fancy Odel department store (see p.116) or the more downmarket House of Fashions (p.116) and Cotton Collection (p.116). Colourful but flimsy beachwear is flogged by shops and hawkers at all the major west-coast resorts – it's cheap and cheerful, but don't expect it to last much longer than your holiday. Most Sri Lankan women now dress Western-style in rather boring skirts and blouses, but you can still find a few shops in

Colombo and elsewhere selling beautiful saris and shalwar kameez (pyjama suits) – these shops are usually easily spotted via their enormous picture windows stuffed with colourfully costumed mannequins.

Books are relatively cheap: new paperbacks are about two-thirds of European and North American prices, and there are also lots of colourful coffee-table books and weird and wonderful works on Sri Lankan history, culture and religion that you won't find outside the island. The Vijitha Yapa bookshop has branches islandwide, and there are a number of other good bookshops in Colombo.

Travelling with children

Sri Lankans love children, and travelling with kids more or less guarantees you a warm welcome wherever you go. Locals will always do whatever they can to help or entertain – there's certainly no need to worry about disapproving stares if your baby starts crying or your toddler starts monkeying around a bit, even in quite posh establishments.

Having said that, travelling with **babies** may prove stressful. Powdered milk is fairly widely available, but disposable nappies and baby food are rare, while things like babysitting services, nursery day-care, changing facilities, high chairs and microwaves for sterilizing bottles are virtually unheard of; car seats will also probably have to be brought from home. Breast-feeding in public, however discreet, is also not something that Sri Lankan women usually do, while prams are virtually useless, since there are no decent pavements to push them on – the common sight of mothers burdened with a tiny baby on one arm and a small child in the other scrambling on and off packed buses or fighting their way across busy roads is one of Sri Lanka's more stomach-churning sights. The heat, and the associated dangers of dehydration, are another concern, not to mention the risks of mosquito-borne diseases such as malaria and dengue fever (for more on which, see p.64).

Older children, however, are likely to get a lot out of a visit to the island. Sri Lanka's beaches are likely to provide the main attraction, with endless swathes of golden sand to muck around on and warm waters to splash about in – though you should always check local swimming conditions carefully and guard carefully against the very real possibility of sunburn and dehydration. Beaches apart, the outstanding kids' attraction is the Elephant Orphanage at Pinnewala, a guaranteed child-pleaser, especially for its cute babies – this is one of the few places in the world where children can see elephants which are even smaller than themselves. There are further elephant-spotting opportunities around Kandy, while a visit to any of the national parks is also likely to stimulate budding zoologists; Yala, where there's a good chance of sighting crocodiles, peacocks, flamingoes and other wacky wildlife, is a particularly good choice. Activity sports, such as banana boating or kayaking at Bentota, may also appeal, while the island's varied forms of transport – whether a tuktuk ride, a train trip through the hill country or a boat cruise along one of the island's rivers or lagoons – should also keep little ones entertained. Energetic kids with a head for heights might also enjoy the challenge of clambering up Sigiriya and its rickety iron staircases. And if you've exhausted all the preceding possibilities, you can always go shopping: there are plenty of fun handicrafts to be had, with gruesome masks, painted elephants and wooden toys aplenty – if you're in Colombo, don't leave without bagging a colourful cuddly stuffed-toy animal from the Barefoot store.

Crime, scams and personal safety

The good news is that Sri Lanka is a remarkably safe place to travel in, and violent crime against foreigners is virtually unheard of – this is still a country where, despite 25 years of brutal civil war, the theft of two bicycles is considered a crime wave. The only bad news is that scams and aggressive touting are widespread in a few places.

Petty theft is less common than in many other parts of Asia (and rarer than in most European and American cities), though you should still take sensible care of your belongings. Pickpockets sometimes work in crowded areas, while thefts from hotel rooms are occasionally reported. Many hotels and guesthouses ask guests to deposit valuables in their safe, and it's sensible to do so when you can. **Muggings** are very rare, though single travellers (especially women) should avoid dark beaches late at night – Negombo and Hikkaduwa have particularly bad reputations. In addition, make sure you keep a separate record of traveller's cheques and credit card numbers (along with the phone numbers needed in case of their loss) plus your passport details; it's worth taking a photocopy of the pages from your passport that contain your personal details.

If you do have anything stolen, you'll need to report it to the **police** – there's little chance that they will be able to recover it for you, but you'll need a report for your insurance claim. Given the fact that you might not find any English-speaking policemen on duty, you might try to get someone from your guesthouse to come along as an interpreter. The process of reporting a crime is usually a laborious affair, with much checking of papers and filling in of forms. Unfortunately, although tourist police offices have been set up in a few parts of the island, they're not much cop.

Dangers

Up until May 2009, the ongoing civil war meant that the whole of **northern Sri Lanka** (meaning anywhere north of Vavuniya) was out of bounds. This is likely to change soon, though potential visitors should still check the latest security situation in the north carefully before visiting. **Eastern Sri Lanka**, by contrast, is now experiencing relative calm, following the expulsion of the LTTE in 2007, though it still pays to check the latest news and consult local information if you plan to visit the region. The biggest source of danger to foreign visitors is currently in **Colombo**, which has recently experienced a spate of bomb attacks, although virtually all these have occurred at locations well off the tourist path, and in any case the situation is likely to have changed by the time you read this. Check the news websites listed on pp.46–47 for latest information. All **other parts of the country** remain unaffected by the civil war, although the possibility of one-off bomb or mine attacks against civilian targets (usually meaning buses) cannot, unfortunately, be ruled out entirely. Having said which, the chances of the average

Travel advisories

For current information on the security situation in Sri Lanka, visit one of the sites listed below.

Australian Department of Foreign Affairs Ⓦ www.dfat.gov.au.

British Foreign & Commonwealth Office Ⓦ www.fco.gov.uk.

New Zealand Ministry of Foreign Affairs Ⓦ www.mfat.govt.nz.

US State Department Ⓦ www.travel.state.gov.

tourist being caught up in an LTTE attack remain extremely small – after 25 years of fighting, the fact is that no foreign tourist has yet been killed as a result of LTTE action. The bottom line is that you're far more likely to drown or be hit by a bus whilst in Sri Lanka, and statistically speaking the country as a whole remains significantly safer for foreign tourists than the London Underground or New York City.

A far more real but altogether more prosaic danger in Sri Lanka is **traffic**. The island has the dubious distinction of being one of the world's top ten offenders when it comes to traffic-related fatalities, and as a pedestrian you're at the very bottom of the food chain in the dog-eat-dog world of Sri Lankan road use. Exercise extreme caution, and treat buses with particular respect.

Drowning is the second-most common cause of death amongst tourists in Sri Lanka (after road accidents). Currents can be strong and beaches may shelve off into deep waters with unexpected steepness – and there are no lifeguards to come and pull you out if you get into trouble. Always ask local advice before venturing in the water anywhere that is obviously not a recognized swimming spot. Conditions can vary radically even within a few hundred metres, so don't assume that because lots of people are swimming at one end of the beach, the other, deserted, end will be safe. The only warning signs of dangerous swimming conditions are the red flags posted on the beaches outside major resort hotels. Sensible precautions include always keeping within your depth and making sure that someone on the shore knows that you're in the water. Never swim under the influence of alcohol – newspaper stories of locals washed out to sea after too many bottles of arrack are an almost weekly occurrence.

Scams and hassles

Sri Lanka has an unfortunate but well-deserved reputation for its **hustlers** and **con artists**, who range from simple gem shop and guesthouse touts to virtuoso scam merchants who run well-oiled schemes to entrap the unwary. At its simplest, you'll encounter low-level hassle from people who

Common scams

Elephant festival in Colombo The capital's Galle Face Green is a well-known hangout for con artists – watch out for their classic chat-up line, "Sri Lanka very hot!". Having engaged you in conversation they will tell you how fortunate you are because there is a big elephant festival happening that very day (unless you've coincided with the Navam Perahera in February – see p.104 – they are lying). They will then whisk you off to see the "festival" (it's usually the temple elephant at the Gangaramaya temple; see p.104) before setting you up for a ludicrously inflated tuktuk fare.

Taking you for a ride Many scams involve gaining your trust, then getting you into a tuktuk to visit some temple/"elephant festival"/handicraft shop or other attraction. Having driven you around for a while, you will be dumped in some remote and seedy part of town at which point the tuktuk driver will demand a wildly inflated fare for the ride. Alternatively, someone you meet on the train tells you there will be no tuktuks at your destination, and rings ahead for one, with the same end result. *Never* get into a tuktuk without agreeing a fare beforehand.

Free tea You are offered free tea by someone claiming to own or work on a plantation, on condition you pay a "small sum" to cover the export duty or postage. Needless to say, the tea never arrives.

Fake charity collectors Often elderly and respectable-looking gents with clipboards and official-looking letters; especially common around the lake in Kandy, but also in Colombo and on beaches everywhere. Real Sri Lankan charities do not collect on the streets.

Foreign coins You are approached by a respectable-looking gent who claims to be collecting foreign coins for his children or local school. You hand over some spare want you to visit their shop, stay in their guesthouse or be your guide (or, alternatively, who want to take you to a shop or guesthouse where they'll receive commission). Tuktuk drivers are the main source of this sort of pressure, although it can come from pretty much anyone with even a few words of English.

The island's **con artists** are a completely different kettle of fish – a breed of often plausible and cunning folk who live by their (often considerable) wits; they're mainly (but not exclusively) found in Colombo, Kandy and Galle. Convincing you of their trustworthiness is an important part of any scam, and con artists will often attempt to boost their own credentials by claiming to be a member of a professional elite (a SriLankan Airlines pilot; a former international cricketer). A standard ploy in Colombo is for con artists to claim to be visiting from the Maldives, thereby implying that they too are visitors and thus to be trusted. Another common introductory ploy is for a con artist to claim to be a cook (or other backroom member of staff) at your hotel, hoping thereby to gain your confidence. Sometimes the lengths to which con artists will go to wheedle themselves into your confidence are uncanny – in Kandy, for instance, visitors walking around the lake are sometimes approached by a respectable-looking gentleman who points out splashes in the lake, explaining that they are caused by water snakes (whereas, in fact, they are caused by a hidden accomplice chucking stones into the lake).

You shouldn't get too paranoid about these characters, but you should be aware that they exist and know how they operate. If you know the basic signs, they're fairly easily spotted; if you don't, you risk being taken for a (potentially expensive) ride. Do keep a sense of perspective, however; it's important not to stop talking to people because you're afraid they're going to rip you off. The vast majority of Sri Lankans that approach you will be perfectly honest, and simply keen to have a chat (or at least find out which country you are from – see p.57). Look out for the classic scams detailed in the box and, if you suspect that you are being set up, simply withdraw politely but firmly from the situation.

currency. Your coins are then passed on to a second person, who approaches you a few minutes later, claiming to have been given the coins some time previously as a tip or whatever, and asking you to change them back into rupees for them, since they are otherwise worthless.

Having a drink You fall into conversation with a friendly local who asks if you would like to have a drink with him. Having taken you to some obscure drinking den, he claims to have forgotten his wallet, leaving you to pay the (usually vastly inflated) bill. Once you've gone, he will return to collect his share of your money from the bar staff.

The card trick Someone asks you where you plan to stay. When you tell them, they produce a business card (purloined) from the relevant establishment and claim that they work there/are related to the owner. They then tell you that the said guesthouse or hotel is closed/full/undergoing renovations, then propose you come with them to their own guesthouse, or one where they earn commission.

Milk powder A plausibly ragged-looking local engages you in conversation and tells you about the shocking poverty he lives in. He insists, however, that he doesn't want any money for himself, but desperately needs a tin of milk powder so that he can at least feed his hungry baby. You are then led to a chemist, where a (surprisingly expensive) tin of milk powder is produced. Once you've left, he'll be back to return the powder and split the proceeds.

Gems Any transaction involving the purchase of gems is potentially risky except in the most reputable outlets. Also see Shopping, p.59.

Health

Sri Lanka is less challenging from a health point of view than many other tropical countries: standards of hygiene are reasonable, medical care is of a decent standard and in significant parts of the island you don't even have to worry about malaria. Nevertheless, the island does play host to the usual gamut of tropical diseases, and it's important to make sure you protect yourself against serious illness. You should start planning the health aspect of your trip well in advance of departure, especially if you're having vaccines for things like rabies or Japanese encephalitis, which need to be administered over the course of a month. Vaccinations and medical advice are available from your doctor or – more conveniently but expensively – a specialist travel clinic. It's also crucial to have adequate medical insurance.

Before travelling you should ensure that you're up to date with the following standard **vaccinations**: diphtheria, tetanus, hepatitis A and polio. Other jabs you might consider are tuberculosis, meningitis and typhoid. Most importantly, you should have adequate protection against **malaria**, assuming you're visiting an affected area (see p.66).

The best way to avoid falling ill is to look after yourself. Eat properly, make sure you get enough sleep and don't try to cram too much strenuous activity into your holiday, especially in the first few days before you've acclimatized to the sun, water and food, and while you're probably still suffering jetlag. If you do get ill in Sri Lanka, standards of medical care are good. Most **doctors** speak English and a significant number have trained in Europe, North America or Australia. All large towns have a hospital, and you'll also find **private medical clinics** in Colombo. If you pay for treatment, remember to get receipts so that you can claim on your insurance policy. All larger towns have well-appointed **pharmacies** (signed by a red cross on a white circle) and can usually produce an English-speaking pharmacist. If stuck, any reputable hotel or guesthouse should be able to put you in touch with a local English-speaking doctor.

For more on **Ayurveda**, Sri Lanka's remarkable home-grown system of holistic medical care, see p.138.

The diseases listed in this section are not the only health hazards in Sri Lanka. For information about **general security** and **road traffic safety** see p.61.

Medical resources for travellers

US and Canada

CDC ⓣ1-800/311-3435, ⓦwww.cdc.gov/travel. Official US government travel health site.

Canadian Society for International Health ⓣ613/241-5785, ⓦwww.csih.org. Extensive list of travel health centres.

International Society for Travel Medicine ⓣ1-770/736-7060, ⓦwww.istm.org. Has a full list of travel health clinics.

Australia, New Zealand and South Africa

Travellers' Medical and Vaccination Centre ⓣ1300/658 844, ⓦwww.tmvc.com.au. Lists travel clinics in Australia, New Zealand and South Africa.

UK and Ireland

Hospital for Tropical Diseases Travel Clinic ⓣ0845/155 5000 or 020/7387 4411, ⓦwww.thehtd.org.

MASTA (Medical Advisory Service for Travellers Abroad) ⓣ0870/606 2782, ⓦwww.masta.org for the nearest clinic.

Travel Medicine Services ⓣ028/9031 5220 (travel medicine clinic).

Tropical Medical Bureau Ireland ⓣ1850/487 674, ⓦwww.tmb.ie.

Water and food

Avoid drinking **tap water** in Sri Lanka. Although it's generally chlorinated and safe to drink, the unfamiliar micro-organisms it contains (compared with what you're used to at home) can easily precipitate a stomach upset. Also avoid ice, unless you're sure that it's been made with boiled or purified water. Mineral water is widely available, although always check that the seal hasn't been broken – it's not unknown for bottles to be refilled with tap water. If you do want to purify your own water, the easiest way it to chemically sterilize it using **water purification tablets** (though these leave an unpleasant taste and do not remove all organisms) or to treat it using **tincture of iodine**, though this also leaves an unpleasant taste (you can buy crystals which remove some of – though not all – the taste). Both tablets and iodine tincture are available in most camping shops. Whatever precautions you take, however, you're still likely to come into contact with local water at various points – your eating utensils will be washed in it, and it will probably be used without your knowledge in things like fruit juices – so it's not worth getting paranoid about.

Though Sri Lankan standards of **food hygiene** are reasonable, it still pays to be careful, and the old traveller's adage usually applies: if you can't cook, boil or peel something, don't eat it (although if you can't peel something, you can always wash it thoroughly in purified water). Another good rule of thumb is to stick to hot food which has been freshly prepared. Avoid salads and anything which looks like it has been sitting uncovered for a while; short eats (see p.44) are particularly likely to be old and to have been poked by everyone in the café. The busier the establishment, the better, since there's less probability that the food's been sitting around all day. Obviously you'll need to use your discretion: the buffet at a five-star hotel has more chance of being OK than a local café's tureen of curry, which has been keeping the flies fat since dawn. Finally, remember that refrigerators stop working during power cuts, so unless you're eating at a place with its own generator, avoid any food (including meat and ice cream) which might have been unfrozen and then refrozen.

Diarrhoea, dysentery and giardiasis

Diarrhoea remains the most common complaint amongst tourists visiting Sri Lanka. It can have many causes, including serious diseases like typhoid or cholera, but in the vast majority of cases diarrhoea is a result of contaminated food or drink and will pass naturally in a few days. Such diarrhoea is also often accompanied by cramps, nausea and vomiting, and fever in more severe cases.

You should seek medical advice if diarrhoea continues for more than five days or if there is blood mixed up in the faeces, in which case you could be suffering from giardiasis or amoebic dysentery (see p.66).

Treatment

One of the biggest problems with diarrhoea, particularly in a hot country like Sri Lanka, is **dehydration**; it's vital you keep topped up with fluids – aim for about four litres every 24 hours (the colour of your urine is the best guide). If you're having more than five bouts of diarrhoea a day or are unable to eat, take **oral rehydration salts** to replace lost salt and minerals. These can be bought ready-prepared in sachets from camping shops; alternatively, you can make your own by mixing eight teaspoons of sugar and half a teaspoon of salt in a litre of purified water. Coconut water is a good alternative, especially if you add a pinch of salt; flat coca-cola or lemonade with a pinch of salt also work. **Children** with diarrhoea dehydrate much more quickly than adults, and it's even more vital to keep them hydrated. If you have to go on a long journey where you won't have access to a toilet, you can temporarily bung yourself up with a blocking drug like lomotil or loperamide, though these simply suppress symptoms and have no curative value. Whilst recovering, stick to bland foods (rice and yoghurt are traditionally recommended, and bananas help replace lost potassium) and get plenty of rest – this is not the moment to go rushing up Adam's Peak.

If you have persistent diarrhoea, you may be suffering from giardiasis or amoebic dysentery. With **giardiasis**, the onset of diarrhoea is slow and the diarrhoea less watery and severe (although associated with severe flatulence). You may also suffer stomach cramps, nausea and a bloated stomach. In **amoebic dysentery**, diarrhoea is severe, with bloody stools and fever. If any of the above symptoms apply, the first thing to do is to get a stool test in order to establish what you're suffering from. Both giardiasis and amoebic dysentery respond to antibiotics – ciprofloxacin is the most commonly prescribed.

Malaria

Of the four strains of malaria, two exist in Sri Lanka. The **vivax** strain accounts for around eighty percent of cases in the island and, though it's extremely unpleasant, it is rarely dangerous and is fairly simple to diagnose and cure (although sufferers may suffer a relapse if the disease isn't properly treated to begin with). The second type, **falciparum**, makes up the other twenty percent of cases and is much more serious, and occasionally fatal if treatment is delayed. One complication of falciparum infection, **cerebral malaria**, is particularly dangerous; symptoms include a reduced level of consciousness, leading to fits, coma and, if untreated, death; in ten percent of cases there may be lasting damage to the nervous system.

Malaria risk in Sri Lanka varies enormously depending on where in the country you are and when you visit. The west and south coasts from Negombo right the way round to Tangalla are virtually malaria-free. Malaria is also absent from the hill country – roughly everywhere from Kandy and above; the mosquitoes responsible for transmitting malaria rarely venture above 1500m. There's a varying risk of contracting malaria elsewhere in the country; check the useful malaria map at Ⓦwww.fitfortravel.nhs.uk/destinations/malariamaps/srilanka.htm.

Avoiding bites

Even if you're on medication, it's important to avoid being bitten, since no antimalarial offers total protection, and mosquitoes in Sri Lanka also transmit other diseases such as dengue fever and Japanese encephalitis. Malarial mosquitoes come out at dusk and remain active throughout the night. Standard avoidance techniques are to wear light-coloured clothing with long sleeves; use a **repellent** containing DEET on exposed parts of your body; and (if your room's not air-conditioned) always sleep under a net. You might also want to spray your clothing with a permethrin spray; burning a mosquito coil in your room or putting one under the table while you eat is also recommended. An alternative to coils is the Pyrethroid tablets which you place on a tray and put in a plug; the electricity heats the tray and vaporizes the Pyrethroid. Citronella oil (available from many chemists in Sri Lanka) is also thought to be good for repelling mosquitoes.

Antimalarial drugs

Ideas about appropriate **antimalarial medication** tend to vary from country to country, and prophylaxis remains a controversial subject; it's important that you get expert medical advice on which treatment is right for you. In addition, resistance to established antimalarial drugs is growing alarmingly – none of the following provides complete protection, so avoiding being bitten in the first place remains important.

The most established regime – widely prescribed in Europe, but not in North America – is a combination of **chloroquine** (trade names Nivaquin or Avloclor) taken weekly either on its own or in conjunction with a daily dose of **proguanil** (Paludrine). You need to start this regime a week before arriving in a malarial area and continue it for four weeks after leaving. **Mefloquine** (Lariam) is a newer and stronger treatment, though not usually prescribed for Sri Lanka. As a prophylactic, you need take just one tablet weekly, starting two weeks before entering a risk area and continuing for four weeks after leaving. Mefloquine is a very powerful and effective antimalarial, though there have been widely reported concerns about its side effects, including psychological problems.

Doxycycline is often prescribed in Australasia. One tablet is taken daily, starting a day or two before entering a malarial zone and continuing for four weeks after leaving. It's not suitable for children under 10 and it can cause thrush in women, while three percent of users develop a sensitivity to light, causing a rash, so it's not ideal for beach holidays. It also interferes with the effectiveness of the contraceptive pill.

Malarone (a combination of Atovaquone and Proguanil) is the most recent drug to come on the market. The bonus is that you only have to start taking it on the day you enter a malarial zone and continue for just a week after leaving, meaning that, although it's expensive, it can prove economical for short trips.

Finally, note that malaria has a typical incubation period of nine to sixteen days, sometimes longer – hence the importance of continuing with the medication once you get home. Initial **symptoms** are virtually indistinguishable from severe flu, coming in three waves: cold, hot and sweating. If you think you might have malaria, have a blood test done as soon as possible.

Sun

The potential health risks associated with the **sun** are easily underestimated – especially since being in it is presumably a major factor in why you decided to come to Sri Lanka in the first place. The tropical sun is probably far stronger than you're used to at home, and can cause various problems. The most obvious is sunburn. Remember that sunlight increases in strength when reflected off water and sand, meaning that you can burn badly even when sea or river breezes keep you feeling cool. You can also burn whilst swimming or snorkelling (some people wear a T-shirt in the water to avoid getting a burnt back), as well as through cloud cover. Sunscreen should therefore always be applied to exposed skin when outdoors. Young children are particularly vulnerable to burns and should be kept out of the sun at all times. Older kids should wear the highest factor sunblock and a hat. For all ages, eyes also need to be protected by proper sunglasses. If you do get sunburnt, take plenty of warm (not cold) showers, apply calamine lotion or aloe vera gel, and drink lots of water.

A common but minor irritant is **prickly heat**, usually afflicting newly arrived visitors. It's caused by excessive perspiration trapped under the skin, producing an itchy rash. Keep cool (a/c is good), shower frequently, use talcum powder on the affected skin and wear loose (ideally cotton) clothing. At its worst, prolonged exposure to the sun and dehydration can lead to **heatstroke**, a serious and potentially life-threatening condition. Symptoms are a lack of sweat, high temperature, severe headaches, lack of coordination and confusion. If untreated, heatstroke can lead to potentially fatal convulsions and delirium. If you're suffering from heatstroke, get out of the sun, get into a tepid shower and drink plenty of water.

Marine hazards

Besides the risks of drowning (see p.62), swimmers are also at a small potential risk of **marine stings**. Jellyfish are common, and some can inflict painful stings; coral scratches and cuts can also be painful (although more of a problem for the coral itself, which dies on contact). Occasionally people develop quasi-allergic reactions to stings; if you start to wheeze or swell up around the face, go to hospital immediately.

The other thing you need to think about is how **clean** the water is: beaches in the vicinity of town centres are obviously prone to pollution. In addition, parts of some beaches are filthy. Look out for broken glass, fishing hooks, syringes and other rubbish; dog shit is also common. If you cut your foot, disinfect it immediately and seek medical advice, since you may need a tetanus booster and/or a hepatitis B vaccine.

Hepatitis

Hepatitis is an inflammation of the liver. The disease exists in various forms, though with a shared range of symptoms, typically jaundiced skin, yellowing of the whites of the eyes, dark urine, pale faeces and a general range of flu-like symptoms. **Hepatitis A** and **hepatitis E** are spread by contaminated food and water. If you become infected, there's little you can do except rest, drink lots of fluids and eat lightly – unfortunately, it can take a couple of weeks or more to shake off the effects. The much more serious **Hepatitis B** can result in long-term liver damage and liver cancer. Like the HIV virus, it's spread via infected blood or body fluids, most commonly through sex or needle sharing, but also by contaminated shaving, tattooing or ear- or body-piercing equipment. **Hepatitis C and D** are similar.

You can (and should) be **vaccinated** against hepatitis A. The hepatitis B vaccine is usually only recommended to those at especially high risk, such as health-care workers. There are no vaccines for other types of hepatitis.

Japanese encephalitis

Japanese encephalitis (JE) is a virus which attacks the brain and is transmitted by mosquitoes which bite at night. It's particularly associated with **rural areas**, as the virus lives in wading birds, pigs and flooded rice fields. The two main areas in Sri Lanka where JE is prevalent are the flat, rice-cultivating areas around the southwest coasts from Colombo to Hambantota, and the northern districts stretching from Kurunegala via Puttalam to Anuradhapura and Polonnaruwa. JE is most prevalent following periods of heavy rainfall resulting in large areas of stagnant water.

JE is an extremely dangerous disease, with mortality rates of up to forty percent (though tourists are only very rarely affected). As with malaria, you won't contract JE if you don't get bitten (see p.66). **Symptoms** include drowsiness, sensitivity to light and confusion. An effective vaccine exists for JE (three shots administered over 28 days), though the standard advice is that it's only worth considering if you're travelling in high-risk areas during the monsoon for a period of over a month, especially if you'll be spending a lot of time in the country and/or camping out a lot. If you're just lounging around on the beach or making a quick visit to the Cultural Triangle, the vaccine's not necessary.

Dengue fever

Dengue fever is another mosquito-borne infection, though in contrast to Japanese encephalitis, dengue is an **urban disease** – Colombo is particularly affected, and it is also present in Galle, Kandy, Ratnapura and Matara. As mosquitoes lay their eggs in water, dengue outbreaks tend to peak during or after periods of rain. There are four subtypes of dengue fever, so unfortunately it's possible to catch it more than once. The disease is typically characterized by the sudden onset of high fever accompanied by chills, headache, a skin rash and muscle or joint pains (usually affecting the limbs and back, hence dengue fever's nickname "break-bone fever"). Dengue is also associated, in around a third of cases, with mild bleeding: typically nosebleeds, bleeding from the gums whilst brushing your teeth or heavier-than-usual menstrual flow. The fever usually lasts three to seven days, while post-viral weakness, lethargy and sometimes depression can persist for anything up to several weeks.

A rare but potentially fatal complication is **dengue haemorrhagic fever** (DHF), which is almost entirely confined to children aged under 15 who have previously been infected with dengue fever. Victims can become pale, clammy and faint, with a rapid pulse and breathing; abnormal bleeding may also be present. Urgent medical attention should be sought.

There is no **vaccine** for dengue fever. Unfortunately, the mosquitoes which transmit dengue bite during the day, making them harder to guard against than malarial mosquitoes. If you think you've contracted dengue fever, go to a doctor – it's easily confused with malaria in its early stages, so you'll need to have a blood test to determine what you've got. Take plenty of fluids, get lots of bed rest, keep any rashes cool and use an antihistamine.

Rabies

Rabies is an **animal disease** which is transmitted to humans by bites, scratches or even by licking; it's usually associated with dogs, but can also be transmitted by cats, monkeys, bats and even domestic livestock – in fact, any warm-blooded animal. Rabies, once symptoms have developed, is invariably fatal. There is, however, an effective vaccine, as well as other precautions you can take if you have been bitten or scratched. You are at risk if you suffer a bite which draws blood or breaks the skin, or if you are licked by an animal on an open wound. Bites to the face, neck and fingertips are particularly dangerous.

The good news is that a safe and effective **vaccine** exists (three shots over 28 days). Casual tourists on short holidays to the island may well feel that they are not sufficiently at risk to go through the hassle of a rabies vaccine, but if you're going for a long period or are likely to be in close contact with animals, you might decide it's worth the trouble. In general, Sri Lankan dogs are fairly well behaved, and it's rare that you'll encounter the sort of aggressive and unpredictable strays (or packs of strays) that you sometimes find in other parts of Asia.

Regardless of whether you've been vaccinated or not, if you're bitten or scratched (or licked on an open wound) by an infected animal, clean the wound thoroughly with disinfectant as soon as possible. Iodine is ideal, but alcohol or even soap and water are better than nothing. If you've already been vaccinated, you'll need two booster shots three days apart. If you haven't been vaccinated, you will need to be given five shots of the rabies vaccine over 28 days (the first must be administered as soon as possible after you've been bitten), along with a single injection of rabies antibody serum.

Other diseases

Typhoid is a gut infection caused by contaminated water or food, and which leads to a high fever accompanied by headaches, abdominal pains and diarrhoea. If left untreated, serious complications may ensue, so seek medical help. Oral and injected vaccines are available and vaccination is recommended if you're visiting the north or the east of the island, especially if you'll be staying in budget accommodation. A vaccination against **meningitis** is also available. This cerebral virus, transmitted by airborne bacteria, can be fatal. Symptoms include a severe headache, fever, a stiff neck and a stomach rash. If you think you have it, seek medical attention immediately. Sri Lanka has experienced occasional outbreaks of **cholera**, although this typically occurs in epidemics in areas of poor sanitation, being transmitted by contaminated water, and almost never affects tourists.

The **tetanus** virus lives in soil and animal faeces; infection is via a cut or scratch on the skin. As befits tetanus's old name of "lockjaw", initial symptoms can be discomfort in swallowing and a stiffness in the jaw and neck, followed by convulsions – potentially fatal. The vaccination is a standard childhood jab in developed countries. **Typhus** is spread by the bites of ticks, lice and mites. Symptoms include fever, headache and muscle pains, followed after a few days by a rash, while the bite itself often develops into a painful sore. A shot of antibiotics will shift it.

Animals and insects

Leeches are common after rain in Sinharaja, Adam's Peak and elsewhere in the hills. They're difficult to avoid, attaching themselves to your shoes and climbing up your leg until they find flesh, and are quite capable of burrowing through a pair of socks. Once latched on, leeches will suck your blood until sated, after which they drop off of their own accord – perfectly painless, but not terribly pleasant. You can make leeches drop off harmlessly with the end of a lighted cigarette or the flame from a lighter, or by putting salt on them. Don't pull them off, however, or bits of leech might break off and become embedded in your flesh, increasing the risk of the bite becoming infected.

Sri Lanka has the dubious distinction of having one of the highest number of **snakebite** fatalities, per capita, of any country in the world, and any form of bite should be treated as quickly as possible. The island boasts five species of poisonous snake, all relatively common, especially in northern dry zones; they include the cobra and the extremely dangerous Russell's viper. Avoid wandering through heavy undergrowth in bare feet and flipflops; wear proper shoes or boots, socks and long trousers. If you're bitten, you should wrap up the limb, as for a sprained ankle, and immobilize it with a splint – this slows down the speed at which venom spreads through the rest of the body; keeping as still as possible also helps. Popular advice recommends catching and killing the snake so that the doctor knows what type of antivenin to administer, although it's unlikely you'll be able to do this, and you'll probably have to settle for a description of the creature. Unfortunately, reliable antivenins have not yet been developed for all types of snake – that for the Russell's viper, for instance, has been developed from the Indian Russell's viper, and is not always effective in treating bites administered by the Sri Lankan sub-species.

STDs, HIV and AIDS

Sexually transmitted diseases (STDs) are common in the chilled-out, uninhibited and scantily clad world of the average Sri Lankan tourist beach. The island has partly shaken off its reputation as a destination for sex tourists, but STDs remain common, and may rise as tourist numbers increase. Practise safe sex, or you might come home with an unwelcome souvenir of your visit.

Compared to other parts of Asia, Sri Lanka has relatively few reported **HIV** and **AIDS** cases – around three to five thousand as of 2005, although there is probably significant under-reporting given the stigma attached to the disease – awareness of AIDS and HIV is poor and the government has its head buried firmly in the sand. Again, there are obvious risks if you have unprotected sex. Contaminated needles are not considered a problem in Sri Lanka, so there's no need to carry your own – but ask to have the packet opened in your presence if you want to check this for yourself. Contaminated blood poses a potentially greater risk – blood transfusions should only be accepted in an absolute emergency.

Costs

Rampant inflation over recent years means that Sri Lanka is no longer the bargain it once was, although prices remain comparable to other places in South and Southeast Asia. How much you spend is entirely up to you. Stay on the beach in a cheap cabana and eat meals in local cafés and you could probably scrape by under US$15 (or €10/£10) a day; check into one of the island's top hotels or villas and add in the cost of tours with personal guides, drivers and transport, and you could easily spend US$500 a day, or more.

If you're **on a budget**, Sri Lanka can still be fairly inexpensive, so long as you stick to using local transport and staying in cheap guesthouses – you can still travel by bus from one end of the island to the other for around US$20 (£14), get a filling meal at local cafés for a couple of dollars, and find a decent double room for US$10–15 (£7–10) per night, or less. Tours or renting a vehicle will obviously bump costs up considerably – a car and driver normally goes for around US$50–60 (£35–40) a day. Entrance fees for archeological sites and national parks can also strain tight budgets – a day-ticket to any one of Anuradhapura, Sigiriya or Polonnaruwa currently costs US$25, while the cost of visiting the country's national parks works out at somewhere around US$80 per couple per day once you've factored in entrance fees and transport.

Note that some hotels and restaurants levy a ten percent **service charge**. In addition, a fifteen percent **government service tax** (GST) is also sometimes added to the bill, while a few top-end places add a one percent Development Tax. The more upmarket the establishment, the more likely it is that one, two or all three of these charges will apply, and it's always worth checking beforehand – the extra twenty-six percent added at a top hotel can add a nasty twist to the bill if you're not expecting it.

Tourist prices

Another nasty surprise is furnished by the island's official **tourist prices**. At all national parks and reserves, and at government-run archeological sites, the authorities operate a two-tier price system whereby foreigners pay a significantly higher entrance fee than locals, sometimes almost a hundred times more than Sri Lankan nationals, as, for instance, at the country's national parks, where locals pay an entrance fee of around US$0.25, while overseas visitors pay around US$25 once various taxes and additional charges have been taken into account. A similar situation obtains at the sites of the Cultural Triangle – at Anuradhapura, for instance, foreigners pay US$25 per day, whilst locals pay nothing (the fact that many of these sites have been restored with funds donated by the international community is, for many visitors, merely another insult). Some visitors oppose this two-tier pricing system in principle; others object not to the basic idea, but to the scale of the difference between the prices. These charges have also damaged the businesses of innumerable Sri Lankan tour guides, who find themselves unable to offer trips to many cultural sites or national parks due to prohibitive entrance charges.

Bargaining

As a tourist, you're likely to pay slightly over the odds for a range of services, from tuktuk fares to items in shops and markets, but **overcharging** is generally less widespread and severe than in some other parts of Asia. Having said that, prices in Sri Lanka are often inherently fluid. Many hoteliers, for instance, chop and change their prices according to demand, while the price of anything from a tuktuk ride to an elephant carving may depend on anything from the time of day to the weather or the mood of the seller. Given this, it's always worth **bargaining**. Remember, though, that the key to effective bargaining is to retain a sense of humour and proportion. There is nothing more ridiculous – or more damaging for local perceptions of foreign visitors – than the sight of a Western tourist arguing bitterly over the final few rupees of a budget room or an item of shopping. The fact is that even the most cash-strapped Western backpacker is, in Sri Lankan terms, extremely rich, as their very presence in the country proves. And however tight one's budget, it's important to realize the difference that even a few rupees can make to a guesthouse owner who is struggling by on a couple of dollars a day.

On the other hand, it's also important not to be outrageously overcharged. Visitors who lack a sense of local prices and pay whatever they're asked contribute to local inflation, pushing up prices both for other tourists and (more importantly) for locals – the implications of just one tourist paying US$10 for a tuktuk ride that should cost US$1 can have serious implications for the local economy.

Tipping

Tipping is a way of life in Sri Lanka – visitors will generally be expected to offer some kind of remuneration for most services, even on top of agreed fees, and the whole business of what to give and to whom can be a bit of a minefield. Many hotels and restaurants add a ten percent service charge to the bill, which should be sufficient unless service has been especially good. If a service charge hasn't been added, a tip won't necessarily be expected, although it is of course always appreciated. If you tour the island by car, your driver will expect a tip of around US$5–10 per day, depending on their level of expertise, though you shouldn't feel obliged to give anything unless you're genuinely pleased with the service you've received (and if you're *not* happy, it's well worth explaining why). If touring a site with an official guide, you should always agree a fee in advance; additional tips should only be offered if you're particularly pleased with the service. When visiting temples, you'll probably be shown around by a resident monk or priest; it's polite to offer them something at the end of the tour – some will take this money themselves (despite Buddhist strictures against clergy handling money); others will prefer you to place it in a donation box. Whatever happens, a dollar or two should suffice. Occasionally, unofficial "guides" (usually bored teenagers or other local hangers-on) will materialize to show you around temples – and will of course expect a tip for their troubles. Again, a dollar or two is almost certainly sufficient. Anyone else who assists you will probably welcome some kind of gratuity, though of course it's impossible to generalize and visitors will have to make (sometimes difficult) decisions about whether to offer money or not.

Travel essentials

Electricity

Sri Lanka's electricity runs at 230–240V, 50 cycles A/C. Round, three-pin sockets are the norm, though you'll also occasionally find square three-pin sockets; adaptors are cheap and widely available. Power cuts are common, especially during periods of low rainfall (much of the island's power is generated by hydroelectricity). Most top-end places have their own generators; if you're staying in budget or mid-range places, a torch is invaluable.

Emergencies

For police assistance in an emergency, call ⓣ119 in Colombo or ⓣ118 anywhere else in the island.

Entry requirements

Nationals of the UK, Ireland, Australia, New Zealand, Canada and the US visiting Sri Lanka for tourist purposes are issued with a free thirty-day **tourist visa** on arrival (the same applies to nationals of most other European countries; if in doubt, check with your nearest embassy in advance or visit ⓦwww.srilanka.travel/entry_formalities.php). This thirty-day visa can be easily extended to three months by visiting the Department of Immigration (Mon–Fri 8.30am–2pm; ⓣ011-259 7511), at 41 Ananda Rajakaruna Mw, Punchi Borella, Colombo 10, on the east side of the city centre past Colombo General Hospital. You can extend your visa as soon as you get to Sri Lanka; the month you're given on arrival is included in the three months. You'll need to bring one passport photo. Fees for three-month visa extensions can be checked at ⓦwww.gov.lk; they're currently US$54 for UK nationals, US$16 for citizens of the Republic of Ireland, US$30 for Australians, US$34.50 New Zealanders, US$50 Canadians, and a hefty US$100 for US citizens. For a list of foreign embassies and consulates in Colombo, see p.118.

In terms of **customs regulations**, entering Sri Lanka you are allowed to bring in 1.5 litres of spirits, two bottles of wine and two hundred cigarettes. Leaving Sri Lanka you are permitted to export up to 10kg of tea duty-free. In theory, you're not allowed to

Sri Lankan embassies and consulates overseas

Australia Level 11, 48 Hunter St, Sydney 2000 ⓣ02/9223 8729, ⓦwww.slcgsyd.com.

Canada 333 Laurier Ave, Ottawa, Ontario KIP 1C1 ⓣ613/233 8449, ⓦwww.srilankahcottawa.org.

New Zealand Contact Australian embassy.

Ireland Contact UK embassy.

UK 13 Hyde Park Gdns, London W2 2LU ⓣ020/7262 1841, ⓦwww.slhclondon.org.

US 2148 Wyoming Ave NW, Washington DC 20008 ⓣ202/483-4025, ⓦwww.slembassy.org.

take out more than Rs.250 in cash, though this is rarely checked. If you want to export **antiques** – defined as anything more than fifty years old – you will need authorization from either the Director of the National Archives (7 Reid Ave, Colombo 7 ⓣ011-268 8757) and the Director General of the Archeology Department (Sir Marcus Fernando Mw, Colombo 7 ⓣ011-269 5255) depending on exactly what it is you want to export. The export of any coral, shells or other protected marine products is prohibited; taking out flora, fauna or animal parts is also prohibited.

Gay and lesbian travellers

There is little understanding of gay issues in Sri Lanka – gays and lesbians are generally stigmatized and homosexuality is technically illegal (although no one has been arrested since 1950), so discretion is advised, and the whole scene remains rather secretive. ⓦwww.geocities.com/srilankangay is a good first port of call for gays and lesbians, with info about contacts, events and meeting places, while ⓦwww.utopia-asia.com/tipssri.htm has further links, as well as listings of gay-friendly accommodation and general travel information. In addition, check out the website of Equal Ground (ⓦwww.equal-ground.org), which organized the island's first-ever Gay Pride celebration in Colombo in mid-2005 and occasionally stages other events.

Getting married in Sri Lanka

Sri Lanka is one of the world's leading honeymoon destinations, and many couples go a step further and actually get married on the island – beach weddings are particularly popular. Arranging the ceremony independently and dealing with the attendant paperwork and bureaucracy can be difficult, however, and it's much easier to leave the details to a specialist operator. Most large hotels and a number of the tour operators listed on pp.30–32 can arrange the whole wedding for you, including (if you fancy) extras like Kandyan drummers and dancers, plus optional elephants and a chorus of local girls.

Insurance

It's essential to take out **insurance** before travelling to cover against theft, loss and illness or injury. A typical travel insurance policy usually provides cover for loss of baggage, tickets and – up to a certain limit – cash or cheques, as well as cancellation or early curtailment of your journey. Most of them exclude so-called dangerous sports unless an extra premium is paid: in Sri Lanka this can mean scuba diving, whitewater rafting, windsurfing and trekking. Many policies can be chopped and changed to exclude coverage you don't need – for example, sickness and accident benefits can often be excluded or included at will. When securing baggage cover, make sure that the per-article limit – typically under £500 – will cover your most valuable possession. If you need to make a claim, you should keep receipts for medicines and medical treatment, and in the event you have anything stolen, you must obtain an official statement from the police.

Internet

Most towns in Sri Lanka now have at least one or two places offering **internet** access, either in proper cybercafés, in communications bureaux or in guesthouses – details of the best places are given throughout the Guide. Costs vary widely, from as little as Rs.1 per minute in Colombo and Kandy up to Rs.6 per minute or more in less well-connected areas. An increasing number of places now have broadband, though many others still have erratic dial-up connections which take forever to load web pages of any complexity.

Laundry

Most guesthouses and hotels offer a **laundry** service. Washing usually takes 24 hours and usually costs around Rs.50–75 for a shirt or blouse and around Rs.100 for a pair of trousers or a light dress. There are no public coin-operated launderettes anywhere in the island.

Mail

Postal services from Sri Lanka are fairly reliable, at least if you stick to airmail, which takes three to four days to reach the UK and US. Surface mail is about half to one-third the cost of airmail, but is so slow and offers so much potential for things to get lost or damaged in transit that it's really not worth bothering with. A postcard to the UK, Australasia and North America costs Rs.20. An airmail parcel to the UK or Australasia costs around US$16 for up to 0.5kg, plus around US$8.35 for each additional 0.5kg up to a maximum weight of 20kg (slightly more expensive to North America). Parcels heavier than 20kg have to be sent by EMS Speed Post (see below). If you want to send a parcel home from Sri Lanka, you must take the contents unwrapped to the post office so that they can be inspected before wrapping (all larger post offices have counters selling glue, string and wrapping paper).

Another option is **EMS Speed Post**, slightly faster (and more expensive) than airmail – a 0.5kg package to the UK costs US$20. Alternatively, a number of reputable international **couriers** have offices in Colombo – try Fedex at 300 Galle Rd, Kollupitiya (ⓣ011-452 2222).

Maps

There are several good **maps** of Sri Lanka. The best and most detailed is the *Rough Guide Sri Lanka Map* (1:500,000); it's also printed on indestructible waterproof synthetic paper so it won't disintegrate in the tropics and can even be used as an emergency monsoon shelter, at a pinch. Another good country map is Nelles' *Sri Lanka* (1:450,000), at a slightly larger scale (although slightly less detailed). The entire island is covered by a series of 92 1:50,000 maps – detailed, but somewhat dated. These are only available from the Survey Dept on Kirulla Road, Havelock Town, Colombo 5 (Mon–Fri 10am–3.30pm); you'll need to show your passport to get in.

Money

The Sri Lankan **currency** is the rupee (abbreviated variously as R., R/ or R/-, and in this book as Rs.). **Coins** come in denominations of 25 and 50 cents, and Rs.1, 2, 5 and 10 (the Rs.1 coin comes in two forms: the old silver coins, and a smaller new bronze version, similar to the UK 1p). **Notes** come in denominations of Rs.10, 20, 50, 100, 200, 500, 1000 and 2000. Try to avoid accepting particularly dirty, torn or disreputable-looking notes, and break big notes and stock up on change whenever you can – don't expect to be able to pay for a Rs.10 cup of tea with a Rs.1000 note.

At the time of writing, the **exchange rate** was around Rs.110 to the US dollar, Rs.150 to the euro, and Rs.170 to the pound sterling; you can check current exchange rates at ⓦwww.xe.com. The Sri Lankan rupee continues to devalue steadily against hard currencies. To guard against the effects of this devaluation, top-end hotels always give their prices either in US dollars or (increasingly) in euros, though you'll be expected to pay in rupees, with the bill converted at the current bank exchange rate. Many other tourist services are also often priced in dollars or euros – anything from entrance tickets at archeological sites to tours, balloon trips or diving courses – though, again, payment will be expected in rupees.

Sri Lanka is well supplied with **banks**. The six main chains (most larger towns will have a branch of at least three or four of these) are the Bank of Ceylon, Hatton National Bank, Sampath Bank, Commercial Bank, People's Bank and Seylan Bank. All are open Monday to Friday from 8 or 9am in the morning until 2 or 3pm in the afternoon, and all shut at weekends. Exchange rates for foreign currency, whether traveller's cheques, cash or making withdrawals by credit or debit card, are fairly uniform across the various banks; you may get fractionally better rates if you shop around, but you won't make any dramatic savings. If you need to change money **outside banking hours**, most top-end hotels change cash or traveller's cheques, though at rates which are up to ten percent poorer than bank rates. Failing this, you could try at local guesthouses or shops – the more tourist-oriented the place you're in, the better your chances, though you'll probably have to accept poor rates. All towns of any consequence now have at least one bank **ATM** which accepts foreign debit and credit cards; details are given throughout the Guide.

Despite the usefulness of plastic, you might still feel it's worth taking at least a few **traveller's cheques**. These can be changed rapidly and painlessly at any bank in Sri Lanka. Sterling-, euro- and dollar-denominated traveller's cheques are all universally accepted, but take a standard brand (Amex, Thomas Cook or Visa) to avoid problems.

You might also want to carry some **cash** with you for emergencies. US dollars, euros, pounds sterling and Australian dollars are all widely recognized and easily changed. New Zealand or Canadian dollars might occasionally cause problems, but are generally accepted in most banks.

Opening hours

Most businesses, including banks and government offices, work a standard **five-day working week** from Monday to Friday 9/9.30am to 5/5.30pm. Major post offices generally operate longer hours (typically 7am–9pm), and stay open on Saturdays as well. Many museums shut on Fridays, while Hindu temples stay shut until around 4pm to 5pm, when they open for the evening puja. Buddhist temples, by contrast, generally stay open at all times.

Phones

Phoning home from Sri Lanka is straightforward, and relatively inexpensive, although if you're planning a long trip and are likely to be making a lot of calls, using your own mobile with a local SIM card (see below) is the most cost-effective option – having said which, some foreign mobile providers have reciprocal arrangements with local operators Dialog and Celltel and offer suprisingly cheap rates using your existing SIM card – you might like to check tariffs before you travel. Without a mobile, the easiest way to make a call is to go to one of the island's innumerable **communications bureaux**, little offices offering phone, fax and photocopying services, and sometimes email as well (look out for signs advertising IDD calls); there will usually be at least a couple on the main street of even the smallest town. You make your call, either from a private cubicle or from a phone at the counter, and then pay the bill at the end. Some places have phones with built-in LCD timers so you can see exactly how long you've been on the line for; in other places they just use a stop watch (in which case it's worth keeping an eye open to make sure it's not fiddled with while you're on the phone). Calls to the UK, Australasia and North America cost from around Rs.60 per minute; calls within Sri Lanka cost around Rs.5 per minute.

There are very few **public payphones** in Sri Lanka – it's generally easier (and quieter) to go to a communications bureau. Another possibility is to phone from your **hotel room**, though this will always cost significantly more than from a communications bureau, and can become positively astronomical in top-end hotels. Finally, a few internet cafés (especially in Colombo) now offer **Webcalls** – international phone calls via the Internet (usually advertised as "Net2Phone"). These are far cheaper than standard phone calls, usually costing around Rs.10 per minute; quality is quite reasonable, albeit not as good as using a proper phone line.

If you want to use your **mobile phone** in Sri Lanka, ask your service provider whether your handset will work abroad and what the call costs are; unsurprisingly, charges are generally steep. Most UK, Australian and New Zealand mobiles use GSM, which works well in Sri Lanka. US mobiles (apart

Calls to and from Sri Lanka

To **call home from Sri Lanka**, dial the international access code (☎00), then the country code (UK ☎44; US & Canada ☎1; Ireland ☎353; Australia ☎61; New Zealand ☎64; South Africa ☎27), then the area code and subscriber number. Note that the initial zero is omitted from the area code when dialling the UK, Ireland, Australia and New Zealand from abroad.

To **call Sri Lanka from abroad**, dial your international access code then the country code for Sri Lanka (☎94), then the area code, minus the initial zero, then the subscriber number.

from tri-band phones) won't work in Sri Lanka. If you're likely to be using your phone much, however, it's generally cheaper to **replace the SIM card** in your phone with a new SIM from a Sri Lankan company. This will give you a Sri Lankan phone number and you will be charged domestic rates – as low as Rs.10 per minute for international calls, and around Rs.5 for local calls. SIM cards cost around US$10, give or take, and are available from the myriad phone shops which have sprung up to cater to the Sri Lankan mobile boom; these places also sell chargers and adaptors for Sri Lankan sockets, and cards with which you can top up your airtime (or look for any shop displaying the relevant sticker). The leading operator is Dialog (Ⓦwww.dialog.lk), although their dominance is now being challenged by several other operators including Tigo (Ⓦwww.tigo.lk), Mobitel (Ⓦwww.mobitel.lk) and Airtel (Ⓦwww.airtel.lk). All now cover pretty much every town of any consequence in the island, although you won't be able to get a signal in some smaller villages.

Photography

Sri Lankans love having their photo taken – though it's obviously polite to ask and, if you're using a digital camera, to show them the results afterwards. A few of the island's more photogenic inhabitants might expect to be paid to be photographed, particularly stilt fishermen, when you can find them, and (occasionally) tea pickers in the highlands. You're not allowed to pose for photographs with Buddha images (i.e. to stand with your back to the image), and photography is also generally not permitted inside Hindu temples. In addition, note that flash photography can potentially damage old murals; if you're asked not to take flash photos, don't. And of course photographing soldiers or military installations is asking for trouble.

There are fairly well-equipped camera shops in most main towns, plus a few places in Kandy and Colombo where you can burn digital images to CD and which also sell memory cards (at Western prices). If you're using slide or black and white **film** it's best to bring it from home. If you buy film in Sri Lanka, check the expiry date on the box and don't buy film which has been left lying around in the sun. Processing is widely available, though won't always match the standards you're used to back home.

Time

GMT plus five hours and thirty minutes.

Tourist information

Considering the important of tourism to the national economy, there are surprisingly few sources of official **tourist information** either in Sri Lanka itself or abroad – only the UK currently boasts a properly equipped overseas tourist office (3rd floor, Devonshire Square, London EC2M 4WD ⓣ0845/880 6333). For detailed information about specific areas, the best sources are the independent tour operators listed on pp.30–32 and staff at hotels and guesthouses.

There are a number of magazines with listings and features of local interest which are worth having a look at – see p.47 for details. In addition to these, the free monthly *Travel Lanka*, available from the tourist office in Colombo (see p.89), contains listings of accommodation, shops, services and transport in the capital and across the island.

Good **online** sources of information include the Sri Lanka Tourist Board's site (Ⓦwww.srilanka.travel) and the excellent Travel Sri Lanka (Ⓦwww.travelsrilanka.com), which has extensive coverage of the island's sights, along with helpful practical information about planning a visit. You might also like to have a browse through Ari Withanage's Sri Lanka pages at Ⓦwww.members.tripod.com/~withanage (created by an expatriate Sri Lankan who now works for the London Fire Brigade) and the eclectic Lanka Library (Ⓦwww.lankalibrary.com), which has loads of background on sites, culture, history and cuisine. For websites dedicated to **current affairs** in Sri Lanka, see p.46.

Travellers with disabilities

Awareness of the needs of disabled people remains extremely low in Sri Lanka, and there's virtually no provision for disabled travellers. Few hotels, restaurants or tourist sites are wheelchair-accessible, although there are plenty of one-storey guesthouses which might be usable – though more by accident than design. Public transport is enough of a challenge for able-bodied passengers, and completely useless for wheelchair users, so you'll need your own vehicle and a driver who is sympathetic to your needs – and even then the lack of specially adapted vehicles can make getting in and out difficult.

Pavements – where they exist – are generally uneven, full of potholes and protected by high kerbs, while the anarchic traffic presents obvious dangers to those with only limited mobility.

Volunteering in Sri Lanka

There are all sorts of voluntary work projects in Sri Lanka – anything from teaching football to mucking out elephants – and a quick trawl on the internet will turn up dozens of possibilities. Note, however, that although volunteering is richly rewarding, it demands a real commitment of time and energy, and most placements cost at least as much as you'd expect to pay on an equivalent-length backpacking holiday on the island, and sometimes rather more. The following organizations give a good idea of what's available.

Global Crossroad US ⓣ1-866/387 7816, UK ⓣ0800/310 1821; ⓦwww.globalcrossroad.com. One- to twelve-week projects, with placements in orphanages and conservation projects, as well as teaching English.

IMPAKT Aid Trust Sri Lanka ⓣ011-250 7099, ⓦwww.impaktaid.com. Well-regarded Sri Lankan specialists working with tsunami survivors and widows.

i to i International Projects UK ⓣ0800/011 1156, ⓦwww.i-to-i.com. Two- to eight-week placements including English teaching, conservation, community projects and post-tsunami rehabilitation work.

Millennium Elephant Foundation Sri Lanka ⓣ035-226 5377, ⓦwww.millenniumelephantfoundation.org. This leading elephant sanctuary near Kandy (see p.228) offers one- to six-month placements. Volunteers are expected to contribute with fundraising, public relations and other administrative support, as well as working with the elephants and the local community.

Outreach International UK ⓣ01458/274957, ⓦwww.outreachinternational.co.uk. Wide variety of three-month placements – anything from turtle conservation to tsunami relief.

Teaching Abroad UK ⓣ01903/708300, ⓦwww.teaching-abroad.co.uk. Placements teaching English and other subjects such as computer skills, working with children, healthcare projects and media internships.

Travellers Worldwide UK ⓣ01903/502595, ⓦwww.travellersworldwide.com. Varied range of projects (two weeks to six months) including English teaching, football coaching and placements at Colombo zoo and Wasgomuwa National Park.

Guide

Guide

1

Colombo and the west coast

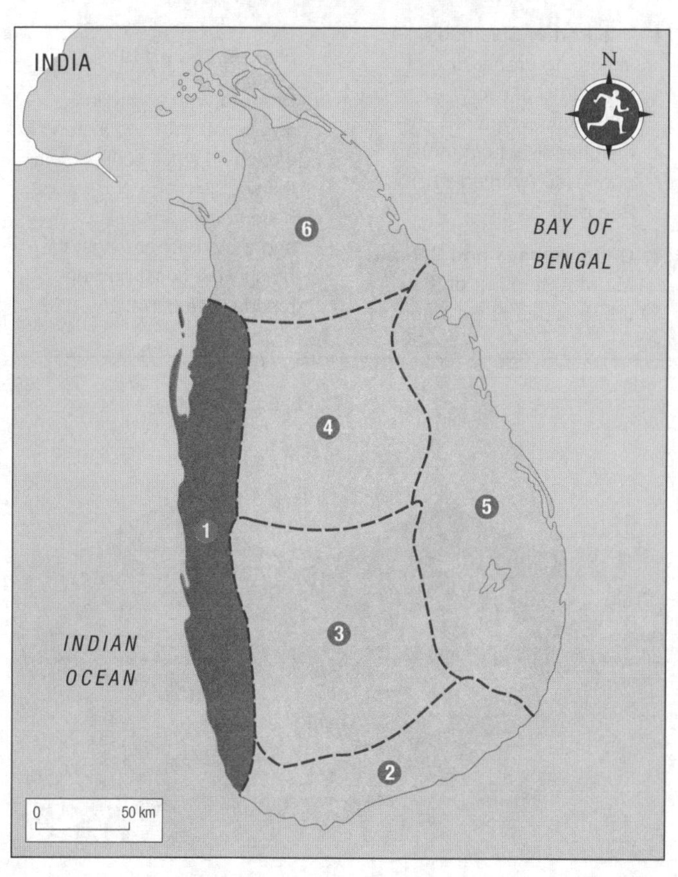

CHAPTER 1

Highlights

* **Bawa hotels** Sample contemporary Sri Lankan style at its most seductive with a stay in one of the many west coast hotels designed by Geoffrey Bawa, the island's foremost twentieth-century architect. **See p.39 & 146**

* **The Pettah** Colombo's absorbing bazaar district, stuffed full of every conceivable type of merchandise, from mobile phones to Ayurvedic herbs. **See p.99**

* **Gangaramaya and Seema Malaka** Step out of the urban melee of Colombo into the serene enclosures of these two contrasting Buddhist temples. **See p.103 & 104**

* **Eating in Colombo** The capital has Sri Lanka's best selection of places to eat by far, from cheap-and-cheerful local cafés to glitzy five-star palaces. **See p.110**

* **Bentota** With an idyllic swathe of sand and a string of elegant small-scale hotels, the southern end of Bentota beach offers an oasis of style and tranquillity amongst the brash west coast package resorts. **See p.142**

▲ Seema Malaka temple, Colombo

1

Colombo and the west coast

Sri Lanka's **west coast** is the island's front door and – via the international airport at Katunayake just outside Colombo – the point of arrival for all visitors to the country. This is Sri Lanka at its most developed and populous: the busiest, brashest, noisiest and most Westernized region in the country, home to the capital city and the principal coastal resorts, which have now all but fused into an unbroken ribbon of concrete which meanders along the seaboard for over a hundred kilometres. The region's **beaches** have traditionally been the driving force behind Sri Lanka's tourist industry, but relentless development has now overwhelmed much of the idyllic Indian Ocean scenery which brought the tourists here in the first place, and for most independent travellers the west coast is largely a place to be negotiated en route to less spoilt parts of the island. A few oases survive amidst the development, however, and if you're after a touch of barefoot beachside luxury, the west coast has Sri Lanka's best selection of top-end places to stay, many of which combine serenity with considerable style.

Situated about two-thirds of the way down the west coast, Sri Lanka's sprawling capital, **Colombo**, is usually low on visitors' list of priorities, but beneath the unprepossessing surface lies an intriguing and characterful city which offers a fascinating microcosm of contemporary Sri Lanka. North of Colombo is the lacklustre resort of **Negombo**, whose proximity to the airport makes it a popular first or last stop on many itineraries.

South of the capital lie the island's main beach resorts. The principal areas – **Kalutara**, **Beruwala** and **Bentota** – are home to endless oversize hotels catering to vacationing Europeans on two-week packages. Pockets of serenity remain, even so, along with some characterful hotels and guesthouses, while the lively little coastal town of **Aluthgama**, sandwiched between Beruwala and Bentota, offers a refreshing alternative to the big resorts. Further south lies **Hikkaduwa**, Sri Lanka's original hippy hangout, now rather past its best, though it does retain a certain down-at-heel charm and (by sleepy Sri Lankan standards at any rate) a refreshingly upbeat atmosphere thanks to the backpackers who still flock here for cheap sun, sand and surf.

The **best time to visit** is from November to mid-April, when the coast is blessed with perfect blue skies and swimming and diving conditions are good. It's perfectly possible to visit during the monsoon months from mid-April to October

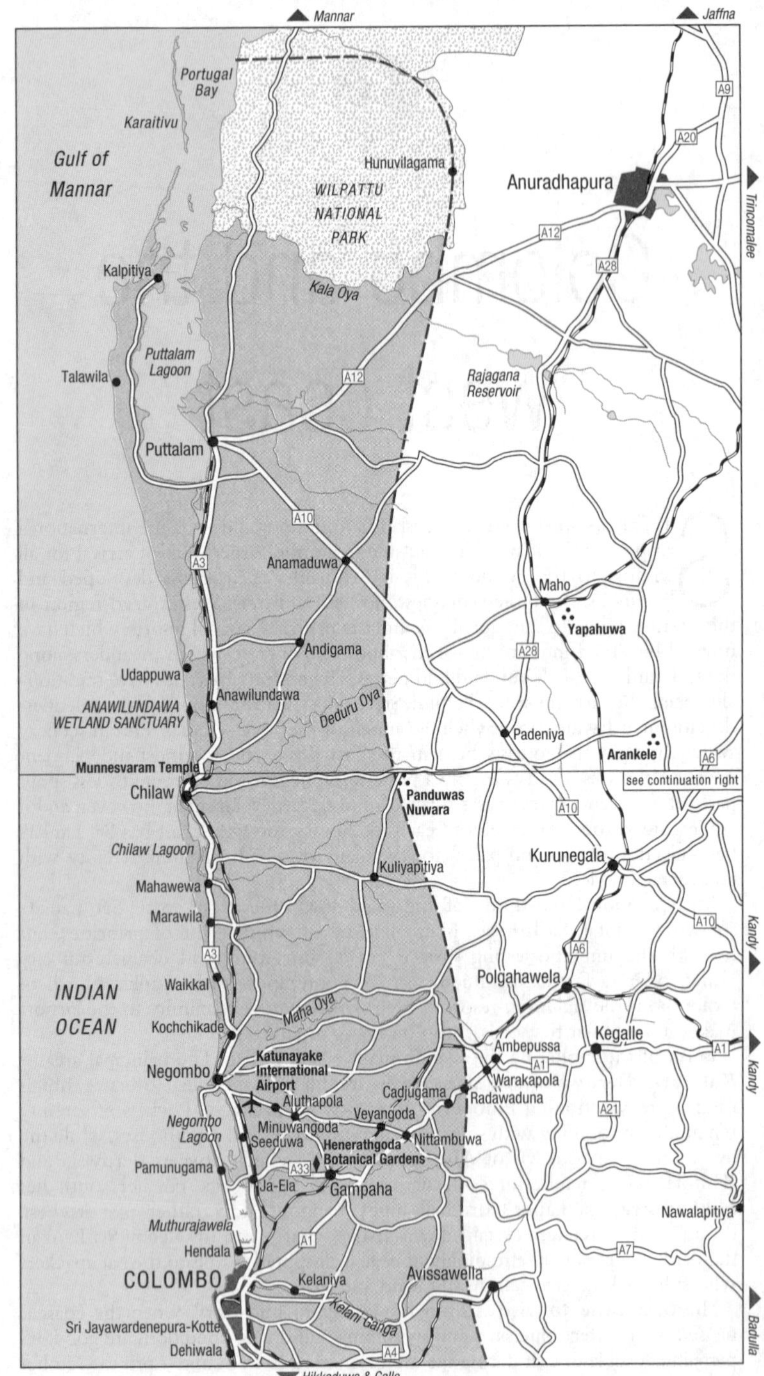
Mannar
Jaffna
Portugal Bay
Karaitivu
Gulf of Mannar
Hunuvilagama
WILPATTU NATIONAL PARK
Anuradhapura
Trincomalee
A9
A20
A12
A28
Kalpitiya
Kala Oya
Puttalam Lagoon
Talawila
A12
Rajagana Reservoir
Puttalam
A10
A3
Anamaduwa
Maho
Yapahuwa
Andigama
A28
Udappuwa
Anawilundawa
ANAWILUNDAWA WETLAND SANCTUARY
Deduru Oya
Padeniya
Arankele
A6
Munnesvaram Temple
Chilaw
Panduwas Nuwara
see continuation right
A10
Chilaw Lagoon
Kurunegala
Kuliyapitiya
Mahawewa
Marawila
A10
Kandy
A6
A3
Polgahawela
Waikkal
INDIAN OCEAN
Maha Oya
Kochchikade
Kegalle
Ambepussa
A1
Kandy
Katunayake International Airport
Negombo
A1
Warakapola
Cadjugama
Radawaduna
Aluthapola
Veyangoda
A21
Negombo Lagoon
Minuwangoda
Seeduwa
Nittambuwa
Henerathgoda Botanical Gardens
Pamunugama
A33
Ja-Ela
Gampaha
Nawalapitiya
Muthurajawela
A1
A7
Hendala
COLOMBO
Kelaniya
Avissawella
Badulla
Kelani Ganga
Sri Jayawardenepura-Kotte
Dehiwala
A4
Hikkaduwa & Galle

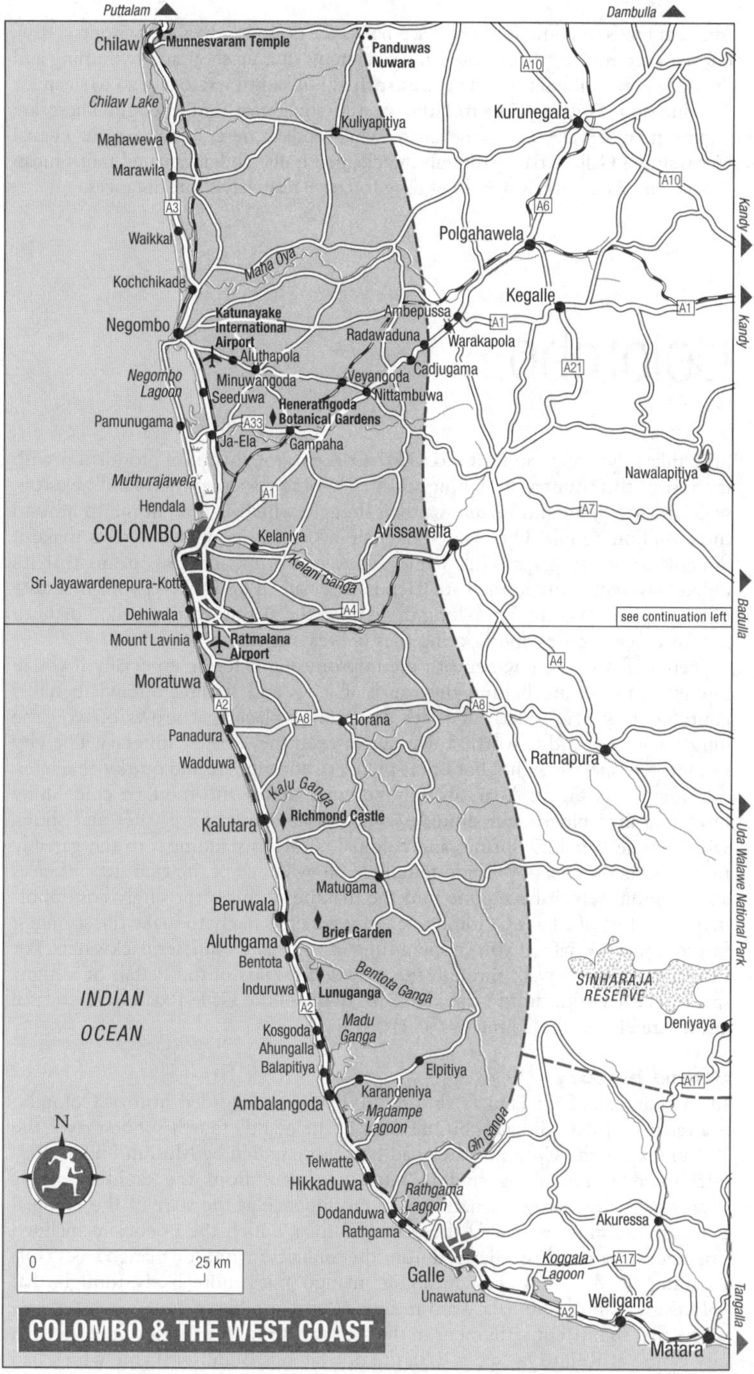

COLOMBO & THE WEST COAST

Puttalam
Dambulla
Chilaw
Munnesvaram Temple
Panduwas Nuwara
Chilaw Lake
Kuliyapitiya
Kurunegala
Mahawewa
Marawila
A10
A3
A6
Kandy
Waikkal
Polgahawela
Maha Oya
Kochchikade
Kegalle
Negombo
Katunayake International Airport
Ambepussa
Radawaduna
Warakapola
A1
Kandy
Aluthapola
Cadjugama
A21
Negombo Lagoon
Minuwangoda
Veyangoda
Seeduwa
Nittambuwa
Heneratgoda Botanical Gardens
Pamunugama
A33
Ja-Ela
Gampaha
Muthurajawela
Nawalapitiya
A1
A7
Hendala
COLOMBO
Kelaniya
Avissawella
Kelani Ganga
Sri Jayawardenepura-Kotte
Badulla
A4
Dehiwala
see continuation left
Mount Lavinia
Ratmalana Airport
A4
Moratuwa
A2
A8
Horana
A8
Panadura
Ratnapura
Wadduwa
Kalu Ganga
Uda Walawe National Park
Kalutara
Richmond Castle
Matugama
Beruwala
Brief Garden
Aluthgama
Bentota
SINHARAJA RESERVE
Bentota Ganga
INDIAN OCEAN
Induruwa
Lunuganga
A2
Deniyaya
Madu Ganga
Kosgoda
Ahungalla
Balapitiya
Elpitiya
A17
Ambalangoda
Karandeniya
Madampe Lagoon
Gin Ganga
N
Telwatte
Hikkaduwa
Rathgama Lagoon
Dodanduwa
Akuressa
Rathgama
0
25 km
Koggala Lagoon
A17
Galle
Tangalla
Unawatuna
Weligama
A2
Matara

(the rain tends to come in short sharp bursts for no more than a few hours a day), but skies can be grey, many hotels and restaurants shut up shop, and swimming and diving become difficult – some places, such as Hikkaduwa, virtually go to sleep for the duration. **Getting around** the west is straightforward enough. There are regular train services along the coast, while endless buses ply the main coastal highway, the Galle Road – though the clogged traffic and antiquated trains mean that it can take a surprisingly long time to cover relatively short distances.

Colombo

Sri Lanka's dynamic capital, **COLOMBO**, seems totally out of proportion with the rest of the country, stretching for fifty kilometres along the island's western seaboard in a long and formless urban straggle which is now home to around three million people. The city's sprawling layout and congested streets make it difficult to get to grips with, while a lack of obvious charms means that it's unlikely to win many immediate friends, especially if (as is likely) your first taste of the capital is via the hour-long drive from the airport through the northern breeze-block suburbs and hooting files of weaving traffic.

There's plenty to enjoy beneath the unpromising exterior, especially if you're interested in getting behind the tourist clichés and finding out what makes contemporary Sri Lanka tick – it's definitely a place that grows on you the longer you stay, and is worth a day out of even the shortest itinerary. The city musters few specific sights, but offers plenty of atmosphere and quirky character: a heady admixture of Asian anarchy, colonial charm and modern chic. Shiny modern office blocks rub shoulders with tumbledown local cafés and shops, while serene Buddhist shrines and colonial churches stand next to the garishly multicoloured towers of Hindu temples – all evidence of the rich stew of races and religions which have gone into the making of this surprisingly cosmopolitan city. Most of all, it's Colombo's energy which is likely to make the strongest impression, especially if you've spent time in the island's quieter backwaters. For sheer adrenaline, a walk through the crowded bazaars of the Pettah or a high-speed rickshaw ride amidst the kamikaze traffic of the Galle Road have no rival anywhere else in the country.

Some history

In the context of Sri Lanka's almost 2500 years of recorded history, Colombo is a relative upstart. Situated on the delta of the island's fourth-longest river, the Kelani Ganga, the Colombo area had been long settled by Muslim traders who established a flourishing trading settlement here from the eighth century onwards, but only rose to nationwide prominence at the start of the colonial period. The Sinhalese called the port Kolamba, which the poetically inclined Portuguese believed was derived from the Sinhalese word for mango trees (*kola* meaning "leaves", and *amba* meaning "mango"); it's more likely, though, that *kolamba* was an old Sinhala word meaning "port" or "ferry".

The first significant settlement in the area was 13km northeast of the modern city centre at **Kelaniya** (see p.109), site of a famous Buddhist shrine which had

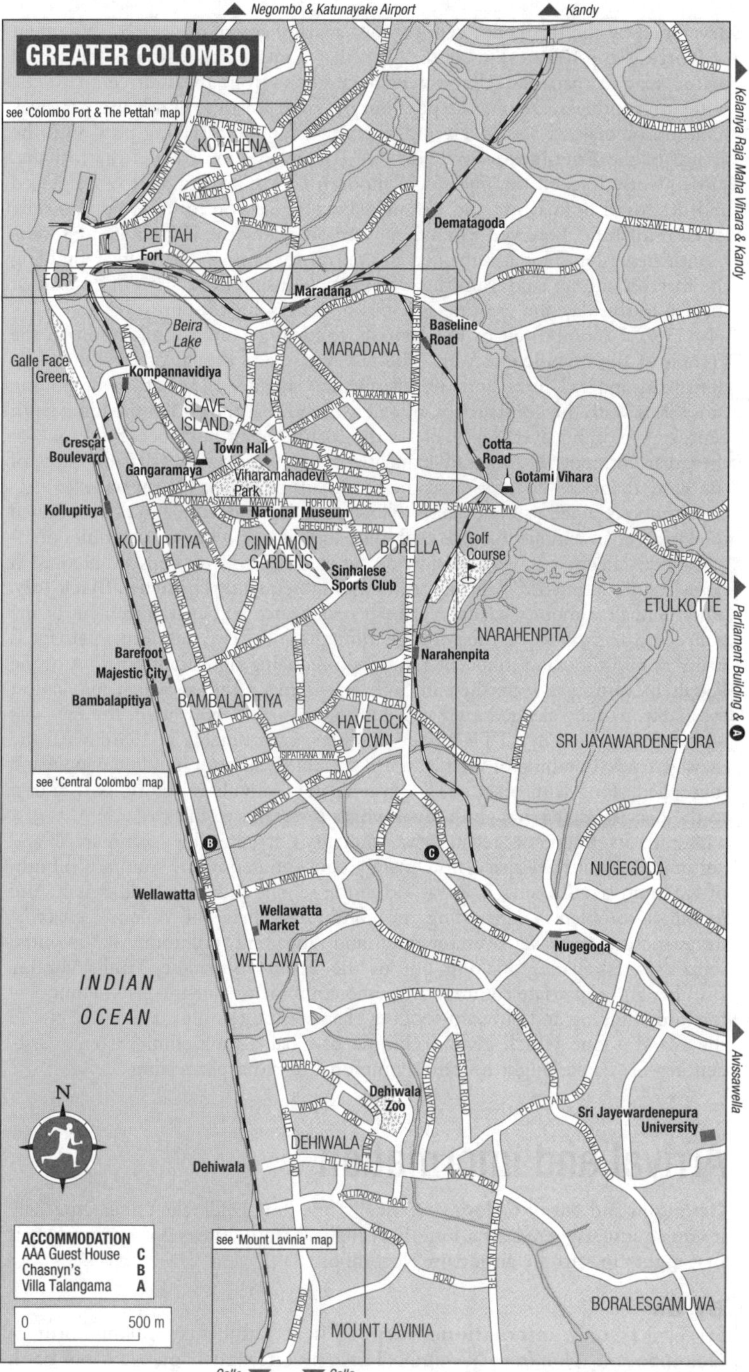
GREATER COLOMBO
Negombo & Katunayake Airport
Kandy
Kelaniya Raja Maha Vihara & Kandy
Parliament Building & A
Avissawella
Galle
Galle
see 'Colombo Fort & The Pettah' map
see 'Central Colombo' map
see 'Mount Lavinia' map
KOTAHENA
PETTAH
FORT
Fort
Maradana
Dematagoda
Baseline Road
Beira Lake
Galle Face Green
Kompannavidiya
SLAVE ISLAND
MARADANA
Town Hall
Viharamahadevi Park
Gangaramaya
Cresçat Boulevard
Kollupitiya
National Museum
KOLLUPITIYA
CINNAMON GARDENS
BORELLA
Sinhalese Sports Club
Golf Course
Cotta Road
Gotami Vihara
ETULKOTTE
NARAHENPITA
Narahenpita
Barefoot
Majestic City
Bambalapitiya
BAMBALAPITIYA
HAVELOCK TOWN
SRI JAYAWARDENEPURA
NUGEGODA
Nugegoda
Wellawatta
Wellawatta Market
WELLAWATTA
INDIAN OCEAN
Dehiwala Zoo
DEHIWALA
Dehiwala
Sri Jayewardenepura University
BORALESGAMUWA
MOUNT LAVINIA
JAMPETTAH STREET
MAIN STREET
NEW MOOR ST
OLD MOOR ST
MESSENGER ST
CENTRAL ROAD
ST ANTHONY'S MW
GRANDPASS ROAD
STACE ROAD
SIRIMAVO BANDARANAIKE MAWATHA
SRI SADDHARMA MW
AVISSAWELLA ROAD
SEDAWATHTHA ROAD
KELANIYA ROAD
KOLONNAWA ROAD
DEMATAGODA ROAD
D.H. ROAD
DANISTER DE SILVA MAWATHA
T.B. JAYA ROAD
DEAN'S ROAD
A RAJAKARUNA RD
E.W. PERERA MAWATHA
WARD PLACE
ROSMEAD PLACE
BARNES PLACE
HORTON PLACE
KYNSEY ROAD
DHARMAPALA MAWATHA
A. COOMARASWAMY MAWATHA
GREGORY'S ROAD
DUDLEY SENANAYAKE MW
SRI JAYAWARDENEPURA ROAD
BUTHGAMUWA ROAD
ELVITIGALA MAWATHA
UNION PLACE
SIR JAMES PEIRIS MW
R.A. DE MEL MAWATHA
5TH LANE
GALLE ROAD
REID AVENUE
BAUDDHALOKA MAWATHA
JAWATTE ROAD
KIRULA ROAD
THIMBIRIGASYAYA ROAD
VAJIRA ROAD
HAVELOCK ROAD
DICKMAN'S ROAD
ISIPATHANA MW
PARK ROAD
NARAHENPITA ROAD
NAWALA ROAD
DAWSON RD
KIRILLAPONE AVE
POHENGODA ROAD
PAGODA ROAD
OLD KOTTAWA ROAD
MARINE DRIVE
W.A. SILVA MAWATHA
HIGH LEVEL ROAD
DUTUGEMUNU STREET
HOSPITAL ROAD
SUNETHRADEVI ROAD
QUARRY ROAD
WAIDYA ROAD
ALLEN AVENUE
KADAWATHA ROAD
ANDERSON ROAD
PEPILIYANA ROAD
HORANA ROAD
HILL STREET
NIKAPE ROAD
PALLIDORA ROAD
KAWDANA ROAD
BELLANTARA ROAD
HOTEL ROAD
ACCOMMODATION
AAA Guest House C
Chasnyn's B
Villa Talangama A
0 500 m
N

developed by the thirteenth century into a major town; the nearby settlement of **Kotte** (see p.109), 11km southeast of the modern city, served as the capital of the island's main Sinhalese lowland kingdom from the fourteenth to the sixteenth centuries. Despite the proximity of both Kelaniya and Kotte, however, Colombo remained a relatively insignificant fishing and trading port until the arrival of the **Portuguese** in 1518. The Portuguese constructed the fort that subsequently formed the nucleus of modern Colombo and, in 1597, attacked and destroyed both Kotte and Kelaniya. Portuguese control of Colombo only lasted until 1656, however, when they were ousted by the **Dutch** after a seven-month siege. The Dutch remained in control for almost 150 years, rebuilding the fort, reclaiming land from the swampy delta using the system of canals that survive to this day, and creating spacious new tree-lined suburbs.

In 1796, Colombo fell to the **British**, following Dutch capitulation to the French in the Napoleonic Wars. The city was made capital of Ceylon, while new road and rail links with Kandy further enhanced the city's burgeoning prosperity. With the construction of a new harbour at the end of the nineteenth century, Colombo overtook Galle as the island's main port, becoming one of the great entrepôts of Asia and acquiring the sobriquet the "Charing Cross of the East" thanks to its location at the crossroads of Indian Ocean trade.

Colombo retained its importance following **independence**, and has continued to expand at an exponential rate ever since, though not without sometimes disastrous side effects. Growing islandwide Sinhalese–Tamil tensions erupted with tragic results in mid-1983, during the month subsequently christened **Black July**, when Sinhalese mobs, with the apparent connivance and encouragement of the police and army, went on the rampage throughout the city, murdering perhaps as many as two thousand innocent Tamils and reducing significant portions of the Pettah to ruins – a watershed in Sinhalese–Tamil relations which led, almost inevitably, to fully fledged civil war. During the **civil war** itself, the city was repeatedly targeted by LTTE suicide bombers, most notably in 1996, when the massive truck-bombing of the Central Bank killed almost a hundred people and succeeded, along with other attacks, in reducing Colombo's historic Fort district to the heavily militarized ghost town which it remains to this day.

Despite its traumatic recent past, the city's irrepressible commercial and cultural life continues apace, now mainly concentrated in the southern suburbs of Kollupitiya and Bambalapitiya, and in the rebuilt and revitalized Pettah. And for all its problems – including the continuing threat of violence, creaking infrastructure, massive overcrowding and appalling pollution – Colombo remains a fascinating melting pot of the island's Sinhalese, Tamil, Muslim, Burgher and expatriate communities, who combine to give the place a uniquely forward-thinking and outward-looking character quite unlike anywhere else in the island – one which gives a glimpse of what a multiethnic, twenty-first-century Sri Lanka might become, communal tensions permitting.

Arrival and information

Getting in and out of Colombo is usually one long gridlocked drag, especially if you've just staggered off a long-haul flight. Many visitors opt to spend their first night close to the airport in Negombo.

By air

Sri Lanka's only **international airport** is at Katunayake, 30km north of Colombo and 10km from Negombo. The arrivals terminal houses various **bank** kiosks, which change money at identical and fairly competitive rates, and a **Sri Lanka Tourist Board** information desk (open 24hr).

Taxis can be booked either at the airport taxi counter next to the tourist information desk or through one of the various travel agents in the booths opposite. Official fares at the airport taxi counter fluctuate constantly. Count on around US$25 for the tediously slow trip into Colombo (1hr or more), US$65 to Kandy (3hr) and US$13 to Negombo (20min); you may be able to get a cheaper deal through one of the travel agents, though don't count on it. Several of these agents also offer very cheap islandwide **tours** with car and driver, although these places don't have the best reputation and you're better off sorting something out in Negombo or Colombo. Free shuttle **buses** run every thirty minutes from just outside the terminal building to Averiwatte bus station, about 1.5km away, from where there are regular services on to Colombo (1hr or more) and Negombo (30min), plus less frequent buses to Kandy.

By train and bus

Arriving by **train**, you'll come in at **Fort Railway Station** (though it's actually in the Pettah, not Fort). It's convenient for the cluster of top-end hotels in Fort and around Galle Face Green, but some way from the city's southern areas, although there are fairly regular suburban trains from here south via Kollupitiya and Bambalapitiya to Mount Lavinia (see p.108).

Arriving by **bus**, you'll come in at one of the city's three **bus stations** – Saunders Place, Bastian Mawatha or the Central Bus Stand – which lie side by side about 500m to the east of Fort station; lack of space in the terminals means that some services drop off passengers in the surrounding side streets. Wherever you're deposited, there are always plenty of tuktuks hanging around.

Information

The city's **tourist office** (Mon–Fri 8.30am–4.15pm; Ⓣ011-243 7055, Ⓦwww.srilanka.travel) is just south of the *Galle Face Hotel* at 80 Galle Rd, Kollupitiya. Staff can assist with general queries and also dish out copies of the free monthly tourist guide, *Travel Lanka*, plus a free (but not very useful) accommodation guide. Other publications to look out for are *Leisure Times*, a monthly **listings magazine** (usually available in Barefoot and Odel; see p.116).

Area numbers and street names

Greater Colombo is divided into fifteen numbered suburbs, and districts are often identified by their **area code** rather than their name. The ones you're most likely to encounter are: Colombo 1 (Fort); Colombo 2 (Slave Island); Colombo 3 (Kollupitiya); Colombo 4 (Bambalapitiya); Colombo 5 (Havelock Town); Colombo 6 (Wellawatta); Colombo 7 (Cinnamon Gardens); and Colombo 11 (Pettah). Mount Lavinia isn't technically part of Colombo, and so isn't included in the numbering system.

The fact that suburbs in the city are known by both name and number is one possible source of confusion. Another is provided by ongoing changes to the city's **street names**. Dozens of streets have now lost their colonial monikers and have been renamed in honour of various polysyllabic Sri Lankan notables. Five of the most important renamings are R.A. de Mel Mawatha (formerly Duplication Rd); Ananda Coomaraswamy Mawatha (Green Path); Dr Colvin R. de Silva Mawatha (Union Place); De Soysa Circus (Lipton Circus); and Ernest de Silva Mawatha (Flower Rd). Many of the new names are only erratically recognized, with the old names still widely used.

City transport

Given how spread out Colombo is you'll need to make liberal use of **public transport** to explore the city. The city boasts a superabundant supply of **tuktuks** – recurrent calls of "Taxi?!" will follow you around the streets wherever you go. **Fares** per kilometre are generally higher here than anywhere else in the country apart from Kandy – Rs.50 per kilometre is a useful rule of thumb, though you may have to bargain hard even to get this. For longer journeys you might find it cheaper to order a metered taxi.

There are plenty of firms operating metered **radio taxis**; these operate city-wide and charge around Rs.65 per kilometre in an air-conditioned car with a minimum charge of around Rs.230. These are excellent value for longer journeys, especially if you can't be bothered to haggle with tuktuk drivers, though you'll have to ring up for one; they can't be found touting for custom on the street. Reputable companies are the excellent Kangaroo cabs (Ⓣ011-2 588 588) and GNTC (Ⓣ011-2 688 688).

Endless lines of antiquated **buses** chunter along Colombo's major thoroughfares, though given the difficulty of working out routes, they're of little use to the casual visitor (and if you've got luggage, forget it). The only time you might want to catch a bus is to get up and down the Galle Road in the southern half of the city between Kollupitiya and Mount Lavinia. Buses tear up and down between Galle Face Green and the southern suburbs literally every few seconds (although southbound buses were being diverted inland along Duplication Rd on their way through Kollupitiya at the time of writing); stops are marked by signs showing a picture of a bus set in a blue border.

Suburban **trains** are a useful way of reaching the southern part of the city, although they can get packed at rush hours (roughly Mon–Fri 7.30–9.30am & 4.30–6.30pm). Trains run roughly every half-hour (less frequently on Sun) from Fort Railway Station, calling at Kollupitiya, Bambalapitiya, Wellawatta, Dehiwala and Mount Lavinia. The journey from Fort to Mount Lavinia takes around half an hour.

▲ Commuter train, Colombo

Accommodation

Colombo has an over-supply of top-end **hotels** aimed at business travellers, plus a growing number of chic boutique hotels. Unfortunately, there's an absolutely chronic shortage of **budget** options. It pays to **book in advance**, especially if you're planning on staying at one of the smaller guesthouses, when you may need to reserve a week or more ahead. Never turn up at a small family-run guesthouse unannounced; you're unlikely to find a vacancy and the owners won't appreciate having unexpected visitors on their doorsteps, especially if you arrive at some ungodly hour of the night or morning.

Fort

The following places are marked on the map on p.98.

Ceylon Continental Janadhipathi Mw ⓣ011-242 1221, ⓦwww.ceyloncontinental.com. Perched right on the oceanfront, this is the smallest and cheapest of Colombo's five-stars, with chintzy orangey-pink decor, old-fashioned rooms (all with at least partial sea views) and a pleasantly intimate atmosphere. Facilities include a big pool (non-guests Rs.700) and a tiny spa. Even by Sri Lankan standards, the staff are frighteningly polite. ❼

Colombo City Hotel 33 Canal Row ⓣ011-534 1962, ⓔcmb_cityhotels@sltnet.lk. Excellent lower mid-range hotel bang in the heart of Fort. The smart modern rooms (some with balconies and views) are very comfortably furnished, with a/c, satellite TV and safe, and there's a breezy rooftop restaurant with fine city views. Excellent value. ❹

Grand Oriental York St ⓣ011-232 0320, ⓔgoh@sltnet. Famous old establishment, with superb port views from its fourth-floor restaurant, though the building itself has lost most of its colonial charm and the setting at the end of a heavily policed road is cheerless. Rooms are decent value, however: characterless but spacious, with satellite TV, fridge, a/c and town or harbour views. ❻

Hilton Sir Chittampalam A. Gardiner Mw ⓣ011-254 4644, ⓦwww.hilton.com. One of Colombo's flasher five-stars, with heavily marbled public areas and heaps of facilities including health club, swimming pool (non-guests an exorbitant Rs.1500) and a good selection of in-house restaurants. Rooms are spread over nineteen floors and get more expensive the higher you go. There are superb views, especially from higher floors, though the decor's drab and rates are usually relatively expensive compared to similar establishments. ❽–❾

YMCA Bristol St ⓣ011-232 5252. The cheapest place in town, this dingy, labyrinthine institution offers a range of very basic doubles with or without private bathroom, very cheap singles (Rs.440) sharing clean communal bathrooms, and a men-only dormitory (Rs.150 per person). No alcohol. Fills up quickly with locals, so book ahead or arrive early. ❶

Galle Face Green

The following places are marked on the map on pp.92–93.

Galle Face Hotel Galle Face Green ⓣ011-254 1010, ⓦwww.gallefacehotel.com. The city's most famous hotel, this oceanfront landmark has bags of colonial charm and slightly quirky character. Rooms in the old building, now known as the Classic Wing, are a bit faded but nonetheless atmospheric (the deluxe rooms are generally better value than the overpriced standard rooms, and avoid those overlooking the noisy Galle Rd). Those in the modern Regency Wing are kitted out in neo-colonial style and combine modern comforts with traditional decor. All rooms come with a/c, satellite TV and minibar, and there's also a romantic seafront bar and restaurant, a small pool (non-guests Rs.1000) and a big spa. Classic Wing ❻, Regency Wing ❼–❾

Holiday Inn Sir M.M. Markar Mw ⓣ011-242 2001, ⓦwww.holidayinn.lk. Tucked away in a quiet side street just off the bottom of Galle Face Green, this pleasantly low-key hotel doesn't have the style of its near neighbours, but offers an excellent location and larger-than-average (albeit slightly drab) and well-equipped rooms at relatively inexpensive rates. There's also a swimming pool (non-guests Rs.200) and the good *Alhambra* Indian restaurant (see p.111). ❻

Taj Samudra 25 Galle Face Centre Rd ⓣ011-244 6622, ⓦwww.tajhotels.com. One of Colombo's smartest hotels, this immense five-star palace is set in lush grounds straddling the eastern side of Galle Face Green. Rooms (some sea-facing) are attractively furnished, if a tad small, and good value at current rates. Facilities include a health club, yoga classes and swimming pool (guests only), plus several excellent restaurants. ❼

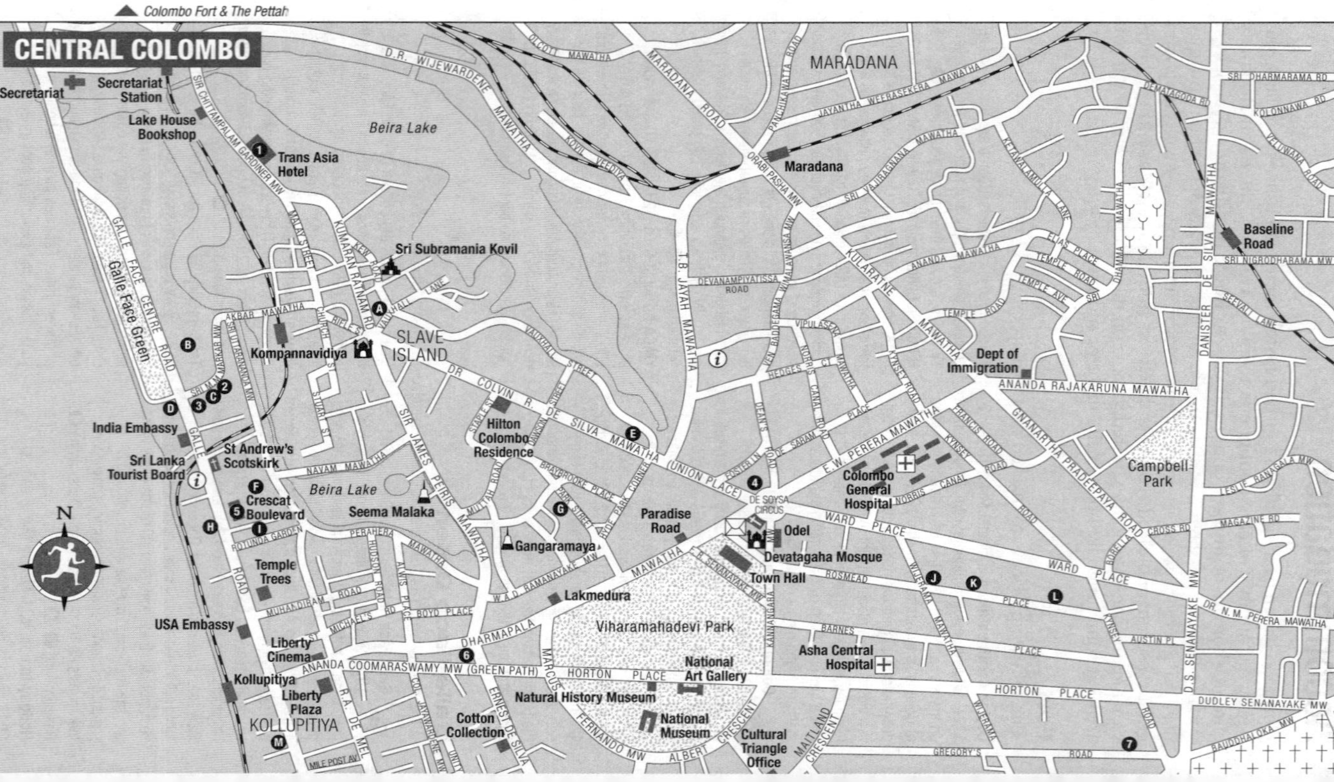
CENTRAL COLOMBO
Colombo Fort & The Pettah
Secretariat
Secretariat Station
Lake House Bookshop
Trans Asia Hotel
Beira Lake
Sri Subramania Kovil
Kompannavidiya
SLAVE ISLAND
Galle Face Green
GALLE FACE CENTRE ROAD
India Embassy
Sri Lanka Tourist Board
St Andrew's Scotskirk
Crescat Boulevard
Seema Malaka
Hilton Colombo Residence
Gangaramaya
Temple Trees
USA Embassy
Liberty Cinema
Kollupitiya
Liberty Plaza
KOLLUPITIYA
Cotton Collection
Natural History Museum
National Museum
National Art Gallery
Viharamahadevi Park
Lakmedura
Town Hall
Devatagaha Mosque
Odel
Paradise Road
DE SOYSA CIRCUS
Colombo General Hospital
Asha Central Hospital
Cultural Triangle Office
Campbell Park
Dept of Immigration
Maradana
MARADANA
Baseline Road
D.R. WIJEWARDENE MAWATHA
T.B. JAYAH MAWATHA
DR COLVIN R. DE SILVA MAWATHA (UNION PLACE)
SIR JAMES PEIRIS MAWATHA
KUMARAN RATNAM RD
SIR CHITTAMPALAM GARDINER MW
MALAY STREET
GALLE ROAD
DHARMAPALA MAWATHA
ANANDA COOMARASWAMY MW (GREEN PATH)
HORTON PLACE
WARD PLACE
E.W. PERERA MAWATHA
GNANARTHA PRADEEPAYA ROAD
ANANDA RAJAKARUNA MAWATHA
KULARATNE MAWATHA
DANISTER DE SILVA MAWATHA
D.S. SENANAYAKE MW
DR. N. M. PERERA MAWATHA
DUDLEY SENANAYAKE MW
MARADANA ROAD
ORABI PASHA MW
R.A. DE MEL
ERNEST DE SILVA
MARCUS FERNANDO MW
ALBERT CRESCENT
MAITLAND CRESCENT
ROSMEAD PLACE
WIJERAMA MAWATHA
KYNSEY ROAD
N

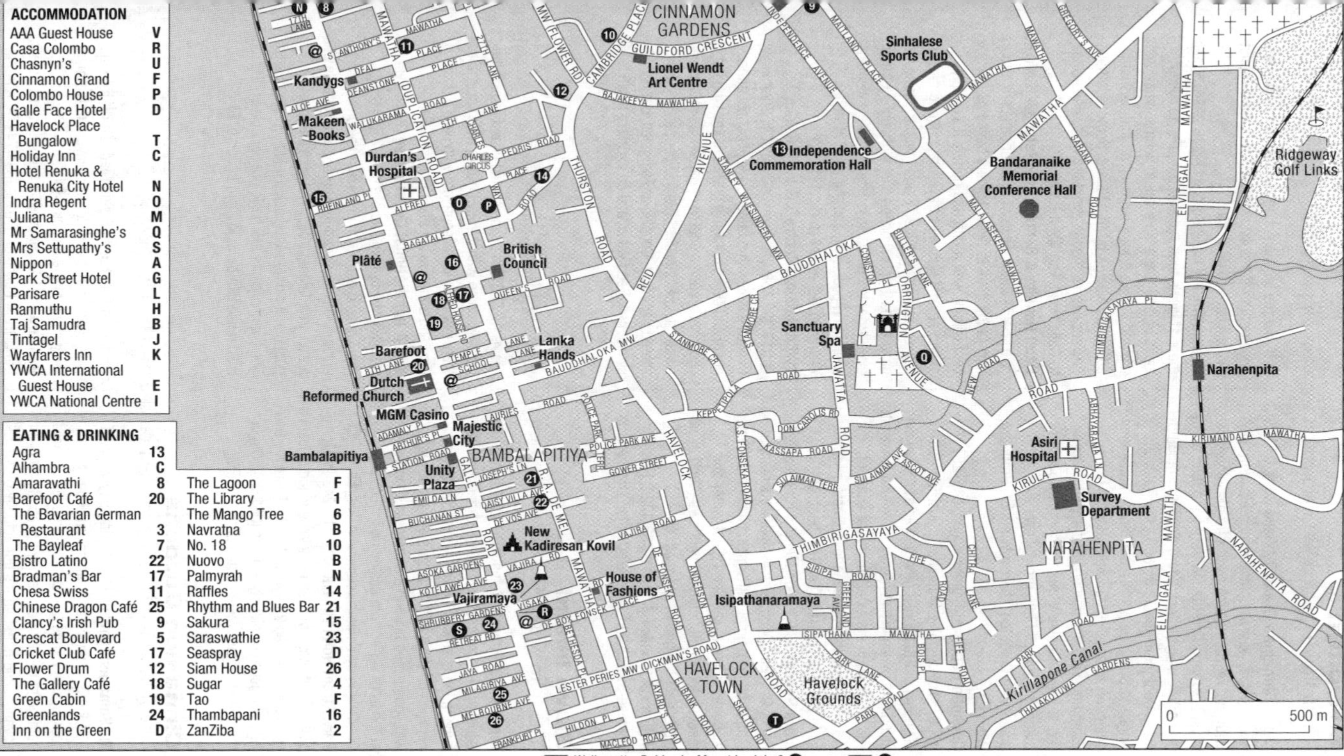
ACCOMMODATION
AAA Guest House V
Casa Colombo R
Chasnyn's U
Cinnamon Grand F
Colombo House P
Galle Face Hotel D
Havelock Place Bungalow T
Holiday Inn C
Hotel Renuka & Renuka City Hotel N
Indra Regent O
Juliana M
Mr Samarasinghe's Q
Mrs Settupathy's S
Nippon A
Park Street Hotel G
Parisare L
Ranmuthu H
Taj Samudra B
Tintagel J
Wayfarers Inn K
YWCA International Guest House E
YWCA National Centre I
EATING & DRINKING
Agra 13
Alhambra C
Amaravathi 8
Barefoot Café 20
The Bavarian German Restaurant 3
The Bayleaf 7
Bistro Latino 22
Bradman's Bar 17
Chesa Swiss 11
Chinese Dragon Café 25
Clancy's Irish Pub 9
Crescat Boulevard 5
Cricket Club Café 17
Flower Drum 12
The Gallery Café 18
Green Cabin 19
Greenlands 24
Inn on the Green D
The Lagoon F
The Library 1
The Mango Tree 6
Navratna B
No. 18 10
Nuovo B
Palmyrah N
Raffles 14
Rhythm and Blues Bar 21
Sakura 15
Saraswathie 23
Seaspray D
Siam House 26
Sugar 4
Tao F
Thambapani 16
ZanZiba 2
CINNAMON GARDENS
Lionel Wendt Art Centre
Sinhalese Sports Club
Independence Commemoration Hall
Bandaranaike Memorial Conference Hall
Ridgeway Golf Links
Kandygs
Makeen Books
Durdan's Hospital
British Council
Plâté
Barefoot
Dutch Reformed Church
Lanka Hands
Sanctuary Spa
Narahenpita
MGM Casino
Majestic City
Bambalapitiya
BAMBALAPITIYA
Unity Plaza
Asiri Hospital
Survey Department
NARAHENPITA
New Kadiresan Kovil
House of Fashions
Vajiramaya
Isipathanaramaya
HAVELOCK TOWN
Havelock Grounds
Kirillapone Canal
0 500 m
Wellawatta, Dehiwela, Mount Lavinia & U
V

Kollupitiya

The following places are marked on the map on pp.92–93.

Cinnamon Grand 77 Galle Rd ⓣ011-243 7437, ⓦwww.cinnamonhotels.com. Vies with the *Taj Samudra* for the title of Colombo's most luxurious five-star, with glitzy public areas and a big array of facilities including a medium-sized pool (non-guests Rs.800), the halcyon Angsana Spa (see p.119) and the capital's best selection of hotel restaurants. Rooms in the Premium Wing are modern and stylish; those in the cheaper Deluxe Wing are comfortable but bland, though all have great views over downtown Colombo. Deluxe Wing ❽, Premium Wing ❾

Colombo House 26 Charles Way ⓣ011-257 4900, ⓔcolombohse@eureka.lk. Just four rather plain and old-fashioned rooms in an attractive old colonial mansion. It's relatively expensive for what you get, though the location amidst some of Colombo's smartest and leafiest streets – very quiet but very central – can't be beat. ❹

Indra Regent 383 R.A. de Mel Mw (Duplication Rd) ⓣ011-257 7405, ⓦwww.indraregent.net. Simple modern hotel with small, functional rooms. All come with a/c, satellite TV, hot water and minibar, though not all have windows – and avoid those near the noisy main road. ❺

Juliana 316 Galle Rd ⓣ011-533 4222. Flashy Chinese-owned and patronized hotel. The decor is naff, but the location is good, and rooms are well equipped for the price, with a/c, hot water, satellite TV, minibar and wi-fi. ❹

Ranmuthu 112 Galle Rd ⓣ011-243 3986. Aimed more at locals than tourists, but in an excellent location, and reasonable value. Rooms (some with a/c and hot water) are large, clean and perfectly adequate, albeit a bit threadbare. Some also have fine sea-views, though avoid the noisy ones close to Galle Road. Fan ❸, a/c ❹

Hotel Renuka & Renuka City Hotel 328 Galle Rd ⓣ011-257 3598, ⓦwww.renukahotel.com. Smart mid-range hotel in two adjoining buildings (each, confusingly, with a different name). It's mainly aimed at local business travellers, offering modern a/c rooms with satellite TV and minibar; many also have at least partial ocean views (though get one away from the noisy Galle Road). There's also small swimming pool, wi-fi and the good in-house *Palmyrah* restaurant (see p.112). ❺

YWCA National Centre 7 Rotunda Garden ⓣ011-232 8589, ⓔnatywca@sltnet.lk. Soothingly tranquil place, with a rather convent-school atmosphere and clean, attractive private rooms with hot water set around a courtyard garden, as well as very cheap double "cubicles" (Rs.550 per person) with shared bathroom. Couples are admitted, but not single men. Good value, and an excellent location. ❸

Slave Island

The following places are marked on the map on pp.92–93.

Nippon 123 Kumaran Ratnam Rd ⓣ011-243 1887. Situated in an interestingly down-at-heel part of town in the characterful, colonnaded Mannings Mansion of 1883, with spacious and reasonably well-maintained fan and a/c rooms (although those at the front suffer from deafening traffic noise). Good value by Colombo standards. Fan ❸, a/c ❹

Park Street Hotel 20 Park St ⓣ011-243 9977, ⓦwww.anilana.com. Elegant new boutique hotel in a sensitively restored 250-year-old villa. There are two very spacious colonial-style suites (US$378/504) in the villa itself, plus more contemporary-looking rooms (US$281) in the converted warehouse at the back. All come with the full array of mod cons, and there's also an Idyllic courtyard with pool, a small gym and attractive bar and restaurant. ❾

YWCA International Guest House 393 Colvin R. De Silva Mw (Union Place) ⓣ011-232 4181. Atmospheric old Dutch colonial mansion with antique furniture scattered around the veranda and a fruit-tree-filled garden, and with plenty of genuine, if rather ramshackle, olde-worlde charm. The twenty rooms are basic but very clean, though road noise can be a problem in some. ❸

Cinnamon Gardens

The following places are marked on the map on pp.92–93.

Mr Samarasinghe's 53/19 Torrington Ave ⓣ011-250 2403, ⓦwww.ranjitsambalama.com. Seven comfortable rooms (a/c or fan; some with shared bathroom) in a modern family house. Ring in advance, and note that it's not actually on Torrington Ave, but on a side road just off it to the east: turn off by the children's playground immediately south of the mosque. ❹

Parisare 97/1 Rosmead Place (no sign; it's behind the UNHCR building) ⓣ011-269 4749. In a family house in a very quiet location in the heart of Cinnamon Gardens, with just three simple but comfortable rooms (although the walls don't reach the ceiling in two of them, meaning that they're cool but not very private). Good single rates. Advance reservations essential. ❸

Tintagel 65 Rosmead Place ⓣ011-460 2121, ⓦwww.tintagelcolombo.com. Superb new boutique hotel set in a stunning colonial mansion which was formerly the family home of the Bandaranaike family, who have provided Sri Lanka with three prime ministers since Independence, including the world's first woman prime minister; S.W.R.D. Bandaranaike was shot here on the veranda in 1959 (see p.427). The mansion has now been lavishly restored by Udayshanth Fernando of Paradise Road (see p.116), with ten spacious and beautiful suites (US$250/380) in muted colours, a picture-perfect little infinity pool, in-house restaurant and a very chic little bar – although, bizarrely, the authorities have refused to give the place an alcohol licence (though guests are welcome to bring their own). ❾

Wayfarers Inn 77 Rosmead Place (no sign) ⓣ011-269 3936, ⓔwayfarer@slt.lk. Set in a quiet residential area, this attractive colonial-style guesthouse has a range of comfortable fan and a/c doubles with satellite TV, hot water and fridge, plus a studio apartment with kitchen (US$37). There's also free internet access and an attractive garden. Advance booking almost always necessary. ❹

Bambalapitiya, Havelock Town and Kirillapone

The following places are marked on the map on p.87 and pp.92–93.

AAA Guest House 49 Lionel Edirisinghe Mw, off Polhengoda Rd, Kirillapone, Colombo 5 ⓣ011-282 8111, ⓦwww.aaalanka.com. One of Colombo's increasingly meagre budget options, with basic but cheap rooms and slightly more upmarket apartments (sleeping up to eight) in a quiet suburban side street. It's a bit of a way from town, although very frequent #138 buses pass close by every couple of minutes, connecting with most points across the city. Ring before you arrive for directions. If you're coming by tuktuk or taxi, ask for Polhengoda Road, near the Apollo Hospital. Fan ❷, a/c ❸, apartments ❹–❺

Casa Colombo 231 Galle Rd, Bambalapitiya ⓣ011-452 0130, ⓦwww.casacolombo.com. Striking new boutique hotel, occupying a two-hundred-year-old mansion given a very contemporary twist, with a mix of colonial chintz and contemporary pazzazz. The twelve funky suites come complete with all sorts of digital mod cons and off-the-wall artworks and bric-a-brac. There's also a small pool and indoor and outdoor dining areas, while the *Icebox* bar (a pure white cube) is as cool as its name suggests – or would be, if the government would actually give the owners an alcohol licence. It's no bargain, however, with rates from around US$300 up to US$735. ❾

Chasnyn's 37A St Peter's Place, Bambalapitiya ⓣ011-258 8583, ⓔharoonmusafer@yahoo.com. Four simple but comfortable and very good-value rooms (sharing two bathrooms) in a quiet and pleasantly old-fashioned house at the southern end of Bambalapitiya. Popular with long-staying guests, so has a very friendly family atmosphere. Advance bookings essential. ❷

Havelock Place Bungalow 6 Havelock Place, Havelock Town (turn down the side road by the petrol station) ⓣ011-258 5191, ⓦwww.havelockbungalow.com. Despite the slightly inconvenient location, this is one of Colombo's more alluring places to stay, set in a pair of intimate and stylishly converted colonial villas which combine old-fashioned charm with all modern amenities (including a/c and wi-fi). There's also a small pool, a beautiful garden and a peaceful garden café. ❼

Mrs Settupathy's 23/2 Shrubbery Gardens (directly behind the Church of Christ), Bambalapitiya ⓣ011-258 7964, ⓔjbs@slt.lk. Cosy and good-value family guesthouse, with six spacious, clean rooms, all with a/c and hot water, and a nice upstairs communal seating area. ❸

Mount Lavinia

The following places are marked on the map on p.109.

Blue Seas 9/6 De Saram Rd ⓣ011-271 6298. Homely and popular guesthouse in a quiet location, with the cheapest decent rooms in Mount Lavinia and a friendly family atmosphere. ❸

Cottage Gardens 42–48 College Ave ⓣ011-271 9692. Five large and attractively furnished detached cottages (each sleeping two) with kitchenette, dotted around a peaceful and very private walled garden. ❹

Ivory Inn 21 De Saram Rd ⓣ0716 812 668. One of Mount Lavinia's best cheapies, with spotless, nicely furnished rooms with private balcony in an attractive modern red-brick building in a quiet location. Fan ❸, a/c ❹

Mount Lavinia Hotel 100 Hotel Rd ⓣ011-271 5221, ⓦwww.mountlaviniahotel.com. Famous old landmark hotel which retains engaging touches of colonial style, despite comprehensive modernization, and enjoys a superb location atop its little oceanfront promontory – although the whole place is often very busy with wedding parties and isn't the most relaxing spot in town. Rooms are modern and fairly characterless, though with all the usual five-star mod cons; most have sea views. There's also a biggish swimming pool, a serene modern beachfront spa, and a huge swathe of idyllic private beach if you want to escape from the hoi polloi (non-guests can use both pool and private beach for Rs.600). ❽–❾

Rivi Ras Hotel 50/2 De Saram Rd ⓣ011-271 7786, ⓦwww.rivirashotel.com. Attractive hotel occupying a series of detached, colonnaded red-brick buildings set in very spacious gardens. Rooms are large and minimally but pleasantly furnished; all have hot water, and a few have a/c and satellite TV. ❹

Tropic Inn 30 College Ave ⓣ011-273 8653, ⓦwww.tropicinn.com. Pleasant and very peaceful small hotel, with attractive wood and wrought-iron decor. Rooms (all with hot water and a/c) are cool, clean, modern and nicely furnished. ❹

The outskirts

The following appears on the map on p.87.

Villa Talagama Hokandara ⓣ011-238 1201, ⓦwww.jetwingeco.com. The ultimate Colombo hideaway, this superb three-room contemporary-colonial-style villa is set in a tranquil location on the edge of the city, a 30min drive from the centre, complete with its own swimming pool and garden overlooking the birdlife-rich Talangama wetlands. ❽ half-board

The City

Colombo is a confusing city. There's no single focal point, and it's more helpful to think of it as a collection of disparate neighbourhoods than as a single, coherent urban space. At the heart of the old colonial city, the moribund and bomb-afflicted **Fort** district, Colombo's former administrative and financial centre, offers a stark reminder of the conflicts which have beset modern Sri Lanka, while to the east and south lie the bustling mercantile district of the **Pettah** and the engaging temples and old-fashioned street life of **Slave Island**. From here, it's a short walk or tuktuk ride to **Galle Face Green** – perfect, after a hard day's exploring, for an evening stroll along the seafront promenade and a sundowner at the historic *Galle Face Hotel*.

South of the Green, the sulphurous **Galle Road** runs through the suburbs of **Kollupitiya** and **Bambalapitiya**, the heart of the modern city, and home to many of Colombo's best shopping and eating venues. Inland, the leafy streets of **Cinnamon Gardens** conceal further places to stay, eat and drink, as well as the tropical oasis of the **Viharamahadevi Park** and the city's excellent **National Museum**. Further south are the more downmarket suburbs of **Wellawatta** and **Dehiwala**, home to the national zoo, and the attractive beachside suburb of **Mount Lavinia**, 10km from the city centre.

Fort

Fort district lies at the heart of old Colombo, occupying (as its name suggests) the site of the now-vanished Portuguese defences. Under the British, Fort developed into the centrepiece of the colonial capital, adorned with handsome Neoclassical buildings and boasting all the necessities of expatriate life in the tropics, right down to the inevitable clocktower and statue of Queen Victoria. Following independence, Fort retained its position as Colombo's administrative and financial hub until the onset of the civil war, when repeated LTTE attacks

– most notably the massive **bomb** that was detonated outside the Central Bank on Janadhipathi Mawatha in 1996 – all but killed off the life of the district. Despite these reverses, the area retains something of its former commercial importance, with myriad banks, airline offices, a clutch of five-star hotels and an optimistically modernist skyline (presided over by the two soaring towers of the unfortunately named World Trade Center), though these tokens of progress give little indication of the ravages of the war years. At street level, central Fort remains one of Sri Lanka's strangest urban spaces, its moribund and eerily deserted streets lined with the grandiose shells of semi-derelict nineteenth-century buildings, and carved up by security barriers and wire-mesh fences into a perplexing maze of blocked-off streets and security checkpoints – significant parts of the district remain closed to visitors thanks to the proximity of the harbour and president's official residence.

Around the clocktower

Thanks to the presence of the President's House, almost the entire western side of Fort (effectively, everything between Janadhipathi Mawatha and the seafront Chaitiya Rd) is currently closed to visitors. Aside from the places described here, the area's few sites of interest are now largely out of bounds. More or less at the centre of the district is the quaint **clocktower-lighthouse**, ignominiously hemmed in on three sides by security fences and now a rather forlorn sight. The clocktower was originally constructed in 1857, apparently at the behest of the punctilious wife of Governor Henry Ward as a result of her exasperation with oriental standards of timekeeping. Ten years later, a lighthouse-style beacon was constructed on top of the clock, and it served simultaneously as timekeeper and as a signal for approaching shipping for a century until the surrounding buildings grew so high that they blocked out the lighthouse's beam (a new lighthouse now stands on the seafront just to the west). East of the clocktower, **Chatham** and **Hospital streets** comprise a strange medley of grandiose but semi-derelict colonial buildings, interspersed with the forlorn shops of jewellers, travel agents and insistent moneychangers, whose shouts of "Change dollar?" are usually the only sign of life hereabouts.

The area north of the clocktower, home to the zealously guarded President's House, is closed to the general public, with the only exit from the clocktower usually being east along Chatham Street to **York Street**, at the edge of the high-security zone. A block north of here, the corner at the junction with Mudalige Mawatha is dominated by the stolidly mercantile frontage of **Cargills** department store, whose expansive red-brick facade is one of Fort's most famous landmarks. Inside, the wood-panelled fittings and display cases look as though they haven't changed since the store's opening in 1906, though the disconcertingly bare shelves appear not to have been restocked since independence.

The port area

Continuing north from Cargills, York Street becomes increasingly down-at-heel before reaching Colombo's **port**, hidden behind high walls and strictly off limits. Until the early twentieth century, the island's main port was Galle, but Colombo's improved road and rail links with the rest of the country and Sri Lanka's strategic location on Indian Ocean sea routes between Europe, Asia and Australasia encouraged the British to invest in a major overhaul of the city's rather unsatisfactory harbour, during which they constructed three new breakwaters (the largest, built in 1885, is over a kilometre long). Opposite the main entrance to the port stands the famous old **Grand Oriental Hotel** – passengers arriving in Colombo would stagger straight off their ocean liner into the palatial hotel foyer, to collapse over

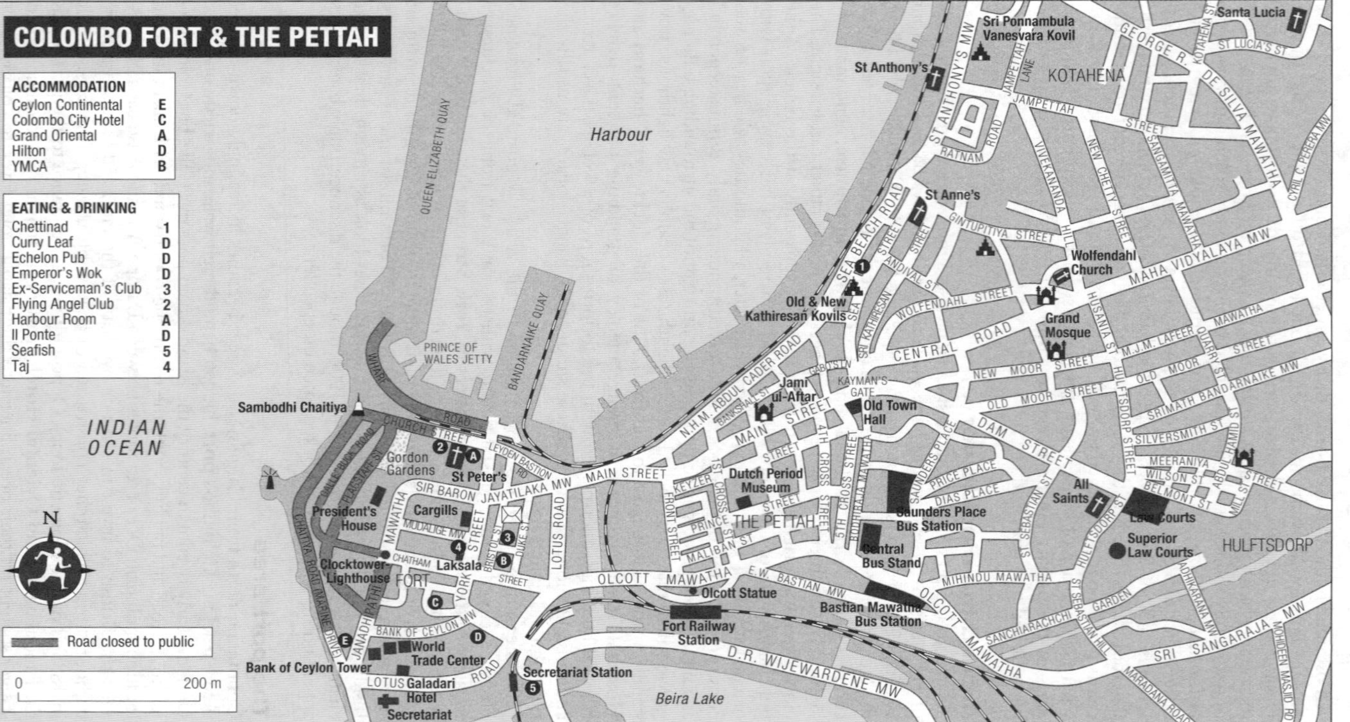
COLOMBO FORT & THE PETTAH
ACCOMMODATION
Ceylon Continental E
Colombo City Hotel C
Grand Oriental A
Hilton D
YMCA B
EATING & DRINKING
Chettinad 1
Curry Leaf D
Echelon Pub D
Emperor's Wok D
Ex-Serviceman's Club 3
Flying Angel Club 2
Harbour Room A
Il Ponte D
Seafish 5
Taj 4
Road closed to public
0
200 m
N
INDIAN OCEAN
Harbour
Beira Lake
QUEEN ELIZABETH QUAY
BANDARNAIKE QUAY
PRINCE OF WALES JETTY
Sambodhi Chaitiya
St Peter's
Gordon Gardens
President's House
Cargills
Laksala
Clocktower-Lighthouse
FORT
World Trade Center
Bank of Ceylon Tower
Galadari Hotel
Secretariat
Secretariat Station
Fort Railway Station
Olcott Statue
Bastian Mawatha Bus Station
Central Bus Stand
Saunders Place Bus Station
Dutch Period Museum
THE PETTAH
Jami ul-Aftar
Old Town Hall
Old & New Kathiresan Kovils
St Anne's
St Anthony's
Sri Ponnambula Vanesvara Kovil
KOTAHENA
Santa Lucia
Wolfendahl Church
Grand Mosque
All Saints
Law Courts
Superior Law Courts
HULFTSDORP
CHURCH STREET
WHARF ROAD
CHAITIYA ROAD (MARINE DRIVE)
GALLE BUCK ROAD
FLAGSTAFF ST
JANADHIPATHI MAWATHA
CHATHAM STREET
SIR BARON JAYATILAKA MW
MUDALIGE MW
YORK STREET
BANK OF CEYLON MW
LOTUS ROAD
BRISTOL ST
DUKE ST
LEYDEN BASTION RD
MAIN STREET
OLCOTT MAWATHA
D.R. WIJEWARDENE MW
FRONT STREET
KEYZER ST
PRINCE ST
MALIBAN ST
1ST CROSS ST
4TH CROSS STREET
5TH CROSS STREET
BODHIRAJA MAWATHA
E.W. BASTIAN MW
N.H.M. ABDUL CADER ROAD
BANKSHALL ST
GABO'S LN
KAYMAN'S GATE
SEA BEACH ROAD
SEA ST
SRI KATHIRESAN ST
ANDIVAL ST
GINTUPITIYA STREET
WOLFENDAHL STREET
CENTRAL ROAD
NEW MOOR STREET
OLD MOOR STREET
DAM STREET
SAUNDERS PLACE
PRICE PLACE
DIAS PLACE
ST SEBASTIAN ST
HULFTSDORP STREET
HUSANIA ST
M.J.M. LAFEER MAWATHA
QUARRY ST
SRIMATH BANDARNAIKE MW
SILVERSMITH ST
MEERANIYA STREET
WILSON ST
BELMONT ST
ABDUL HAMID ST
MILL ST
MIHINDU MAWATHA
SANCHIARACHCHI GARDEN
ST SEBASTIAN HILL
ADHIKARANA MW
SRI SANGARAJA MW
MOHIDEEN MASJID RD
MARADANA ROAD
MAHA VIDYALAYA MW
VIVEKANANDA HILL
NEW CHETTY STREET
SANGAMITTA MAWATHA
GEORGE R. DE SILVA MAWATHA
CYRIL C. PERERA MW
ST LUCIA'S ST
KOTAHENA ST
JAMPETTAH STREET
JAMPETTAH LANE
ST ANTHONY'S MW
RATNAM ROAD

a revivifying cocktail. Little of the establishment's former colonial splendour remains, though its *Harbour Room* restaurant-bar affords marvellous port views.

The area east of the hotel is currently out of bounds, though you can go through the checkpoint to visit **St Peter's Church** (daily 7am–5pm), next door to the hotel. Occupying an old Dutch governor's residence of 1680, it was converted into a church in 1821, its plain little Neoclassical facade squeezed into a narrow space between surrounding buildings. The interior is almost completely bare, the only decoration being the wall memorials to various British notables who ended their lives in Ceylon – a strangely time-warped and atmospheric little spot, which seems a million miles away from the decaying Sri Lankan streets outside.

Southern Fort and Marine Drive

Heading straight back down York Street for 500m brings you to the southern end of Fort, whose modern high-rises offer a sharp contrast to the colonial appearance of the rest of the district. Southern Fort is dominated by a triumvirate of five-star **hotels**, the slender, cylindrical **Bank of Ceylon Tower** and the twin towers of the **World Trade Center**, whose glassy facades and expanses of bland concrete embody Sri Lanka at its most forward-looking and internationalist. These prestigious commercial symbols were repeatedly targeted by LTTE bombers during the civil war, and although most of the damage has now been patched up, the bombed-out remains of the Mercantile Bank, at the bottom end of Janadhipathi Mawatha, provide a sombre reminder of the events of January 31, 1996, when a truck laden with 200kg of explosives exploded outside the Central Bank opposite, killing 91 people and injuring over 1500 – the most devastating of all the LTTE's various attacks against Colombo.

The Pettah and Kotahena

East of Fort, the helter-skelter bazaar district of the **Pettah** is Colombo's most absorbing area, and feels quite unlike anywhere else in Sri Lanka. The crush and energy of the gridlocked streets, with merchandise piled high in tiny shops and on the pavements, holds an undeniable, chaotic fascination, although exploring can be a slow and rather exhausting process, made additionally perilous by the barrow boys and porters who charge through the crowds pulling or carrying enormous loads and threatening the heads and limbs of unwary tourists.

Shops in the Pettah are still arranged in the traditional **bazaar layout**, with each street devoted to a different trade: Front Street, for example, is full of bags, suitcases and shoes; 1st Cross Street is devoted to hardware and electrical goods; 3rd Cross Street and Keyzer Street are stuffed with colourful fabrics, and so on. The wares on display are fairly mundane – unless you're a big fan of Taiwanese household appliances or fake Barbie dolls – although traces of older and more colourful trades survive in places.

Unlike the rest of Colombo, the district retains a strongly **Tamil** (the name Pettah derives from the Tamil word *pettai*, meaning village) and **Muslim** flavour, as evidenced by its many pure veg and Muslim restaurants, quaint mosques, Hindu temples and colonial churches (many Sri Lankan Tamils are Christian rather than Hindu). Even the people look different here, with Tamil women in gorgeous saris, Muslim children dressed entirely in white and older men in brocaded skullcaps – a refreshing change from the boring skirts and shirts which pass muster in the rest of the city.

Fort Railway Station to the Jami ul-Aftar

On the south side of the Pettah stands Colombo's principal train terminus, **Fort Railway Station**, a rambling Victorian barn of a building. In front of the station stands a statue of **Henry Steel Olcott** (1842–1907), the American Buddhist and co-founder (with Madame Blavatsky, the celebrated Russian clairvoyant and spiritualist), of the Theosophical Society, a quasi-religious movement which set about promoting Asian philosophy in the West and reviving oriental spiritual traditions in the East, to protect them from the attacks of European missionary Christianity. The society's utopian (if rather vague) objectives comprised a mixture of the scientific, the social, the spiritual and the downright bizarre: the mystical Madame Blavatsky, fount of the society's more arcane tenets, believed that she had the ability to levitate, render herself invisible and communicate with the souls of the dead, as well as asserting that the Theosophical Society was run according to orders received from a group of "masters" – disembodied tutelary spirits who were believed to reside in Tibet. In 1880, Blavatsky and Olcott arrived in Ceylon, formally embracing Buddhism and establishing the **Buddhist Theosophical Society**, which became one of the principal driving forces behind the remarkable worldwide spread of Buddhism during the twentieth century. Olcott spent many of his later years touring the island, organizing Buddhist schools and petitioning the British colonial authorities to respect Sri Lanka's religious traditions, though his most visible legacy is the multicoloured Buddhist flag (composed of the five colours of the Buddha's halo) which he helped design, and which now decorates temples across the island.

A couple of blocks north of the station on Prince Street, amongst some of the most densely packed of the Pettah's bazaars, the **Dutch Period Museum** (Tues–Sat 9am–5pm; Rs.500) occupies the old Dutch town hall, a fine colonnaded building of 1780. The mildly interesting displays on the Dutch colonial era feature the usual old coins, Kandyan and Dutch artefacts, military junk and dusty European furniture, plus a couple of miserable-looking waxworks of colonists dressed in full velvet and lace despite the sweltering heat. The main attraction, however, is the wonderfully atmospheric mansion itself, whose groaning wooden floors and staircases, great pitched roof and idyllic garden offer a beguiling glimpse into the lifestyle enjoyed by the eighteenth century's more upwardly mobile colonists.

Return to 2nd Cross Street and fight your way north for two blocks to **Main Street**, the district's principal thoroughfare, usually a solidly heaving bedlam of vehicles and pedestrians, with porters weaving through the throng pushing carts piled high with every conceivable type of merchandise. On the far side of the road is Colombo's most eye-catching mosque, the **Jami ul-Aftar**, a gloriously kitsch red-and-white construction of 1909 which rises gaudily above the cluttered shops of Main Street like a heavily iced cake.

The Old Town Hall to Sea Street

Continue east from the Jami ul-Aftar past a memorably malodorous fish market before reaching the intersection known as **Kayman's Gate** – the name probably refers to the crocodiles which were once kept in the canals surrounding Slave Island and in the fort moat to deter slaves from attempting to escape. Kayman's Gate is dominated by the fancifully Moorish-style **Old Town Hall** of 1873. Following an incarnation as a public market, the building was reopened in 1984 as a now-defunct municipal museum. The wrought-iron market building to one side still houses various marooned pieces of industrial and municipal hardware – including a steamroller, old street signs and a former van of the Colombo Public Library – which you can peek at through the railings. The doors into the town hall itself are usually left open, allowing you to walk up the fine Burma teak staircase to the old council chambers, whose austere wooden fittings and stalled fans exude a positively *Marie Celeste*-like charm. The small room next door houses a petrified huddle of waxwork figurines sitting around a table re-enacting a council meeting of yesteryear – unquestionably one of Colombo's most surreal sights.

The fruit and veg sellers who line the western side of the town hall building make this one of the most photogenic sections of the Pettah, while just behind lies another half-submerged remnant of colonial times in the form of an elaborate wrought-iron **market building**, now occupied by a miscellany of shops. Just behind here, **4th Cross Street** is usually full of colourful lorries loading and unloading: great sacks of chillies clutter the pavements, while merchants sit behind huge ledgers and piles of spices inside the picturesque little office-warehouses that line the street.

North of the town hall, the crowds begin to thin. The south side of **Gabo's Lane** is home to a few easily missed shops selling Ayurvedic ingredients: outlandish-looking sacks and pallets sit outside shops stuffed with bark, twigs and other strange pieces of vegetable matter. North of here, **Sea Street**'s eye-catching selection of fluorescent Sinhala signs advertise a long line of small jewellers' shops, usually full of local women haggling over ornate gold rings, earrings and necklaces. Sea Street's middle section is dominated by the colourful **New Kathiresan** and **Old Kathiresan kovils**, whose three gateways fill one side of the street with a great clumpy mass of Hindu statuary. The temples are dedicated to the war god Skanda and are the starting point for the annual Vel Festival (see p.50); they're usually shut during the day, but become a hive of activity after dark, when bare-chested, luxuriantly bearded priests conduct evening puja amidst the hypnotic noise of drumming and dense swirls of smoke.

Kotahena

Continuing north along Sea Street and St Anthony's Mawatha, you enter the adjacent suburb of **Kotahena**, home to numerous colonial churches and small but brightly coloured Hindu temples. Walking north along St Anthony's Mawatha, you'll pass a string of colourful shops selling Hindu and Christian religious paraphernalia before reaching **St Anthony's Church**, where people of all faiths come to pay homage to a statue of St Anthony which is said to work miracles in solving family problems.

A fifteen-minute walk from St Anthony's, along Jampettah, Kotahena and St Lucia's streets, lies the cathedral of **Santa Lucia**, perhaps the most imposing church in Sri Lanka. Built between 1873 and 1910, and sporting a stately grey classical facade inspired by St Peter's in Rome, it seats some six thousand people, though not since the pope conducted a service here in 1994 has it been even half full. Inside, the tombs of three French bishops of Colombo are about as exciting as it gets. Two further Neoclassical buildings – a Benedictine monastery and a convent – sit by the cathedral, creating an unexpectedly impressive architectural ensemble in this slightly out-of-the-way corner of the city.

Back on Jampettah Street, just east of St Anthony's, head south up Vivekananda Hill to reach the Dutch Reformed **Wolfendhal** (or Wolvendaal) **Church** of 1749, Colombo's oldest and one of Sri Lanka's most interesting Dutch relics. The rather severe Neoclassical exterior conceals an attractive period-piece interior complete with old tiled floor, simple stained glass, wicker seating and wooden pews, organ and pulpit. There are lots of memorials on the walls, plus numerous finely carved eighteenth-century floor tablets in the south transept commemorating assorted Dutch officials, including various governors whose remains were moved here from Fort in 1813. The whole structure exudes a sense of beautiful quiet and longevity which seems to have survived in a curious bubble amidst the ramshackle surrounding streets. Ask the caretaker to show you the church's impressive collection of old Dutch church silver, if he's around.

The area just south of here is dotted with a number of small, fanciful-looking mosques – the largest (but plainest) is the **Grand Mosque** on New Moor Street, the most important in the city, which hides behind shyly latticed orange walls. The large and striking modern building with the hat-shaped roof you can see from here is the **Superior Law Courts** (the original Neoclassical courts stand stolidly next door, two dumpy little buildings with dour Doric facades). Opposite the law courts rises the soaring spire of the pale grey Gothic Revival church of **All Saints**.

Galle Face Green

Running along the seafront south of Fort, the grassy sweep of **Galle Face Green** is one of the city's few open public spaces, bounded to the north by the modern towers of Fort and to the south by the sprawling facade of the *Galle Face Hotel*. The Green was created by Sir Henry Ward, governor from 1855 to 1860 (an easily missed memorial plaque to him stands halfway along the promenade, in which the Green is "recommended to his successors in the interest of the Ladies and Children of Colombo"), and such is its place in the city's affections that even the rail line south – which elsewhere runs straight down the coast – was rerouted inland to avoid it. The Fort end of the Green is bounded by the ponderous Neoclassical **Secretariat**, now dwarfed by the *Galadari* hotel and the World Trade Center towers which rise behind it. Statues of independent Sri Lanka's first four prime ministers stand in front; in the centre is a purposefully moustachioed D.S. Senanayake, the first post-independence PM, who died in 1952 from injuries sustained when he fell from his horse on the Green.

A turn along the Green's seafront promenade makes a pleasantly salty stroll, with the waves crashing a few feet below and breezy views along the coast and out to sea, where lines of gargantuan tankers and container ships line up waiting to enter the harbour. Late in the day is the best time to visit, when half the city seems to come here to gossip, fly kites and eat the curious-looking snacks served up by the line of hawkers stretched out along the front.

▲ Galle Face Green at dusk

Unfortunately, the Green is also plagued with **con artists** preying on tourists staying at the various nearby hotels – see p.62 for more details.

Slave Island

Immediately east of Galle Face Green is the area known as **Slave Island** – not actually an island, it's encircled on three sides by **Beira Lake**, an inland waterway whose various sections are connected by stagnant, pea-green canals. This is a ramshackle but personable district, dotted with a number of intriguing religious structures and retaining colourful pockets of local life. The name dates back to its Dutch-era title, **Kaffir Veldt**, from the African slaves (Kaffirs) who worked in the city – at one time there were as many as four thousand of them here. After a failed insurrection in the seventeenth century, the Dutch insisted that all slaves were quartered overnight in the Kaffir Veldt, and stocked the surrounding waterways with crocodiles in order to discourage attempts to escape.

Parts of Slave Island preserve a ramshackle charm, especially around Rifle Street, Akbar Mawatha and Malay Street, dotted with scruffy little cafés and assorted churches and mosques, the latter built during the British colonial era for soldiers from Malaya serving in the British army, who were garrisoned on the island. Indian troops were also stationed here, and it was for them that the **Sri Subramanian Kovil**, one of central Colombo's most imposing Hindu temples, was built. The entrance, just off Kumaran Ratnam Road, is marked by a towering *gopuram*, a great mountain of kitsch masonry flanked with incongruously Victorian-looking miniature clocktowers. The temple is dedicated to the god Subramanian (or Kataragama, as he is known to the Sinhalese; see p.216), whose peacock symbol you will see at various places inside. The interior follows the standard pattern of Sri Lankan Hindu temples, with an inner shrine constructed from solid stone enclosed within a shed-like ambulatory, and an eclectic array of images including conventional Hindu gods – many blackened images of the maleficent Durga amongst them – alongside curious little statues of the Buddha, dressed up like a Hindu deity in robes and garlands. The temple, like all in Colombo, is usually closed except during the morning and evening pujas (around 8–9am & 5–6pm), when you're free to wander around inside.

Seema Malaka

Just south of the Sri Subramanian Kovil, the streets open up to reveal the southern arm of **Beira Lake** – not a thing of any great beauty, though it's surrounded by fine old trees and provides welcoming breezes throughout the day, as well as attracting pelicans, egrets and cormorants. Two of the city's most interesting Buddhist temples lie close to one another on the lake's eastern side. The more modern, the **Seema Malaka**, is attractively situated at the end of a causeway jutting out into the middle of the lake – an unexpected and beautiful sight against the drab tower blocks behind. Designed by Sri Lanka's foremost twentieth-century architect, Geoffrey Bawa (see p.146), this unusual temple is used for inaugurations of monks from the nearby Gangaramaya temple – though it was actually paid for by a Colombo Muslim who, having fallen out with his co-religionists, decided to revenge himself by endowing a Buddhist shrine. Set on three linked platforms rising out of the lake, Seema Malaka's novel structure was apparently inspired by the design of Sri Lankan forest monasteries such as those at Anuradhapura and Ritigala, which feature similar raised platforms linked by bridge-like walkways. The buildings are roofed with lustrous blue tiles, with a small bo tree and delicately carved kiosk on the outer platforms standing either side of the larger central structure, an intricately latticed wooden pavilion lined inside and out by two rows of delicate Thai Buddhas in various mudras.

Gangaramaya

Just east of the Seema Malaka lies the older **Gangaramaya** temple, established during Sri Lanka's nineteenth-century Buddhist revival and now one of Colombo's most important shrines. It's also the focus of the major **Navam Perahera** festival, held on poya day every February, when up to fifty elephants descend on the place. Although only established in 1979, this has quickly grown to be one of the most popular peraheras in Colombo. The resident **temple elephant** can also often been seen in the main courtyard – and provides an unintentional prop for city con-artists trying to invent non-existent "elephant festivals" (see p.62).

The temple itself is probably the most bizarrely eclectic in the country, home to a strange hotch-potch of objects from Sri Lanka and abroad, with statues of Thai Buddhas, Chinese Bodhisattvas and Hindu deities presented to the temple by well-wishers scattered randomly here and there. The heart of the temple comprises a serene, and relatively traditional, group of buildings clustered around a central courtyard with a small dagoba at its centre. To one side of the courtyard, a venerable old **bo tree** grows out of a raised platform draped in prayer flags. Across the courtyard lies the principal **image house**, its base supported by dwarfs (symbols of prosperity) in various contorted positions. Inside, the entire building is occupied by an eye-popping *tableau vivant*, centred on a gargantuan orange Buddha sitting majestically in the meditation posture, flanked by elephant tusks and surrounded by dozens of other larger-than-life Buddhas and devotees bearing garlands – thoroughly kitsch, but undeniably impressive. Between the bo tree and image house stands the temple's beautiful old **library**, housed in a richly decorated wooden pavilion, with shelves stacked full of antique ola-leaf manuscripts and a range of foreign Buddha images from Thailand and China. To the rear of the courtyard stands an incongruous Chinese-style **pavilion**, topped with a flamboyant gilded roof, next to a tier of stacked-up Buddha statues from Thailand and a couple of **vintage cars** presented to the temple over the years.

Next to the entrance, the temple **museum** (Rs.100; no set hours) fills a large room with an astonishing treasure trove of weird and wonderful bric-a-brac, ranging in size from the "world's smallest Buddha statue" (visible through a magnifying glass) to a stuffed elephant. The overall effect is rather like an enormous Buddhist car-boot sale, with objects of great delicacy and value alongside pieces of pure kitsch, such as a banana carved out of ivory.

Viharamahadevi Park and the museums

Just south of the Gangaramaya temple stretches the city's principal open space, **Viharamahadevi Park**, (daily 6am–6pm; free) originally called Victoria Park but renamed with characteristic patriotic thoroughness in the 1950s after the famous mother of King Duttugemunu (see p.362). The park makes a welcome spot to crash out in between forays to nearby museums and temples, and boasts gorgeous tropical trees, plentiful birdlife and the occasional visiting elephant; it's also a magnet to local courting couples, who sit discreetly snogging under umbrellas. At the northern end of the park lies lively **De Soysa Circus** – still widely known by its old name of Lipton Circus – one of central Colombo's major intersections and home to a couple of the city's best shops (see p.116), the huge Osu Sala state pharmacy and the eyecatching **Devatagaha Mosque**, a big, white Moorish-looking structure that adds a quaint touch of architectural whimsy to the otherwise functional junction. Immediately south of here, facing the park, stands Colombo's **Town Hall**, built in 1927 – a severely functional white Neoclassical structure that's something like a cross between the US Capitol and a municipal waterworks. Opposite, a large **gilded Buddha** stares fixedly at the town hall.

The National Museum

Just south of the park are Colombo's three state museums, most notably the extensive **National Museum** (daily except Fri 9am–5pm; Rs.500; no phones or cameras allowed), set in an elegant white Neoclassical building dating from 1877 and boasting a large and absorbing collection of Sri Lankan artefacts from prehistoric times to the colonial era. Recent renovations to the ground floor have significantly increased the museum's appeal, though the upstairs rooms remain very much a work in progress. Note that both the National Museum and Natural History Museum (see p.106) can currently only be entered from Albert Crescent to the south; absurdly, there's no access from Horton Place on the park side of the museum area.

The **entrance lobby** is dominated by a famous eighth-century limestone Buddha from Anuradhapura – a classic seated image in the meditation posture whose simplicity, serenity, lack of decoration and very human features embodies much that is most characteristic of Sri Lankan art. Turn right from here to reach **room 1**, which offers a good overview of Sri Lankan **prehistory**, although the exhibits themselves are fairly modest, a reflection of the paucity of archeological remains so far uncovered. Exhibits include a few human bones, the fossilized shells of assorted snails (which apparently formed a significant part of the diet of early Sri Lankans) and the teeth of extinct species of rhino and hippo which formerly roamed the island – along with conjectural artistic impressions of what these early wild beasts and even wilder humans would have looked like.

Return to the entrance lobby, beyond which **rooms 2 to 5** are home to the museum's finest collection of artefacts, which show the full range of Sri Lankan artistry from the Anuradhapura period through to the Kandyan era, all backed up with extensive and interesting documentation. Room 2 is devoted to **Buddha images** and related iconography, showing changing representations of the master through the centuries, starting with early symbolic portrayals – sacred footprints (*sri pada*), dagobas – followed by portraits of the master in wood and stone, exemplifying the transition in Buddhist art from the abstract to the figurative. Another important strand in Sri Lankan art is shown by the superb collection of **Hindu images** in room 3, most of them twelfth-century bronzes from the Shiva Devale no. 1 at Polonnaruwa, proof of the strength of Hindu influence on this avowedly Buddhist city. Figures include a fine Shiva nataraja (dancing Shiva) and several voluptuous, wasp-waisted Parvatis – all of which look hauntingly exotic and extremely Indian compared to the chaste Buddha images in the previous room.

The exhibits in rooms 4 and 5 leap abruptly into the **Kandyan era**, with a range of luxury items showing the incredibly intricate levels of craftsmanship, in a variety of materials, which were achieved by the kingdom's artisans, including minutely embossed brass plates, delicately carved ivory figurines and ola-leaf manuscripts – look out in particular for the stunning silver sword made for Bhuvanekabahu I, of Gampola (room 4), with its jewel-encrusted dragon's head handle. Most impressive, however, is the glittering **regalia** of the kings of Kandy (room 5) – one of the museum's highlights – which was surrendered to the British during the handover of power in 1815 and kept in Windsor Castle until being returned by George V in 1934.

Exiting room 5 brings you to a small **veranda** which is home to a display of "urinal stones", including a superb example from Anuradhapura – sumptuously decorated carvings on which monks would formerly have relieved themselves in order to demonstrate their contempt for worldly riches. Beyond here lies the large **room 6**, or "Stone Antiquities Gallery", home to an impressive selection of eroded pillars, friezes and statues salvaged from archeological sites across the island, and ranging in time from third-century Anuradhapura through to various colonial coats of arms and tombstones. The majority of pieces come from Anuradhapura and Polonnaruwa, and include a sequence of pillar inscriptions which were commonly used to record administrative decrees and grants of land, along with numerous carvings and statues ranging from Hindu gods to Buddhist moonstones, all excellently captioned and explained.

The **first floor** is currently undergoing extensive refurbishment and was closed at the time of writing, though it's planned to incorporate galleries devoted to coins, jewellery and crafts, bronzes, anthropology, painting, ceramics and epigraphy.

The Natural History Museum and National Art Gallery

Just behind the National Museum, the **Natural History Museum** (daily except Fri; Rs.300) fills three gloomy and labyrinthine floors with exhibits ranging from stuffed leopards and pickled snakes to quaintly didactic presentations on the island's ecology and economy ("Easy Ways To Make Agricultural Chemical Safe for You And Everyone Else", and the like). It all looks like the sort of thing you'd have expected to find in Communist Bulgaria, although the vast quantity of stuffed animals posed in moth-eaten pomp is enough to turn a conservationist's hair grey.

Next door to the Natural History Museum (and accessible from Horton Place), Sri Lanka's **National Art Gallery** (daily except Fri 9am–5pm; free) comprises a single large room full of twentieth-century paintings by Sri Lankan artists (along with assorted portraits of various island notables), showing the influence of a range of European styles and including several rather Matisse-like canvases by George Keyt (1901–93), Sri Lanka's foremost twentieth-century painter. Sadly there are no labels, and exhibits are roped off, so you can't get close enough to read the signatures or even look at the paintings in any detail, meaning that the whole experience is rather unedifying.

Cinnamon Gardens

South and east of Viharamahadevi Park stretches the smart suburb of **Cinnamon Gardens**, named for the plantations which flourished here during the nineteenth century. The capital's most sought-after area, the leafy streets here preserve their aura of haughty Victorian privilege – along with their colonial street names – and are lined with elite colleges and enormous old mansions (most now occupied by foreign embassies and government offices) concealed behind dauntingly high walls. There's not actually much to do or see here, though there are a couple of places to stay and eat. The heart of the district is formed by the rectangle of streets between Ward Place and Gregory's Road, the latter home to a whole string of embassies in spectacularly opulent colonial residences. South of here, Maitland Place runs down to the **Sinhalese Sports Club**, whose engagingly old-fashioned stadium, complete with antiquated manually operated scoreboard, serves as Colombo's venue for Test cricket. Just south of here at the end of Independence Avenue lies the bombastic **Independence Commemoration Hall**, an overblown stone replica of the wooden Audience Hall at Kandy.

Southern Colombo

Immediately beyond Galle Face Green, **Galle Road** runs purposefully south, bisecting a string of coastal suburbs – **Kollupitiya**, **Bambalapitiya**, **Wellawatta** and **Dehiwala** – before reaching Mount Lavinia. Much of the commercial activity driven out of Fort by repeated bombings has now established itself in this part of the city, moving Colombo's centre of gravity decisively southwards and transforming Galle Road – the area between Kollupitiya and Bambalapitiya especially – into the city's de facto high street.

It's a far from pleasant sight, however: choked with traffic for fourteen hours a day, enveloped in a constant film of smog and accompanied by a perpetual cacophony of screeching bus horns – the overall filthiness being made all the more obvious by the enticing sight of the Indian Ocean just a couple of hundred metres away down countless side roads. There's no way you could possibly consider Galle Road a tourist attraction, but it offers a good example of contemporary Sri Lanka at its most diverse: garish cinema hoardings stand next to serene Buddhist temples and colonial colleges, while shiny modern office blocks and air-conditioned shopping malls rub shoulders with ramshackle cafés and tiny lock-up shops, all boasting plenty of noisy character and, in places, even a strange, smelly sort of charm.

Running parallel to the Galle Road on its landward side, R.A. de Mel Mawatha – still almost always referred to by its former name of **Duplication Road** – is leafier and more salubrious, edged by smart shops and restaurants though still busy with traffic during the day.

Kollupitiya, Bambalapitiya and Wellawatta

Immediately south of Galle Face Green, Galle Road has a decidedly military atmosphere, with the heavily fortified compounds of the US and Indian embassies and **Temple Trees**, the prime minister's official residence, all but hidden behind sandbagged gun emplacements and high walls topped by army watchtowers. The only spot of architectural relief is supplied by the quaint Gothic **St Andrew's Scotskirk** of 1842, just north of Temple Trees. Continuing south, Colombo's ordinary commercial life resumes as Galle Road passes through central **Kollupitiya**, with strings of cafés, banks and assorted shops. Many of the buildings here are functionally nondescript, with lots of the reflective glassy facades favoured by modern Sri Lankan architects, though the occasional dog-eared little café, colourful sign or curious shop survives amongst the bland modern office blocks.

There are more flashes of character in the helter-skelter commercial suburb of **Bambalapitiya**. Following the decline in Fort's fortunes, the area around Bambalapitiya Junction (where the Galle Road meets Bauddhaloka Mawatha) has now to all intents and purposes become the centre of modern Colombo. It's a slightly anarchic mix of the old and new, ranging from the large Majestic Plaza shopping mall to little lopsided shops selling bits of rope or packets of spices, while a series of determinedly local cafés and South Indian restaurants brighten the fume-filled Galle Road with their fanciful signs. This is one of the busiest areas of Colombo: the pavements are clogged during daylight hours with office workers, beggars and tuktuk drivers touting for custom, while the handcarts of *vadai*-sellers and modest piles of merchandise laid out by street hawkers – anything from Buddha posters to recycled computer innards – add to the congestion.

The Galle Road becomes progressively more ramshackle and down-at-heel as it continues south into the suburb of **Wellawatta**, popularly known as "Little Jaffna" thanks to its large Tamil population. This is one of the most characterful suburbs in southern Colombo, an interesting area full of colourful local cafés and picturesque (in a grubby kind of way) shops selling saris, "fancy goods" and all sorts of other paraphernalia – the whole area is very lively by night, and makes for an interesting stroll at any time.

Dehiwala Zoo

Some 10km south of Fort in the suburb of Dehiwala, the national **Zoo** (daily 8.30am–6pm; Rs.500) is home to a good range of Sri Lankan, Asian, African and South American wildlife housed in mostly tolerable conditions – hopefully, ongoing renovations will eventually put paid to the few distressingly small cages for some of the monkeys and big cats (plans to relocate some of the zoo's animals to a new site next to Pinnewala Elephant Orphanage over the next couple of years have also been floated). Sri Lankan species here include cute sloth bears, monkeys, porcupines, jungle- and fishing-cats, lots of birds and a number of leopards, part of the zoo's good collection of **big cats**, which also includes jaguars, lions, tigers and cheetahs. The zoo is also home to a number of Asian and a couple of African **elephants**; they can be seen performing during the infamous "elephant dance" (daily at 4.30pm) during which these surprisingly agile pachyderms perform various party tricks to the never-failing delight of local schoolchildren and other elephant-fanciers.

The zoo's large assortment of **monkeys** includes examples of all the native primates, such as purple-faced leaf monkey, grey langur and toque macaque. There's also a wide array of other mammals, from African giraffes and springboks or South American guanacos and tapirs to Australian red-necked wallabies and giant red kangaroos – plus a cage full of rabbits. There's also an excellent collection of **birdlife**, including some fabulously large and fluffy owls, lots of cockatoos and macaws (including an astonishing – and very rare – hyacinth macaw) and toucans. There's a huge walk-in aviary full of Sri Lankan species; a good place to practise your bird-spotting skills. In addition to the caged birdlife, a flooded quarry at one end of the zoo serves as a magnet to Colombo's aquatic birds, which are fed daily at 3.30pm. Egrets, herons and pelicans from all over the city flock here – a fine sight at feeding times, when hundreds swoop down onto the water. If you feel like some food yourself, there's a **restaurant** inside the zoo, as well as plenty of kiosks selling drinks and snacks.

To **reach the zoo**, catch any bus running south along Duplication Road/Galle Road to the suburb of Dehiwala, and then either walk or take a tuktuk.

Mount Lavinia

Ten kilometres south of Colombo Fort, the leafy beachside suburb of **Mount Lavinia** is bounded by the small headland (the so-called "Mount") that is one of the few punctuating features on the coastline near the capital. The area supposedly takes its name from a certain Lavinia, the lady friend of British Governor Sir Thomas Maitland, who himself established a residence here in 1806.

Maitland's residence was subsequently expanded by successive governors before being turned into the **Mount Lavinia Hotel**, now one of the most venerable colonial landmarks in Sri Lanka and the main reason most foreign visitors come here. Even if you can't afford to stay at the hotel, there are a few other pleasant small-scale guesthouses nearby, and the suburb's proximity to the international airport makes it a handy first or last stop on a tour of the island – or a convenient bolthole if you just want to escape the madness of central Colombo for a day or two.

Mount Lavinia is also home to Colombo's closest half-decent **beach**, and on Sunday afternoons half the city seems to come here to splash around in the water, play cricket and smooch under umbrellas. The proximity of the city means that the water is borderline for swimming, while the beach itself is a bit messy, with piles of fishing tackle scattered here and there. It's not an idyllic tropical seashore by any means, but does have a decent stretch of sand and a certain scruffy charm, especially at night, with the lights of the towers in central

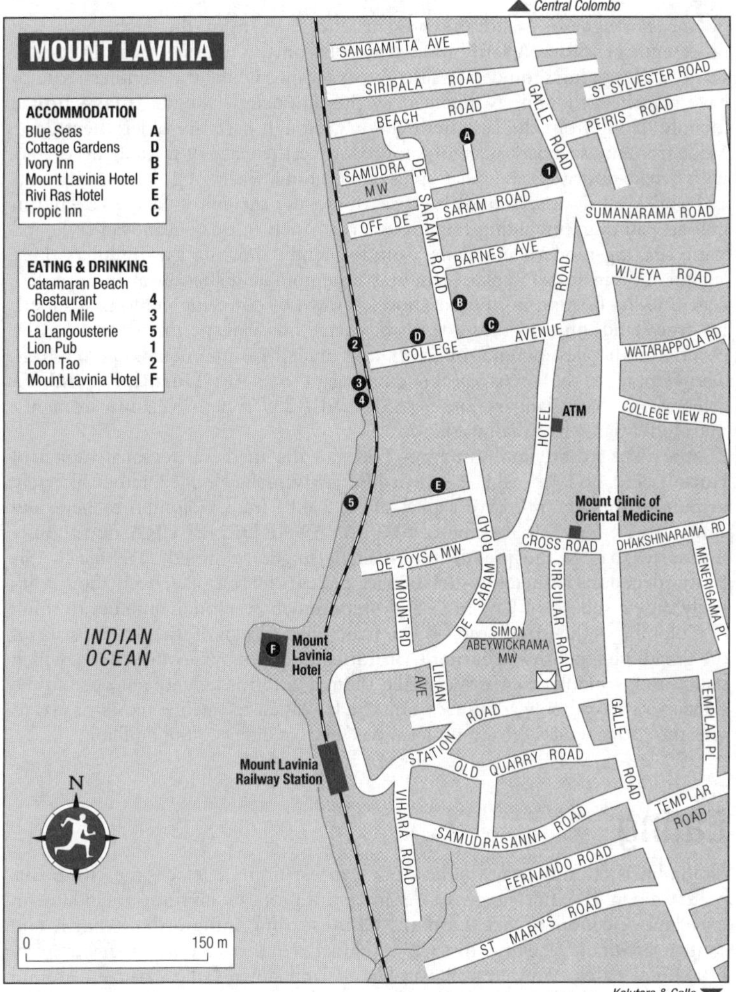

Colombo twinkling away to the north, and the more modest illuminations of the *Mount Lavinia Hotel* framing the beach to the south.

Mount Lavinia has a good spread of **places to eat**, some of them quite swish. Both the beach and the *Mount Lavinia Hotel* are attractive spots for an evening meal, although it's a bit of a trek down the Galle Road unless you're staying in one of the southern suburbs. Plenty of taxi and tuktuk drivers hang out around the hotel until late at night, so you won't have any problems getting home.

Kelaniya and Kotte

Ten kilometres east of Fort lies Colombo's most important Buddhist shrine, the **Kelaniya Raja Maha Vihara** – the Buddha himself is said to have taught at this spot on the last of his three visits to the island. Various temples have stood on the present site – earlier structures were destroyed first by the Indians, then by the Portuguese – and the present one dates from the eighteenth and nineteenth centuries. A fairly modest dagoba (in the unusual "heap of paddy" shape, with sloping shoulders) marks the exact spot where the Buddha is said to have preached, though it's upstaged by the unusually elaborate **image house** (mainly dating from the twentieth century, though parts are older), next door. Made from unusual dark orange-coloured stone, the exterior is richly decorated, with ornate doorways and pillars, plus entertaining friezes of galloping elephants and pop-eyed dwarfs around the base. Inside, the shrine's walls are covered in myriad paintings, including numerous strip panels in quasi-Kandyan style and some striking modern murals by Soliyas Mendis showing the Buddha's three legendary visits to Sri Lanka, including a memorable depiction of an incandescent Buddha floating in mid-air above a crowd of cowering demons. A superb **bo tree** stands on the other side of the image house, its perimeter wall usually covered with piles of floral offerings and draped in innumerable prayer flags. The temple is the focus of the extravagant two-day **Duruthu Perahera** celebrations every January. Buses #224 and #235 run to Kelaniya from just outside Bastian Mawatha bus station.

Some 7km inland southeast from Fort lies the medieval regional capital of **Kotte** (see p.421). In 1984, President J.R. Jayawardene decided, rather bizarrely, to transfer the administrative capital of Sri Lanka from Colombo to here, and also to revive Kotte's old name of **SRI JAYAWARDENEPURA** (fortuitously similar to that of the president himself, it might be noted). Technically, Sri Jayawardenepura is therefore the official capital of Sri Lanka, even though it's really only a suburb of Colombo, and pretty much everyone continues to think of Colombo as the island's capital. The main physical sign of the suburb's status is the grandiose modern **Parliament Building**, designed by Geoffrey Bawa, which stands in the middle of an artificial lake, though unfortunately it's not open to the public, so you can only admire it from afar. It's easiest to catch a tuktuk or taxi to visit the parliament; there are no local bus services direct to the building.

Eating

Colombo is far and away the best place to eat in Sri Lanka – the city boasts pretty much the full range of Asian and European cuisines, including an excellent selection of **Sri Lankan**, **Chinese** and **Indian** (both north and south) restaurants. If your stomach's acclimatized, there are innumerable lively little **local cafés** – clustered all over Slave Island, down Galle Road and around the Pettah – which really come alive after dark. **Lunch packets** are sold by pavement stalls and cafés all over the city – a decent-sized helping of simple rice and curry costs around Rs.100.

Many of the restaurants listed below close from around 2.30 or 3pm until 6.30 or 7pm, while a few only open in the evening. We've given telephone numbers for those places where it's advisable to book ahead.

Fort and Pettah

Eating in Fort is basically a choice between the various smart restaurants in the five-star *Hilton*, *Ceylon Continental* and *Galadari* hotels (those in the *Hilton* are easily the best) and the down-at-heel little local cafés in the streets outside. If none of the place listed below appeal, you could also try the uninspiring *Deli Market* food court, on the third floor of the World Trade Center, which does a rather unexciting and overpriced range of pastas, pizzas and other Western standards.

The following are marked on the map on p.98.

Chettinad 293 Sea St, Pettah. This no-frills local's café makes a good lunch stop in the depths of the Pettah, dishing up delicious and dirt-cheap South Indian food – *dosas, vadais, uttapam* – in an authentically Subcontinental atmosphere, complete with banana-leaf "plates", metal utensils and a colourful display of sweets in the entrance.

Curry Leaf *Hilton* hotel, Sir Chittampalam A. Gardiner Mw, Fort ☎011-249 1000. Tucked away in the *Hilton* grounds in a rather naff faux-jungle village construction. The nightly buffet (Rs.2250) is pricey but provides Colombo's best introduction to the full range of Sri Lankan cuisine – string hoppers, hoppers, *kottu rotty, wattalapan*, plus all sorts of rice and curries, as well as fresh seafood. Open evenings only.

Emperor's Wok *Hilton* hotel, Sir Chittampalam A. Gardiner Mw, Fort ☎011-249 1000. Showy Chinese restaurant whose Hong Kong and Chinese chefs cook up an enormous range of Cantonese and Sichuan dishes (starting at around Rs.850), from shark's fin and abalone to bean curd and shredded duck, along with all the usual standards, plus special set lunch and dim sum menus. Gets busy, so best to book.

Il Ponte *Hilton* hotel, Sir Chittampalam A. Gardiner Mw, Fort ☎011-254 4644. Informal Italian restaurant in the far corner of the *Hilton*'s grounds, with seating either in an indoor a/c section or outside by the pool. The small menu features pizzas, panini, pastas and salads, plus Australian steaks, burgers, Italian ice cream and tiramisu. It's all pretty low-key, but the food is good, and the thin-crust pizzas (from around Rs.1000) are the best in Sri Lanka.

Seafish 15 Sir Chittampalam A. Gardiner Mw, Fort. This low-key little restaurant is the place for good and relatively inexpensive fish and seafood, and there are also a few meat, noodle and pasta options, plus curries. Mains from around Rs.625.

Taj York St, Fort. A fun and lively place at lunchtimes, when local office workers pile in for the cheap and good burianis, rice and curry, and short eats (much prodded). It's also the only cheapie in Fort that stays open in the evenings.

Around Galle Face Green

The following are shown on the map on pp.92–93.

Alhambra *Holiday Inn*, Sir M.M. Markar Mw. Long-running North Indian restaurant (despite the Moorish name and decor), with a solidly prepared and refreshingly inexpensive range of North Indian standards, including Mughlai dishes, biryanis and tandooris, plus plenty of vegetarian options. Mains from around Rs.375.

The Bavarian German Restaurant 11 Galle Face Court 2, Galle Rd. A rustic interior full of chunky wooden furniture provides a suitably Bavarian setting for hearty Central European dishes like goulash, pickled beef, pepper steak, Wiener schnitzels, and bratwurst, plus a few seafood, pasta and vegetarian options. Most mains Rs.1100–1200.

Navratna *Taj Samudra* hotel, Galle Face Centre Rd ☎011-244 6622. Colombo's swankiest Indian restaurant, offering an inventive selection of regional dishes from across the Subcontinent – anything from Goan fish curry to Rajasthani *ghatta* (dumplings) – plus an excellent vegetarian selection. Mains from around Rs.800.

Kollupitiya

The following are shown on the map on pp.92–93.

Amaravathi Mile Post Ave. Functional but deservedly popular a/c restaurant serving up an eclectic and inexpensive medley of dishes from Sri Lanka and India (both north and south) ranging from curries and *kottu rotty* through to *dosas* and tandooris. Mains from Rs.300.

Barefoot Café Barefoot, 704 Galle Rd. Set in the beautiful courtyard at the back of Colombo's most personable shop (see p.116), with outdoor seating and a small menu of moderately priced café-style fare, plus excellent daily lunch specials and desserts, and live music most Sundays. Open Mon–Sat 10am–7pm, Sun 11am–4pm.

Chesa Swiss 3 Deal Place, corner of R.A. de Mel Mw (Duplication Rd) ☎011-257 3433. Chic Swiss restaurant in a gorgeous colonial villa, with garden or indoor a/c seating, offering a good selection of nourishing creations ranging from fondues and rosti to pickled beef and barley soup as well as Australian steaks, venison and a reasonable vegetarian selection. Mains from around Rs.1000. Open evenings 7–11pm only.

Crescat Boulevard Galle Rd. The food court in the basement of Colombo's smartest shopping mall teems with fast-food outlets dishing up everything from Mongolian to Sri Lankan, Indian, Chinese and Malaysian cuisine, plus pizza, pasta, wraps and ice cream.

Cricket Club Café 34 Queen's Rd, off R.A. de Mel Mw (Duplication Rd). This shrine to cricket is deservedly popular with expats, tourists and locals alike, with memorabilia ranged around the walls and nonstop matches on the TV. The food is tasty, unpretentious and excellent value (mains from around Rs.270), with a bistro-style menu of burgers, steaks and veggie dishes, all named after famous men in white (Ganguly's grill, Freddie's fillet o' fish, and so on).

Flower Drum 26 Thurston Rd. Recently given a suave modern makeover, this long-established Chinese restaurant serves up a reliable selection of Cantonese standards, including a better-than-average seafood selection, although there's relatively little for vegetarians. Most mains around Rs.600.

Gallery Café 2 Alfred House Rd. Colombo's most stylish café, occupying a beautiful villa which once housed the offices of architect Geoffrey Bawa, and good for a drink and some people-watching as well as a meal. The outer courtyard hosts temporary art and photographic exhibitions, plus a small shop (see p.116), while the inner courtyard is home to the café itself, with open-air seating and a big menu of reasonably prepared international dishes (from around Rs.950) – anything from fish and chips to prawn curry – and a huge range of calorie-busting puddings.

Green Cabin 453 Galle Rd. Cheap and cheerful local place on Galle Rd serving up tastier-than-average rice and curry, *lamprais* and other Sri Lankan offerings, plus *kottu rotty* and hoppers in the evening.

The Lagoon *Cinnamon Grand* hotel, 77 Galle Rd ⓣ011-243 7437. Colombo's best seafood, served up in a bright glass-sided restaurant permeated with salty marine smells. Choose what you want from the superb display of fish and seafood (including all sorts of fish, and prawns the size of small lobsters), and have it prepared in any one of over 25 different cooking styles, ranging from Sri Lankan and Indian to Chinese, Thai and Continental. Mains from around Rs.800.

Palmyrah *Hotel Renuka*, 328 Galle Rd. This unpretentious basement restaurant is one of Colombo's better places for Sri Lankan cuisine, with tasty and inexpensive curries, hoppers, *pittu* and *kottu rotty*, plus a few traditional Jaffna specialities including rich meat and fish *poriyals*. Mains from around Rs.300.

Raffles 35 Bagatale Rd ⓣ011-255 9846, ⓦwww.rafflescolombo.com. Set in a gracious old colonial house, this relaxed restaurant dishes up a well-prepared array of international meat, fish and vegetarian dishes – anything from lemongrass chicken or beef shashlik to mushroom strudel. Mains from around Rs.600.

Sakura 14 Rheinland Place. Cheerful little Japanese café complete with fake cherry blossom, red lanterns and kitsch ornaments. Seating is either at the counter or in a tatami room around the back, and there's a big selection of reasonably priced, fairly authentic Japanese fare, with mains from around Rs.400.

Tao *Cinnamon Grand* hotel, 77 Galle Rd ⓣ011-243 7437. The beautiful gardens of the *Cinnamon Grand*, with twinkling fairy lights and floodlit palm trees, provide an idyllic setting for superb fusion cuisine which blends Sri Lankan, Asian and European influences. The inventive and beautifully prepared food ranges from mainstream seafood and meat dishes to more unusual mixes like the combination plate of red curry chicken, grilled lamb chops and spiced tiger prawns. Mains from around Rs.1000. Open 7–11pm.

Thambapani 496/1 R.A. de Mel Mw (Duplication Rd). Serene and intimate little restaurant with open-air and indoor seating and a wide-ranging menu of island cuisine: an eclectic mix of local and colonial influences – mainly seafood, plus grills, pies, pasta and a decent selection of Sri Lankan options, including curries, *lamprais*, *pittu* and hoppers. Mains from around Rs.550.

Cinnamon Gardens

The following are shown on the map on pp.92–93.

Agra Off Independence Ave ⓣ011-472 3333. Lively new Indian restaurant with one of the prettiest interiors in the city and a fine selection of classic North Indian and Mughlai cuisine, including plenty of veg, non-veg and seafood tandooris at very reasonable prices. Mains from around Rs.600.

The Bayleaf 79 Gregory's Rd ⓣ011-269 5920. Smart Italian restaurant in a gracious colonial villa on one of Colombo's most exclusive streets, with seating inside and out. The menu features a big selection of home-made pastas, plus a few meat and fish options, while the cocktails are reckoned to be some of the best in the city. Mains from around Rs.1000.

The Mango Tree 82 Dharmapala Mw ⓣ011-587 9790. Sleek North Indian restaurant with attractively muted modern decor and a well-prepared range of meat, seafood and vegetarian dishes with the emphasis on tandooris, tikkas, kebabs and hearty Punjabi-style cuisine. Mains from around Rs.600.

No. 18 18 Cambridge Place ⓣ011-269 4000. Ultra-chic modern café-restaurant with seating either in the minimalist interior or the garden outside and a menu featuring Asian and Italian fusion cuisine, plus assorted meat and fish dishes, including Australian steaks – though very little for vegetarians. Mains from around Rs.900.

Bambalapitiya

The following are shown on the map on pp.92–93.

Chinese Dragon Café 11 Milagiriya Ave, off Galle Rd. Friendly restaurant in a rambling old mansion tucked away off Galle Road. The extensive menu includes a decent range of Chinese standards along with a few Thai- and Malaysian-style dishes, plus local favourites like chillie crab and devilled chicken. Mains from Rs.400.

Greenlands 3A Shrubbery Gardens, off Galle Rd. A Colombo institution, hidden away in an old colonial house, this sedate South Indian vegetarian restaurant offers a big range of excellent, dirt-cheap food including *vadais* (masala, ulundu, curd), *dosas* (paper, ghee, onion) and other goodies including *idlis*, *pooris* and *bonda* (a kind of bhaji). Very popular, so service can be slow. Lurid piles of Indian sweets – *laddu, burfi, Mysorepak* – are sold at the entrance.

Saraswathie Galle Rd. This long-established, no-nonsense South Indian vegetarian restaurant is ultra-cheap, interestingly hectic and offers a quintessential slice of Colombo life. Food includes various types of *dosa* (plain, masala, onion, ghee), string hoppers, veg burianis, potato curry, *idlis* and *vadais*, all at virtually giveaway prices – you can stuff yourself stupid for around a dollar.

Siam House 17 Melbourne Ave. The best Thai food in the city with a big menu featuring all the usual favourites – red and green curries, fish curries, spicy salads, *pad thai* – all with plenty of flavour, and not a little fire too. Mains from around Rs.600.

Mount Lavinia

The following are shown on the map on p.109.

Catamaran Beach Restaurant Low-key beach-shack with tables on the sand under a palm-thatched roof, serving good cheap snacks and seafood, plus the usual noodles, rice and devilled dishes.

Golden Mile The ritziest place on the beach, with a beautiful oceanside location and seating either outside on the sand or inside the big two-storey wooden building. Food is mainly fish and seafood, plus a few meat and veggie options, with mains from around Rs.600

La Langousterie Attractive open-air restaurant, set in a beachfront pavilion and with a decent range of well-prepared and moderately priced seafood and Sri Lankan dishes for around Rs.500.

Loon Tao Rustic beach restaurant specializing in Chinese seafood, with a vast menu offering fish and seafood in every conceivable style – Sichaun, Cantonese, Thai, Malaysian – as well as an extensive range of meat and vegetarian options. Mains from around Rs.650.

Mount Lavinia Hotel There are a range of eating options at this landmark hotel. The *Governor's Restaurant* does a vast and better-than-average buffet spread nightly, though the number of guests can mean it's a bit like eating in the middle of a rush hour. Alternatively, the informal and more sedate *Seafood Cove* (open evenings only) on the hotel's private beach offers a range of freshly caught fish, cooked to suit. Even if you don't eat here, it's worth coming for a drink at the *Lighthouse Bar* above the sea – gorgeous at sunset.

Drinking, nightlife and entertainment

Colombo's **nightlife**, never the brightest in Asia, has nosedived into virtual nonexistence over the past couple of years thanks to a mixture of draconian anti-noise legislation and the tense security situation in the capital – venture out anytime after 9pm and you're likely to be stopped at least a couple of times by obstreperous gun-toting soldiers, and the whole city has the feeling of somewhere under a curfew – hardly conducive to late-night partying.

All the following places are shown on the map on pp.92–93, unless otherwise stated.

Bars and pubs

Bistro Latino R.A. de Mel Mw (Duplication Rd), Bambalapitiya. Latin-themed venue, with passable Mexican food, a decent drinks list and weekly salsa sessions.

Bradman's Bar *Cricket Club Café*, 34 Queen's Rd, off R.A. de Mel Mw (Duplication Rd), Kollupitiya. Cosy little pub-style bar at one of the city's most popular cafés (see p.112); gets packed with expats and locals most nights.

Clancy's Irish Pub 29 Maitland Crescent, Cinnamon Gardens. Lowbrow but consistently popular pub-cum-club which just goes on and on while fancier venues boom and bust. There's live music (Wed–Sat), DJs (Mon) and a weekly quiz (usually Tues), plus passable pub food and Guinness in cans – although otherwise it's about as Celtic as chicken tikka masala. Rs.300–500 entrance for men, depending on the night; free for ladies. Closed Sun.

Echelon Pub *Hilton* hotel, Fort. Big, comfortable English-style pub, with sports TV and regular live music in the evenings. See map, p.98.

Ex-Serviceman's Club Bristol St, Fort. The down-at-heel bar and beer garden here serves up the cheapest beer in Colombo, and is usually full of voluble locals getting smashed on Johnnie Walker – unaccompanied ladies may feel uncomfortable. See map, p.98.

Flying Angel Club (Mission to Seafarers) 26 Church St, Fort. This homely and friendly little club (it looks like someone's sitting room) next to St Peter's Church is aimed mainly at visiting sailors, but is a pleasant spot for a beer or soft drink, and also has internet access (Rs.100 per hr). See map, p.98.

Galle Face Hotel Galle Face Green. Romantic, colonial-style veranda bar overlooking the courtyard of this atmospheric old hotel, with the Indian Ocean breaking just beyond. Wildly popular with honeymooners.

Harbour Room *Grand Oriental Hotel*, York St, Fort. Restaurant-bar on the fourth floor. The food is nothing special, but it's worth coming for a drink for the magnificent views over the port below, particularly spectacular after dark. See map, p.98.

Inn on the Green *Galle Face Hotel* (though entered from outside, on the Galle Rd opposite the *German Restaurant*), Kollupitiya. Surprisingly successful stab at a traditional English pub, complete with dartboard, sports TV and a weekly quiz night. There's also a big selection of local and imported tipples, cheap beer (including draught Tetleys) and decent pub food.

Lion Pub Galle Rd, Mount Lavinia. Entered via a gaping lion's mouth, this popular drinking hole attracts Sri Lankans and Westerners alike, with pleasant outdoor seating, cheap beer and a party atmosphere – expect spontaneous outbreaks of singing from boozed-up locals. See map, p.109.

Rhythm and Blues Bar 19/1 Daisy Villa Ave, R.A. de Mel Mw (Duplication Rd), Bambalapitiya. Relaxed and completely unpretentious bar-cum-live music venue, open daily from 7.30pm, with a mix of live bands and DJs, plus a couple of pool tables and a long drinks list.

Nightclubs

Almost all Colombo's tiny handful of **nightclubs** are hidden away in top-end hotels. Guests get in free, as do visiting ladies; blokes usually have to pay Rs.500–1000. Most places stay open till around 4am; don't expect anything much to be happening before 11pm. Popular places at present include the small and rather unexciting lounge bar-cum-club *ZanZiba*, 32B 1/1 Sir M.M. Markar Mw, Kollupitiya (closed Sun & Mon), which is about as good at Colombo nightlife gets at the moment, with a young Sri Lankan and foreign clientele and DJs nightly churning out mainstream R&B, house and electro. *Sugar*, 447 Union Place (above the now defunct *H2O* club; Fri & Sat only; free) attracts a slightly older and mainly Sri Lankan crowd.

There are also nightclubs inside most of the big hotels. These include *The Library* at the *Trans Asia* (more a bar-lounge than a club – though there's also a small dancefloor and the atmosphere can get slightly lively later on) and *Nuovo*, at the *Taj Samudra*.

Cinema, theatre and performing arts

Colombo's only modern **cinema** is the Majestic, on the fourth floor of the Majestic City mall (see opposite); it shows the latest Hollywood blockbusters on its one and only screen (4–5 screenings daily; Rs.250). The dog-eared Liberty Cinema, opposite Liberty Plaza, sometimes shows Hollywood blockbusters, while the British Council (see p.118) occasionally screens more highbrow Western and Sri Lankan films. Named after the famous Sri Lankan photographer and musician, the **Lionel Wendt Art Centre** (☎011-269 5794) on Guildford Crescent in Cinnamon Gardens stages a varied programme of dance, music and drama, and also hosts regularly changing exhibitions, mainly photographic.

Shopping

Colombo has a good range of shops, and a day trawling through the city's handicrafts emporia and chic boutiques can be an enjoyable way to end a visit and offload surplus rupees. You'll find the best of Sri Lanka's modest traditional **handicraft** production on sale at various places around the city, as well as at characterful modern shops, such as Barefoot, which offer chic contemporary takes on traditional designs – everything from stationery and stuffed toys to fabrics and kitchenware – and all at bargain-basement prices. The only fly in the soup is the fact that in virtually all establishments (except Barefoot) you'll be tailed obsessively during your browsing by the shops' under-employed sales assistants – though whether this is so that they can be of immediate service when required or because they suspect all foreigners of being closet shoplifters remains unclear. Colombo also boasts an excellent selection of **bookshops**, a plethora of **jewellers** and, of course, plenty of **tea shops**.

When buying handicrafts, remember that the export of **antiques** (classified as any object more than fifty years old) is prohibited without a licence. See p.73 for more details.

Gems and jewellery

There are gem and jewellery shops all over the city, particularly along Sea Street in the Pettah and on Levels 4 and 5 of the World Trade Center in Fort at the so-called Sri Lanka Gem and Jewellery Exchange, which is also home to a useful **gem-testing laboratory** (Mon–Fri 9am–4.45pm) run by the National Gem and Jewellery Authority. Staff here can tell you whether a stone is what it's claimed to be, and if it's natural, but they don't offer valuations. Tests are carried out on the spot and are free (you can buy a basic certificate of authenticity for Rs.287, or a more detailed one for Rs.862). The obvious drawback is that it will be difficult to get something tested without buying it first, although you might be able to persuade Colombo jewellers to send a representative with you and the gem(s) before you part with your cash.

Department stores and shopping malls

Cargills York St, Fort. The grand old lady of Colombo department stores, worth a look for its atmospheric colonial interior, although there's singularly little to actually buy. Part of the shop is now home, ignominiously, to a branch of *KFC*, while there's a good little supermarket at the back, with an excellent array of arrack.

Crescat Boulevard Galle Rd, Kollupitiya, next to the *Cinnamon Grand* hotel. Sri Lanka's ritziest mall – if you've spent some time out in the sticks, you might appreciate the crisp a/c and bland consumerism of it all. Home to branches of the Vijitha Yapa Bookshop, Mlesna and Dilmah tea shops, as well as a Keells supermarket, a good food court (see p.111) and the smart icafe internet café (see p.118).

Majestic City Galle Rd, Bambalapitiya. Formerly the city's flagship shopping centre until the opening of Crescat. It's now looking very dated, but retains a loyal following amongst Colombo's teenage mall rats. Lots of shoe and clothes shops (including branches of Odel and Cotton

Collection), a big Cargills supermarket, internet café, an OK basement food court and Colombo's best cinema.

Odel 5 Alexandra Place, just off De Soysa Circus (Lipton Circus), Cinnamon Gardens Ⓦ www.odel.lk. A popular expat haven, this chic emporium stocks a good range of clothes, along with assorted homeware and all sorts of other stuff. There's also a Dilmah Tea Shop and a good bookshop (see opposite), plus branches of *Délifrance* and the *Nihonbashi Sushi Bar*. There's another branch at Majestic City, though it only sells clothes.

Clothes

Cotton Collection 26 Ernest de Silva Mw (Flower Rd), Cinnamon Gardens. Small but always busy shop selling cut-price rejects from Sri Lanka's garment industry along with its funky own-label clothes, including fun T-shirts, colourful ladieswear and lots of kids clothes. There are branches in Majestic City (see p.115) and the *Hilton* hotel.

House of Fashions R. A. de Mel Mw (Duplication Rd), Bambalapitiya, on corner of Visaka Rd. Huge and incredibly popular store which acts as a clearing house for the surplus production of Sri Lanka's massive garment industry, with three floors stuffed full of all sorts of clothing and sportswear at giveaway prices, including Western labels at under a tenth of their retail price back home. Can be a bit hit and miss, though, depending on which orders have been over-fulfilled recently, while taller and larger foreigners may struggle to find much that fits.

Handicrafts and souvenirs

Barefoot Galle Rd, Bambalapitiya Ⓦ www.barefoot.lk. Colombo's most interesting and original shop, and a serene retreat from the pollution and noise of Galle Road (the sense of escape is enhanced by the deliberate lack of street-facing windows). It's best known for its vibrantly coloured woven fabrics, which are sold on their own or made into all sorts of objects including clothes, tablecloths, fabric-covered stationery, marvellous soft toys (grown-ups will love them too), and much more besides. There's also an excellent little bookshop (see opposite) and café (see p.111). Interesting temporary exhibitions are often held here as well, while a local weaver can often be seen at work in the courtyard at the back.

Gallery Café Alfred House Rd, Kollupitiya. The small shop at this chic café (see p.112) has a stylish assortment of assorted knick-knacks, including cute minimalist elephant sculptures, fabrics, photo frames and leatherbound books, plus some beautiful coffee-table books.

Kandygs Galle Rd, Kollupitiya. Downmarket alternative to the famous Barefoot, selling its own range of brightly coloured cotton fabrics either loose by the yard or made up into tablecloths, pillowcases, cushion covers, bags, toys and so on.

Lakmedura Dharmapala Mw, Cinnamon Gardens. Basic selection of masks, the usual lurid elephants, wooden toy cars and other handicrafts, plus a decent array of tea and an unusually large quantity of horrible metal objects.

Laksala York St, Fort. The flagship store of the national chain of government-run handicrafts shops, this cavern of kitsch is worth visiting just to get an idea of the tat that often passes for Sri Lankan craftsmanship: shiny orange Buddhas, shoddy masks, herds of gruesomely coloured wooden elephants and similar monstrosities. Other offerings include woodcarvings, metalware, a mixed selection of batiks, jewellery, tea and drums.

Lanka Hands Bauddhaloka Mw, Bambalapitiya. An upmarket alternative to the ubiquitous Laksala, selling similarly touristy stuff, but of a somewhat higher quality. Wares include decent woodcarvings, brasswork, lacquered bowls, a mixed bag of batiks, and better-than-average *kolam* masks. Also has a reasonable selection of Western and Sri Lankan CDs upstairs.

Paradise Road 213 Dharmapala Mw, Cinnamon Gardens Ⓦ www.paradiseroadsl.com. Set in a lovely, chintzy colonial villa, this is one of the top names in Colombo chic, stocking a range of superior household items alongside miscellaneous bric-a-brac and souvenirs. There's also a nice little café upstairs. They have a second branch around the corner from the *Gallery Café* (see above), called Paradise Road Studio.

Plâté 580 Galle Rd, Kollupitiya. This engagingly old-fashioned emporium sells a weird mishmash of clothes, art supplies, handicrafts and miscellaneous bric-a-brac, but is of interest mainly for its good selection of old prints and postcards of Sri Lanka, from US$10 and up, sold on the top floor.

Tea

There are **tea** shops all over Colombo. The main chain is the Mlesna Tea Centre, which has branches at Majestic City (see p.115), Crescat Boulevard (see p.115),

Liberty Plaza in Kollupitiya, and the *Hilton* (see p.91). Other outlets include Dilmah, at Odel (see opposite) and Crescat Boulevard; and the Tea Shop, on Sir M.M. Markar Mawatha next to the *Holiday Inn*. The city's various Cargills and Keells supermarkets also have extensive selections.

Bookshops

New English-language **books** are sold in Sri Lanka for about two-thirds of the retail price in Europe and North America, though the stock is often rather dog-eared. All the city's bookshops also offer huge selections of Sri Lanka-related titles, ranging from gorgeous coffee-table volumes to arcane tomes on a baffling range of historical, cultural and religious topics. The best selection can be found on Galle Road between Kollupitiya and Bambalapitiya; there are also small bookshops in most of the big hotels.

Barefoot Galle Rd, Bambalapitiya Ⓦwww.barefoot.lk. The bookshop here manages to cram an excellent range of titles into a relatively small space, including the city's best selection of English-language fiction, plus lots of gorgeous coffee-table books and loads of volumes on Sri Lankan art, culture and history.

Lake House Bookshop Sir Chittampalam A. Gardiner Mw, Slave Island. Large bookshop with a huge selection of Sri Lanka-related volumes, plus a passable selection of English-language novels.

Makeen Books 430–432 Galle Rd. Decent selection of English-language novels and Sri Lanka-related titles.

Odel De Soysa Circus (Lipton Circus). Excellent outlet in the city's flashest department store, particularly good for glossy coffee-table tomes, and with a decent selection of local and foreign magazines.

Vijitha Yapa The island's main bookshop chain has branches in the basement of Unity Plaza (next door to Majestic City; see p.115), Crescat Boulevard (see p.115) and Thurston Rd, and a small branch at the British Council (p.118); in addition, a new branch inside the *Galle Face Hotel* should have opened by the time you read this. The first three branches have a good range of books on Sri Lanka, plus a big selection of English-language novels – mainly bodice-rippers, but with a few more worthwhile titles. A good selection of guidebooks, a few magazines and some stationery are also stocked; the Crescat Boulevard branch sells English newspapers and a few magazines.

Listings

Airline tickets George Travel (see p.119) is a good source of discounted international airline tickets.

Airlines, international Cathay Pacific, 186 Vauxhall St, Slave Island ⓣ011-233 4145; Emirates, Hemas House, 75 Braybrooke Place, Slave Island ⓣ011-230 0200; Indian Airlines, Bristol Complex, 4 Bristol St, Fort ⓣ011-232 6844; Malaysia Airlines, 81 York St, Fort ⓣ011-234 2291; Qatar Airlines, 2nd Floor, West Tower, World Trade Center, Fort ⓣ011-557 0000; SriLankan Airlines, Levels 19–22, East Tower, World Trade Center, Fort ⓣ019-733 3723 (reservations), ⓣ019-733 5500 (reconfirmations), ⓣ019-733 2377 (flight information); Thai Airways, JAIC Hilton, Union Place, Slave Island ⓣ011-230 7100.

Airport ⓣ011-225 5555 or 011-225 2861. Flight information ⓣ01973 2677.

Ayurveda There's a surprising lack of Ayurveda facilities in Colombo (although an increasing number of spas – see p.119). The best place in town is the Mount Clinic of Oriental Medicine, 6A Cross Rd, Mount Lavinia (ⓣ011-272 3464, Ⓔmtclinic@sti.lk); it's run by a doctor qualified in both Ayurveda and Chinese medicine, and the main emphasis is on the serious treatment of chronic conditions, rather than on "soft" Ayurveda massages and baths. A hundred different therapies are offered – perhaps the largest range of anywhere in Sri Lanka – including no fewer than 25 different types of Ayurvedic massage and four Chinese, plus medieval-sounding treatments including blood-letting and cauterization with fire (so-called "moxibustion"), as well as the rare *ashtakarma* (eightfold treatment). Individual treatments from around US$25.

Banks and exchange There's at least one bank on virtually every city block across Colombo; all change cash and traveller's cheques, and the majority now have 24hr ATMs; most accept Visa, and around half now also accept MasterCard.

British Council 49 Alfred House Gardens, Kollupitiya ⓣ011-452 1521, ⓦwww.britishcouncil.org/srilanka (Tues–Sun 9am–5.30pm). Has a good library, a small cafeteria and a branch of the Vijitha Yapa bookshop chain; also stages occasional talks, readings, concerts and exhibitions.

Bus information Central Transport Board ⓣ011-258 1120; Central Bus Station ⓣ011-232 8081.

Car rental Most people opt to hire a car with driver, most easily done through your hotel or via one of the tour operators listed on pp.30–32. There are also plenty of companies offering self-drive cars. Reliable options for both car with driver and self-drive include Malkey Rent-A-Car (see p.32; ⓦwww.malkey.lk) and Quickshaws (ⓦwww.quickshaws.com). Alternatively, check out George Travel (see "Travel agents", oppsoite).

Couriers Fedex, 300 Galle Rd, Kollupitiya (just north of the *Juliana* hotel).

Cricket Test matches are played at the Sinhalese Sports Club (SSC), centrally located on Maitland Place in Cinnamon Gardens. The BCCSL shop (Board of Cricket Control of Sri Lanka; ⓣ011-471 4599) here sells tickets for forthcoming internationals. One-day internationals are played at the Premadasa Stadium, Maligawatha, Dematagoda. Tickets are available direct from the stadia.

Cultural associations Alliance Française, 11 Barnes Place, Cinnamon Gardens ⓣ011-269 4162; British Council (see above); Goethe Institute, Gregory's Rd, Cinnamon Gardens ⓣ011-269 4562; Indian Cultural Centre, 133 Bauddhaloka Mw, Bambalapitiya ⓣ011-250 0014.

Cultural Triangle tickets You can buy these at the Central Cultural Fund office on the corner of Maitland Crescent and Independence Ave, Cinnamon Gardens (Mon–Fri 9am–4.30pm).

Customs Customs House, Times of Ceylon Building, Fort ⓣ011-247 0945.

Department of Immigration Ananda Rajakaruna Mw, Maradana ⓣ011-532 9000.

Department of Wildlife Conservation Has recently moved to a new address in a hopelessly inconvenient location on the edge of Colombo at 382 New Kandy Rd, Malabe, on the road past Talangama ⓣ011-256 0380, ⓔdirector@dwlc.lk.

Diving Underwater Safaris, 25C Barnes Place, Cinnamon Gardens (ⓣ011-269 4012, ⓦwww.underwatersafaris.org) is the oldest diving school in Sri Lanka, offering PADI courses and reef and wreck dives at local sites.

Embassies and consulates Australia, 21 Gregory's Rd, Cinnamon Gardens ⓣ011-246 3200; Canada, 6 Gregory's Rd, Cinnamon Gardens ⓣ011-522 6232; India, 36–38 Galle Rd, Kollupitiya ⓣ011-242 1605; Malaysia, 33 Bagatelle Rd, Kollupitiya ⓣ011-255 4681; Maldives, 23 Kaviratne Place, Wellawatta ⓣ011-258 7827; Thailand, 9th Floor, Green Lanka Towers, 48/46 Nawam Mw, Slave Island ⓣ011-230 2500; UK, 389 Bauddhaloka Mw, Cinnamon Gardens ⓣ011-539 0639; US, 210 Galle Rd, Kollupitiya ⓣ011-249 8500.

Emergencies Police ⓣ119 (islandwide) or ⓣ011-243 3333 (Colombo); fire and ambulance ⓣ011-242 2222.

Golf The beautiful Royal Colombo Golf Club is a short drive from the city centre at 223 Model Farm Road, Colombo 8 ⓣ011-269 5431, ⓦwww.rcgcsl.com. Green fees are US$35/50 per day (weekdays/weekends).

Hospitals and health clinics If you need an English-speaking doctor, first ask at your hotel or guesthouse (or at the nearest large hotel). For more serious problems, head to one of the city's reputable private hospitals. These include Asiri Hospital, Horton Place, Cinnamon Gardens ⓣ011-269 6412; Apollo Hospital, Narahenpita ⓣ011-453 0000; and Durdans Hospital, 3 Alfred Place, Kollupitiya ⓣ011-257 5205.

Internet access Reliable places (from north to south) include: Flying Angel Club (Mission to Seafarers), Church St, Fort (daily 8am–8pm; Rs.100 per hr); Berty's, Galle Rd, Kollupitiya (Mon–Sat 7–9pm; Rs.80 per hr); icafe, Ground Floor, Crescat Boulevard, Galle Rd, Kollupitiya (daily 9am–9.30pm; Rs.180 per hr); Jawsons, 3rd Floor, Majestic City, Bambalapitiya (daily 10am–7.30pm; Rs.80 per hr); Enternet Box, corner of Galle Rd and De Fonseka Place, Bambalapitiya (daily 8.30am–8.30pm; Rs.50 per hr).

Left luggage There's a left-luggage office (signed "cloak room"; daily 5am–10pm) at Fort Railway Station, outside the station to the left of the entrance.

Maps Survey Department, Kirula Rd, Havelock Town (see p.74).

Pharmacies Union Chemists (7am–11pm; open 365 days a year); or the City Dispensary (daily 8.30am–8.30pm), both close by at the eastern end of Union Place. There's another large City Dispensary (same hours) on Bambalaptiya Junction, Galle Rd, and there are also well-stocked pharmacies in Cargills on York St, Fort, and in the basement of Majestic City, Kollupitiya.

Phones There are clusters of communications bureaux on pretty much every main road all over the city. A few of the internet places listed above (try Berty's) do Net2Phone calls (around Rs.10 per min to the UK, US and Australia).

Photos The reliable Millers Colour Lab (Kodak Express) has branches in Majestic City (see p.115) and on York St in Fort (in the street-facing side of

the Cargills building; see p.115) and offer all the standard digital and print services, including burning digital images to disk (Rs.2 per image).
Post office The main post office on Bristol St in Fort (Mon–Sat 7am–6pm) offers free poste restante service (post is held for only fourteen days). There are agency post offices all over the city, especially along Galle Rd.
Spas There are good spas at the *Galle Face* and *Mount Lavinia* hotels. Right in the city centre, the tranquil new Angsana City Club and Spa, Crescat City (next to the *Cinnamon Grand* hotel; ⓣ011-242 4245, ⓦwww.angsanaspa.com), offers a range of massages, facials manicures, pedicures and hairdressing, and has treatment rooms for couples, steam bath and sauna, as well as a gym, café and a large rooftop infinity swimming pool, which you can use if you have a treatment. Alternatively, the soothing little Sanctuary Spa, at 47/1 Jawatta Rd, Havelock Town (ⓣ011-250 1269, ⓦwww.sanctuaryspas.com) has well-equipped facilities (including jacuzzi and steam room) and a range of treatments including aromatherapy, hot stone therapy, Swedish, Indonesian, Balinese and Thai massage, wraps, facials, manicures and pedicures. Advance bookings essential.
Supermarkets The main chains are Cargills, which has branches at York St, Fort (see p.115) and in the basement of Majestic City (see p.115); and Keells, in the basement of Crescat Boulevard (see p.115).
Swimming Many of the city's hotel pools can be used by non-guests for a fee. See the listings on pp.91–96 for details.
Train information Fort Railway Station ⓣ011-243 1281, enquiries ⓣ011-243 4215.
Travel agents George Travel, 82 Bristol St, Fort (opposite the YMCA) ⓣ011-293 9782, mobile ⓣ0776 504 855, ⓔgeorge_trv@yahoo.com. Small but long-established travel agent offering cheap car-and-driver transfers and tours islandwide. Also a good source for cheap air fares.

Moving on from Colombo

As you'd expect, Colombo has the island's best transport connections: the capital is at the centre of the island's **rail** network, while a vast range of **buses** depart from one of the three bus stations to pretty much everywhere in the country.

By train

Colombo is the hub of the Sri Lankan rail system, with direct services to many places in the country – see box on p.120 for timetables. The principal terminus, **Fort Railway Station** can be somewhat anarchic, especially during rush hours. Different ticket windows sell tickets to different destinations – if in doubt, check with the helpful enquiries window (no. 10) by the entrance on the left. The **Railway Tourist Information Service**, outside next to the main entrance (Mon–Fri 9am–5pm, Sat 9am–3pm; ⓣ011-244 0048) is a useful source of general information and arranges tours (see p.32).

If you're taking the **train to Kandy**, be sure to sit on the south side of the train (ie on the right as you face the front of the train) – you'll get much better views.

By bus

All **long-distance buses** out of Colombo leave from one of the Pettah's three bus stands. Note that the journey times given below are necessarily approximate and are based on travel in an express private bus. Normal private services and, especially, CTB buses may take significantly longer.

The southernmost of the three bus stands, **Bastian Mawatha** handles private buses to Kandy, Nuwara Eliya, the airport and south along the coast; it's cramped but relatively orderly, with several wire-mesh information kiosks if you get stuck. Private buses leave from here to the airport (every 15min; 50min), Kandy (every 10–15min; 3hr) and Nuwara Eliya (every 30min; 4hr 30min). Private services south along the coast depart roughly every fifteen minutes to Galle (2hr 30min)

Principal train departures from Colombo Fort

Note that train timetables are subject to constant change, so if possible it's always best to check latest departure times before travelling (call ⓣ011-243 1281 or 011-243 4215 or visit ⓦwww.bluehaventours.com). In addition to the services listed below, there are regular trains from Colombo north to **Negombo** (15 daily; 1hr–1hr 30min) plus trains to **Chilaw** (11 daily; 2hr 40min–3hr) and **Puttalam** (4 daily; 3hr 30min–4hr 30min). Inter-city services are marked with an asterisk (*).

West and south coast

Colombo	06.50	08.35	10.30	14.05	15.50	16.40	17.25	18.00	19.30
Galle	09.55	11.20	13.25	17.40	18.35	19.15	20.45	21.10	00.00
Matara	11.00	13.10	14.25	19.05	19.30	20.10	–	22.25	–

All services call at Kalutara South (approximately 1hr from Colombo), Aluthgama (1hr 20min), Ambalangoda (1hr 50min) and Hikkaduwa (2hr 10min). All Matara trains also call at Weligama.

Colombo to Kandy

Colombo	07.00*	10.30	12.40	15.35*	16.35	17.40
Kandy	09.30	13.50	16.10	18.05	20.00	21.00

Hill country trains

Colombo	05.45	08.35*	09.45	22.00
Peradeniya	08.36	10.50	12.30	23.15
Nanu Oya	12.30	14.10	15.45	03.30
Badulla	16.00	–	19.05	07.30

All services to Badulla call at Hatton (for Adam's Peak; approximately 2hr 30min from Kandy), Nanu Oya (for Nuwara Eliya; 4hr), Haputale (5hr 30min), Bandarawela (6hr) and Ella (6hr 30min).

Cultural Triangle and east coast

Colombo	05.45	08.45	10.40	13.45	16.20*	19.15*	21.30	22.00
Anuradhapura	10.30	–	16.05	19.00	20.15	–	03.05	–
Polonnaruwa	–	15.10	–	–	–	01.25	–	06.10
Trincomalee	–	16.05	–	–	–	–	–	06.25
Batticaloa	–	18.33	–	–	–	04.00	–	09.20

All Anuradhapura services call at Kurunegala (2hr–2hr 30min).

and Matara (3hr 30min), travelling via Kalutara (1hr), Beruwala, Aluthgama and Bentota (1hr 30min–1hr 45min), Ambalangoda (2hr) and Hikkaduwa (2hr 15min). For Weligama and Midigama, catch a Matara bus. There are also slighty less frequent departures for destinations beyond Matara, including Tangalla (4hr 30min), Hambantota (5hr), Tissamaharama (5hr 30min) and Kataragama (6hr), though you may find it easier to catch a Matara bus and change there.

Saunders Place Bus Station handles all other long-distance private buses. These include services to Negombo (every 10min; 1hr), Kurunegala (every 15min; 2hr), Dambulla (every 20min; 4hr), Anuradhapura (every 30min; 5hr), Polonnaruwa (every 30min; 6hr), Ratnapura (every 15min; 3hr), Haputale (every 30min; 6hr), Bandarawela (every 20min; 6hr 30min), Badulla (hourly; 7hr), Trincomalee (hourly; 7hr), Batticaloa (4 daily; 9hr), Pottuvil/Arugam Bay (2 daily; 10hr). This station is utterly chaotic, and potentially quite dangerous, with far too many vehicles jockeying for position in too small a space. Watch your back. There's little signage or order to the place – you'll have to ask around to find your bus.

The **Central Bus Stand** handles all CTB bus departures islandwide. It's well laid out and spacious, although you're unlikely to use it, since it's generally much quicker to take a private bus.

By car

Cars with driver can be hired (expensively) through the travel desks at any of the major hotels or (more cheaply) through a local travel agent (see listings, pp.30–32) or car-hire agent (see p.118). Count on around US$25 for a trip to the airport, and US$60–70 for transfers or day tours to Galle and Kandy.

By air

The easiest way to reach the **international airport** is to hire a taxi (see p.90). Alternatively, there's an **airport bus** from Bastian Mawatha station (every 15min; 1hr 15min) which will take you to the bus station at Averiwatte, from where a shuttle service takes you the final 1.5km to the airport itself.

Sri Lanka's **domestic airport** is at **Ratmalana**, south of Mount Lavinia. This is where flights to **Jaffna** leave from when they're running – the tourist office (see p.89) will let you know if services are currently operational, and whether they're willing to take foreigners. There have also been flights to Trincomalee in the past, though these are currently suspended. Check with the tourist office for the latest information.

North of Colombo

The coast **north of Colombo** is much less developed than that to the south. The main draw hereabouts is the beach at the old colonial town of **Negombo**, conveniently close to the international airport. North of here lie the personable but little-visited fishing towns of **Chilaw** and **Puttalam** and a swathe of beautifully unspoilt coastline, though this whole area has suffered due to its proximity to the front line of the civil war and its leading attraction, the extensive **Wilpattu National Park**, is currently off limits due to security concerns.

Negombo and around

Sprawling **NEGOMBO** is of interest mainly thanks to its proximity to the international airport, just 10km down the road – many visitors stagger off long-haul flights straight into one of the beach hotels here, or stay here as a last stop before flying home; it's also a good place to arrange onward tours and transport. Negombo's beach is very wide in places, but can feel rather shabby if you've visited any of the more pristine resorts further south. A couple of miles south of the beach, scruffy **Negombo Town** offers an interesting introduction to coastal Sri Lankan life, with a lively pair of fish markets, a few colonial remains and hundreds of colourful wooden boats.

The Negombo area is also the heartland of **Christian Sri Lanka**, as borne out by the enormous churches and florid wayside Catholic shrines scattered about the town and its environs. The people of Negombo are **Karavas**, Tamil and Sinhalese fishermen who converted en masse to Catholicism during the mid-sixteenth century under the influence of Portuguese missionaries, taking Portuguese surnames and becoming the first of Sri Lanka's innumerable de Silvas, de Soysas,

Mendises and Pereras. The **Dutch** made the town an important commercial centre, building a canal (and a fort to guard it) on which spices – particularly the valuable cinnamon which grew profusely in the surrounding areas – were transported from the interior to the coast prior to being shipped abroad.

Thanks to its position between the rich ocean waters and the Negombo Lagoon inland, Negombo has also developed into one of the most important **fishing ports** on the island. Fishing still dominates the local economy, with the sea providing plentiful supplies of tuna, shark and seer, while the lagoon is the source of some of the island's finest prawns, crabs and lobster. The Karavas are also famous for their unusual fishing boats, known as **oruwas**, distinctive catamarans (a word derived from the Tamil *ketti-maran*) fashioned from a hollowed-out trunk attached to an enormous sail. Hundreds of these small vessels remain in use even today, and make an unforgettable sight when the fleet returns to shore.

Arrival

Negombo's position near the airport guarantees a steady year-round flow of tourists, although things become fairly sleepy – and some shops and restaurants close down – from mid-April to late October. The resort area sprawls for a considerable distance along the coast, dividing broadly into two areas: the **town** itself, and **Negombo beach**. The latter straggles north for several kilometres and is backed by the long main drag, **Lewis Place** (which later turns into **Porutota Road**): a ramshackle thoroughfare dotted with endless shops, cafés and guesthouses.

The **bus** and **train** stations are close to one another in the town centre, some way from most of Negombo's accommodation. A tuktuk from either station to Lewis Place/Porutota Road should cost around Rs.150–200, but you might have to bargain hard; drivers here are used to taking advantage of newly arrived tourists.

Note that the **milk powder scam** (see p.63) is a particular favourite in Negombo at present. Expect to be approached at least once.

▲ Church of Perpetual Hope

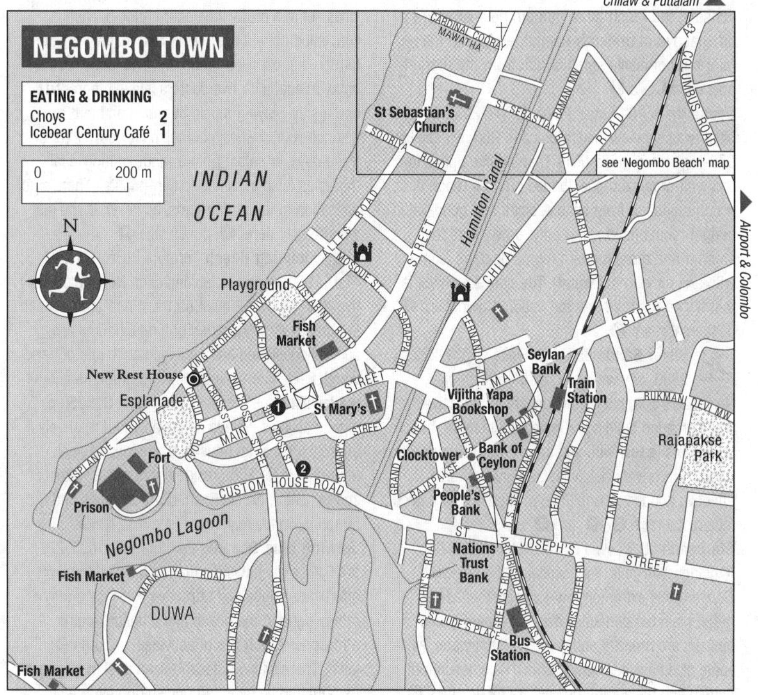

Accommodation

There's heaps of **accommodation** in Negombo, though the easy custom generated by its proximity to the airport means that standards are indifferent – the larger **hotels** here service an endless supply of all-inclusive package tourists who appear to demand nothing more of Sri Lanka than cheap beer, execrable quasi-European cuisine and ping-pong tournaments. The good news for budget travellers is that some of Negombo's nicest places to stay are also the cheapest. Most of the **budget** places are clustered along Lewis Place; more **upmarket** options are concentrated to the north along Porutota Road.

Other than the *New Rest House* (see Negombo Town map, above), all accommodation below appears on the Negombo Beach map on p.126.

Budget

Dephani 189/15 Lewis Place ⓣ031-223 8225, ⓔdephanie@slt.lk. One of Negombo's most attractive guesthouses – sleepy and homely, with a beautiful garden running down to the beach. Rooms are neat and clean, with big frame-nets and attractive old-fashioned wooden furniture. ❷–❸

The Icebear 103 Lewis Place ⓣ031-223 3862, ⓦwww.icebearhotel.com. Tranquil and comfortable Swiss-owned place with a range of attractively furnished rooms (most with a/c; all with hot water) of various sizes and prices scattered around an idyllic beachfront garden. ❸–❹

Jeero Guest House 239 Lewis Place ⓣ031-223 4210, ⓔsilversands@dialogsl.net. Small, good-value family place in a neat modern house – the four rooms (two sea-facing) are spacious, nicely furnished and come with hot water. The helpful owner is a CTB-registered guide (see p.125). ❷

New Rest House 14 Circular Rd, Negombo town ⓣ031-222 2299. The best option in Negombo town itself, set in an imposing old colonial-era seafront villa. Rooms in the old wing are absolutely huge, very dark and decidedly spooky.

Those in the much more modern new wing are a bit shabby but perfectly habitable, despite the faint but pervasive smell of fish from the market outside. ❶, a/c ❸

Ocean View 104 Lewis Place ⓣ031-223 8689, ⓦwww.oceanview-negombo.com. Run by excellent CTB-registered guide Mark Thamel (see opposite), this well-organized guesthouse offers a range of accommodation from simple, clean and good-value budget rooms (cold water only) downstairs to smarter and more modern rooms upstairs (some with a/c; all with hot water). The only drawback is that it's on the road, not the beach. Downstairs ❶, upstairs ❷, a/c ❸

Silver Sands 95 Lewis Place ⓣ031-222 2880, ⓦwww.silversands.go2lk.com. Negombo's best budget option, set in attractive white arcaded buildings running down to the beach. The rooms (a few with a/c) are old but scrupulously clean, with private balconies and unusual but effective hooped mosquito nets. There's also a good little restaurant. ❷–❸, a/c ❹

Starbeach 83/3 Lewis Place ⓣ031-222 2606, ⓔgoldenst@cga.lk. Very similar to the adjacent *Dephani*, this extremely low-key guesthouse has rather plain but perfectly adequate rooms (those upstairs are breezier and come with hot water, while some also have sea views), plus a nice beachfront garden and restaurant. Downstairs ❶, upstairs ❷, or ❸ with sea view.

Moderate and expensive

Brown's Beach Hotel Lewis Place ⓣ031-555 5000, ⓦwww.aitkenspencehotels.com. Large but homely resort hotel, with spacious and attractive public areas backing onto the beach. Accommodation is either in smallish standard rooms in the main building or in smart, recently refurbished beachside rooms and cabanas. Facilities include a huge pool (non-guests Rs.400), a children's playground and a rustic little Ayurveda centre. ❼

Camelot Beach Hotel 345 Lewis Place ⓣ031-222 2318. Ageing but reasonably well maintained and well-priced package hotel with bright, comfortable a/c rooms and a nice big pool (non-guests Rs.500). ❺

Golden Star Beach Hotel 163 Lewis Place ⓣ031-531 0818, ⓦwww.goldenstarbeach.com. Comfortable medium-scale beachfront hotel with spacious and well-maintained modern rooms (all with a/c; most also have sea views), plus an attractive pool (non-guests Rs.350) and beachfront bar. ❺

Jetwing Ayurveda Pavilions Porutota Rd ⓣ031-227 6719, ⓦwww.jetwing.com. Luxurious little hideaway with twelve gorgeous miniature villas set in a pretty little ochre huddle, each concealed behind high walls with its own private garden and open-air bathroom. The focus here is on Ayurveda, with two doctors, eleven therapists and a sitar-playing music therapist on hand to balance your *doshas*; courses cost from €210 for three days, or select from a range of individual therapies (also available to non-guests). There's no obligation to take treatments, however, if you just want to stay here. ❼, queen villa ❽

Jetwing Beach Porutota Rd ⓣ031-227 3500, ⓦwww.jetwing.com. Negombo's only five-star, set at the quiet northern end of the beach in attractively landscaped grounds. Rooms are superbly designed and equipped, with lots of dark wood, white linen, glass-walled bathrooms and all the facilities you'd expect for around US$250 a night. Facilities include a heavenly (but relatively affordable) spa, an unusual tree-studded pool (non-guests Rs.750), resident naturalist, water-sports centre, excellent childcare facilities and the tempting *Sands* restaurant (see p.127). ❾

Jetwing Blue Oceanic Porutota Rd ⓣ031-227 9000, ⓦwww.jetwing.com. Big beachside resort offering spacious and attractive sea-facing a/c rooms right on the beach and a holiday-camp atmosphere, with lots of activities and organized jollity. There's also a decent-sized pool (non-guests Rs.500) and a cheap but uninspiring Ayurveda centre. ❻

Paradise Holiday Village 154/9 Porutota Rd ⓣ031-227 4588, ⓦwww.paradiseholidayvillage.com. Bright, modern hotel with spacious and sparklingly clean tiled rooms and apartments (all with a/c, wi-fi, minibar, fridge, satellite TV and safe), a medium-size pool and cheery blue and white decor. Popular with pilots. ❺, apartment ❻

Sunset Beach 5 Senaviratna Mw, Lewis Place ⓣ031-222 2350, ⓦwww.hotelsunsetbeach.com. This pleasantly understated hotel is one of Negombo's more appealing mid-range options. All rooms are sea-facing and come with optional a/c (US$10 supplement); they're quite simple but bright, with tiled floors and big French windows opening onto private balconies. Medium-size pool (non-guests Rs.300). ❺

Villa Araliya 154/10 Porutota Rd, Kochchikade ⓣ0712 728 504, ⓔvilla.aralia@wow.lk. One of Negombo's most characterful places to stay (though slightly away from the beach), set in a pair of rambling red-brick buildings around a neat garden and swimming pool. Rooms (all with a/c) are attractively furnished in contemporary colonial style; no two are exactly the same, so have a look around before choosing. ❺

The Town

Negombo town preserves a clutch of colonial remnants and some lively splashes of local life that can fill an interesting couple of hours. The heart of the old town is situated on the tip of a peninsula enclosing the top of the Negombo lagoon. Close to the western end of the peninsula lie the very modest remains of the old Dutch **fort**, mostly demolished by the British to make way for the prison that still stands behind the gateway. There's little to see beyond an increasingly weed-covered archway emblazoned with the date 1678 and a very short section of ramparts topped with a miniature clocktower added by the British, and even these have now been partially obscured by rows of ugly new concrete car shelters.

Continuing east, Custom House Road takes you past the northernmost arm of the Negombo lagoon, with myriad multicoloured fibreglass boats tied up under huge tropical trees. A couple of hundred metres down the road, a bridge crosses to the diminutive island of **Duwa**, home to the town's second fish market and offering photogenic views of long lines of colourful wooden boats tied up along the waterside. Duwa is also the venue for a Passion play, staged here every Easter.

A further 150m along Custom House Road, head north to reach one of Negombo's finest churches, **St Mary's**, a grandiose pink Neoclassical edifice, constructed over fifty years from 1874 onwards, which towers aristocratically above the low-rise streets. The interior is decorated with dozens of colourful statues of po-faced saints and tableaux showing the Stations of the Cross – the importance ascribed to religious images in both Catholicism and Hinduism was doubtless a useful factor in persuading the local Karavas to switch allegiance from one faith to the other. North of here, the **Dutch canal** (known here as Hamilton Canal) arrows due north, continuing all the way to Puttalam. Once the major conduit for Dutch trade in the area, it now looks rather forlorn – you can walk along the towpath for a couple of hundred metres, but no further. Alternatively, head just north of St Mary's to reach Negombo's principal **fish market**, occupying a crumbling concrete pavilion surrounded by ramshackle clapboard shacks and piles of fishing nets.

Tour operators and guides in Negombo

Negombo is a good starting point from which to arrange onward **tours** and **transport**. All the larger hotels and various tour operators along the main road can arrange day-tours or transfers to Kandy, Colombo, Pinnewala Elephant Orphanage or pretty much anywhere else you fancy (count on around US$65 to Kandy, half that to Colombo) or longer tours islandwide. One of the more reliable general operators is **Alma Tours**, in Negombo Beach at 217 Lewis Place (Ⓣ031-487 3624), which can arrange islandwide trips and all sorts of vehicle hire, including self-drive vans (Rs.3000 per day), car or van with driver ($50 per day all-inclusive), motorbikes (100–250cc; Rs.1000–1500 per day) and good-quality Japanese bicycles (Rs.200 per day). Negombo is also the centre of operations for **Jetwing** (see p.32), who own no fewer than five of the town's hotels – tours can be arranged either through individual hotels or the Jetwing office opposite the *Blue Oceanic* hotel.

There are also several reputable independent CTB-registered **guides** in town, including the excellent Mark Thamel at the *Ocean View* guesthouse (see opposite), Terry at the *Jeero* guesthouse (see p.123) and Lakshman Bolonghe (a.k.a. "Lucky") at 146 Lewis Place, just south of Alma Tours (Ⓣ031-223 3733, Ⓔlucky_tour55@hotmail.com). All offer islandwide trips customized to suit for around US$60–70 per day all-inclusive for two people. Lucky also leads specialist birdwatching excursions, including interesting half-day trips to Chilaw (Rs.5000 for 2–3 people), whose position on the border between wet and dry zones makes it an excellent place for birdlife.

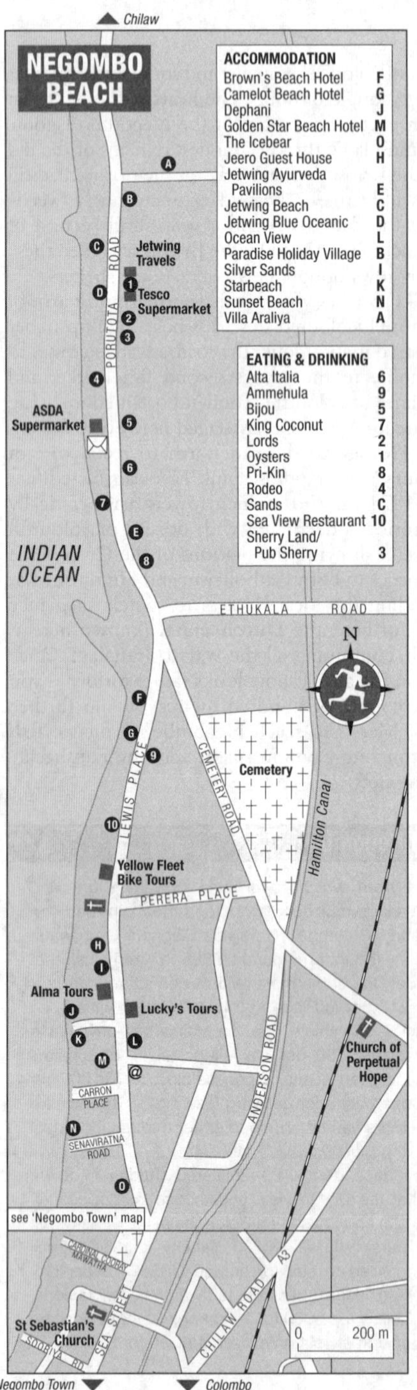

The beach

A couple of kilometres north of the old town lies Negombo's **beach** area: a long sequence of hotels and guesthouses strung out along the sand or the main thoroughfare of **Lewis Place** (**Porutota Road** at its northern end). The beach scene here is rather desultory. The whole resort is too spread out to really have any central focus or atmosphere, and visitors tend to stay in their hotel slumped out around the pool – not altogether surprising, since the exposed nature of the coast here means that the sea is often rough and not great for swimming, and none too clean, either. The stretches of sand outside the main resorts are raked and cleaned daily, but the sections in between are still very much the province of the local Karavas, with crowds of fishermen mending their nets and kids playing cricket, accompanied by the occasional pig rooting around in the rubbish that litters the tar-stained sands.

Local boatmen sometimes hang out on the beach touting for custom and offering **oruwa trips** either out to sea or into the Negombo lagoon (count on around Rs.1000 for 1hr), while some guesthouses and tour operators, including Alma Tours (see p.125), arrange **boat trips** along the Dutch canal north of Negombo (around Rs.4000 for 3hr for two people). These usually include a visit to a coir factory and some low-level birdwatching along with the chance to watch local toddy tappers at work, and perhaps to sample some of the resulting brew – Negombo's very own booze cruise. None of these trips, however, is as interesting at the boat ride through the nearby Muthurajawela wetlands (see p.129).

The **watersports** centre at the *Jetwing Beach* hotel (ⓣ031-227 3500) offers sailing, surfing, windsurfing and kitesurfing tuition, and also has kayaks, sailing boats, boogie-boards and other equipment for hire.

Eating and drinking

Negombo's location between the sea and the Negombo lagoon, source of some of the island's finest prawns and crabs, makes it a good place for **seafood**, while the number of tourists passing through means it also has one of Sri Lanka's better selections of **places to eat** – although disappointingly, most are strung out along the main road, rather than on the beach itself.

As for **drinking**, *Rodeo* is usually the liveliest place in town, while the football-themed *Oysters* and *Pub Sherry* nearby can also get lively; the latter has a big list of cocktails, plus imported and local spirits and beers including rum, tequila, Corona beer, Red Bull and – yes – sherry. For somewhere a bit more tranquil, head to the peaceful beachside bar at the *Golden Star* hotel – particularly beautiful at sunset.

All the places below appear on the Negombo Beach map (opposite) apart from *Choys* and the *Icebear Century Café*, which are shown on the Negombo town map on p.123.

Alta Italia 36 Porutota Rd. Pleasant Italian-managed place which makes a decent stab at producing authentic Italian cuisine in the tropics. Offerings include gnocchi, risotto, lasagne, pizzas and heaps of pasta dishes (Rs.400–500), plus tiramisu and Italian coffee.

Ammehula 286 Lewis Place. Lively and colourfully decorated little place (though tables are a bit close to the road) dishing up a decent selection of moderately priced tourist standards, including fresh seafood, rice and curry, pastas and so on. Mains from Rs.400.

Bijou 44 Porutota Rd. This homely Swiss-managed place has a tempting menu of excellent Central European dishes like pepper steak, Wiener schnitzel and fondues (order in advance), plus a range of perfectly prepared seafood. Most mains Rs.650–850. Often closed out of season.

Choys Custom House Road, Negombo town. A handy lunchstop in the old town, this modern a/c restaurant serves up a reasonable range of Chinese and seafood dishes, plus pizza, pasta and a few curries. Mains from around Rs.500.

Icebear Century Café Main St, on corner of 3rd Cross St, Negombo town. Set in a gorgeously renovated colonial mansion in the heart of the old town, this pretty little café is one of Negombo's most unexpected and enjoyable surprises, serving up shakes, juices, sandwiches, soups and cakes, plus breakfasts, business lunches and high teas, along with excellent coffee.

King Coconut 11 Porutota Rd. A hungry-looking T-rex with snarling mouth welcomes you to one of Negombo's few independent beachfront restaurants (although it's on a rather shabby bit of sand). The pizzas (from Rs.430) are passable (though far from authentic), and there's also Chinese food, pasta and the usual range of meat dishes.

Lords Porutota Rd. This chic modern restaurant brings a welcome dash of style to Negombo's scruffy main road, with sleek decor and beautifully presented cuisine. The wide-ranging menu offers all sorts of tempting international fare, including a good vegetarian selection, ranging from Thai fish cakes and crispy lemon chicken to button mushroom, cashew nut and raisin curry. Mains from around Rs.800.

Pri-Kin 10 Porutota Rd. Reliable and long-established restaurant dishing up a good range of seafood and Chinese dishes, plus Sri Lankan standards and tourist favourites like the inevitable Wiener schnitzel. Mains from around Rs.350.

Sands *Jetwing Beach* hotel ⓣ031-227 3500. The open-air poolside restaurant at Negombo's smartest hotel offers some of the town's best food, plus a romantic setting within muffled earshot of crashing breakers. The long international menu features plenty of fish, seafood and steaks, plus a good little selection of unusual Sri Lankan curries. The vegetarian selection is feeble, however. Mains from around Rs.900.

Sea View Restaurant Lewis Place. Popular little streetside restaurant offering a well-prepared range of tourist standards, including lots of fish and seafood options at bargain prices, with most mains between Rs.300 and Rs.400.

Sherry Land 74 Porutota Rd. This relaxing little garden restaurant-cum-bar does a bit of everything – rice and curry, Chinese, salads and snacks – though the main emphasis is on seafood. Mains from around Rs.600.

Listings

Ayurveda Ayurveda treatments are available at the beautiful (though expensive) *Ayurveda Pavilions*, as well as *Jetwing Beach*, *Brown's Beach* and *Jetwing Blue Oceanic* hotels – see the hotel listings on p.124 for more details.
Banks There are numerous banks in Negombo town, but none in the beach area. The ATMs at the People's Bank, Seylan Bank and Bank of Ceylon all accept foreign Visa cards; that at the Nations Trust Bank accepts foreign MasterCards.
Bookshop There's a modest branch of the Vijitha Yapa bookshop near the train station.
Internet Numerous places along Lewis Place and Porutota Road in the beach area offer internet access, though they're all pretty small-scale and tend to come and go quickly. The best-equipped option is the internet café (Rs.180 per hr; daily 8am–10.45pm) in the H20 centre on Lewis Place, just south of the *Golden Star Beach Hotel*. Net2Phone calls (usually around Rs.10 per min) are also available at a number of these places.
Motorbike rental Alma Tours (see box, p.125) and Yellow Fleet Bike Tours, 264 Lewis Place, both have a range of bikes from around Rs.1000 per day.
Post office Main Street, Negombo town. There's also a handy agency post office on Porutota Road just south of the ASDA Supermarket.
Shopping There are heaps of handicraft shops all along the main road (itinerant hawkers also sell along the beach) – the best selection is along Porutota Road around the *Jetwing Blue Oceanic* hotel.
Swimming pools Most hotels allow non-guests to use their pools for a fee. See the accommodation listings on pp.123–124 for details.

South and east of Negombo

South of Negombo, the main coastal highway runs through an unbroken swathe of ugly modern development all the way to Colombo, though you can escape the fumes and concrete by taking the **old coastal road** through Pamunugama and Hendala, which runs along the narrow spit of land dividing

Moving on from Negombo

All Negombo's guesthouses should be able to arrange **taxis**; the trip to the international airport currently costs around Rs.1200; to Kandy, around Rs.6500. For details of **tours** from Negombo, see the box on p.125.

The **bus station** was being rebuilt at the time of writing, but should have reopened by the time you read this. Express minibuses leave every 10–15 minutes to **Colombo** (1hr) and the **airport** (20min). There are departures to **Kandy** (3hr 30min) roughly every thirty minutes in the morning, less frequently in the afternoon. Alternatively, change at Kurunegala (buses every 30min; 2hr 15min) or Kegalle (every 30min; 2hr 30min) – the route via Kegalle is more direct. Kegalle is also where you need to alight for the Pinnewala Elephant Orphanage. Heading north of Negombo, there are regular services to **Chilaw** (every 15min; 1hr 15min). To reach the Cultural Triangle, take a bus to **Kurunegala**, from where there are regular onward services to **Dambulla** and **Anuradhapura**. There are also currently once-daily morning services to Aluthgama, Kataragma and Hatton.

The **train** service between Negombo and Colombo is frustratingly slow, taking between one hour and one hour thirty minutes to cover the forty kilometres to the capital, and often with an hour or more between services; it's easier and just as quick (or quicker) to catch the bus. Heading north, there are services to **Chilaw** (11 daily; 1hr 15min) and **Puttalam** (4 daily; 2hr 45min). If you want to reach **Kandy** by train without travelling via Colombo, head to **Veyangoda** about 25km inland (around 45min and Rs.1800 by tuktuk; also served by infrequent buses), and pick up the train from there.

If you're **driving** from Negombo to Colombo, it's well worth travelling via the more scenic **coastal road** through Pamunugama and Hendala (see above), rather than along the main road.

Negombo Lagoon from the ocean. This bumpy little palm-fringed road is infinitely preferable to the main highway, with occasional glimpses of the sea and an eye-catching sequence of florid, improbably grandiose nineteenth-century Catholic churches. The whole area is incredibly tranquil considering its proximity to Colombo, and the last few miles of road are particularly lovely, running alongside the Dutch canal, with colourful little wooden boats tied up along the banks. Then, at Elakanda Junction in the suburb of Hendala, the road turns a corner and deposits you suddenly back on the main coastal highway amongst the mayhem of the northern Colombo suburbs.

Most of this section of coast is edged with passable stretches of beach, and there are several **places to stay** if you really want to get away from it all – though apart from lying on the sand and visiting the **Muthurajawela** wetlands, there's really absolutely nothing to do. The friendly *Villa Temple Flower* (☎011-223 6755; ❸, a/c supplement US$5), 10km south of Negombo and a three-minute walk from the sea, has a beautiful setting in a flower-filled garden with pool, though the rooms are rather dark and musty, and relatively expensive. Alternatively, the *Palm Village Hotel* (☎011-479 5114; ❺), 15km south of Negombo, offers good-value accommodation in an old and plain but not unappealing resort hotel with a nice beachfront setting and pool, and comfortably equipped sea-facing rooms with air-conditioning, hot water and satellite TV.

Muthurajawela

Around 15km south of Negombo (and 20km north of Colombo), at the southern end of the Negombo lagoon and close to the southern edge of the airport, **Muthurajawela** comprises a considerable area of saltwater wetland which attracts a rich variety of water-loving **birds**, including various species of colourful kingfisher, assorted herons, egrets, moorhen, duck, painted stork and many others, as well as crocodiles, macaque monkeys and a large population of water monitors. The small Muthurajawela **visitor centre** (☎011-483 0150) is the starting point for rewarding two-hour boat trips (daily 7am–4pm; Rs.800 per person including guide) through the wetlands; it's best to ring in advance to make sure there's a boat available when you arrive, especially on Sundays, when lots of locals visit. Trips take you up along the idyllic old Dutch canal before reaching the Negombo lagoon itself, which you'll skirt whilst exploring the surrounding wetlands and mangroves.

The trip from Negombo, including transport and boat tour, costs around Rs.1800 in a tuktuk, or Rs.2800 in a car, and can be arranged through most of the town's guesthouses and travel agents. Alternatively, catch a train to Ja-Ela, on the main Colombo to Negombo line, and take a tuktuk from there for the three-kilometre trip to the visitor centre; turn west off the main Colombo highway down Bopitiya Road (signposted to the *Villa Palma* hotel).

East of Negombo

Some four kilometres east of Negombo, the eye-catching **Angurukaramulla Temple** serves as a rare beacon of Buddhism in an overwhelmingly Christian area. The temple is best known for its huge Buddha statue, built in 1980 and showing the master seated in the *samadhi* (meditation) pose. There are also various garish Buddhist *tableaux vivants* to admire, along with a ramshackle subsidiary building filled with portraits or statues of all the major Sinhalese kings, topped with an unusual modern *vatadage* (circular shrine).

Further inland, the **Aluthapola Temple** is said to date back to the reign of King Valagamba, creator of the famous temples at Dambulla. Like Dambulla,

Aluthapola is a cave temple, built into the side of a huge rock outcrop and sheltering a large reclining Buddha said to date back to 1792, though heavily restored since. Climb up to the top of the outcrop above, where there's an old Dutch survey tower and mesmerizing views over the endless green treetops of the so-called "Coconut Triangle" (the area between Negombo, Puttalam and Kurunegala). Sunset is particularly beautiful. Aluthapola is around 15km from Negombo, on the road between Kimbulapitiya and Minuwangoda. Tuktuk drivers in Negombo offer a combined tour of this and Angurukaramulla Temple, plus a Negombo city tour, for around Rs.2000.

Some 15km further inland from Aluthapola, just outside the town of Gampaha on the main Colombo–Kandy railway, the historic **Henerathgoda Botanical Gardens** (daily 7.30am–5pm; Rs.600) are famous as the place where rubber was first grown in Asia, during the 1870s, using seeds smuggled out of Brazil – some of the original trees can still be seen in situ. The rest of the gardens have recently received some long-overdue care and attention, and are well worth a brief visit, although admittedly nowhere near as extensive or spectacular as those at Peradeniya.

If you want **to stay** hereabouts, the stylish new *The Wallawwa* boutique hotel (Ⓣ0773 864 384, Ⓦwww.thewallawwa.com; ❽–❾), tucked away just down the road from Henerathgoda in the village of Kotugoda (15min drive from the airport, 25min from Negombo), occupies a sleekly converted old *walauwa* (manor house). Rooms are elegantly designed and come with rainshowers, four-poster beds, widescreen TVs and wi-fi, and there's also a spa and a top-notch restaurant. It's also conveniently close to the main roads to Colombo, Kandy and Dambulla.

North of Negombo

North of Negombo, the coastline becomes increasingly rocky and wild, with narrow beaches and crashing waves that make swimming impossible for most of the year. Not surprisingly, the area remains largely undeveloped, although there are a pair of good hotels at **Waikkal**. Further north lies the bustling fishing town of **Chilaw** and the interesting **Munnesvaram Temple**, one of the island's most important Hindu temples. North of Chilaw is the fishing town of **Puttalam**, beyond which lies the extensive **Wilpattu National Park**.

Waikkal to Mahawewa

Twelve kilometres north of Negombo, the small village of **WAIKKAL** is a major **tile-making** centre, thanks to the good clay found hereabouts, and the area is dotted with quaint tile factories sporting tall chimneys attached to barn-like buildings with sloping sides and huge roofs, with great mounds of freshly baked tiles stacked up beneath them. The village also has a couple of good **places to stay**. The best is the *Ranweli Holiday Village* (Ⓣ031-227 7359, Ⓦwww.ranweli.com; ❺), an idyllic eco-friendly resort squeezed in between the ocean and the canal, with rustic but stylish rooms set in low red-brick buildings connected by covered walkways. Activities include yoga and Ayurveda courses, boat trips on the canal and birdwatching with the hotel's excellent guides. The other place here is the *Club Hotel Dolphin* (Ⓣ031-227 7788, Ⓦwww.serendibleisure.com; ❼), a huge, family-oriented resort which straggles along the coast for the best part of a kilometre, though it manages to feel surprisingly intimate even so, and retains a certain elegance despite its size.

Activities include boat trips, kayaking, horseriding and birdwatching, while the extensive facilities include two swimming pools; the impressive larger one is, allegedly, the longest in South Asia.

Twenty kilometres north of Negombo, the strongly Catholic village of **MARAWILA** has several large churches and produces good batiks – a trade introduced by the Dutch from Indonesia. There's another small strip of rather wild and rocky beach here, and a cluster of uninspiring hotels, including the large and charmless *Club Palm Bay* resort (Ⓣ032-225 4956; £102 double all inclusive with drinks) and a couple of cheaper options, though there's no real reason to stay here given the proximity of Waikkal and Negombo.

Beyond Marawila, organized tourism ceases, as the beautiful coastal road runs north through an endless succession of fishing villages, past toppling palms, Christian shrines and cemeteries, palm shacks and prawn hatcheries. A few kilometres north of Marawila is **MAHAWEWA**, also renowned for its batiks. There are various tiny "factories" dotted around the village if you want to buy, or just watch how the cloth is made.

Chilaw and around

Some 32 kilometres north of Negombo lies the predominantly Catholic fishing town of **CHILAW** (pronounced, Portuguese-style, "chilao"), home to a big fish market and dominated by the eye-catching, orange-pink **St Mary's Cathedral**. **Buses** run from Negombo to Chilaw every half-hour or so, and there are also more sporadic train services up the coast.

Some 4km east of Chilaw, the **Munnesvaram Temple** is one of the four most important Shiva temples on the island and an important pilgrimage centre. Its origins are popularly claimed to date back to the mythical era of the *Ramayana* (see box below), though the original temple was destroyed by the Portuguese, and the present building dates from the British era. A lively local **festival** is celebrated here each year in either August or September, with fire-walking; tour operators in Negombo might be able to give you information about precise timings.

Munnesvaram follows the usual plan of Sri Lankan Hindu temples, with a solidly built inner shrine of stone enclosed within a larger, barn-like wooden structure, its stout outer walls painted in the traditional alternating red and white stripes. The

Rama, Shiva and Munnesvaram

According to legend, **Munnesvaram temple** was established by none other than **Rama** himself, after he defeated and killed Rawana, as related in the *Ramayana*. Following the final battle with Rawana, Rama was returning to India in his air chariot (the *Dandu Monara*, or "Wooden Peacock" – often claimed to be the earliest flying machine in world literature – whose stylized image formerly adorned the tailfins of all Air Lanka planes) when he was overcome by a sudden sense of guilt at the bloodshed occasioned by his war with Ravana. Seeing a temple below he descended and began to pray, whereupon Shiva and Parvati appeared and ordered him to enshrine lingams (symbolic of Shiva's creative powers) in three new temples: at Konesvaram in Trincomalee, Thirukethesvaram in Mannar, and at Munnesvaram.

The belief that these three temples were thus established by Rama – an incarnation of the great Hindu god Vishnu – lends each an additional aura of sanctity, though the fact that they were created to enshrine a trio of lingams serves as a subtle piece of propaganda asserting the superiority of Shiva over his greatest rival in the Hindu pantheon. The paradox is that, despite Sri Lanka's close association with Vishnu in his incarnation as Rama, almost all the island's Hindu temples are dedicated to Shiva, or to deities closely related to him, and hardly any to Vishnu himself.

darkly impressive **inner shrine** (*cella*) is very Indian in style; a large gilded *kodithambam* (a ceremonial pillar carried in procession during the temple festival, and a standard element of all Sri Lankan Hindu temples) stands in front of the entrance door. Inside the shrine is the temple's main Shiva lingam and a gold figure of Parvati, festooned in garlands. The **outer building** is a fine old wooden structure, slightly adulterated by bits of modern bathroom-style tiling. To the left of the entrance are various chariots used to carry images and other paraphernalia during temple festivities; more festival chariots can be found at the rear of the inner shrine, including a peacock (for Skanda), a Garuda (Vishnu) and a lion (Parvati). On the other side of the inner shrine are images of various gods – Vishnu flanked by Garuda and Hanuman; Sarasvati playing a sitar; Kali killing a buffalo; and Lakshmi. The huge chariot used in the festival is usually parked in the courtyard outside.

Some 10km north of Chilaw lies the lushly beautiful but little-visited **Anawilundawa Wetland Sanctuary** (open access; free). The sanctuary consists of an ancient "cascading irrigation tank system", dating from the twelfth century AD and designed to irrigate surrounding paddy fields, along with a stretch of beach. Paths crisscross the sanctuary and you can wander freely between lotus-strewn tanks and the wide and beautifully unspoilt stretch of empty beach by the Hamilton Canal.

If you want to stay hereabouts, the appealingly rustic *The Mudhouse* eco-retreat (Ⓣ0773 016 191, Ⓦwww.themudhouse.lk; ❽ full board), around 30km northeast of Chilaw near the town of Anamaduwa, is set within two hectares of jungle beside a lotus-strewn lake, with accommodation in simple but comfortable huts made entirely of natural local materials.

Puttalam and around

North of Chilaw, you enter the dry zone, the luxuriant palm trees giving way to more arid scrubland and dry forest. **PUTTALAM** (pronounced "Pootalam") sits 50km from Chilaw near the southern end of the enormous Puttalam Lagoon, and is of interest mainly as a transit point on the little-travelled (at least by tourists) road between Negombo and Anuradhapura.

About 8km short of Puttalam, a small side road branches off along the narrow spit of land bounding the extensive Puttalam Lagoon to reach the remote town of **KALPITIYA**. Flanked by sea and lagoon on three sides, the town has a watery, end-of-the-world feeling, though all that may change shortly if government plans to establish a new US$4 billion luxury resort here, complete with golf course and airstrip, bear fruit. In the meantime, there's an old Dutch fort (currently occupied by the army, so access in limited) and the remains of the fine old St Peter's Kirk to explore. The town is also beginning to feature on the itineraries of adventurous kitesurfers, and is gaining a reputation as one of the best places in the island to see **dolphins** (and also sometimes whales). Trips can be arranged through *Alankuda Beach* (Ⓣ060-232 4855, Ⓦwww.alankuda.com; ❾), an appealing new boutique resort set on a beautiful strip of unspoilt beach and offering an unusual blend of the traditional and the modern, with rustic wattle-and-daub cabanas, a couple of villas and a stunning seafront pool. It's not cheap, with rates from US$300 per night, although this does include all meals and activities. En route to Kalpitiya you'll also pass the important Catholic shrine at the nineteenth-century church of **St Anne**, almost on the seafront at the village of **Talawila**, site of an important festival in March and again in July/August.

Some 25km north of Puttalam, **Wilpattu** is the largest national park in Sri Lanka, and was one of the most popular until its position close to the front line of the civil war led to its closure in 1985. It finally reopened in 2003, but has been closed again since 2006, when a landmine killed seven Sri Lankan tourists in the park.

South of Colombo

Heading south out of Colombo, the fulminating Galle Road passes through a seemingly endless succession of ragtag suburbs before finally shaking itself clear of the capital, though even then a more or less continuous ribbon of development straggles all the way down the coast – according to Michael Ondaatje in his celebrated portrait of Sri Lanka, *Running in the Family*, it was said that a chicken could walk along the roofs of the houses between Galle and Colombo without once touching the ground. The endless seaside buildings mean that although the road and rail line run close to the coast for most of the way, you don't see that much of the sea, beaches or actual resorts from either.

Beyond Colombo, the towns of **Moratuwa** and **Panadura** have both now been pretty much absorbed by the capital; the former is a major carpentry and furniture-making centre, and you might see lines of chairs and other furniture set out alongside the road for sale.

Kalutara and around

Just over 40km from Colombo, bustling **KALUTARA** is the first town you reach travelling south that retains a recognizably separate identity from the capital. It's one of the west coast's largest settlements, but the long stretch of beach north of town remains reasonably unspoilt, dotted with a string of upmarket hotels that make a decent first or last stop on a tour of the island, given Kalutara's relative proximity to the international airport (although it's still a tedious two hour-plus drive by the time you've negotiated Colombo).

Sitting next to the broad estuary of the Kalu Ganga, or "Black River", from which it takes its name, Kalutara was formerly an important spice-trading centre, controlled at various times by the Portuguese, Dutch and British. Nowadays, it's more famous as the source of the island's finest **mangosteens** (in season June–Sept). Kalutara announces its presence via the immense white dagoba of the **Gangatilaka Vihara**, immediately south of the long bridge across the Kalu Ganga. The dagoba was built during the 1960s on the site of the former Portuguese fort, and has the unusual distinction of being the only one in the world that is entirely hollow. You can go inside the cavernously echoing interior, whose walls are ringed by a strip of 75 murals depicting various scenes from the Buddha's life; windows above the murals offer fine views of the Kalu Ganga and out to sea. Outside, the line of donation boxes flanking the roadside are fed with huge quantities of small change by local motorists, who stop here to say a prayer and offer a few coins in the hope of a safe journey – if you've spent much time travelling along the anarchic Galle Road, you'll understand why.

The remainder of the temple buildings are situated in a compound on the other side of the road, featuring the usual bo tree enclosures and Buddha

The best season for **diving** and **swimming** on the west coast is roughly November to mid-April; at other times, heavy breakers and dangerous undertows mean that it can be risky to go in beyond chest height. For more about swimming and other marine hazards, see p.62 and p.67.

shrines. It's a lively complex, and a good place to watch the daily rituals of Sri Lankan Buddhism: the Buddha images here are "fed" three times a day (rather like the package tourists at the nearby resorts); devotees place food in boxes in front of the images, as well as offering flowers, lighting coconut-oil lamps, tying prayers written on scraps of cloth to one of the bo trees (sometimes with coins wrapped up inside them) or pouring water into the conduits which run down to water the bo trees' roots.

A few kilometres inland along the lagoon-side road immediately south of the Gangatilaka temple, near the village of Palatota, stands the imperious **Richmond Castle** (daily 9am–4pm; Rs.100). A striking hybrid of Indian and British architectural styles, the house was built at the end of the nineteenth century by a wealthy landowner and spice-grower Don Arthur de Silva Wijesinghe Siriwardena; it now serves as an educational centre for underprivileged local children. Sitting proud atop a hill at the centre of a 42-acre estate, the two-storey mansion is constructed on a lavish scale – two entire shiploads of teak from Burma were used during its construction, some of which can be seen in the finely carved wooden pillars in the main hall. Hotels sometimes arrange trips to the house by canoe down the old Dutch canal – a pretty journey between nodding palm trees which is at least half the fun of a visit to the house.

Kalutara's **beach** extends north of the bridge all the way to the village of **WADDUWA**, some 8km distant, backed by a string of large but discreetly spread-out resort hotels. The coast is edged with a fine – if in places rather narrow – swathe of golden sand, and remains surprisingly unspoilt and quiet given the proximity of Colombo, although (as along much of the west coast) the sea can be rough, and most people swim in their hotel pools.

Practicalities

The **bus stand** is a few minutes' walk south of the Gangatilaka Vihara on Main Street. Services head up and down the Galle Road every ten to fifteen minutes heading north to Colombo (1hr–1hr 20min) and south to Aluthgama (30–45min), Ambalangoda (1hr–1hr 20min), Hikkaduwa (1hr 15min–1hr 45min) and Galle (1hr 45min–2hr 30min). The **train station**, Kalutara South, is 100m west of the bus stand; see p.120 for timetable details. There are several **banks** a few hundred metres further south along Main Street; the **ATMs** at the Commercial and Sampath (Visa and MasterCard) and Seylan (Visa only) banks accept foreign cards.

Most people **eat** in their hotels in Kalutara, although the new *Cinnamon Tree* restaurant, on the roadside close to the *Hibiscus Beach Hotel*, serves up a good rice and curry, as well as a few Western dishes, in attractive wooden surroundings screened off from the view (if not the noise) of Galle Road's thundering traffic. Otherwise, there are a few very informal beachside cafés along the southern section of the beach.

Accommodation

Most **accommodation** in Kalutara straggles up the beach north of the lagoon, spreading from Kalutara itself to **Wadduwa**. Distances are given from the bridge across the Kalu Ganga at the north end of Kalutara. There are a number of rather dismal **budget guesthouses** (❷) in the impoverished fishing village at the southern end of the beach, but if funds are tight it's really much better to press on south to Aluthgama or Hikkaduwa.

Kalutara

Hibiscus Beach Hotel 3.5km north of Kalutara ⓣ034-508 2222, ⓦwww.hibiscusbeachhotel.com. Well-run and upwardly mobile resort attractively set in a palm grove threaded with colonnaded walkways. The comfortable, wood-furnished rooms all have TV and minibar, while the superior split-level villas boast gorgeous, partly open-air bathrooms with private pools and jacuzzis. Rooms ❼, villas ❾

Kani Lanka Resort and Spa 1.5km south of Kalutara ⓣ034-222 6537, ⓦwww.kanilanka.com. Stylish, Geoffrey Bawa-designed resort hotel in a breezy location on a narrow spit of land between the ocean and the Kalutara lagoon, with fine views over the town to one side and the ocean to the other. Rooms are elegantly furnished in minimalist style, and diversions include catamaran-sailing, kayaking and windsurfing on the adjacent lagoon. There's an attractive but pricey spa attached. ❼

Ramada Resort Kalutara 5km north of Kalutara ⓣ034-222 8484, ⓦramadainternational.com. One of the west coast's larger and more overblown resort hotels, with accommodation either in attractively furnished rooms or large beachfront cottages, ambitiously styled as "cabanas". Both come with all mod cons, and there's also a wide pool, sauna, health centre and floodlit tennis court. ❻

Royal Palms 3km north of Kalutara ⓣ034-222 8113, ⓦwww.tangerinehotels.com. Upmarket resort hotel, with an enormous, serpentine pool, engagingly restyled with a fun Raj-period theme. Rooms are opulently furnished with teak floors and silk cushions, and mod cons include flat-screen TVs and generously stocked minibars. There's also a gym, tennis court and Ayurveda centre (actually in the *Tangerine Beach Hotel* next door). ❽

Tangerine Beach Hotel 3km north of Kalutara ⓣ034-223 7295, ⓦwww.tangerinehotels.com. A caparisoned elephant statue, marooned within a lotus pond in the striking hexagonal foyer, hints at the tongue-in-cheek bombast of this resort hotel. Playful architectural details include garlanded cows and some splendidly carved wooden doors, while splashes of saffron and fuschia break up the overall whitewash. Rooms (some with sea views) are cheerful and good value. ❼

Wadduwa

The Blue Water 11km north of Kalutara ⓣ038-223 5067, ⓦwww.bluewatersrilanka.com. This large Geoffrey Bawa-designed five-star resort manages to combine size and understated style, with classically simple buildings set behind a vast, imaginatively landscaped pool and beautifully screened by a grove of coconut palms. The attractive rooms have all mod cons and sea-facing balconies or terraces, and there's also a gorgeous little spa. ❾

Reef Villa 8km north of Kalutara ⓣ038-228 4442, ⓦwww.reefvilla.com. Wadduwa's first genuine boutique hotel is a sumptuous mix of colonial charm and modern luxuries. Set in a lush three-acre garden, each of the seven enormous, high-ceilinged suites is beautifully furnished in an updated Raj-era style, featuring antique canopied beds and Indian ceiling punkah fans, plus granite waterfall showers. Facilities include massage treatments, an enticing pool and tennis courts. ❾

Siddhalepa Ayurveda Health Resort 7km north of Kalutara ⓣ038-229 6967, ⓦwww.ayurvedaresort.com. One of Sri Lanka's best-known Ayurveda resorts, run by the company responsible for producing much of the island's Ayurvedic medicines. The residential Ayurveda courses are complemented with yoga and meditation classes, and the atmosphere is pleasantly low-key, with comfortable accommodation, the best in themed chalets styled after various types of island architecture. Full-board only, and treatments not included in rates. ❼

Beruwala to Balapitiya

Starting some 15km south of Kalutara, the beaches at **Beruwala** and **Bentota** are home to Sri Lanka's biggest concentration of resort hotels, catering particularly to a German and, increasingly, Russian clientele. This is the best-established package-holiday area on the island, and some parts, notably the main stretch of beach at Beruwala, have largely sold out to the tourist dollar – if you're looking for unspoilt beaches and a taste of local life, this isn't necessarily the place to find them. There are exceptions, however, including a cluster of excellent (though relatively expensive) hotels at the quiet southern end of Bentota, and a handful of attractive (and much cheaper) guesthouses on the beautiful lagoon which backs the busy little town of **Aluthgama**, sandwiched between Bentota

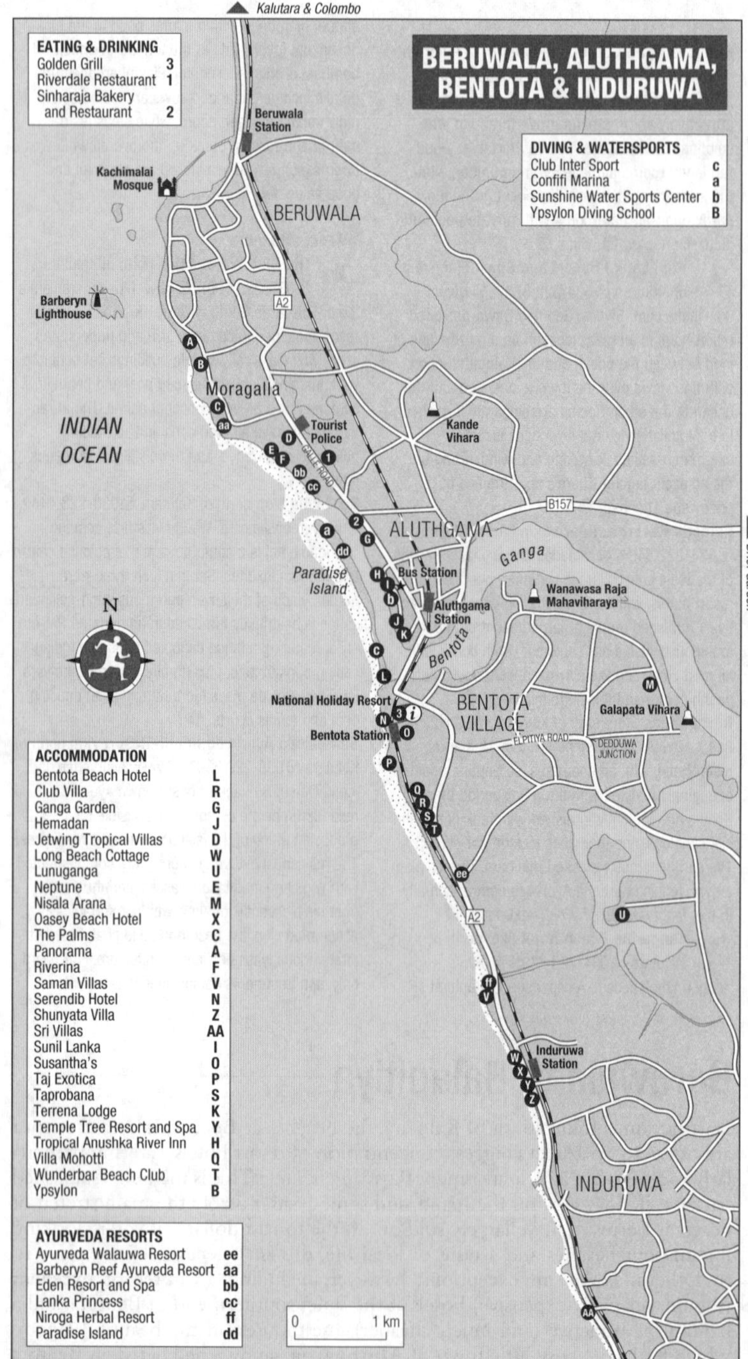
Kalutara & Colombo
BERUWALA, ALUTHGAMA, BENTOTA & INDURUWA
EATING & DRINKING
Golden Grill 3
Riverdale Restaurant 1
Sinharaja Bakery and Restaurant 2
DIVING & WATERSPORTS
Club Inter Sport c
Confifi Marina a
Sunshine Water Sports Center b
Ypsylon Diving School B
Beruwala Station
Kachimalai Mosque
BERUWALA
Barberyn Lighthouse
A2
Moragalla
INDIAN OCEAN
Tourist Police
GALLE ROAD
Kande Vihara
B157
ALUTHGAMA
Brief Garden
Ganga
Paradise Island
Bus Station
Wanawasa Raja Mahaviharaya
Aluthgama Station
Bentota
N
National Holiday Resort
BENTOTA VILLAGE
Galapata Vihara
Bentota Station
ELPITIYA ROAD
DEDDUWA JUNCTION
ACCOMMODATION
Bentota Beach Hotel L
Club Villa R
Ganga Garden G
Hemadan J
Jetwing Tropical Villas D
Long Beach Cottage W
Lunuganga U
Neptune E
Nisala Arana M
Oasey Beach Hotel X
The Palms C
Panorama A
Riverina F
Saman Villas V
Serendib Hotel N
Shunyata Villa Z
Sri Villas AA
Sunil Lanka I
Susantha's O
Taj Exotica P
Taprobana S
Terrena Lodge K
Temple Tree Resort and Spa Y
Tropical Anushka River Inn H
Villa Mohotti Q
Wunderbar Beach Club T
Ypsylon B
Induruwa Station
INDURUWA
AYURVEDA RESORTS
Ayurveda Walauwa Resort ee
Barberyn Reef Ayurveda Resort aa
Eden Resort and Spa bb
Lanka Princess cc
Niroga Herbal Resort ff
Paradise Island dd
0 1 km
Kosgoda, Balapitiya & Galle

and Beruwala. Heading south from Bentota, things become progressively more low-key through the villages of **Induruwa**, **Kosgoda** (where you'll find a night-time turtle watch scheme) and **Balapitiya**, with tranquil stretches of sand and a series of (mainly upmarket) hotels and guesthouses.

Many of the hotels here are the work of local architect **Geoffrey Bawa** (see p.146) – it's well worth splashing out to stay in one of his classic creations, whose artful combination of nature and artifice offers an experience both luxurious and aesthetic. Needless to say, most people come here to loaf around on the beach, but there are plenty of distractions, including a wide range of **diving** and **watersports** (see box, p.145) as well as **boat trips** on the Bentota Ganga and the beautiful estates at **Brief Garden** and **Lunuganga**. In addition, the area is a major centre for **Ayurvedic treatments**; most of the larger hotels offer massages and herbal or steam baths, and there are also a number of specialist resorts (see box, p.140), as well as a number of well-established **spas**.

Beruwala

BERUWALA is Sri Lanka's resort destination par excellence, perfect if you're looking for an undemanding tropical holiday with hot sun, bland food and characterless accommodation. Big resort hotels stand shoulder to shoulder along the main section of the broad and still attractive **beach** – Beruwala's so-called "Golden Mile" – often separated by stout fences and security guards from contact with the ordinary life of Sri Lanka outside. Until recently, it hasn't been a lot of fun if you have chosen to venture outside your hotel grounds, thanks to the hordes of yelling touts, handicraft-wallahs and gem merchants descending on any tourist that dares set foot on the beach. However, there are signs that Beruwala's beach areas are beginning to improve: aware how bothersome, and financially damaging, this plaguing of tourists can be, some of the Golden Mile's more forward-looking beach hotels have joined forces to retrain and organize Beruwala's roving touts – now renamed "beach operators" – issuing them with licences (and smart branded T-shirts) and cutting down on numbers. Generally, outside these hotels (which include the *Riverina*, *Neptune* and *The Palms*, listed on p.139) you can expect to be left in peace to flop on the beach, and if you want to venture further afield, the beach operators can be useful sources of information and tours. Over the next few years, all of Beruwala's hotels are likely to join in the scheme, and in time even the security fences should come down.

There's cheaper accommodation available north of the Golden Mile, where things are generally quieter and you may have the relatively unspoilt (though narrower) swathe of sand to yourself. There are lifeguards all along the main stretch of Beruwala beach in season (Nov–April); flags outside the resort hotels indicate whether it's safe to swim or not. Beruwala suffered significantly in the **tsunami**, and though most places have long since been restored, a few badly damaged resort hotels north of the main strip remain unrenovated.

North of the resorts, scruffy **Beruwala town** is where Sri Lanka's first recorded Muslim settlement was established, during the eighth century. On a headland overlooking the harbour at the northern end of town, the **Kachimalai Mosque** is believed to mark the site of this first Arab landing, and to be the oldest on the island. Containing the shrine of a tenth-century Muslim saint, it's an important pilgrimage site at the end of Ramadan.

Practicalities

Beruwala's **train and bus stations** are in Beruwala town proper, two to four kilometres north of the various resorts and guesthouses (the train station is served only by irregular, slow services). It's easiest to go to Aluthgama and get a

Ayurveda: the science of life

Ayurveda – from the Sanskrit, meaning "the science of life" – is an ancient system of healthcare which is widely practised in India and Sri Lanka. Its roots reach back deep into Indian history – descriptions of a basic kind of Ayurvedic medical theory are found as far back as the second millennium BC, in the sacred proto-Hindu texts known as the Vedas.

Unlike allopathic Western medicines, which aim to determine what's making you ill, then destroy it, Ayurveda is a holistic system which regards illness as the result of a derangement in a person's basic make-up. The Ayurvedic system holds that all bodies are composed of varied combinations of five basic **elements** – ether, air, fire, water and earth – and that each body is governed by three **doshas**, or life forces: **pitta** (fire and water); **kapha** (water and earth); and **vata** (air and ether). Illness is seen as an imbalance in the proportions of three influences, and specific diseases are considered symptoms of more fundamental problems. Ayurvedic treatments aim to rectify such imbalances, and Ayurveda doctors will typically examine the whole of a patient's lifestyle, habits, diets and emotional proclivities in order to find the roots of a disease – treatment often consists of establishing a more balanced lifestyle as much as administering specific therapies.

With the developed world's increasing suspicion of Western medicine and pharmaceuticals, Ayurveda is gaining a growing following amongst non-Sri Lankans – it's particularly popular with Germans, thousands of whom visit the island every year specifically to take Ayurvedic cures. Genuine courses of Ayurveda treatment need to last at least a week or two to have any effect, and treatment plans are usually customized by a local Ayurveda doctor to suit the needs of individual patients. Programmes usually consist of a range of herbal treatments and various types of baths and massages prescribed in combination with cleansing and revitalization techniques including yoga, meditation, special diets (usually vegetarian) and abstention from alcohol. Some of the more serious Ayurveda resorts and clinics offer the **panchakarma**, or "five-fold treatment", comprising the five basic therapies of traditional Ayurveda: therapeutic vomiting; purging; enema; blood-letting; and the nasal administration of medicines – a rather stomach-turning catalogue which offers the serious devotee the physical equivalent of a thorough spring-cleaning. A few places offer other yet more weird and wonderful traditional therapies such as treatments with leeches and fire ("moxibustion").

Although a sizeable number of people visit Sri Lankan Ayurvedic centres for the serious treatment of chronic diseases, the majority of treatments offered here are essentially cosmetic, so-called "soft" Ayurveda – **herbal** and **steam baths**, and various forms of **massage** are the overwhelming staples, promoted by virtually every larger resort hotel along the west coast. These are glorified beauty and de-stress treatments rather than genuine medicinal therapies, and whether there's anything truly Ayurvedic about many of them is a moot point, but they're enjoyable enough, if you take them for what they are and don't confuse them with genuine Ayurveda.

The principles of Ayurveda spill over into many other Sri Lankan products. "Ayurveda tea" is ubiquitous, while local toiletries, beauty products and food may often contain Ayurvedic ingredients – even basic spices such as salt, pepper, nutmeg, coriander and turmeric are claimed to have Ayurvedic benefits, if used correctly. In addition, you'll occasionally see **Ayurveda pharmacies**, intriguing places with long shelves closely packed with jars full of herbs, roots and other vegetable matter. Such medicines generally remain cheaper than imported Western medicines, and the treatment of choice for many Sri Lankans, although the fact that many ingredients only grow wild, and in small quantities, has created a national shortage of some remedies.

tuktuk from there. The larger hotels all **change money** or traveller's cheques at lousy rates; if you want a bank (or a post office), you'll have to go down the road to Aluthgama. The **tourist police** office is on the east side of the Galle Road, just north of *Jetwing Tropical Villas*.

Accommodation and eating

Some of Beruwala's **hotels** only take guests on an all-inclusive basis; this usually includes unlimited quantities of local booze. The Western **food** served up in buffets in the resort hotels is generally execrable – you're usually much better off sticking to the Sri Lankan offerings – while your dining experience is unlikely to be improved by the shockingly bad live "music" which many hotels insist on inflicting on their guests while they eat. If you get totally fed up with buffet food, the plush new *Riverdale Restaurant*, on the land-side of Galle Road, offers a wide à la carte menu, from reasonably priced rice and curry to New Zealand lamb chops; it also has a small separate bar and coffee shop. Otherwise you're limited to a few cheap and cheerful cafés along the beach, though the food is generally pretty average.

For **Ayurveda resorts** in Beruwala, see the box on p.140.

Accommodation

Jetwing Tropical Villas ⓣ034-227 6157, ⓦwww.jetwing.com. One of the west coast's more unusual and appealing hotels, this imaginatively designed four-star makes a virtue of its unpromising location slightly away from the beach on Galle Road, with a quadrangle of intimate low-rise buildings enclosing a pool and a superb garden stuffed full of trees and birdlife. The split-level rooms are beautifully furnished, and there's a heavenly new teak-and-bamboo spa, discreetly hidden away in the trees. ❻

Neptune ⓣ011-230 8408, ⓦwww.aitkenspencehotels.com. This long-running, rather Andalucian-looking establishment, with whitewashed buildings enclosing neat gardens, is one of Beruwala's most popular resort hotels, though it's beginning to look a little worn. Facilities include a big T-shaped pool and treatments at the adjacent *Neptune Ayurveda Centre*, and the rooms (all with a/c) are slightly more characterful than others hereabouts. ❻

The Palms ⓣ034-227 6041, ⓔresvthepalms@sltnet.lk. Peacefully hidden away behind a vast swathe of coconut palms, this good-value four-star is one of Beruwala's better post-tsunami renovations. The spacious, sea-facing rooms, each with large beds and pressed white linen, snake along an attractive section of beach and there's a large pool and Ayurveda centre. ❻

Panorama ⓣ034-227 7091. The cheapest accommodation in the town, with nine good-value rooms set in a family home above a narrow strip of beach – all are clean and comfortable, while four have partial sea views. ❸

Riverina ⓣ034-227 6044, ⓦwww.riverinahotel.com. This plush four-star is probably the nicest of the beachside resorts, with curving white buildings set around palm-studded gardens. The spacious rooms come with satellite TV and minibar (though none have sea views), and there's an attractive Ayurveda centre with very reasonably priced treatments. Activities include minigolf, horse-riding trips along the beach (Rs.2000 for 30min), and a well-conceived "Miniclub" kids' play area. ❽

Ypsylon ⓣ034-227 6132, ⓦwww.ypsylon-srilanka.de. Laid-back German-owned guesthouse at the quieter northern end of Beruwala beach with bright and comfortable modern rooms, all sea-facing and with hot water (some also have a/c for US$7 extra). Also has a small pool and a breezy restaurant, and the Ypsylon Diving School (p.145) is on site. ❹

Aluthgama and around

Dividing Beruwala from Bentota, the lively little town of **ALUTHGAMA** offers a welcome dose of everyday life amidst the big resorts, and remains refreshingly unaffected by the local package-tourist industry. The main street is a colourful succession of trades: a fish market straggles part way up its west side, with all sorts of seafood lined up on benches supervised by machete-wielding fishmongers, while at the south end of the road, local ladies flog great piles of lurid factory-made cloth. A photogenic vegetable market is held just south of here, past the Nebula supermarket – Mondays are particularly lively.

The town is also home to one of Sri Lanka's **tallest Buddha statues**, completed in 2007. Seated in *bhumisparsha* mudra ("earth witness" pose) atop a lotus pedestal, the colorrus looms imposingly (and impassively) over the pretty white buildings of the hilltop **Kande Vihara**, which also encompass an ornate Baroque eighteenth-century image house, a relic chamber with some well-preserved Kandyan-era murals – and plays home to a pair of resident elephants and a herd of deer. The temple is about 1km inland from Aluthgama; heading north towards Beruwala, turn right (opposite *Club Bentota*) just before the bridge over the narrow Kaluwamodera Ganga.

Aluthgama's other attraction is its good and relatively cheap selection of **guesthouses**; these places aren't actually on the beach, but slightly behind it

Ayurveda and health resorts in Beruwala and Bentota

Ayurveda Walauwa Resort Bentota ⓣ034-227 5372, ⓦwww.sribudhasa.ch. In a high-walled compound on the land side of the Galle Road, this looks a bit like a prison from the outside, though the tree-filled interior is leafy, shady and peaceful, with soothingly old-fashioned rooms in a beautiful old *walauwa* (manor). Six-day Ayurveda courses cost US$1000 per person including accommodation (based on two people sharing), Ayurveda meals and all treatments. ❽ full-board (excluding treatments)

Barberyn Reef Ayurveda Resort Beruwala ⓣ034-227 6036, ⓦwww.barberynresorts.com. The oldest of the area's Ayurveda resorts, and still one of the best. Seekers of physical and mental wellbeing will appreciate the low-key ambience, with a variety of crisp, immaculate and good-value rooms set in tranquil, shaded grounds laden with frangipani. Courses go for around US$660 per week on top of accommodation; room rates include vegetarian Ayurvedic meals and free yoga and meditation classes. ❼ full-board (excluding treatments)

Eden Resort and Spa Beruwala ⓣ034-227 6075, ⓦwww.edenresortandspa.com. Glitzy resort, full of five-star indulgence, that doubles as a spa and health club. The huge list of treatments includes hydrotherapy, herbal baths, reflexology, pedicures, shiatsu, beauty treatments and free yoga lessons, and there's also a vast pool which flows almost into the main restaurant, plus gym and outdoor jacuzzi. For all its luxury though the place has the sanitized atmosphere of an upmarket shopping mall. ❾

Lanka Princess Beruwala ⓣ034-227 6711, ⓦwww.lankaprincess.com. Large and smart German-owned place offering cosmetic (rather than medicinal) Ayurveda treatments in a luxurious, albeit rather bland, resort setting; some more hardcore treatments are also available. A six-day "wellness cure" goes for around US$650 per person, plus accommodation. ❾ full-board (excluding treatments)

Niroga Herbal Resort Bentota ⓣ034-227 0312, ⓦwww.nirogaayurvedaresort.com. Next to *Saman Villas*, this homely and friendly ten-room Ayurveda resort is one of the cheapest around, with good-value twelve-day all-inclusive courses for around US$1200 per person which also encompass (Spartan) accommodation, Ayurvedic meals and eight days' free yoga. The emphasis here is on the treatment of specific complaints – anything from obesity to alcohol addiction – with treatment plans personally customized after an initial doctor's consultation. ❽ full-board, inclusive of treatments

Paradise Island Bentota ⓣ034-227 5354, ⓦwww.sribudhasa.ch. Sister establishment to the *Ayurveda Walauwa*, in a fine location near the tip of Paradise Island, though the actual hotel is rather unprepossessing. Six-day complete treatment courses go for US$1296 per person including accommodation (based on two people sharing) and meals. ❽ full-board (excluding treatments)

across the beautiful lagoon at the mouth of the Bentota River – in many ways just as attractive a location as the oceanfront, especially at night, when the lights of the northern Bentota resorts twinkle prettily in the darkness across the waters. Most guesthouses have their own boats to shuttle you quickly across the lagoon to the beach opposite, depositing you on the spit of land known as Paradise Island (see p.142); otherwise it's a ten-minute walk, or a quick tuktuk ride, to the nearest section of beach at Bentota.

Practicalities

Aluthgama is the area's major transport hub, with **train and bus stations** close to one another towards the northern end of the town centre. Count on Rs.150 for a tuktuk to places in Bentota and the main section of Beruwala beach, or Rs.200 to the latter's northern end. **Leaving Aluthgama**, buses head north and south along the Galle Road every ten to fifteen minutes; for details of train services, see p.120. North of the bus station, there are several **banks** with ATMs accepting foreign cards, including Hatton National Bank and Commercial Bank, next to a well-stocked branch of Cargills supermarket, and Sampath Bank, a little further north. Various scruffy shops at the southern end of the main road through Aluthgama stock a surprisingly good selection of **handicrafts**, principally *kolam* masks and woodcarvings; it's also worth checking out the well-stocked Aluthgama Wood Carvers shop, just off Galle Road opposite the *Terrena Lodge* guesthouse.

Accommodation and eating

If you're taking a tuktuk to any of the guesthouses along River Avenue, note that it's more often known as Ceysands Road (though, even more confusingly, the road's official name is L.T.P. Manju Sri Mawatha). All the guesthouses listed below do decent though quite pricey **food** – the *Tropical Anushka River Inn* is more reasonable than most and dishes up a fine rice and curry for Rs.450. Aluthgama town has various cheap bakeries and rice and curry places, including the cheerful *Sinharaja Bakery and Restaurant* at the north end of town, which has short eats and snacks downstairs, and simple noodle and rice lunches and dinners upstairs – a refreshing and package-tourist-free pocket of local life.

Accommodation

Ganga Garden Off Galle Rd, behind the *Sinharaja Bakery* ⓣ034-428 9444, ⓦwww.gangagarden.com. UK-owned lagoon-side guesthouse. The simple rooms (all with a/c and hot water) are relatively expensive, but scrupulously maintained, while the ornate communal veranda and the surrounding gardens are exquisite. ❹

Hemadan 25 River Ave ⓣ034-227 5320, ⓔhemadan@wow.lk. One of the most appealing guesthouses in Aluthgama, with a pleasantly soporific atmosphere and a neatly kept garden running down to the lagoon. The best rooms – spacious and attractively furnished with high ceilings – are those overlooking the narrow courtyard; they're also cheaper than the more run-of-the-mill ones on the lagoon. ❸

Sunil Lanka River Ave ⓣ034-558 2535. This sociable place has bright, comfortable and attractively furnished rooms with enormous beds arranged around a cute little courtyard garden, leading down to a breezy platform restaurant right on the water. A/c costs a bargain Rs.250 extra. ❸

Terrena Lodge ⓣ034-428 9015, ⓔterrena_lodge@yahoo.com. Austrian-owned place in a fine location overlooking the lagoon, with pleasant, good-sized rooms with hot water. ❸

Tropical Anushka River Inn 97 River Ave ⓣ034-227 5377, ⓦwww.anushka-river-inn.com. Six clean and very comfortable rooms, beautifully furnished in teak, with a/c and hot water in a friendly guesthouse on the edge of the lagoon – the restaurant leans right out over the water. There's a small Ayurveda centre at the top, fanned by swaying palms, with very reasonable treatments, a breezy roof terrace and good food too. Not cheap, though you should be able to negotiate a discount on a quiet day. ❹

Moving on from Aluthgama

Moving on from Aluthgama there are buses every ten to fifteen minutes north to **Colombo** (1hr 30min–2hr) via Kalutara (30–45min) and south to **Galle** (1hr 30min–2hr); via Ambalangoda (30–45min) and Hikkaduwa (45min–1hr). There are also regular trains up and down the coast – see p.120 for timetables.

Around Aluthgama: Brief Garden

About 10km inland from Aluthgama, the idyllic **Brief Garden** (daily 8am–5pm; Rs.500 including guided tour) comprises the former house and surrounding estate of the writer and artist **Bevis Bawa**, elder brother of the architect Geoffrey Bawa; the name alludes to Bawa's father, who purchased the land with the money raised from a successful legal brief. Bevis Bawa began landscaping the five-acre gardens in 1929 and continued to work on them almost up until his death in 1992, creating a series of terraces which tumble luxuriantly down the hillside below the house – Bevis's work here served as an important inspiration to brother Geoffrey in encouraging him to embark on a career in architecture and landscape design. The gardens are nice for a stroll, but the main attraction is the **house**, a low-slung orange building stuffed with quirky artworks, some by Bawa himself, plus several pieces (including two entertaining aluminium sculptures and a big mural of Sri Lankan scenes) by the Australian artist Donald Friend, who came to Brief for a week's visit and ended up staying five and a half years. Other exhibits include a fascinating collection of photographs of the imposing Bawa himself (he was six foot seven inches tall), both as a young man serving as a major in the British Army and as one of Sri Lanka's leading social luminaries, posing with house guests such as Laurence Olivier and Vivien Leigh.

Bentota

South of Aluthgama, **BENTOTA** offers a further clutch of package resorts, plus an outstanding selection of more upmarket places. The **beach** divides into two areas. At the **north** end, facing Aluthgama, lies **Paradise Island** (as it's popularly known), a narrow spit of land beautifully sandwiched between the choppy breakers of the Indian Ocean and the calm waters of the Bentota lagoon, though sadly it's heavily developed and covered in a sequence of big and rather pedestrian hotels. Backing Paradise Island, the tranquil **Bentota Ganga** provides the setting for Sri Lanka's biggest range of watersports (see p.145), along with interesting boat trips up the river. The **southern end of Bentota beach** (south of Bentota train station) comprises a wide swathe of sand backed by dense thickets of corkscrew palms – one of the most attractive beaches on the island, although somewhat spoilt by the unsightly amounts of litter that get dumped here. This is also where you'll find one of Sri Lanka's finest clusters of top-end hotels and villas, set at discreet intervals from one another down the coast.

Despite the number of visitors, Bentota beach remains surprisingly quiet, particularly south of the station. Unlike Hikkaduwa or Unawatuna, there's virtually no beachlife here, and the oceanfront lacks even the modest smattering of impromptu cafés, handicraft shops and hawkers you'll find at Beruwala – it's this somnolent atmosphere which either appeals or repels, depending on which way your boat's pointing. If you're staying at Aluthgama or Beruwala and fancy a day on the beach here, you can eat and drink at all the guesthouses and hotels listed on pp.143–144; most also allow non-guests to use their pools for a modest fee.

Arrival and information

Bentota has its own **train station**. Some (but not all) express services stop here; alternatively, get off at Aluthgama and catch a tuktuk. If arriving by **bus**, it's easier to get off at the terminal in Aluthgama unless you know exactly where you want to be set down. The *Bentota Beach Hotel* publishes a list of licensed **taxi** rates, for both local and island-wide trips; **tuktuks** should be (at least) thirty percent cheaper. The rather moribund **National Holiday Resort** shopping complex, just south of the *Bentota Beach Hotel*, is home to a range of touristy little shops, as well as a Bank of Ceylon (with an ATM accepting foreign Visa cards), a post office and a useless **information centre** (Mon–Fri 9am–5pm).

Accommodation and eating

Bentota is one of the most expensive places **to eat** on the island. As is usual hereabouts, most people keep to their guesthouses or hotels for meals, but if you want to venture out, the most appealing place is the beautiful restaurant at *Club Villa*, whose small but reasonably priced menu features a well-prepared mix of Sri Lankan and international dishes. Alternatively, you could try the popular and unpretentious *Golden Grill* restaurant in the National Holiday Resort complex, which does a decent and fairly reasonable range of tourist standards, including steaks and seafood; or choose from the broader menu (pizza, pasta and plenty of fish), at cheap and cheerful *Susantha's*. Bawa enthusiasts might also consider booking themselves in for lunch (US$26) or tea on the terrace (US$20) at the master's former country retreat at *Lunuganga* (advance reservations required on ⓣ034/428 7056).

For **Ayurveda resorts** in Bentota, see the box on p.140.

Accommodation

Bentota Beach Hotel ⓣ034-227 5176, ⓦwww.johnkeellshotels.com. One of the west coast's oldest resort hotels, and the first designed by Geoffrey Bawa (see p.146); the distinctive pagoda-style main building still serves as a local landmark. Bawa's innovative designs have been much tampered with, sadly, though elements of the original conception survive, such as the stunning batik ceiling in reception and the frangipani-studded courtyard pool. What remains is a slightly bland but perfectly acceptable four-star, surrounded by large, rambling grounds and with comfortable rooms that have either sea or lagoon views. The attached Club Inter Sport (see p.145) provides a big range of watersports and an Ayurveda centre. ❽

Club Villa ⓣ034-227 5312, ⓦwww.club-villa.com. One of Sri Lanka's most personable small hotels, this intimate Geoffrey Bawa-designed establishment occupies a tranquil location at the southern end of Bentota beach. The fifteen rooms occupy a cluster of serene colonial-style modern buildings enlivened with strategically placed artworks and colourful furnishings, which manage to combine memorable design with a pleasing sense of homeliness. There's also a small swimming pool and an attractive restaurant. Half- and full-board rates only – though still good value compared to similar places nearby. ❽

Lunuganga ⓣ034-428 7056, ⓦwww.lunuganga.com. Now an exquisite boutique hotel and restaurant, Geoffrey Bawa's former country house and its extensive gardens (see p.145) offer a privileged insight into the estate to whose beautification Bawa devoted most of his adult life. There are six sublime rooms: three in the main house (US$234–375), plus Bawa's converted private art gallery (US$411) and the two-room Cinnamon Hill House (US$524). ❾

Nisala Arana ⓣ0777 733 313, ⓦnisalaarana.com. Homely new boutique hotel in an extensive secluded fruit and palm garden, 3km inland from the beach. Accommodation is in three colonial-style two-suite villas: the gorgeously restored nineteenth-century bungalow (whole house US$440); treetop Mango Wing; and newer Coconut Wing (both US$180 per room). Local tours are run in an open-top Morris Minor. ❽

Saman Villas ⓣ034-227 5435, ⓦwww.samanvilla.com. Luxurious boutique hotel, superbly situated on a isolated headland 3km south of Bentota bridge. The swimming pool – seemingly suspended in mid-air above the sea – is spectacular, while the elegantly designed rooms come with every conceivable mod con (including private plunge pools in deluxe rooms) – as you'd expect for approaching US$400 a night. There's also a gorgeous spa – probably the prettiest in Sri Lanka. ❾

Serendib Hotel ⓣ034-227 5248, ⓦwww.serendibleisure.com. Serene and very low-key Geoffrey Bawa-designed resort, occupying a classically simple white building on Bentota beach. The brightly furnished rooms (all with a/c) are good value compared to the competition, and there's also a pool and a very reasonably priced spa. ❼

Susantha's ⓣ034-227 5324, ⓦwww.hotelsusanthas.com. Set immediately behind the train station around a shady courtyard garden, this excellent guesthouse is one of Bentota's cheapest options – although still relatively expensive by Sri Lankan standards. All rooms are clean and nicely furnished, and it's only a few hundred rupees extra for a/c, a breezy balcony – and a minibar dangerously full of beer. There's also a decent restaurant, plus bargain treatments in the frill-free Ayurveda centre, featuring an ingeniously designed (if rather uncomfortable-looking) steam bath. ❹

Taj Exotica ⓣ034-227 5650, ⓦwww.tajhotels.com. Set in magnificent isolation on a beautiful headland at the southern end of Bentota beach, this vast hotel, all gleaming marble, rather overwhelms its tranquil natural setting, although it has plenty of swanky and rather ostentatious style, and the full range of five-star comforts and facilities, including an attractive spa – but at this price you might prefer one of the smaller, more intimate establishments further down the beach. ❾

Taprobana ⓣ034-428 7088, ⓦwww.anilana.com. Beautiful villa in shades of orange and pink with nine rooms, stylishly if rather minimally furnished in a kind of modern colonial idiom and set around a small swimming pool. The emphasis is on style, tranquillity and privacy: there are no TVs or minibars in the rooms, and the entire place feels more like a private home than a guesthouse. ❽

Villa Mohotti (aka *The Villa*) ⓣ011-460 2060, ⓔinfo@tintagelcolombo.com. Closed for renovations at the time of writing, this gorgeous 1880s colonial mansion, with extensions by Geoffrey Bawa, should have reopened by the time you read this. Rooms are widely spread out, so there's plenty of privacy, and are very elegantly furnished. Sensitive upgrading will retain the essence of Bawa but add more public areas, a massage room and no doubt plenty of extra luxuries. Bookings currently via *The Villa*'s sister hotel, *Tintagel* in Colombo: check the latter's website for direct contact details (see p.95). ❽–❾

Wunderbar Beach Club ⓣ034-227 5908, ⓦwww.hotel-wunderbar.com. A lot livelier than its more luxurious neighbours – the informal open-air restaurant, complete with Bob Marley posters, would look more at home in Hikkaduwa. Accommodation is in huge and pleasantly furnished a/c rooms with very high ceilings and big balconies, though they're not cheap; some have TV, minibar and sea views too. There's also a pool. ❺

Bentota village

Sprawling under an endless canopy of palm trees between the lagoon and the land-side of the busy coastal highway, sleepy **Bentota village** has a smattering of low-key sights, although the place is full of opportunistic locals hanging around waiting to pounce on tourists – harmless but tiresome. You might be offered a village tour, which could include seeing a local toddy tapper in action or a visit to one of the village's many small coir factories, where coconut husks are turned into rope (you'll see huge piles of coconut husks piled up around the village, waiting for processing).

There are also two village temples. At the eastern end of the village, next to the lagoon, is the **Wanawasa Raja Mahaviharaya**, a large and unusually ugly building full of kitsch pictures, dayglo statues and a memorable model of Adam's Peak equipped with a kind of flushing mechanism which sends water streaming down the mountainsides at the tug of a lever. Further south, also on the lagoon-side, is the much more attractive **Galapata Vihara**, a venerable temple which dates back to the twelfth century and sports interesting wall paintings, peeling orange Buddhas and a large boulder outside carved with a long extract from the *Mahavamsa*, written in Pali.

Bentota River safaris

The Bentota lagoon is the last section of the broad **Bentota River** (Bentota Ganga), a popular spot for boat safaris along the river, which meanders inland for a few kilometres from the Bentota bridge before losing itself in another

Diving and watersports

The calm waters of the Bentota lagoon provide a year-round venue for all sorts of **watersports** including waterskiing (around US$10 for 15min), jetskiing (US$20 for 15min), speed-boating (US$30 for 15min), sailing (US$12 per hr), windsurfing (US$7 per hr), canoeing (US$7 per hr), lagoon boat trips (see opposite), deep-sea fishing (US$100 for four people) and banana-boating (US$5 per person; minimum of about five people). The places listed below are the main operators, but almost every hotel and guesthouse in the area seems now to have some kind of watersports centre attached, offering all sorts of deals. Bentota also has good **diving**, and one of the best selections of dive schools in the country.

Club Inter Sport contact via the *Bentota Beach Hotel* ⓣ034-227 5176. This all-purpose house of fun offers a bit of everything: waterskiing, jetskiing, windsurfing (tuition and board rental), sailing (with or without tuition), speedboating, deep-sea fishing and banana-boating, and has PADI-registered dive instructors in season.

Confifi Marina next to *Club Bentota* ⓣ034-558 1416, ⓦwww.lsr-srilanka.com. Diving and watersports centre offering a full range of dives and courses, plus snorkelling trips, waterskiing, jetskiing, windsurfing, boat trips, banana-boating, tube-riding and canoeing.

Sunshine Water Sports Center Aluthgama, just north of the *Hemadan* guesthouse ⓣ034-428 9379 or 0777 941 857, ⓦwww.sunshinewatersports.net. Full range of watersports, and particularly good for windsurfing and waterskiing, with tuition available from two former Sri Lankan champions. Other offerings include jetskiing, body-board hire, snorkelling trips, deep-sea fishing, Bentota river cruises and lagoon- and sea-kayaking, as well as rather expensive diving. Rough Guide readers are promised a ten percent discount.

Ypsylon Diving School ⓣ034-227 6132, ⓦwww.ypsylon-srilanka.de. One of the area's longest-established dive schools, offering the usual range of single dives, PADI courses, night dives, introductory "discovery" dives and wreck dives.

mazy lagoon dotted with tiny islands and fringed with tangled mangrove swamps. These trips aren't the greatest natural adventure you're likely to have: the boats themselves are usually noisy and smelly, and the standard of guiding pretty hopeless. Even so, you should see a fair selection of aquatic birds – herons, cormorants and colourful kingfishers – as well as a few water monitors, while your boatman might also ferry you right in amongst the mangroves themselves, a mysterious and beautiful sight as you drift though still, shaded waters beneath huge roots. Obviously, the longer the trip and the further upriver you travel, the more unspoilt the scenery becomes – you're unlikely to see much of interest on a one-hour trip. Longer excursions usually include extras such as trips to coconut factories or handicrafts shops, and you may also be taken to visit the Galapata Vihara (see opposite).

Trips can be arranged through some Bentota or Aluthgama guesthouses and hotels, or through the area's many watersports centres (see box above). The standard tour lasts three hours and costs around Rs.600 per person in a group of at least four.

Lunuganga

Further inland up the Bentota River lie the magical house and gardens of **Lunuganga**, one of the west coast's most beguiling attractions, rambling over two small hills surrounded by the tranquil waters of Dedduwa Lake. Lunuganga was the creation of seminal Sri Lankan architect Geoffrey Bawa (see p.146) who acquired the estate – at that time nothing more than "an undistinguished bungalow surrounded by 25 acres of rubber trees" (according

Geoffrey Bawa (1919–2003)

We have a marvellous tradition of building in this country that has got lost. It got lost because people followed outside influences over their own good instincts. They never built right "through" the landscape...You must "run" with the site; after all, you don't want to push nature out with the building.

Geoffrey Bawa

One of the twentieth century's foremost Asian architects, **Geoffrey Bawa** was born in 1919 to a wealthy family of Colombo Burghers (see p.172), the small but colourful community of English-speaking Sri Lankans of European descent who have played such an important role in the modern nation's cultural life. Bawa's own family boasted English, Dutch, German, Sinhalese and Scottish ancestors, a heady cocktail of cultures which mirrors the eclectic mix of European and local influences so apparent in his later architectural work.

Bawa spent a large proportion of his first forty years abroad, mainly in Europe – indeed he seems to have considered himself more Western than Sri Lankan for much of his early life. Having studied English at Cambridge and law in London, Bawa finally dragged himself back to Sri Lanka and followed his father and grandfather into the legal profession, though without much enthusiasm – his only positive experience of the law seems to have been driving around Colombo in his Rolls-Royce whilst wearing his lawyer's robes and wig. After scarcely a year he threw in his legal career and went to Italy, where he planned to buy a villa and settle down.

Fortunately for Sri Lanka, the villa didn't work out, and Bawa returned and stayed with his brother Bevis at his estate at Brief Garden (see p.142), which Bevis had been busily landscaping and improving. Inspired by his brother's house and garden, Bawa decided to do something similar himself, and soon purchased a nearby estate which he christened **Lunuganga** (see p.145). This was the turning point in Bawa's life, and the pleasure he found in working on Lunuganga convinced him to swap careers. Another trip to England to train as a professional **architect** ensued, and having finally qualified (at the advanced age of 38), Bawa returned to Colombo and flung himself into his work.

Bawa's early leanings were modernist, encouraged by his training in London and by his close working relationship with the Danish architect Ulrik Plesner, a keen student of functional Scandinavian design. The style of his early buildings is often described as "**Tropical Modernism**", but local conditions gradually changed Bawa's architectural philosophy. The pure white surfaces favoured by European modernists weathered badly in the tropics, while their flat rooflines were unsuitable in monsoonal climates – and in any case, shortages of imported materials like steel and glass encouraged Bawa to look for traditional local materials.

to his biographer David Robson) – in 1948, and gradually transformed it over the subsequent five decades, inspired by the example of his brother Bevis's work at Brief Garden (see p.142). The original house was systematically modified and expanded and new gardens created in place of the old rubber plantation, with intertwining terraces, a sculpture gallery and strategically placed artworks, opening up at moments to reveal carefully planned vistas, such as that over Cinnamon Hill, framing the distant Katakuliya temple. Like much of Bawa's work, Lunuganga manages to feel both captivatingly artful and refreshingly natural at the same time, while the various buildings offer an intriguing overview of the Bawa style in miniature, from the tiny little hip-roofed "Hen House", built sometime during the 1970s, to the serene Cinnamon Hill House of 1992.

If you want to explore the house in more depth then you'll need to stay here (see p.143), but Lunuganga's gardens are now open for **tours** (daily 9am–5pm;

The result was a style in which the strong and simple forms of modernism were beautifully softened and enriched by local influences and landscapes. Bawa revived the huge overhanging tiled roofs traditionally used by colonial architects in the tropics, whose broad eaves and spacious verandas offered protection against both sun and rain, while buildings were designed with open interconnecting spaces to obviate the need for air-conditioning. The use of local materials, meanwhile, allowed his buildings to blend seamlessly with their setting and to age gracefully. His former offices in Colombo, now the *Gallery Café* (see p.112), are a good example of this, with airy interior courtyards, a largely open-plan layout and the use of rustic local materials and objects throughout.

Bawa also worked hard to ensure that his buildings sat harmoniously within the landscape (he often designed to fit around existing trees, for example, rather than cut them down), and attempted to blur the distinction between interior and exterior spaces so that architecture and landscape became joined – perhaps most spectacularly at the **Kandalama Hotel**, which appears to grow out of the jungle-covered ridge against which it's set. Bawa's architecture also provided a showcase for other local artists. Sculptures and murals by the outstanding Laki Senanayake are a prominent feature of many Bawa buildings (such as the extraordinary staircase at the *Jetwing Lighthouse Hotel*; see p.163), while the batik artist Ena de Silva and designer Barbara Sansoni, the founder of the famous Colombo shop Barefoot (see p.116), were also frequent contributors.

The arrival of package tourism in the 1960s brought with it the need for modern hotels, a genre with which Bawa became inextricably associated (a list of his principal hotels appears on p.39). His first major effort, the **Bentota Beach Hotel**, established a style which hotels all over the island would subsequently follow. The main wooden pavilion, topped by a hipped roof, used natural local materials throughout and paid distant homage to traditional Kandyan architecture in its overall shape and conception; at its centre lay a beautifully rustic courtyard and pond set within a cluster of frangipani trees, giving the sense of nature not only being around, but also inside the building (sadly, subsequent alterations have changed many of these telling details, although the broad plan of the place survives intact).

Around a dozen other hotels followed – most notably the *Kandalama* and the *Lighthouse* – as well as the mammoth new **Sri Lankan Parliament** building in Kotte and **Ruhunu University** at Matara. Not surprisingly, Bawa's architectural practice became the largest on the island during the 1970s, and most of Sri Lanka's finest young architects started their careers working for him. Many took his influence with them when they left, and buildings (hotels especially) all over the island show the trappings of the Bawa style, executed with varying degrees of competence and imagination.

Rs.1250). The estate is about 6km inland from Bentota along the Elpitiya road; if you're driving yourself, turn right at Dedduwa Junction (after 4km) and ask locally for "Geoffrey Bawa's house". You can combine a visit to the gardens with tea on the terrace or lunch (see p.143).

Induruwa

Immediately south of Bentota, the straggling village of **INDURUWA** is backed by a stretch of wide and beautiful beach which, compared to the more developed stretches of sand further north, remains clean and mercifully tout-free, while an offshore reef makes swimming safer here than in most places further up the coast. This winning combination is attracting more and more visitors to its increasingly upmarket accommodation, though the general atmosphere remains deeply somnolent.

Frequent **buses** run up and down the Galle Road past the various hotels and guesthouses; if arriving by bus try to get the conductor to put you off in the right place – the hotels are spread out and can be difficult to spot from the road as you whizz past. There's a **train station** in the middle of the village too, but only slow services stop here. You'll probably **eat** where you're staying, although the hotels and guesthouses of southern Bentota, including *Club Villa* (see p.143), are only a short tuktuk ride away if you want to venture out.

Accommodation

The following places are shown on the map on p.136.

Long Beach Cottage ⓣ034-227 5773, ⓔhanjayas@yahoo.de. This cosy, laid-back beachside guesthouse, tenderly looked after by an enchanting elderly Sri Lankan/German couple, has operated pretty much unchanged for over thirty years. The spotlessly white rooms are comfortable and a real steal – other guesthouses offer half as much for twice the price. ❷

Oasey Beach Hotel ⓣ034-229 0422, ⓦwww.oaseybeachhotel.com. Comfortable mid-range hotel close to Induruwa station in a breezy spot on a clean stretch of beach. Spacious a/c rooms are nicely furnished if a little characterless, with TV, minibar and big, curved balconies overlooking the ocean. There's also an Ayurveda centre and small pool. ❻

Shunyata Villa ⓣ034-227 1944, ⓦwww.shunyata-villa.net. Idyllic boutique guesthouse in serene modern beachfront premises. Rooms sport deliciously cool Zen-like decor, with white walls, and rock-crystal jacuzzi bathrooms, and come with a/c, CD player and minibar (but no TV). There's also a nice little pool and Ayurveda treatments, which are administered in a homely little palm-leaf shack in the beautiful garden. ❼

Sri Villas ⓦwww.srivillas.com. Three very stylish and spacious modern villas (sleeping 4–8; US$320–530), built behind an enticing thirty-metre lap pool and set on a half-kilometre stretch of deserted beach. Each villa is quite individual but all are liberally sprinkled with beautifully crafted furniture, colourful fabrics and local artworks. If you're popular (and rich) enough, the whole property is available for rent. ❾

Temple Tree Resort and Spa ⓣ034-227 0700, ⓦwww.templetreeresortandspa.com. Beguiling new boutique hotel of sleek lines and chic simplicity. Floor-to-ceiling windows lend the minimalist rooms, finished in natural palm, and ice-cool granite bathrooms (sporting sunken jacuzzi tubs) a Californian touch, and there's a gorgeous pool and delightful little spa. The inventive Asian-fusion cuisine is fabulous too. ❾

Kosgoda and Balapitiya

About 8km south of Induruwa, the four-kilometre stretch of beach close to the village of **KOSGODA** is the most important **sea turtle nesting site** along the west coast. All five species of turtle that visit Sri Lanka's beaches lay eggs here, and the **Turtle Conservation Project** (TCP; ⓣ038-567 0168, ⓦwww.tcpsrilanka.org), in association with the Wildlife Department, has set up a community-based watch scheme along a one-kilometre stretch to protect the eggs from poaching by local villagers.

Turtle watches (Rs.600; donation only if you don't see a turtle) currently take place nightly from 8pm, starting from the TCP's beach hut just behind the *Kosgoda Beach Resort*, though the scheme periodically stops running: it's best to call in advance to check. As at the longer-established programme at Rekawa on the south coast (see p.205), local villagers (often former beach touts) have been trained as guides, and keep lookout along the beach in anticipation of the first, laboured arrival. During the season (Jan–May), if you're patient (the turtles may not pitch up till the early hours), you should get to witness the awesome spectacle of at least one nesting turtle, shattered from its epic journey, fighting its way up the beach. On April nights, the peak month, the appearance of up to eight or even ten of creatures is not unusual; outside these

Turtle hatcheries

A familiar sight along the Galle Road between Bentota and Hikkaduwa, particularly in Kosgoda, are the numerous battered signs for an ever-growing multitude of **turtle hatcheries** set up in recent years in response to the rapidly declining numbers of turtles visiting Sri Lanka's beaches. Staffed by volunteers, and funded by tourist donations, the hatcheries buy the turtles' eggs (at above market value) from local fishermen and rebury them in safe locations; once hatched, the babies are kept in concrete tubs for a few days before being released into the sea. Despite the hatcheries' (mostly) laudable aims however, questions marks have long been raised over their effectiveness – it is almost impossible to replicate the turtles' natural incubation and hatching conditions, and as a consequence the overwhelming majority succumb to disease or predators – and there is little evidence that they have helped to reverse the turtles' declining fortunes. Whether the introduction in 2009 of stricter government regulation of the hatcheries' practices – setting maximum quotas for the number of eggs they are allowed to retain – succeeds in improving the turtles' predicament still remains to be seen.

months, luck plays a greater role and it's not uncommon to go two or three nights without a sighting.

A further 8km south of Kosgoda, and about 5km north of Ambalangoda, the village of **BALAPITIYA** is the starting point for interesting boat safaris along the **Madu Ganga**, a good place to spot water monitors and a wide array of birdlife, including myriad colourful kingfishers. There are also no fewer than 64 islands along this stretch of river, one of which is home to a large Buddhist temple adorned with lurid modern paintings and sculptures. Ninety-minute boat trips along the river cost around Rs.2000 per person, if you can make your own way to the river. Local hotels can arrange round-trips.

Accommodation

Heritance Ahungalla Ahungalla, 6km south of Kosgoda (and 9km north of Ambalangoda) ⓣ091-226 4041, ⓦwww.aitkenspencehotels.com. Boasting one of Sri Lanka's largest and most spectacular pools, which blends almost imperceptibly with the ocean, this vast five-star resort sprawls along a considerable section of unspoilt beach. Originally designed by Geoffrey Bawa, it's luxurious but surprisingly intimate and low-key, with attractive landscaping, stylish rooms and a fine (if pricey) Balinese-run spa. ❽

Kosgoda Beach Resort Kosgoda ⓣ091-226 4848, ⓦwww.kosgodabeachresort.lk. This plush and appealingly low-key resort enjoys a tranquil setting between the ocean and Kosgoda lagoon, with attractively furnished rooms in a mix of low-slung colonial-style chalets and pretty brick cottages. There are mod cons aplenty, and a fine pool that curves through the pretty palm-studded gardens. ❾

The River House Balapitiya ⓣ011-769 500, ⓦwww.anilana.com. Occupying a fine position above the Madu Ganga, this superb villa houses five large, very stylish suites ($286–373), each with a private garden and plunge pool. An exquisite blend of traditional craftsmanship and modern comforts. ❾

Ambalangoda and around

Some 25km south of Bentota, the bustling, workaday coastal town of **AMBALANGODA** is the island's major production centre for the demonic wooden **masks** which leer at you from doorways and handicrafts shops across the island. These were originally designed to be worn by performers in exorcism ceremonies and *kolam* dances (see box, p.151), and although the dances themselves are now rarely performed, the masks have acquired a new lease of life as souvenirs, while many locals hang a Gurulu Raksha mask outside their houses to ward away demons (the Gurulu is a fearsome mythical bird which is believed to prey on snakes and related demonic beings). Masks are made out of the light and easily carved Sri Lankan balsa wood, *kaduru* (*Nux vomica*), and come in all sorts of different sizes, costing anything from a few hundred rupees up to several hundred dollars – larger masks can take up to six weeks to carve and paint. Some masks are artificially aged to resemble antiques, their colours skilfully faded to a lustrous, mellow patina which makes a more aesthetic alternative to the lurid, day-glo tones of the standard items.

The Town

The main outlets for masks are the two museums-cum-shops which face one another across the coastal highway at the northern end of the town centre, and were set up by two sons of the late mask-carver Ariyapala Wijesuriya, who was largely responsible for establishing Ambalangoda as a centre of mask-carving. The larger of the two is the **Ariyapala and Sons Mask Museum** (daily 8.30am–5.30pm; donation), comprising two interesting and well-laid-out sections downstairs focusing on *kolam* dances and *sunni yakuma* healing dances respectively, with masks and photos of performances. The shop upstairs sells the island's biggest selection of masks, featuring all the characters you'll have encountered in the museum. The quality here can be variable, however: masks are churned out in the workshop next door (which you can also visit) in industrial quantities for the endless tour groups that stop here, and you might find better craftsmanship in the smaller workshops around town, in Hikkaduwa, or even in Kandy or Colombo.

Just across the road, the second shop-museum, **Ariyapala Traditional Masks** (daily 8.30am–6pm; donation), is less interesting. The small, dusty downstairs display features large puppets of the last king of Kandy, Sri Wickrama Rajasinha, and his queen, plus a gruesome *tableau vivant* showing the execution of the family of Prime Minister Ehelepola. The items for sale upstairs are of a similarly variable standard to those over the road. There are a number of other mask-making workshops dotted around the northern end of town, the best being **Southland Masks** (daily 8am–5pm), at 353 Main St (the side road which runs

▲ Masks, Ambalangoda

Low-country dancing

The masks you'll see at Ambalangoda (and elsewhere around the island) were originally produced to be worn by performers in low-country (southern) dances, either in devil dances or *kolam*. Many Sri Lankans still believe that diseases and illness can be caused by demons, and the purpose of the **devil dance** – more strictly known as an exorcism ceremony (*bali*) or healing dance (*sunni yakuma*) – is to summon up the demons who are causing a person sickness, make offerings to them and then politely request that they leave their victim in peace. There are various groups of demons – five *yakka* demons, twelve *pali* demons and eighteen *sanni* demons; each is believed to be responsible for certain diseases, and each is represented by its own mask, which is worn by a dancer during the exorcism ceremony (all 35 individual masks are sometimes combined into a single enormous medicine mask). Devil dances are still occasionally performed in rural villages, although you'd have to be very lucky to see one.

The origins of the **kolam** dance-drama are popularly claimed to date back to the mythical Queen Menikpala, who whilst pregnant developed a craving to witness a theatrical performance. Vishvakarma, the god of craftsmen and artists, is said to have given the king the first *kolam* masks and the plot of the entire entertainment. The traditional *kolam* performance features a sequence of dances held together by a rather tenuous plot based around the visit of the pregnant Queen Menikpala and her husband, King Maha Sammatha, to a village. The performance traditionally comprises a medley of satirical and royal dances, featuring characters such as the king's drunken drummer, a lecherous village clerk, assorted village simpletons, a couple of propitious demons, a lion and, of course, the royal couple themselves. Unfortunately, complete *kolam* performances are no longer staged, so it's impossible to experience this unique Sri Lankan medley of folk tale, demonic superstition and history (laced with a touch of Buddhism) – though you can at least still enjoy the masks.

As well as *kolam* and devil dances, the south is also home to a range of populist **folk dances** – though nowadays you're more likely to see them performed in one of Kandy's nightly cultural shows (see p.253) than anywhere in the south itself. Popular dances include the stick dance (*leekeli*), harvest dance (*kulu*), pot dance (*kalageldi*) and the ever-popular *raban* dance, during which small *raban* drums (they actually look more like thick wooden plates than musical instruments) are spun on the fingers or on sticks balanced on the hands or head – an experienced performer can keep as many as eight *rabans* twirling simultaneously from various parts of his or her body.

behind the Ariyapala and Sons Mask Museum), which has a fine selection of beautifully crafted masks in a wide range of designs.

Dance performances are staged around half a dozen times a year at the nearby **Bandu Wijesuriya School of Dance** (Ⓣ091-225 8948, Ⓔban2dance@yahoo.com). If no performance is scheduled, you can usually visit the school to see students rehearsing (Mon–Fri at around 3.30pm; Sat 8am–4pm; donation) or even enrol in dance classes yourself.

Masks and dancing aside, Ambalangoda also boasts a fine swathe of almost completely untouristed **beach** and a very picturesque new fishing harbour. It's also worth wandering down **Main Street**, an interesting and relatively traffic-free little thoroughfare whose southern end is lined by attractive shops selling everything from huge sacks of rice to shiny new motorbikes, and whose pavements are taken over most days by a lively fish, fruit and veg market.

Practicalities

Buses run up and down the coast along the Galle Road every fifteen minutes or so. If you need to **change money**, there is a Bank of Ceylon on Main Street

Moving on from Ambalangoda

Moving on from Ambalangoda there are buses along the coast every ten to fifteen minutes north to **Colombo** (2hr–2hr 30min) via Aluthgama (30–40min) and Kalutara (every 15min; 1hr–1hr 30min) and south to **Galle** (1hr–1hr 20min) via Hikkaduwa (20–30min). The bus station has neatly labelled bays inside, though many buses simply stop on the road outside. There are also regular **trains** – see the timetable on p.120.

just west of the bus station, and branches of the Seylan and Commercial banks south of the bus station along Galle Road; the ATMs at all three accept foreign cards. For **food**, the *Nirodh Tourist Restaurant*, on Main Street opposite the Bank of Ceylon, is a pleasant spot with standard tourist grub at standard prices, although rather popular with local flies.

Ambalangoda has a couple of excellent **places to stay**. Overlooking the pretty new harbour breakwater, the attractive and well-run *Shangrela Beach Resort* at 38 Sea Beach Rd (ⓣ091-225 8342, ⓦwww.shangrela.de; ❸) has spacious, bright and good-value tiled rooms (fan and a/c) and a lush garden; they also run local boat trips. Also good is the *Sumudu Tourist Guest House* (ⓣ091-225 8832; ❹), at 418 Main St, just down the side road behind the main mask museum. This very friendly family-run establishment has six simple but pleasant, high-ceilinged rooms (fan and a/c), some with hot water, in a characterful old colonial villa.

Around Ambalangoda

About 6km inland from Ambalangoda at the village of Karandeniya, the obscure **Galagoda Sailathalaramaya temple** (no set hours; donation of around Rs.250–500 requested) is the unlikely home of Sri Lanka's longest reclining Buddha, measuring some 35m in length (the precise dimensions remain unknown, since it's considered blasphemous to measure it), which fills the entire length of an extremely ramshackle building at the back of the temple. The statue is said to be more than two hundred years old and has now lost most of its original red and saffron paint, though its delicately moulded features – with wide-awake eyes and aquiline nose – remain perfectly preserved. Karandeniya is on the Elpitiya road; the temple itself is off the main road down a tiny road on the left (no sign).

Hikkaduwa and around

Back in the 1970s, **HIKKADUWA** was Sri Lanka's original hippy hangout, a budget travellers' alternative to the fancier resort hotels at Beruwala and Bentota. Nearly four decades later, it embodies the worst aspects of the unconstrained development that has ravaged the coastline all the way from Negombo to Unawatuna. Years of unplanned building have reduced the beach to a narrow ribbon of sand, while the once-beautiful Coral Sanctuary has become a circus of boats chasing traumatized fishes through a labyrinth of dead coral. And just a few yards inland, running the length of the town, the noxious Galle Road is the province of psychotic bus drivers who scream along at insane speeds, filling the ocean-fresh air with clouds of smog and making the simple act of stepping outside your guesthouse a potentially life-threatening experience.

As trashy as it may be, however, Hikkaduwa preserves a kind of ramshackle, down-at-heel charm which still appeals to some. Compared to somnolent Bentota or Beruwala it still has a bit of atmosphere, with plenty of restaurants and shops to tempt you out of your guesthouse, and a crowd of predominantly young and independent travellers who give the place a liveliness that's lacking in most of the island's other beach towns. There are signs, too, that Hikkaduwa is finally waking up to its plight. The aftermath of the tsunami saw a significant amount of rebuilding around town, with many of the hotels and guesthouses refurbishing and generally smartening up their acts. And the town received a further boost in 2008, when it staged its first **beach festival** (Ⓦwww.srilanka.travel/hikkaduwa), a five-day rave in July/August featuring international DJs that's destined to become an annual fixture.

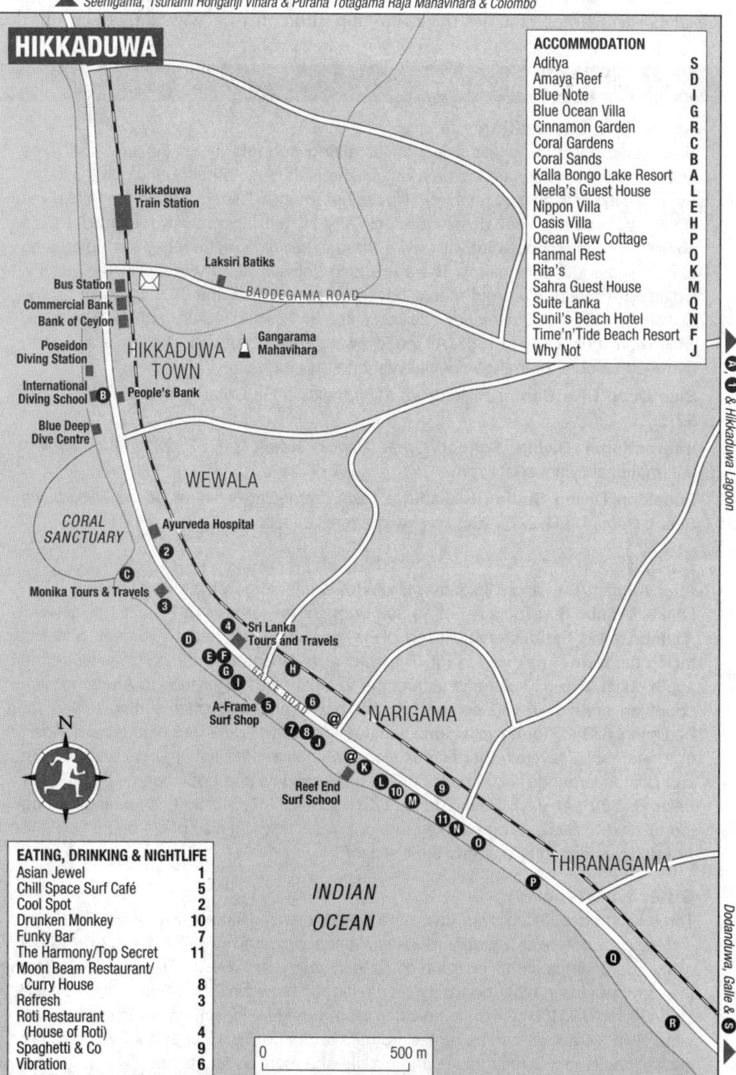

Arrival and accommodation

The **bus** and **train** stations are at the northern end of Hikkaduwa town. A tuktuk from here to Wewala will cost around Rs.80, to Narigama around Rs.100 and to Thiranagama around Rs.120.

Virtually every building in Hikkaduwa seems to offer **accommodation** of some kind, with a series of guesthouses straggling for several kilometres down the coast. Noisy and shabby **Hikkaduwa town** itself, at the northern end of the beach, was formerly the centre of the area's tourist industry, and still boasts a fair number of faded and uninspiring hotels. The beach here is a lot wider than that further south, however, and there's also safe swimming here thanks to the offshore reef. South of *Coral Gardens* hotel stretches the more appealing area of **Wewala**, effectively the

Watersports at Hikkaduwa

Diving and snorkelling

Hikkaduwa has the largest selection of **diving schools** in Sri Lanka – the three operators listed below are the best-established, although other outfits come and go. As usual, the dive season runs from November to April. There's a good range of dives close by, including **reef dives** down to 25m at the labyrinthine Hikkaduwa Gala complex, a well-known spot with swim-through caves, and the rocky-bottomed area of Kiralagala (22–36m deep). There are also some sixteen **wrecks** in the vicinity, including a much-dived old steam-driven oil tanker from the 1860s known as the *Conch*; the *Earl of Shaftesbury* sailing ship, wrecked in 1848; and the *Rangoon*, which sank near Galle in 1863. All the following also rent out **snorkelling** equipment, and may be able to arrange specialist snorkelling trips.

Blue Deep Dive Centre Hikkaduwa town, next to the *Coral Reef Hotel* ⓣ091-491 5975.

International Diving School *Coral Sands Hotel* ⓣ0722 231 683, ⓦwww.internationaldivingschool.com.

Poseidon Diving Station Hikkaduwa town, immediately south of the *Hikkaduwa Beach Hotel* ⓣ091-227 7294, ⓦwww.divingsrilanka.com.

Surfing

After Arugam Bay and Midigama, Hikkaduwa has some of the best **surfing** in Sri Lanka. Mambo Surf Tours A-Frame Surf Shop in Narigama (ⓣ091-545 8132, ⓦwww.mambo.nu) is the best-established place for surfing info and equipment, and sits facing the town's main surf point. They can arrange one-day surfing tours along the south coast, two-day surf and safari trips to Yala, plus longer trips to Arugam Bay – count on around US$50 per person per day – and also offer surfing tuition for beginners (US$35 for however long you need); they also do 24hr board repairs. Apart from Mambo's, several other places along the beach offer tuition, trips and rent out surf boards (around Rs.300 per hr or Rs.1000 per day) and body boards (Rs.200 per hr or Rs.700 per day); Reef End Surf School (ⓣ0777 043 559, ⓔreefend@yahoo.com), next to *Rita's*, is one of the more popular ones, and also offers budget trips to Arugam Bay during Hikkaduwa's off-season.

Other watersports

Three kilometres inland from town, the broad, breezy **Hikkaduwa lagoon** has vast watersports potential: Spunky Monkey Wakeboardcamp (ⓣ0779 613 926, ⓦwww.wakeboardcamps.com), in front of *Kalla Bongo Lake Resort* (see p.156), offers five-day courses in **wakeboarding** on the lagoon between October and May (around US$480, or US$100 per day), and can also arrange windsurfing, wakeskating and waterskiing. **Canoes** can be rented from *Kalla Bongo* (Rs.150 per hr) if you'd rather explore the lagoon's mangroves and birdlife at a more sedate pace.

heart of tourist Hikkaduwa, with the biggest concentration of rooms, food and other amenities. If you want something quieter (especially in season, when Wewala can get pretty busy), the areas of **Narigama** and **Thiranagama** offer increasing isolation and peace the further south you go.

Most of Hikkaduwa's accommodation is squeezed into the narrow strip of land between the beach and the Galle Road, meaning that many places suffer from traffic noise – the further you can get from the road, the better. In addition, the majority of places are built end-on to the beach to maximize the use of the available space, so in most places you don't get any sea views. Pretty much everywhere can provide **meals**, and many places have cute, if small-scale, oceanside restaurants. **Out of season**, rooms rates can fall by as much as fifty percent, though this is of largely academic interest, since apart from festival time Hikkaduwa during the monsoon is best avoided: from mid-April to the beginning of November many places close for repairs, and the entire town has all the charm and atmosphere of a building site.

Hikkaduwa town

Coral Sands 326 Galle Rd ⓣ091-227 7513, ⓦwww.coralsandshotel.com. The only one of the old hotels in Hikkaduwa town worth considering, this rambling, marine-themed resort has had a new lease of life since taking over the former *Blue Corals* next door. Renovations are gradual – and it still feels like two hotels – but the best of the rooms are bright and comfortably furnished, with a/c, TV and minibars. The bonus is the wide beach and the safe ocean swimming; there are also two good-sized pools, a diving centre (see opposite) and a large, though ostentatiously fenced-off, garden. ❻

Wewala

Amaya Reef ⓣ091 438 3244, ⓦwww.amayaresorts.com. Eye-catching hotel whose bold, sweeping, yellow facade promises a bit more style than most other places in town. Rooms are compact but sleekly designed in cheerful tones, with flat-screen TVs and sea-view terraces, though there are signs of wear and tear, and the food is disappointing. Still, the broad pool (non-guests Rs.500) is probably Hikkaduwa's finest. ❻

Blue Note ⓣ091-438 3052, ⓦwww.eureka.lk/bluenote. Well-run place with spotless and comfortable (TV, minibar and optional a/c) concrete bungalows ranged around a sandy courtyard next to the beach. There's also a decent roadside bar-café with cheap draught beer and satellite TV news and sport, plus a quieter beachside restaurant. ❹, a/c ❺

Blue Ocean Villa ⓣ091-227 7566, ⓦwww.blueoceanvilla.com. Intimate modern place with a Mediterranean feel, painted in pleasing shades of blue and peach. Rooms (fan or a/c) are spacious, high-ceilinged and immaculately maintained; best-value are the two breezy sea-facing rooms upstairs (and make sure you get a room away from the road). ❹

Coral Gardens ⓣ091-227 7188, ⓦwww.johnkeellshotels.com. Large mid-range hotel looking like a cross between a Chinese pagoda and a multistorey car park. Rooms are spacious, with a/c and at least a partial sea view – perfectly comfortable, albeit perfectly anonymous. Facilities include a pool (non-guests Rs.250), gym and Ayurveda centre. ❻

Nippon Villa ⓣ091-438 3095, ⓔwewala@sltnet.lk. Inviting modern hotel in cheery strains of blue and orange set around a pleasant two-storey courtyard with a pool (non-guests Rs.200). There's a mix of good-value, spotless rooms; some have TV, minibar and four-posters, and the larger ones at the front have sea views. ❸–❹

Oasis Villa ⓣ091-492 7597, ⓦwww.theoasisvilla.com. Tucked away from the traffic in a lush garden plot a few metres inland off Galle Road, this attractive whitewashed place is a good option for self-caterers, with some apartments with kitchenettes (US$35) alongside the mix of nicely furnished, good-sized rooms (fan or a/c). ❹

Time'n'Tide Beach Resort ⓣ091-227 7781, ⓦwww.time-n-tide.com. Behind the questionable shade of lime-green, this bright, newly refurbished place has comfortable rooms, with attractive wood beds, and pretty terraces and balconies. The level of luxury increases as you go up – the high-ceilinged rooms at the top have a/c, satellite TV and internet facility. ❹–❺

Why Not ⓣ0775 233 548. Small, simple but very cheap rooms with neat, tiled bathrooms, plus a large and rather funky beachside restaurant. ❷

Narigama and Thiranagama

Cinnamon Garden ⓣ091-227 7081, ⓔcinnamongardenhotel@wow.lk. This part-UK-owned guesthouse occupies a pair of attractive, low-slung, colonial-style buildings overlooking a sizeable garden and the sea, with a breezy open-air restaurant and spacious, high-ceilinged rooms (some with a/c). ❹

Neela's Guest House ⓣ091-438 3166, ⓔneelas_sl@hotmail.com. Long-established and very welcoming guesthouse in a good location on one of the wider stretches of beach south of Hikkaduwa. The comfortable and well-maintained rooms here are good value (especially the cheaper downstairs ones), and there's also a pleasant beachside restaurant. ❷–❹

Ocean View Cottage ⓣ091-227 7237, ⓦwww.oceanviewcottage.net. Comely guesthouse in a sea-facing modern block overlooking a grassy garden and decent-sized pool (non-guests Rs.200). The big, gleaming-white rooms (most with a/c) have hot water, minibar and attractive balconies, and there's internet for Rs.3 per min. ❹, a/c ❺

Ranmal Rest ⓣ091-227 5474, ⓦwww.ranmal-rest.com. Long-established family-run place occupying two cheery yellow blocks built around a garden with a good range of rooms, all with terrace or balcony. Nicest in the main building are the high-ceilinged rooms with colonial-style furnishings upstairs, but most characterful of the lot are the two all-wood beachfront cabanas (US$60). His parents are charming but really it's cheeky little Braveen that runs the show. ❺

Rita's ⓣ091-227 7496, ⓦwww.ritas.net.ms. This long-running guesthouse went slightly upmarket following the tsunami, with a corresponding hike in prices; simpler rooms remain good value, though the smarter ones with a/c and hot water (including some at the front with fabulous sea views) are rather expensive. Also has a breezy restaurant. Fan ❸, a/c ❺

Sahra Guest House ⓣ091-227 6093 or 0773 542 880, ⓔanildmp@yahoo.com. Recently revamped budget option in an attractive, two-storey pagoda-shaped building. Rooms are simple, with rather ageing furniture, but comfortable and very cheap. ❷

Suite Lanka ⓣ091-227 7136, ⓦwww.suitelanka.de. Refreshing oasis of olde-worlde charm, with bijou rooms and a pair of stylish suites opening out onto a shady garden, all kitted out with colonial-style furniture (including unusual high beds). Also has a small pool. ❻

Sunil's Beach Hotel ⓣ091-227 7186, ⓔsunilsd@sltnet.lk. This large and slightly old-fashioned hotel is one of the better mid-range options in town. Rooms are a bit past their best, but are clean and spacious; rates include a/c. There's also a pool and a decent in-house bar and restaurant. ❹

Around Hikkaduwa

Aditya Rathgama, 5km south of Hikkaduwa ⓣ011-259 3068, ⓦwww.aditya-resort.com. One of Sri Lanka's most intimate and personable small luxury hotels, set in a shady, hammock-strewn garden on its own stretch of deserted beach. Each of the twelve enormous suites is a harmonious and colourful blend of indoor and outdoor space, with cool, deliciously light interiors featuring distinctive antiques and artwork from across the Subcontinent, plunge pools and private garden areas or expansive balconies overlooking the ocean. There's also a fine (and not outrageously priced) restaurant, glorious pool, gym, library and a seductive, antique-filled spa. Exquisite luxury but on a homely scale. ❾

Kalla Bongo Lake Resort Baddegama Rd, 3km inland ⓣ091-438 3234, ⓦwww.kallabongo.com. Occupying a spacious hilly garden plot with magnificent views over the broad Hikkaduwa lagoon, this chilled-out new place is already a popular hangout for the young Hikkaduwa crowd. Rooms are in two blocks: cheaper ones in the lower building overlook the cute raised pool, while those in the upper block have funky white beds and spectacular views. There's also an open-air restaurant, cosy lagoon-side bar and watersports with the attached Spunky Monkey Wakeboardcamp (see p.154). ❺

The town and beaches

You're unlikely to want to spend any longer than you have to in chaotic **Hikkaduwa town**, a run-down and depressing place epitomized by the shattered Coral Sanctuary (see opposite), which lies at its southern end. The area's tourist industry has largely fled south of here, to the villages of **Wewala** and **Narigama**, where a long string of hotels and guesthouses line up along the oceanfront. Unplanned development has taken its toll here too, eating away at the beach and producing some memorable eyesores, but vestiges of the beach's original charm remain, in the palm-shack restaurants and other improvised buildings built up by cash-strapped local entrepreneurs out of a motley assortment of left-over materials. Further south, the **Thiranagama** area is quieter still, with a pleasantly broad stretch of sand and a few stilt fishing posts.

The Coral Sanctuary

Hikkaduwa's **Coral Sanctuary**, situated at the north end of town, was established in 1979 (and subsequently upgraded to national park status in 2002) to protect the small, shallow area of reef, never more than a few metres deep, which stretches from the beach a couple of hundred metres out to sea, and is now enclosed and protected by a string of rocks. Sadly, the once-beautiful coral here is now almost completely dead, bleached a skeletal white thanks to the depredations of the local boatmen, who after decades of polluting and abusing the gardens have succeeded in transforming this natural wonder into an ecological disaster area – although it at least escaped significant further damage during the tsunami. You'll see a few specks of colour here and there on reviving clumps of coral, but the gardens are now interesting principally for their rich populations of tropical **fish** – indeed the death of the coral has increased levels of algae in the water, and thus the number of feeding fish, including myriad colourful species such as parrotfish, unicornfish, trunkfish, angelfish, grunts, fusilierfish and balloonfish. Around full moon time you may also be fortunate enough to see **turtles**, a majestic sight, though as soon as one is spotted, every boatman in the vicinity is likely to go chasing after the poor creature.

A popular way of seeing the sanctuary is to take a trip in one of the innumerable **glass-bottomed boats** (around Rs.700 per six-person boat for 30min) but it's not a great experience: visibility through the glass is generally poor, whilst the flotilla of boats chasing round the waters in search of big fish and turtles lends all the charm of a marine motorway. **Snorkelling** is much more eco-friendly, and you'll see more, although the number of boats tearing around can make it a bit unnerving. You can rent snorkelling equipment from one of the dive centres listed on p.154; count on around Rs.400 for a couple of hours and check carefully for leaks. Alternatively, various shops along the main road also hire out gear.

Eating and nightlife

The nicest **place to eat** in Hikkaduwa is, of course, the beach – though unfortunately most of the town's restaurants are strung out along the smelly Galle Road. Standards at most places are very average, with a handful of honourable exceptions; in addition to those places listed below, you might also book into for intimate meal at *Aditya* (see opposite), which has a small but appetizing menu of pan-Asian and Pacific Rim dishes.

The town has a certain amount of tourist-inspired **nightlife** during the season, with a number of crashed-out places to drink along the beach, though a recent government ban on amplified noise outdoors after 10pm has quietened things down considerably. Most nights out in Hikkaduwa are in any case fairly impromptu and mainly revolve around drinking, though a couple of places have worked around the ban and organize "party" nights: currently the most happening venue is *Vibration*, on the land-side of Galle Road near the *Moon Beam Hotel*; Friday is the big night, with percussion bands and DJs in the garden out back, while on Saturdays the funky (by Sri Lankan standards) basement bar transforms into a club. Other places to look out for include the perennially popular, laid-back *Chill Space Surf Café*, next to the A-Frame Surf Shop which has a new indoor dancefloor (with Saturday disco); and the tiny *Funky Bar*, right over the waves a little further south, which hosts Saturday beach barbecues, and keeps going till the last person leaves.

Restaurants

Asian Jewel Baddegama Rd, 3km inland from town ⓣ091-493 1388. The veranda restaurant at this welcoming British-run boutique hotel, close to Hikkaduwa lagoon, is ideal if you've had your fill of rice and curry. The menu would look comfortably at home in an English pub – cottage pie, fish and chips, even Sunday roasts – but all the dishes are well prepared and genuine, using imported ingredients, and diners can use their inviting pool. A guilty pleasure.

Cool Spot Wewala. Cute little place that's been dishing up big portions of dirt-cheap grub to locals and tourists alike for almost forty years, from snacks and milkshakes to basic rice and noodle dishes.

Drunken Monkey Narigama, just south of *Neela's* guesthouse. Popular and pleasantly crashed-out beach café, set in an attractive two-storey wooden building right on the sands, with a decent range of cheap tourist standards. Service is chronically slow, so you've got plenty of time to lie back and listen to the waves.

The Harmony/Top Secret *The Harmony Guest House*, Narigama. Chilled-out and very popular beachside café, with mats and scatter cushions laid out on the sand beneath funky low Moroccan-style lanterns, plus the (occasionally hopping) *Top Secret* beach bar. Food is the standard offering of cheap favourites.

Moon Beam Restaurant *Moon Beam Hotel*, Narigama. One of the nicest beach restaurants, in a big wooden pavilion with a rustic bar in the centre, with a long menu of well-prepared dishes (mains around Rs.800) served in big portions. The same team run the similarly themed *Curry House* next door, which offers an excellent range of equally good Sri Lankan curries (around Rs.750), with a particularly fine choice for vegetarians.

Refresh Wewala. Set on a romantic, lantern-dotted terrace running down to the sea, Hikkaduwa's most popular independent restaurant has a menu the size of a telephone directory, offering everything from gazpacho to falafel and gnocchi to nachos. With success though has come a hike in prices and a drop in standards: with mains averaging Rs.900, it's certainly atmospheric but undeniably overpriced.

Roti Restaurant (House of Roti) Wewala. Unassuming little café serving up *rotty* in over a hundred different combinations (Rs.60–160), from simple banana *rotis* to more ambitious concoctions featuring decidedly untraditional ingredients like salami and avocado.

Spaghetti & Co Thiranagama. Italian-owned and -managed place, set in a colonial-style villa and garden on the land-side of the Galle Rd and offering a good range of well-prepared pasta and enjoyable pizzas (at half the price of *Refresh*). From 6pm.

Listings

Ayurveda There are numerous little ad hoc Ayurveda centres dotted around Wewala and Thiranagama, though they're all very low-key compared with the flashy resorts at Beruwala and Bentota. The Ayurveda Hospital, just north of *Cool Spot* café, is the best and most authentic place (if you don't mind the rather gloomy treatment rooms), offering a range of very cheap standard therapies including oil and herbal baths.

Banks and exchange There are branches of the Commercial Bank, the Bank of Ceylon and the People's Bank dotted along the main road south of Hikkaduwa's bus station; all have ATMs accepting foreign cards. If you're staying in Wewala and want to avoid traipsing up to Hikkaduwa, Sri Lanka Tours and Travels (see opposite) changes cash and traveller's cheques at bank rates.

Bicycle rental A number of places along the main road have knackered old bikes for rent; try those in front of the Netflora Internet Café (see opposite; Rs.150 per day).

Car and motorbike rental Sri Lanka Tours and Travels (see opposite) hires out cars or jeeps for US$40 per day self-drive, or US$60 per day with driver. They also have a range of mopeds and

Moving on from Hikkaduwa

Moving on from Hikkaduwa there are buses roughly every ten to fifteen minutes north along the coast to **Colombo** (2hr 15min–3hr) via Ambalangoda (20–30min), Aluthgama (45min–1hr) and Kalutara (1hr 15min–1hr 45min), and south to **Galle** (30–45min). Note that many buses heading north don't leave from the bus station itself, but from the ocean-side of the main road, about 50m south of the station. There are also regular **trains** up and down the coast – see the timetable on p.120.

motorbikes for Rs.500–2000 per day, depending on size; you don't need a licence, but you'll have to leave your passport or plane ticket (should you have one) as a deposit.

Handicrafts A load of places along the Galle Rd offer all sorts of collectables, including plenty of *kolam* masks (the quality is actually often as high here as in Ambalangoda) and more unusual wooden sculptures. Laksiri Batiks, 400m down Baddegama Rd, behind the bus station (just before the Gangarama Mahavihara), has a batik factory and a decent range of pieces from around US$5, as well as clothes and sarongs.

Internet Half a dozen places along the Galle Rd offer internet access for Rs.3 per min. Both Netflora Internet Café, opposite *Why Not*, and Xperiment Net Café, just north of *Rita's*, have modern terminals, fast connections and stay open till 11pm or later. Wi-fi is available at the big hotels and at *Chill Space Surf Café*.

Post office Baddegama Rd, 150m east of the bus station (Mon–Sat 8am–6pm)

Travel agents Monika Tours and Travels (Ⓣ0773 372 144, Ⓔmonika_shyamali@hotmail.com), next to *Refresh*, and Sri Lanka Tours and Travels (Ⓣ0772 965 270, Ⓔkingslyperera@hotmail.com), opposite *Nippon Villa*, are two of the more reliable places, offering islandwide guided tours, though neither is cheap: tours go for around US$100 per person per day, including transport and accommodation.

Around Hikkaduwa

There are several interesting Buddhist temples **around Hikkaduwa**, all easily reachable by tuktuk or bicycle (though be *very* careful cycling along the treacherous Galle Rd). Also close by are a pair of beautiful mangrove-fringed lagoons, fun to explore by boat: the eponymous Hikkaduwa lagoon and its counterpart south of town, inland from **Dodanduwa**.

North of Hikkaduwa

The closest temple to town, just 500m inland from the bus station along Baddegama Road, is the **Gangarama Mahavihara**, an attractive modern Buddhist temple perched atop a large terrace, whose pretty ensemble of neat white buildings is often busy with devout locals, including many old ladies in white saris making offerings at the bo tree and various shrines – a far cry from the bedlam of Hikkaduwa town just down the road.

About 2km north of town lies the diminutive **Seenigama Temple**, an eye-catching little white building squeezed onto a tiny island just offshore. Unusually, the temple is dedicated to Dewol, a malevolent deity who is approached by those seeking revenge.

Hikkaduwa was badly hit by the 2004 tsunami, and the scruffy stretch of coast north of town is one of the few areas where evidence of the disaster remains. Around 500m north of Seenigama (on the land-side of the main coastal road) stands the **Tsunami Honganji Vihara**, erected with Japanese assistance as a memorial to those who perished in the tragedy and unveiled on December 26, 2006, the second anniversary of the catastrophe. The centrepiece of the memorial is a towering, eighteen-metre-high Buddha statue standing on a platform at the centre of a small lake – the tallest standing Buddha in Sri Lanka and supposedly modelled on one of the images at Bamian in Afghanistan which were destroyed by the Taliban in 2001. The location of the memorial is telling, just a couple of minutes' walk from where the *Samudra Devi* ("Queen of the Sea") train, en route to Matara, was washed away by the tsunami, killing at least 1700 people – the world's worst-ever railway disaster, and a potent symbol of the tsunami's terrible destructive power.

Just north of the vihara, turn right (there's a rather battered sign for a non-existent Tsunami Museum) to reach the **Purana Totagama Raja Mahavihara**, or Telwatta Monastery, across the rail tracks a few hundred metres inland. This was a celebrated centre of learning as far back as the fifteenth century – the great teacher and poet Sri Rahula Maha Thera, celebrated both for his verse and for his powers of exorcism, lived here; he's commemorated with a bright modern copper statue. The original temple was destroyed by the Portuguese; the present buildings date from 1805, an atmospheric complex with well-preserved murals, peeling reclining Buddhas and fine *makara toranas*.

South of Hikkaduwa

Around 4km south of Hikkaduwa, the traffic-plagued town of **DODANDUWA** is home to the chintzy little **Kumarakanda Vihara**, looking for all the world like a Baroque Portuguese church rather than a Buddhist temple. The temple is on the inland side of the Galle Road just north of the rail line, from where a long flight of steps leads up to the principal shrine, which contains a reclining Buddha and various modern murals.

Inland from here (take the road immediately south of the temple and ask for directions) a sylvan country lane runs to **Rathgama lagoon**, one of the many that dot the southwestern coast. The Blue Lagoon Boat House down by the waterside offers **lagoon trips** (Rs.1600 for two people for 2hr) in primitive wooden catamarans – late afternoon is the best time to see birds and other wildlife, including monkeys. They'll also take you to the two retreats on the lake, one for men, one for women. You may be offered similar trips but at much higher prices by touts at Dodanduwa.

2

The south

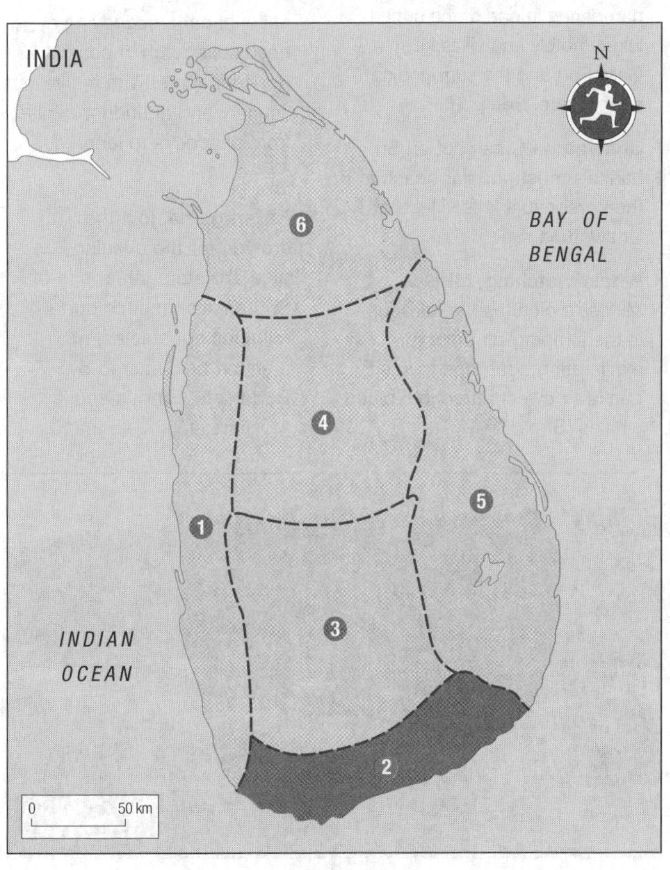

CHAPTER 2 Highlights

* **Galle** Sri Lanka's most perfectly preserved colonial town, its time-warped streets lined with historic Dutch villas hidden behind enormous ramparts. See p.165

* **Historic hotels and villas** Enjoy a splash of hedonistic pampering in one of the superb luxury hotels and villas in Galle Fort and the surrounding countryside. See p.170

* **Unawatuna** Crash out on Sri Lanka's most popular beach at the personable little village of Unawatuna. See p.178

* **Whale-watching, Mirissa** Mirissa's picturesque harbour is the jumping-off point for exhilarating boat trips to see Sri Lanka's newest attraction: blue whales. See p.192

* **Mulkirigala** Southern Sri Lanka's outstanding historical attraction, with a sequence of beautifully decorated cave temples carved into the flanks of a spectacular rock outcrop. See p.204

* **Yala** Sri Lanka's foremost national park, occupying a beautiful stretch of coastal dry-zone forest with marvellous scenery and abundant wildlife, from peacocks to leopards. See p.213

* **Kataragama** Join the crowds for the evening puja at Kataragama, one of Sri Lanka's most colourful religious spectacles, at a shrine held sacred by Buddhists, Hindus and Muslims alike. See p.215

▲ Unawatuna

2

The south

In many ways, **the south** encapsulates all that is most traditional about Sri Lanka. Stretched out along a great arc of sun-baked coastline from Galle in the west to Tissamaharama in the east, the area remains essentially rural: a land of a thousand sleepy villages sheltered under innumerable palms, where the laid-back pace of life still revolves around coconut farming, rice cultivation and fishing (the last still practised in places by the distinctively Sri Lankan method of stilt-fishing – one of the island's emblematic images). Culturally, too, the south remains relatively conservative and inward-looking, a bastion of Sinhalese traditions exemplified by the string of temples and giant Buddha statues which dot the coast, and by the colourful peraheras and festivals celebrated throughout the region, which culminate in the exuberant religious ceremonies enacted nightly at the ancient shrine of Kataragama. The tranquillity of the southern coastal strip was shattered by the 2004 tsunami, although rebuilding has been swift, and – in tourist areas at least – you'll see little physical evidence of the disaster now.

The south's physical distance from the rest of the island, and from the hordes of Indian invaders who periodically overran the north, meant that the ancient kingdom of **Ruhunu** (or Rohana) – a name still often used to describe the region – acted as a bastion of traditional Sinhalese culture. In later centuries, despite the brief importance of the southern ports of Galle and Matara in the colonial Indian Ocean trade, Ruhunu preserved this separation, and with the rise of Colombo and the commercial decline of Galle and Matara in the late nineteenth century, the south became a relative backwater – as it remains, despite the more recent incursions of tourism and government plans for economic development.

The region's varied attractions make it one of Sri Lanka's most rewarding areas to visit. Gateway to the south – and one of its highlights – is the atmospheric old port of **Galle**, Sri Lanka's best-preserved colonial town. Beyond Galle stretch a string of picture-perfect beaches – **Unawatuna**, **Thalpe**, **Weligama**, **Mirissa** and **Tangalla** – whose relative inaccessibility has protected them from the swarms of package tourists who inundate the west coast. Nearby, the little-visited town of **Matara**, with its quaint Dutch fort, offers a further taste of Sri Lanka's colonial past, while ancient **Tissamaharama** makes a good base from which to visit two of the country's finest national parks: the placid lagoons and wetlands of **Bundala**, and **Yala**, famous for its elephants and elusive leopards. Beyond Tissamaharama lies the fascinating religious centre of **Kataragama**, whose various shrines are held sacred by Buddhists, Hindus and Muslims alike.

Getting around the south is straightforward: most of the places covered in this chapter are strung out along the main coastal highway, and principal towns are served by innumerable buses; in addition, the southern coastal railway

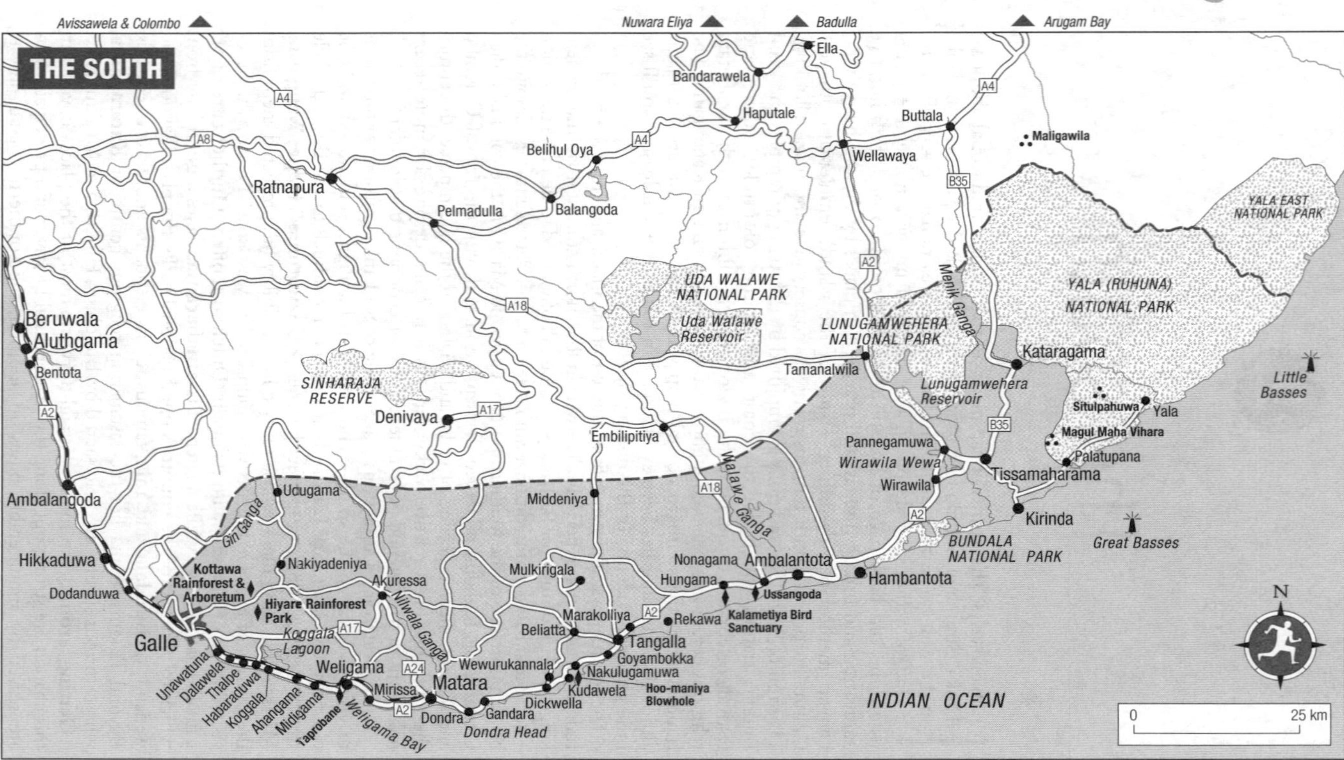
THE SOUTH
Avissawela & Colombo
Nuwara Eliya
Badulla
Arugam Bay
Colombo
Ella
Bandarawela
Haputale
Buttala
Maligawila
Wellawaya
Belihul Oya
Ratnapura
Pelmadulla
Balangoda
A4
A8
B35
A2
A18
A17
A24
YALA EAST NATIONAL PARK
YALA (RUHUNA) NATIONAL PARK
UDA WALAWE NATIONAL PARK
Uda Walawe Reservoir
Menik Ganga
LUNUGAMWEHERA NATIONAL PARK
Lunugamwehera Reservoir
Kataragama
Tamanalwila
Little Basses
Beruwala
Aluthgama
Bentota
SINHARAJA RESERVE
Deniyaya
Embilipitiya
Situlpahuwa
Yala
Magul Maha Vihara
Palatupana
Pannegamuwa
Wirawila Wewa
Tissamaharama
Wirawila
Ambalangoda
Udugama
Middeniya
Walawe Ganga
Kirinda
Great Basses
Gin Ganga
BUNDALA NATIONAL PARK
Hikkaduwa
Kottawa Rainforest & Arboretum
Nakiyadeniya
Akuressa
Mulkirigala
Nonagama
Ambalantota
Hambantota
Dodanduwa
Hiyare Rainforest Park
Nilwala Ganga
Hungama
Ussangoda
Marakolliya
Rekawa
Kalametiya Bird Sanctuary
Beliatta
Tangalla
Galle
Koggala Lagoon
Weligama
Wewurukannala
Goyambokka
Nakulugamuwa
Matara
Unawatuna
Dalawela
Thalpe
Habaraduwa
Koggala
Ahangama
Midigama
Taprobane
Mirissa
Kudawela
Hoo-maniya Blowhole
Dickwella
Gandara
Dondra
Dondra Head
Weligama Bay
INDIAN OCEAN
N
0
25 km

Principal trains in the south

Note that train timetables are subject to constant change, so if possible it's always best to check latest departure times before travelling at the nearest station (or online at ⓦwww.bluehaventours.com). For details of services **south from Colombo to Galle and Matara**, see p.120.

Matara	04.20	05.20	05.50	13.10	14.05
Galle	05.30	06.30	07.30	14.15	15.30
Colombo	08.15	09.00	10.05	17.05	18.40

All services from Matara also call at Weligama (roughly 30min from Matara), Hikkaduwa (1hr 30min), Ambalangoda (1hr 45min), Aluthgama (2hr 15min) and Kalutara (3hr).

connects Galle, Weligama and Matara with Colombo. **Weather** in the south follows two general patterns, though in recent years these have become increasingly inconsistent. The part of the south lying in the **wet zone** (from Galle to Tangalla) is affected by the southwest monsoon, with rainfall traditionally heaviest during May and June, and generally good weather from November through to mid-April; the much more arid **dry zone** area (east of Hambantota) is affected by the northeast monsoon and receives most of its rainfall from October to February, but is largely rain-free for the rest of the year.

Galle and around

Perched on the coast close to the island's southernmost point, the venerable port of **GALLE** (pronounced "Gaul") has grown from ancient origins into Sri Lanka's fourth largest city. At the heart of modern Galle – but strangely detached from it – lies the old Dutch quarter, known as the **Fort**. Sri Lanka's best-preserved colonial townscape, the Fort is enclosed within a chain of huge bastions which now guard the area from modernization as effectively as they once protected Dutch trading interests from marauding adventurers.

The Fort has an understated, sleepy charm, its low-rise streets lined with old churches and Dutch colonial villas, many of which retain original street-facing verandas, their white plaster now stripped by sea breezes and weathered to a peeling grey. There's not actually much to see (a few unusual museums excepted): the main pleasure here is just ambling round the atmospheric old streets and walls, savouring the easy pace of life and refreshing absence of traffic – you won't find a quieter town anywhere else in the island.

In recent years, the town has witnessed an extraordinary influx of cash, as expats (mainly British) and members of the Colombo elite have bought up and renovated many of the Fort's historic properties, converting them into sumptuous hotels and luxurious private villas. The growing number of creative-minded foreigners who now call Galle home has lent the Fort an unexpectedly cosmopolitan air, and brought a lively roster of arts festivals unparalleled across the rest of the island, including the annual **Galle Literary Festival**, which attracts literary luminaries from far and wide.

Some history

Galle is thought to have been the Biblical **Tarshish**, from whence King Solomon obtained gold, spices, ivory, apes and peacocks, and the combination

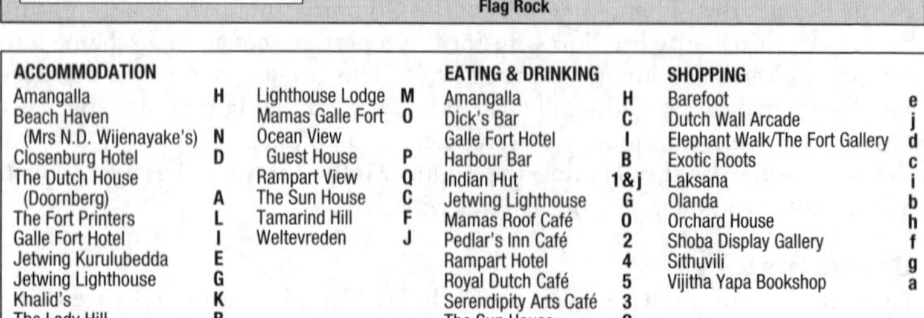
GALLE
a
A, B & C
D, 1
Kottawa Rainforest & Arboretum, Hiyare Rainforest Park, Samakanda & Matara
E, F, G & Hikkaduwa
NEW TOWN
DICKSON RD
MAIN STREET
SEA STREET
Train Station
Selaka Building
P&J City
Sampath Bank
Hatton National Bank
Bank of Ceylon
Police
Bus Station
COLOMBO ROAD
HAVELOCK PLACE
H.W. AMARASURIYA MW
Dharmapala Park
Dutch Channel
Galle International Cricket Stadium
ESPLANADE ROAD
Moon Bastion
Sun Bastion
Galle Harbour
Fish Market
Clocktower
Main Gate
Star Bastion
Bank of Ceylon
Army Camp
National Museum
BAUDDHALOKA MAWATHA
Hall de Galle
Zwart Bastion
Maritime Museum
Police Station
Aeolus Bastion
MIDDLE STREET
CHURCH STREET
Dutch Reformed Church
QUEEN'S STREET
Old Gate
Graffiti Wall
District Court
Queen's House
Akersloot Bastion
RAMPART STREET
LIGHTHOUSE STREET
CHURCH CROSS STREET
FRONT ST
All Saints' Church
Tourist Police
BAY STREET
Sudharmalaya Vihara
Commercial Bank
Historical Mansion Museum
Clippenberg Bastion
SUDHARMALAYA ST
PAPPAWA STREET
THE FORT
Aurora Bastion
Neptune Bastion
PEDLAR STREET
LEYN BAAN STREET
HOSPITAL STREET
NEW LANE
Triton Bastion
RAMPART STREET
Meeran Jumma Mosque
Point Utrecht Bastion
0 200 m
Flag Rock
ACCOMMODATION
Amangalla H
Beach Haven (Mrs N.D. Wijenayake's) N
Closenburg Hotel D
The Dutch House (Doornberg) A
The Fort Printers L
Galle Fort Hotel I
Jetwing Kurulubedda E
Jetwing Lighthouse G
Khalid's K
The Lady Hill B
Lighthouse Lodge M
Mamas Galle Fort O
Ocean View Guest House P
Rampart View Q
The Sun House C
Tamarind Hill F
Weltevreden J
EATING & DRINKING
Amangalla H
Dick's Bar C
Galle Fort Hotel I
Harbour Bar B
Indian Hut 1&j
Jetwing Lighthouse G
Mamas Roof Café 0
Pedlar's Inn Café 2
Rampart Hotel 4
Royal Dutch Café 5
Serendipity Arts Café 3
The Sun House C
SHOPPING
Barefoot e
Dutch Wall Arcade j
Elephant Walk/The Fort Gallery d
Exotic Roots c
Laksana i
Olanda b
Orchard House h
Shoba Display Gallery f
Sithuvili g
Vijitha Yapa Bookshop a

of its fine natural harbour and strategic position on the sea routes between Arabia, India and Southeast Asia made the town an important trading emporium long before the arrival of the Europeans. In 1589, the Portuguese established a presence here, constructing a small fort named Santa Cruz, which they later extended with a series of bastions and walls. The **Dutch** captured Galle in 1640 after a four-day siege, and in 1663 expanded the original Portuguese fortifications to enclose the whole of Galle's sea-facing promontory, establishing the street plan and system of bastions which survive to this day, as well as introducing marvels of European engineering such as an intricate subterranean sewer system which was flushed out daily by the tide and is still in use today.

The **British** took Galle in 1796 during the islandwide transfer of power following Dutch defeat in the Napoleonic Wars (see p.424) – ironically, after all the ingenuity and labour they had invested in the town's defences, Galle was finally surrendered with hardly a shot being fired. The city continued to serve as Ceylon's principal harbour for much of the eighteenth century, but Colombo's growing commercial importance and improvements to its harbour gradually eroded Galle's trade. By the early twentieth century, Galle had become an economic backwater, lapsing into a tranquil decline which happily, if fortuitously, allowed the old colonial townscape of the Fort to survive almost completely intact.

In the years **since independence**, Galle has recovered some of its lost dynamism. Despite playing second fiddle to Colombo, Galle's port still receives significant quantities of shipping; there are usually a few enormous container ships parked offshore waiting to dock, while the LTTE considered the city's naval base sufficiently important to launch a suicide attack against it in 2006. Wealthy expats have now restored many of Galle's colonial villas, and Sri Lanka's Central Cultural Fund is renovating many of the Fort's public buildings and monuments (with help from the Dutch government), while 2009 saw the completion of a project to convert the Fort's old Dutch warehouses into a polished new maritime museum – a fitting tribute to the town's rich seafaring traditions.

Arrival and information

There are two parts to Galle: the old town or **Fort**, within the ramparts of the old Dutch fort, and the **new town** to the north, home to the bus and train stations and virtually all the town's commercial activity. A tuktuk from either the train or bus station (both right in the middle of the new town) to any of the Fort guesthouses shouldn't cost more than Rs.100. Galle has more than its fair share of **touts** and **con artists** – all the usual cautions (see p.62) apply. None of the Fort's guesthouses is clearly signed, so if you take a tuktuk to reach one, check the address to make sure you're actually being taken to the right place; some guesthouse owners will pick you up from the bus station if you ring in advance.

Galle festivals

Proof of Galle's burgeoning cultural credentials is provided by the string of new festivals established here over the last few years. Pride of place goes to the **Galle Literary Festival** (Jan/Feb; ⓦwww.galleliteraryfestival.com), founded in 2007, which has already established itself as a major item on the global literati circuit – the 2009 festival attracted a string of luminaries ranging from Colin Thubron through to Thomas Keneally and Germaine Greer. The success of the lit-fest led to the creation of the **Galle Art Trail** (Oct/Nov; ⓦwww.gallearttrail.com) art festival and the nascent **Galle Film Festival** (ⓦwww.gallefilmfestival.com). See the various websites for full details.

Tours in and around Galle

The octopus-catcher; the crazy "fort jumpers", who hurl themselves off the precipitous Flag Rock; the porcupine-keeping army camp soldiers...An amble through the Fort's sleepy backstreets is an obligatory part of visiting the city, but for an opportunity to peep behind the crumbling Dutch facades and meet some of the town's engaging residents, it's well worth joining one of the insightful guided walks led by Juliet Coombe and Daisy Perry, authors of *Around the Fort in 80 Lives* (see p.460). Themed **walking tours** of the Fort (Rs.1500; 1hr 30min; ⓣ0776 838 659), starting from either the *Serendipity Arts Café* or the gallery at 60 Leyn Baan St, are adapted to individual interests, whether wildlife (including a derelict house full of bats), history (visiting the otherwise inaccessible Fort prisons and clambering *inside* the ramparts), architecture (comparing villas luxury and decrepit) – or simply meeting some of the characters featured in the book.

Venturing further afield, highly enjoyable guided **bike rides** are run in the lush countryside around Galle by Idling Tours (ⓣ0777 906 156). Trips, on good-quality mountain bikes, range from a gentle two- to three-hour pedal along little-used tracks through paddy fields and inland villages, finishing with lunch at *Why Beach* (see p.185; Rs.1800), to the exhilarating all-day Samakanda Big Burn, with a challenging ride up to *Samakanda* (see p.178) for lunch, followed by birdwatching on Hiyare reservoir and a freewheeling forty-kilometre descent to the beach (Rs.7600); prices include meals and snacks. Custom-made tours can also be arranged.

For **information**, a new visitor centre at the Maritime Archeology Museum in Fort should be open by the time you read this. Alternatively, the Tourist Information Centre (Mon–Fri 9am–4.30pm; ⓣ091-224 7676), in the park opposite the train station, is staffed on an ad hoc basis by English-speaking guides, and provides free general information. For tours of the Fort, see the box above.

Accommodation

Galle has an excellent selection of both budget and luxury accommodation, though few mid-range places. The Fort is home to one of the best selection of reasonable family-run **guesthouses** in Sri Lanka, offering sociable lodgings and good home-cooking. At the other end of the price scale, there are a number of outstanding top-end **hotels** and boutique guesthouses, both within the Fort and beyond, as well as a glut of elegant villas (see box, p.170), offering luxurious lodgings – some in historic surroundings.

The Fort

Amangalla 10 Church St ⓣ091-223 3388, ⓦwww.amanresorts.com. Occupying the premises of the former *New Oriental*, Galle's most famous colonial hotel, this superb Aman resort has remained extremely faithful to that famous old establishment's decor and style, with sensitively updated rooms and facilities (including the exquisite Baths spa and gorgeous residents-only *Sunset Bar*) which manage discreetly to combine olde-worlde charm with the last word in contemporary luxury. Rates vary (sometimes quoted in excess of US$600) but currently start at around US$350 per night. ❾

Beach Haven (Mrs N.D. Wijenayake's) 65 Lighthouse St ⓣ091-223 4663, ⓦwww.beachhaven-galle.com. Very welcoming and sociable guesthouse right in the middle of the Fort offering a varied range of good-value fan and smarter a/c rooms. There's also a pleasant upstairs sitting area and communal veranda overlooking the street – good for idle people-watching – tasty home-cooked meals, plus internet and free wi-fi. ❷–❸, a/c ❹

The Fort Printers 39 Pedlar St ⓣ091-224 7977, ⓦwww.thefortprinters.com. Beautifully renovated former colonial mansion with whitewashed rooms, heavy teak floorboards and timber ceilings – the austerity leavened with brightly coloured fabrics and some fine modern artworks. There's also a neat and compact walled garden, and a small natural-style pool. ❽

Galle Fort Hotel 28 Church St ⓣ091-223 2870, ⓦwww.gallefortthotel.com. Set in a spectacularly restored former gem merchant's mansion, this UNESCO Heritage Award-winning hotel is every bit as memorable as nearby *Amangalla*, and much more affordable, with rates from roughly US$200 per night. Accommodation is in a mix of elegant rooms and enormous suites, all individually designed by the hotel's Australian owners, with tasteful neo-colonial decor enlivened by imaginative personal touches. There's also superb food (see p.175), and an atmospheric bar and pool. ❾

Khalid's 102 Pedlar St ⓣ0773 177 676, ⓔkhalidgalle@aol.com. Long-established guest-house set in a beautifully restored colonial house. Rooms all have fan, hot water and balconies. Levels of upkeep are variable, however, and overall it's pricey for what's on offer – room 4 is best, though rooms 1 and 2 (with ocean views) come at a premium. No alcohol but decent food and free internet and wi-fi. ❸–❹

Lighthouse Lodge 62B Lighthouse St ⓣ091-545 0514, ⓦwww.geocities.com/euagalle. Three bright and homely rooms, with modern furnishings (good beds), a/c and cable TV, at the top of a rather cramped family house; one has a roomy street-side balcony, ideal for watching the sleepy goings-on beneath. ❸–❹

Mamas Galle Fort 76 Leyn Baan St ⓣ091-222 6415, ⓦwww.mamas-galle-fort.com. Occupying a beautifully restored old colonial house, with two airy and spacious "luxury" rooms with a/c – comfortable enough, though a bit overpriced unless you negotiate – and two very small but cheap and neat singles (Rs.1100). There are also herbal treatments, cooking courses and a breezy rooftop café (see p.175). ❺

Ocean View Guest House 80 Lighthouse St ⓣ091-224 2717, ⓔjewelgem@sltnet.lk. Set in an immaculately restored colonial villa, this beautiful family home is one of the Fort's more upmarket guesthouses. Rooms (all with hot water and a/c, some with sea views) are pleasantly wood-furnished, though some are rather small for the price. There's also a cute rooftop garden (with real grass) and wi-fi. No alcohol. ❺

Rampart View 37 Rampart St ⓣ091-492 8781, ⓦwww.gallefortrampartview.com. Modern house right by the ramparts with four spacious and clean rooms (with a/c for an extra Rs.500) with hot water, a nice little breezy verandh, plus a grassy rooftop terrace with great views out over Flag Rock. Free wi-fi. ❸

Weltevreden 104 Pedlar St ⓣ091-222 2650. Welcoming but peaceful family-run place set in an attractive ochre-painted Dutch house arranged around a beautiful, flower-filled courtyard garden. Rooms (some with TV) are a little dark, but modern, comfortable and good value, and there's tasty home-cooking available. ❷–❸

Outside the Fort

Closenburg Hotel Megalle ⓣ091-222 4313, ⓦwww.closenburghotel.com. Occupying a rambling nineteenth-century villa tucked away in a bay 3km east of Galle, this fine old hotel has a mix of atmospheric and old-fashioned fan rooms complete with chunky teak furniture, and more modern a/c rooms with sea-facing balconies. ❼

The Dutch House (aka Doornberg) 23 Upper Dickson Rd ⓣ091-438 0275, ⓦwww.thedutchhouse.com. Opposite *The Sun House* and under the same management, this meticulously restored Dutch villa of 1712 has four huge suites complete with reproduction antique furniture and all the amenities you'd expect at US$400-plus a night. Outside there's an immaculately manicured garden with croquet hoops, and a gorgeous L-shaped infinity pool. ❾

Jetwing Kurulubedda Mahamodera ⓣ091-222 3744, ⓦwww.jetwing.com. Reached via a short but atmospheric boat ride through the mangroves from *Jetwing Lighthouse* (see below), this magical hideaway feels out in the wilds – though you're just on the edge of the city. There are just two luxurious eco-lodges (around US$530 full board), beautifully designed in dark wood and featuring lap-style plunge-pools and open terraces enveloped by the tree canopy – chic outdoor living rooms that double up as private birdwatching platforms. Full board only. ❾

Jetwing Lighthouse Dadella ⓣ091-222 3744, ⓦwww.jetwing.com. On the main road 2km west of town, this very stylish – albeit hugely expensive (around US$550 per night) – Geoffrey Bawa-designed hotel is perched on a rather wild stretch of coast in an elegantly understated, slightly Tuscan-looking ochre building. The sixty rooms are masterpieces of interior design, complete with all mod cons, and there are plenty of facilities, including two pools, a gym and an attractive spa. Good food, too (see p.176). ❾

The Lady Hill 29 Upper Dickson Rd ⓣ091-224 4322, ⓦwww.ladyhillsl.com. Galle's best mid-range option, set in a modern five-storey building atop the highest hill in Galle. Rooms are on the small side, but come with a/c, minibar, TV and private balconies from where (on higher floors especially) there are superlative views over the town, coast and hills inland – all good value. There's also a small swimming pool, fine rooftop bar and wi-fi. ❺

Villas along the south coast

The past decade has seen a massive explosion in Sri Lanka's **holiday villa** market, with literally hundreds of properties being offered by owners keen to jump onto a potentially lucrative bandwagon. The biggest concentration of villas is in and around Galle (including upwards of twenty historic houses available in the Fort alone, and a dense concentration in Thalpe, about 10km east), though properties dot the coastline as far as Tangalla, and increasing numbers of tea plantation bungalows in the hill country are also becoming available (see p.268). There's plenty of choice, with villas sleeping anything between two and sixteen people and ranging in price from less than US$100 per night in low season up to US$2000 for a large villa over Christmas and New Year. Many occupy stunning natural settings, often on unspoilt stretches of private beach, while some show contemporary Sri Lankan design at its finest. In all, the emphasis is on intimacy, style and self-indulgence.

A good place to start browsing is ⓦwww.villasinsrilanka.com, while ⓦwww.srilankainstyle.com, www.boutiquesrilanka.com and www.reddottours.com also have a big selection of properties; all the villas below – just a selection of some of the best properties – can be viewed and booked online via one (or more) of these agencies. Prices quoted for high season; during low season rates drop by up to fifty percent, or even more.

Ambassador's House Galle Fort. Beautiful and rather grand colonial-era villa, tastefully reworked and elegantly furnished throughout in modern-colonial style. Sleeps ten. US$500 per night.

Auraliya Thalpe. Beguiling modern beach villa occupying a trio of Dutch-style pavilions set around a spectacular pool. Sleeps twelve. US$850 per night.

The Beach House Tangalla. Serene Dutch-style residence opening out onto a gorgeous sweep of beach, with a magnificent ocean-facing terrace and sizeable pool. Sleeps ten. US$960 per night.

The Beach Hut Dalawela. Idyllic romantic retreat with bags of style. The gorgeous main bedroom, overlooking a neat pool and wide sandy beach, is ideal for honeymooners. Sleeps up to four. US$400 per night.

The Fort House Galle Fort. Lovingly restored and characterful former merchant's house retaining many original features, with a small courtyard pool. Sleeps eight. US$450 per night.

Kadju House Tangalla. Intimate modern villa, perched at the top of a sloping cashew-nut grove with superb bay views and a spectacular rooftop infinity pool. Sleeps eight. US$1000 per night.

The Last House Tangalla. The last house designed by Geoffey Bawa displays all the hallmarks of the architect's best work: grace, serenity and an unerring sense of proportion. Sleeps ten. US$1000 per night.

OneTwoFive Thalpe. Superb modern villa situated on a beautiful stretch of private beach (complete with stilt fishermen), with huge bedrooms, plus a fun eight-bed bunk room for kids. Sleeps up to sixteen. US$500 per night.

SaffronsBeachVilla Habaraduwa, near Koggala. Architecturally stunning, state-of-the-art villa on a great expanse of beach. Decor is high camp throughout (with a touch of Bond villain), from the Mao cushion covers to the koi carp pond. Guests also have use of the owner's private SaffronsEcoIsland on Koggala lake. Sleeps six. US$1000 per night.

Tamarind Hut Kalahe. Delightfully rustic, but still luxurious, wattle-and-daub house set on a coconut plantation "island" a few kilometres inland from Unawatuna. Sleeps four. US$200 per night.

Taprobane Island Weligama. One of Sri Lanka's ultimate romantic fantasies: undisturbed use of the island's only private offshore island (see p.189) and a resident staff of six. Sleeps ten. US$1750 per night.

The Sun House 18 Upper Dickson Rd ☎091-438 0275, ⓦwww.thesunhouse.com. One of Sri Lanka's most magical places to stay, set in a restored 1860s planter's villa perched on a hillside and offering memorable views across a sea of palm trees. Rooms (from around US$220) are lovingly furnished and brimful of character (albeit a couple are rather small); best is the beautiful Cinnamon Suite, occupying the whole first floor of the main house. There's also marvellous food (see p.176) and a small pool set in an enchanting, frangipani-studded garden. ❾

Tamarind Hill Dadella ☎091-222 6568, ⓦwww.anilana.com. Elegant new boutique hotel, 2km west of town, occupying a stylishly refurbished nineteenth-century *walauwa*. Highlights are the vast, colonial-style Admiral's and Captain's suites, which take up an entire floor of the imposing main building. Rooms (from around US$210), enclosing the neat garden courtyard, are less grand but equally full of exquisite design touches; behind, the fine pool stretches out towards a lush canopy of palms. ❾

The Fort

The principal entrance to the Fort is through the **Main Gate**, one of the newest parts of the fortifications, having been added by the British in 1873 to allow easier vehicular access. The section of ramparts facing the new town is the most heavily fortified, since it protected the Fort's vulnerable land-side. The Dutch substantially enlarged the original Portuguese fortifications here, naming the new defences the **Sun**, **Moon** and **Star bastions**. The sheer scale of theses bastions is brutally impressive, if not particularly aesthetic – a fitting memorial to Dutch governor Petrus Vuyst (1726–29), who was largely responsible for their construction and whose cruelty and abuse of power was such that he was eventually recalled to Jakarta and executed by the Dutch authorities. The ugly clocktower on top of the bastions was erected by the punctilious British in 1883.

The National Museum to All Saints' Church

From the Main Gate, go left at the roundabout to reach one of the Fort's two main north–south thoroughfares, the atmospheric **Church Street** (originally Kerkstraat), named after a long-demolished Dutch church. An attractive old

▲ Old Gate, Galle

colonial building near the top of the street holds the **National Museum** (Tues–Sat 9am–5pm; Rs.300), a wildly over-optimistic name for three dark rooms of rather sorry-looking exhibits which give only the faintest sense of the exotic and luxurious items which would formerly have passed through Galle's harbour; save your money. The large and rather stately white building next door to the museum was originally built for the Dutch governor in 1684; it was subsequently converted into the venerable *New Oriental Hotel* in 1863 and then, following a massive makeover, reopened in 2005 as the ultra-luxurious **Amangalla** hotel (see p.168) – though the exterior has survived almost unchanged.

Almost next door, the atmospheric and beautifully restored **Dutch Reformed Church** (or Groote Kerk) is Galle's most absorbing colonial building. Built on the site of an earlier Portuguese Capuchin convent, the present structure was completed around 1755. The graceful and slightly Italianate lines of the facade belie the severity of the **interior**, in which the only decorative concessions are the enormous canopy over the pulpit (presumably for acoustic effect) and the attractive organ loft, reached by an elegant flight of balustraded stairs. The floor is covered in ornately carved **memorials** to the city's Dutch settlers, the earlier examples in Dutch (moved here from two earlier Dutch cemeteries which were

Dutch Burghers

Many of the tombstones which cover the floor and fill the churchyard of the Dutch Reformed Church bear Dutch names – Jansz, De Kretser, Van Langenberg and the like – dating from the colonial period right up to modern times. These commemorate the families of Sri Lanka's smallest, and oddest, minority: the **Dutch Burghers** – Sri Lankans of Dutch or Portuguese descent.

At the time of Independence the community numbered around fifty thousand, based mainly in Colombo, and exerted a strong influence on the country, having held major government posts under the British as well as running many of the island's trading companies. However, their numbers declined significantly in the 1950s, when as many as half the country's Burgher families, disillusioned by Sinhalese nationalist laws based on language and religion, left for Australia, Canada or Britain.

Despite their Dutch (or Portuguese) ancestry, the Burghers have for centuries spoken English as their first language. Burgher culture preserves strong Dutch elements, however, and they would be horrified to be confused with the British, despite a certain amount of intermarriage over the years (not only with the British, but also with the Sinhalese and Tamils). Not that there is really such a thing as a single Burgher culture or community. Many of the wealthier Burghers arrived in Ceylon as employees of the Dutch East India Company, while working-class Burghers, more often from Portugal, came to help build the railways and settled largely on the coast between Colombo and Negombo. And to make things a little more confused, there are thousands of Sri Lankans with Dutch or Portuguese names, adopted during the years of occupation, yet who have no connection at all with Europe.

In recent years, the Burghers have made their mark in Sri Lanka, and beyond, in the arts. **Geoffrey Bawa** (see p.146), arguably Asia's greatest twentieth-century architect, belonged to the community (though his family, in typical Burgher style, also claimed Malay descent). **George Keyt** (1901–93), Sri Lanka's foremost modern painter, was also a Burgher, as are two of the leading contemporary Sri Lankan artists, **Barbara Sansoni**, founder of the Barefoot company in Colombo (see p.116), and designer **Ena de Silva**. Overseas, the best-known Burgher is Canada-based novelist **Michael Ondaatje**, author of the Booker Prize-winning *The English Patient*, whose memoir of island life, *Running in the Family*, gives a wonderful picture of Burgher life in the years before independence.

dismantled by the British in 1853), later ones in English, many of them bearing witness to the lamentably brief life expectancy of Ceylon's early European colonists. Most striking, however, is the carved memorial, hanging on the southern wall, to **E.A.H. Abraham**, Commander of Galle, complete with a miniature skull, a medieval-looking armoured helmet and the remains of his baptism shirt.

A few steps further down the road is the dilapidated but still functioning **post office**, whose Dickensian-looking interior is worth a peek. Diagonally opposite stands **Queen's House**, originally the offices of the Dutch city governor (it's still sometimes called the Old Dutch Government House) and now belonging to *Amangalla*. Immediately south of here is the Fort's principal Anglican place of worship, **All Saints' Church**, a Romanesque basilica-style structure whose stumpy steeple provides one of the area's most distinctive landmarks. The church was begun in 1868 on the site of a previous courthouse – the town's gallows might (as a sign outside gruesomely points out) have stood on the site of the current high altar; otherwise, the bare interior gives disappointingly little insight into the history of the British in Galle.

The Maritime Museum to the Historical Mansion Museum

From All Saints', retrace your steps for a few metres then turn right down Queen's Street to reach the **Maritime Museum**, unveiled in 2009 and replacing an earlier incarnation which met a watery end during the tsunami. The museum occupies the **Great Warehouse**, one of Galle's most striking buildings: a long, barn-like ochre structure punctuated by barred windows behind black shutters, which housed ships' provisions and valuable commodities such as cowries, sappan wood and cinnamon. Not yet complete at the time of visiting, the museum looks to provide a fittingly comprehensive overview of Galle's marine and maritime history, with five galleries of exhibits including replicas and models of old seafaring vessels, from Moorish trading boats to British naval ships, along with a well-executed life-size diorama of the south's iconic stilt fishermen, and – perhaps most impressive – the thirteen-metre carcass of a whale, which hangs from the ceiling in the main room.

At the far end of the Maritime Museum stands the **Old Gate**, the only entrance to the Fort until the construction of the Main Gate in 1873. The fully restored arch on the Fort side of the gate is dated 1669 and inscribed with the coat of arms of the **VOC** (Vereenigde Oost-indische Compagnie, or Dutch East India Company), showing two lions holding a crest topped by the inevitable cockerel; the distinctive VOC symbol at its centre – with the O and C dangling off the arms of the V – is reckoned to be one of the world's oldest corporate logos. The mossy arch on the exterior, port-facing side is decorated with the date 1668 and a newly buffed-up British crest, emblazoned with the words "Dieu et mon droit", which was added after the British took charge of the town in 1796. Just north of here, the capacious, three-gabled **Hall de Galle** is one of the principal venues for the town's growing number of arts festivals.

Back inside the ramparts, the car park in the northeastern corner of the Fort is almost completely surrounded by handsome old Indian rain trees, one of which is being dramatically engulfed by an enormous banyan. Should you be overcome with poetic sentiments you can unleash them on the **graffiti wall** nearby, which was unveiled for the first Galle Art Trail (see p.167) and looks set to stay. Immediately south of here, the top of **Leyn Baan Street** (Rope Walk St) is home to dozens of lawyers' offices, one or two of them still sporting their picturesque old hand-painted signs.

A couple of minutes' walk down the road, the entertaining **Historical Mansion Museum** (daily 9am–6pm; closed for prayers Fri noon–2pm; optional donation) is the result of the efforts of a certain Mr Gaffar, who for over forty years has accumulated an enormous collection of antiques, bric-a-brac and outright junk. The overall effect this Aladdin's cave of curiosities is strangely compelling, even when it becomes obvious that at least part of the aim of the entire museum is to lure you into Mr Gaffar's gem shop. The museum also employs a number of local artisans – including a lacemaker, gem-cutter and jewellery-maker – who can be seen at work in the courtyard, and whose creations are also sold in the shop.

The ramparts

The **fort ramparts** continue along the ocean-facing side of **Hospital Street**, a block east of the Historical Mansion Museum. They're largely hidden behind buildings until the junction with Pedlar Street, though you can see parts of the **Zwart Bastion** (Black Fort), which incorporates the remains of the original Portuguese fortress of Santa Cruz, making it the town's oldest surviving section of fortification. Its neighbour to the south, the **Ackersloot Bastion** (1789) is named after the birthplace of Admiral Wilhelm Coster, the Dutch captain who captured Galle from the Portuguese in 1640. Capping Hospital Street is **Point Utrecht Bastion**, topped by a slender white **lighthouse** of 1938; the ruined structure standing below it was a British powder magazine. From the lighthouse you can climb down to a small section of **beach** while heading west, and overlooking the lighthouse, is the large, early twentieth-century **Meeran Jumma Mosque**, which looks every inch a Portuguese Baroque church (it's actually built on the site of the former Portuguese cathedral), with only a couple of tiny minarets and a token scribble of Arabic betraying its true function. The mosque stands at the heart of Galle's **Muslim quarter**, whose white-robed and skull-capped inhabitants form a distinctive part of life in the old town's streets.

From the lighthouse, a neat path leads along the top of the ramparts to the Neptune Bastion on the Fort's western side; though the path fizzles out as you reach the green north of here, you can continue over the ramparts all the way to the main town-facing bastions – a beautiful stroll, particularly at sunset.

At the southernmost point of the Fort, **Flag Rock** is the most imposing of Galle's bastions – the name derives from the Dutch practice of signalling approaching ships to warn them of offshore hazards hereabouts (the warning signals would have been backed up by musket shots, fired from the huge Pigeon Rock, which you can see just offshore). If you're lucky, you might have timed your arrival to watch the clearly potty "**fort jumpers**" in action, who (anticipating a Rs.500 tip) fling themselves freestyle off the bastion down the sheer thirteen-metre drop into the terrifyingly narrow space between the rampart and the deadly rocks just offshore.

The section of ramparts beyond here gives a clear idea of how the original Dutch fortifications would have appeared. Look closely at the stones and you'll see that many are actually formed from coral, which was hewed and carted into place by slaves. The next bastion along, the **Triton**, comes alive around dusk, as the townsfolk turn out en masse to promenade along the walls and take in the extraordinary red-and-purple sunsets enjoyed by this part of the coast.

Continuing north, the **Neptune** and **Clippenberg bastions** give increasingly fine views over the Fort, with the stumpy spire of All Saints' prominent amongst the picturesque huddle of red rooftops. Closer to hand stands the neat white dagoba of the 1889 **Sudharmalaya Vihara**, looking bizarrely out of place amidst its colonial surroundings and worth a quick visit. The path peters out north of here as the **Aeolus Bastion** is still in military use, meaning that you'll have to descend briefly from the walls and detour around it. Just beyond here, the modest **tomb** of a Muslim saint lies in solitary splendour beneath the ramparts. From here you can continue up to the Star Bastion and back across to the Main Gate.

The new town

Exiting the Fort by the Main Gate, you'll have a fine view of Galle's compact **Galle International Cricket Ground**, occupying the site of the former British racecourse, and one of Sri Lanka's three principal Test match venues. To the east, the **harbourside** is normally busy with fishing boats, their owners noisily bartering over piles of tuna, seer and crab. Beyond here the **new town** straggles northwards in an indeterminate confusion of hooting buses and zigzagging rickshaws. The most interesting place for a wander is the relatively traffic-free section of **Main Street** past the junction with Sea Street, where lines of small shops and local pavement traders cut a colourful dash.

Eating and drinking

The ongoing gentrification of the Fort has given Galle a long-overdue injection of culinary sophistication, and there's now a good range of **restaurants**, although most are expensive. If you're on a budget, several of the Fort's guest-houses dish up good local cooking, as do a handful of delightfully homespun **cafés**, most of which offer lunchtime rice and curry as well as Western light meals and snacks. Several of the town's hotels make an atmospheric venue for a sunset **drink**, while it's easy enough to head out to Unawatuna or Dalawela for an evening's lounging by the beach; a tuktuk should cost around Rs.200 each way, and (in Unawatuna at least) there are plenty hanging around for the return trip until quite late at night.

Cafés

Mamas Roof Café 76 Leyn Baan St. Breezy rooftop café occupying an attractive plant-dotted terrace and serving Sri Lankan and Western food, plus tea and snacks. The sun-soaked and rather precarious platform above offers the best views of the eastern side of the Fort.

Pedlar's Inn Café 92 Pedlar St. Attractive little café in an old Dutch villa, with streetside seating on the veranda. A good place for simple Western breakfasts, sandwiches or coffee and a cake; the chocolate brownies are particularly delicious.

Royal Dutch Café 72 Leyn Baan St. Next to *Mamas*, this tiny, three-table veranda café makes a good stop for a pot of ginger tea (or lunchtime rice and curry if prebooked) and to hear the stories of owner Fazal, a fount of knowledge about the Fort. The attached batik and sari shop is also worth a quick browse.

Serendipity Arts Café 100 Pedlar St. Popular and chilled-out spot, with interesting photos on the walls plus books and magazines to browse. There's a good range of wholesome soups, salads and sandwiches, as well as Sri Lankan dishes, or indulge yourself with ice cream and Mars Bar sauce or the "naughty" dish of the day. Also hosts excellent walks (see p.168) and occasional book readings.

Restaurants

Amangalla 10 Church St. Even if you can't afford to stay here, this superbly revamped landmark hotel is worth visiting for a meal to lap up something of its dreamy atmosphere. Light lunches go for around US$9, or come for afternoon tea on the veranda, or an evening meal of finely prepared Sri Lankan or international cuisine (mains US$20–30).

Galle Fort Hotel 28 Church St. Food is a major attraction at this gorgeous hotel, which dishes up some of the best non-Sri Lankan cooking you'll find on the island (as well as a gourmet nine-course Sri Lankan "curry tiffin"; order 24hr in advance). Light lunchtime meals go for around US$6, while the daily changing gourmet evening menu (4–5 courses for US$27.50) features the best fish from the market and delicately flavoured contemporary pan-Asian cooking, rounded off with the best puddings in the Fort.

Indian Hut 83 H.K. Edmond Mw, Thanipolgaha Junction, 2km northeast from Galle, and 54 Rampart St, Fort. A 10min (Rs.200) tuktuk ride inland from the Fort, the main branch of this fun rip-off of *Pizza Hut*, popular with families and bedecked with a pond spanned by cutesy little bridges, offers a welcome glimpse of tourist-free local life. The tiny new Fort branch occupies a covered balcony above the Dutch Wall Arcade (see below). Food features a decent range of cheap and well-spiced Indian, Pakistani and Chinese dishes, but there's no booze.

Jetwing Lighthouse Dadella, 2km west of Galle. This beautiful hotel provides the five-star setting for some excellent but reasonably priced Sri Lankan and international cuisine, either in the stylish *Cinnamon Room* restaurant (count on US$15–25 for a two-course meal with drinks) or the less formal *Cardamom Café* (open 24hr).

The Sun House 18 Upper Dickson Rd ⓣ091-438 0275. The candlelit garden veranda of this magical colonial villa provides an incomparably romantic setting for daily-changing three-course set meals (around US$30), featuring fabulous Sri Lankan cuisine with Indian, Malay, Dutch and Portuguese influences – anything from chilli-roasted mahi-mahi fillet in lemongrass sauce to Cajun shark with mango salsa. Book by 1pm for dinner.

Bars

Dick's Bar *The Sun House*, 18 Upper Dickson Rd. This intimate and sociable lounge-style bar is the toast of Galle's expat community, with a good range of international beers, single malts and an impressive array of (pricey) cocktails – accompanied by SLappas, an enterprising local twist on tapas, or a selection of home-made traditional British pies.

Galle Fort Hotel 28 Church St. The perfect place to indulge your Somerset Maugham fantasies, the *Galle Fort*'s beautiful veranda bar is the most memorable place in town for a drink, with a long list of expertly mixed cocktails.

Harbour Bar *Lady Hill Hotel*, 29 Upper Dickson Rd. It's well worth the climb up to this hilltop hotel bar before dark, when there's a marvellous view on one side out over the red-tiled roofs of the Fort and, on the other, across miles of palm trees stretching away inland to the Hill Country. Drinks are reasonably priced.

Rampart Hotel 31 Rampart St. Though they also serve (average) food, the main attraction here is the pleasantly breezy location overlooking the western ramparts, making it the ideal venue for a sunset beer.

Shopping

The rush of cash into Galle has sparked a miniature consumer revolution in town, with an increasing number of funky little boutiques and galleries springing up around the Fort.

Barefoot 49 Pedlar St. Galle outpost of the famous Colombo shop, stocking the same distinctive range of clothing, fabrics, stationery, toys and books.

Dutch Wall Arcade 54 Rampart St. Modelled on Olanda, this rampart-side old Dutch warehouse houses a fascinating collection of colonial-era bric-a-brac – cigarette cases, typewriters, sewing machines and the like – picked up from local houses and laid out in glass cabinets.

Elephant Walk/Fort Gallery 36 Church St. Eclectic selection of quality handicrafts and other knick-knacks including clothes, old prints, scented candles, wood carvings and kitchenware; the upstairs gallery is rather less inspiring.

Exotic Roots 32 Church St. Attractive little boutique showcasing the paintings and pottery of owner Catherine Hewapathirana, featuring colourful modern takes on traditional Sri Lankan subjects like elephants and stilt fishermen.

Laksana 30 Hospital St. One of the more reputable and reliable jewellers in Galle, stocking an interesting selection of antique silver items along with assorted coins, watches, daggers and other colonial-era bric a brac.

Olanda 30 Leyn Baan St. This atmospheric shop is almost a sight in its own right, occupying a huge old Dutch warehouse stuffed full of bits and pieces of colonial furniture and other objects salvaged from local villas, from chairs and wardrobes to carriages and candelabra, as well as more portable items including attractive pottery, snuff-boxes, telescopes, gramophones and beautiful old hanging lamps.

Orchard House Hospital St. Attractive renovated Dutch shophouse, selling a good range of teas, spices and all sorts of associated paraphernalia, plus linen clothing and very popular hand-painted bags.

Shoba Display Gallery 67A Pedlar St. Women's cooperative showcasing the dextrous skills of local

lacemakers, who have provided lace for costumes used in various British period dramas. There's also a selection of ready-made items for sale, including bags and cute children's clothing.
Sithuvili 56 Leyn Baan St. Half a dozen absorbing rooms of Sri Lankan art and crafts by Ambalangoda artist Janaka de Silva, including a good range of masks and well-executed reproductions of Kandyan-style temple paintings.
Vijitha Yapa 12 H.W. Amasuriya Mw. Galle branch of national bookshop chain with a reasonable selection of English-language titles.

Listings

Banks There are branches of Sampath Bank, Hatton National Bank and the Bank of Ceylon clustered together around the junction of Gamini Mw and H.W. Amarasuriya Mw in the new town; the ATMs at all three accept foreign Visa and MasterCards. In the Fort, there are ATMs accepting foreign cards at the branches of the Bank of Ceylon on Middle St, and the Commercial Bank on Church St.
Hospital General Hospital ⓣ091-222 2261.
Internet Many of the Fort's guesthouses have internet and wi-fi, or try Café 59, Church St (8.30am–10.30pm; Rs.2 per min). In the New Town, try Infolink Computer Systems (daily 8.30am–7.30pm; Rs.100 per hr), on the third floor of the Selaka Building near the bus station.
Pharmacies Try Steuart Remedica, on the ground floor of the Selaka Building immediately north of the bus station.
Photography Selaka Colour Lab, on the first floor of the Selaka Building, is the town's main Kodak agent. There's also a (nameless) Fuji agent at the entrance to the P&J City Building.
Police The tourist police have an office on Hospital St in the Fort (open 24hr).
Post The main post office (Mon–Sat 7am–9pm), in the new town on Main St, has a well-organized poste restante section, plus an EMS mail service and stationers. There's also a dilapidated sub-post office in the Fort on Church St, just south of the Dutch Reformed Church.
Spas The superb Baths spa at *Amangalla* is open to non-guests, with steam rooms, saunas and gorgeous hydrotherapy pools, as well as a full range of massages and treatments; they also offer a full fourteen-day Ayurveda programme. The spa at the *Jetwing Lighthouse* has a similarly comprehensive list of treatments.
Supermarket There's a Cargills supermarket in the P&J City Building in the new town immediately north of the bus station.

Moving on from Galle

Galle's **bus station** is fairly straightforward to navigate, with well-labelled bays. Services in both directions along the main **coastal road** leave roughly every fifteen minutes; express air-conditioned minibuses leave every fifteen minutes for **Colombo** (3hr–3hr 30min) via **Hikkaduwa** (30min), **Aluthgama** (1hr 30min) and **Kalutara** (2hr 15min). Long-distance services heading east usually originate in Colombo rather than Galle, meaning that you can't count on getting a seat. If you're heading to **Tangalla** (2hr 30min), **Hambantota** (3hr 30min) or **Tissamaharama** (4hr 15min) you may find it quicker to catch a bus to **Matara** (every 15min; 1hr 15min) and change there, rather than waiting for a through bus (on which you might struggle to find a seat). There are also a few direct buses to **Kataragama** (5 daily; 5hr); otherwise, change at Matara and/or Tissa.

The easiest way to get to **Kandy** from Galle is to return to Colombo. To reach **Sinharaja**, you'll need to take a bus to **Akuressa** (every 10min; 1hr) then change for **Deniyaya** (every 30min); there are also three direct buses from Galle to Deniyaya (4hr). Reaching the southern **hill country** from Galle is a laborious process; there's currently a once-daily service departing in the morning to **Badulla** (8hr) via **Bandarawela**, and at least one service daily to **Nuwara Eliya** (8hr). Alternatively, catch the bus to **Tissa**, then another to **Wellawaya**, from where there are frequent services to Ella, Haputale and Badulla – this is a long day's journey, however.

For **train** timetables, see p.165.

Around Galle

Around 16km from the city along the road to Udugama, the compact **Kottawa Rainforest and Arboretum** (8am–5pm; Rs.660) provides an easily accessible introduction to the Sri Lankan rainforest, with a wide one-kilometre walking trail shaded by giant dipterocarps towering up to 45m high. Resident mammals include purple-faced langurs and giant squirrels, plus rather more shy muntjac and sambur, and there's an impressive array of colourful endemic birds and (rather less polychromatic) reptiles. Leeches can be ferocious in the wet season, so bring appropriate gear. Buses run every fifteen minutes or so between Galle and Udugama, taking about half an hour to reach Kottawa; the ticket office is by the side of the road, near the 14km post. Informative guided tours are run by Rainforest Rescue International (Rs.2250–3000 per person, depending on group size; ⓣ071-950 0234, ⓦwww.rainforestrescueinternational.org), whose website lists a host of other possibilities for exploring Galle's rainforests. Prices include transport, guide, entry fees and lunch.

You'll need your own transport to reach **Hiyare Rainforest Park** (8am–5pm; Rs.100), around 8km from Kottawa and 4km off the Galle–Udugama road back towards the city. Centrepiece of the park is the picturesque Hiyare Reservoir, while the surrounding rainforest is home to a small population of rare hog deer and over fifty species of birds. It's also a major focus for reforestation, and a nursery has also been established here as part of Sri Lanka's Trees for Life scheme (ⓦwww.responsibletourismsrilanka.org). You're invited to plant a tree yourself on a guided tour of the forest (Rs.1000; ⓣ0773 683 880), which also includes transport, a boat ride on the reservoir, guided walk along the forest trails, guide and entry fees.

The low-lying hills inland from Galle are also home to one of Sri Lanka's most inspirational eco-tourism projects, **Samakanda** (ⓦwww.samakanda.org), a sixty-acre organic farm and eco-retreat developed on the site of an abandoned tea estate by British environmentalist Rory Spowers, who recorded the trials involved in its creation in the highly readable *A Year in Green Tea and Tuk-Tuks* (see p.461). Defined as a "bio-versity", it's an exemplary model of sustainable living, with plenty of community involvement and minimal environmental impact, and there's heaps to do here, from nature hikes and bikes rides in the surrounding hills to week-long courses involving yoga, tea picking and learning about organic cultivation. Accommodation is in a pair of comfortable solar-powered bungalows (sleeping 4–6; US$150–200; minimum two nights), and food is a major part of the fun – you can either cater for yourself (using self-picked ingredients), fire up the outdoor clay pizza oven or barbecue, or (Dec–April only) dine on Rory's gourmet cuisine. *Samakanda* can be visited as a day-trip (Rs.500; book in advance) and for meals (from Rs.1000); *Samakanda* lies beyond Kottawa around 22km north of Galle, on the Udugama road, close to village of Nakiyadeniya.

Unawatuna and around

Five kilometres southeast of Galle, the ever-expanding village of **UNAWATUNA** is now firmly established as Sri Lanka's most popular resort for independent travellers – and with good reason. Set snugly in a pretty semicircular bay, picturesquely terminated by a dagoba on the rocky headland to the northwest, the beach remains idyllic, while the sheltered bay gives safe year-round swimming, and a group of rocks 150m offshore further breaks up waves (though it can still get a bit rough during the monsoon).

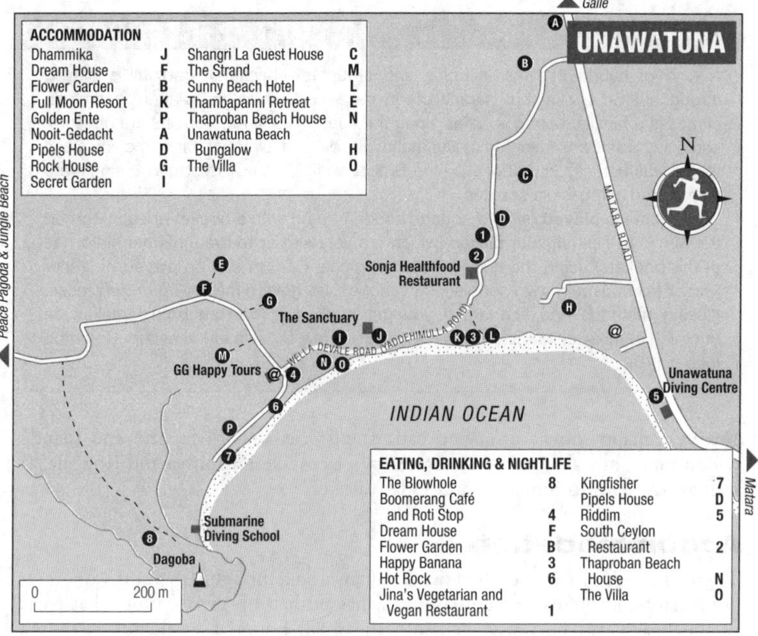

It's far from unspoilt, of course. New hotels and guesthouses continue to spring up and much of the beach has now disappeared under a string of restaurants, while in recent years Unawatuna has begun to compete with Hikkaduwa as Sri Lanka's beach-party capital, with noisy discos thumping out beats along parts of the beach during the season. At other times, Unawatuna recaptures some of its former sleepiness, managing to be lively enough without being trashy, and at any time of year you can at least stay up eating and drinking on the beach until fairly late at night, a rare pleasure in early-to-bed Sri Lanka. The resort remains busy all year round, making it a good place to visit if you're on the west coast during the monsoon.

Arrival and information

Unawatuna is hidden away off the coastal Matara Road some 5km east of Galle. Take any bus heading east from Galle and ask to be dropped at the turn-off for the village, **Wella Devale Road** (also known as Yaddehimulla Rd and Beach Access Rd), which runs from the Matara Road for 500m down to the beach (no buses actually go into the village itself). The village isn't signposted at all and is very easy to miss – if you're arriving by bus make sure the conductor knows where you're getting off (coming from Galle the turning is just after the prominently signposted *Nooit-Gedacht*, on the right-hand side of the road). A **tuktuk** to or from Galle costs around Rs.200.

If you want a **bank**, you'll have to go to Galle. The cheapest places to get **online** are currently the internet café at the *Surf City Guest House* (daily 8.30am–9.30pm; Rs.200 per hr), or GG Happy Tours (same times; Rs.4 per min); *Thaproban Beach House*'s restaurant is the place to head for free **wi-fi**.

For general information about the area and other travel services, try the helpful **GG Happy Tours** in the middle of the village (ⓣ091-223 2838,

Carrom

A kind of hybrid of pool, marbles and draughts (checkers), **carrom** is played throughout Sri Lanka, but particularly in the south, where the clatter of wooden pieces is a familiar sound in cafés along the coast. The game's origins are obscure: some say that it was invented by the maharajas of India, although many Indians claim that it was actually introduced by the British, while Burma, Egypt and Ethiopia are also touted as possible sources.

The game is **played** using a square wooden board with a pocket at each corner; the aim is to flick all your pieces (which are very similar to draughtsmen) into one of the pockets, using the heavier "striker" piece. Carrom can be played by either four or (more usually) two people, and various rules govern the set-up of the pieces, flicking methods and scoring. If you get hooked, a **carrom board** makes an unusual, if bulky, souvenir – there are usually a few for sale at Laksala in Colombo (see p.116).

Ⓦwww.gghappytours.com), who can arrange car-and-driver hire and island-wide tours. They also run tours to nearby places like Balapitiya and Koggala, as well as day-trips to Sinharaja and Uda Walawe.

Accommodation

There are heaps of **places to stay** in Unawatuna, though the resort's ongoing popularity and increasing gentrification has pushed up prices. Note that parts of the beach can be noisy well into the small hours at weekends as there's usually a late-night disco going on, and you'll in any case usually pay over the odds for a beachfront location; the best-value accommodation is in any case away from the water.

Seasonal variations and fluctuations in demand keep prices fluid, though there are few steals. High season runs roughly from November to mid-April; outside this period rates fall by up to thirty percent in many places, though at any time of year it's worth bargaining if trade is quiet.

Budget

Golden Ente Ⓣ091-224 8034. Behind the unpromising exterior – a rather ugly oversized pink box – this is the one of the best budget options, with basic but spacious and good-value rooms, each with individual terrace or balcony. ❷

Nooit-Gedacht Ⓣ091-222 3449, Ⓦwww.sriayurveda.com. Set in a delectable if crumbling colonial mansion of 1735, this budget Ayurveda resort has bags of character and a very mixed assortment of rooms – most are stately but rather gloomy period pieces; a few are bright and modern and come with a/c. The Ayurveda centre here is one of the best on the south coast, offering the usual baths and massages, plus more serious courses of treatment; a one-week course costs around US$650, inclusive of accommodation and all treatments. RG readers are offered a ten percent discount. ❷, a/c ❹

Rock House Ⓣ091-222 4948, Ⓔrockhouse2002@hotmail.com. The better of two adjacent, identically named guesthouses is the one set further back from the road, with a range of bright, modern rooms of varying size and standard, including three apartments (US$40) in Unawatuna's highest building, audaciously perched atop a rock with fabulous views down to the bay across a sea of palms. ❷–❸, a/c ❹

The Strand Ⓣ091-222 4358, Ⓦwww.homestay-strand.net. A mishmash of rooms of various styles, sizes and standards (some with hot water, one with a/c; best is "The Nest") set in an attractive old 1920s colonial-style house and surrounding modern buildings, all scattered around a tranquil (if rather untidy) garden. The charming owner is full of fascinating (if heartrending) tsunami stories. ❸–❺

Sunny Beach Hotel Ⓣ091-438 1456. One of Unawatuna's originals, this modern two-storey building is set right above the beach, with a breezy seafront terrace restaurant. Rooms are a mixed bag, but the best are spacious and good value – ask to see a few. ❷

Mid-range and expensive

Dhammika ☎091-222 6582, Ⓦwww.hotel-dhammika.com. Friendly and well-run place in the centre of the village with unimpeded views (apart from the overhead cables) across the bay. Spacious and attractively furnished rooms all come with satellite TV, hot water and large sea-view balconies; some also have a/c (US$5 extra). Excellent value. ❹

Dream House ☎091-438 1541. Italian-owned establishment set in a very attractive old colonial villa, with four characterful (if rather small) rooms with wooden floors and period furniture, plus Italian cooking – very pleasant, but a bit overpriced. ❻

Flower Garden ☎091-222 5286, Ⓦwww.hotelflowergarden.com. Idyllic (if rather pricey) little hideaway set in an abundant flower-filled garden at the top of Wella Devale Rd, with accommodation in neat little chalets with hot water and optional a/c. There's also a small Ayurveda centre, a decent-sized pool and good European cuisine. ❺, a/c ❻

Full Moon Resort ☎091-223 3091, Ⓦwww.fullmoonvillage.com. Attractive guesthouse right on the beach, with bright yellow-and-blue concrete cabanas and a range of pleasant rooms (some with a/c), plus a good seafront restaurant with an Italian slant. Can be noisy, though, when there's a disco (currently Fri) at next-door *Happy Banana*. ❹, a/c ❺

Pipels House ☎0776 369 721, Ⓦwww.pipels.com. Neat and homely little Danish-owned guesthouse, with just four compact rooms (sharing bathrooms), attractively kitted out in colourful fabrics; best is the top-floor apartment with a private balcony. ❺

Secret Garden ☎0776 973 175, Ⓦwww.secretgardenvilla.lk. Exactly as the name suggests, with a tiny door leading into a wonderful concealed walled garden full of trees, birds and the occasional monkey. Accommodation is either in the old colonial villa (a mix of beautifully furnished suites and rooms) or in the less characterful modern bungalow, and there's a serene new yoga dome. Bungalow ❺, villa ❻

Shangri La Guest House ☎091-438 4252, Ⓦwww.shangrila.lk. Set in rambling, shady hammock-strewn gardens 200m from the beach, this South African/Sri Lankan-owned guesthouse is deservedly popular. There's an excellent range of accommodation, from spotless, homely rooms in the main house to attractive wooden cabanas with open-air showers, plus a pair of two-bedroom cottages, each sleeping four (US$35).

Diving, snorkelling and surfing at Unawatuna

Unawatuna has a modest range of **watersports** on offer, with two good diving schools: **Submarine Diving School** (☎091-438 0358, Ⓦwww.submarinediving.xail.net), at the western end of the beach, and **Unawatuna Diving Centre** (☎091-224 4693, Ⓦwww.unawatunadiving.com; Oct–April only), around the bay to the east. Both offer the usual range of PADI courses, plus single and introductory dives and wreck and deep dives (there are no fewer than eight wrecks in the vicinity, including an old wooden English ship, the *Rangoon*, lying at a depth of 30m), though they're rather more expensive than in nearby Hikkaduwa. Diving is best between October and April.

You can **snorkel** off the beach at Unawatuna, although it's not wildly exciting; you might see a few colourful tropical fish, and there's a little patch of live coral where the waves break in front of the Submarine Diving School. The best two snorkelling spots are **Rock Island**, about 1km offshore, and around the headland facing Galle at **Jungle Beach**, where you'll find live coral and fish. For the former you'll need to hire the Submarine Dive School's **glass-bottomed boat** (Rs.2800 for two people or Rs.3800 for four, including snorkelling gear, for a couple of hours), which can also be used to reach Jungle Beach (Rs.1500 per person). Alternatively, Jungle Beach is reachable by tuktuk, or by foot (though it's a convoluted 45-min walk, and very easy to get lost; ask for directions locally). Submarine rent out expensive snorkelling equipment (Rs.200 per hr or Rs.1000 per day), as do a couple of cheaper shacks on the beach nearby. Check all equipment carefully, as there are plenty of dud masks and snorkels in circulation.

A lot of locals **surf** at Unawatuna, though the waves aren't nearly as good as at nearby Hikkaduwa or Midigama. Boards can be rented on the beach near the diving school, though they're expensive (Rs.350 per hr or Rs.1500 per day).

There's also cheap internet, a pool table and decent food. ❹

Thambapanni Retreat ⓣ091-223 4588, ⓦwww.thambapannileisure.com. Inviting hotel tucked away in thick jungle at the foot of Rumassala a few minutes' walk from the beach. Standard rooms have a/c and are comfortable enough, although the more expensive "deluxe" and "superior" ones (also with satellite TV and minibar) are much more characterful; best is the ice-cool "Cave House", built onto the open rock. There's also a small swimming pool, Ayurveda centre, sauna and yoga classes. ❺–❼

Thaproban Beach House ⓣ091-438 1722, ⓦwww.thambapannileisure.com. Much-loved Unawatuna landmark, right on the beach in the middle of the village, that's looking prettier than ever following a major refurb. The attractive rooms are all equipped with a/c, minibar and balcony – smarter ones, elegantly furnished in light wood and bamboo, add a touch of boutique style. There's also internet, wi-fi and an excellent restaurant. Fills up quickly, so book ahead. ❺–❻

Unawatuna Beach Bungalow ⓣ091-222 4327, ⓔunawatunabeachbungalow@yahoo.com. One of the nicer small guesthouses in Unawatuna, set just behind the beach (and the drab *Unawatuna Beach Resort*). The comfortable modern rooms (a/c is an extra Rs.1000) have pristine bathrooms and hot water. ❹

The Villa ⓣ091-224 7253, ⓦwww.villa-unawatuna.com. Right on the beach in Unawatuna's most shamelessly kitsch building – it's like staying in an enormous cuckoo clock. The six rooms are quite small but nicely equipped with big walk-in nets, colonial-style furniture and colourful blue bathrooms, as well as a/c, hot water, minibar, phone and satellite TV; all have sea views. Also has a good restaurant. ❻

The village and beach

Unawatuna **beach** is small and intimate: a graceful semicircular curve of sand not much more than a kilometre from start to finish, enclosed by headlands at either end. It's easy to spend days here, idling purposelessly between the beach's many cafés and the ocean and enjoying the easy pace of life, which seems to strike just the right balance between liveliness and somnolence. For the energetic, there are various **watersports** on offer (see box, p.181), while for the more indolent, roving masseurs hang around the beach (though some look thoroughly disreputable, and assaults have been reported), along with wandering ladies flogging sarongs and beachwear. At the northern end of the beach, a footpath leads up to a small **dagoba** perched on the rocks above the bay, offering fine views over Unawatuna and north to Galle.

Behind the beach, **Unawatuna village** is, in places at least, a surprisingly attractive place. Its recreational possibilities have long been recognized, the village having originally developed as a country retreat for Dutch merchants and administrators living in Galle – the flouncy colonial villas built by them and their British successors still give parts of Wella Devale Road a surprisingly chintzy look.

Tucked discreetly away in a shady garden behind the *Dhammika* hotel, The Sanctuary (ⓣ0773 078 583; book in advance) is a blissful spot for some open-air pampering, with reasonably priced **Ayurveda treatments**; there are equally professional herbal massages at the *South Ceylon Restaurant*, which also runs free daily group **yoga and meditation** classes (call Siri Goonasekera on ⓣ091-224 5863). The *Sonja Healthfood Restaurant* next door runs excellent one-day **cookery courses** (Rs.3000; book a day in advance; ⓣ0779 615 310), offering a rare opportunity to get behind an apron and learn some of the secrets of Sri Lankan chefs. The courses begin at 11am with a visit to the market, after which you'll grind and mix spices then prepare five traditional dishes. Dinner is served at 5.30pm; you can invite one guest free, and other people can come along for Rs.250.

Eating and drinking

Unawatuna is easily the best of the south-coast resorts for food, with dozens of inviting **restaurants** lining the beachfront and Wella Devale Road – fish and seafood are predictably excellent. Invariably romantically candlelit at night, any of the beachfront places are an atmospheric choice for a longer (or stronger) **drink**, though *Kingfisher* and crashed-out *Riddim*, next to Unawatuna Diving Centre at the eastern end of the bay – a great place for sunset cocktails – stand out. Both these places – as do a number of others, including *Happy Banana* – host regular **discos** in season; ask around when you arrive.

The Blowhole Cute little thatched restaurant right at the western end of the beach, dishing up well-prepared rice and curry and other standards. The real draw though is the rickety wooden terrace atop the rocks behind – a great place to watch the sun set over the ocean.

Boomerang Café and Roti Stop Cheap and cheerful snack stop, doling out delicious *roti* and sandwiches with all sorts of fillings.

Dream House ⑦091-438 1541. Some of the south coast's best Italian cooking is served up in the salubrious surroundings of this upmarket guesthouse when the Tuscan owners are in residence (Dec–March only), using imported ingredients. Book in advance.

Flower Garden Attractive open-sided restaurant, serving an excellent range of beef steaks, plus plenty of pasta and fish and an extensive wine list.

Happy Banana This lively beachfront restaurant has long been one of the most popular venues in town, particularly on Fridays when it hosts a barbecue and disco. There's a long menu of sandwiches, salads and more substantial fare.

Hot Rock The best of several similarly named (and almost indistinguishable) venues at the western end of the beach. Wholesome food, including *jaffles* (toasties) and stacked sandwiches, plus cheap beer and good music in a romantic setting.

Jina's Vegetarian and Vegan Restaurant *Zimmer Rest.* Run by the former chef at the *South Ceylon* (see opposite), with a very similar menu (and at identical prices) of vegan and vegetarian dishes – everything from Indian *puri* to (veggie) shepherd's pie. It's also a good stop for a tasty sandwich (made with home-baked bread) and home-roasted organic coffee. Order before 4pm.

Kingfisher Perched above a colourful part of the beach always busy with local families, this tiny coconut-thatched place has a devoted following for its broad-reaching menu and laid-back ambience. Seafood is a particular speciality, though they're equally strong on light bites such as wraps and salads. The scatter-cushioned chill-out zone next door is a wonderfully indolent spot for a drink. Also hosts a weekly disco (Sat) and occasional beach parties.

Pipels House Delightfully pretty little walled-garden café, dishing up a simple but wholesome menu of reasonably priced home-made snacks; the burgers, wrapped in home-baked bread, are fully of meaty goodness, and the ice cream and chocolate cake are to die for.

South Ceylon Restaurant In a quaint rickety wooden building on the main road through the village, this place does an unusual selection of international vegetarian dishes ranging from gado-gado and moussaka to enchiladas and lasagne – not always totally authentic, but generally tasty and good value, with pretty much everything under Rs.450.

Thaproban Beach House Perennially popular, and deservedly so, for its quality cooking, polished service and touch of sophistication. The menu is the most diverse in the village, ranging from spatchcock to paella, while the pizzas are Unawatuna's best – and they do a more than decent breakfast fry-up. Dine either in the welcoming, lantern-lit main restaurant or right over the waves on the beachfront terrace.

The Villa Pleasant and quietly civilized beachfront restaurant serving an interesting range of dishes, from teriyaki chicken to mutton *rogan josh*. Also does Sri Lankan breakfasts (order the day before).

Moving on from Unawatuna

If you're **heading west** from Unawatuna, it's easiest to take a tuktuk to Galle and pick up a bus or train there (see p.165 & p.177 for details). **Heading east**, you should be able to flag down a bus to Weligama, Mirissa or Matara along the main Matara Road, though the local tuktuk drivers will tell you a pack of lies about buses not stopping at Unawatuna in an attempt to get you into their vehicle. If you wave at anything that passes, something will probably stop for you sooner or later – you'd be unlucky to wait more than fifteen minutes. If you do succumb to the tuktuk drivers, the ride to Weligama shouldn't cost more than Rs.600.

Around Unawatuna: Rumassala

Unawatuna's most striking natural feature is **Rumassala**, an incongruously grand outcrop of rock whose sides rise up sheer behind the village; it's popularly claimed to be a fragment of the chunk of mountain carried from the Himalayas by the monkey god **Hanuman**. As recounted in the *Ramayana*, Hanuman was sent by Rama to collect a special herb from the Himalayas which was needed to save the life of Rama's wounded brother, Lakshmana. Arriving in the Himalayas, the absent-minded Hanuman realized he had forgotten the name of the required plant, so ripped up an entire chunk of mountainside in the hope that the necessary plant would be found somewhere on it. He then carried this fragment of mountain back to Sri Lanka, dropping a bit in Ritigala, in the north of the island, and another piece at Unawatuna. The rock still sports a large collection of medicinal herbs as well as entertaining troupes of boisterous macaque monkeys, Hanuman's latter-day relatives, who periodically descend from the rock to raid the villagers' papaya trees.

Around the headland from Unawatuna, high up on the Rumassala hillside, is a gleaming white **peace pagoda** – actually an enormous dagoba – constructed by Japanese Buddhists in 2004. The views from here, particularly at sunset, are magical, with the mosque and clocktower of Galle Fort clearly visible in the distance to the west and, to the east, the carpet of thick jungle that separates the pagoda from Unawatuna. The peace pagoda is a fifteen-minute drive across Rumassala's beautiful countryside from Unawatuna (Rs.500 in a tuktuk), though it's much more easily (and prosaically) accessed from the Matara Road – there's a turning at the 120km post just opposite the cement factory.

Dalawela to Midigama

Beyond Unawatuna the coast becomes increasingly soporific, as the main coastal highway heads through the small villages of **Dalawela** and **Thalpe** to the workaday town of **Koggala**, home to a few absorbing sights, before reaching the little surfing village of **Midigama**, which boasts some of the best waves in Sri Lanka.

This section of coast is also the best place to witness one of Sri Lanka's most emblematic sights, **stilt fishermen**. The stilts consist of a single pole and crossbar planted out in the sea, on which fishermen perch whilst casting their lines when the currents are flowing in the right direction (most likely to happen between Oct and Dec, especially at sunset). Positions are highly lucrative thanks to the abundant supplies of fish, even close to shore, and are handed down from father to son.

Dalawela and Thalpe

A few kilometres beyond Unawatuna, the beautiful and unspoilt beaches at **DALAWELA** and **THALPE** are becoming increasingly popular with visitors who are turned off by the relative hustle and bustle of Unawatuna. Dalawela is home to a handful of good mid-range guesthouses and hotels while a succession of high walls on the ocean-side of the Matara road at Thalpe, 2km further on, conceals a raft of luxury beachfront villas belonging to (mostly) foreigners and available for rent; there are also a few small upmarket hotels. Accommodation aside, there's very little to either village apart from the beach and a few clusters of fishing stilts – perfect for Robinson Crusoe types who enjoy counting palm trees.

Sri Lankan Buddhism

Buddhism runs deep in Sri Lankan life. The island was one of the first places to convert to the religion, in 247 BC, and has remained unswervingly faithful in the two thousand years since. As such, Sri Lanka is often claimed to be the world's oldest Buddhist country, and the religion's trappings are apparent everywhere, most obviously in the island's myriad temples and festivals, as well as in its large and highly visible population of monks.

Temple of the Tooth, Kandy ▲

Buddhist monk at prayer ▼

Temples and worship

Despite the long influence of the West on Sri Lanka, Buddhism continues to permeate the practical life and spiritual beliefs of the majority of the island's Sinhalese population. Buddhist **temples** can be found everywhere, often decorated with superb shrines, statues and murals. The sight of orange-robed **monks** (see opposite) is another of the island's enduring visual images, more commonly seen at temples, though also frequently encountered out and about, adding a splash of religious colour to the passengers aboard a crowded bus or walking serenely through the urban hustle and bustle of a noisy town centre.

Buddhist places of pilgrimage and festivals also play a vital role in sustaining the faith. The island's major sites of **Buddhist pilgrimage** – the Temple of the Tooth at Kandy, the revered "footprint" of the Buddha at Adam's Peak and the Sri Maha Bodhi at Anuradhapura (see p.241, p.294 & p.362) – attract thousands of pilgrims year-round. The timing of pilgrimages is often linked to significant dates in the Buddhist calendar, which is punctuated by a further round of Buddhist holidays and festivals. These range from the monthly full-moon Buddhist holidays, or **poya days**, during which the pious retreat to their local temples to meditate and pray, to more elaborate **festivals**, often taking the form of enormous **processions** (peraheras), when locals parade along the streets, sometimes accompanied by elaborately costumed elephants. Nowhere are these processions more extravagant than during the magnificent **Esala Perahera** in Kandy (see p.232), one of Sri Lanka's – indeed Asia's – most visually spectacular pageants.

The Sangha

Even if you don't go near a temple, you won't travel far in Sri Lanka without seeing a shaven-headed Buddhist monk clad in striking orange or red robes. Collectively known as **the Sangha**, the island's twenty thousand or so monks form one of the most visible and distinctive sections of Sri Lankan society, and serve as living proof of the island's commitment to the Buddhist cause.

Young boys are traditionally chosen to be monks if they show a particular religious bent, or if their horoscope appears favourable – although many are given to the Sangha by poor Sinhalese families in order to provide them with a decent standard of living and an education. Young novices generally enter the Sangha at around 10 years old (sometimes younger), going to live and study in a monastery and largely severing their ties with home. Following full ordination at around 20, monks are expected to commit themselves to the Sangha for life, although in practice a fair number fail to last the course and return to secular society.

Once ordained, monks traditionally live in **village temples**, relying on their local communities for food and material support, in return for which they act as teachers and spiritual mentors. In practice, however, many have proved somewhat less retiring than the monastic ideal requires. A significant number are actively involved in **politics**, commanding considerable popular support for their stridently anti-Tamil rhetoric and presenting a significant political obstacle to all hopes of achieving a lasting peace in the island.

For more on Sri Lanka's monks, see p.442.

▲ Statues in Cave 2, Dambulla

▼ Roadside Buddhist shrine

▼ Sacred Bo Tree, Anuradhapura

The golden Buddha at Dambulla ▲

Prayer flags, Anuradhapura ▲

Ruvanvalisaya, Anuradhapura ▼

Temple terms

No two Sri Lankan temples are exactly alike, and the island's shrines range in style and scale from rudimentary cave temples buried in thick jungle through to the magnificent remains of great monastic foundations which once supported thousands of monks. Despite their myriad sizes and shapes, however, virtually all share the same three basic features: a **dagoba** (stupa; see p.445); a **bo tree**; and an **image house** containing a statue of the Buddha, usually along with likenesses of other deities. Larger temples may have **additional shrines** to other gods considered important by Sri Lankan Buddhists – Vishnu (considered a protector of Buddhism in Sri Lanka) is the most frequently encountered, although other deities from the Hindu pantheon such as Ganesh and Pattini can also sometimes be seen, while the eternally popular Kataragama (see p.216) is also well represented. Temples in the Kandy area sometimes have a **digge**, or drummers' hall, in which musicians and dancers rehearse. You might also see examples of a **vatadage**, a circular image house comprising a dagoba covered in a roof, while monastic temples will have a **poyage**, a building in which the resident monks assemble on full-moon (poya) days to recite scriptures and confess breaches of the monastic code. For more on Buddhist temples, see p.446.

As well as purely Buddhist temples, or viharas, there are also numerous **devales**, independent shrines dedicated to other gods such as Vishnu, Kataragama, Pattini or Saman – nominally Buddhist, though often showing a strong dash of Hindu influence too. These shouldn't be confused with **kovils**, which are purely Hindu temples, and have no connection with Buddhism at all. All Buddhist temples are freely open to **visitors**, whether Buddhist or not, provided the few basic rules outlined on p.56 are followed.

Dalawela and Thalpe are also hugely popular with Galle's expats, who flock here for the two lively beach hangouts. The rustic beachfront restaurant at ✱ *Wijaya Beach* is usually packed out from lunchtime onwards, dishing up a creative range of specials and the south coast's best pizza, as well as good beers and cocktails. Backing onto a gorgeous coral-sheltered stretch of beach a few kilometres on (close to the 127km post), *Why Beach Club and Restaurant* (Tues–Sat; ⓣ0776 980 000) is an equally genial place to chill during the daytime, strewn with funky open-air sofas and serving up quality Mediterranean cuisine, tasty finger-food and a fine array of cocktails from the well-stocked bar until 7pm. It's also open for dinner on Wednesday and Thursday, and on other nights if booked in advance.

Accommodation

Amanda Beach Villas Dalawela, 1.5km past Unawatuna ⓣ091-493 0683, ⓔsterne@sltnet.lk. Classy new hotel with a striking ochre facade reminiscent of a Dutch church. Overlooking a neat garden and the beach, the four stylish rooms have attractive four-posters and plenty of mod cons. Guests can use the pool at the more downbeat sister hotel, *Sun Shine Inn*, across the road. ❼

Apa Villa Thalpe, 3.5km past Unawatuna ⓣ091-228 3320, ⓦwww.villa-srilanka.com. This beautiful beachfront property comprises three stunning colonial-style villas, containing seven minimally furnished but very stylish suites (each sleeping two), set in spacious gardens around a gorgeous pool. A sister property, *Illuketia*, lies 5km inland in a beautifully re-created plantation house with six slightly cheaper suites. ❽–❾

Frangipani Tree Thalpe, 3km past Unawatuna ⓣ091-228 3711, ⓦwww.thefrangipanitree.com. Intimate new boutique hotel arranged around a spectacular lap pool that extends the length of the immaculate frangipani-studded lawn. Suites are stylish and minimalist, with built-in cement furniture and outdoor bath tubs, and facilities include a tennis court and beach spa. ❾

Shanthi Guest House Dalawela, 2km past Unawatuna ⓣ091-438 0081, ⓦwww.shanthiguesthouse.com. Large, modern guest-house in an attractive beachfront location right next to the village's main cluster of stilt-fishing posts, with a natural swimming pool formed by a protective reef. There's a big selection of rooms of varying standards (all with hot water, some with a/c), plus simpler wood or concrete cabanas, and bikes for hire. ❸, a/c ❹

Sri Gemunu Beach Resort Dalawela, 2km past Unawatuna ⓣ091-228 3202, ⓦwww.sri-gemunu.com. Next door to the *Shanthi*, the stilt-fishing posts and the natural pool, this attractive and very friendly modern beach hotel has comfortable standard rooms with hot water and shared balcony, plus deluxe rooms with a/c, TV, minibar and private balcony. Half-board rates only: fan ❺, a/c ❻

Star Light Hotel Thalpe, 3km past Unawatuna ⓣ091-228 2216, ⓔstarlight@sltnet.lk. Rather glitzy modern hotel with fourteen big and very smartly furnished a/c rooms, plus a pool – good value, though some rooms are very close to the main road and it's a few minutes' walk away from the beach. ❺

Wijaya Beach Dalawela, 2.5km past Unawatuna ⓣ091-228 3610. The nicest budget place in Dalawela, with a friendly and laid-back atmosphere. Rooms are modern, tiled and very comfortable, and there's a terrific beachfront restaurant and safe swimming, thanks to a reef just offshore. *Wijaya Beach* is easy to miss: coming from the west, if you've reached the drab *Point de Galle* you've gone too far. ❹

Koggala and around

Around 12km beyond Unawatuna lies the small and unprepossessing town of **KOGGALA**, dominated by a pair of military themed constructions with two very different purposes: a military airbase, hurriedly built here during World War II against the threat of Japanese attack, and the spectacular new *Fortress* hotel. The town is also home to one of the island's more rewarding museums, erected in honour of the famous Sinhalese writer **Martin Wickramasinghe**, and close to the fascinating **Handunugoda Tea Plantation** and **Kataluwa Purvarama Mahavihara** temple, while **Koggala Lagoon** is just a couple of kilometres away: dotted with islands and fringed with mangroves, it's good for birds and boat trips, although factories associated with the nearby Free Trade Zone have sullied the waters somewhat. You might be able to arrange a boat or catamaran trips here locally (ask around at the museum or one of the hotels); count on around US$35 for two people for a three-hour trip.

Koggala and its environs are also home to two of the island's most stunning **hotels**. The forbiddingly austere outer walls of *The Fortress* (ⓣ091-438 0909, ⓦwww.thefortress.lk; ❾) gives little indication of the hedonistic extravagance within. Housed in two sweeping colonial-style wings, each of the 49 split-level suites (from US$340) and apartments is a luxurious confection of state-of-the-art amenities and designer chic. Facilities include a spectacular 74-metre infinity pool, the sensuous Lima Spa and three first-class restaurants, including the outrageously over-the-top fine-dining *Wine3* – proud purveyor of a US$14,500 dessert: a rather surreal boast for sleepy little Koggala.

There's more luxury – though without the hubris – a few kilometres inland from Koggala at the enchanting *Kahanda Kanda* (ⓣ091-223 6499, ⓦwww.kahandakanda.com; ❾) perched in a magnificent (and pleasantly cool) position above Koggala lagoon. This is one of Sri Lanka's most beguiling small hotels, each of its five eclectic suites (from around US$410) – housed in a series of imaginatively landscaped pavilions – an individual masterpiece of original design. The food is superb (and well worth the trip even if you're not staying: lunch Rs.2500; dinner Rs.3250), and facilities include a fabulous infinity pool, gym and massage room, but the emphasis is on privacy, intimacy and tranquillity.

Back in the real world are Koggala's pair of mid-market resort hotels, the better of which is the *Koggala Beach* (ⓣ091-228 3243, ⓦwww.koggalabeach.com; ❻), a rather faded but not unattractive resort with tidily refurbished sea-facing rooms; the room-only rate is quite good value, but watch the outrageous US$25 surcharge for breakfast.

Martin Wickramasinghe Museum

Directly opposite *The Fortress*, the excellent **Martin Wickramasinghe Museum** (daily 9am–5pm; Rs.200) is inspired by – and partly devoted to – the life, works and ideas of Martin Wickramasinghe, one of the most important Sinhalese cultural figures of the twentieth century. A prolific writer, Wickramasinghe penned fourteen Sinhala-language novels and eight collections of short stories, plus some forty non-fiction books on subjects ranging from Buddhism to cultural anthropology – all of which played an important part in establishing Sinhala as a viable literary alternative to English at a time when the language was particularly threatened by Western influence. Wickramasinghe was deeply attached to Koggala and remained very much a local boy at heart – his birthplace and grave (both now part of the museum) lie just a few metres apart – although the traditional rural village which he grew up in (and idealized in his work) has now largely vanished.

The site is divided into several different sections. The excellent **Folk Museum** houses an absorbing selection of exhibits pertaining to the daily practical and spiritual life of the Sinhalese – everything from catching a fish to chasing off malevolent spirits. Displays include various Buddha statuettes, assorted Kandyan costumes, cute cow bells, implements used in traditional industries such as rubber collection, toddy tapping and cinnamon gathering, along with the wooden rattles and bows and arrows used to scare birds from paddy fields. You'll also find an excellent collection of traditional masks depicting assorted characters, including an unusual pair of red-faced British officers and a couple of "sand boards" – trays of sand which were used to practise writing – the Sri Lankan equivalent of a blackboard.

Behind the museum is a display of traditional modes of transport, including a high-speed bull-racing cart, while at the rear of the grounds stands the **house** in which Wickramasinghe was born and grew up with his nine sisters. The **Hall of Life**, attached to the house, is devoted to Wickramasinghe's life, though it gives disappointingly little information on the man himself. Wickramasinghe's simple **grave** stands right by the side of the house.

Kataluwa Purvarama Mahavihara

Around 5km beyond Koggala lies one of the south's most absorbing temples, the **Kataluwa Purvarama Mahavihara**. The temple is interesting principally for the remarkable Kandyan-style **wall paintings** in the main shrine, dating from the late nineteenth century – a resident monk will probably materialize to explain some of the most notable panels. The four walls were painted by different artists in competition (no one seems to know who won) and illustrate various Jatakas and other cautionary Buddhist tales, peopled with detailed crowds of meticulously executed figures including various colonial bigwigs and – strangely enough – a rather lopsided, characteristically dour Queen Victoria, placed here to commemorate her support for native Buddhism in the face of British missionary Christianity. The inner shrine (mind your head: the doors are built purposefully low to force you to bow as you enter the presence of the Buddha) contains further Buddha figures, as well as a black Vishnu and a blue Katargama.

The temple lies about 3km inland from the coastal highway; various side roads (a couple of them signed) lead to it from the main road, though the road layout is slightly confusing, so you'll have to ask for directions locally.

Handunugoda Tea Estate

The **Handunugoda Tea Estate** (7am–6pm; free), around 4km inland from the Kataluwa junction, is renowned locally for the remarkably high quality of its teas given such low altitude. It's particularly celebrated as one of Sri Lanka's few producers of highly prized white tea – a silverish-white brew with a very delicate flavour. It's also one of the planet's most expensive brews, retailing at around US$1400 per kilo. Rubber and cinnamon, as well as coconuts, are also grown here, and guided tours of the plantation provide an informative overview of the production and treatment of all four crops; the highlight is a tea-tasting session of over twenty varieties (with cake) at the main plantation bungalow overlooking the estate.

Ahangama and Midigama

The road from Koggala to Midigama runs close to the ocean for much of the way, in many places squeezing the beach into a narrow ribbon of sand between the tarmac and the waves. A few kilometres beyond Koggala, the town of **AHANGAMA** is famous for having the greatest concentration of **stilt fishermen** along the entire coast, and also has some decent surf. Thanks to the proximity to the highway to the sea, this is one of the few areas along the south coast where there's still evidence of tsunami damage.

A couple of kilometres further on, the scattered village of **MIDIGAMA** has some of the best surfing in the island, though the village is very small and sleepy and apart from at its far eastern end the beach is rather narrow and exposed – unless you're here to surf, there's not a lot to do. West of tiny Midigama village, a clutch of low-key guesthouses straggle along the beach and road (which are very close together here); the quaint little clocktower at the village's centre makes a useful landmark when you're trying to work out where to get off the bus. *Subodanee* and a few other guesthouses rent out **surfboards** at around Rs.300 per hr or Rs.1100 per day.

Accommodation

Note that the surfer-oriented places in Midigama tend to close during the low season (mid-April to Oct), or are turned upside down with repairs. The following are listed in the order you reach them travelling from west to east.

Ahangama

Kabalana Beach Hotel 500m past the 133km post ⓣ091-228 3294, ⓦwww.kabalana.com. Ahangama's smartest option, close to its best surfing point and set on a fairly broad section of beach. Standard rooms (in the main building) and beach-front cabanas are all furnished in a heavily colonial idiom – antique-style furniture and crisp white linen – with rather more modern a/c, satellite TV and minibar, and there's a good-sized pool. ❻–❼

Ahangama Easy Beach At the 136km post ⓣ091-228 2028, ⓦwww.easybeach.info. Norwegian-run, this prettily flower-bedecked guest-house has a mix of smart (a/c and non-a/c) modern rooms and a/c concrete cabanas. There's also an attractive restaurant with a broad-ranging menu, internet and wi-fi, plus surfboards for rent, though the beach is rather narrow. Rooms ❹, cabanas ❺

Midigama

Villa Gaetano 750m beyond the 137km post, just beyond the river ⓣ091-228 3968, ⓦwww.internet-window.de/gamini. Well-run hotel offering modern, comfortable and very good-value rooms with hot water, minibar and a/c (US$4 supplement). There's also a pleasant restaurant with an imaginative menu (excellent seafood), internet access, snorkelling gear (turtles can sometimes be seen just offshore, along with various tropical fish) and an extremely informative owner who can point you towards various local attractions. ❸

Surfer's Dream/Sita's Garden 500m past *Villa Gaetano* (not signposted) ⓣ091-228 3968. Opposite a small dagoba down a short track inland off the main road, tiny *Surfer's Dream* has four very simple and cheap rooms and a small restaurant. *Sita's Garden* comprises a rather smarter pair of all-wood cabanas across the rail line behind. Both are owned by *Villa Gaetano*. ❶–❸

Subodanee Down the side road from the clocktower, diagonally opposite the train station ⓣ091-228 3383. Cheap and cheerful surfers' place with a mix of basic budget rooms (some with shared bath), smarter modern tiled doubles, plus some pricier new cabanas a couple of minutes' walk inland. There's also a decent range of food. Rooms ❶–❷, cabanas ❹

Ram's Surfing Beach At the 139km post, 300m east of the clocktower ⓣ041-225 2639. Very friendly surfers' place with a mix of cheap and basic rooms and smarter modern doubles, plus a popular restaurant, though it's right on the main road so can be noisy. ❶–❷

Villa Tissa 200m after the 140km post, 100m off the main road ⓣ041-225 3434, ⓦwww.villatissa.com. Very attractive and peaceful small hotel set in three interconnecting reproduction Dutch-style villas at the picturesque eastern end of Midigama Bay, with stilt posts and a safe, reef-protected swimming area just offshore. Rooms are beautifully furnished in colonial style, and the attractive veranda restaurant features a varied Sri Lankan and Western menu. There's also a lovely pool in the neatly tended garden. Good value. ❻

Weligama

Twenty-three kilometres east of Unawatuna, the sleepy fishing town of **WELIGAMA** ("Sandy Village") meanders around a broad and beautiful bay, dotted with rocky outcrops and fringed with fine golden sand. It's an attractive spot, which has never really caught on as a destination for foreign tourists – though this may change with the arrival of a pair of upmarket resort hotels. For now, however, things remain pretty somnolent and there's not much to do other than stare at the sea – which may be exactly what you're after.

Weligama itself is surprisingly attractive as Sri Lankan towns go: quiet and relatively traffic-free, its modest commercial centre trailing off into lush streets

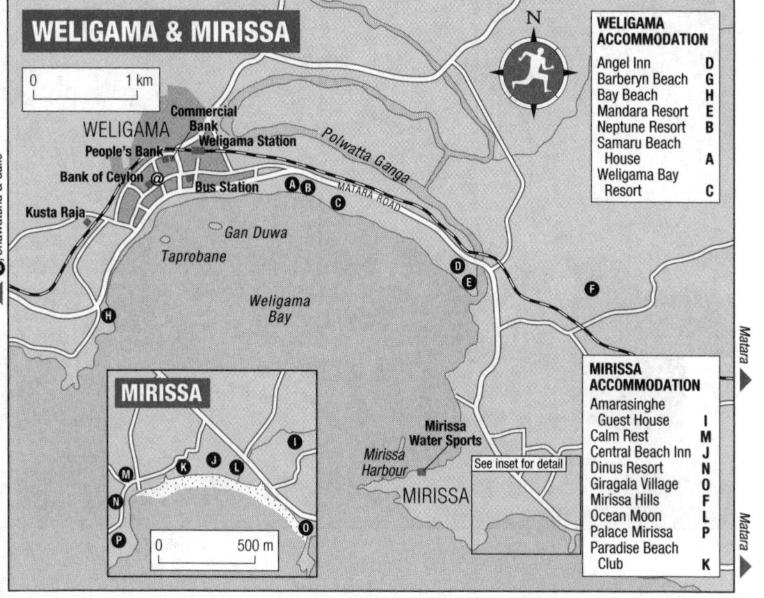

of pretty gingerbread villas decorated with ornate *mal lali* wooden fretwork, while along the well-tended seafront road ladies sit out in front of their houses hunched over pieces of lace, a local speciality since Dutch times. At the western edge of town, near the rail line, stands a large megalith carved (probably sometime during the eighth or ninth centuries) with a three-metre figure known as **Kusta Raja**, the "Leper King", usually thought to show an unknown Sinhalese monarch who was miraculously cured of leprosy by drinking nothing but coconut milk for three months. An alternative theory claims it as a depiction of a Mahayana Bodhisattva, possibly Avalokitesvara or Samantabhadra – a claim lent credence by the carvings of meditating Buddhas in the figure's tiara.

The waters of **Weligama Bay** are relatively exposed, and suffer from pollution close to the town – ask at your guesthouse about where's safe to swim. The bay's most prominent feature is the minuscule island of **Taprobane**, just offshore, virtually invisible under a thick covering of luxuriant trees. The island was owned during the 1930s by the exiled French Count de Maunay, who built the exquisite white villa that still stands, its red-tiled roof poking up through the trees; the whole lot is available for rent (see p.170). The prettiest part of the bay is around Taprobane, where dozens of colourful outrigger **catamarans** pull up on the beach between fishing expeditions; you may be able to negotiate a trip round the bay with one of the local fishermen.

If you want to get out into the water, you can arrange **diving** through Bavarian Divers at the *Bay Beach* hotel (see p.190; ⓣ041-225 2708, ⓦwww.cbg.de/bavariandivers), a German-run diving school offering the standard range of PADI courses plus dives to local sites including coral reefs, the underwater rocks of the Yala Rock complex and the wreck of the SS *Rangoon*, which sank just outside Galle harbour in 1863. There's also some good **surfing** in the centre of the bay between December and April; equipment can be rented from *Neptune Resort* and *Samaru Beach House*, both of which also offer lessons for around

▲ Fishing boats at Weligama

Rs.1000. Several of the guesthouses also offer **boat trips** on the Polwatta Ganga, which flows behind the town a few hundred metres inland.

Practicalities

Buses stop at the well-signed bus station in the centre of Weligama, a block inland from the bay. Weligama is also a major stop on the Matara–Colombo railway; the **train station** is in the town centre a block inland from the bus station. There are branches of the Commercial Bank, People's Bank and Bank of Ceylon in the town centre, each of which has **ATMs** accepting foreign cards. The small **post office** is directly opposite the train station. Most of the hotels and guesthouses offer **internet** access, though there's cheaper online access at Weligama Nenasala (8.30am–5.30pm; Rs.50 per hr), on the first floor of the orange building next to the Bank of Ceylon on Main Street (no English sign).

Weligama has a good range of **accommodation**, spread out along the beach. There's nowhere much to eat in town, though all the hotels and guesthouses offer **food**. The places below are marked on the map on p.189.

Accommodation

Angel Inn ⓣ041-225 0475. Spacious and sparklingly clean white rooms (a/c or non-a/c) in an attractive three-storeyed guesthouse, plus four cutesy (though rather more basic) wooden cabanas, unusually sited on the road side rather than the beach, and a garden with a small pool leading down to the beach. Excellent value. ❸

Barberyn Beach 4km west of Weligama ⓣ041-225 2994, ⓦwww.barberynresorts.com. An offshoot of the long-established *Barberyn Reef* in Beruwala, this beautiful Ayurveda resort has sixty rooms in extensive beachfront grounds and a huge range of treatments for around US$90 per day. Full board only. ❼

Bay Beach ⓣ041-225 0201, ⓦwww.baybeachhotel.com. Once Weligama's smartest option, this rather faded resort hotel occupies a superb location at the top end of the bay, with marvellous views of myriad colourful fishing boats moored just offshore. Rooms are bit dated but comfortable and come with TV and individual terrace; there's also a pool and a breezy restaurant. ❺

Mandara Resort ⓣ041-567 6762, ⓦwww.mandararesort.com. Weligama's most stylish option (though not its most expensive) has a

Moving on from Weligama

Few **bus** services originate in Weligama (most are in transit between Galle, Matara and Colombo), so you'll have to take your chances with what's passing through. There should be at least one bus in each direction every fifteen minutes, with services west to **Galle** (45min) and **Colombo** (3hr 45min) and east to **Matara** (30min), **Tangalla** (1hr 45min), **Hambantota** (3hr) and **Tissamaharama** (3hr 20min). For **train** services, see the timetable on p.165 for details.

gorgeous position at the eastern end of the bay. It's designed on a sub-Bawa template, with breezy public areas leading through a long, narrow pool, while the spacious rooms (with DVD player and sound system) are furnished in attractive, minimalist style; the best have a good-sized plunge pool or jacuzzi. ❽–❾

Neptune Resort ⓣ041-225 0803, ⓦwww.neptune-resort.com. Bright and welcoming place, with spacious, well-furnished rooms in striking hexagonal-shaped two-storey cabanas (some with a/c for an extra Rs.1000), or (cheaper) in the attractive main building. There's also an appealingly rustic, coir-canopied restaurant, plus internet, wi-fi, surfboard rental and boat trips on the Polwatta Ganga. Rooms ❹, cabanas ❺

Samaru Beach House ⓣ041-225 1417. Probably the top budget option in town, right on the beach with spotless modern rooms outside the main building or darker and simpler rooms inside – all are excellent value. There are also surfboards (Rs.1000 per day) and bikes (Rs.400 per day) for rent. ❷–❸

Weligama Bay Resort ⓣ041-225 3920, ⓦwww.weligamabayresort.com. Weligama's glitzy new Czech-run five-star feels like it's been airlifted straight from Beruwala. Rooms, in two neat lines of villas leading down to an inviting beachside pool, are beautifully furnished and stuffed full of mod cons, though overall it's a bit lacking in class: ideal for those who can't live without Playstations, Ferrero Rocher and Premier League football. ❾

Mirissa

A couple of kilometres beyond Weligama, the picture-perfect swathe of sand at the village of **MIRISSA** was formerly the island's most famously "undiscovered" beach. The days when you could expect to have the place almost to yourself are long gone, but although the village now attracts a steady stream of visitors, its beach remains one of the prettiest in the island, with a narrow strip of sand backed by a dense thicket of coconut palms which manage to camouflage most signs of human presence.

Mirissa is also the starting point for trips to view Sri Lanka's most exciting new wildlife attraction – **blue whales**, which between December and April can be seen just a few kilometres offshore (see box, p.192). With whale-watching still in its infancy, trips are for now run only by **Mirissa Water Sports** (ⓣ0773 597 731, ⓦwww.mirissawatersports.com; Rs.5750 per person for 2hr; Rs.3250 per person per additional hour; minimum four people), though as word spreads this is likely to change. Boats leave from the village's picturesque harbour, in the southeastern corner of Weligama Bay around 1km west of Mirissa beach, and can be arranged via any of the guesthouses in town.

The fact that all the guesthouses here are concentrated in a much smaller area than in Weligama means that Mirissa is a bit livelier, though it's still pretty comatose. There's reasonable **swimming**, though conditions vary considerably along different parts of the beach, so it's worth asking at your guesthouse about where's safe to swim before venturing into the water. You can also **snorkel** here, though you won't see much apart from the occasional pretty fish. Snorkelling "safaris" and numerous **other watersports**, including sport fishing and sea kayaking, as well as cruises around the bay and beyond, can be arranged with Mirissa Water Sports.

On the trail of the whale

Sri Lanka has often been mooted as a possible **whale-watching destination**, with numerous sightings of these giant mammals reported over the years at various places around the island. When it actually came to putting together whale-watching trips, however, local tour operators were stumped. The lack of properly equipped vessels was one problem, as was the commonly held belief that the best place for spotting whales was in the waters around the troubled city of Trincomalee, which has been off limits for long periods during the past three decades. And tour operators and wildlife enthusiasts who did go out looking for whales generally felt like they were searching for needles in a very large and very wet haystack.

This, at least, was the situation until 1999, when **Dr Charles Anderson**, a British marine biologist living in the Maldives, proposed a theory that there was an annual migration of blue and sperm whales between the Bay of Bengal and around the coast of Sri Lanka to the Arabian Sea (heading west in April, and returning in the opposite direction in Dec/Jan). He also suggested that the best place to look for the whales would be around Dondra Head, at the southernmost point of the island. This is where the continental shelf on which Sri Lanka sits is at its narrowest, with ocean depths of 1km within 6km of the coast – ideal whale country.

The spooky accuracy of Anderson's theory was rapidly borne out by staff at **Mirissa Water Sports** (see p.191), a new company set up in the wake of the tsunami, whose crew began recording a long string of whale sightings which seemed to confirm the dramatic discovery that Sri Lanka was sitting alongside one of the world's great cetacean migratory routes. By April 2008, two of the island's largest tour operators, including eco-tourism leaders Jetwing, had begun to offer trips, and were optimistically announcing Sri Lanka as one of the world's top two or three whale-watching destinations. The figures so far seem to bear them out (for a log of the latest sightings, check out Ⓦwww.jetwingeco.com/index.cfm?section=page&id=1081), with sightings of these huge but strangely elusive creatures almost guaranteed from December through until April, and the possibility of seeing both sperm and blue whales (not to mention spinner dolphins) in a single trip.

For more on the island's whales and dolphins, see p.455.

Practicalities

Mirissa village is mostly packed into a compact area between the harbour to the west, headland to the south and Matara road to the north and east. **Buses** whizz up and down the Matara road every few minutes; when arriving, make sure the conductor knows to let you off, since Mirissa is easily missed. When leaving, you'll have to flag something down along the main road. The village has its own **train** station, though as only slow services stop here and it's a bit of a way from the village, it's easier to catch the bus. **Internet** access is sporadically available at the village's various guesthouses; ask around to see who's got a machine that's currently in working order.

There are no culinary treats in Mirissa, but if you want to eat away from your guesthouse the village boasts a few simple but acceptable **beach cafés**, all offering the usual seafood dishes, noodles and rice and curry. The following places are all marked on the map on p.189.

Accommodation

Amarasinghe Guest House 500m inland from the coastal highway, signposted from almost opposite the *Ocean Moon* guesthouse Ⓣ041-225 1204, Ⓦwww.geocities.com/chanamirissa. Some distance from the beach, but the idyllic rural location, surrounded by lush gardens full of birds and the occasional monkey, is ample compensation. Accommodation is in a range of rooms (in the family house) and bungalows (in the garden) of varying sizes and prices. Free internet. ❶–❸

Calm Rest ⓣ041-490 7984, ⓔrangasuleshana@yahoo.com. One of the nicest guesthouses in Mirissa, with a few smallish but comfy rooms plus some attractively rustic cabanas, all set in a pretty garden. There's also an attractive open-air restaurant. Rooms ❸, cabanas ❹
Central Beach Inn ⓣ041-225 1699. Budget guesthouse with neat, clean and simple rooms in functional concrete chalets, and larger but rather dark cabanas – all set in attractive flowering gardens. Rooms ❶, cabanas ❷
Dinus Resort ⓣ041-225 3610, ⓔdinumirissa@yahoo.com. Newly expanded guesthouse at the western end of the bay, with a decent mix of accommodation: cheap rooms in the simple main house, and pricier but more attractive ones in the striking new orange-and-white building, which has good views of the bay from its upper storey. ❷–❹
Giragala Village ⓣ041-225 0496, ⓦwww.geocities.com/giragala. Refreshingly breezy location on the grassy defile at the eastern end of the beach, with simple but comfortable rooms in functional concrete accommodation blocks dotted around spacious grounds. Sheltered by Giragala rock, the bay here is safe for swimming. ❹
Mirissa Hills ⓣ041-225 0980, ⓦwww.mirissahills.com. Set on a working cinnamon plantation in lush countryside around 2km inland from the beach, this superb new retreat has a range of stylish, beautifully furnished accommodation. Room rates at The Bungalow, a restored *walauwa*, and The Museum – where Sri Lanka's first cinnamon museum will open in 2010 – are very reasonable. The highlight is the gorgeous hilltop "Mount Cinnamon" villa (sleeps eight; US$850 per night), complete with exquisite contemporary Sri Lankan artwork (including an extraordinary screen by Laki Senanayake; see p.146) and a magnificent panorama of the surrounding countryside. ❻
Ocean Moon ⓣ041-225 2328. Friendly place with a selection of comfortable and reasonably priced modern concrete cabanas and a few cheaper and more basic rooms. Rooms ❶, cabanas ❷
Palace Mirissa ⓣ041-225 1303, ⓦwww.palacemirissa.com. Set in a magnificent position on the headland overlooking Mirissa Bay, this is the smartest option within walking distance of the beach. Scattered amongst rambling gardens, accommodation is in spacious and attractive – but expensive – stilted concrete cabanas, all with a/c, TV and ocean views. There's also a banana-shaped pool and very average food. Half-board rates only. ❼
Paradise Beach Club ⓣ041-225 1206, ⓔmirissa@sltnet.lk. Finally restored to full capacity after a long lay-off following the tsunami, this popular, laid-back but rather pricey establishment is the closest Mirissa gets to a proper resort. Accommodation is either in simple, slightly cramped concrete cabanas scattered around attractive gardens by the beach, or the newer, more comfortable and more expensive two-storey block behind. The main drawback is the average buffet food and compulsory half-board. ❺

Matara and around

Close to the southernmost point of the island, the bustling town of **MATARA** (pronounced "*maat*-rah" the middle syllable is virtually elided) provides a taste of everyday Sri Lanka that may (or may not) be welcome if you've spent time in the coastal resorts. Standing at the terminus of the country's southern rail line, the town is an important transport hub and a major centre of commerce – a lively place given a youthful touch by the presence of students from **Ruhunu University**, 3km east of town. Matara preserves a few Dutch colonial buildings, an atmospheric old fort area and an attractive seafront (though you wouldn't want to swim here). A couple of kilometres either side of town, the low-key beachside suburbs of **Polhena** and **Medawatta** offer good snorkelling and surfing respectively, while the area **around Matara** boasts a couple of mildly interesting and little-visited sights, including the giant Buddha and unusual underground temple at **Weherehena** and the town of **Dondra**, whose slender lighthouse marks the island's southernmost point.

Matara itself (from Mahatara, or "Great Harbour") is an ancient settlement, though no traces of anything older than the colonial era survive. The Portuguese used the town intermittently, but it was the Dutch, attracted by the deep and sheltered estuary of the Nilwala Ganga, who established a lasting presence here, fortifying the town and making it an important centre for cinnamon and elephant trading.

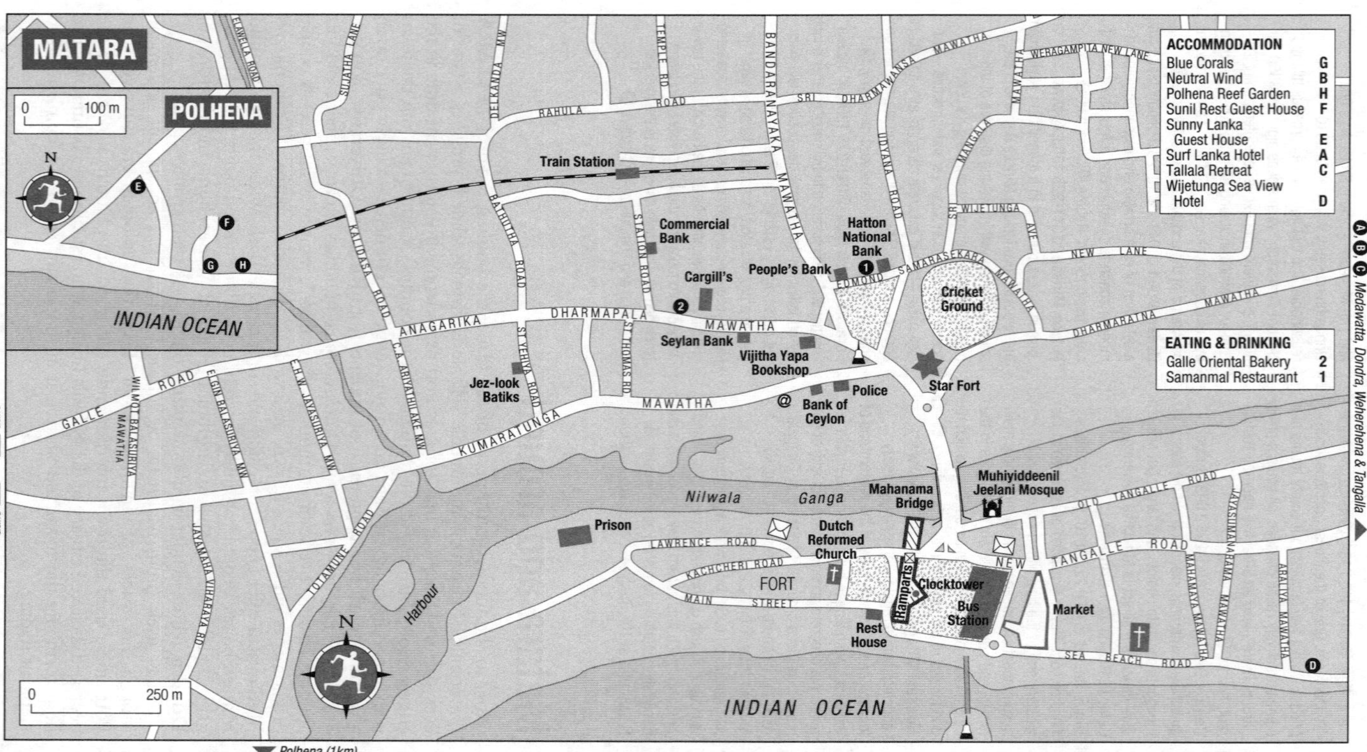
MATARA
POLHENA
0 100 m
N
E
F
G
H
INDIAN OCEAN
ACCOMMODATION
Blue Corals G
Neutral Wind B
Polhena Reef Garden H
Sunil Rest Guest House F
Sunny Lanka Guest House E
Surf Lanka Hotel A
Tallala Retreat C
Wijetunga Sea View Hotel D
EATING & DRINKING
Galle Oriental Bakery 2
Samanmal Restaurant 1
A, B, C, Medawatta, Dondra, Weherehena & Tangalla
Train Station
Commercial Bank
Cargill's
People's Bank
Hatton National Bank
Cricket Ground
Star Fort
Seylan Bank
Vijitha Yapa Bookshop
Police
Bank of Ceylon
Jez-look Batiks
Muhiyiddeenil Jeelani Mosque
Mahanama Bridge
Nilwala Ganga
Prison
Dutch Reformed Church
FORT
Ramparts
Clocktower
Bus Station
Market
Rest House
Harbour
INDIAN OCEAN
0 250 m
Galle
Galle
Polhena (1km)
ELAWELLA ROAD
SUJATHA LANE
DELKANDA MW
TEMPLE RD
RAHULA ROAD
BANDARANAYAKA MAWATHA
SRI DHARMAWANSA MAWATHA
WERAGAMPITA NEW LANE
MAWATHA
MANGALA
UDYANA ROAD
SRI WIJETUNGA AVE
NEW LANE
SAMARASEKARA MAWATHA
EDMOND
DHARMARATNA MAWATHA
STATION ROAD
KALIDASA ROAD
BATHUTHA ROAD
ANAGARIKA DHARMAPALA MAWATHA
ST THOMAS RD
ST YEHIYA ROAD
C.A. ARIYATHILAKE MW
E.H.W. JAYASURIYA MW
ELGIN BALASURIYA MW
WILMOT BALASURIYA MAWATHA
GALLE ROAD
KUMARATUNGA MAWATHA
JAYAMAHA VIHARAYA RD
TOTAMUNE ROAD
LAWRENCE ROAD
KACHCHERI ROAD
MAIN STREET
OLD TANGALLE ROAD
NEW TANGALLE ROAD
JAYASUMANARAMA MAWATHA
MAHAMAYA MAWATHA
ARALIYA MAWATHA
SEA BEACH ROAD

Arrival

Matara's large and unusually well-organized **bus station** is next to the old ramparts, south of the river, and convenient for *Wijetunga Sea View Hotel*. The **train station** is just north of the town centre. A tuktuk from either terminal to Polhena shouldn't cost more than Rs.250, or Rs.200 to Medawatta. For information on moving on from Matara, see the box on p.197.

There are various banks scattered across town with **ATMs** that accept foreign Visa and MasterCards. The smart modern **post office** is opposite the north end of the bus station; you can make international **phone calls** here. The best place for **internet** access is Dimuthu Internet Café, at 33/1 Kumaratunga Mw (daily 9am–6pm; Rs.40 per hr), about 200m west of the Buddhist temple on the corner with Angarika Dharmapala Mawatha. There's a decent Vijitha Yapa **bookshop** 100m west or so along Dharmapala Mawatha, and a Cargill's Food City **supermarket** (and pharmacy) in the old Broadway Cinema, 200m further west.

Accommodation

Matara town suffers from a chronic lack of **places to stay**, and many foreign visitors choose to stay in the suburbs of **Polhena**, a couple of kilometres west of town, or **Medawatta**, about 1.5km east, both of which have a reasonable range of cheap accommodation.

Matara town

Wijetunga Sea View Hotel Beach Rd ⓣ041-223 4700, ⓔwijetunga@yahoo.com. Central Matara's cheeriest option, with brand-new, bright-blue a/c rooms. Recently returned from Italy, the owner has brought back a hint of Mediterranean chic – and serves pasta alongside the usual suspects in the restaurant. Fan ❸, a/c ❹

Polhena

Blue Corals ⓣ0777 600 803. Three good-value modern tiled rooms in a tall blue building close to the beach. The owner, Nishantha, runs snorkelling (see p.197) and diving trips, and can also arrange boat tours along the Nilwala Ganga (Rs.5000 per six-person boat) and rent out motorbikes (Rs.700 per day) and bikes (Rs.150, or free for guests). ❶

Polhena Reef Garden ⓣ041-222 2478, ⓔprgh@sltnet.lk. Polhena's poshest option, with spacious if rather old-fashioned a/c rooms with hot water and private balconies. A new pool should be ready by the time you read this. ❹, a/c ❺

Sunil Rest Guest House ⓣ0777 611 787, ⓔsunilrestpolhena@yahoo.com. Polhena's friendliest, liveliest and best-organized guesthouse, with a range of inexpensive and comfortable rooms (if you're not put off by the bright shade of pink), including some on the beach. There's also a music room – fun for bashing around on Sri Lankan instruments – TV/DVD room, regular barbecues, plenty of trips, bikes for hire (Rs.100 per day) and internet (Rs.50–60 per hr). ❶–❷

Sunny Lanka Guest House ⓣ041-222 3504, ⓔsunnyamare@yahoo.com. One of Polhena's budget stalwarts. Rooms are large, clean and rather bare, but very good value at the price. ❶

Medawatta

Neutral Wind ⓣ0777 621 160. Small, friendly, family-run place next to *Surf Lanka*, popular with long-term surfers, with clean rooms in a cheerfully painted house. ❷

Surf Lanka Hotel ⓣ041-222 8190, ⓦwww.surf-lanka.com. The smartest place in Medawatta, with a range of bright and spacious rooms in an airy if rather functional white building right above Secret Point; more expensive ones have a/c, TV and jacuzzi tubs. ❹–❻

Around Matara

Talalla Retreat Gandara, 11km east of Matara ⓣ041 225 9171, ⓦwww.talallaretreat.com. Wonderfully tranquil Australian-owned retreat, set in extensive coconut-palm gardens just 50m from a two-kilometre stretch of unspoilt beach. Accommodation is in attractive two-storey chalets supported on slender columns, and you'll feel at one with the elements: upper rooms eschew glass in favour of slatted bamboo blinds, and there are outdoor marble bathrooms throughout. The food is good, too – limited in range but well prepared and wholesome – and treatments in the simple spa are reasonably priced. ❼

The Town

As at Galle, Matara divides into two areas: the **modern town** and the old Dutch colonial district, known as the **Fort**. The two are separated by the **Nilwala Ganga**, a fine and remarkably unspoilt swathe of water, edged by thick stands of palm trees and spanned by the town's most impressive modern construction: the six-lane **Mahanama Bridge**, constructed with Korean help and unveiled in 2007 on the third anniversary of the tsunami.

The Fort and seafront

Matara's main **Fort** lies on the narrow spit of land south of the river, its eastern side bounded by a long line of stumpy **ramparts**, built by the Dutch in the eighteenth century and topped by the inevitable ugly white British clocktower of 1883. At the north end of the ramparts, a dilapidated **gateway** (dated 1780) marks the original entrance to the Fort, from which a short walk across an untidy green brings you to the restored **Dutch Reformed Church**, one of the earliest Dutch churches in Sri Lanka – a large and rather austere gabled structure almost invisible beneath its huge pitched roof. The rest of the Fort comprises an interesting district of lush, tree-filled streets dotted with fine old colonial-era houses in various stages of picturesque disrepair – some are surprisingly palatial, with big colonnaded facades and sweeping verandas – although sadly a combination of unrestrained traffic and insensitive development is beginning seriously to erode the area's atmospheric character. At the far west end of the Fort, the peninsula tapers off to a narrow spit of land at the confluence of the Nilwala Ganga and the sea, where there's a pretty new harbour.

Head back towards the ramparts along the Fort's Main Street, passing Matara's dilapidated old *Rest House*, which was destroyed by the tsunami and sadly shows no sign of reopening. East from here, the **seafront** has been prettified since the tsunami with park benches and a promenade, and makes an attractive place for a stroll if you don't mind the hooting traffic of the main road. Opposite the bus station, a rather wobbly new pedestrian suspension bridge (this time provided by the Japanese) leads across to the red-tiled roofs of a tiny **island temple**, of no great architectural merit in itself but a peaceful spot with wonderful views of the ocean behind. A few paces east of the bus station, Matara's cacophonous indoor morning **market** is worth a quick foray, its stalls piled high with bug-eyed fish and fruit and veg in all manner of shapes.

Heading north towards the river, the striking white building at the southern end of the Mahanama Bridge is the **Muhiyiddeenil Jeelani** mosque, though it looks far more like a Portuguese Baroque church than a place of Islamic worship.

The Star Fort and the new town

Cross the bridge to the far side of the river to reach Matara's other Dutch stronghold: the diminutive **Star Fort**, a quaint little hexagonal structure built to protect the river crossing to the main Fort area and surrounded by a dirty-green moat in which the Dutch once kept crocodiles. Thoroughly cleaned and restored to its original hues, the entrance gate is emblazoned "Redoute Van Eck 1763", commemorating the governor under whose administration it was constructed, and sports a fully working wooden drawbridge. The caretaker will take you up onto the less than intimidating ramparts for fine views over Matara's attractive cricket ground (which takes all of thirty seconds) and show you around the minuscule interior, which comprises a couple of empty rooms, a central well and rainwater drain edged with coral paving stones, and two tiny prison cells to either side of the gate, each of which was allegedly used to hold up to 25 inmates.

North of here, the **new town** sprawls away in all directions. Turn left beyond the prominent Buddhist temple to head down **Anagarika Dharmapala Mawatha**, the area's principal thoroughfare, a heaving, gridlocked confusion of vehicles and pedestrians. About 500m west along here, an unprepossessing house in a small side street hides **Jez-look Batiks** (☎041-222 2142), one of the best batik workshops in the south, run by the personable Jezima Mohamed, who will make up your own designs if you fancy. They also make gorgeous silk and even jute batiks, as well as clothes.

Polhena and Medawatta

A couple of kilometres west of the centre of Matara, the rather down-at-heel beachside suburb of **Polhena** has some good **snorkelling** straight off the beach, with lots of colourful fish and a small section of live coral; swimming conditions and visibility are best outside the monsoon period. Snorkelling equipment can be rented from *Sunil Rest* for Rs.200 per day, and the knowledgeable local snorkelling guides Titus (c/o *Hotel TK Green Garden*; ☎041-222 2603) and Nishantha (c/o *Blue Corals*) charge Rs.400 (including equipment) for two-hour trips.

At the picturesque eastern end of Matara Bay, about 1.5km east of the town, another low-key suburb, **Medawatta**, is popular with long-term surfers who come here to ride waves of up to 4m at **Secret Point**, best between November and March. Surfboards (Rs.1000 per day) can be hired from the *Surf Lanka* hotel.

Eating

There's not much choice when it comes to **eating** in Matara. The most characterful place in town is the *Galle Oriental Bakery*, on Anagarika Dharmapala Mawatha, a pleasantly old-fashioned local establishment with charmingly antiquated, white-smocked waiters. The very cheap food includes rice and curry, plus short eats, though with enough chilli in them to reduce you to tears.

Moving on from Matara

Matara is the south's major transport hub. The **bus station** is unusually orderly, with clearly marked bays and a helpful information office (although it's not signposted) in the outside corridor in the corner near the statue of a woman holding a baby. Eastbound services leave from the eastern side of the terminal; westbound services from the west. There are 24-hour services to **Colombo** (4hr–4hr 30min), with intercity expresses leaving every fifteen minutes and also calling at **Weligama** (30min) and **Galle** (1hr 15min). Heading east, there are services every fifteen minutes to **Tissamaharama** (3hr) via **Tangalla** (1hr 30min) and **Hambantota** (2hr 30min), though few direct buses to **Kataragama** (5 daily; 3hr 30min) – it's easiest to change at Tissa. Matara is also a good place from which to head up to the hill country. There are two buses daily to **Nuwara Eliya** (8hr), plus three daily services to **Bandarawela** (6hr) and **Ratnapura** (4hr) and one to **Badulla** (6hr). If you're heading to **Sinharaja**, there are frequent buses to **Akuressa** (every 10min; 45min), where you'll need to change for Deniyaya (there are also a few direct buses to Deniyaya, 3hr). There are also regular buses to **Embilipitiya** (every 20min; 2hr 30min) and a once-daily service to **Monaragala** (5hr). As ever, it pays to check the latest schedules in the information office in advance.

Matara stands at the end of the southern **rail** line from Colombo; see p.165 for details of services.

Alternatively, try the *Samanmal Restaurant*, immediately north of the cricket ground. This serves primarily as a local drinking hole, although the Sri Lankan-style Chinese food is cheap and surprisingly good – even though it's so gloomy inside you can hardly see what you're eating.

Around Matara

A few kilometres east of Matara and a couple of kilometres inland, the tiny village of **WEHEREHENA** is home to one of the island's largest Buddha statues, the focal point of a sprawling modern temple complex constructed on the site of a hidden underground temple built in the seventeenth century to escape the evangelical attentions of the Portuguese. Thirty-nine metres tall and set within a rather ugly shelter, the giant Buddha figure itself, shown in the seated *samadhi* position, is a thing of impressive size, if no particular beauty. Most of the temple is actually buried underground, with endless corridors decorated with around twenty thousand cartoon-style depictions of various Jatakas. Right underneath the giant Buddha, a monk will take your donation (Rs.100 is "suggested") and point out a mirror below in which you can see reflected a cache of precious gold and stone Buddhas buried in an underfloor vault. From here steps lead up to the giant Buddha itself – you can climb all the way up to the head, although there's not much to see. A big **perahera** is held here on the Unduvap poya day in early December.

The temple is a twenty-minute bus ride from Matara. Take **bus #349** from the central aisle (east side) of the bus station; departures are every thirty minutes. Alternatively, a tuktuk will cost around Rs.500 return, including waiting time.

Dondra

Around 5km southeast of Matara, the sleepy little town of **DONDRA** was formerly one of the south's most important religious centres, known as **Devi Nuwara** ("City of the Gods") and housing a great temple dedicated to Vishnu, amongst the most magnificent on the island until it was destroyed by the Portuguese in 1588. Nothing of the temple now survives apart from one ancient shrine, the **Galge**, a small, plain rectangular structure thought to date back to the seventh century AD, making it the oldest stone building in Sri Lanka. The shrine lies half a kilometre inland from the main crossroads in the middle of Dondra; turn left down a narrow lane just after the clocktower. After 400m you'll reach a rather flouncy modern white temple; the Galge lies up a short flight of steps in a grassy field on the slope immediately above.

The diminutive Galge pales into insignificance next to modern Dondra's main temple, the sprawling roadside **Devi Nuwara Devalaya**, right in the middle of town by the main road, complete with a huge standing Buddha (a copy of the Aukana Buddha – see p.355). One of the south's major festivals, the **Devi Nuwara Perahera**, is held at the temple every year on the Esala poya day (late July/early Aug).

Just over a kilometre south of town, the fifty-metre-high **Dondra lighthouse**, built in 1889, marks the **southernmost point** in Sri Lanka. You can climb the 222 steps to the top of the lighthouse (daily 9am–6.30pm; Rs.500, though you may be able to bargain this down) for huge views up and down the coast and a close look at the beam's beautifully maintained colonial machinery, still used to illuminate Dondra Head for the benefit of local shipping. Look south of here, and there's nothing but sea between you and Antarctica, over ten thousand miles distant.

To reach Dondra, take any **bus** heading eastwards out of Matara; you'll have to either walk or catch a tuktuk to the lighthouse itself.

Tangalla and around

Strung out along one of the south's most beautiful stretches of coastline, **TANGALLA** (or **Tangalle**) is amongst the region's more developed beach destinations, with a string of simple guesthouses – and a handful of upmarket hotels and villas – dotted along the coves and beaches which line the oceanfront here. Tourism has never taken off quite as much as the entrepreneurial locals would like, however, and although the substantial tsunami damage the resort suffered has now for the most part been repaired, Tangalla remains resolutely low-key compared to the resorts further west. What gives Tangalla added appeal, however, is the number of rewarding attractions in the surrounding countryside, including the **Hoo-maniya blowhole**, the giant Buddha and gaudy shrines of **Wewurukannala**, and the magnificent rock temples of **Mulkirigala**, all of which can be combined into a rewarding half-day excursion. In addition, the nearby beach at **Rekawa** is Sri Lanka's premier site for turtle-watching, while dedicated ornithologists might also fancy a trip to the little-visited **Kalametiya Bird Sanctuary**, home to a rich selection of marine birdlife, which can be combined with a visit to the mysterious plateau at **Ussangoda**.

Arrival

Buses stop at the bus station right in the middle of town by the clocktower. The Commercial Bank, People's Bank and Hatton National Bank in the

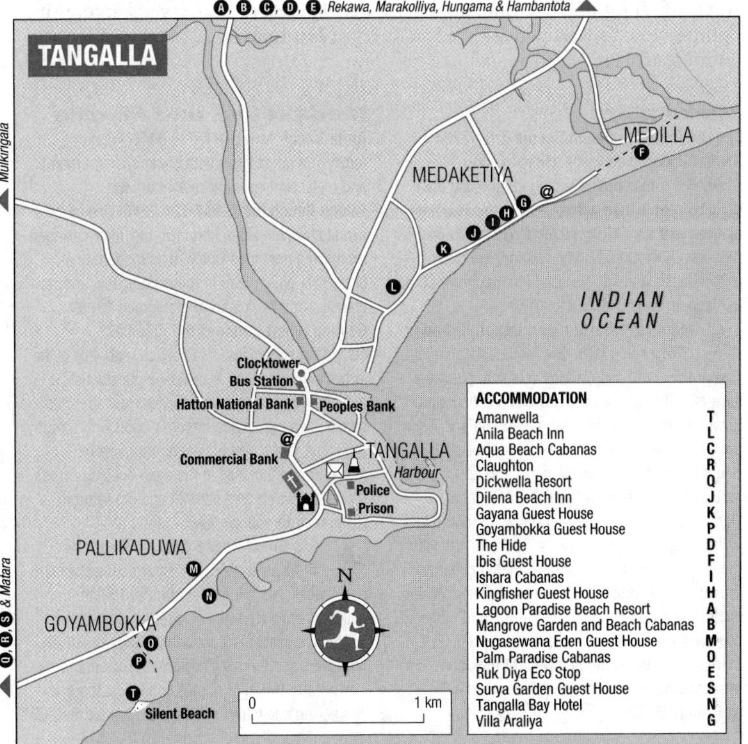

middle of town all have **ATMs** which accept foreign cards. Sawsiri Communications, on the southern side of the town centre (Mon–Sat 7.30am–5pm, Sun 7.30am–1pm; Rs.90 per hr), provides (slow) **internet** access; alternatively you can get online at *Gayana* and *Blue Horizon* guesthouses (both Rs.100 per hr), at either end of Medaketiya beach. Most of the guesthouses also rent out **bicycles** (Rs.200–250 per day).

Moving on from Tangalla there are services roughly every fifteen minutes west to Matara (1hr 30min), Weligama (1hr 45min), Galle (2hr 30min) and Colombo (5hr–5hr 30min); east to Hambantota (1hr 30min) and Tissamaharama (2hr); and north to Embilipitiya (1hr 30min).

Accommodation

Almost all accommodation in Tangalla is strung out along the beaches which stretch for several kilometres to either side of the workaday town of Tangalla itself. The biggest concentration of budget guesthouses is north of Tangalla at **Medaketiya**, while, further north, **Medilla** and particularly Kapuhenwala beach at **Marakolliya** (accessed by car from the main road only) boast some more characterful alternatives. South of Tangalla there are further options at **Pallikaduwa** and **Goyambokka** – the rustic accommodation at the latter is significantly more expensive, though given the idyllic setting you might be prepared to cough up the extra rupees.

If you're looking for something more upmarket, there are a handful of excellent options (plus some outstanding villas; see box, p.170) on the coast **west of Tangalla** en route to Dickwella. There are also several interesting options close to Kalametiya Bird Sanctuary at **Hungama**, 22km east of Tangalla en route to Hambantota.

Marakolliya

Lagoon Paradise Beach Resort ⓣ047-224 2509, ⓦlagoonparadisebeachresort.com. Occupying a memorable setting in rambling palm gardens next to the Rekawa lagoon, this is a fine alternative if the *Mangrove Garden* is full. Accommodation is in spacious and comfortable rooms and cabanas, and kayaks can be rented for trips on the lagoon. Rooms ❸, cabanas ❹

Mangrove Garden and Beach Cabanas ⓣ0777 906 018, ⓦwww.beachcabana.lk. One of the south coast's most magical places to stay, making full use of its superb position close to where the Rekawa lagoon meets the sea. There are two locations, a few hundred metres apart. Bounded on three sides by water and accessed by rope ferry across the lagoon, the *Mangrove Garden* is marginally the smarter, with rooms in stylish, high-ceilinged chalets. Back on "dry" land, the idyllic beachside wood-and-thatch cabanas are equally enchanting (*douze points* for guessing where the bathroom is). Catamarans and pedaloes are available to rent to explore the lagoon, and there's safe swimming in a natural rock pool, an attractive restaurant, and night-time turtle-watching. ❹–❺

Medaketiya and Medilla

Anila Beach Inn ⓣ047-224 0446. Friendly family-run guesthouse with cheap modern rooms and a pleasant open-air restaurant. ❶

Dilena Beach Inn ⓣ047-224 2240. One of the nicest cheapies along here: two big, high-ceilinged rooms in a neat little Dutch-style modern brick bungalow, plus a third in the main house, and an equally attractive platform restaurant. ❶–❷

Gayana Guest House ⓣ047-224 0477. Straddling both sides of the beach road, this is the largest, smartest and best set-up guesthouse in Medaketiya, though on a rather narrow stretch of beach. Clean a/c modern rooms, each with balcony, are either in the breezy beachfront block or (cheaper and fan only) in the main building across the road. There's also internet and big seafront restaurant. ❸–❹, a/c ❺

Ibis Guest House ⓣ047-567 4439, ⓦibis.jangan.ch. Medilla's most welcoming guesthouse, set in a pair of attractive white buildings amid a hammock-slung sandy garden. Rooms are spacious, comfortable and attractively furnished, and there's a chilled-out restaurant, internet (Rs.150 per hr), plus good local tours and snorkelling and windsurfing equipment for rent. ❹

Ishara Cabanas ⓣ0777 548 795. Four simple but funkily furnished rooms in a cute matching pair of concrete cabanas, each with little terraces/balconies, set a little way back from the beach. ❷

Kingfisher Guest House ⓣ047-224 2472. Friendly guesthouse with an informative owner and rather dark and basic but very cheap rooms, some with shared bath. Also a reasonable restaurant. ❶

Villa Araliya ⓣ047-224 2163. Medaketiya's most characterful place to stay, with a friendly dog and two nice bungalows set in abundant gardens and another room inside the main house, all furnished in quasi-colonial style. ❷, bungalows ❸

Pallikaduwa

Nugasewana Eden Guest House ⓣ047-224 0389, ⓦwww.nugasewana.com. Not a great setting, right on the main road, but the rooms (all with hot water, some with a/c) in this pleasant modern guesthouse are comfortable and spacious. Fan ❸–❹, a/c ❹

Tangalla Bay Hotel ⓣ047-224 0346, ⓦwww.tangallabayhotel.com. This memorably ugly hotel sits on top of one of the town's loveliest promontories like an enormous concrete wart. The interior is modelled on a ship, and is kind of fun, in a rather gloomy way, and the setting above the ocean is gorgeous. Rooms are fresh and clean, if a bit dated; all have hot water; a/c is available for a US$5 supplement and a TV for an extra US$10. There's also a small pool and attached diving centre. ❺–❻

Goyambokka

Amanwella ⓣ047-224 1333, ⓦwww.amanresorts.com. Set on Goyambokka's Godellawela Beach (or "Silent Beach", as it's generally known), this utterly captivating, shamelessly luxurious resort offers a model of how beach hotels in Sri Lanka should be done, with a stylishly understated, low-impact design which blends magically with the surrounding palm trees and water. The rooms are works of art in themselves, with all mod cons including large plunge pools and superb ocean views through huge French windows, and there's a sensational infinity pool overlooking the beach. Room rates vary dramatically: anything between US$400 and US$800 per night. ❾

Goyambokka Guest House ⓣ047-224 0838. The cheapest in Goyambokka, this intimate little guesthouse is set in a pretty house fronted by flower-filled gardens. Lovely from the outside, and with an attractive open-air restaurant, although the rooms are disappointingly basic and gloomy. ❸–❹

Palm Paradise Cabanas ⓣ047-224 0842, ⓦwww.palmparadisecabanas.net. Very popular place, set in beautiful beachside gardens, with accommodation in rustic – though rather gloomy and expensive – wooden cabanas. There's safe swimming nearby, a decent range of food, plus pricey internet access (but free wi-fi), Ayurvedic massages and bike rental. Half-board rates only in high season. ❻

West of Tangalla

Claughton Nilwella, 11km west of Tangalla ⓣ071-272 5470, ⓦwww.srilankayellowpages.com/claughton. Beautiful Geoffrey Bawa-designed establishment in a fabulous position on a breezy headland overlooking a harbour and the broad sweep of Nilwella beach. Rooms are an elegant blend of colonial and contemporary, and there's a spectacularly sited pool; the whole villa can be rented for around US$500–550 per night. ❼

Dickwella Resort Dickwella, 17km west of Tangalla ⓣ041-225 5271, ⓦwww.dickwella.net. First-rate Italian-owned resort in a superb location on a headland flanked by two gorgeous beaches, with stylish and luxuriously appointed rooms scattered around extensive gardens in a series of attractive Mediterranean-style white buildings. Diving and other watersports are available, and there's a large salt-water swimming pool, a new (and rather pricey) spa, and high-quality food including a Neapolitan-standard pizzeria. Half-board rates only. ❾

Surya Garden Guest House Seenimodera, 6km west of Tangalla ⓣ041-492 1258, ⓦwww.srilanka-vacanze.com. Laid-back Italian-owned guesthouse close to a fine stretch of beach, with accommodation in stylish bungalows with outdoor bathrooms, plus some simpler rooms, dotted around shady gardens. The rustic restaurant serves good Italian food. Rooms ❸, cabanas ❺

East of Tangalla: Hungama

AquaBeach Cabanas ⓣ047-492 0554, ⓦwww.aqua-beach.com. Set in a sandy palm garden on an endless stretch of deserted beach, this tranquil retreat has just four simple but very comfortable wooden cabanas, plus a seawater swimming pool, yoga pavilion and regular "wellness" programmes. Half-board only. ❻

The Hide ⓣ047-222 7148, ⓦwww.thehide.net. Beautifully restored old colonial mansion within walking distance of Kalametiya and set in a neatly planned garden brimful with fruit trees and herbal plants. The three high-ceilinged rooms are lovingly furnished with an interesting collection of antiques, and there's also a saltwater pool and excellent local food (no alcohol). Eighty percent of profits are ploughed back into local community projects. ❼–❽

RukDiya Eco Stop ⓣ047-567 2566. Rustic but clean family-owned guesthouse, with good (and very cheap) local food. The engaging owners coordinate an excellent programme of community-based local tours (see p.206), including camping trips to Kalametiya, and rent out bikes (Rs.300) and mopeds (Rs.700). ❶–❷

The town and beaches

Tangalla's beaches stretch for several kilometres either side of **Tangalla town**, a busy but unremarkable provincial centre with a dusty selection of shops and cafés plus the obligatory clocktower and anarchic bus station. The most developed section of coast, though still very somnolent, is to the north of town, along **Medaketiya and Medilla beaches**, a long, straight swathe of golden sand lined with a string of guesthouses opened in anticipation of a flood of tourists who have yet to arrive. Beyond Medilla, around 4km northeast of Tangalla town, the coastline tapers to little more than a sandspit at idyllic Kapuhenwala beach in **Marakolliya**, backed by the mangrove-fringed Rekawa lagoon.

Though just as sleepy, the coast immediately south of town, known as **Pallikaduwa**, is quite different in character, made up of a sequence of beautiful rocky coves – much more scenic than Medaketiya and Medilla, but with little sand. The rocky shoreline here has prevented building directly on the beach, so most of Pallikaduwa's accommodation is set back behind the main road. The most scenic section of Tangalla coastline can be found a couple of kilometres further south at the village of **Goyambokka**, with a superb rocky promontory flanked by two gorgeous beaches – to the west of the headland, Godellawela Beach (or "Silent Beach", as it's popularly known) is an absolute picture, though you'll have to share it with guests from the superb *Amanwella* hotel.

Eating

Eating is something of a disappointment in Tangalla – unless you fancy a splurge at *Amanwella* – and you'll probably end up having meals at your guesthouse (though in most instances the cooking's unlikely to consist of much more than boringly prepared fish or stodgy rice and curry). Some of the bigger guesthouses offer a broader menu: north of Tangalla town, try the restaurants at *Mangrove Beach Cabanas* or *Ibis Guest House*, or, south of town, the *Palm Paradise Cabanas* in Goyambokka. South of here, the Italian-slanted *Il Camino*, at the *Surya Guest House*, offers a range of pasta dishes, plus a few *secondi piatti*, if ordered a day in advance.

Swimming, snorkelling and diving at Tangalla

Swimming in Tangalla can be hazardous: Kapuhenwala, Medaketiya and Medilla beaches shelve steeply into the sea and there are dangerous currents in places, although the coves south of town at Pallikaduwa and Goyambokka are pleasantly sheltered. Always check at your guesthouse before venturing into the water: conditions vary considerably even within a few hundred metres – and the fact that the various beaches are often idyllically deserted means that there might not be anyone around to help if you get into trouble. Many of the guesthouses in town rent out **snorkelling** equipment, the best area for which is by the navy base in the middle of Tangalla town, close to the *Rest House*, which still boasts a few bits of live coral. **Diving** can be arranged through the Tangalle Diving Centre (ⓣ0776-277 622, ⓦwww.tangalledivingcentre.com) at the *Tangalla Bay Hotel*.

Around Tangalla

A rewarding half-day trip from Tangalla combines the **Hoo-maniya blowhole**, the **Wewurukannala** temple with its enormous Buddha statue and the absorbing rock temples of **Mulkirigala**. All local guesthouses should be able to arrange a combined round-trip by tuktuk to these three places, perhaps including the lace-making cooperative at **Dickwella**; the current going rate is around Rs.2500 for two people. Other interesting local excursions include evening trips to spot turtles coming ashore at **Rekawa**, while Tangalla can also be used as a base for visits to the little-visited wetlands of the **Kalametiya Bird Sanctuary** and the curious red-soil plateau at **Ussangoda**, en route to Hambantota.

Hoo-maniya blowhole

Around 8km west of Tangalla, the village of Kudawela is home to the **Hoo-maniya blowhole** (Rs.100) – the fanciful name derives from the low, booming "Hoo" sound which it produces prior to spouting water. The blowhole is formed from a deep, narrow cleft in the cliff, around twenty metres deep and a metre wide, which funnels plumes of water up into the air in great jets by some mysterious action of water pressure – it's most impressive during the monsoon (May–Sept; June is reckoned to be best), when the jets can reach heights of fifteen metres. At other times it can be slightly underwhelming, though a push-button contraption at the new **visitor centre** gives an entertaining re-creation of the blowhole's jetstream even when the real thing's decided not to perform.

To reach the blowhole by public transport, take a direct **bus** from Tangalla to Matara along the coast road and ask to be put off at the turn-off to Kudawela, just beyond the village of Nakulugamuwa, from where it's 2km on foot or by tuktuk.

Wewurukannala and Dickwella Lace

Around 8km beyond Hoo-maniya, 2km inland from the village of **Dickwella**, the entertainingly kitsch temple at **Wewurukannala** (Rs.100) is home to the largest Buddha statue on the island, a fifty-metre concrete colossus constructed in the late 1960s. The rather supercilious-looking Buddha is shown in the seated posture, draped in orange robes with his head crowned by a gaudy, polychromatic *siraspata* (the Buddhist equivalent of the halo) – supposedly representing the flame of wisdom, though on this occasion it looks more like an enormous dollop of ice cream. Immediately to the rear of the statue is a seven-storey building, which the Enlightened One appears to be using as a kind of backrest. You can walk up the steps inside the building, past a big collection of cartoon-style Jataka paintings, and peer into the Buddha's head.

The main **image house** dates from the late nineteenth century and contains an impressive ensemble of huge Buddhas in various poses. Outside and to the left of the main shrine is the oldest part of the temple, a small shrine some 250 years old, decorated with faded murals and housing a seated clay Buddha. Next door, another image house houses a kind of Buddhist **chamber of horrors** showing the punishments awaiting wrongdoers in the afterlife. The gruesome collection of life-size statues here depict unfortunates being sawn in half, boiled in oil and impaled on stakes by rather jolly-looking devils. The corridor past the statues shows a long series of paintings (many unfinished): the upper panels depict various sins – everything from slapping your mother to urinating in front of a temple – the corresponding panel underneath shows the relevant punishment. You have been warned. Back in Dickwella village, diagonally opposite the

Dickwella Resort, it's worth stopping by at **Dickwella Lace** (daily 9am–5pm), a women's cooperative set up to protect and revive the art of *beeralu*, or bobbin lace-making, one of the area's traditional industries. The poorest women from around fifty local villages are trained up here, and provided with the skills to earn an income from their craft. As well as demonstrations of lace-making techniques, there's also a small lace museum, and beautifully designed bags, tablecloths and linen on sale.

Buses to Matara via Beliatta pass directly by Wewurukannala temple. Alternatively, take a bus to Matara along the main coast road and get off at Dickwella, from where it's a couple of kilometres on foot or by tuktuk.

Mulkirigala

Sixteen kilometres north of Tangalla lies the remarkable temple-monastery of **Mulkirigala** (daily 6am–6pm; Rs.100), the only monument in the south to rival the great ancient Buddhist sites of the Cultural Triangle. Mulkirigala (sometimes spelt Mulgirigala) consists of a series of **rock temples** carved out of the face of a huge rock outcrop which rises sheer and seemingly impregnable for over two hundred metres out of the surrounding palm forests; the temples date back to the third century BC, but were completely restored during the eighteenth century under the patronage of the kings of Kandy. The overall effect is rather like a cross between the far better known Dambulla and Sigiriya, though even if you've visited those sites, climbing Mulkirigala is worth it, both for the temples themselves and for the magnificent panoramas out over the surrounding countryside.

Immediately beyond the ticket office lies **terrace one**, home to two rock temples and a small dagoba; the unusual structures standing on elephant feet outside are oil lamps dating from the turn of the twentieth century. The temple nearest the entrance contains a reclining Buddha, plus paintings (along the side wall nearest the entrance) of Vishnu, Kataragama (by the door) and Vibhishana (the demonic blue figure with fangs), while the wall between the two doors into the first temple is decorated with pictures of *arhats* (enlightened Buddhist monks). The second cave here is one of Mulkirigala's finest, with beautifully executed Kandyan-style paintings dating back to the eighteenth-century restoration – the wall between the two doors, decorated with Jataka stories, is particularly striking.

Retrace your steps past the ticket office to reach the steep flight of steps that lead up to **terrace two**, with a single rock temple housing a reclining Buddha flanked by two disciples. Further steps lead up to **terrace three**, the most interesting section of the complex. There are four temples here, ranged side by side, with a small rock pool at the left-hand end. Immediately behind the pool is the smallest of the four temples (you have to go through the adjacent temple to reach it), the so-called **Naga** or **Cobra temple**, named after the fearsome snake painted on the door at the rear.

The next temple along sports a gaudy reclining Buddha in its inner shrine, while the third temple, known as the **Raja Mahavihara**, is Mulkirigala's finest. The vestibule, paved with old Dutch floor tiles and supported by Kandyan-style wooden pillars, contains an antique chest which was once used to hold ola-leaf manuscripts of religious and other texts. It was in this chest, in 1826, that the British official and antiquarian **George Turnour** discovered a clutch of ancient manuscripts which enabled him to translate the *Mahavamsa* (see p.415), the first time Sri Lanka's famous historical chronicle had been deciphered in the modern era. The shrine itself holds yet another sleeping Buddha, its feet intricately decorated. The fantastically kitsch final temple is home to Mulkirigala's only *parinirvana* Buddha – that is to say a dead, rather than a merely sleeping, Buddha (see p.445), surrounded by a lurid tableau of grieving figures.

Next to the Raja Mahavihara, steps lead up again, past a set of treacherously narrow and steep rock-cut steps to **terrace four**, at the very summit of the site. There's not much to see here, apart from two young bo saplings, both grown from cuttings taken from the famous tree at Anuradhapura, and a small dagoba at the top of the site; the main attraction is the wonderful views – scramble down the path behind the dagoba onto the open rock for an unobstructed panorama over a sea of palms.

You're free to explore the site by yourself, though if you want a tour, a resident **guide** will show you around for a tip. To get to Mulkirigala by public transport, take a bus from Tangalla to Beliatta (every 15min; 30min), and then change on to a Middeniya-bound #338, from which it's another half-hour to the site.

Rekawa

The two-kilometre beach at **REKAWA** village, 10km east of Tangalla, is home to one of the most important **sea turtle nesting sites** in Sri Lanka, visited by five different species which lay their eggs in the sand here most nights throughout the year. The nesting sites along the beach are currently protected by the Turtle Conservation Project (TCP; ⓣ0777-810 508, ⓦwww.tcpsrilanka.org), which conducts research into visiting turtles, pays local villagers to protect eggs from poachers and trains some as tourist guides.

Turtle watches are held nightly, with villagers keeping watch up and down the beach for their arrival – when one appears (the vast majority are green turtles), it first crawls across the beach, away from the sea, leaving behind a remarkable trail which looks as if a one-wheeled tractor has driven straight up out of the water. This takes an exhausting thirty minutes, since turtles are very badly adapted for travel on land. Having reached the top of the beach, the turtles then spend about another 45 minutes digging an enormous hole; you'll hear periodic thrashings and the sound of great clouds of sand being scuffed up. As laying begins, you're allowed in close to watch, although all you actually see is the turtle's backside with eggs – looking just like ping-pong balls – periodically popping out in twos and threes. The eggs are then taken by staff to be re-buried in a secure location. The turtle then rests, fills in the hole and eventually crawls back down to the sea. It's an epic effort, the sight of which makes the whole evening-long experience (just about) worthwhile.

Turtle watches start at around 8pm from the TCP hut on Rekawa beach. The **best time** to see the animals is between January and April; periods when there's a full or fullish moon are also good throughout the year, because there are both more turtles and more light to see them by. Rekawa's record is apparently 23 turtles in one night, and most nights at least one will appear, though you might have to wait until around midnight for a sighting. The villagers levy a Rs.600 fee (or just a donation at the end of an unsuccessful evening), while a tuktuk from Tangalla will cost Rs.1000.

Kalametiya and Ussangoda

Roughly equidistant between Tangalla and Hambantota, the little-visited **Kalametiya Bird Sanctuary** (best Nov–March) comprises an area of coastal lagoons and mangroves, similar to that found in Bundala, and rich in marine and other birdlife. Access to the sanctuary is from the village of **Hungama**, where three-hour birdwatching tours of the sanctuary, combined with a catamaran or outrigger canoe trip on picturesque **Lunama lagoon**, can be arranged with the excellent *RukDiya Eco Stop* (see p.202; Rs.1000 per person), a community-based initiative which offers a number of other rewarding local tours.

A trip to Kalametiya can be combined with a visit to the mysteriously barren landscape at **Ussangoda**, around 5km east. This large, flat plateau (claimed in legend as a landing place of Rawana) is famous for its scorched, brick-coloured soil, widely believed to have been caused by a meteor strike in ancient times, which supports hardly any vegetation. The plateau is bordered to the south by sheer cliffs which drop to a fine sweep of beach, regularly visited by turtles and one of the few around here that's safe for swimming. To reach Ussangoda, turn off the Hambantota road after the 221km post towards the *Ussangoda Beach Resort* (actually a simple restaurant), from where it's a two-kilometre walk; vehicles are not permitted. It can also be accessed by foot from the beach backing Lunama lagoon.

Hambantota

The area dividing Tangalla and Hambantota marks the transition between Sri Lanka's wet and dry zones, where the lush palm forests of the southwest give way to the arid and scrub-covered savannah that characterizes much of the island. Some 53km beyond Tangalla, the dusty provincial capital of **HAMBANTOTA** is the unlikely beneficiary of a remarkable economic regeneration programme, focused around the dredging of a Chinese-sponsored shipping port (see box below); while in May 2009 the town was announced as the site of the island's second international airport. Though you won't see much evidence of the port, its scale is apparent by the fact that the main coastal highway now takes a thirteen-kilometre diversion inland to make room for it. There's not much in Hambantota itself to appeal to tourists, though the town can be used as a base to visit Kalametiya Bird Sanctuary and a couple of other seldom-visited attractions to the west, or Bundala or Yala to the east.

Hambantota was originally settled by Malay seafarers (the name is a corruption of "Sampan-tota", or "Sampan Port", alluding to the type of boat in which

Hambantota, the tsunami and the string of pearls

The changing skyline of sleepy Hambantota's arid hinterland, specked with cranes and giant wind turbines, attests to a remarkably ambitious programme of development focused around the construction of a vast new **shipping port** – quite a contrast to Sri Lanka's usually languid pace of progress. Closer than Colombo to the busy shipping lanes between East Asia and the Middle East (and with Trincomalee's political future still uncertain), Hambantota's deep lagoon had been earmarked as a potential site for a new port since the late 1990s, but it wasn't until the 2004 tsunami that serious development became a real possibility. The **tsunami** hit Hambantota, already one of the south's poorest towns, harder than almost any other urban centre in the country, sweeping most of what was in its path up to a kilometre inland and killing over a thousand in a matter of minutes. The massive subsequent relief effort, involving the relocation of some five thousand people to a hurriedly constructed housing project a few kilometres inland, received substantial help from local boy Prime Minister **Mahinda Rajapakse**, who drew criticism for appropriating over US$800,000 of the government's tsunami-relief funds into his private "Helping Hambantota" fund. Within a year, Rajapakse swept to power as president, fighting in part on a manifesto promising rapid economic development of the south. Rajapakse pushed forward negotiations with the Chinese government to agree terms for the port: a source of future employment and industry for Hambantota, and a link in China's "string of pearls" strategy to dominate Asia's sea lines. The first phase of the US$1 billion construction project began in 2007, and though it won't be fully operational for many years to come, the port looks set to receive its first ship in 2011.

they arrived) and the town still has the largest concentration of Malay-descended people in Sri Lanka, with a correspondingly high proportion of Muslims and mosques – you really notice the call to prayer here. A few inhabitants still speak Malay, and although you probably won't notice this, you're likely to be struck by the occasional local face with pure Southeast Asian features. Hambantota is also famous as the **salt** capital of Sri Lanka. Salt is produced by letting seawater into the **lewayas**, the sometimes dazzlingly white saltpans which surround the town, and allowing it to evaporate, after which the residue is scraped up and sold.

The Town

Hambantota's modest attractions are easily covered in an hour's walk. Starting from the lively **fish market** opposite the bus station, follow the coastal road south, edging the pretty breakwater-protected **harbour** – Hambantota's best feature. The views over the beach, usually lined with colourful fishing boats, and along the coast to the grand, saw-tooth hills around Kataragama away in the distance are magnificent, though the beach itself is scruffy, and strong currents and a deep ocean shelf just offshore make swimming dangerous.

Beyond here, the road meanders around the headland to the attractive old *Rest House*. Nearby sits a neglected old British **martello tower**, and a black-and-white-striped **lighthouse**, which retains its network of internal ladders; if you're nimble enough, you can climb to the top for some fine views. The clutch of government buildings nearby were formerly home to Hambantota's British government agents, amongst them **Leonard Woolf**, who spent several years here in the pay of the Ceylon Civil Service – his name is recorded on a board outside the District Secretariat – before returning to England, where following his marriage he published the classic *The Village in the Jungle*, an extraordinarily depressing tale of life in the Sri Lankan backlands.

Practicalities

Buses stop at the terminal right in the middle of town. There are branches of Hatton National Bank, just up from the harbour on Main Street, and the People's Bank, opposite the *Rest House*; the former has an **ATM** which accepts foreign cards. **Internet** access is available at Hiroda Communications (8.30am–8pm; Rs.50 per hr) on Bazaar Street, one block along Main Street from the bus stand. **Moving on from Hambantota** there are buses roughly every fifteen minutes west to Tangalla (1hr 30min), Matara (2hr 30min), Weligama (3hr), Galle (3hr 30min) and Colombo (6hr); east to Tissamaharama (45min–1hr); and north to Embilipitiya (1hr 30min).

Hambantota is not awash with **places to eat**. Aside from the hotel restaurants you might try *Jade Green*, opposite the *Peacock Beach Hotel*, which does short eats and a decent lunchtime rice and curry buffet, or the hard-to-miss *Kuma Restaurant*, which takes up almost the entire first floor of the vast vegetable market just south of the bus stand; its outdoor terrace is great for watching the goings-on in the fishing harbour below. For a **drink**, try the breezy *Lihiniya Bar* at the *Peacock Beach Hotel*.

Accommodation

Oasis Ayurveda Beach Resort Sisilasagama, 7km west of Hambantota ⓣ047-222 0650, ⓦwww.oasis-ayurveda.de. Set in pleasant gardens between a lagoon and beach, this comfortable Ayurveda-focused resort has light and airy rooms housed in the breezy main building or discreetly hidden-away chalets, each with TV, minibar and bathtubs. Activities include squash and yoga, and there's a gym, large pool and Ayurveda centre. ❻

Peacock Beach Hotel 1km along the road to Tissa ⓣ047-222 0377, ⓦpeacockbeachonline.com. Hambantota town's most upmarket option, close to the beach and set behind luxuriant gardens with a pool tucked to one side. The sea-facing rooms, all with a/c and TV, are bland but perfectly comfortable; the cheaper ones have balconies. Local tours are run in an open-top double-decker bus. ❻

Rest House ⓣ047-222 0299. Beautifully located on a headland overlooking the harbour, with views of the parched coastline and distant hills. Rooms in the atmospheric old wing are huge and stuffed full of lovely furniture; cheaper ones in the "new" wing are much less characterful, and expensive for what you get. ❹, a/c ❺

San Rose Marry Rd, 1km from the centre ⓣ047-222 0103. Probably the best budget option in Hambantota, overlooking a lotus pond in a quiet part of town, though there's nowhere to eat. All its rooms are huge, and the smarter ones upstairs are tiled and modern. ❷–❸

Bundala National Park

Accessed around 15km east of Hambantota (and a similar distance west of Tissa), **Bundala National Park** is one of Sri Lanka's foremost destinations for **birdwatchers**, protecting an important area of coastal wetland famous for its abundant aquatic (and other) birdlife, as well as being home to significant populations of elephants, crocodiles, turtles and other fauna. Although it doesn't have quite the range of wildlife or scenery of nearby Yala National Park, Bundala is much quieter, and makes a good alternative if you want to avoid Yala's crowds.

The park stretches along the coast for around twenty kilometres, enclosing five shallow and brackish **lagoons**, or *lewayas* (they sometimes dry up completely during long periods of drought) separated by thick low scrubby forest running down to coastal dunes. Almost two hundred bird species have been recorded here, their numbers swelled by seasonal visitors, who arrive between September and March. The lagoons attract an amazing variety of

▲ Flamingoes, Bundala National Park

aquatic birds, including ibis, pelicans, painted storks, egrets and spoonbills, though the most famous visitors are the huge flocks of **greater flamingoes**. The Bundala area is the flamingoes' last refuge in southern Sri Lanka, and you can see them here in variable numbers throughout the year; their exact breeding habits remain a mystery, though it's thought they migrate from the Rann of Kutch in northern India. Flamingoes apart, the park's most visible avian residents are its many **peacocks** (or Indian peafowl, as they're correctly known): a memorable sight in the wild at any time, especially when seen perched sententiously amidst the upper branches of the park's innumerable skeletal *palu* (rosewood) trees.

Bundala is also home to 32 species of **mammals**, including civets, mongooses, wild pigs and giant Indian palm squirrels, as well as black-naped hares, though the most commonly seen mammals are the excitable troupes of grey langur **monkeys**. There are also a few **elephants**, including around ten permanent residents and some twenty semi-resident; larger seasonal migratory herds of up to sixty, comprising animals that roam the Yala, Uda Walawe and Bundala area, also visit the park. All five species of **turtle** (see p.454) lay their eggs on the park's beaches, although there are currently no turtle watches. You'll probably also come across large **land monitors** and lots of enormous **crocodiles**, which can be seen sunning themselves along the sides of the park's lagoons and watercourses.

Bundala is about twenty minutes' drive from either Hambantota or Tissa – drivers charge around US$40 for the jeep trip from either town (see p.211 for information on jeep drivers in Tissa). The **entrance fee** is currently US$8 per person, plus the usual additional charges and taxes (see p.55), paid at the park's well-organized new **visitor centre**. The **best time to visit** is between September and March, when the migratory birds arrive; early morning is the best time of day, though the park is also rewarding in late afternoon. Take binoculars, if you have them.

Tissamaharama

Beyond Bundala National Park the main highway turns away from the coast towards the pleasant town of **TISSAMAHARAMA** (usually abbreviated to **Tissa**). Tissa's main attraction is as a base for trips to the nearby national parks of Yala and Bundala or the temple town of Kataragama, but it's an agreeable place in its own right, with a handful of monuments testifying to the town's important place in early Sri Lankan history when, under the name of **Mahagama**, it was one of the principal settlements of the southern province of Ruhunu. Mahagama is said to have been founded in the third century BC by a brother of the great Devanampiya Tissa (see p.416) of Anuradhapura, and later rose to prominence under **Kavan Tissa**, father of the legendary Dutugemunu (see p.362). A cluster of dagobas and a beautiful tank dating from this era lend parts of Tissa a certain distinction and a sense of history which makes a pleasant change from the run-of-the-mill towns which dot much of the southern coast.

Arrival

Buses stop at the new bus station in the middle of the town; a tuktuk to the guesthouses around Tissa Wewa will cost Rs.50–60. There are branches of various **banks** along Main Street, each with ATMs accepting foreign cards. For **internet**

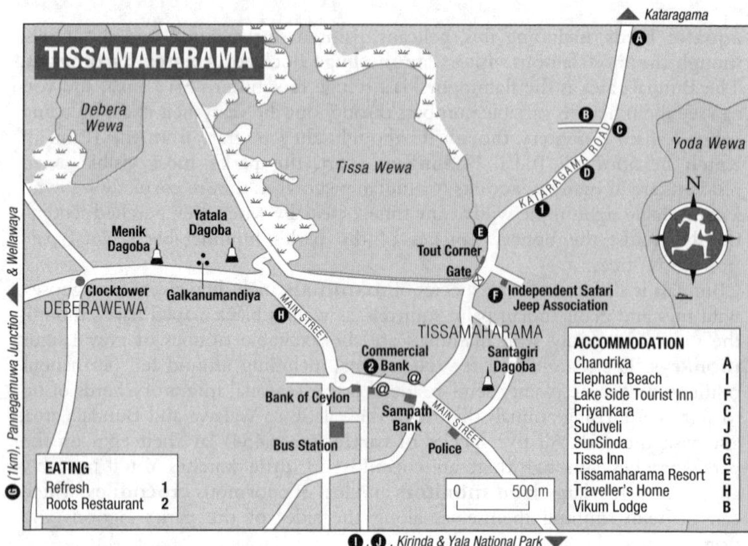

access try Sakura Communications (daily 7.30am–10pm; Rs.50 per hr), next to the Commercial Bank, which also has free wi-fi; failing that, make for Nemasala, opposite Sampath Bank (daily 9am–6.30pm; Rs.70 per hr).

Accommodation

Accommodation in Tissa is split into three quite separate areas. A kilometre north of the town proper, the area around the placid waters of the **Tissa Wewa** is easily the nicest base, and has the widest selection of hotels and guesthouses – the ones we list in the area are all north of the lake, on (or just off) the Kataragama road. There are also a couple of recommendable alternatives away from the lake in **Tissa town** itself, and in the village of **Deberawewa**, about 2km west. There are also two possibilities near the small temple town of **Kirinda** (15km from Tissa, and very close to Yala).

Tissa Wewa

Chandrika ⓣ047-223 7143, ⓦwww.chandrikahotel.com. Pleasantly old-school mid-range hotel, if a bit far from the action, with comfy rooms (with TV and optional a/c for US$5) facing a pretty palm-studded garden which leads down to an inviting pool. ④, a/c ⑤

Lake Side Tourist Inn ⓣ047-223 7216, ⓦwww.tissalakeside.com. Homely, old-fashioned hotel with an airy lake-facing restaurant, pool and comfortably furnished, well-maintained rooms; all have hot water, and a few have a/c, TV and/or (restricted) lake views. Fan ③, a/c ④

Priyankara ⓣ047-223 7206, ⓦwww.priyankarahotel.com. The poshest spot in town, but very reasonably priced. All rooms have a/c, TV and balcony; it's well worth paying the extra US$10 for one of the brighter, smarter deluxe rooms. There's good, moderately priced food, too, and a lovely pool from which you can gaze at the birdlife in the paddies. ⑥

SunSinda ⓣ047-223 9078, ⓔsterne@sltnet.lk. Smart and surprisingly inexpensive modern hotel with cheerful orangey decor and pretty rooms furnished in a kind of ethnic-minimalist style. All come with a/c, hot water and balcony (though not much of a view). There's also a large but shallow pool. ⑤

Tissamaharama Resort (also known as the *Tissamaharama Rest House*) ⓣ047-223 7299, ⓦwww.ceylonhotels.lk. Right next to Tissa Wewa, this has the most scenic position in town, though it's rather overpriced. Rooms (all with a/c) are comfortable if dated, and superior rooms have TV, minibar and fine lake views; there's also a good-sized pool (non-guests Rs.200). ❺

Vikum Lodge ✆047-223 7585. Tissa's most personable guesthouse, slightly out of the way, but well worth the walk. Rooms (all with hot water, some with a/c) are unusually bright and well maintained, and are arranged around a pretty garden courtyard (good for bird-spotting) with a little vine-covered restaurant in the centre. Excellent value. ❷, a/c ❸

Tours from Tissa

A horde of local operators offer a wide range of trips from Tissa. Easily the most popular are the half- and full-day trips to **Yala** and **Bundala national parks**, which are best started at either 5.30am or 2.30pm, to be in the parks for dawn or dusk. Some operators also offer **overnight camping trips** to Bundala (though not currently to Yala); these usually leave at 3.30pm and return at 10.30am the next morning and include two park drives, plus tent, dinner, breakfast and tea. Staying the night in the park gives you the chance to see nocturnal animals, including snakes, crocs, owls, wild pigs, porcupines (rare) and nocturnal birds. You can arrange similar trips to stay around the edge of the Yala, just outside the boundaries; the terrain is similar, and you might see a bit of wildlife, but by and large this is a watered-down experience compared to visiting the park itself, and costs the same for the jeep.

Another popular option is the half-day excursion to the rock temple at **Situlpahuwa** followed by a visit to **Kataragama** for the evening puja. The journey to Situlpahuwa passes through the fringes of Yala (though you don't have to pay the entrance fee), so you might spot some wildlife en route, but this is much less interesting than a proper trip to the main portion of the park. Some drivers also offer a combined tour of five different local **tanks**, including Tissa Wewa, Deberawewa and Wirawila Wewa, all rich in birdlife (assuming they haven't dried up, as happens frequently in periods of low rainfall). The third national park nearby, **Lunugamwehera**, was closed at the time of writing, though is likely to reopen at some point, perhaps before the end of 2009.

Tour operators and prices

Almost all the town's guesthouses and hotels can fix up tours, though it may be marginally cheaper to organize one yourself with one of the drivers at **tout corner**, by the archway at the southeastern corner of Tissa Wewa. Tissamaharama's 170-plus strong rabble of jeep safari drivers is now loosely organized into a syndicate, the **Independent Jeep Safari Association** (✆0776 310 215), with a sporadically open office on the side road opposite tout corner. Obviously standards vary, but the association does contain some switched-on individuals and by going with a registered driver (who should have an ID card and a numbered badge on the side of his jeep) you should be guaranteed at least a basic level of training and English. For more about choosing a driver, see p.55.

Prices are fixed by the Jeep Safari Association – some would argue artificially high – though you might save Rs.500–1000 booking direct with a driver if business in quiet, as he can then avoid paying commission to a third party. Alternatively, *Traveller's Home* guesthouse usually undercuts standard prices, and might be worth a call (see p.212). A half-day trip to Yala or Bundala currently costs around US$40, or US$80 for a full day, plus tip. Other half-day trips – such as to Situlpahuwa combined with Kataragama or around five different local lakes also cost US$40. These prices are for a jeep seating up to six or seven people, so obviously it becomes cheaper if you can get a group together. Overnight camping trips to Bundala or around Yala's edges cost around US$100 per person, excluding entrance fees.

It has been known for rogue drivers to collect the Yala entrance fee from their passengers, then to drive them around the edge of the park on the pretence that they're inside it, allowing the driver to pocket the hefty entrance fee. You should only ever hand over entrance fees at the park's visitor centre, to the relevant official.

Tissa town and Deberawewa

Tissa Inn Deberawewa, 1.5 km west of the Deberawewa clocktower ⓣ047-223 7233, ⓦwww.tissainn.com. Good-value if slightly old-fashioned hotel set in sprawling gardens, with a homely, low-key atmosphere and twelve clean and comfortable rooms (with optional a/c for US$10 extra). ❸

Traveller's Home ⓣ047-223 7958, ⓔtravellershome@sltnet.lk. Friendly guest house with six good-value doubles, plus a couple of other more expensive and less appealing rooms (one with a/c). The owner is also a good source of information about Yala and can arrange daytime and camping tours. Free bikes for rent. ❶–❸

Kirinda

Elephant Reach 1.5km outside Kirinda towards Tissa ⓣ047-567 7544, ⓦwww.elephantreach.com. Low-key but comfortable safari-themed hotel, with accommodation in mud-coloured brick chalets (plus a handful of rooms in the main building). Rooms sport TV and minibar, and there's a games room and pool. ❼

Suduveli 2km outside Kirinda towards Tissa ⓣ0722 631 059. This friendly and homely little guesthouse offers a good place to crash out for a day or two, with accommodation either in very good-value rooms in the main house (a couple with shared bathroom) or in cute cabanas (including one family cabana) in the rambling gardens. There are free bikes for guests, cheap motorbike rental and a free tuktuk from Tissa, plus jeep hire for Yala trips. Rooms ❶, cabanas ❸

The Town

Modern Tissa is a bustling but unremarkable local commercial centre – essentially a single thoroughfare, **Main Street**, lined with banks, shops and little cafés. Refreshingly compact, the town is bounded on its northern side by a beautiful expanse of paddy fields, in the middle of which stands the most impressive of Tissa's various dagobas, the **Santagiri** (or Sandagiri) **dagoba**, allegedly built by Kavan Tissa in the second century BC and now restored to its original glory, with a "bubble"-shaped dome topped by an unusually large and lavishly decorated harmika and broad spire – a strangely squat and top-heavy-looking construction quite unlike any other dagoba in the island. About a kilometre north of the modern town lies the beautiful **Tissa Wewa**, an expansive artificial lake thought to have been constructed in the second or third century BC – the shore nearest the town is often busy with crowds of people bathing (including the occasional tourist) and flocks of aquatic birds including bitterns, herons and egrets skimming across the waters. A beautiful walk leads along the massive **bund** (embankment) which bounds the lake's southern shore, lined by majestic old Indian rain trees which were planted throughout the island by the British to provide shade along major trunk roads; you should be able to fix up a **boat trip**

Moving on from Tissa

Tissa is a major terminus for buses travelling east along the coastal road, which stop here before heading back west (hence you should be able to get a seat). Services depart roughly every fifteen minutes for **Hambantota** (45min–1hr), **Tangalla** (2hr), **Matara** (3hr), **Weligama** (3hr 20min), **Galle** (4hr–4hr 30min) and **Colombo** (7hr), though most are old CTB rustbuckets; if you're heading back to Colombo, you might find it faster and more comfortable to change onto an express bus in Matara. Tissa is also a convenient place to head up into the hills, though to get there you may have to change buses at **Pannegamuwa**, a small town located on a major road intersection 5km west of Tissa, and/or at **Wellawaya** (hourly; 2hr), from where there are plenty of buses to **Ella** or **Haputale**. There are also a few services to **Monaragala** (5 daily; 2hr), from where you can catch a bus to Arugam Bay.

If you're staying around Tissa Wewa and going to **Kataragama** (every 10min; 20–30min), there's no need to go into the bus station in town; just stand on the main road here, which is also the road to Kataragama, and flag down anything that passes.

on the lake – wonderful for birdlife – along here (around Rs.600 per hr). At the far end a track leads to the smaller adjacent lake of **Debera Wewa**, another haven for birdlife, its surface prettily covered in water lilies.

From the southwest corner of the Tissa Wewa, a short walk along the road back towards the town centre brings you to two large dagobas dating back to the second century BC – each once probably formed part of a large monastery, though little now survives above ground. The first of these, the **Yatala dagoba**, is surrounded by a wall faced with sculpted elephant heads and may once have housed the Tooth Relic (see p.243). There's a small and only erratically open **museum** here, containing a very modest selection of carvings and masonry rescued from local archeological sites. Continue down the road for 400m or so to reach the **Menik dagoba**. The small cluster of pillars you pass en route is all that remains of the **Galkanumandiya**, thought to be some kind of monastic building.

Eating

All Tissa's guesthouses and hotels do **food**; probably the best is served in the charmingly understated dining room of the *Priyankara* hotel, with a small but varied menu of well-prepared dishes. Virtually every tourist piles in at some point to the enormously popular *Refresh*, with a menu as vast as in its sister establishment in Hikkaduwa; the food's not bad but with mains starting at around Rs.1000 it's hard not to feel you're paying for the restaurant's success. In town, the scruffy little *Roots Restaurant*, just off Main Street, has a reasonable selection of cheap Chinese and Sri Lankan food.

Yala National Park

Around 20km southeast of Tissamaharama lies the entrance to **Yala National Park** (properly known as Yala West or Ruhunu National Park), Sri Lanka's most visited wildlife reserve. Yala covers an area of 1260 square kilometres, although four-fifths of this is designated a Strict Natural Reserve and closed to visitors. On the far side of the Strict Natural Reserve is Yala East National Park (see p.399), which is only accessible via Arugam Bay (though was closed at the time of writing). There's no public transport to Yala, and you're only allowed into the park in a vehicle, so you'll have to hire a jeep.

To avoid disappointment, it's important to understand what Yala is, and what it isn't – if you expect vast herds of elephants and other large mammals, with leopards dangling from every tree, you'll inevitably be disappointed. In addition, there's no limit to the number of vehicles allowed inside the park, and it can sometimes seem impossibly busy, with posses of belching jeeps careering around in frantic pursuit of elusive elephants or leopards. Despite this, Yala can be a richly rewarding place to visit. The park's dry-zone **landscape** is strikingly beautiful, especially when viewed from the vantage points offered by the curious rock outcrops which dot the park. From these you can look out over a seemingly endless expanse of low scrub and trees dotted with brackish lakes next to the dune-covered coastline – particularly magical from Situlpahuwa. In addition, the park's wildlife has its own distinctive charm, with huddles of colourful painted storks perched on the edge of lagoons between the supine shapes of dozing crocodiles; fan-tailed peacocks kicking up clouds of dust while monkeys chatter in the treetops; or the incongruously conjoined sight of elephants marching sedately through the bush while rabbits scamper through the undergrowth.

The park's most famous residents are its elusive **leopards**. Sightings are reasonably common, though you'll stand a much better chance of spotting one if you spend a full day in the park, which allows you to reach less touristed areas. Much more visible are the resident **elephants**. Other resident **mammals** include sambar and spotted deer, wild boar, wild buffaloes, macaque and langur monkeys, sloth bears, jackals, mongooses, pangolins, porcupines, rabbits and (rare) wild cats, as well as plentiful **crocodiles**. Yala is also rich in **birdlife**. Around 130 species have been recorded here, including many migrants escaping the northern winter. Peacocks are ubiquitous throughout the park, while you should also spot at least a couple of jungle fowl, a singularly inelegant, waddling creature, like a feral hen, which has been adopted as the national bird of Sri Lanka.

Yala also has a certain historic interest. The remains of extensive settlements that once dotted the area during the Ruhunu period can still be seen, most notably the monastery at **Situlpahuwa**, which may once have housed over ten thousand people and remains an important site of pilgrimage en route to nearby Kataragama. The temple comprises two rock-top dagobas separated by a small lake; there's a faded Pali inscription at the base of the first rock. The main draw, though, is the temple's lost-in-the-jungle setting and the marvellous views it affords of pretty much the entire park, with scarcely a single sign of human presence interrupting the majestic swathe of scrub and forest receding into the saw-tooth hills further away up the east coast. South of Situlpahuwa are the very modest remains of the first-century BC **Magul Maha Vihara**. Although these two temples lie within the national park, you can visit them without paying the entrance fee; combined with Kataragama, they make a good half-day excursion from Tissa.

Practicalities

For details of arranging a **jeep from Tissa** to Yala, see p.211. Entrance costs US$15, plus the usual additional fees (see p.55). Yala is usually **closed annually** from September 1 to October 15.

The **entrance** to the park is at Palatupana, 27km from Tissa (about a 45min drive), where there's a well-designed and informative new **visitor centre**. All vehicles entering the park are assigned an obligatory tracker. You're meant to stay inside your vehicle (except on the beach), keep your jeep's hood up, stick to roads and avoid all noise, although you are allowed to drive freely around the park, following whichever track takes your fancy. **Birdwatching** is good year-round, though from October to March visitors have the added bonus of seeing thousands of migratory species arrive to escape the northern winter. **Elephants** can also usually be seen, though they can be a bit easier to spot during the dry season (May–Aug), when they congregate around the park's waterholes. **Leopards** can be seen year round, though they might be slightly easier to spot during the latter part of the dry season, when the ground vegetation dies back. Adult leopards are mainly active from dusk until dawn. Most daytime leopard sightings are of cubs and sub-adults, who are dependent on their mother for food. These confident and carefree young animals can provide hours of viewing, often showing themselves to visitors in the same spot for several days running.

If you want to **stay** in the countryside around the park your best option is the luxurious *Yala Village* (Ⓣ047-223 9450, Ⓦwww.johnkeellshotels.com; ❼), a couple of kilometres from the park entrance, which has appealing air-conditioned chalets with wildlife-themed decor and satellite TV (if you get bored of looking for elephants from the hotel's elevated observation deck) scattered around ten acres of jungle between the sea and lagoon.

Kataragama

Nineteen kilometres further inland from Tissa lies the small and remote town of **KATARAGAMA**, one of the three most venerated religious sites in Sri Lanka (along with Adam's Peak and the Temple of the Tooth at Kandy), held sacred by Buddhists, Hindus and Muslims alike – even Christians sometimes visit in search of divine assistance. The most important of the town's various shrines is dedicated to the god **Kataragama** (see box, p.216), a Buddhist-cum-Hindu deity who is believed to reside here.

Kataragama is easily visited as a day-trip from Tissa, but staying the night means you can enjoy the evening puja in a leisurely manner and imbibe some of the backwater charm and laid-back rural pace here. The town is at its busiest during the **Kataragama festival**, held around the Esala poya day in July or August. The festival is famous for the varying forms of physical mortification with which some pilgrims express their devotion to Kataragama, ranging from crawling from the river to the Maha Devale to gruesome acts of self-mutilation: some penitents pierce their cheeks or tongue with skewers; others walk across burning coals – all believe that the god will protect them from pain. During the festival devotees flock to the town from all over Sri Lanka, some walking along the various pilgrimage routes which converge on Kataragama from distant parts

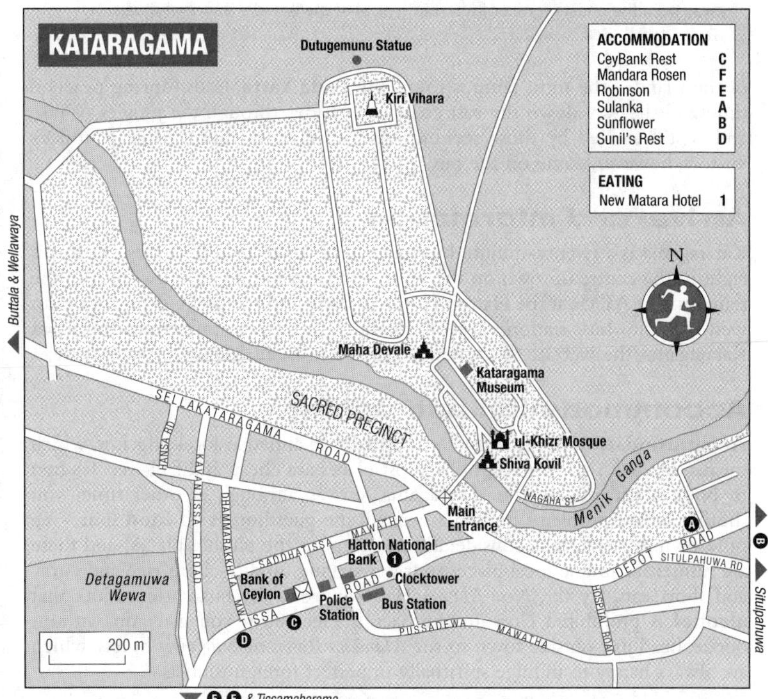

Kataragama

Perhaps no other deity in Sri Lanka embodies the bewilderingly syncretic nature of the island's Buddhist and Hindu traditions as clearly as the many-faceted **Kataragama**. The god has two very different origins. To the Buddhist Sinhalese, Kataragama is one of the four great protectors of the island. Although he began life as a rather unimportant local god, named after the town in which his shrine was located, he gained pan-Sinhalese significance during the early struggles against the South Indian Tamils, and is believed to have helped Dutugemunu (see p.362) in his long war against Elara. To the Hindu Tamils, Kataragama is equivalent to the major deity **Skanda** (also known as Murugan or Subramanian), a son of Shiva and Parvati and brother of Ganesh. Both Buddhists and Hindus have legends which tell how Kataragama came to Sri Lanka to battle against the *asuras*, or enemies of the gods. Whilst fighting, he became enamoured of Valli Amma, the result of the union between a pious hermit and a doe, who became his second wife. His cult waned amongst the Sinhalese following the accession of Tamils to the throne of Kandy, but was subsequently revived amongst the island's plantation Tamils, who considered Kataragama a manifestation of the god Skanda. Despite Kataragama's confused lineage, modern-day visitors to the shrine generally pay scant attention to the god's theological roots, simply regarding him a powerful deity capable of assisting in a wide range of practical enterprises.

Kataragama is often shown carrying a **vel**, or trident, which is also one of Shiva's principal symbols. His colour is red (devotees offer crimson garlands when they visit his shrines) and he is frequently identified with the peacock, a bird which was sacrificed to him. Thanks to his exploits, both military and amorous, he is worshipped both as a fearsome warrior and as a lover, inspiring an ecstatic devotion in his followers exemplified by the *kavadi*, or peacock dance (see p.218), and the ritual self-mutilations practised by pilgrims during the annual Kataragama festival (see p.215) – a world away from the chaste forms of worship typical of the island's Buddhist rituals.

of the island – the most famous route, the **Pada Yatra**, leads (during peaceful times) all the way down the east coast from Jaffna, through the jungles of Yala, and is still tackled by those seeking especial religious merit. Most of today's visitors, however, come on the bus.

Arrival and information

Kataragama is a twenty-minute bus journey north of Tissa. The **bus station** is right in the centre of town on the Tissa Road, a five-minute walk south of the temples. The ATMs at the Hatton National Bank and Bank of Ceylon, both just west of the bus station, accept foreign cards. For **information** about Kataragama, the website Ⓦwww.kataragama.org is an absolute treasure trove.

Accommodation and eating

Accommodation in Kataragama is virtually all aimed at local pilgrims, which means that, with a few exceptions, most places are cheap and frill-free. It's best to book ahead during the Kataragama festival, although at other times you shouldn't have problems finding a bed. All the guesthouses do **food** (pure-veg only, owing to religious considerations, except in the plusher places) and there are numerous simple local places in town serving up dirt-cheap rice and curry and short eats; try the *New Matara Hotel*, opposite the bus station. Note that **alcohol** is prohibited close to the Sacred Precinct: if you can't do without booze, head just outside town to the *Mandara Rosen* or *Sunflower* hotels, which are always happy to indulge spiritually imperfect foreign tourists.

CeyBank Rest Tissa Rd ☎011-254 4315. Rooms here are good value – clean, quiet and spacious, with nice private balconies and hill views – unless you opt for expensive a/c. It tends to fill up most weekends and holidays with Bank of Ceylon employees, but there's usually space at other times. ❷, a/c ❹

Mandara Rosen Tissa Rd, Detagamuwa, 1.5km out of town ☎047-223 6030, Ⓦwww.rosenhotelsrilanka.com. This smart four-star looks a bit out of place in sleepy Kataragama, but makes an excellent and very affordable base from which to explore the area. Rooms – in an unusual and rather picturesque building modelled on a traditional pilgrim's rest house – come with a/c, satellite TV and minibar; there's also a decent-size swimming pool complete with underwater music. ❻

Robinson Tissa Rd, Detagamuwa, 1km out of town ☎047-223 5175, Ⓔrobinsonhotel@dialogsl.net. Pleasant modern hotel set in shady gardens, with cheerily painted, bright and comfortable (if rather pricey) rooms, all with TV and a/c. ❹

Sulanka Depot Rd ☎047-223 5227. Large but peaceful traditional rest house ranged around shaded gardens. Its pleasantly old-fashioned rooms (a few with a/c) are likely to have been upgraded by the time you read this, with a probable increase in prices. Half-board (and pure-veg food) only. ❸, a/c ❹

Sunflower Depot Rd, 1km out of town ☎047-223 5611, Ⓦwww.hotelsunflowerlk.com. One of Kataragama's plusher options, set in neat gardens, with spacious and comfortable – if slightly bland – modern rooms, each with TV and a/c. There's also a shallow pool. ❺

Sunil's Rest Tissa Rd ☎047-567 7172. Two very clean rooms in an attractive, friendly, family guest-house. ❸

The town and Sacred Precinct

Kataragama town spreads out over a small grid of tranquil streets shaded by huge Indian rain trees – outside poya days and puja times, the whole place is incredibly sleepy, and its quiet streets offer a welcome alternative to the dusty mayhem that usually passes for urban life in Sri Lanka. During the **evening puja** (see box, p.218), Kataragama is magically transformed. Throngs of pilgrims descend on the Sacred Precinct, while the brightly illuminated stalls which fill the surrounding streets do a brisk trade in garlands, fruit platters and other colourful religious paraphernalia, as well as huge slabs of gelatinous oil cake and other unusual edibles.

The town is separated by the Menik Ganga ("Gem River") from the so-called **Sacred Precinct** to the north, an area of beautiful parkland overrun by inquisitive grey langurs and dotted with myriad shrines; pilgrims take a ritual bath in the river before entering the precinct itself. The first buildings you'll encounter are the **ul-Khizr mosque** and the adjacent **Shiva Kovil** – the former houses the tombs of saints from Kyrgyzstan and India and is the main focus of Muslim devotions in Kataragama.

Continue up the main avenue, past a string of gaudy minor shrines, to reach the principal complex, the **Maha Devale**. This exhibits a quintessentially Sri Lankan intermingling of Hindu and Buddhist, with deities and iconography from each religion – trying to work out where one religion begins and the other ends is virtually impossible, and certainly not something which troubles the pilgrims who congregate here every night. The main courtyard is surrounded by an impressive wall decorated with elephant heads, and is entered through an ornate metal gate – both wall and gate are decorated with peacocks, a symbol of the god Kataragama. Inside are three main shrines. Directly opposite the entrance gate is the **principal shrine**, that of Kataragama himself – lavishly decorated, although surprisingly small. **Kataragama** himself is represented inside not by an image, but simply by his principal symbol of a *vel*, or trident. The two rather plain adjacent shrines are devoted to **Ganesh**, often invoked as an intermediary with the fearsome Shiva, and the **Buddha**.

Back towards the main entrance to the complex are two **stones** surrounded by railings, one marked by a trident, the other with a spear – supplicants bring

The evening puja

Kataragama's Sacred Precinct springs to life at **puja** times. Flocks of pilgrims appear bearing the fruit platters as offerings to Kataragama, and many smash coconuts in front of his shrine (see below). As the puja begins, a long queue of pilgrims line up to present their offerings, while a priest makes a drawn-out sequence of obeisances in front of the curtained shrine and a huge ringing of bells fills the temple. Musicians playing oboe-like *horanavas*, trumpets and drums perambulate around the complex, followed by groups of pilgrims performing the **kavadi**, or peacock dance, spinning around like dervishes whilst carrying *kavadi*s, the semicircular hoops studded with peacock feathers after which the dance is named. The music is strangely jazzy, and the dancers spin with such fervour that it's not unusual to see one or two of the more enthusiastic collapsing in a dead faint on the ground. Eventually the main Kataragama shrine is opened to the waiting pilgrims, who enter to deposit their offerings and pay homage to the god, while others pray at the adjacent Buddha shrine or bo trees.

The evening puja starts at 7pm. There's another early-morning puja at around 5am (except on Sat), and a mid-morning one at around 11am, though these are pretty low-key compared to the evening ceremonies.

coconuts here as offerings to Kataragama, sometimes setting fire to the coconut first, then holding it aloft while saying a prayer, before smashing it to pieces on one of the stones. It's considered extremely inauspicious if your coconut fails to break when you throw it on the stone, which explains the concentration and determination with which pilgrims perform the ritual. North of the main enclosure stands a secondary complex of subsidiary shrines, including ones to Vishnu and to Kataragama's wife, Valli Amma. Next to the Maha Devale, the scandalously overpriced new **Kataragama Museum** (8am–5pm; US$5) houses various bits of religious statuary and other paraphernalia, but really isn't worth the money.

From the rear of the Maha Devale, a road leads 500m past further lines of stalls selling lotus flowers to the **Kiri Vihara**, an alternative focus for Buddhist devotions at Kataragama – it's basically just a big dagoba, its only unusual feature being the two sets of square walls which enclose it – but it's a peaceful place, surrounded by parkland and usually far less busy than the Maha Devale. A modern statue of King Dutugemunu astride his faithful elephant Kandula stands just behind.

3

Kandy and the hill country

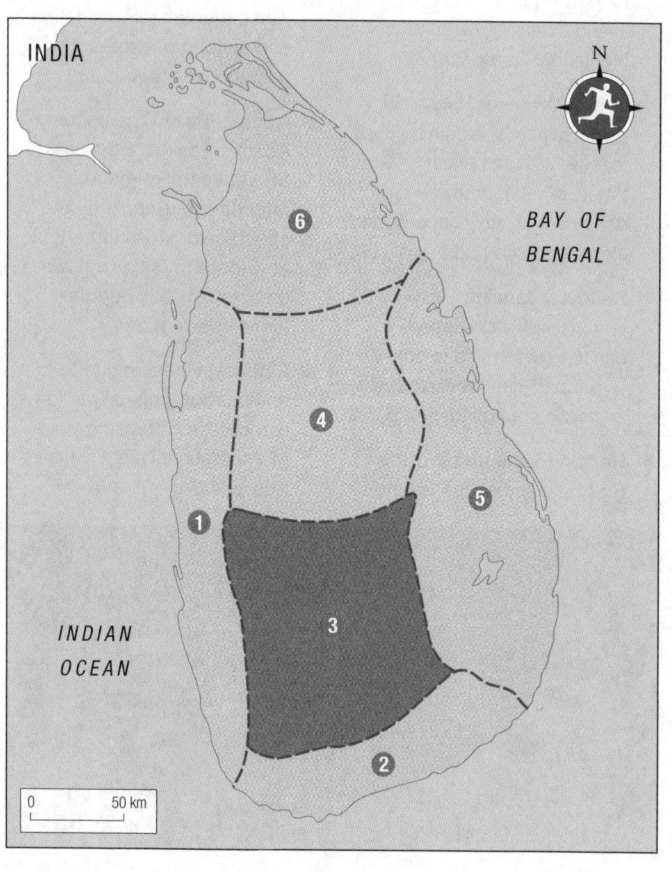

CHAPTER 3 **Highlights**

* **Pinnewala Elephant Orphanage** Home to the world's largest troupe of captive pachyderms. See p.227

* **Kandy** The last independent capital of the Sinhalese, hidden away amidst the island's beautiful central highlands. See p.230

* **Esala Perahera, Kandy** Sri Lanka's most spectacular festival, with immense processions of drummers, dancers and richly caparisoned elephants. See p.232

* **Kandyan dancing** Watch lavishly costumed dancers performing to an accompaniment of explosively energetic drumming. See p.253

* **Horton Plains and World's End** Hike across the uplands of Horton Plains to the vertiginous cliffs of World's End, which plunge sheer for almost a kilometre to the plains below. See p.276

* **Ella** The island's most beautifully situated village, with superb views, country walks through tea plantations and a string of excellent guesthouses. See p.282

* **Adam's Peak** The ascent of Adam's Peak is the classic Sri Lankan pilgrimage, offering the island's most spectacular view and a look at a footprint said to have been left by the Buddha himself. See p.294

* **Sinharaja** This unique tract of undisturbed tropical rainforest is a botanical treasure trove of international significance. See p.305

▲ Kandyan dancing

3

Kandy and the hill country

Occupying the island's southern heartlands, the sublime green heights of the **hill country** are a world away from the sweltering coastal lowlands – indeed nothing encapsulates the scenic diversity of Sri Lanka as much as the short journey by road or rail from the humid urban melee of Colombo to the cool altitudes of Kandy or Nuwara Eliya. The **landscape** here is a beguiling mixture of nature and nurture. In places the mountainous green hills rise to surprisingly rugged and dramatic peaks, whose craggy grandeur belies the island's modest dimensions; in others, the slopes are covered in carefully manicured tea gardens whose neatly trimmed lines of bushes add a toy-like quality to the landscape, while the mist and clouds which frequently blanket the hills add a further layer of mystery.

The hill country has been shaped by two very different historical forces. The northern portion, around the historic city of **Kandy**, was home to Sri Lanka's last independent kingdom, which survived two centuries of colonial incursions before finally falling to the British in 1815. The cultural legacy of this independent Sinhalese tradition lives on today in the city's distinctive music, dance and architecture, encapsulated by the **Temple of the Tooth**, home to the island's most revered Buddhist relic, and the exuberant **Kandy Esala Perahera**, one of Asia's most spectacular festivals.

In contrast, the character of the southern hill country is largely a product of the British colonial era, when tea was introduced to the island, an industry which continues to shape the economy and scenery of the entire region. At the heart of the tea-growing uplands lies the town of **Nuwara Eliya**, which preserves a few quaint traces of its British colonial heritage and provides the best base for visiting the misty uplands of **Horton Plains** and **World's End**. To the south, in Uva Province, a string of small towns and villages – **Ella**, **Bandarawela** and **Haputale** – offer marvellous views and walks through the hills and tea plantations. At the southwestern corner of the hill country lies the town of **Ratnapura**, the island's gem-mining centre and a possible base for visits to the **Sinharaja** reserve, a rare and remarkable pocket of surviving tropical rainforest, **Uda Walawe National Park**, home to one of the island's largest elephant populations, and **Adam's Peak**, whose rugged summit, bearing the imprint of what is claimed to be the Buddha's footprint, remains an object of pilgrimage for devotees of all four of the island's principal religions.

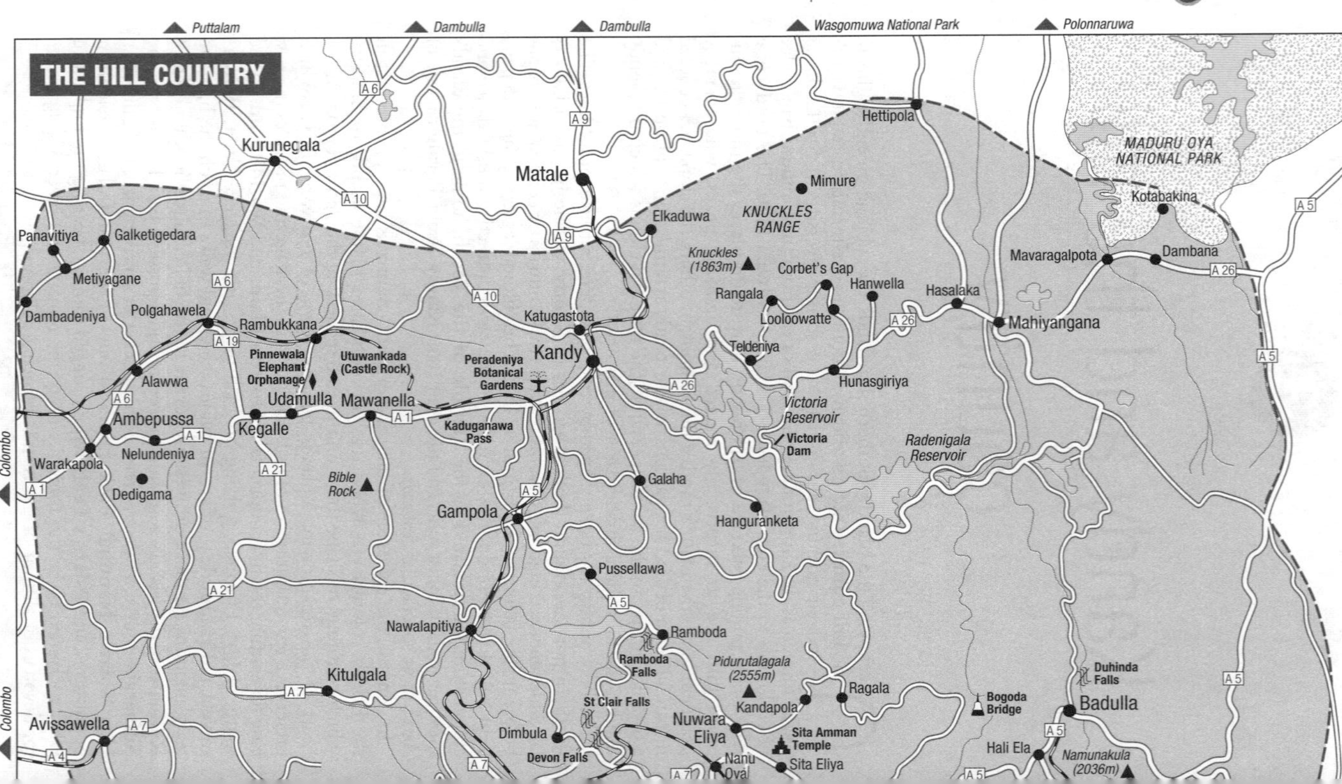
THE HILL COUNTRY
Puttalam
Dambulla
Dambulla
Wasgomuwa National Park
Polonnaruwa
Batticaloa
Colombo
Colombo
MADURU OYA NATIONAL PARK
Kotabakina
Dambana
Mavaragalpota
Mahiyangana
Hettipola
Mimure
KNUCKLES RANGE
Knuckles (1863m)
Corbet's Gap
Hanwella
Hasalaka
Rangala
Looloowatte
Teldeniya
Hunasgiriya
Victoria Reservoir
Victoria Dam
Radenigala Reservoir
Elkaduwa
Matale
Kurunegala
Panavitiya
Galketigedara
Metiyagane
Dambadeniya
Polgahawela
Rambukkana
Pinnewala Elephant Orphanage
Utuwankada (Castle Rock)
Alawwa
Udamulla
Mawanella
Ambepussa
Kegalle
Nelundeniya
Warakapola
Dedigama
Bible Rock
Katugastota
Kandy
Peradeniya Botanical Gardens
Kaduganawa Pass
Galaha
Hanguranketa
Gampola
Pussellawa
Nawalapitiya
Ramboda
Ramboda Falls
Pidurutalagala (2555m)
Ragala
Kitulgala
St Clair Falls
Kandapola
Nuwara Eliya
Sita Amman Temple
Sita Eliya
Nanu Oya
Dimbula
Devon Falls
Avissawella
Bogoda Bridge
Duhinda Falls
Badulla
Hali Ela
Namunakula (2036m)
A 1
A 4
A 5
A 6
A 7
A 9
A 10
A 19
A 21
A 26

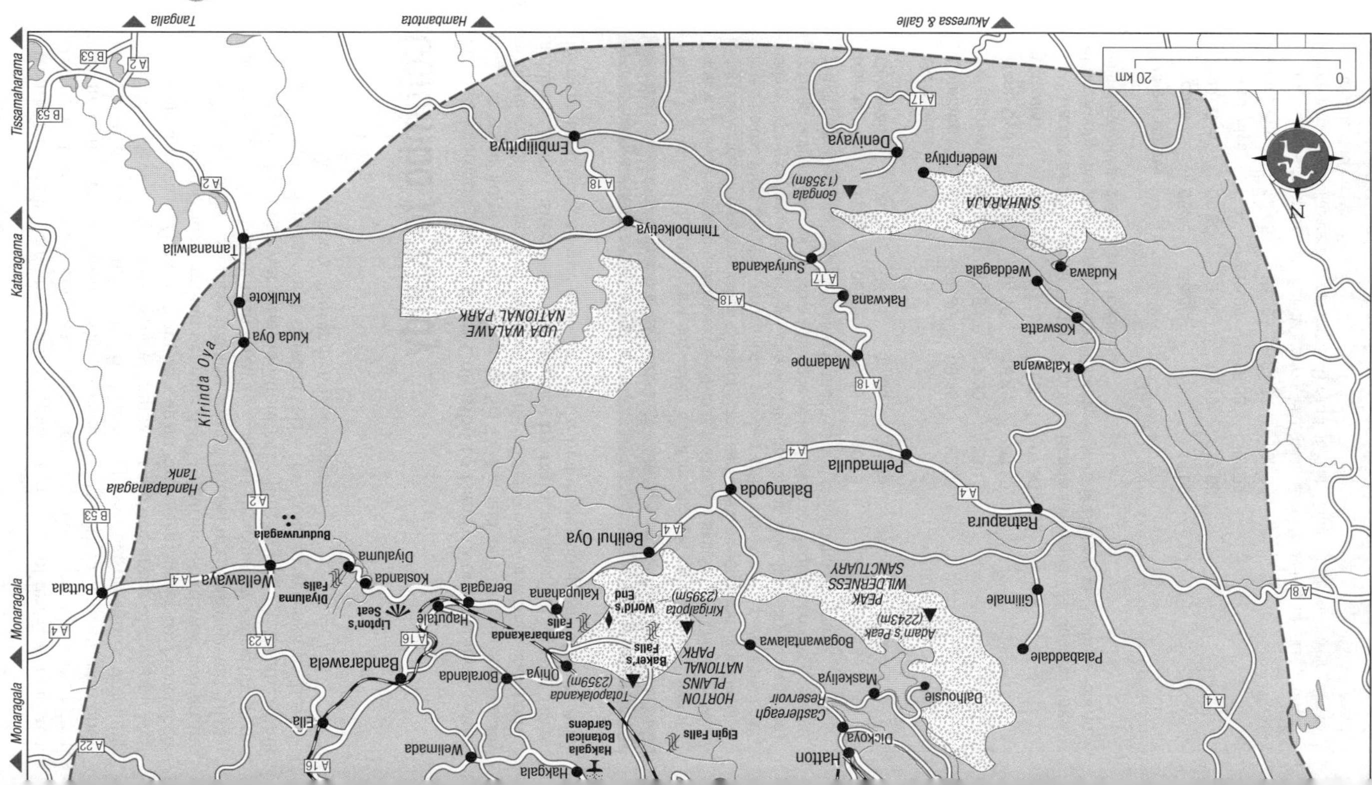
Monaragala
Monaragala
Kataragama
Tissamaharama
Tangalla
Hambantota
Akuressa & Galle
Buttala
Wellawaya
Handapanagala Tank
Kirinda Oya
Buduruwagala
Diyaluma Falls
Diyaluma
Koslanda
Lipton's Seat
Haputale
Beragala
Kalupahana
Bambarakanda Falls
Ella
Bandarawela
Welimada
Boralanda
Ohiya
Hakgala
Hakgala Botanical Gardens
Totapolakanda (2359m)
Baker's Falls
World's End
Elgin Falls
HORTON PLAINS NATIONAL PARK
Kirigalpota (2395m)
Belihul Oya
Balangoda
Hatton
Dickoya
Castlereagh Reservoir
Maskeliya
Bogawantalawa
PEAK WILDERNESS SANCTUARY
Adam's Peak (2243m)
Dalhousie
Palabaddale
Gilimale
Ratnapura
Pelmadulla
Madampe
Rakwana
Suriyakanda
Thimbolketiya
Embilipitiya
Kuda Oya
Kitulkote
Tamanalwila
UDA WALAWE NATIONAL PARK
Gongala (1358m)
Deniyaya
Mederipitiya
SINHARAJA
Kalawana
Koswatta
Weddagala
Kudawa
A 2
A 4
A 8
A 16
A 17
A 18
A 22
A 23
B 53
0
20 km
N

Weather in the hill country is unpredictable at the best of times, and different areas enjoy slightly different climatic conditions depending on where they lie in relation to the two monsoons. As a very general rule of thumb, the driest months throughout the hill country are from January to April (sometimes stretching from Dec–May). There's usually heavy rainfall at the beginning of the southwest monsoon from May/June to July, and again from September to November/December. August, however, can be quite dry. The further southwest you go, the wetter things usually become – the area around Ratnapura, Sinharaja and Adam's Peak receives more rainfall than anywhere else in the country, especially at the beginning of the southwest monsoon from May/June to July. The southeast hill country – Ella, Haputale and Bandarawela – by contrast receives its heaviest rainfall from September to November/December.

Colombo to Kandy

The 110-kilometre journey **from Colombo to Kandy** is one that most visitors make at some point during a tour of Sri Lanka, and one which dramatically encapsulates the scenic contrasts between the island's coastal lowlands and interior highlands. Many visitors make the journey **by train**, a classic rail journey (sit on the right-hand side en route to Kandy for the best views) along one of south Asia's

Principal trains in the hill country

Note that railway timetables are subject to constant change, so it's always best to check latest departure times before travelling at the nearest station (or online at Ⓦwww.bluehaventours.com). In addition to the principal services between Kandy and Badulla listed below, there are also various local services which cover only a part of the line; again, timings change frequently – check at the nearest station. Inter-city services are marked with an asterisk (*). Note that none of the Colombo–Badulla services goes via Kandy; you'll have to catch a train to Peradeniya and pick up the train there.

Kandy	05.00	06.10*	06.35	10.25	15.00*	15.30
Colombo	08.15	08.45	10.00	13.45	17.35	18.45

Up trains

Colombo	05.45	08.35*	09.45	22.00
Peradeniya	08.36	10.50	12.30	23.15
Nanu Oya	12.30	14.10	15.45	03.30
Badulla	16.00	–	19.00	07.30

All Badulla services call at Hatton, Haputale, Bandarawela and Ella. Journey times from Kandy are approximately 2hr 30min to Hatton, 5hr 30min to Haputale, 6hr to Bandarawela and 6hr 30min to Ella.

Down trains

Badulla	05.45	08.50	–	18.00
Nanu Oya	09.30	12.30	15.15*	22.00
Peradeniya	–	17.00	18.33	02.27
Colombo	15.45	19.30	21.00	05.30

All services from Badulla call at Hatton, Haputale, Bandarawela and Ella. Journey times from Badulla are approximately 1hr to Ella, 1hr 30min to Bandarawela, 2hr to Haputale and 5hr to Hatton.

most spectacularly engineered tracks, first opened in 1867, which weaves slowly upwards through long tunnels and along narrow ledges blasted by Victorian engineers out of solid rock, with vertiginous drops below. Despite the pleasures of the train trip, however, the journey **by road** (another legacy of British engineering skills, completed in 1825) is in many respects more spectacular, as the main highway rolls uphill and down, before making the final, engine-busting climb up into Kandy, giving a much more immediate sense of the hills' scale and altitude than the rail line's carefully graded ascent – although the long slog through the interminable suburbs of Colombo and Kandy is an undoubted drag.

East from Colombo

Heading inland from Colombo along the Kandy road, the interminable urban sprawl continues for the best part of 25km until you pass the turn-off to the large town of Gampaha. Beyond here, a series of roadside villages exemplify the continuing tendency for Sri Lankan villages (especially in the Kandyan region) to specialize in a particular craft or crop. These include, in order, **Belummahara** (pineapples, stacked up in neat racks by the roadside), **Nittambuwa** (rambutans, when in season), **Cadjugama** (cashew nuts) and **Radawaduna** (cane furniture) (see map, p.84). Cadjugama, in particular, attracts a steady trade from passing tourists, who stop to sample the cashew nuts which are collected wild in the nearby jungle and sold by ladies along the road, although prices are high and the atmosphere is hassly and unappealing.

Dedigama

Some five kilometres beyond Cadjugama, around the village of **Warakapola** (roughly at the halfway point between Colombo and Kandy), the appearance of steep-sided, forest-covered hills marks the gradual beginnings of the hill country. A few kilometres beyond Warakapola, at Nelundeniya, a side road from the main highway heads 4km south through a verdant landscape of rubber trees, paddy fields and banana palms to the sleepy village of **DEDIGAMA**. The village was formerly the capital of the semi-autonomous southern kingdom of **Dakkinadesa** and served as one of the island's capitals for a decade or so during the reigns of the brothers Bhuvanekabahu IV (1341–51) and Parakramabahu V (1344–59), who ruled simultaneously from Dedigama and Gampola, although sources disagree on which king reigned from which city. (A pillar inscription erected by Bhuvanekabahu can be found in the grounds of the modern Kota Vihara temple in the middle of the village, though its substance – the pardoning of a rebellion – suggests how slight his hold on power actually was.) The place is better known, however, for its associations with **Parakramabahu the Great** (see p.340), king of Polonnaruwa, who was born here and who later succeeded to the throne of Dakkinadesa – although he quickly hot-footed it off to Panduwas Nuwara, where he established a new capital before launching his bid for islandwide power.

Parakramabahu is popularly credited with having created Dedigama's major sight, the huge **Suthighara Cetiya**, just past the Kota Vihara, whose impressive remains – comprising the huge base and lower portion of a dagoba on a high, three-tiered base – seem totally out of scale with the tiny modern-day village. Next to the dagoba, the **Dedigama Museum** (daily except Tues 8am–4pm; donation) contains an interesting cache of objects recovered from the dagoba's relic chamber, and that of a second, but now vanished, dagoba, including a fine sequence of tiny and delicately carved gold-plated Buddhas and an unusual elephant-topped oil lamp. There are also full-size models of the dagoba's upper and lower relic chambers, and a model of the *yantragala* (relic tray) which was once filled with the semi-precious stones and crystal reliquaries.

Dambadeniya and around

Another, longer, detour can be made by heading north from Warakapola to a second, and much more significant, former seat of Sinhalese power, some 10km north of the highway at the village of **DAMBADENIYA**, the first of the short-lived Sinhalese capitals which was established following the fall of Polonnaruwa. The new capital was founded by **Vijayabahu III** (1232–36) and also served as the seat of his son, **Parakramabahu II** (1236–70), whose long reign saw a brief renaissance in Sinhalese political power. Parakramabahu II succeeded in expelling the Indian invader Magha with Pandyan help, and his forces re-occupied the shattered cities of Anuradhapura and Polonnaruwa, though this purely symbolic victory was followed by further turmoil, and his son, Vijayabahu IV (1270–72), lasted only two years before being assassinated by Bhuvanekabahu, who moved the capital to Yapahuwa.

The main attraction here is the rambling **Vijayasundara Vihara** ("Beautiful Vijaya Temple", named in honour of Vijayabahu III, who founded it). A rough-and-ready structure supported by crude stone columns covered in spots of moss and dusty old wooden beams, the attractively rustic central shrine formerly housed the island's famous Tooth Relic, which was kept here in a room on the upper storey (reached via a rickety wooden staircase), its exterior walls decorated with faded paintings under sections of cut-away plaster. Inside, Kandyan-era strip paintings show various scenes including the Tooth Relic procession and a vivid depiction of the Jataka story of King Dhamsonda, in which the Buddha, in a previous incarnation, can be seen jumping into the mouth of a hungry demon to assuage its hunger. There's also an impressive bo tree, while fragments of very ancient stone carvings, probably dating back to the thirteenth century, are scattered around the temple, including the guardstones flanking the entrance to the so-called subsidiary shrine next to the central shrine. A statue, said to be of Parakramabahu II, stands on the far side of the complex. The resident head monk is happy to show visitors around and enjoys striking a pose for photographs, but is also wont to solicit excessively large donations – a few dollars should suffice.

A couple of minutes' drive from the Vijayasundara Vihara are the remains of Dambadeniya's **Royal Palace**, sitting atop a large granite outcrop dotted with rock-cut pools and approached by a fine stone staircase. Not much remains of the palace itself, however, bar some simple brick foundations, though the setting, surrounded by bird-filled jungle, is atmospheric.

Panavitiya

A few kilometres north of Dambadeniya, the village of **PANAVITIYA** is home to an interesting little **ambalana** (rest house), built to provide shelter for travellers along the road (this was the old highway to Anuradhapura). The tiny but intricately carved rosewood structure is richly decorated with assorted Kandyan-style carvings, similar to those found at the Embekke Devale and Padeniya Raja Mahavihara, including a mahout with elephant and stick, wrestlers, dancers and drummers, demons, coiled snakes, peacocks and many other human and animal figures, framed in decorative bands of lotus rosettes and coiled rope motifs. Unfortunately, termites have gobbled up significant chunks of the original wood, which accounts for the clumsy lumps of filler which hold parts of the structure together.

The turn-off to Panavitiya is in the village of **Metiyagane**: from here, turn north along Panavitiya Danggolla Road for around 2km, then turn left at the black archeological department sign to Panavitiya. The *ambalana* is a few hundred metres further along.

Pinnewala Elephant Orphanage and around

Back on the main road, the highway climbs steeply to the bustling town of **KEGALLE**, crammed into a single hectic main street along the side of an elevated ridge – the top of the cute yellow clocktower is said to be modelled on the hat of a British governor. Just beyond Kegalle, and some 40km west of Kandy, a turn-off heads to the **Pinnewala Elephant Orphanage** (daily 8.30am–6pm; Rs.2000, video cameras Rs.500 extra), one of Sri Lanka's most popular tourist attractions. First set up in 1975 to look after five orphaned baby elephants, Pinnewala has now mushroomed to a population of more than eighty, making it the world's largest collection of captive elephants. The animals here range in age from newborns to elderly matriarchs, and include orphaned and abandoned elephants, as well as those injured in the wild (often in conflicts with farmers), amongst them famous residents such as the three-legged Sama, who stood on a land mine, and the blind Raja (the orphanage's oldest elephant, aged 65). In addition, the orphanage's population is constantly augmented by new arrivals born in captivity: one or two elephants are born here every year, and the babies here are without doubt the tiniest and cutest you're ever likely to see. The adult elephants work in the orphanage itself, earning their keep by helping with various chores, such as collecting food.

It's best to time your visit to coincide with one of the three daily **feeding sessions** (9.15am, 1.15pm & 5pm), an entertaining sight as the older elephants stuff their faces with trunkloads of palm leaves, whilst the orphaned youngsters guzzle enormous quantities of milk out of oversized baby bottles (for Rs.250, you can feed an elephant one bottle of milk yourself). Twice a day (10am–noon & 2–4pm), the elephants are driven across the road to the Ma Oya river for a leisurely bath – you can observe their antics from the riverbank or, in greater comfort and for the price of an expensive drink, from the terraces of the *Pinnalanda* or *Elephant Park Hotel* restaurants above the river.

Plans to establish a new national **zoo** at Pinnewala over the next couple of years have also been mooted, which would involve moving some of the animals currently housed in the Colombo zoo in Dehiwala (see p.108) into a new site next to the orphanage.

Shit happens: pachyderm paper

One of the most novel wildlife initiatives in Sri Lanka in recent years has been the invention of **pachyderm paper**: paper made from elephant dung. As well as their many remarkable abilities, elephants are also a kind of paper factory on legs. During feeding, they ingest a huge amount of fibre which is then pulped in the stomach and delivered in fresh dollops of dung, ready prepared for the manufacture of paper. The dung is dried in the sun and boiled, and the resultant pulp used to make high-quality stationery with an artistically textured finish. The texture and colour vary according to the elephants' diet, while other ingredients including tea, flowers, paddy husks and onion peel are also added according to the required finish. More than just a novelty stationery item, pachyderm paper could prove an important source of income to locals – and thus a significant help in conservation measures.

You can see the paper being made and buy a range of pachyderm paper products at the **Pinnawala Elephant Dung Paper Products** factory, on the side road to the elephant bathing spot near *Greenland Guesthouse*. Elephant paper is also available at the small shop by the elephant bathing spot, at the Millennium Elephant Foundation (see p.228) or online at ⓦwww.paperhigh.com.

Practicalities

Pinnewala is on a side road a few kilometres north of the road between Colombo and Kandy, just to the east of Kegalle, near the 82km post. By far the easiest way to reach it is **by taxi** from Kandy; count on US$25–30. You could conceivably visit by **tuktuk** from Kandy (around US$20), though it's a smelly and uncomfortable ride, and not worth the small saving. The orphanage is also reachable by public transport from Kandy. By **bus**, take a service from the Goods Shed terminal towards Kegalle (every 15min; 1hr) and get off at Udamulla, a few kilometres short of Kegalle. From here, catch a bus for Rambukkana and get off at Pinnewala (every 20min; 10min). By **train**, catch a service to Rambukkana (served by slow trains from Kandy to Colombo, approximately 5 daily; 1hr 40min), 3km from the orphanage, from where you can either hop on a bus or take a tuktuk. The orphanage could also be visited from **Colombo**: take one of the regular buses from the Bastian Mawatha terminal to Kegalle, or a train from Fort Railway Station to Rambukkana (around 5 daily from Colombo; 2hr 30min). From **Negombo**, a day-trip to the orphanage by taxi will cost around US$50. There's a handy Hatton National Bank in the village, whose **ATM** accepts foreign Visa and MasterCards.

There are lots of **handicraft shops** around the village (especially along the road leading from the orphanage to the river) with a wide range of stock, including leather goods and elephant paper (which is also sold at the orphanage) – see box on p.227. There are also heaps of **spice gardens** en route to Pinnewala.

Accommodation

Elephant Park ⓣ035-226 6171, ⓦwww.pinnalanda.com. The nicest option is the village, in an unbeatable riverside location. Rooms (all a/c and with hot water) are comfortable and modern, and some also have beautiful river views right above the elephant bathing spot. ❹

Elephant View ⓣ035-226 5292, ⓔeleview@sltnet.lk. Comfortable modern rooms with a/c and hot water either in its main building on the side road to the elephant bathing spot or in a separate annexe on the main road through the village (in the former *Pinnawala Village Hotel*). ❹

Greenland Guest House ⓣ035-226 5668, ⓔpinnawala@msn.com. The cheapest place in the village, tucked away on the side road leading to the elephant bathing spot, and with a range of slightly spartan fan and a/c rooms. Fan ❷, a/c ❸

Ralidiya Hotel ⓣ035-226 5321, ⓦwww.ralidiyahotel.com. On the main road through the village, this place is aimed mainly at local wedding parties, but also has three small and rather overpriced river-facing fan rooms. ❹

The Millennium Elephant Foundation

A few kilometres down the road from Pinnewala back towards Kandy, the **Millennium Elephant Foundation** (also known as the "Elephant Bath"; daily 8am–5pm; Rs.600; ⓦwww.millenniumelephantfoundation.org) has a rather more didactic aim than Pinnewala – indeed the two places complement one another rather neatly. With the exception of the young Pooja, who was born at the foundation in 1986 (the only birth here to date), the nine elephants here are all retired working beasts. Guides will tell you everything you need to know about elephants and demonstrate how they are trained to work; you can also help clean them and interact with them, and it's possible to do voluntary work with the foundation's mobile veterinary unit – see the website for details. The foundation was also instrumental in introducing pachyderm paper (see p.227) to the Sri Lankan market.

The small **museum** here is full of elephant skulls and (remarkably heavy) bones, along with a few poster displays.

Pinnewala to Kandy

Back on the main road to Kandy there are immediate views of the dramatically steep and densely forested mountain of **Utuwankanda** (also known by its British name of Castle Rock), the former stronghold of the infamous robber **Saradiel** (see box below). The road then climbs steeply again, giving increasingly grand views of craggy, densely wooded hills, including the prominent, flat-topped **Bible Rock** to the right, which acquired its pious name thanks to dutiful local Victorians on account of its resemblance to a lectern.

Past Bible Rock the road enters **Mawanella**, beyond which there are more spice gardens and another steep climb as the road hairpins ever upwards, with increasingly spectacular views, to the top at the famous viewpoint at **Kadugannawa**

Saradiel: Sri Lanka's Robin Hood

The spectacular rock-topped peak of Utuwankanda is famous in local legend as the hideout of the great Sri Lankan folk hero, **Deekirikevage Saradiel** (or Sardiel), who terrorized traffic on the main Kandy to Colombo highway throughout the 1850s and early 1860s, and whose exploits in fleecing the rich whilst succouring the poor have provoked inevitable comparisons with Robin Hood, whose flowing locks and predilection for remote forest hideouts Saradiel shared.

Saradiel's life of crime began early. Having been expelled from his temple school for assaulting a local rich kid, and following a spell as a barrack boy with the Ceylon Rifle Regiment in Slave Island, Saradiel launched into a fully fledged career of highway robbery. An initial flurry of thefts ended when, following the fatal stabbing of a police informer, Saradiel was arrested and taken back to Colombo to be tried for murder – though having arrived in the capital he managed to pull off the first of several daring escapes by climbing the prison wall and jumping off the roof.

Returning to Utuwankanda, Saradiel continued his career of banditry, protected by the thickness of the surrounding jungles, out of which he would swoop to prey on passing traffic. His gang waylaid carriages, regularly disrupting traffic on the Kandy road and forcing the British authorities to strengthen local police forces, though they remained unable to track down and capture the elusive highwayman – at one point they threw a drag-net around Utuwankanda, but once again Saradiel eluded capture in spectacular fashion by stampeding a herd of buffaloes and hanging onto one of the galloping beasts.

Saradiel was eventually lured to Mawanella and captured by a detachment of the Ceylon Rifles following a shoot-out, during which his companion, Mammalay Marikkar, had shot dead a certain Constable Shaban, the first Sri Lankan police officer to die in action – an event still commemorated annually by the island's police. Saradiel and Mammalay Marikkar were taken to Kandy, sentenced to death, and hanged on May 7, 1864. Thousands thronged the streets of the city to catch a glimpse of the notorious criminal, but were surprised to see a slim and pleasant-looking figure rather than the ferocious-looking highwayman they had expected – a police statement described him as 5ft 3in tall, with long hair and hazel eyes.

Despite terrorizing the area around Utuwankanda, it is said that Saradiel never robbed the poor – and that he often distributed his earnings amongst those most in need. The picturesque legend may have gained something in the telling in the 140 years since his death, and in his career of mayhem and murder Saradiel perhaps more closely resembles another rebellious nineteenth-century British colonial outlaw, Ned Kelly, rather than the peaceable Robin Hood. Whatever the truth, as a lone Sinhalese bandit who succeeded in disrupting the well-oiled machinery of British rule – and in consistently evading the consequences – Saradiel still commands a certain respect, and perhaps even affection, in the minds of Sri Lankans right up to the present day.

Pass, the most dramatic point along the entire highway, with spectacular views of Bible Rock and surrounding peaks – a panorama which brings home to ruggedness and scale of the hill country terrain and makes you realize why the Kingdom of Kandy was able to survive against European interference for so long. The road up cuts through a short rock-hewn tunnel before reaching the top of the pass, where there's a rather grand monument to British engineer **W.F. Dawson** (d.1829), who oversaw the construction of the Kandy road. A bit further on you'll pass the **Highway State Museum**, a rather grand name for a collection of five old colonial-era steamrollers, plus a replica of the Bogoda Bridge, laid out along the side of the road.

Beyond Kadugannawa town the long urban sprawl leading into Kandy begins – a tediously slow journey, especially during the morning and evening rush hours. The fantastically crowded little town of Pilimatalawa follows soon after, merging also seamlessly into Kiribathgoda and then Peradeniya, home to Kandy's university and famous botanical gardens (see p.255), on the outskirts of Kandy proper.

Kandy and around

Situated amidst precipitous green hills at the heart of the island, **KANDY** is the proud bastion of an independent Sinhalese tradition which preserved its freedom through two and a half centuries of attacks by the Portuguese and Dutch. Kandy's unique cultural heritage is everywhere apparent – in its music, dance and architecture – while the city is also home to the country's most important religious shrine, the **Temple of the Tooth**, as well as its most exuberant festival, the **Esala Perahera**. Kandy maintains a somewhat aristocratic air, enhanced by its scenic highland setting and its pleasantly temperate climate. And though the modern city, Sri Lanka's second largest, has begun to sprawl considerably, the twisted topography of the surrounding hills and the lake at its centre ensure that Kandy hasn't yet overwhelmed its scenic setting, and retains at its heart a modest grid of narrow, low-rise streets which, despite the crowds of people and traffic, retains a surprisingly small-town atmosphere.

Some history

Kandy owes its existence to its remote and easily defensible location amidst the steep, jungle-swathed hills at the centre of the island. The origins of the city date back to the early thirteenth century, during the period following the collapse of Polonnaruwa, when the Sinhalese people drifted gradually southwards (see p.419). During this migration, a short-lived capital was established at **Gampola**, just south of Kandy, before the ruling dynasty moved on to Kotte, near present-day Colombo. A few nobles left behind in Gampola soon revolted, and sometime during the fifteenth century moved their base to the still more remote and easily defensible town of **Senkadagala**. Senkadagala subsequently became known by the sweet-sounding name of **Kandy**, after Kanda Uda Pasrata, the Sinhalese name for the mountainous district in which it lay (although from the eighteenth century, the Sinhalese often referred to the city as **Maha Nuwara**, the "Great City", a name by which it's still sometimes known today).

By the time the Portuguese arrived in Sri Lanka in 1505, Kandy had established itself as the capital of one of the island's three main kingdoms (along with Kotte and Jaffna). The Portuguese swiftly turned their attentions to Kandy, though their first expedition against the city ended in failure when the puppet ruler they placed on the throne was ousted by the formidable **Vimala Dharma Suriya**, the first of many Kandyan rulers who tenaciously resisted the European invaders. As the remainder of the island fell to the Portuguese (and subsequently the Dutch), the Kandyan kingdom clung stubbornly to its independence, remaining a secretive and inward-looking place, protected by its own inaccessibility – Kandyan kings repeatedly issued orders prohibiting the construction of bridges or the widening of footpaths into the city, fearing that they would become conduits for foreign attack. The city was repeatedly besieged and captured by the Portuguese (in 1594, 1611, 1629 and 1638) and the Dutch (in 1765), but each time the Kandyans foiled their attackers by burning the city to the ground and retreating into the surrounding forests, from where they continued to harry the invaders until they were forced to withdraw to the coast. Despite its isolation, the kingdom's prestige as the final bastion of Sinhalese independence was further enhanced during the seventeenth and eighteenth centuries by the presence of the **Tooth Relic** (see p.243), the traditional symbol of Sinhalese sovereignty, while an imposing temple, the **Temple of the Tooth**, was constructed to house the relic.

It had long been the tradition for the kings of Kandy to take South Indian brides descended from the great Vijayanagaran dynasty, and when the last Sinhalese king of Kandy, Narendrasinha, died in 1739 without an heir, the crown passed to his Indian wife's brother, Sri Viyjaya Rajasinha (1739–47), so ending the Kandyan dynasty established by Vimala Dharma Suriya and ushering in a new Indian **Nayakkar** dynasty. The Nayakkar embraced Buddhism and cleverly played on the rivalries of the local Sinhalese nobles who, despite their dislike of the foreign rulers, failed to unite behind a single local leader. In a characteristically Kandyan paradox, it was under the foreign Nayakkar that the city enjoyed its great Buddhist revival. **Kirti Sri Rajasinha** came to the throne in 1747 and began to devote himself – whether for political or spiritual reasons – to his adopted religion, reviving religious education, restoring and building temples and overseeing the reinvention of the **Esala Perahera** (see p.232) as a Buddhist rather than a Hindu festival. These years saw the development of a distinctively Kandyan style of architecture and dance, a unique synthesis of local Sinhalese traditions and southern Indian styles.

Having gained control of the island in 1798, the **British** quickly attempted to rid themselves of this final remnant of Sinhalese independence, although their first expedition against the kingdom, in 1803, resulted in a humiliating defeat. Despite this initial reverse, the kingdom survived little more than a decade, though it eventually fell not through military conquest but thanks to internal opposition to the excesses and cruelties of the last king of Kandy, **Sri Wickrama Rajasinha** (ruled 1798–1815). As internal opposition to Sri Wickrama grew, the remarkable **Sir John D'Oyly**, a British government servant with a talent for languages and intrigue, succeeded in uniting the various factions opposed to the king. In 1815, the British were able to despatch another army which, thanks to D'Oyly's machinations, was able to march on Kandy unopposed. Sri Wickrama fled, and when the British arrived, the king's long-suffering subjects simply stood to one side and let them in. On **March 2, 1815**, a convention of Kandyan chiefs signed a document handing over sovereignty of the kingdom to the British, who in return promised to preserve its laws, customs and institutions.

Within two years, however, the Kandyans had decided they had had enough of their new rulers and **rebelled**, an uprising which soon spread across the entire hill

The Esala Perahera

Kandy's ten-day **Esala Perahera** is the most spectacular of Sri Lanka's festivals, and one of the most colourful religious pageants in Asia. Its origins date back to the arrival of the **Tooth Relic** (see p.243) in Sri Lanka in the fourth century AD, during the reign of Kirti Siri Meghawanna, who decreed that the relic be carried in procession through the city once a year. This quickly developed into a major religious event – the famous Chinese Buddhist Fa-Hsien, visiting Anuradhapura in 399 AD, described what had already become a splendid festival, with processions of jewel-encrusted elephants. Occasional literary and artistic references suggest that these celebrations continued in some form throughout the thousand years of upheaval which followed the collapse of Anuradhapura and the Tooth Relic's peripatetic journey around the island. Esala processions continued into the Kandyan era in the seventeenth century, though the Tooth Relic lost its place in the procession, which evolved into a series of lavish parades in honour of the city's four principal deities: Vishnu, Kataragama, Natha and Pattini, each of whom had (and still has) a temple in the city.

The festival took shape in 1775, during the reign of **Kirti Sri Rajasinha**, when a group of visiting Thai clerics expressed their displeasure at the lack of reverence accorded to the Buddha during the parades. To propitiate them, the king ordered the Tooth Relic to be carried through the city at the head of the four temple processions. A pattern that endures to this day. Sri Rajasinha's own enthusiastic participation in the festivities, and that of his successors, also added a political dimension – the Nayyakar kings of Kandy (who were from South India) probably encouraged the festival in the belief that by associating themselves with one of Buddhism's most sacred relics, they would reinforce their dynasty's shaky legitimacy in the eyes of their Sinhalese subjects. The Tooth Relic itself was last carried in procession in 1848, since when it's been considered unpropitious for it to leave the temple sanctuary – its place is now taken by a replica.

The festival

The ten days of the festival begin with the **Kap Tree Planting Ceremony**, during which cuttings from a tree – traditionally an Esala tree, though nowadays a Jak or Rukkattana are more usually employed – are planted in the four *devales* (see p.247), representing a vow (*kap*) that the festival will be held. The procession (perahera) through the streets of Kandy is held nightly throughout the festival: the first five nights, the so-called **Kumbal Perahera**, are relatively low-key; during the final five nights, the **Randoli Perahera**, things become progressively more spectacular, building up to the last night (the Maha Perahera, or "Great Parade"), featuring a massive cast of participants including as many as a hundred brilliantly caparisoned elephants and thousands of drummers, dancers and acrobats walking on stilts, cracking whips, swinging fire pots and carrying banners, while the replica casket of the Tooth Relic itself is carried on the back of the **Maligawa Tusker** elephant (see p.246).

Following the last perahera, the **water-cutting ceremony** is held before the dawn of the next day at a venue near Kandy, during which a priest wades out into the Mahaweli Ganga and "cuts" the waters with a sword. This ceremony symbolically releases a supply of water for the coming year (the Tooth Relic is traditionally believed to protect against drought) and divides the pure from the impure – it might also relate to the exploits of the early Sri Lankan king, **Gajabahu** (reigned 174–196 AD), who is credited with the Moses-like feat of dividing the waters between Sri Lanka and India in order to march his army across during his campaign against the Cholas.

After the water-cutting ceremony, at 3pm on the same day, there's a final **"day" perahera**, a slightly scaled-down version of the full perahera. It's not as spectacular as the real thing, though it does offer excellent photo opportunities.

The procession

The perahera is a carefully orchestrated, quasi-theatrical event – there is no spectator participation here, although the astonishing number of performers during later nights give the impression that most of Kandy's citizens are involved. The perahera actually comprises five separate processions, which follow one another around the city streets: one from the Temple of the Tooth, and one from each of the four *devales* – a kind of giant religious conga, with elephants. The exact route changes from day to day, although the procession from the Temple of the Tooth always leads the way, followed (in unchanging order) by the processions from the Natha, Vishnu, Kataragama and Pattini *devales* (Natha, as a Buddha-to-be, takes precedence over the other divinities). As its centrepiece, each procession has an elephant carrying the insignia of the relevant temple – or, in the case of the Temple of the Tooth, the replica Tooth Relic. Each is accompanied by other elephants, various dignitaries dressed in traditional Kandyan costume and myriad dancers and drummers, who fill the streets with an extraordinary barrage of noise. The processions each follow a broadly similar pattern, although there are slight differences. The Kataragama procession – as befits that rather unruly god (see p.216) – tends to be the wildest and most freeform, with jazzy trumpet playing and dozens of whirling dancers carrying *kavadis*, the hooped wooden contrivances, studded with peacock feathers, which are one of that god's symbols. The Pattini procession, the only one devoted to a female deity, attracts mainly female dancers. The beginning and end of each perahera is signalled by a deafening cannon shot.

Perahera practicalities

The perahera is traditionally held over the last nine days of the lunar month of Esala, finishing on Nikini poya day – this usually falls during late July and early August, though exact **dates** vary according to the vagaries of the lunar calendar, and the festival authorities sometimes opt for slightly different dates depending on practical or astrological considerations. Dates can be checked on Ⓦwww.srilanka.travel and www.daladamaligawa.org, but be aware that these aren't usually confirmed until about three months before the event; the latter site also has lots of background information on the festival.

Accommodation during the Esala Perahera can get booked up months in advance, and prices in most places can double or triple (although the slump in Sri Lankan tourism over the last couple of years has seen far fewer overseas tourists visiting the procession, leading to correspondingly lower accommodation prices). If you get stuck for somewhere to stay, the tourist office should be able to help you out; in addition, many locals rent out rooms during the festival. Note that the entire city more or less shuts down during the latter stages of the perahera – from mid-afternoon, the centre fills with spectators, the streets are cordoned off and all businesses close.

The perahera itself begins between 8pm and 9pm. You can see the parade for free by grabbing a spot on the **pavement** next to the route. During the early days of the perahera it's relatively easy to find pavement space; during the last few nights, however, you'll have to arrive four or five hours in advance and then sit in your place without budging – even if you leave for just a minute to go to the toilet, you probably won't get your spot back. Not surprisingly, most foreigners opt to pay to reserve one of the thousands of **seats** which are set out in the windows and balconies of buildings all along the route of the perahera (sometimes in unnervingly precarious positions); this obviously guarantees you a place, and something to sit on, although you'll still have to be in it a couple of hours before the perahera begins or you risk not being able to get through the crowds that throng the pavements. On the last three or four nights seats start at US$10–20 for the cheapest spots (usually on the upper floors of streetside buildings and with restricted views) and go for US$50 or more for good street-level positions with unrestricted views – while the very best seats can go for considerably more than this; on earlier nights a good seat will cost US$20–30. If possible, check exactly which seat you're being offered before handing over any cash, and beware of unscrupulous touts who might simply disappear with your money – it's safest to book a seat through your guesthouse or hotel.

country. The British were obliged to call for troops from India and exert their full military might in order to put down the uprising. Fears of resurgent Kandyan nationalism continued to haunt the British during the following decades – it was partly the desire to be able to move troops quickly to Kandy which prompted the construction of the first road to the city in the 1820s, one of the marvels of Victorian engineering in Sri Lanka. Despite the uncertain political climate, Kandy soon developed into an important centre of British rule and trade, with the usual hotels, courthouses and churches servicing a burgeoning community of planters and traders. In 1867, the **railway** from Colombo was completed, finally transforming the once perilous trek from the coast into a comfortable four-hour journey, and so linking Kandy once and for all with the outside world.

Post-colonial Kandy has continued to expand, preserving its status as the island's second city despite remaining a modest little place compared to Colombo. It has also managed largely to avoid the Civil War conflicts which traumatized the capital, suffering only one major LTTE attack, in 1998, when a **truck bomb** was detonated outside the front of the Temple of the Tooth, killing over twenty people and reducing the front of the building to rubble.

Arrival and information

Kandy's **train station** and the main **Goods Shed bus station** sit next to one another on the southwest edge of the city centre. Note that the city's tuktuk drivers are possibly the most rapacious in Sri Lanka and you may have to pay well over the odds to reach your hotel. The **tourist office** (daily 9am–4pm; ⓣ081-222 2661), near the entrance to the Temple of the Tooth, is a useful source of information about the city and surrounding area, as well as for the latest bus timetables. The **Cultural Triangle Office** (daily 9am–5pm; ⓣ081-222 2738), housed in the same building, sells Cultural Triangle tickets (see p.314) and also has a few books for sale on Kandy and Cultural Triangle sites.

Accommodation

There's a huge selection of **accommodation** in all price ranges in and around Kandy – many of the smarter places listed below are featured on ⓦwww.kandyhotels.com. The **temperature** in Kandy is markedly cooler than along

Hassles in Kandy

Kandy has a well-deserved reputation for **hassle**, **touts** and **con artists**, and unfortunately the situation seems to be getting worse. Easily the worst place for hassle is the main road along the south side of the lake en route to Saranakara Road, which is plagued by opportunistic young men who hang around hoping to embroil passing tourists in whatever wallet-emptying scheme they've recently dreamt up, whether accompanying you on a shopping trip, taking you for an overpriced tuktuk ride or any of the other scams listed on p.62. Other local scams which have recently emerged include attempts to take tourists on visits to local "tsunami schools" or offering you the chance to meet the "head priest" at the Temple of Tooth. The only good news is that these time-wasters are generally so amateurish that's its transparently obvious what they're really after.

▲ Departures board, Kandy train station

the coast – you probably won't need air-conditioning, but you probably will want hot water (all the following places have this unless stated otherwise). In general, the better the view, the further from town – and the more taxing the walk from the centre.

Most of the town's **budget** accommodation is clustered on just two roads: **Saranankara Road**, which climbs steeply up from the southern side of the lake, about ten minutes' walk from the town centre, and **Rajapihilla Mawatha**, which winds erratically around the hillside above – there's a useful **shortcut** up to Rajapihilla Mawatha via the steps from the lakeside to Royal Palace Park (see p.241), and another tiny footpath between the top of Saranankara Road (starting next to *Highest View* guesthouse) and Rajapihilla Mawatha. There are no **top-end** options in Kandy itself, but plenty scattered around the beautiful countryside surrounding the city.

Meals are available at all the places listed below, and most can also arrange tours (see p.254 for more details).

Budget

Blinkbonnie Tourist Inn 69 Rajapihilla Mw ⓣ081-222 2007, ⓔblinkbonnie@yahoo.com. Perched high above town, and with fine views from its terrace restaurant. Rooms are modern and comfortable; all have hot water and some sort of view, and some have a/c. There's also internet access, free pick-up from bus or train stations and motorbike rental (guests only; Rs.2000 per day). ②–④

Blue Haven 30/2 Poorna Lane, Asigiriya ⓣ081-222 9617, ⓦwww.bluehaventours.com. In a pleasantly semi-rural setting on the edge of town, with comfortable rooms, an attractive upstairs veranda and a terrace restaurant looking out over the tree tops – a good choice if you want to escape the tourist scene of Saranankara Rd. Good value at current rates, and Rough Guide readers are promised a further ten percent discount. Fan ②, a/c ③

Expeditor 41 Saranankara Rd ⓣ081-223 8316, ⓦwww.expeditorkandy.com. Smart modern guesthouse, owned by Kandy's leading tour guide (see p.254), with a wide range of rooms, from a couple of downstairs cheapies with shared bathroom to smart upstairs en-suite rooms with high wooden ceilings and fine lake views – all are nicely furnished, very comfortable and scrupulously maintained. Good home-cooking, too. ①–③

Freedom Lodge 30 Saranankara Rd ⓣ081-222 3506, ⓔfreedomomega @yahoo.com. Homely family-run guesthouse, with smart, extremely comfortable and very good-value

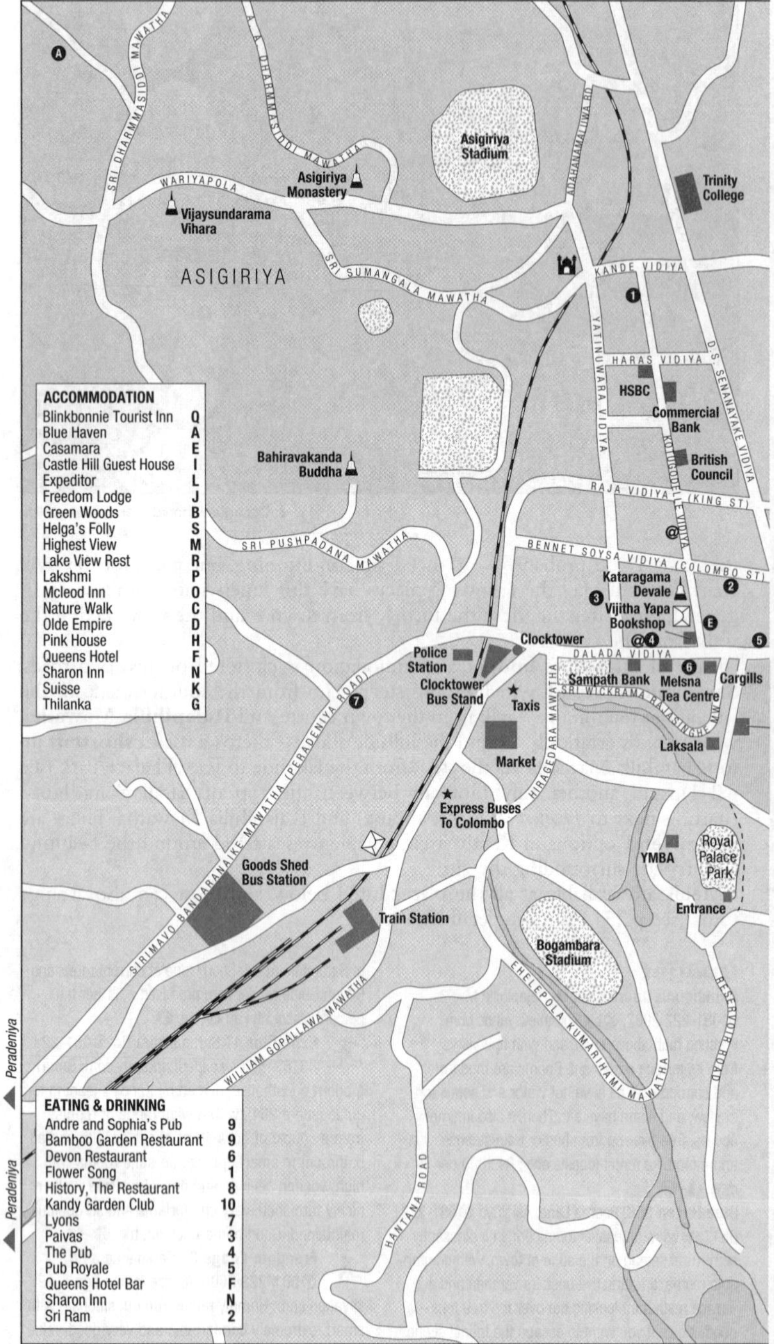

A
SRI DHARMMASIDDI MAWATHA
A. A. DHARMMASIDDI MAWATHA
Asigiriya Stadium
ADAHANAMALUWA RD
Trinity College
WARIYAPOLA
Asigiriya Monastery
Vijaysundarama Vihara
SRI SUMANGALA MAWATHA
ASIGIRIYA
KANDE VIDIYA
1
YATINUWARA VIDIYA
D.S. SENANAYAKE VIDIYA
HARAS VIDIYA
HSBC
Commercial Bank
KOTUGODELLE VIDIYA
British Council
Bahiravakanda Buddha
RAJA VIDIYA (KING ST)
SRI PUSHPADANA MAWATHA
BENNET SOYSA VIDIYA (COLOMBO ST)
Kataragama Devale
2
3
Vijitha Yapa Bookshop
E
4
5
Clocktower
Police Station
DALADA VIDIYA
Clocktower Bus Stand
Sampath Bank
6
Melsna Tea Centre
Cargills
SRI WICKRAMA RAJASINGHE MW
Taxis
HIRAGEDARA MAWATHA
7
Market
Laksala
Express Buses To Colombo
Royal Palace Park
YMBA
Entrance
SIRIMAVO BANDARANAIKE MAWATHA (PERADENIYA ROAD)
Goods Shed Bus Station
Train Station
Bogambara Stadium
WILLIAM GOPALLAWA MAWATHA
EHELEPOLA KUMARIHAMI MAWATHA
RESERVOIR ROAD
HANTANA ROAD
Peradeniya
Peradeniya
Tea Museum
ACCOMMODATION
Blinkbonnie Tourist Inn Q
Blue Haven A
Casamara E
Castle Hill Guest House I
Expeditor L
Freedom Lodge J
Green Woods B
Helga's Folly S
Highest View M
Lake View Rest R
Lakshmi P
Mcleod Inn O
Nature Walk C
Olde Empire D
Pink House H
Queens Hotel F
Sharon Inn N
Suisse K
Thilanka G
EATING & DRINKING
Andre and Sophia's Pub 9
Bamboo Garden Restaurant 9
Devon Restaurant 6
Flower Song 1
History, The Restaurant 8
Kandy Garden Club 10
Lyons 7
Paivas 3
The Pub 4
Pub Royale 5
Queens Hotel Bar F
Sharon Inn N
Sri Ram 2

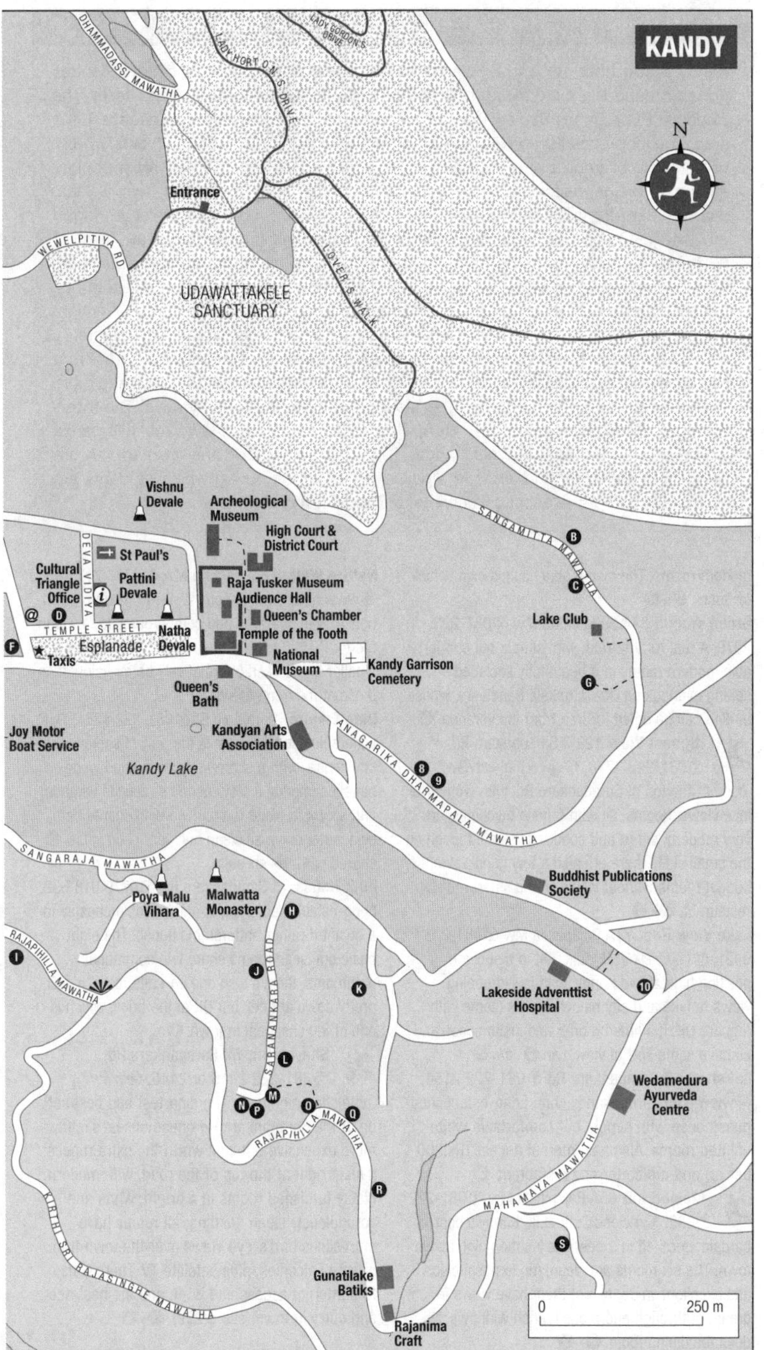
KANDY
N
DHAMMADASSI MAWATHA
LADY HORTON'S DRIVE
LADY GORDON'S DRIVE
Entrance
WEWELPITIYA RD
UDAWATTAKELE SANCTUARY
LOVER'S WALK
Vishnu Devale
Archeological Museum
High Court & District Court
St Paul's
Cultural Triangle Office
Pattini Devale
Raja Tusker Museum
Audience Hall
Queen's Chamber
Temple of the Tooth
DEVA VIDIYA
TEMPLE STREET
Natha Devale
Esplanade
Taxis
National Museum
Kandy Garrison Cemetery
Queen's Bath
SANGAMITTA MAWATHA
Lake Club
Joy Motor Boat Service
Kandyan Arts Association
Kandy Lake
ANAGARIKA DHARMAPALA MAWATHA
SANGARAJA MAWATHA
Poya Malu Vihara
Malwatta Monastery
Buddhist Publications Society
RAJAPIHILLA MAWATHA
SARANANKARA ROAD
Lakeside Adventtist Hospital
Wedamedura Ayurveda Centre
MAHAMAYA MAWATHA
KIRTHI SRI RAJASINGHE MAWATHA
Gunatilake Batiks
Rajanima Craft
0
250 m

Meditation

Kandy is the best place in Sri Lanka to study **meditation**, with numerous centres dotted around the surrounding countryside (though none right in the city itself). The Buddhist Publications Society (see p.254) has a full list of all the various centres in the area. The long-established **Nilambe Meditation Centre** (☎0777 804 555 or 0777 811 653, Ⓦwww.nilambe.org) is the place most used to dealing with – and most popular among – foreign visitors, set in a beautifully tranquil spot in the hills near Galaha, around 22km from Kandy. You can just turn up (though you might prefer to ring in advance just to be sure there's space) and there's no minimum length of stay. The cost is Rs.400 per day, including basic food and lodging. All levels are welcome, from novices to experienced meditators. To reach the centre, take the Galaha/Deltota bus from #633 from Kandy and ask the conductor to put you off at Nilambe Office Junction, from where it's a 45-minute walk. Bring a torch – there's no electricity at the centre.

The **Dhamma Kuta Vippassana Meditation Centre**, at Hindagala, 7km from Peradeniya (☎081-238 5774, Ⓦwww.beyondthenet.net/dhammakuta) caters to more experienced meditators, with courses lasting three, ten and twenty days. The **International Buddhist Meditation Centre** (☎060-280 1871, Ⓦwww.rockhillsrilanka.com), at Hondiyadeniya, Wegirikanda, 10km from Kandy on the road to Nuwara Eliya, runs challenging courses in Vipassana meditation during which students are required to adopt the ascetic lifestyle of a Buddhist monk.

modern rooms. The owner also has his own vehicle for tours. ❷–❸

Green Woods 34A Sangamitta Mw ☎081-223 2970. A real rural retreat, with simple but comfortable modern rooms in a beautifully secluded setting overlooking Udawattakele Sanctuary, whose birdlife can be ogled for free from the veranda. ❷

Highest View 129/3 Saranankara Rd ☎081-223 3778, Ⓦwww.highestview.com. At the top of Saranankara Rd, with wonderful lake views. Rooms, all with private balconies, are very modern, smart and spotlessly clean, though on the small side. There are also a few good-value budget rooms without views, and a smart roof-top restaurant. ❷–❸

Lake View Rest 71A Rajapihilla Mw ☎081-223 9421, Ⓔlakeview@sltnet.lk. Set in a sublime position high above Kandy, with jaw-dropping views to lake and city below. Rooms (some with a/c) are OK, if a little bit drab and institutional, and all have some sort of view. Fan ❸, a/c ❹

Lakshmi 57 Saranankara Rd ☎081-222 2154, Ⓦwww.palmgardenkandy.com. Long-established guesthouse with simple but comfortable white-painted rooms. Also has internet access (Rs.200 per hr) and a nice terrace restaurant. ❸

Mcleod Inn 65A Rajapihilla Mw ☎081-222 2832, Ⓔmcleod@sltnet.lk. Kandy's best bargain, perched in a peerless location high above town. The six rooms are clean, modern, spacious and excellent value; two of them have views to dream of through enormous French windows, as does the dining room. ❷–❸

Nature Walk 9 Sangamitta Mw ☎0777 717 482, Ⓦwww.naturewalkhr.com. Well-run modern guesthouse, with spacious and comfy rooms (a few with a/c for Rs.500 extra); those at the back are a bit smaller and darker, but relatively better value, than those at the front. ❷–❸

Olde Empire 21 Temple St ☎081-222 4284. This venerable establishment is the only cheapie in the city centre, with a charmingly antiquated wood-panelled interior, a picturesque streetside veranda, and six basic white rooms (two with shared bath; cold water only), all clean and very good value. ❶ shared bath, ❷ en-suite

Pink House 15 Saranankara Rd ☎0779 018 552. Long-established, popular and sociable cheapie in a quaint if rather battered old house. The eight basic but clean rooms share two communal bathrooms; there's also one en-suite room. It's all pretty down at heel, but OK at the price, which is one of the cheapest in town. ❶

Sharon Inn 59 Saranankara Rd ☎081-222 2416 or 2446, Ⓦwww.hotelsharoninn.com. The smartest and best set up of the Saranankara Rd guesthouses, slightly more expensive but well worth the extra rupees. It's set right at the top of the road, with modern, nicely furnished rooms in a bright, white and scrupulously clean building; all rooms have marvellous bird's-eye views over the town from private balconies, plus satellite TV. There's also free internet access and wi-fi, and the best rice and curry in town (see p.252). ❸–❹

Moderate and expensive

Hotel Casamara 12 Kotugodelle Vidiya ⓣ081-222 4688, ⓔcasamara@senfini.com. The most centrally located hotel in Kandy, and much nicer than its grotty exterior would suggest, offering well-equipped modern rooms with a/c, satellite TV and minibar. ❺

Castle Hill Guest House 22 Rajapihilla Mw ⓣ081-222 4376, ⓔayoni@sltnet.lk. Characterful colonial villa set in gorgeous gardens high above the lake and town, offering one of the best of Kandy's many memorable views. There are just four rooms: the two at the front are a bit bare, but with lovely views and big enough to swing a sackful of cats in; the two at the back are smaller and rather gloomy. ❹

Helga's Folly Off Mahamaya Mw ⓣ081-223 4571, ⓦwww.helgasfolly.com. Utterly maverick and magical place, set high above Kandy in a rambling old house whose former house guests have included Gandhi, Nehru and Laurence Olivier, not to mention Stereophonics frontman Kelly Jones, who penned a song in honour of the place. The extraordinary interior is a riot of colourful invention, with each room decorated in a different theme and colour, from the eye-popping yellow lounge, with petrified dripping candles, deer heads, Indonesian puppets and colonial photos, to the individual bedrooms (all a/c), each with a unique design featuring any combination of wacky murals, colonial furniture and unusual objets d'art – at least in the more expensive rooms, though the cheaper standard rooms are relatively disappointing given the price. Facilities include a small cinema and a (very shallow) pool. ❼–❾

Queens Hotel Dalada Vidiya ⓣ081-222 2813, ⓦwww.queenshotel.lk. Dating back to the 1860s, this venerable hotel is one of central Kandy's most famous landmarks, and still has a certain olde-worlde style. The spacious rooms (most with a/c) have plenty of colonial character – unfortunately all but nine of them overlook busy roads and are rather noisy. Good value nonetheless, and there's also a pool (non-guests Rs.200) plus a pleasantly old-fashioned in-house bar and restaurant. ❺

Hotel Suisse Sangaraja Mw ⓣ081-223 3024, ⓦwww.hotelsuisse.lk. Famous old hotel which served as Mountbatten's Southeast Asian headquarters during World War II. It's becoming a bit shabby, and often hosts noisy weddings, but rates are surprisingly inexpensive, and rooms (some lake facing; all with a/c and minibar) are spacious and comfortable, with vaguely colonial decor. The attractive public areas include a cosy bar, a billiards room and a pool (non-guests Rs.150). ❺

Thilanka 3 Sangamitta Mw ⓣ081-223 2429, ⓦwww.thilankahotel.com. Set high above the lake, with outstanding views and a large neon sign which disfigures the Kandyan skyline on a nightly basis. Choose between the attractively old-fashioned standard rooms and smarter deluxe rooms with a/c. Activities and facilities include yoga classes, a rustic and reasonably priced Ayurveda centre and the most spectacularly situated swimming pool in town (non-guests Rs.200). Excellent value. ❺–❻

Around Kandy

Amaya Hills 7km southwest of Kandy ⓣ081-223 3521, ⓦwww.amayaresorts.com. The highest hotel in the immediate vicinity of the city, this large pink edifice offers superlative views out over the hills, comfortable rooms with Kandyan-themed decor, a large pool (though it's quite cool up here), a gorgeous-smelling Ayurveda centre and wi-fi throughout. ❻

Chaaya Citadel 2km west of Kandy ⓣ081-223 4365, ⓦwww.johnkeellshotels.com. Occupying an attractive perch above the Mahaweli Ganga, this low-rise four-star is the best value – and perhaps also the best looking – of the big hotels around Kandy, with spacious and stylish rooms (all with minibar, safe, satellite TV and balcony) and a large pool. ❼–❽

Earl's Regency 4km east of Kandy ⓣ081-242 2122, ⓦwww.aitkenspence.com. Large and very well run – if somewhat characterless – five-star in a fine position overlooking the Mahaweli Ganga. All rooms are attractive and well appointed, and the more expensive ones boast sweeping hill or river views. There's also a large U-shaped pool, a spa and gym. ❼–❽

Jetwing Hunas Falls Elkaduwa, 27km north of Kandy ⓣ081-247 0041, ⓦwww.jetwing.com. One of the most spectacularly located hotels in Sri Lanka, perched way up in the hills on the western edge of the Knuckles Ranges, a bumpy 1hr drive from Kandy. There's a strong eco-tourism focus, with walks led by expert resident naturalists into the stunning surrounding countryside, and it's all surprisingly luxurious, despite the remote setting, with excellent food and plush rooms. ❼

Kandy House Gunnepana, 5km west of Kandy ⓣ081-492 1394, ⓦwww.thekandyhouse.com. Magical boutique guesthouse, 20min drive from central Kandy, set in a wonderfully atmospheric old traditional Kandyan *walauwa* (manor house) amidst thick jungle full of wild spices. Rooms are furnished with antique-style furniture, four-poster beds, Victorian bathtubs and are colourful contemporary silk and cotton fabrics, and are surrounded by gorgeous landscaped gardens running down to a beautiful little infinity swimming pool. ❽–❾

Kandy Samadhi Centre Kukul Oya Rd, 25km west of the city ⓣ081-447 0925, ⓦwww.thekandysamadhicentre.com. Beautiful and serene retreat, a 50min drive west of the city in an unspoilt area of mountainous jungle. The emphasis is on simplicity and tranquillity, with elegantly simple rustic decor and rooms scattered amongst thirteen individual pavilions. Ayurveda, shiatsu and reiki treatments are available, and all food is home-grown and organic (no meat or alcohol). ❹–❻

Mahaweli Reach 4km north of Kandy ⓣ081-447 2727, ⓦwww.mahaweli.com. Large, long-established hotel in a fine riverside setting by the Mahaweli Ganga. Rooms are beginning to look rather dated, and the whole place is showing signs of age, but it's not without a certain old-fashioned charm, and offers all the facilities you'd expect, given that it's one of only two five-stars in Kandy. ❼

Rangala House Rangala, 25km west of Kandy ⓣ081-240 0294, ⓦwww.rangalahouse.com. Modern boutique guesthouse in a beautiful location up in the Knuckles Range, 50min drive from Kandy and very convenient for the nearby Victoria Golf Club. The atmosphere is very homely – it's more like staying in someone's country house than in paying accommodation. ❼

Stone House Lodge 42 Nittawella Rd, 2.5km north of Kandy ⓣ081-223 2769, ⓦwww.stonehouselodge.lk. Small, upmarket guesthouse in a laid-back semi-rural setting, with an intimate and welcoming atmosphere and wonderful views of the hills from the immaculate garden. The four rooms are beautifully furnished in colonial style – and the master bedroom is a real work of art. ❻–❼

Villa Rosa Asigiriya, 2km west of Kandy ⓣ081-221 5556, ⓦwww.villarosa-kandy.com. Beautiful boutique hotel in a stunning location high above the Mahaweli Ganga a couple of kilometres west of town, with spacious and stylish rooms. The attractively soothing orangey-pink decor complements the very serene atmosphere, with the emphasis on "spiritual tourism" – facilities include meditation and yoga platforms and an attractive little Ayurveda centre (open to non-guests). ❼–❽

The City

Kandy's centrepiece is its large artificial **lake**, created in 1807 by Sri Wickrama Rajasinha in an area of the town previously used for paddy fields. Although nowadays considered one of Kandy's defining landmarks, at the time of its construction the lake was regarded by the city's put-upon inhabitants as a huge white elephant, and proof of their king's unbridled delusions of grandeur – a number of his subjects who objected to labouring on this apparently useless project were impaled on stakes on the bed of the lake. Rajasinha named the lake the **Kiri Muhuda**, or Milk Sea, and established a royal pleasure house, or "harem", on the island in the centre; the more practically minded British subsequently converted it into an ammunition store, but also added the attractive walkway and parapet that encircles the lake. Despite the traffic which blights the southern shore (especially during Kandy's anarchic rush hour), the walk round the perimeter offers memorable views of the city, with the long white lakeside parapet framing perfect reflections of the Temple of the Tooth and old colonial buildings around the *Queen's Hotel*. If you want to get out onto the water, the **Joy Motor Boat Service** (daily 8.30am–6.30pm), at the western end of the lake, offers fifteen-minute spins around the lake, or transfers to the *Hotel Suisse*, for Rs.1500 per boat (seating up to fifteen people).

The south side of the lake is dotted with assorted religious buildings. These include the **Malwatta Monastery**, with its distinctive octagonal tower, built in imitation of the Pittirippuva at the Temple of the Tooth on the opposite side of the lake. The temple is reached from the lakeside through an impressive stone arch decorated with creatures both real (lions, geese, birds) and imaginary (toranas, centaurs). A tiny circular monks' bathing house stands right by the lakeside pavement, close to the gate.

A hundred metres along the lakeside road back towards town (go up the broad steps to the building signed Sri Sangharaja Maha Pirivena) is another cluster of monastic buildings belonging to the **Poya Malu Vihara**, including an interesting square colonnaded **image house**, with a colourfully painted upper storey and a finely carved stone doorway very similar to one in the Temple of the Tooth's main shrine.

From the southwestern corner of the lake, steps ascend to the entrance to Rajapihilla Mawatha and the entrance to the modest **Royal Palace Park**, also known as Wace Park (daily 9am–4.30pm; Rs.100), another of Sri Wickrama Rajasinha's creations. The small ornamental gardens at the top of the park provide an unlikely setting for a Japanese howitzer, captured in Burma during World War II and presented to the city by Lord Mountbatten (who had his wartime headquarters here in the *Hotel Suisse*) – a thoroughly useless and unattractive gift. Beyond the ornamental gardens, a series of terraced footpaths wind down a bluff above the lake, offering fine views of the water and Temple of the Tooth – usually chock-full of snogging couples hiding in every available corner.

There are better views over the lake and into the green ridges of hills beyond from **Rajapihilla Mawatha**, the road above the park – the classic viewpoint is from the junction of Rajapahilla Mawatha and Kirthi Sri Rajasinghe Mawatha, from where one can look down over the entire town below, laid out at one's feet as neatly as a map.

The Temple of the Tooth

Posed artistically against the steep wooded hills of the Udawattakele Sanctuary, Sri Lanka's most important Buddhist shrine, the **Temple of the Tooth**, or Dalada Maligawa (daily 6am–8pm; Rs.500, camera permit Rs.150, video Rs.300; Ⓦ www.sridaladamaligawa.lk and www.daladamaligawa.org), sits on the lakeshore just east of the city centre. The temple houses the legendary **Buddha's Tooth** (see box, p.243), which arrived here in the sixteenth century after various peregrinations around India and Sri Lanka. Nothing remains of the original temple, built around 1600. The main shrine of the current temple was originally constructed during the reign of Vimala Dharma Suriya II (1687–1739) and was rebuilt and modified at various times afterwards, principally during the reign of Kirti Sri Rajasinha (1747–81). It was further embellished during the reign of Sri Wickrama Rajasinha, who added the moat, gateway and Pittiripuwa; the eye-catching golden roof over the relic chamber was donated by President Premadasa in 1987.

The temple was badly damaged in 1998 when the LTTE detonated a massive **truck bomb** outside the entrance, killing over twenty people and reducing the facade to rubble. Restoration work was swift and thorough, however, and there's little visible evidence left of the attack, although crash barriers now prevent vehicular access to the temple, and all visitors have to pass through stringent security checks.

Guides of varying standards hang around at the entrance; count on around Rs.250 for a thirty-minute tour; some are very informative, but check how good their English is first, and always agree a price before starting. **Pujas** (lasting around 90min) are held at 6am, 9am and 6.30pm. Tourists now tend to outnumber locals at the evening puja – you might prefer to go to one of the morning pujas. The main attraction of the puja is the noisy drumming which precedes and accompanies the ceremony, most of which is performed behind closed doors – although at the end of the puja the upstairs room housing the Tooth Relic is opened to the public gaze. You're not actually allowed into the

▲ The Temple of the Tooth

Tooth Relic chamber, but you are permitted to file past the entrance and look inside for a cursory glance at the big gold casket that holds the relic.

Note that buying a ticket for the temple also allows you access to the **Raja Tusker Museum** and **Audience Hall** (see p.245), as well as the **Sri Dalada Museum**.

The Pittirippuva and outer buildings

The temple's exterior is classically plain: a rather austere collection of unadorned white buildings whose hipped roofs rise in tiers against the luxuriant green backcloth of the Udawattakele Sanctuary. The most eye-catching exterior feature is the octagonal tower, the **Pittirippuva**, projecting into the moat that surrounds the temple; strictly speaking, it's not part of the temple at all. Sri Wickrama Rajasinha used the upper part as a platform from which to address his people, and it's now where all new Sri Lankan heads of state give their first speech to the nation.

The entrance to the temple proper is through the **Maha Vahalkada** (Great Gate), which was formerly the main entrance to the royal palace as well as the temple. A sumptuous carving of Lakshmi stands by the entrance – a curious touch of Hinduism in such an important Buddhist shrine. Once through the gateway, turn right and walk up further steps covered by a canopy painted with lotuses and pictures of the perahera. The **ticket office** is at the top of the steps by the entrance to the temple proper, via a gorgeously carved stone door adorned with a moonstone, guardstones and topped by a *makara torana* archway.

The shrine

The interior of the temple is relatively modest in size, and something of an architectural hotchpotch. In front of you lies the **Drummers' Courtyard** (Hewisi Mandapaya), into which is squeezed the two-storey **main shrine** itself. The shrine is a rather curious construction: some portions have been lavishly embellished (the three doors, for instance), but many of the painted roundels on the walls have been left unfinished, and the stone pillars which support the upper storey are utterly plain, giving the whole thing the effect of a job only half done – although the overall effect is still undeniably impressive.

The most intricate carving is on the two stone side doors, while the main doors are fashioned of gorgeously decorated silver, though they're usually hidden behind a curtain except during pujas. The walls are decorated with a colourful and intricate confusion of entwined geese (a symbol of union or marriage), lotuses, vines and lions, and dotted with painted medallions (some unfinished) of the **sun and moon**, a symbol of the kings of Kandy which can be found all over the city – the image of the twinned heavenly orbs was designed to represent both the light-giving and the eternal nature of their rule. A more quirky touch is supplied by numerous paintings of **hares** curled up inside some of the moons (see box, p.244). What's perhaps strangest about all this decoration, however, is its largely royal and secular content: Buddha images, in this holiest of Sri Lankan temples, are notable largely by their absence.

From the drummers' courtyard, a set of stairs to the left (as you face the main shrine) leads to the upper level; halfway up you'll pass the casket in which a replica of the Tooth Relic is paraded during the Esala Perahera, along with golden "flags" and ceremonial fans which are also used during the procession, and a small dagoba. At the top of the steps is the **Pirit Mandapa** (Recitation Hall), a rather plain space whose unusual latticed wooden walls lend a faintly Japanese air (though the lino-clad floor is hideous). This leads to the entrance of the **Tooth Relic chamber** itself, on the upper level of the main shrine. You

The Buddha's Tooth

Legend has it that when the Buddha was cremated in 543 BC at Kushinagar in North India, various parts of his remains were rescued from the fire, including one of his **teeth**. In the fourth century AD, as Buddhism was declining in India in the face of a Hindu revival, the Tooth was smuggled into Sri Lanka, hidden (according to legend) in the hair of an Orissan princess. It was first taken to Anuradhapura, then to Polonnaruwa, Dambadeniya and Yapahuwa. In 1284, an invading Pandyan army from South India captured the Tooth and took it briefly back to India, until it was reclaimed by Parakramabahu III some four years later.

During these turbulent years the Tooth came to assume increasing political importance, being regarded not only as a unique religious relic but also as a symbol of Sri Lankan sovereignty – it was always housed by the Sinhalese kings in their capital of the moment, which explains its rather peripatetic existence. After being reclaimed by Parakramabahu III, it subsequently travelled to Kurunegala, Gampola and Kotte. In the early sixteenth century, the Portuguese captured what they claimed was the Tooth, taking it back to Goa, where it was pounded to dust, then burnt and cast into the sea (Buddhists claim either that this destroyed Tooth was simply a replica, or that the ashes of the Tooth magically reassembled themselves and flew back to Sri Lanka). The Tooth finally arrived in Kandy in 1592 and was installed in a specially constructed temple next to the palace, later becoming the focus for the mammoth Esala Perahera.

The exact nature and authenticity of the Tooth remains unclear. Bella Sidney Woolf, writing in 1914 when the Tooth was still regularly displayed to the public, described it as "a tooth of discoloured ivory at least three inches long – unlike any human tooth ever known," unconsciously echoing the sentiments of the Portuguese visitor, a certain de Quezroy, who in 1597 claimed that it actually belonged to a buffalo. Whatever the truth, the Tooth remains an object of supreme devotion for many Sri Lankans. Security concerns mean that it is no longer taken out on parade during the Esala Perahera, though it is put on display in the Temple of the Tooth for a couple of weeks once or twice every decade.

Hares in the moon

The paintings of hares in the moon shown on the exterior of the Tooth Relic shrine refer to one of the most famous of the **Jataka** stories, describing the previous lives of the Buddha before his final incarnation and enlightenment. According to the Jataka story of the Hare in the Moon, the future Buddha was born a hare. One day the hare was greeted by an emaciated holy man, who begged him – along with a fox and a monkey, who also happened to be passing – for food. The fox brought a fish, the monkey some fruit, but the hare was unable to find anything for the holy man to eat apart from grass. Having no other way of assuaging the ascetic's hunger, the hare asked him to light a fire and then leapt into the flames, offering his own body as food. At this moment the holy man revealed himself as the god Indra, placing an image of the hare in the moon to commemorate its self-sacrifice, where it remains to this day.

The Jataka fable may itself be simply a local version of a still more ancient Hindu or Vedic myth – traditions referring to a hare in the moon can be found as far away as China, Central Asia and even Europe, while the story also appears, in slightly modified form, in one of the Brothers Grimm fairy tales.

can't actually go into the relic chamber, and the entrance is railed off (except during the temple pujas), although you can make out some of the details of the fantastically ornate brass doorway into the shrine, framed in silver and decorated in a riot of embossed ornament, with auspicious symbols including dwarfs, some holding urns of plenty, plus more entwined geese, peacocks, suns and moons and dagobas. Paintings to either side of the door show guardstone figures bearing bowls of lotuses, surmounted by *makara toranas*.

The **interior** of the Tooth Relic chamber is divided by golden arches into three sections, though the chamber is kept shut except during pujas, and even then you'll only be able to get a brief glimpse as you're hurried past the door. The Tooth Relic is kept in the furthest section, the **Vedahitina Maligawa** (Shrine of Abode), concealed from the public gaze in a dagoba-shaped gold casket which is said to contain a series of six further caskets, the smallest of which contains the Tooth itself.

On the far side of the Pirit Mandapa, another flight of stairs leads back down to the courtyard, passing a striking gilded Buddha from Burma and further objects used in the perahera.

The Alut Maligawa

From the rear of the Drummers' Courtyard, steps lead up to the **Alut Maligawa** (New Shrine Room), a large and undistinguished building completed in 1956 to celebrate the 2500th anniversary of the Buddha's death. The interior, as if to compensate for the lack of Buddhist imagery in the main section of the temple, is filled with a glut of Buddha statues, many donated by foreign countries, which offer an interesting opportunity to compare Asian variations of traditional Buddhist iconography. From left to right the images are from China (white marble); Sri Lanka (a classically simple orange ceramic figure); Japan (a golden figure with black hair and a large golden halo); Japan again (sandalwood, backed by elaborate flames of enlightenment); Thailand (the main central image; a gilded seated figure surrounded by the stylized flames of enlightenment); Korea (black hair); Taiwan (a small gold figure); India (white marble with a large backrest); and finally Sri Lanka again (a large gold standing figure). Beneath the central Thai image is a holographic Buddha face from France, set in a minute dagoba, which turns its head to follow you as you move around the room.

A sequence of 21 **paintings** hung around the chamber's upper walls depict the story of the Tooth Relic from the Buddha's death to the present day. The Buddhas below were a gift from Thailand to commemorate the fiftieth anniversary of Sri Lanka's independence.

The Sri Dalada Museum

Exit the back door of the Alut Maligawa and follow the signs up to the **Sri Dalada Museum** (Tooth Relic Museum; entrance included in ticket), situated on the first and second floors of the building and devoted to anything and everything concerned with the Tooth Relic itself. The **first floor** is dominated by a sequence of large and solemn busts of all the *diyawardene nilambe* (temple chiefs) from 1814 to 1985. Other exhibits include photos of the damage caused by the 1998 bombing, fragments of murals destroyed in the blast, a selection of (mainly colonial) documents relating to the Tooth Relic and Kandy, and a few old fabrics, including a selection of the enormous handkerchiefs designed for the royal noses of the kings of Kandy.

The more interesting **second floor** is largely occupied by the bewildering assortment of objects offered to the Tooth Relic at various times. These include all sorts of bowls and vases, fans, fancy jewellery, incense burners, foreign coins and votive offerings, including several given by former Sri Lankan presidents. The highlight is the gorgeous silk Buddha footprint which is said to have been offered to the temple in the reign of Kirti Sri Rajasinha by a visiting Thai monk on behalf of the king of Siam.

The Royal Palace and around

The Temple of the Tooth originally lay at the heart of the sprawling **Royal Palace**, a self-contained complex of buildings immediately surrounding the temple and housing various royal residences, audience chambers and associated structures. Significant sections of the original palace complex survive, although it's difficult to get a very clear sense of how it would originally have looked, thanks to the many additions and alterations made to the area since 1815. Several of the buildings are now used as museums, and although none is of outstanding individual interest, taken together they provide a tantalizing glimpse of what the former royal precinct would have looked like – the best overview of the complex is from the Vishnu Devale (see p.249).

The layout of the surviving palace buildings is rather confusing. Two of its buildings – the **Audience Hall** and **Raja Tusker Museum** – can only be reached by going through (and buying a ticket for) the Temple of the Tooth. The others, including the **National** and **Archeological museums**, are reached by walking around the outside of the temple along the lakeside (or alternatively by walking around from the Vishnu Devale).

The Audience Hall and Raja Tusker Museum

Immediately north of the temple (and reached via a side exit from it, or from the exit from the Sri Dalada Museum) lies the imposing **Audience Hall**, an impressively complete Kandyan pavilion set on a raised stone plinth, open on all sides and sporting characteristic wooden pillars, corbels and roof, all intricately carved. The hall originally dated from 1784, though it was set on fire during the British attack of 1803 – the conservation-minded British invaders obligingly put out the fire and subsequently restored the building. It was here that the Kandyan chiefs signed the treaty that handed over power to the British on March 2, 1815.

Just north of the Audience Hall, in another handsome old palace building adorned with hipped roof, guardstones and moonstone, stands the **Raja Tusker**

Museum (daily 8.30am–4.30pm; free entrance with Temple of the Tooth ticket), devoted to the memory of Sri Lanka's most famous elephant, **Raja**. The main attraction is the stuffed remains of Raja himself, now standing proudly in state in a glass cabinet. Raja died in 1988 after fifty years' loyal service as Kandy's **Maligawa Tusker** – the elephant which carries the Tooth Relic casket during the Esala Perahera. Such was the veneration in which he was held that his death prompted the government to order a day of national mourning, while the animal's remains are now an object of devotion to many Sinhalese, who come to pray at Raja's glass case. The museum also has photos of Raja in various peraheras, plus sad snaps of him surrounded by anxious vets during his last illness in 1988.

No single elephant has yet proved itself able to fill Raja's considerable boots, and at present the role of Maligawa Tusker is shared between various different elephants. All Maligawa Tuskers must fulfil certain physical requirements. Only male elephants are permitted to carry the relic and, most importantly, they must be **Sathdantha** elephants, meaning that all seven parts of their body – the four legs, trunk, penis and tail – must touch the ground when they stand upright. In addition, the elephant's tusks must be formed in the curved shape of a traditional winnow, and it must have a flat back and reach a height of around twelve feet. It is proving increasingly difficult to find such "high-caste" elephants locally, although the temple already owns several suitable beasts, including ones donated by notables including various prime ministers of Sri Lanka and India, as well as the king of Thailand.

The National Museum and around

The other surviving buildings of the royal palace lie outside the Temple of the Tooth enclosure. Just south of the Temple lies the **Queen's Bath** (Ulpenge), a grand but now rather dilapidated structure built over the lake, rather like a boathouse; the upper storey was added by the British.

Beyond the Queen's Bath (and immediately behind the Temple of the Tooth, though not directly accessible from it) lies the Kandy branch of the **National Museum** (Tues–Sat 9am–5.30pm; Rs.500, camera charge Rs.160), set in a low white building which was formerly the Queen's Palace (or "King's Harem", as it's sometimes described). The museum contains a treasure trove of mementoes of Kandyan life before the coming of the Europeans, with many exhibits attesting to the high levels of skill achieved by local craftsmen, with a plethora of minutely detailed ivory objects (look for the cute figurines of various Kandyan bigwigs) along with lots of jewellery, fabrics, bracelets and ear ornaments. Look out too for the intriguing selection of **water clocks**: small copper bowls with a tiny pinhole in the bottom: floated on water, they sink after precisely 24 minutes, the equivalent to one Sinhalese hour, or *paya* (in a neat but coincidental reversal of Western time-keeping, the Sinhalese divided each day into sixty hours of 24 minutes).

Next door to the National Museum sits the relatively modest **Queen's Chamber**, a discreet low white structure with tiny balustraded windows and stone pool inside. Just past here lies the large Neoclassical **High Court** built by the British – the courtroom is open on two sides so you can watch proceedings within (though you're not allowed to take photographs or write notes). Not far beyond is the **District Court**, housed in an old-style Kandyan pavilion and again open on two sides.

Past the District Court lies the **Archeological Museum** (daily except Tues 8am–5pm). The museum is situated in the long, low white building that was formerly the **King's Palace**, built by Vimala Dharma Suriya (1591–1604). The palace's ornate main doors are decorated with the Kandy kings' sun and moon symbol, while the interior of the gateway is adorned with lions and geese (the latter symbolizing purity). Inside, the museum holds a mildly interesting collection of assorted pots, bits of masonry, fragments of carved stones and old wooden pillars. Note that the museum doesn't issue its own entrance tickets, being covered by the Cultural Triangle combined ticket (see p.314). If you don't have one of these, you'll have to tip whoever lets you in and shows you around.

A tiny path continues from here around to the Vishnu Devale (see p.249).

The Kandy Garrison Cemetery

Back on the lakeside just beyond the National Museum, a signposted turning points up to the evocative **Kandy Garrison Cemetery** (Mon–Sat 8am–1pm & 2–6pm; donation), established in 1817, shortly after the British seized control of Kandy, to provide a final resting place for expired British colonists. Having fallen into complete dereliction, the cemetery has recently been painstakingly restored and now offers a moving memorial to Ceylon's former colonial master. Shockingly few of the people buried here made it to the age of 30, and even those who avoided the usual hazards of tropical diseases and hostile natives found unusual ways to meet their maker, such as John Spottiswood Robertson (died 1856), trampled to death by a wild elephant; David Findlay (died 1861), killed when his house collapsed on top of him; or William Watson Mackwood (died 1867), who somehow managed to impale himself on a stake whilst dismounting from his horse.

The most notable interree, however, is **Sir John D'Oyly**, the remarkable colonial official who brokered the surrender of the city to the British in 1815. D'Oyly was one of the most fascinating figures in the history of colonial Ceylon – at once a supreme diplomat who manipulated the Kandyan nobility with almost Machiavellian genius, and also a kind of proto-hippy who became a strict vegetarian, avoided European society and devoted himself to the study of Sinhala and Buddhism. As an observer remarked in 1810: "He lives on plantain, invites nobody to his house, and does not dine abroad above once a year. When I saw him…I was struck with the change of a Cambridge boy into a Cingalese hermit." Despite his brilliant orchestration of the bloodless coup at Kandy, D'Oyly's subsequent attempts to protect the Kandyans from British interference and Christian missionaries were little appreciated, and by the time of his death from cholera in 1824, he had become a lonely and marginalized figure – not that you'd realize it, judging by the size of his memorial, the largest in the cemetery, topped by a broken Greek pillar. It's on your left as you come in, quite close to the entrance.

The devales

Kandy traditionally lies under the protection of four gods, each of whom is honoured with a temple in the city. Three of these temples, the **Pattini**, **Natha** and **Vishnu** *devales*, sit next to one another just in front of the Temple of the Tooth – a fascinating and picturesque jumble of shrines, dagobas and bo trees. The fourth *devale*, dedicated to **Kataragama**, lies a couple of blocks west in the city itself. Besides their obvious artistic merits, the *devales* offer a fascinating lesson in the way in which Hindu and Buddhist beliefs shaded into one another in Kandy, as throughout Sri Lankan history: two of the four devales are dedicated to adopted Hindu gods, while the principal shrine of the Natha *devale* is housed in a building which wouldn't look out of place in South India.

The four *devales* are technically covered by the Cultural Triangle Ticket (see p.314), though it's extremely unlikely that you'll be asked to produce one.

Pattini Devale

The **Pattini Devale** is the simplest of the four temples. The cult of the goddess **Pattini** (see box below) was introduced from South India in the second century AD by King Gajabahu (reigned 174–196 AD); she remains a popular deity amongst poorer Sri Lankans, thanks to her lowly origins. Her golden ankle bracelet, brought back from India by Gajabahu, is said to be kept here (though you can't see it). Entering from Deva Vidiya, you're confronted by the **Wel-Bodhiya**, a huge bo tree, perched on an enormous, three-tiered platform; it's believed to have been planted by **Narendrasingha**, the last Sinhalese king of Kandy, in the early eighteenth century. The actual shrine to Pattini is off to the right, set in a modest little enclosure entered through gorgeous embossed brass doors decorated with the usual sun and moon symbols, *makara toranas* and guardstone figures. The shrine itself is set in a small but beautiful Kandyan wooden pavilion, and is usually the most popular of all the *devales* amongst visiting worshippers. To either side stand subsidiary shrines to the Hindu deities Kali and Mariamman – the latter, like Pattini, is a female deity of humble South Indian origins who is believed to protect against disease. You'll probably be approached by a temple flunkey at this point asking for a donation; he'll most likely show you a book in which previous donations are listed, many of which appear to have been wildly inflated by the addition of surplus zeros.

Natha Devale

From the Pattini Devale, a gate leads directly through to the **Natha Devale**. **Natha** is the most purely Buddhist of the gods of the four *devales*, and thus the most important in the city, being considered a form of the Mahayana Bodhisattva **Avalokitesvara**, who is still widely worshipped in Nepal, Tibet, China and Japan. Natha was thought to have influence over political events in the kingdom – new kings of Kandy were obliged to present themselves at the shrine on attaining the throne – although the god's exalted status means that his shrine is far less popular with the hoi polloi than that of humble Pattini next door.

Away to your right at the end of the enclosure is the **Natha Shrine** itself, built by Vikramabahu III in the fourteenth century, and thus the oldest building

Pattini

Pattini (originally named Kannaki) was a humble Indian girl from the city of Madurai who married a certain **Kovalan**, an errant spouse with a weakness for dancing girls. Despite Pattini's considerable charms, the feckless Kovalan abandoned his wife and bankrupted himself in pursuit of one particular amour until, ashamed and penniless, he returned to Pattini to beg forgiveness. The pliable Pattini welcomed him back without even a word of reproach and handed over her last possession, a golden ankle bracelet, for him to sell. The unfortunate Kovalan did so, but was promptly accused of stealing the bracelet by the king's goldsmith and executed. The distraught Pattini, legend states, descended upon the royal palace, tore off one of her breasts, caused the king to drop dead and then reduced his palace to ashes before being taken up into the heavens as a goddess.

Pattini's cult was originally introduced to Sri Lanka by King Gajabahu in the second century BC, but enjoyed its heyday during the Kandyan era, when the kingdom's Hindu rulers revived her cult and built her Kandy temple. Pattini is now revered as the ideal of the chaste and devoted wife: pregnant women come her to pray for a safe delivery (rather inexplicably, since Pattini was childless), while she is also thought to protect against infectious diseases such as chicken pox, smallpox and measles.

For more on Pattini, visit ⓦwww.pattini.org.

in Kandy. This low stone gedige (South Indian-style stone shrine), topped with a small *shikhara* dome at its end, is very reminiscent in style of similar temples at Polonnaruwa, and shows strong Indian influence (the fact that the city's most Buddhist deity sits in its most Hindu-style temple is entirely characteristic of the syncretic nature of Kandyan culture). The shrine is fronted by a much later pavilion sporting beautifully carved wooden pillars. In the middle of the enclosure stands a **Buddha shrine**, with two elaborately railed bo trees to the rear. Exit the temple through the archway to the north, its exterior wall richly carved and painted with *makara torana* and guardstone figures.

Vishnu Devale

Directly ahead of here stands a wooden pavilion, through which steps lead up into the third of the *devales*, the **Vishnu Devale** (also known as the Maha Devale, or "Great Temple"). The first building you come to is an open-sided **digge** pavilion, in which drummers and dancers would formerly have performed in honour of the deity – you can still occasionally see trainee dancers being put through their paces here. Past the *digge*, further steps leads up to the main **Vishnu shrine**. The Vishnu image here is thought to come from Dondra on the south coast, though it's usually hidden behind a curtain; ceremonial objects used in Esala Perahera stand ranged along the sides of the shrine. Behind and to the left of the Vishnu shrine stands a subsidiary shrine to **Dedimunda** (a local god of obscure origins), his image framed by a gorgeously embossed gilded arch featuring the ubiquitous sun and moon motif.

The rest of the city

Just north of the tourist office lies **St Paul's Church**, a quaint, ochre-coloured neo-Gothic structure built in 1843, which offers a homesick and thoroughly incongruous memento of rustic English nostalgia amidst the myriad Buddhist monuments which cover this part of town – indeed the irreverent insertion of such a large Christian building into such a sacred Buddhist precinct says much about British religious sympathies (or lack of). The **interior** is a piece of pure English Victoriana, with beautiful wooden pews, floor tiles decorated with floral and fleur de lys patterns, wooden rood screen and choir stalls, naff stained glass, brass eagle lectern and a grand piano, all tenderly preserved. The various monuments date back to the 1840s, recording deaths in parts of the empire as far flung as Bombay, Port Said, Wei-Hai-Wei and South Africa. Opposite here, the walls of the buildings are all but buried underneath a surfeit of **signs** in English and Sinhala advertising the services of local lawyers, whose offices stand along the street, occupying a former Victorian-era army stables and barracks.

West of here lies the **city centre** proper, where you'll find the fourth of the city's principal *devales*, the **Kataragama Devale**, entered through a lurid blue gateway on Kotugodelle Vidiya (though it's surprisingly easy to miss amidst the packed shopfronts). This is the most Hindu-influenced of Kandy's temples, right down to the pair of resident Brahmin priests who serve here. The attractive central Kataragama shrine is topped by a broad wooden roof and protected by two intricately gilded doors, with a pair of Buddha shrines behind and to the left. The right-hand side of the enclosure has a very Indian flavour, with a line of shrines housing images of Durga, Krishna, Radha, Ganesh and Vishnu – those at the back have ornate gold doors with tiny bells on them which devotees ring to attract the gods' attention.

The centre of the modern city spreads out around the Kataragama Devale, confined, thanks to the hilliness of the surrounding terrain, to a compact and crowded grid of streets lined with small shops and honeycombed in places with tiny alleyways. The most interesting area is along the eastern end of Bennet Soysa Vidiya (generally known by its old name of Colombo St), where fruit and veg sellers sell their wares from the narrow and congested pavements. At the far end of Dalada Vidiya stands Kandy's unusually ornate **clocktower**, with golden elephant friezes and a cute, hat-like top.

The Bahiravakanda Buddha and Asigiriya

West of the town centre, the immense white **Bahiravakanda Buddha** stares over the city centre from its hilltop perch. The statue was constructed at the behest of the religiously minded **President Premadasa**, who also contributed the striking golden roof of the principal shrine of the Temple of the Tooth, as well as various other religious edifices around the island – though these many pious acts didn't save him from being blown to smithereens by an LTTE suicide bomber in 1993. To reach the statue, take the side turning off Sri Pushpadana Mawatha opposite a flag-festooned bo tree (signposted to the circuit bungalow). From here, it's a stiff ten-minute climb to the top. Foreigners pay Rs.100 to get into the enclosure, although the views are just as good from outside.

On the north side of the Bahiravakanda hill lies the **Asigiriya monastery**, along with the Malwatta Monastery the most important in Kandy. Founded in the fourteenth century, it is the oldest religious foundation in the city. There's a small but picturesque quadrangle of rustic buildings here, with the chapter house in the middle. If you arrive during the evening puja (around 4.30pm), or succeed in button-holing a passing monk, you may be able to get inside to see the monastery's large reclining Buddha and collection of ola-leaf manuscripts.

Immediately northeast of here lies the **Asigiriya Stadium**, one of Sri Lanka's three venues for Test match cricket, shoe-horned into a small hollow beneath towering hills – often and rightly described as one of the most beautiful cricket grounds in the world.

Udawattakele Sanctuary

On the opposite (north) side of the lake, providing a dense green backdrop to the Temple of the Tooth, **Udawattakele Sanctuary** (daily 6am–6pm; Rs.661) was formerly a royal reserve, subsequently preserved and protected by the British. The sanctuary sprawls over two kilometres of densely forested hillside, with imposing trees, plenty of birdlife, snakes, and a few mammals including monkeys, porcupines and pigs – as well as lots of leeches if it's been raining. Two main two paths, Lady Horton's Drive and Lady Gordon's Road (both named after the wives of British governors) wind through the reserve, with a few smaller paths and nature trails branching off them. The entrance to the park is a steep hike from town: go up past the post office along Kandy Vidiya and then Wewelpitiya Road; the easy-to-miss entrance is next to the Sri Dalada Thapowanaya temple.

Eating, drinking and entertainment

Kandy is, sadly, something of a culinary desert, though it does at least have a decent selection of **bars and pubs**.

Restaurants and cafés

Bamboo Garden 29A Anagarika Dharmapala Mw. Part of *Andre and Sophia's Pub* (see p.252), this lively restaurant-cum-bar has a big menu of Sri Lankan-style Chinese food, with almost 150 dishes covering all the meat, veg and seafood Cantonese

Robert Knox and seventeenth-century Kandy

In 1660, a party of English sailors who had gone ashore near the mouth of the Mahaweli Ganga were taken prisoner by soldiers of the king of Kandy, Rajasinha II. Among them was a 19-year-old Londoner named **Robert Knox**. Knox's subsequent account of his nineteen years as a hostage of the king was eventually published as *An Historical Relation of Ceylon*, a unique record which offers a fascinating snapshot of everyday life in the seventeenth-century Kingdom of Kandy. The book later served as one of the major sources of Daniel Defoe's *Robinson Crusoe*, and something of Knox's own industrious (if rather dour) character may have crept into Defoe's self-sufficient hero.

Upon arriving in Kandy, Knox was surprised to discover that he and his shipmates were not the only European "guests" being detained at Rajasinha's pleasure – also in Kandy were prisoners of war, shipwrecked sailors, army deserters and assorted diplomats. Knox seems to have admired many of the qualities of his hosts, though he did object (as have so many subsequent Western travellers to Asia) that "They make no account nor conscience of lying, neither is it any shame or disgrace to them, if they be catched in telling lies; it is so customary." He also recorded (with puritan disapproval) the kingdom's liberal attitude to sex: "Both women and men do commonly wed four or five times before they can settle themselves." Married women appeared free to have affairs with whoever took their fancy, so long as they were of an equal social rank, sometimes even leaving their husbands at home to look after the children. When important visitors called, husbands would offer them the services of their wives and daughters "to bear them company in their chamber". Men were allowed to have affairs with lower-caste women, but not to sit or eat with them. Polyandry, in which a wife was shared between two or more brothers, or in which one man married two or more sisters, was also accepted, while incest was reputedly common amongst beggars. If nothing else, the kingdom's sex drive was impressive. As Knox observed of the Kandyan women: "when their Husbands are dead, all their care is where to get others, which they cannot long be without."

In terms of material possessions, the life which Knox recorded was simple. Most Kandyans contented themselves with the bare necessities of life, encouraged in a life of indolence by the fact that the moment they acquired anything it was taken away by the king's mob of tax collectors. Justice was meted out by a court of local chiefs, but appeared to favour whoever was able to present the largest bribe – those convicted of capital offences were trampled to death by an elephant.

Despite being a prisoner, Knox and his fellow "guests" were free to live a normal life and, as time passed, to wander around the kingdom at will – although all escape routes were cut off by the dense jungle which surrounded the kingdom, while the only paths through and out were heavily guarded. Europeans enjoyed favoured status under Rajasinha II, even though many of them showed a loutish disregard for local customs and spent most of their time drunk – indeed the Europeans' major contribution to the development of Kandyan society was to help break down the taboos against beef and alcohol – although Knox himself kept a puritanical distance from such goings-on. Most eventually took Sinhalese wives and settled down to raise families, injecting a substantial splash of European blood into the Kandyan gene pool, although Knox steadfastly resisted all native female charms – he appears to have been a rather dour character, and perhaps something of a misogynist. He supported himself by a mixture of small-scale farming, knitting caps and peddling; in the latter guise Knox wandered all over the kingdom, acquiring the intimate knowledge of its geography that finally allowed him and a companion to escape to the Dutch-controlled north – the only Europeans to succeed in finding their way out of the maze of the Kandyan kingdom.

standards – reasonably prepared. Most mains around Rs.450.

Devon Restaurant 11 Dalada Vidiya. Incessantly popular no-frills modern restaurant with a good selection of Sri Lankan staples, including hoppers at breakfast, plus burianis, *lamprais* and devilled dishes, with most mains under Rs.300. Portions are large, though the food can be excessively hot. There are also separate sections with Chinese and North Indian menus, plus a big cake shop in the entrance. Closes at 8pm.

Flower Song Kotugodelle Vidiya. Neat modern Chinese restaurant, with a long list of Cantonese standards and other Sri Lankan-style Chinese dishes. The cooking can be decidedly hit and miss, however. Most mains around Rs.600.

History, The Restaurant 27A Anagarika Dharmapala Mw. This slightly bizarre themed place offers one of the island's more peculiar dining experiences, in a modern restaurant plastered with colonial-era photos of Sri Lanka, with a slide-show of further old photos projected onto a wall. The food is surprisingly cheap and good, however, with an international menu ranging from burgers and pasta to rice and curry, plus a decent wine list. Most mains Rs.300–400.

Lyons 27 Peradeniya Rd. Popular local restaurant with a Sri Lankan-cum-Chinese-cum-Continental menu, though it's best known for its big range of feisty devilled dishes (from Rs.275).

Paivas Yatinuwara Vidiya. This scruffy-looking place won't win any design awards, but offers a decent selection of cheap and tasty North Indian standards (evenings only) – the vegetarian dishes are particularly good value at under Rs.200 – along with various Chinese dishes (from Rs.300).

The Pub 36 Dalada Vidiya. Very tourist-oriented place, with dim lighting and smart decor, plus MTV and international sports on the big-screen TV. The pub-style menu features a short and eclectic selection of reasonably prepared international dishes including pastas, fish, pork chops and steak (though hardly any vegetarian options). Also a good spot for a drink (see below). Mains from around Rs.450.

Sharon Inn 59 Saranankara Rd. The best rice and curry in town (Rs.650), served daily at 7pm and offering an interesting spread of fifteen or so dishes, often featuring unusual Sri Lankan vegetables.

Sri Ram 87 Bennet Soysa Vidiya (Colombo St). Colourful, batik-filled little restaurant with a big, inexpensive menu of well-prepared South Indian standards including thalis, *dosas* and idlis, as well as more unusual Chettinad (Tamil Nadu-style) veg and meat curries. Mains from around Rs.200. No alcohol.

Pubs and bars

Andre and Sophia's Pub 29A Anagarika Dhamapala Mw. Popular drinking spot (it's where the enormous red neon "PUB" sign is, visible from anywhere within about ten miles) set high above the lake, with good views by day and a lively crowd of locals and tourists by night.

Kandy Garden Club East end of the lake. No-frills drinking hole in an atmospheric old colonial building at the end of the lake. The temporary membership fee of Rs.100 gets you access to a pair of snooker tables and some of the cheapest beer in the city.

The Pub Dalada Vidiya. The outdoor terrace overlooking Dalada Vidiya is one of the nicest spots in town for a drink, and there's a decent (though relatively pricey) list of draught, local and imported beers and spirits.

Pub Royale Dalada Vidiya. Unpretentious wood-pannelled bar with cheapish beer, and a fun place to observe the chaos of the city traffic, especially during the evening rush hour.

Queens Hotel Bar Dalada Vidiya. Atmospheric, colonial-style drinking hole under an enormous veranda at the back of the stately *Queens Hotel*, with an old wooden bar, armchair seating and long rows of fans whirling gently overhead.

Cultural shows

Three places in town put on nightly shows of Kandyan **dancing and drumming**. All are touristy but fun, with a fairly standard range of dances, generally including snippets of both southern as well as Kandyan dances and usually culminating in a spot of firewalking. The biggest, ritziest and most popular is at the **Kandyan Arts Association** (daily at 5.30pm; Rs.500), on the north side of the lake just east of the Temple of the Tooth – a big, very touristy place whose flashy but fun shows draw coach parties galore. The **YMBA** (daily at 5.30pm; Rs.500), at the west end of Rajapihilla Mawatha, offers a similar programme but in a much more intimate atmosphere. The show at the **Lake Club** (daily at 5.30pm; Rs.500), east of the town centre on Sangamitta Mawatha, is midway in scale between the YMBA and Kandyan Arts Association, but not as good as either.

Kandyan dancing and drumming

Kandyan dancing and drumming is Sri Lanka's iconic performing art, featuring carefully choreographed displays accompanied by pulsating barrages of massed drumming, with performers clad in elaborate traditional Kandyan costume. The art form originated as part of an all-night ceremony in honour of the god Kohomba, an elaborate ritual featuring some fifty dancers and ten drummers. This ceremony flourished under the patronage of the kings of Kandy and reached such heights of sophistication that it was eventually adopted into local religious ceremonies, becoming a key element in the great Esala Perahera festival. Many temples in the Kandyan area even have a special columned pavillion, or **digge**, designed specifically for performances and rehearsals by resident dancers and drummers.

Kandyan dancing

There are five main **types of Kandyan dance**. The four principal genres are the *ves*, *pantheru*, *udekki* and *naiyandi*, all featuring troupes of flamboyantly attired male dancers clad in sumptuous chest plates, waistbands and various other neck, arm and leg ornaments which jangle as the dancers move about. The most famous is the **ves** dance, which is considered sacred to the god Kohomba. It's at once highly mannered and hugely athletic, combining carefully stylized hand and head gestures with acrobatic manoeuvres including spectacular backflips, huge high-kicking leaps and dervish-like whirling pirouettes. In the more sedate **pantheru** dance, the turbaned performers play small tambourines, whilst during the **udekki** dance they beat tiny hourglass-shaped drums.

The fifth and final style of Kandyan classical dance is the **vannam**. This began life as songs, before evolving into stylized dances, each of which describes a certain emotion or object from nature, history or legend – the most popular are the various animal-derived *vannams*, including those inspired by the movements of the peacock (*mayura*), elephant (*gajaga*), lion (*sinharaja*) and cobra (*naga*). *Vannams* are usually performed by just one or two dancers (and sometimes by women), unlike other Kandyan dances, which are ensemble dances featuring four or five performers, always men.

As well as the traditional Kandyan dances, the city's cultural shows usually include examples of a few characteristic **southern dances** such as the *kulu* (harvest dance) and the ever-popular *raban* dance – for more on which, see p.151.

Kandyan drumming

All genres of dance are accompanied by **drumming**, which can reach extraordinary heights of virtuosity. The archetypal Sri Lankan drum is the *geta bera* (literally "boss drum"), a double-headed instrument carried on a strap around the drummer's waist and played with the hands. *Geta bera* are made to a fixed length of 67cm, with different types of skins (monkey and cow, for example) at either end of the drum to produce contrasting sounds. The double-headed *daule* drum is shorter but thicker, and is played with a stick in one hand and the palm of the other. The *tammettana bera* is a pair of tiny drums (a bit like bongos) which are tied together and played with a pair of sticks. You might see examples of all three during the larger cultural shows in Kandy, where the dancing is accompanied by troupes of between four and eight drummers. A *horanava* (a kind of Sri Lankan oboe) is sometimes added to the ensemble, providing a simple melodic accompaniment. The rhythmic coordination and ensemble achieved by these musicians in the absence of any conductor is remarkable, and even if the finer points pass you by, the headlong onslaught of a Kandyan drum ensemble in full flight leaves few people unmoved, providing a fitting musical accompaniment to the gymnastic fireworks of the dancing itself.

Like the dancers they accompany, Kandyan drummers perform in **traditional costume**, dressed in a large sarong, a huge red cummerbund and a white tasselled turban – significant musical points are marked by a toss of the head, sending the tassel flying through the air in a delicate accompanying flourish.

Listings

Ayurveda A number of hotels in and around Kandy have Ayurveda centres or offer treatments: those at the *Earl's Regency*, *Amaya Hills*, *Thilanka* and *Villa Rosa* (see listings on pp.239–240) are all reputable and well run. Alternatively, the well-set-up Wedamedura Ayurveda Centre at 7 Mahamaya Mw (Ⓣ081-447 9484, Ⓦwww.ayurvedawedamedura.com) offers the usual steam and herbal baths, as well massages, reflexology, pedicures and aromatherapy, and full panchakarma treatments. A resident Ayurveda doctor offers consultations and treatment plans, and you can arrange complete courses including accommodation and meals.

Banks and exchange There are heaps of banks in the city centre, the majority on Dalada Vidiya. The following have ATMs which accept foreign cards (all Visa and MasterCard, except where noted): Bank of Ceylon (MasterCard only), Dalada Vidiya; Sampath Bank, Dalada Vidiya; People's Bank, Dalada Vidiya (Visa only); HSBC, Kotugodelle Vidiya; Commercial Bank, Kotugodelle Vidiya.

Bookshops Vijitha Yapa Bookshop, right in the city centre on Kotugodelle Vidiya, has a reasonable selection of English-language books, including lots of tomes about Sri Lanka. The Buddhist Publications Society, near the eastern end of the lake, has an enormous selection of Buddhist titles and books on Sri Lankan history.

British Council 88/3 Kotugodelle Vidiya Ⓣ081-222 2410, Ⓦwww.britishcouncil.org/srilanka (Tues–Sun 9am–5.30pm).

Golf The magnificent eighteen-hole, par-73 course at the Victoria Golf Club (Ⓣ0712 743 003, Ⓦwww.srilankagolf.com) is around 20km east of Kandy at Rajawella, tucked into a scenic spot between the Knuckles Range and the Victoria Reservoir. Green fees are US$35 per day.

Handicrafts A huge new shopping centre is currently under construction by the west end of the lake, which will doubtless furnish all sorts of new shopping possibilities when open. For the moment, the two biggest places are the dismal Laksala at the west end of the lake, and the much better Kandyan Arts and Crafts Association towards the eastern end, which has a big range of reasonably produced and priced regional arts and crafts; local artisans can also be seen at work around the veranda here, plying looms, brushes and needles. There's also some reasonable stuff at a couple of places on Rajapahilla Mw: Kandy Souvenirs at no. 61 has a fairly wide range of woodcarvings, metalwork, leatherwork, *kolam* masks and jewellery, while Gunatilake Batiks, at no. 173A, has a big stock of batiks, and Rajanima Crafts, next door at no. 173, has a wide selection of *kolam* masks and some fine Buddha and elephant carvings in sandlewood, teak and mahogany – you can also watch craftsmen at work in the factory next door. There are a couple of big crafts shops (and many jewellers) along Peradeniya Rd en route to the Botanical Gardens, although if you've a real interest in local artisanal traditions, head out to the Matale Heritage Centre (see p.315).

Hospital Lakeside Adventist Hospital (Ⓣ081-222 3466 or 081-223 4605), on the lakeshore 100m

Tours from Kandy

The main **taxi stand** (minivans and cars) is opposite the Clocktower Bus Stand at the west end of the centre. Drivers charge around US$25–30 to Pinnewala, US$20–25 for the three-temples circuit; and around US$35 for the two combined.

Almost all the city's guesthouses can arrange **tours**; count on US$50–60 per day for the hire of a car and driver. Alternatively, contact the reliable and inexpensive Blue Haven Tours and Travels at 1st floor, 34 Bennet Soysa Vidiya (Colombo St) (Ⓣ081 220 1525, mobile Ⓣ0777 372 066, Ⓦwww.bluehaventours.com).

The vastly experienced **Sumane Bandara Illangantilake**, c/o the *Expeditor Inn* (see p.235; Ⓣ081-490 1628 or 223 8316, Ⓦwww.srilankatrekkingexpeditor.com), offers islandwide tours, plus trips around Kandy including an unusual off-road version of the three-temples walk (see p.258). Sumane is also the island's leading guide to the Knuckles Range, an authority on the Veddhas (see p.266), and can arrange visits to pretty much anywhere you might fancy going. For tours, count on around US$65 per person per day full-board, excluding entrance fees. Sumane's pupil, Ravi Desappriya (Ⓦwww.srilankatrekking.com) is another good local guide, organizing a similar range of trips.

beyond the *Hotel Suisse*; there's also a dental clinic here.
Internet access The best place is the cheap and well-equipped Sumathi Information Technologies (daily 8am–8pm; Rs.70 per hr), on Kotugodelle Vidiya. Failing this, there are a couple of little places next to the DHL office near the southern end of D.S. Senanayake Vidiya.
Pharmacy Sri Lanka Pharmacy, 39 D.S. Senanayake Vidiya (Mon–Sat 8.30am–7.30pm).
Post office The main post office is opposite the train station (Mon–Sat 7am–9pm). In the city centre, try the Seetha Agency Post Office (daily 7am–10pm), 29 Kotugodelle Vidiya, a couple of doors south of the Kataragama Devale, or the Senkadagala Sub-Post Office, just behind the Tourist Office.
Supermarket Cargills, Dalada Vidiya (daily 8am–9pm).
Tea Mlesna Tea Centre, opposite *The Pub* on Dalada Vidiya, has a reasonable selection, as does Cargills on Dalada Vidiya.

Around Kandy

The countryside around Kandy is full of attractions, comprising an interesting blend of the cultural and the natural – elephants, historic temples, hill walking and more. Top of most visitors' list is a trip to the famous **Pinnewala Elephant Orphanage** (covered on p.227), usually followed by a visit to the idyllic **Peradeniya Botanical Gardens**. There's also a fascinating collection of Kandyan-era **temples** scattered around the countryside, while the dramatic but little-visited **Knuckles Range** boasts some of the island's finest wilderness trekking.

Peradeniya Botanical Gardens

Set 6km southwest of Kandy in a loop in the Mahaweli Ganga lie the expansive **Peradeniya Botanical Gardens** (daily 7.30am–5.45pm; Rs.600), the largest and finest gardens in Sri Lanka, covering almost 150 acres and stuffed with a bewildering variety of local and foreign tree and plant species. The history of the site dates right back to the fourteenth century, when Wickramabahu III established a royal residence here. The park itself was created during the eighteenth century by King Kirti Sri Rajasinha to serve as a pleasure garden for the Kandyan nobility. It was transformed into a botanical garden by the British in 1821 during the enterprising governorship of Edward Barnes, who had Sri Lanka's first tea trees planted here in 1824, though their full commercial potential wasn't to be realized for another half-century.

The versatile talipot

The **talipot palm** is one of Sri Lanka's botanical celebrities, an arboreal oddity that flowers just once in its life, after about fifty to seventy years, producing what is claimed by some to be the largest cluster of flowers in the world, as the whole of the top of the tree sheds its leaves and turns into an enormous green efflorescence, sometimes reaching almost ten metres in height.

The enormous leaves of the mature talipot have also proved particularly useful. In Kandyan times they were used to construct shelters (three or four leaves sewn together produce a passable tent) or to serve as umbrellas – "one single Leaf being so broad and large, that it will cover some fifteen or twenty men, and keep them dry when it rains," according to Robert Knox. Talipot leaves are best known, however, as the source of **ola leaf**, the local alternative to paper, which was manufactured in Sri Lanka and India from as early as 500 BC. The efficacy of ola is proved by the fact that some ola-leaf manuscripts have survived over five hundred years, and have proved far more durable in the tropical climate than paper.

There are around ten thousand trees in the gardens. Lots are labelled, though unfortunately many of the signs have weathered away to illegibility, while others show only the tree's Latin name – not much help unless you're an expert botanist. The area around the entrance is largely given over to small-scale flora, including an **orchid house**, a **flower garden** and a tiny and rather unimpressive **Japanese garden**, where the most interesting sight is a bizarre-looking snake creeper, whose tangled aerial roots look just like a writhing knot of vipers.

Running from the entrance, the principal thoroughfare, stately **Royal Palm Avenue**, bisects the gardens, heading in an arrow-straight line from the entrance to the Mahaweli Ganga at the far northern end, via the **Great Circle**

Moving on from Kandy

Thanks to its position roughly in the centre of the island, Kandy is within fairly easy striking distance of pretty much everywhere in the country, although if you're heading to the south coast, it's normally easiest to go back to Colombo and start from there. Heading south into the **hill country**, the train connects Kandy with most places you're likely to want to go, while to the north, all the sites of the **Cultural Triangle** are no more than two to three hours away by road. For details of tours and taxis from Kandy, see p.254.

By train

Regular trains connect Kandy with Colombo in one direction, and with the southern hill country in the other. The ride through the hills up to Nanu Oya (for Nuwara Eliya), Haputale, Ella and Badulla is unforgettable; it's well worth trying to bag a seat in the **observation car** (see p.35). Travelling to Colombo, sit on the south side of the train (the left-hand side, as you face the front) for the best views. Note that not all trains between Colombo and the hill country actually call at Kandy; some go via **Peradeniya**. **Timetables** for the principal train services from Kandy are given on p.224.

By bus

Most long-distance **bus** services depart from Kandy's main bus station, the memorably chaotic **Goods Shed Bus Terminal** opposite the train station (the **Clocktower Bus Stand**, south of the clocktower at the west end of the city centre, is used for local departures only). It's very difficult to make sense of the vast scrum of buses: if you can't find the one you're looking for, ask at one of the two wire-mesh information kiosks in the middle of the terminal.

Heading west, there are express services to **Colombo** (every 10–15min; 3hr), which leave from the roadside on Station Road about halfway between the Goods Shed terminal and the clocktower. Buses to **Negombo** (4 daily; 3hr 30min) leave from the main road opposite the Goods Shed terminal. There are occasional direct private buses to the international **airport** (check at the bus station or tourist office for latest times). Alternatively, all buses to Negombo pass the turn-off to the airport, about 2km from the terminal itself. Another possibility is to take a (non-inter-city) Colombo train to **Veyangoda**, then catch a bus or tuktuk for the thirty-minute trip to the airport.

Heading north, there are regular buses to **Anuradhapura** (every 30min; 4hr), **Polonnaruwa** (every 30min; 3hr 45min) and **Dambulla** (every 20min; 2hr), plus one bus direct to **Sigiriya** daily at 8am (2hr 30min; otherwise change at Dambulla). All buses to Polonnaruwa travel via **Habarana** and **Giritale**.

There are also services south to **Nuwara Eliya** (every 45min; 2hr 30min), **Ratnapura** (3 daily; 3hr 30min) and **Badulla** (hourly; 5hr 30min). For **Ella**, you'll probably have to travel via Badulla, and for **Haputale** via Nuwara Eliya and/or Bandarawela; in both instances it's far easier to take the train. There are also regular buses to **Trincomalee** (every 45min; 6hr); **Kurunegala** (every 15min; 1hr 30min) and **Kegalle**, for Pinnewala (every 15min; 1hr).

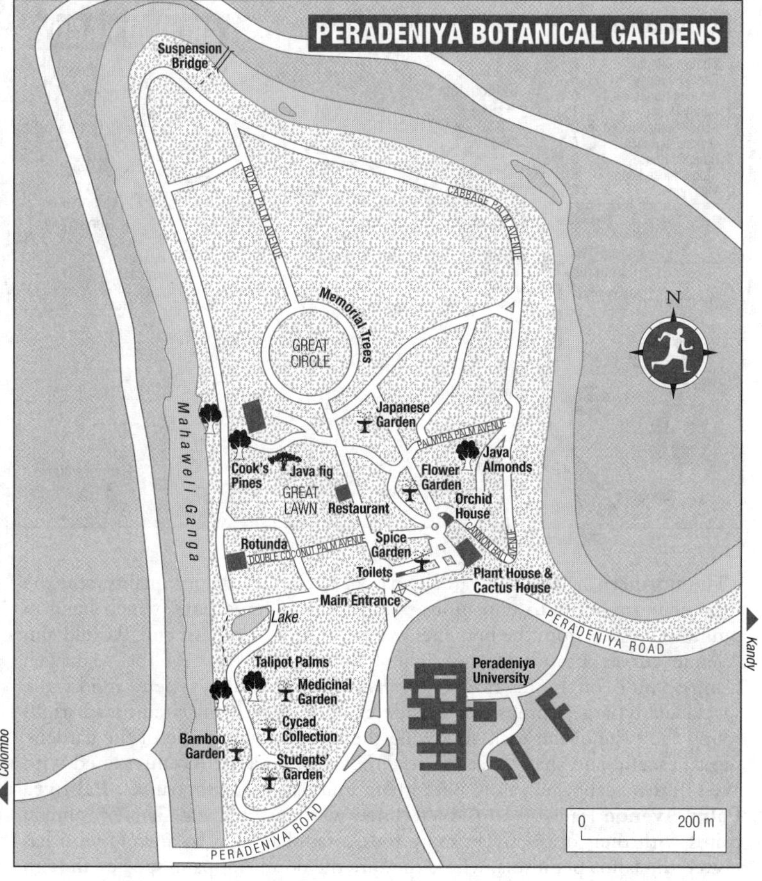

at the centre. The eastern side of the Great Circle is dotted with a sequence of **memorial trees** planted at various times by assorted international bigwigs, ranging from a couple of princes of Wales (1875 and 1922) and the czar of Russia (1891 – the tree has lasted rather longer than the czar) through to Joseph Tito (1959) and various post-independence Sri Lankan prime ministers and presidents.

To the west of the avenue stretches the **Great Lawn**, home to Peradeniya's most majestic sight: a huge Javan fig whose sprawling roots and branches create a remarkable natural pavilion. (There's also an overpriced **restaurant** near here, and cheaper drinks in a kiosk next door.) Running along the southern side of the Great Lawn, **Double Coconut Palm Avenue** is flanked with coco de mer trees, rather stumpy and unimpressive-looking things, though their massively swollen coconuts – which can weigh up to 20kg – are the world's largest and heaviest fruit. There are also a few stunning kauri pines here from Queensland (they're actually broadleaved trees, not pines). A long line of strangely twisted Cook's pines run along the east side of the lawn.

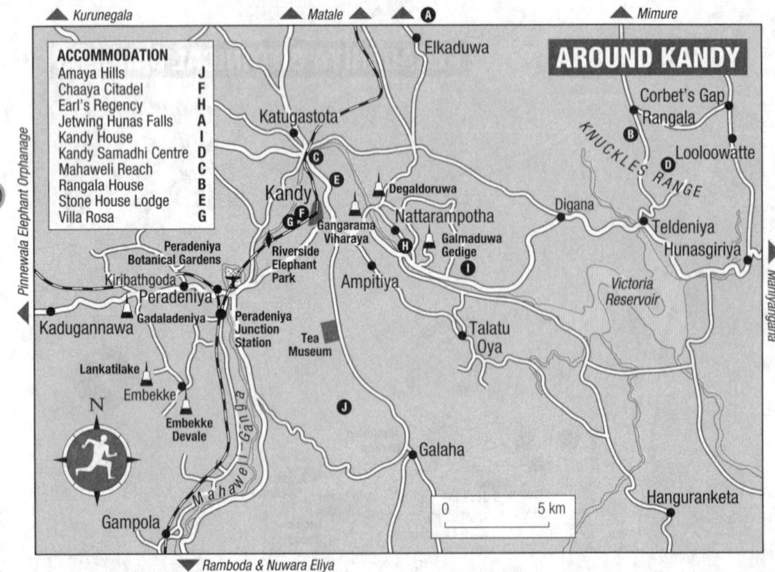

The northern half of the gardens has an altogether wilder quality, and the trees here are home to enormous populations of **fruit bats**, which hang in ominous clusters from the branches overhead. At its northern end, Royal Palm Avenue curves around to the right, following the bank of the Mahaweli Ganga; you'll often see troupes of **macaque monkeys** here amidst the spectacularly large clumps of riverside bamboo. A pleasant circuit leads right round the edge of the park, following the river through some of the gardens' most peaceful and shady areas to reach **Cabbage Palm Avenue**, lined with West Indian cabbage palms with their unusual, greenish trunks. **Palmyra Palm Avenue** leads off to the left, lined with very tall and slender Palmyra palms with their distinctively spiky tops, a familiar sight to anyone who has visited the Jaffna peninsula, where they are the dominant palm species, though they're relatively uncommon elsewhere in the island. South of here is a marvellous group of **Java almonds**, whose huge buttressed roots line the side of the path. Returning to Cabbage Palm Avenue and continuing south brings you to **Cannon Ball Avenue**, lined with beautiful cannon ball trees, wreathed in creepers from which hang the characteristically large, round fruits, after which the militaristic British named the tree. The Sinhalese (who call them *sal* trees) hold their beautiful flowers sacred, since they appear to comprise a tiny dagoba, shaded by a cobra's hood and surrounded by tiny florettes, which are thought to represent a crowd of worshippers. Beyond here, the avenue curves around away from the river, before returning you to the Orchid House and entrance.

South of the Great Lawn lies a small but picturesque **lake**, covered in water-lilies and overlooked by a classical rotunda and an enormous clump of giant bamboo. Continuing south brings you to a didactic but dull little area of carefully laid out medicinal and aquatic plants, plus various types of grass. Next to these is a line of far more striking **talipot palms** (see box, p.255), identifiable by the unusual criss-cross bark pattern at the foot of the trunk (the remains of old leaves) and by their enormous leaves – the trees as a whole look rather like enormous toilet brushes. Beyond here, at the southernmost edge of the gardens, is the pretty little **Students' Garden**, surrounded by weird cycads and ferns.

A tuktuk to the gardens will cost around Rs.1000 return from Kandy, including waiting time. Alternatively, frequent buses leave the Clocktower Bus Stand for Peradeniya.

Close to the entrance lies **Peradeniya University**, one of the island's most illustrious places of higher education.

The three-temples loop

The countryside around Kandy is dotted with dozens of historic Kandyan-era **temples**. Few see any foreign visitors, and setting off into the local backwaters in search of these legacies of the Kandyan kingdom makes a wonderful alternative to joining the hordes flocking to Pinnewala or Peradeniya. The most interesting of these temples are the **Embekke Devale**, **Lankatilake** and **Gadaladeniya**, which lie some 10km west of Kandy and make a rewarding day-trip – they are often combined into a round-trip by vehicle or foot, known as the **three-temples loop** (a further trio of temples is described on p.261). All three temples were constructed during the fourteenth century, in the early days of the nascent Kandyan kingdom, when the region was ruled from Gampola and Tamil influence was strong. They can all be visited (albeit with some difficulty) by bus or, far more conveniently, by taxi (count on around US$20–25 for the round-trip). The best way to visit, however, is to walk at least part of the way between the three, starting at the Embekke Devale and finishing at the Gadaladeniya (or vice versa).

Embekke Devale

To reach the **Embekke Devale** (Rs.200), and the start of the walk, take bus #643 from the Clocktower bus station (every 20min; 1hr). You'll be dropped off in **Embekke village**, from where it's a one-kilometre walk to the temple: turn right onto the tiny road opposite the red postbox, then follow it straight ahead as it switchbacks up over a steep hill.

Dating from the fourteenth century, the rustic little Embekke Devale, dedicated to Kataragama, is famous principally for the fine pavilion (the *digge*) fronting the main **shrine**, with its intricately decorated wooden pillars – apparently brought here from another temple at Gampola. Each of the myriad pillars bears a different design, a marvellously carved assortment of peacocks, entwined swans, wrestlers, dragons, dancers, horsemen, soldiers and Bodhisattvas (shown as composite figures: part man, part fish, part bird). One of the most famous panels depicts an elephant and lion fighting; another shows what looks curiously like a Habsburg double-headed eagle. Two quaint lions flank the entrance to the main Kataragama shrine behind, which is topped by a delicate pagoda-tower. To the left of the main building stands an unusual **granary**, raised on stones above the ground to protect its contents from wild animals; to the right, a subsidiary shrine with sumptuously carved wooden doors houses a Buddha and a fine (but difficult to see) wooden statue of a peacock, a bird traditionally associated with Kataragama.

Lankatilake

From Embekke Devale, retrace your steps back up the road towards Embekke Village. At the top of the hill, about 200m from the temple, the road forks. Go left here, climbing a steep hill and continuing for 500m through the edge of the village. At the end of the village you reach a gorgeous bo tree and paddy fields, with a huge rock outcrop to your right. Continue straight along the road for a further 500m until the road forks. Keep right here and continue over the brow of a hill, from where you'll catch your first, magical sight of the **Lankatilake temple** (Rs.200) rising out of the tea plantations ahead. Continue ahead, ignoring another road to the left, through further paddy fields. You can take a shortcut immediately below the temple by walking along the wall across the paddy fields by an electricity pylon (follow the locals); alternatively, continue along the road till you reach the temple's access road, which leads off on the left. Both wall and road lead to the base of the temple.

From here, a magnificent flight of rock-cut steps leads precipitously up to the temple itself, giving glorious views of the surrounding hills. Lankatilake is perhaps the finest temple in the district: an imposingly solid-looking structure built on a huge rock outcrop and painted a faint blue rather than the usual white. It was founded in 1344, and its architecture is reminiscent of the solid, gedige-style stone temples of Polonnaruwa rather than the later and more decorative Kandyan-style wooden temples. The building was formerly four storeys tall, though the uppermost storeys collapsed in the nineteenth century and were replaced by the present, rather ill-fitting wooden roof. The gloomy central **shrine**, with eighteenth-century Kandyan paintings, is magically atmospheric: narrow but tall, and filled with a great seated Buddha under a huge *makara torana*, above which rise tiers of decidedly Hindu-looking gods. The massive exterior walls contain a sequence of small shrines containing statues of Saman, Kataragama, Vishnu and Vibhishana, punctuated by majestic low-relief carvings of elephants. To the left of the temple, a large rock inscription in Pali records the details of the temple's construction.

If you want to reach Lankatilake by **bus** directly from Kandy, take service #666 or #643 from the Goods Shed bus station (every 30min; 1hr).

Gadaladeniya

Returning to the road by the pylon, continue along to the left. The road hairpins quickly up to reach a larger road and another village. Turn left along the main road and continue for about 3km, keeping right whenever the road forks, to reach the **Gadaladeniya temple** (Rs.200). This part of the walk is less special – the road is bigger and there's more traffic, although there are plenty of tuktuks around if you get bored. The area is a major centre of metalworking, and you'll pass dozens of shops selling traditional oil lamps, looking something like a cross between a miniature spire and an overblown cake stand.

Gadaladeniya dates from the same year – 1344 – as Lankatilake. The principal **shrine**, built on a rock outcrop at the top end of the site, has a pronounced South Indian appearance (it was designed by a Tamil architect, one Ganesvarachari), and the style of the corbelled roof and carvings of dancers, drummers and the two quaint elephants which flank the entrance is strongly reminiscent of the temples at the great Hindu capital of Vijayanagar in Karnataka. The interior houses a fine gold Buddha (with oddly close-set eyes) under a marvellous *makara torana*, plus a subsidiary Vishnu shrine. The whimsical subsidiary shrine, in the middle of the compound, consists of a cruciform building, each wing housing a tiny Buddha shrine and topped by a minuscule dagoba, with the entire structure being surmounted by a larger dagoba – a unique local take on the traditional Indian-style *shikhara* dome.

To **return to Kandy**, carry on down the road for a further ten minutes to reach the main Colombo–Kandy highway. Buses back to Kandy pass every minute or so – just flag one down. To reach Gadaladeniya directly from Kandy, take any of the numerous non-express buses heading west along the road to

Kegalle, Colombo or Kaduganawa and ask to be set down at the Gadaladeniya turn-off (it's a couple of kilometres beyond Kiribathgoda, and before you reach Kadugannawa).

Temples east of Kandy

There's a further trio of interesting temples just east of the city, dating from the Buddhist renaissance which the Kandyan kingdom experienced under Kirti Sri Rajasinha (see p.231), who built all three.

Gangarama Viharaya

About two kilometres east of Kandy (head east along the Mahiyangana road, then turn north towards Madawela) on the banks of the Mahaweli Ganga, lies the **Gangarama Viharaya**. This small monastery is notable mainly for its fine two-storey **image house**, decorated with Kandyan-era paintings and home to an eight-metre-tall standing Buddha statue, carved out of the natural rock outcrop around which the shrine is built. (You can see the rock outcrop poking out of the back of the image house, carved with an extensive rock inscription in Sinhala recording details of the temple's construction.) The walls inside are decorated with the usual hundreds of tessellated sitting Buddhas, while the lower sections of the wall show Jataka stories and scenes from the Buddha's life, delicately painted in characteristic Kandyan style in narrow panels using a predominantly bright-red palette. A small **digge** stands opposite the entrance to the image house.

Degaldoruwa

A couple of kilometres further along the road to Gangarama lies **Degaldoruwa**, the most interesting of this group of temples. Built into a large rock outcrop, the temple consists of three small connected chambers: the first two – the *digge* and antechamber – are built outside the rock and topped by crumbling old wooden roofs, while the third, the main shrine, is hollowed out of the rock itself, and invisible from the outside. The **digge** has a few old wooden pillars and a couple of drums hanging from the rafters; it's unusual in being directly attached to the rest of the temple, rather than occupying a separate pavilion, as is usually the case. Old wooden doors lead into the **antechamber**, which preserves a fine moonstone and a sequence of murals showing scenes from the Jataka stories, painted in five vivid red panels.

The doors leading from here into the **main shrine** have metal fittings which were formerly studded with jewels. The principal image is a large reclining Buddha; the pillow on which the Buddha's head rests is inlaid with a glass copy of a huge amethyst – according to tradition, the painters who decorated the shrine worked by the light generated by this enormous jewel. The murals here are some of Sri Lanka's finest, though they're rather dark and difficult to make out, having until recently been covered in a thick layer of soot from fires lit inside the shrine – a tiny square of black wall has been left just next to one of the doors to show what the walls looked like before restoration. The wall opposite the reclining Buddha is painted with Jataka scenes and pictures of dagobas at Sri Lanka's principal pilgrimage sites, but the finest painting is on the ceiling, a magnificent depiction of the **Buddha's battle with Mara**, dating from the 1770s and 1780s, and rivalling the far better-known example at Dambulla.

Outside stands a belfry, apparently built in imitation of a Christian church tower. Steps to the left of the temple lead up to a large platform, where a stupa and bo tree stand facing one another above the temple.

Galmaduwa Gedige

Return to the main Mahiyangana road and continue east for about five kilometres to reach the village of **Kalapura**, home to the extremely unusual **Galmaduwa Gedige**. The bizarre shrine here is enclosed in a cloister-like stone structure (the gedige) and topped by a stone pyramid – an odd but endearing Kandyan version of a traditional South Indian temple. Apparently, the gedige was left unfinished, and its exact purpose remains unclear (the image house at the back was only added during a restoration in 1967). Old ola-leaf manuscripts suggest that the innermost section was originally built as a jail to contain a single prisoner of noble birth who had offended the king, and that the surrounding ambulatory was added later.

Tea Museum

South of Kandy, the small Hantana Road climbs steeply up into the hills through run-down tea estates, with sweeping views back to Kandy. Four kilometres along the road is the mildly interesting **Tea Museum** (daily 8.15am–4.45pm; Rs.180), housed in an attractively converted tea factory. The ground and first floors hold various imposing pieces of colonial-era machinery collected from defunct factories around the hill country, including assorted engines, rollers, sifters, drying furnaces, fans, withering trays and even a tractor, plus a cute little working model of a tea factory. The second floor has displays on two of Sri Lankan tea's great pioneers, with a small collection of the frugal personal effects (pipe, plate and walking stick) of James Taylor, who established the island's first commercial tea estate, and a display on the much more flamboyant career of Thomas Lipton (see p.457), who did so much to publicize Sri Lankan tea and create a demand for it in the kitchens of Britain. There are also exhibits of other tea-related colonial-era bits and pieces, including Sri Lanka's oldest packet of tea, dating from 1944 and "Guaranteed by the Ceylon Tea Propaganda Board". The top floor has a small café serving tea and cakes, plus assorted tea and handicraft shops.

East and south of Kandy

The hill country **east of Kandy** remains largely off the tourist map and far less developed than the area to the west of the city – a refreshingly untamed area of rugged uplands which still preserves much of its forest cover. Two main highways run east from Kandy to Mahiyangana. The more circuitous but smoother **southern road** meanders around the south side of the **Victoria Reservoir and Dam**, opened in 1989 as part of the huge Mahaweli Ganga Project and one of the island's major sources of electricity. A **visitors' centre**, just off the highway, offers fine views of the spectacular dam itself. Much of the densely forested area around the reservoir is protected as part of the Victoria-Randenigala Sanctuary (no entrance), and you might even spot the occasional elephant sticking its trunk out of the forest while you're travelling down the road.

Around 8km south of the main road lies the sleepy little town of **HANGURANKETA**, a former refuge of the kings of Kandy, who built a large palace here to which they would retreat during times of internal rebellion or external threat. The original palace was destroyed by the British during the rebellion of 1818 (or 1803, according to some sources) and its remains used to construct the **Potgul Maliga Vihara** ("Temple Library"), which is home to an important collection of ola-leaf manuscripts, protected in their sumptuous original copper and silver covers. The temple as a whole is a good example of the high Kandyan style, with a fine central image house surrounded by smaller shrines and an unusual, mural-covered dagoba.

The Knuckles Range

The second of the two main roads east from Kandy, the rougher but more dramatic **A26**, twists and turns through the hills, skirting the northern edge of the Victoria Reservoir and running around the southern outliers of the **Knuckles Range**, the hill country's last great unspoilt wilderness, though its tourist potential remains largely untapped. The rugged peaks of the Knuckles (Dumbara Hills) – named by the British for their resemblance to the knuckles of a clenched fist – cover a rugged and still largely untouched area of great natural beauty and biodiversity. The steeply shelving mountain terrain reaches 1863m at the summit of the main Knuckles peak itself (the sixth highest in Sri Lanka) and includes stands of rare dwarf cloudforest. The area is home to leopard, various species of deer (sambhur, barking and mouse), monkeys (purple-faced langur and macaque), giant squirrels, rare species of lizard such as the horned black-lipped lizard, and an exceptionally fine collection of endemic bird species. The most straightforward approach to the Knuckles is from the main Kandy to Mahiyangana road. Some 27km east of Kandy, at **Hunasgiriya**, a left turn leads via **Rangala** into the range, hairpinning up via the village of Looloowatte (1065m) to **Corbet's Gap**, from where there are magnificent views of the main Knuckles directly ahead.

The areas of the range above 1000m are now a World Heritage Conservation Area, and an **entrance fee** of Rs.661 per person per day is now charged at entrances to the area. There are all sorts of intriguing but still largely unexplored trekking possibilities in the Knuckles, although you'll really need to go with a guide if you plan on doing any extended walks. Local wildlife and walking authority Sumane Bandara Illangantilake (see p.254) offers a rewarding forty-kilometre, three-day hike through the hills, either camping or staying in village homes, and visiting unspoilt and remote places like the secluded village of **Mimure**, in the main valley of the Knuckles Range, said to be the most traditional in Sri Lanka, where life continues much as it has done for generations (electricity only arrived in the village in late 2008). Alternatively, for a shorter taste of the area, he runs a twenty-kilometre one-day trek from Matale around the western flanks of the range. Treks cost roughly US$65 per person per day. In addition, a few of the tour operators listed on pp.30–32 and other local guides in Kandy are gradually beginning to offer visits to the area.

East to Mahiyangana

East of Hunasgiriya, the A26 gives increasingly fine views of the Knuckles Range to the north, with sheer rockfaces towering above the road and further craggy peaks rising beyond – Sri Lanka at its most alpine. Another thirty minutes' drive brings you to the dramatic escarpment at the eastern edge of the hill country, from where there are marvellous views of the dry-zone plains almost a kilometre below. The highway descends through a precipitous sequence of seventeen numbered hairpins – this stretch of the A26 is popularly known as Sri Lanka's most dangerous road, and although it's fairly small beer compared to Himalayan or Andean highways, the local bus drivers do their best to keep the adrenaline flowing. At the bottom of the hills, the village of **Hasalaka** is the starting point for the 45-kilometre road north to the little-visited Wasgomuwa National Park (or continue through Mahiyangana and on through Girandurukotte – see p.350 for more).

Around 7km further east from Hasalaka, the small town of **MAHIYANGANA** (pronounced "my-*yan*-gana") is famous in Buddhist legend as the first of the three places in Sri Lanka which the Buddha himself is said to have visited (the others are Kelaniya and Nainativu). The large **Rajamaha Dagoba**, a kilometre or so south of town, is held to mark the exact spot at which the Buddha preached, and is also believed to enshrine a lock of his hair. The dagoba's origins are lost in antiquity; it's said to have been rebuilt by King Dutugemunu, and has been restored many times since. The present bell-shaped structure, picturesquely backdropped by the hill country escarpment, sits atop a large platform studded with elephant heads and approached by an impressively long walkway. The town's other eye-catching building is the striking replica of the famous **Mahabodhi**

▲ Rajamaha Dagoba, Mahlyangana

Stupa at Bodhgaya in India, erected at the behest of the late President Premadasa, which sits next to the main road on the west side of town.

Mahiyangana is something of a crossroads town on the bus routes between Polonnaruwa, Kandy, Badulla, Monaragala and Ampara. There are a couple of pleasant mid-range **places to stay** just outside town on the road to the scenic Sorabora (or Horabora) Lake: the newly built *Sorabora Village Inn* (ⓣ055-225 7149; ❷, a/c ❸); and the neat, modern *Sorabora Gedara* hotel (ⓣ055-225 8308, ⓦwww.soraboragedarahotel.com; ❹–❺), which has comfy air-conditioned doubles, a new swimming pool, plus bar and restaurant. There are also a few cheaper but acceptable options along the river, close to the replica of the Mahabodhi Stupa. The nicest is the *New Rest House* (ⓣ055-225 7304; ❸), with spacious if slightly shabby and expensive rooms, plus good food. Immediately to the north and south (respectively), are the cheaper but very basic *Rest House* (055-225 7299; ❶) and the slightly cleaner *Venjinn Guest House* (ⓣ055-225 7151; ❷, a/c ❸).

Alternatively, the smaller and more characterful *The Nest*, about 2km east of town on Padiyathalawa Road (ⓣ0777 652 670, ⓦwww.nest-srilanka.com; ❸), has four comfortable rooms with optional air-conditioning (Rs.500 extra); there's good Sri Lankan food, and the owner can organize trips to local Veddha villages.

Northeast of Mahiyangana lies the huge **Maduru Oya National Park**, covered on p.391.

East of Mahiyangana: Kotabakina

The country east of Mahiyangana is one of the last strongholds of Sri Lanka's ever-diminishing number of **Veddhas** (see box, p.266), who live in the area around the village of **Dambana**, some 25km further along the A26. From Dambana, a rough track leads north a couple of kilometres to the principal Veddha village of **KOTABAKINA** ("King's Village"; also often but erroneously referred to as Dambana, though properly speaking this name refers to the Sinhalese village on the main highway). The village itself is a beautifully sylvan spot, with picturesque little bamboo-framed, mud-walled huts hemmed in by lush paddy fields. Men will be welcomed to the village with the traditional double-handed handshake, after which you can have a look round and talk to the village chief (one of the five sons of Tissahami) and other male villagers – striking-looking people, with wispy uncut beards, shoulder-length hair and brightly polished little axes, which they carry, dwarf-fashion, over their shoulders. You won't meet any women, however, since all females retreat to their huts so as not to be seen by outsiders, and will stay there for the duration of your visit. You'll need to pick up an **interpreter** en route to the village, however (there are usually lots of volunteers offering their services for a consideration), since the Veddhas cannot – or perhaps will not – speak either English or standard Sinhalese, but stick doggedly to their own "Veddha language" (although whether it's a proper language or merely a strange sub-dialect of Sinhalese remains a moot point; native Sinhalese speakers can usually understand around a third of it).

Although undeniably interesting, visits to Kotabakina can also, sadly, be gratingly false. The Veddhas are used to entertaining passing coach parties with displays of dancing, singing, fire-making and bow-and-arrow shooting, and have become adept at extracting large sums of money for their services. Visits can be rather demeaning for all concerned, and may well end in unedifying disputes over money. If you do agree to watch some dancing or whatever, make sure you agree a sum in advance, and don't expect to pay less than about US$30 for the pleasure, or perhaps significantly more. Even if you don't, expect to hand over US$5–10 to look around the village (plus a few

The Veddhas

The **Wanniyala-aetto** ("People of the forest"), more usually known by the name of **Veddhas** (meaning "hunter"), were the original inhabitants of Sri Lanka, and are ethnically related to the aborigines of India, Sumatra and Australia. The Veddhas may have arrived in the island as far back as 16,000 BC, and developed a sophisticated matrilineal hunter-gatherer culture based on ancestor worship and an intimate knowledge of their forest surroundings, the latter allowing them to coexist in perfect harmony with their environment until the arrival of the Sinhalese in the fourth century BC. Veddhas feature extensively in early Sinhalese legend, where they are described as *yakkas*, or demons, and this common perception of them as demonic savages has persisted through the centuries. One memorably smug Victorian colonial official described them as a:

strange and primitive race [whose] members are but a degree removed from wild beasts. They know nothing of history, religion or any art whatever. They cannot count, know of no amusement save dancing, and are popularly supposed not to laugh. During the Prince of Wales's visit, however, one of those brought before him managed to grin when presented with a threepenny piece. The Veddhas have, however, of late years shown some signs of becoming civilised under British influence.

Faced by successive waves of colonizers, the Veddhas were forced either to assimilate with the majority Sinhalese or Tamils, or retreat ever further into their dwindling forests. Despite the best attempts of successive British and Sri Lankan governments to "civilize" them, however, an ever-diminishing population of Veddhas still cling obstinately to their traditions – about 350 pure Veddhas are now left in seven villages, mainly in the area east of Mahiyangana, and a small number have attempted to continue their traditional hunter-gatherer existence (even if they now use guns rather than bows and arrows), and also farm rice and other crops to supplement their diet and income. The creation of national parks, alongside government development and resettlement schemes and agricultural projects, have further encroached on traditional Veddha lands – in recent years they have campaigned vigorously for recognition and for the right to continue hunting on land now protected by the Maduru Oya National Park. Some "reserved" areas have now been set aside for their use, though their struggle for proper recognition continues.

For more on the Veddhas, see Ⓦwww.vedda.org.

dollars for your interpreter). Alternatively, you might be able to find some cut-price Veddhas along the main A26 at **Mavaragalpota**, a few kilometres back toward Mahiyangana, who offer similar displays at about a quarter of the price. Fake Veddhas have also been known to offer their services to unwary tourists along the road and around the temple in Mahiyangana. Having said which, you might consider that the whole experience is already sufficiently ersatz, and that a few imposter Veddhas more or less won't make much difference. If you have a genuine interest in the Veddhas, Sumane Bandara Illangantilake (see p.254) has good connections with them, speaks their language (or "language"), and can arrange visits to Kotabakina on a more rewarding and equitable footing.

South from Kandy to Nuwara Eliya

The journey south from Kandy to Nuwara Eliya is spectacular both by train and by bus. The **bus** is far more direct and significantly quicker, cutting up through the hills and swinging round endless hairpins, passing the magnificent waterfalls at the village of **RAMBODA** en route, which plunge over the cliffs in two adjacent hundred-metre cataracts. There's good-value **accommodation** here at the functional but comfortable *Ramboda Falls Hotel* (Ⓣ052-225 9582, Ⓦwww.rambodafall.com; ❺), close to – and offering a good view of – the Ramboda Falls, as well as of a second, smaller set of falls right next to the hotel. There's more upmarket accommodation at the atmospheric *Lavender House* (Ⓣ052-225 9928, Ⓦwww.thelavenderhouseceylon.com; ❾), a fine old tea planter's villa with five rooms beautifully furnished in traditional colonial style. From Ramboda, it's a short drive on to Labookelie Tea Factory (see p.275) and Nuwara Eliya.

The **train** is significantly slower, but makes for a quintessentially Sri Lankan experience, as the carriages bump and grind their way painfully up the interminable gradients towards Nuwara Eliya (and occasionally lose traction and slither a yard or so back downhill again). The track climbs slowly through pine and eucalyptus forest into a stylized landscape of immaculately manicured tea plantations which periodically open up to reveal heart-stopping views through the hills, nowhere more so than above the village of **Dimbula**, at the centre of a famous tea-growing area, where the line passes high above a grand, canyon-like valley between enormous cliffs.

The southern hill country

The **southern hill country** is the highest, wildest and – for many visitors – the most beautiful part of Sri Lanka. Although the area was an integral part of the Kandyan Kingdom, little physical or cultural evidence survives from that period, and most of what you now see is the creation of the British colonial period, when the introduction of **tea** here changed the economic face of Sri Lanka forever. The region's attractions are self-explanatory: a whimsical mixture of ruggedly beautiful scenery and olde-worlde colonial style, with sheer green mountainsides, plunging waterfalls and mist-shrouded tea plantations enlivened by quaint British memorabilia – clunking railways, half-timbered guesthouses, Gothic churches and English vegetables – while a further, unexpected twist is added by the colourful Hindu temples and saris of the so-called "Plantation Tamils", who have been working the tea estates since colonial times.

Nuwara Eliya and around

Sri Lanka's highest town, **NUWARA ELIYA** lies at the heart of the southern hill country, set amidst a bowl of green mountains beneath the protective gaze of Sri Lanka's tallest peak, Pidurutalagala (2555m). Nuwara Eliya (pronounced, as one word, something like "Nyur-*rail*-eeya") was established by the British in the nineteenth century, and the town and surrounding area continue to be touted as Sri Lanka's "Little England" – a remnant of the old country stuck in the heart of the tropics. The reality, however, is that Nuwara Eliya is far less of a period piece than the publicity would have you believe, although the town still boasts a triumvirate of fine old colonial hotels, along with scattered

Tea estate bungalows

For a true taste of the colonial lifestyle of old Ceylon, you can't beat a stay in one of the sumptuous **tea estate bungalows** that dot the southern highlands. Originally built for British estate managers in the nineteenth and early twentieth centuries, many offer beautiful and atmospheric lodgings, often in spectacular locations. The **Tea Trails** network (ⓣ011-230 3888, ⓦwww.teatrails.com; all ❾ full-board) comprises four superb bungalows of contrasting characters, all in working tea estates in the vicinity of Adam's Peak. The recently established **Tapro Spa** (ⓣ011-267 8389, ⓦwww.taprospa.com) network comprises another three attractive bungalows (US$250/450 full board) on the Labookelie estate (see p.275) near Nuwara Eliya, plus another near Kalutara. Other possibilities include Warwick Gardens (ⓣ060-253 2284, ⓦwww.jetwing.com; US$156/201/215), on its own six-acre estate near Ambewella, about 20km south of Nuwara Eliya; and the *Kirchhayn Bungalow*, on the Aislaby Estate near Bandarawela (ⓣ057-492 0494, ⓦwww.kirchhaynbungalow.com; ❽), a characterful old bungalow owned by the last remaining British planting family in Sri Lanka. Further properties can be found at ⓦwww.boutiquesrilanka.com and ⓦwww.reddottours.com.

atmospheric villas and fusty guesthouses whose misplaced architecture – a mixture of jaunty seaside kitsch and solemn faux-Tudor – lend some parts an oddly English (or perhaps Scottish) air, like a crazily transplanted fragment of Brighton or Balmoral, an illusion heightened by the luxuriant green spaces of the golf course, racecourse and Victoria Park. The memory of England lives on, too, in the small-scale market-gardening which is still one of the mainstays of the modern town's economy – the odd spectacle of dark-skinned Tamil men dressed up like English farm labourers in padded jackets and woolly hats, whilst carting around great bundles of turnips, swedes, marrows, radishes and cabbages, is one of Nuwara Eliya's characteristic sights, adding a pleasantly surreal touch to the town's out-of-focus English nostalgia.

And yet, despite the faint traces of colonial magic which still cling to parts of the town, Nuwara Eliya is a frustratingly contradictory – and, for many visitors, disappointing – place. Much of it is now a functional and unappealing expanse of concrete shopping arcades and traffic intersections. The stress of altitude causes vehicles here to belch out great noxious clouds of fumes, making a mockery of Nuwara Eliya's claim to be Sri Lanka's "Garden City", while the unpredictable weather can dampen even the brightest spirits. That said, if you take it with a pinch of salt, Nuwara Eliya still has a certain charm, especially if you can afford to stay in one of the town's nicer hotels, and it also makes an excellent base for **excursions** into the spectacular surrounding countryside and tea estates.

Some history

Although there's evidence of Kandyan involvement in the region, Nuwara Eliya is essentially a British creation. The Nuwara Eliya region was "discovered" by the colonial administrator John Davy in 1819, and a decade later Governor **Edward Barnes** recognized its potential, founding a sanatorium and overseeing the creation of a road from Kandy, which he hoped would encourage settlement of the area. Barnes's plans slowly bore fruit, and during the 1830s the town gradually developed into a commercial and coffee-planting centre, with a largely British population. In 1847, **Samuel Baker** (who later distinguished himself by discovering Lake Albert in Africa and helping to identify the sources of the Nile) had the idea of introducing English-style agriculture to the area, laying the foundations for the town's important market-gardening industry:

Spring in Nuwara Eliya

A popular resort amongst Sri Lankans, Nuwara Eliya is at its busiest during the Sinhalese–Tamil **new year** in April, when spring comes to the hill country, the flowers bloom and the Colombo smart set descends. For ten days the town gets overrun and accommodation prices go through the roof, while visitors are entertained by a succession of events, including horse racing, golf tournaments, motor-cross (motorcycles), clay-pigeon shooting and a mini-carnival.

vegetables grown here are still exported all over the island, whilst many of the area's local Tamil tea plantation workers supplement their incomes by growing vegetables in their own allotments.

With the gradual failure of the coffee crop during the 1870s, local planters turned their attention to the beverage which would radically change the physical and social face of the region: **tea**. The first experimental plantation was established in 1867 by Sir James Taylor at the Loolecondera Estate, between Kandy and Nuwara Eliya, and its success led to Nuwara Eliya becoming the centre of Sri Lanka's tea-growing industry. British influence went beyond quaint architecture and golf, however. Whereas the coffee industry had required only seasonal labour, tea required year-round workers, and this led to the arrival of massive numbers of Tamil migrant workers from South India – the so-called **Plantation Tamils** – who settled permanently in the area and decisively changed the region's demographic make-up; about sixty percent of the population here is now Tamil.

Arrival

Nuwara Eliya doesn't have it's own **train station**; the nearest stop is at **Nanu Oya**, about 5km down the road. Buses to Nuwara Eliya meet all arriving trains (despite what touts might tell you); alternatively, there are usually plenty of minivan-taxis hanging around. Arriving **by bus**, you'll end up at the bus station in the middle of town.

There's a small **tourist information office** just south of the bus station (daily 9am–5pm; ⓣ052-222 3555). They have internet access and are a useful source of information about the latest bus times, and can put you in touch with local guide-drivers.

Accommodation

More than anywhere else in Sri Lanka, your choice of accommodation in Nuwara Eliya is likely to have a decisive influence on how much you enjoy your visit. It's well worth prising open your wallet in order to stay at one of the town's patrician **old colonial hotels**, and even if you can't afford one of these top-end places, there are plenty of attractive **mid-range alternatives**. These are usually much better value than the town's almost uniformly overpriced **budget options**. It's also worth remembering that Nuwara Eliya is geared up as much for Sri Lankan visitors as for foreigners – come the weekend or holiday periods, many cheaper places get overrun by parties of hormonal schoolboys or pissed-up locals. Wherever you stay, make sure you've got reliable hot water and plenty of blankets. The better places either include heaters in their room rates or offer to rent them out; some places also have fireplaces in their rooms and will light a fire for you for small fee.

Prices can fluctuate to reflect local holidays. Many places hike rates at weekends, especially over "long" weekends when the Friday or Monday is a

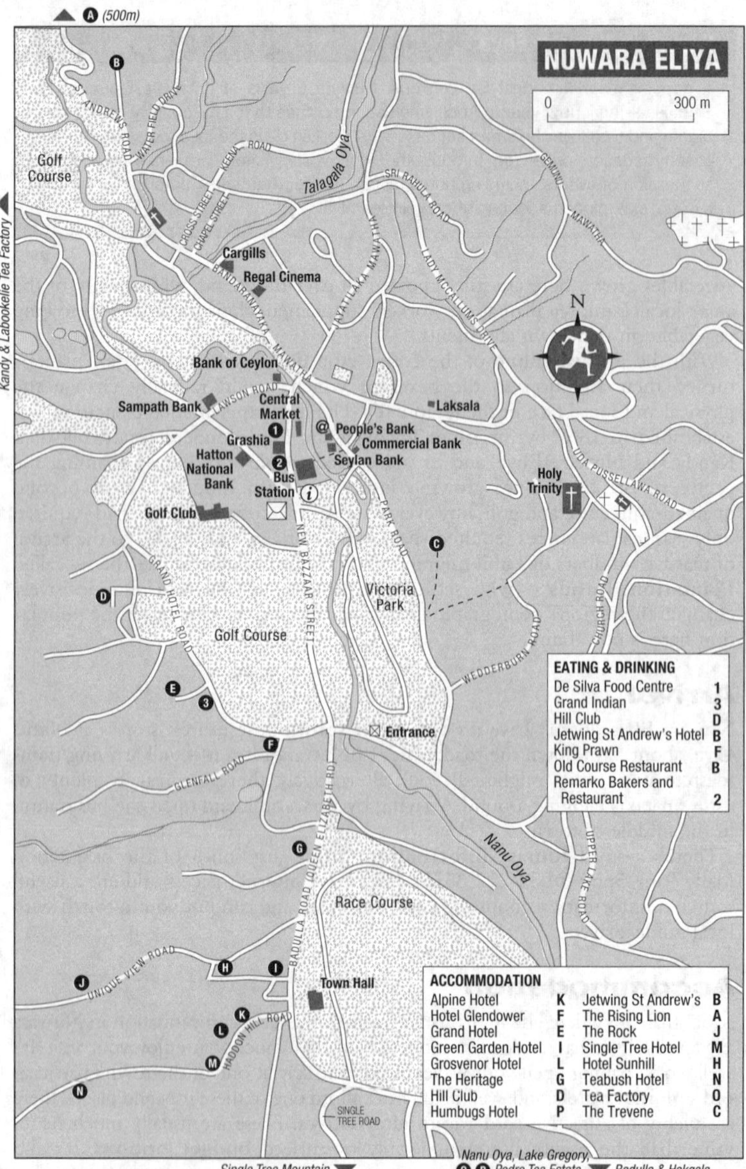

poya day. Rates also rise steeply during December and Christmas, and over the "mini-season" during the school vacations in August, while rates in most places can triple or quadruple during the April **new year** period (roughly from April 10–30; see box, p.269). The price codes given below are for basic weekday room rates outside these peak times.

Food is available in all the following places.

Budget and moderate

Alpine Hotel 4 Haddon Hill Rd ⓣ052-222 3500, ⓦwww.alpineecotravels.com. Modern mid-range hotel with smart if characterless rooms, all comfy and pleasantly furnished, with swish bathrooms (most with bathtubs), satellite TV and heater. The cheaper rooms in the Colonial Wing are a bit smaller and darker, but relatively better value. Colonial Wing ❹, Standard Wing ❺

Hotel Glendower 5 Grand Hotel Rd ⓣ052-222 2501, ⓔglendower22@sltnet.lk. The top mid-range option in town, this welcoming half-timbered establishment makes an excellent halfway alternative to the town's posh hotels, with plenty of period character, including a cosy pub-style bar, a pleasant lounge and billiards table and an excellent in-house Chinese restaurant (see p.273). Rooms are bright, comfortable and characterful; all but one have bathtubs. ❹

Green Garden Hotel 16A Unique View Rd ⓣ052-223 4166, ⓔgreengardenhotel@yahoo.com. Friendly little family-run guesthouse with smallish but cosy rooms (including some with satellite TV and balconies) and a homely little restaurant. Rates are a bit on the high side, but the owners might be open to bargaining if business is slow. ❸

Grosvenor Hotel 6 Haddon Hill Rd ⓣ052-222 2307. Atmospheric small hotel in an old colonial building with a rather English-country-house feel. Rooms are large and quite smart, with reproduction colonial furniture; some also have fireplaces – staff will kindle a warming blaze for you on request. The attractive public areas include a cosy lounge with lots of big leather armchairs and a nice old-fashioned restaurant. ❹

The Heritage Badulla Rd ⓣ052-223 5750. Set in an aristocratic old country house – a former British governor's residence – and still boasting a bit of colonial ambience. Standard rooms ("Garden Wing") are drab and overpriced; deluxe ones ("Colonial Wing") are much nicer, with wooden floors, colonial-style furniture and satellite TV. Standard ❹, deluxe ❺

The Rising Lion 3 Sri Piyatissapura Mw ⓣ052-222 2083. Located on a hill above the north end of town at an altitude of around 2600m, this small guesthouse claims to be the highest place to stay in Sri Lanka, offering memorable views and comfortable rooms with fireplace and satelite TV (a couple also have superb views). Nice, if a bit overpriced. ❹ with view, ❸ without

The Rock 60 Unique View Rd ⓣ052-222 3096. Modern guesthouse, a steep 10min walk up the hill from town, though compensated for by fine views. Rooms are spacious and clean, with pretty pink floral decor, and there's also a pleasant bar and restaurant. ❹

Single Tree Hotel 1/8 Haddon Hill Rd ⓣ052-222 3009, ⓔsingletreehtl@sltnet.lk. Comfortable and relatively good-value guesthouse with cosy rooms (some with satelite TV) and lots of wood panelling – it's a bit like being in an enormous sauna. Also has internet access (Rs.4 per min) and is a good place to arrange tours (see p.275). ❷–❸

Hotel Sunhill 18 Unique View Rd ⓣ052-222 2878, ⓔsunhill@itmin.com. One of Nuwara Eliya's larger and better budget places. Standard rooms are bright and reasonably comfy, though it's worth paying the small surcharge for one of the smarter "deluxe" rooms, with TV and good views. ❸

Teabush Hotel 29 Haddon Hill Rd ⓣ052-222 2345, ⓦwww.lankashopping.com/teabush.htm. Small hotel set in a gracious colonial bungalow. Rooms are comfy and pleasantly chintzy, with old wooden furniture, satellite TV and heater. There's a comfortable lounge to crash out in and a nice restaurant and bar with panoramic views. Unfortunately, it's also significantly overpriced at current rates. ❻

The Trevene 17 Park Rd ⓣ060-252 0606, ⓦwww.hoteltrevenenuwaraeliya.com. Top-notch new guesthouse, set in an atmospheric colonial bungalow complete with cosy old lounge and sunny veranda. Rooms at the front have attractive old wooden floors and period furniture; those at the back are simpler and cheaper. Good value. ❸–❹

Expensive

Grand Hotel Grand Hotel Rd ⓣ052-222 2881, ⓦwww.tangerinehotels.com/thegrandhotel. Doughty half-timbered pile, over a century old, which appears to have been lifted wholesale from a golf course in Surrey. The gorgeous public areas are painfully redolent of Blighty, with gracious old wooden decor and creaking furniture. Rooms (of various standards and prices) are relatively less memorable, but retain traces of their original colonial character. Facilities include two good restaurants, a health centre, gym, sauna and massage centre. ❻

Hill Club Off Grand Hotel Rd ⓣ052-222 2653, ⓦwww.hillclubsrilanka.com. Founded in 1876, this baronial-looking stone and half-timbered structure is Sri Lanka's most famous exercise in nostalgia, with one of the island's best-preserved colonial interiors, complete with a cosy lounge, billiards room, a pair of bars and a fine old dining room – although recent renovations have eroded a little of its idiosyncratic personality. Rooms are characterful and homely, with creaky wooden floors, dark

▲ Grand Hotel, Nuwara Eliya

wood furniture and bathtubs; superior ones have (rather incongruous-looking) satellite TV and minibar. Even if you're not staying it's worth coming for dinner or a drink (see p.273). ❻–❼

Jetwing St Andrew's 10 St Andrew's Drive ⓣ052-222 2445, ⓦwww.jetwing.com. Set in a late Victorian former country club overlooking a swathe of immaculate lawn and the golf course, this serene colonial-style hotel is the smartest place in town. Rooms are spacious, well-equipped and pleasantly old-fashioned, while public areas – including an oak-panelled restaurant (see opposite), billiards room and cosy lounge – retain a delightful Edwardian ambience. ❼

Around Nuwara Eliya

Humbugs Badulla Rd, Hakgala, 10km southeast of Nuwara Eliya ⓣ052-222 2709. Homely rooms plus gorgeous views down the escarpment into the massed hills of Uva Province. The pleasant little café does a big line in strawberries – fresh strawberries and cream in season, strawberry milkshakes and strawberry preserves – plus a few other simple snacks and meals. ❸

The Tea Factory Kandapola, 14km east of Nuwara Eliya ⓣ052-222 9526, ⓦwww.aitkenspencehotels.com. Set on a hilltop surrounded by rolling tea estates, this spectacular five-star hotel was created out of the old Hethersett Estate Tea Factory, which closed in the 1970s. The factory's original exterior has been completely preserved, with corrugated-iron walls and green windows, and it's not until you step inside the stunning interior atrium that you realize the place isn't a working factory at all, although there's still plenty of old machinery lying around, giving the place a look which is at once industrial and futuristic. Rooms are stylish and extremely comfortable, with stunning views to all sides, and there are loads of facilities, including a plush spa. ❼

The Town

Nuwara Eliya's attractions are relatively modest – the real highlight here is the surrounding countryside. The town is dominated by the thickly forested mountain of **Pidurutalagala** (whose tongue-twisting name was transformed by the linguistically challenged British into the cod-Spanish Mount Pedro). Sadly, the mountain's summit has been taken over by the government – it now houses the island's major air-traffic control centre – and is out of bounds.

The centre of town, strung out along **New Bazaar Street**, is now a featureless procession of concrete shops, though it's worth sticking your nose into the determinedly local **Central Market**, a picturesque little covered alleyway of fruit and veg stalls alongside some smelly fish stands.

South of here, the workaday **Victoria Park** (daily 7am–6.30pm; Rs.60) boasts a few neatly maintained trees and shrubs, and some of the tallest eucalyptuses you'll ever see. The park also has an unusual ornithological distinction: despite its proximity to the polluted town centre, it's something of an ornithological hotspot, being visited by a number of rare Himalayan migrant **birds**, including the Kashmir flycatcher, Indian blue robin and the pied thrush, as well as Sri Lankan endemics such as the Sri Lanka white-eye, yellow-eared bulbul and the dull-blue flycatcher. Note that you can only get into the park through the single **entrance** on its southern side.

Opposite the park, Nuwara Eliya's sylvan **golf course** (see p.274) adds a further welcome splash of green, while to the south lies the town's scrubby **racecourse**, the scene of Sri Lanka's only horse-racing meetings, held here in April, August and December; each meeting lasts for a day, with ten to fifteen races. Beyond the racecourse, shabby **Lake Gregory** marks the town's southern end; you can follow footpaths around the banks, but it's not a particularly inspiring walk.

If you want to get a bird's-eye view out over the surrounding hills, there's a pleasant short walk, starting near the racecourse, to **Single Tree Mountain**. Go straight up the road immediately before the *Clifton Inn*, and walk up through tea plantations to the electricity station at the top, from where (in clear weather) there are marvellous views out to Hakgala and beyond.

Eating and drinking

There are several decent **restaurants** in the larger hotels, offering good food and heaps of colonial charm. Many of the guesthouses and hotels also have convivial little **bars** – those at the *Hill Club* and *St Andrew's Hotel* are particularly appealing, while at the south end of town you can choose between those at the *Glendower* and *Sunhill* hotels.

De Silva Food Centre New Bazaar St. This lively upstairs restaurant does good, no-nonsense Chinese and Sri Lankan food, with almost everything on the menu for under Rs.400. Entrance is through the café downstairs, which has a fine array of cakes and short eats.

Grand Indian *Grand Hotel*, Grand Hotel Drive. Set at the foot of the hotel's driveway, this smart little café dishes up passable North and South Indian standards (mains Rs.300–500) at lunch and dinner (noon–3pm & 6.30–10pm), and snacks at other times. The attached pastry shop is a decent place for a cup of tea and a cake.

Hill Club Off Grand Hotel Drive. Dining at this atmospheric old hotel offers a heady taste of the colonial lifestyle of yesteryear, complete with discreetly shuffling, white-gloved waiters. Dinner is served between 7 and 10.30pm: you'll need to pay the temporary club membership fee (Rs.100) and wear a jacket and tie to eat in the main dining room (or drink in the mixed bar) – if you don't have your own you can borrow the requisite clobber from the club wardrobe's tasteless selection of 1970s leftovers; ladies are expected to don "formal dress". Food is either a five-course set dinner with fine-dining pretensions (US$22) or a selection of à la carte international dishes (mains from around US$10). Retreat to the lounge afterwards for the coffee and brandy. There's also a set lunch (daily noon to 2.30pm; US$16), or just come for a drink in one of the two cosy bars. Confirmed misogynists should note that the erstwhile men-only bar has now been transformed into a "casual bar" and thrown open to the fairer sex. Even more controversially, you now don't even need to wear a tie to go in it.

King Prawn *Hotel Glendower*, 5 Grand Hotel Rd. One of the island's better Chinese restaurants, with an extensive menu of well-prepared chicken, beef, pork, fish and vegetarian Cantonese-style dishes prepared with a hint of Sri Lankan spice. Mains from Rs.500.

Old Course Restaurant *St Andrew's Hotel*, 10 St Andrew's Drive. Set in the oak-panelled dining room of Nuwara Eliya's smartest hotel, the *Old Course* serves up a well-prepared and beautifully presented choice of local and international dishes, including a good vegetarian selection. You can watch your dinner being prepared in the open-plan kitchen and choose wine from Sri Lanka's only walk-in wine cellar. Mains from around US$10.

Remarko Bakers and Restaurant New Bazaar St. Cheap and cheerful little bakery-cum-restaurant with evening and lunchtime rice and curry and buriani buffets, short eats, rolls and cakes, along with a small selection of à la carte curries, seafood and Western dishes (Rs.250–350).

Listings

Banks and exchange The ATMs at the Commercial, Sampath, Bank of Ceylon and Hatton banks accept foreign Visa and MasterCards; those at the Seylan and People's banks accept Visa only.

Golf The gorgeous, 120-year-old Nuwara Eliya Golf Club course (☎052-222 2835, ⓦwww.negolf.lk) winds through the town centre, beautifully landscaped with magnificent old cypresses, pines and eucalyptus. A round (including green fees, club hire, caddy and balls) costs around US$65 on weekdays and US$70 at weekends.

Internet Access is available at the tourist information centre by the bus station (9am–5pm daily; Rs.100 per hr) and at S&S Computers and the Institute of Computer Technology, both of which are upstairs in the shopping complex on the north side of the People's Bank, behind the bus station (both Rs.60 per hr; daily 8.30am–7pm).

Pharmacy There's a well-stocked pharmacy at Cargills supermarket.

Phones There are several places along New Bazaar St offering IDD calls.

Police The police station (☎052-222 2222) is next to the big road intersection at the north end of New Bazaar St.

Post The post office (Mon–Sat 7am–8pm) occupies a bowel-tighteningly ugly pink and half-timbered monstrosity on New Bazaar St, just south of the town centre.

Supermarkets Cargills on Bandaranayaka Mw (daily 9am–9pm) has a decent selection of food and drink, plus a Mlesna Tea Centre; the Grashia supermarket on New Bazaar St is also passable.

Taxis Can be found lined up along New Bazaar St.

Around Nuwara Eliya

The main reason for visiting Nuwara Eliya is to get out into the surrounding countryside, which boasts some of the island's highest and most dramatic scenery. The most popular and rewarding trip is to Horton Plains and World's End (see p.276), though there are other options closer to town, as well as some wonderful **walks** through the surrounding hills. You might also consider a trip to the stunning and spectacularly located **Tea Factory** hotel (see p.272), virtually a sight in its own right, and a good spot for some lunch followed by a walk in the beautiful surrounding estates.

The Pedro and Labookelie tea estates

If you're interested in finding out more about the local tea industry, the **Pedro Tea Estate** (daily 8.30am–6pm; tours are free, though you're encouraged to have a drink in the café afterwards), set beneath a flank of Mount Pedro about 3km east of Nuwara Eliya, offers a convenient introduction. The factory building and tea fields are less picturesque than others in the highlands (there's

Moving on from Nuwara Eliya

There are regular private and CTB buses to **Kandy** (every 30min; 2hr 30min–3hr), **Badulla** via Welimada (every 30–45min; 3hr) and the train station at **Nanu Oya** (every 30min; 15min), plus less frequent services to **Colombo** (5 daily; 4hr 30min) and **Hatton** (7 daily; 2hr) and a once-daily service daily to **Matara** and **Galle** (8–9hr), leaving around 8am. There are also occasional services to **Bandarawela** and **Ella** (4 daily; 3hr 30min–4hr), though if heading towards either of these places, or **Haputale**, it's far easier to take the **train** (see timetables on p.224).

Tours from Nuwara Eliya

There are lots of interesting destinations within easy striking distance of Nuwara Eliya. The most popular is **Horton Plains National Park**, though there are plenty of other possible destinations. You could also, at a push, use Nuwara Eliya as a base for visiting **Adam's Peak** – you'll need to leave at 10pm to arrive at Dalhousie at around 12.30am, then start climbing at 2am in order to reach the summit for dawn.

The best place to organize local tours is **Single Tree Hotel** (see p.271), who lay on a range of activities including tea factory visits, guided mountain-biking, horse riding, fishing, canoeing and an interesting full-day waterfall tour, visiting no fewer than sixteen cascades – a good way to get to see some of the hidden corners of the surrounding hill country. As a very rough rule of thumb, count on around US$25–30 for a half-day tour, or US$50–60 for a full day, including guiding and vehicle. The return trip to Horton Plains usually costs around US$30 per vehicle; the journey to Horton Plains and then on to Haputale or Ella will cost around US$55, as will the trip to Adam's Peak. They can also arrange longer, islandwide tours on request, and can put you in touch with several good walking guides, including the excellent Raja (Neil Rajanayake), who can take you on various one-day walks throughout the area including a fine hike up to Uda Radella (15km), one of the finest viewpoints on the island; an exhilarating downhill walk from Ohiya to Haputale (15km); another one-day walk from Bomburuwela (4km from Nuwara Eliya) to Welimada (17km); and a twenty-kilometre hike up Great Western mountain, near Nanu Oya. Email ©nuwaraeliyatrekkingclub@hotmail.com for more information and count on around US$50 per person per day inclusive of guiding and transport.

rather too much suburban clutter, and pylons straggle impertinently across the views), but the easy accessibility and informative resident guide make it a worthwhile short excursion. Established in 1885, the estate remained under British ownership until being nationalized in 1975 (it was re-privatized in 1985); its factory is still home to a few impressive pieces of old British machinery, some still in operation. Bus #715 bus to Kandapola (every 30min) goes past the factory, or catch a tuktuk.

Around 20km north of Nuwara Eliya lies the expansive **Labookelie Tea Estate**, set in gorgeous rolling countryside at an elevation of around 2000m. The estate is part of the Mackwoods conglomerate, a famous old mercantile firm founded by William Mackwood in 1841. The Labookelie tea gardens are much more photogenic, and the countryside much more unspoilt, than at the Pedro estate, and the whole place is well set up for visitors, with free **tours** of the busy factory and a swish café in which to sup a cup of the resultant brew whilst nibbling a cake. Labookelie is also fairly easy to reach, since all buses from Nuwara Eliya to Kandy pass right by the entrance.

Hakgala Gardens and the Sita Amman Temple

Hakgala Botanical Gardens (daily 8am–5pm; Rs.600) lie beneath the towering **Hakgala Rock** some 10km southeast of Nuwara Eliya, with majestic views across the hills of Uva Province receding in tiers into the distance. The rock is allegedly one of the various pieces of mountain scattered by Hanuman on his return from the Himalayas (see p.184) – its name, meaning "Jaw Rock", refers to the fact that Hanuman apparently carried the mountain in his mouth. The gardens were first established in 1861 to grow **cinchona**, a source of the anti-malarial drug quinine, and were later expanded to include a wide range of foreign species. They're also well known for their **roses** (in bloom from April to Aug).

The gardens sprawl up the steep hillside, ranging from the anodyne ornamental areas around the entrance to the far wilder and more interesting patches of forest up the hill where you'll find many majestic Monterey cypresses from California, plus fine old cedars, a section of enormous tree ferns, stands of Japanese camphor, and pines and eucalyptus, including a shaggy cluster of bark-shedding Australian melaleucas. This is also one of the best places in the island to spot endemic montane **bird** species, including the dull-blue flycatcher, Sri Lanka whistling thrush and Sri Lanka bush warbler. You might also catch a glimpse of the elusive **bear monkeys** that live here. To reach Hakgala, take any **bus** heading to Welimada or Badulla (every 15min; 20min).

Head back along the main road towards Nuwara Eliya for about 1.5km to reach the **Sita Amman Temple**, said to be built at the spot where Rawana held Sita captive, as related in the *Ramayana* (although the same claim is also made for the Rawana Cave in Ella; see p.284) – the strange circular depressions in the rock by the adjacent stream are supposed to be the footprints of Rawana's elephant. The small temple – the only one in Sri Lanka dedicated to Sita – boasts the usual gaudy collection of statues, including a couple of gruesome Kali images, though there's not really much to see.

Waterfalls west of Nuwara Eliya

The area west of Nuwara Eliya around the tiny village of **DIMBULLA** is one of the most scenically spectacular parts of the island, though its tourist potential remains almost totally unexploited. The easiest way to get a taste of the area is to go on one of the "waterfall tours" run by the *Single Tree Hotel* in Nuwara Eliya (see box, p.275), which usually include the Ramboda falls (see p.266) along with several picturesque cascades in the Dimbula area – notably the broad, two-tiered **St Clair Falls** and the taller and more precipitious **Devon Falls**, which lie less than two kilometres apart just north of (and clearly visible from) the A7 highway.

Horton Plains and World's End

Perched on the very edge of the hill country midway between Nuwara Eliya and Haputale, **Horton Plains National Park** covers a wild stretch of bleak, high-altitude grassland bounded at its southern edge by the dramatically plunging cliffs that mark the edge of the hill country, including the famous **World's End**, where the escarpment falls sheer for the best part of a kilometre to the lowlands below. Set at an elevation of over two thousand metres, Horton Plains are a world apart from the rest of Sri Lanka, a misty and rainswept landscape whose cool, wet climate has fostered the growth of a unique but fragile ecosystem. Large parts of the Plains are still covered in beautiful and pristine stands of **cloudforest**, with their distinctive umbrella-shaped keena trees, covered in a fine cobweb of old man's beard, whose leaves turn from green to red to orange as the seasons progress. The Plains are also one of the island's most important watersheds and the source of the Mahaweli, Kelani and Walawe rivers, three of the island's largest.

The Plains' **wildlife** attractions are relatively modest. Herds of elephants formerly roamed here, until they were all shot by colonial hunters, while around 45 leopards still live in the area around the park, though you'll have to be incredibly lucky to see one. The park's most visible residents are its herds of sambar deer, while you might see rare bear-faced (also known as purple-faced) monkeys. The park is also one of the best places in the island for **birdwatching**, and an excellent place to see montane endemics such as the dull-blue flycatcher, Sri Lanka bush warbler, Sri Lanka whistling thrush and the pretty yellow-eared bulbul. You'll probably also see beautiful lizards, some of them boasting outlandishly fluorescent green scales, though their numbers are declining as the result of depredations by crows, attracted to the park (as to so many other parts of the island) by litter left by loutish visitors.

Exploring the park

Horton Plains is bisected by a single road running between Pattipola (on the park's Nuwara Eliya side) and Ohiya (Haputale side); **entrance fees** (see p.55) are collected at ticket offices next to this road on either side of the park. If approaching from Nuwara Eliya, you'll pay at the entrance on the Pattipola side of the park; if approaching from Haputale, you'll pay at the entrance on the Ohiya side. (Note that although the road is publicly owned and maintained, both locals and tourists now have to pay the national park entrance fee just to drive along it, even if you've no intention of going walking in the Plains themselves – the latest and most spectacular in the Department of Wildlife Conservation's long list of dubious money-making rackets.) It's a three-kilometre drive from either entrance up to the smart new **visitors' centre**, which has some interesting displays on the Plains' history, flora and fauna. The centre is also the starting point for the main, nine-kilometre **circular trail** around the park, walkable in two to three gentle hours. There's also a much longer (22km return) trek to the top of **Kirigalpota** from here, as well as an easy shorter trail (6km return) to the summit of **Totapolakanda**, which starts a few kilometres back down the main road to Nuwara Eliya.

From the visitors' centre, the main circular trail around the park leads for 500m through rolling plains covered in patana grass and dotted with rhododendron bushes; the altitude here is over 2000m and the air quite thin, so don't be surprised if you feel a bit short of breath – fortunately, most of the main trail is more or less flat. This opening section of the trail gives a good view of the park's strange patchwork flora, with alternating stretches of bare patana grassland interspersed with densely wooded cloudforest. According to legend, the grasslands were created by Hanuman during the events described by the *Ramayana*. Tradition states that Hanuman, to avenge the kidnapping of Sita, tied a burning torch to his tail and swept it across the plains, creating the areas of treeless grassland which can still be seen today, although the prosaic explanation is that they're the result of forest clearances by prehistoric farmers – these areas were still being used to grow potatoes as recently as the 1960s.

Beyond the grasslands, the path leads for 2km through a superb stretch of cloudforest: a tangle of moss-covered keena trees and nellu shrubs, along with many medicinal herbs and wild spices such as pepper, cardamom and cinnamon. Another couple of kilometres brings you to the edge of the cliffs which bound this section of the park and the first viewpoint, **Small World's End**. Past here, the path continues through another 1.5km of cloudforest, dotted with numerous clumps of dwarf bamboo, before reaching **World's End** proper (2140m). From here, the cliffs plunge almost vertically for 825m, revealing enormous views across much of the southern island: you can see the coast on a clear day – the large lake in the near distance is at Uda Walawe National Park. There are also marvellous views along the craggy peaks which line the escarpment, including Sri Lanka's second and third highest, Kirigalpota (2395m) and Totapolakanda (2359m), which stand at the edge of the park (and which are reachable by the trails mentioned above). Another 200m beyond World's End,

▲ Baker's Falls, Horton Plains

the path turns inland towards Baker's Falls. If you ignore this turning for a moment and continue along the cliff edge for a further 100m you'll reach another viewpoint from the overhanging rock ledge – it's said that no fewer than ten star-crossed couples have leapt to their deaths from here over the years.

From here, retrace your steps back to the main track and follow it as it loops back towards the visitors' centre, through open patana grassland with cloud-forest set back on both sides. A couple of kilometres from World's End you pass **Baker's Falls** (named after Samuel Baker; see p.268). It's a steep and slippery scramble down to the beautiful little falls themselves, after which you'll have to scramble back up again – if the altitude hasn't already got to you, it probably will here. The final couple of kilometres are relatively humdrum, crossing open patana grassland back to the entrance, enlivened during the early morning by the resonant croaking of thousands of frogs in the surrounding grasses and trees.

Just outside the entrance to the park on the Ohiya side, a track leads off the road to **Poor Man's World's End**, named back in the good-old days when it was possible to come here to enjoy the view without having to pay the national park entry fee. The viewpoint is reachable along the plantation road which divides the national park itself from the Forestry Department land on the other side; look for the DWC stone post roughly 1km before the Ohiya-side ticket office. It's a five-minute walk to the viewpoint, although you can carry on along the plantation road for several kilometres, a superb little hike through tea plantations strung out along the edge of the ridge. It's a fine panorama, offering an interestingly different perspective on the dramatically plunging escarpement, and there are further sensational views of World's End from the road beyond here as it plunges down towards Ohiya.

One other way of getting into Horton Plains was formerly to do the extremely taxing walk up from **Belihul Oya**, at the foot of the escarpment – a very steep 11km trek. Unfortunately, at the time of writing the path had been closed, though it may reopen at some point in the future.

Practicalities

The park is open daily from 6am to 4pm; entry costs US$16 per person, plus US$8 per group "service charge". If you haven't come with a guide, it's fairly easy to find your own way around, although you might appreciate having someone explain the local flora – you may be able to pick up a guide at the entrance, but don't count on it. The Plains can get very cold and wet: take a thick sweater, stout shoes, something waterproof, and food and drink; hot drinks are available at the tiny café at the beginning of the main track.

You can reach Horton Plains from either **Nuwara Eliya** or **Haputale**. Note that the view from World's End is generally obscured by mist from around 10am onwards, especially during the rainy months from May to July, so you'll have to arrive early to stand a realistic chance of seeing anything. In practice this means that you'll have to **hire a vehicle**. The return trip with waiting time from either Nuwara Eliya or Haputale takes around ninety minutes and currently costs around Rs.2000 per vehicle. Most drivers will suggest you leave around 5.30am to reach the park by 7am, and World's End by 8.30am – it's well worth the brief pain of dragging yourself out of bed to do this. The drive from Nuwara Eliya is particularly beautiful, with trees poking their heads out of the mist in the valleys; just before you reach the park there's a stunning dawn view of Adam's Peak (prettiest during the pilgrimage season from December to May, when the lights on the mountain are illuminated).

If you're completely strapped for cash, it's possible to reach the park by public transport, though this also involves a long and strenuous walk. The easiest place to start is **Haputale**; catch a train to **Ohiya station**, from where it's an 11km walk (around 3hr uphill, and 2hr back down) up the road to the national park entrance, a pleasant hike with fine views. Make sure you check latest train times before starting out to make sure you don't get stranded.

There are a few **places to stay** dotted around the edge of the park, including a trio of remote options around Bambarakanda Falls, covered on p.294.

Badulla and around

Set on the eastern edge of the hill country, the bustling modern town of **BADULLA** is capital of Uva Province and an important transport hub – you might pass through en route between the hill country and the east coast. If you do get stuck here overnight, there are a couple of modest attractions to while away a few hours. Thought to be one of the oldest towns on the island, Badulla became a major centre on the road between Polonnaruwa and the south, though the old town has vanished without trace. Badulla thrived under the British, developing into a vibrant social centre complete with racecourse and cricket club, though there's almost nothing left to show from those days now.

Easily the most interesting building in town is the eighteenth-century **Kataragama Devale** (entrances on Lower St and Devale St). The Kandyan-style **main shrine**, made almost entirely of wood, is entered via a colonnaded walkway leading to a cluster of finely carved columns and an elaborate door topped by a carving of buxom figure in a tiara, flanked by two elephants – possibly a bodhisattva. Inside, the principal image of Kataragama is, as usual, hidden behind a curtain, flanked by statues of a pink Saman holding an axe and flag, and Vishnu, bearing a conch shell and bell. The shrine's exterior is decorated with a faded, probably Kandyan-era painting of a perahera and rounded off with a little wooden pavilion tower. There's a smaller subsidiary shrine to **Pattini** (see p.248) to the right of the main shrine, with another finely carved wooden door, pillars and the slight remains of old murals below a layer of modern plaster.

At the southern end of town stands the **Muthiyagana Vihara**, whose origins are believed to date back two thousand years to the reign of Sri Lanka's first Buddhist king, Devanampiya Tissa. It's a tranquil, if unremarkable, spot, though you might get a sighting of the resident elephant in the grounds. Elephants are unlikely to be seen in the vicinity of the modest little **St Mark's Church**, one of the few mementoes of Badulla's colonial-era past, flanking the roundabout at the northern end of King Street. Inside, a prominent tablet memorializes the infamous soldier and sportsman **Major Thomas William Rogers**, who is said to have shot well over a thousand elephants before being torched by a timely bolt of lightning at Haputale in 1845. The memorial concludes, appropriately enough, with the traditional biblical homily, "In the midst of life we are in death" – a sentiment with which Major Rogers, who single-handedly despatched so many of island's most majestic and intelligent creatures, would no doubt have agreed.

Practicalities

The **bus station** is bang in the middle of Badulla on King Street; the **train station** is about a kilometre due south of here on the edge of town. There are branches of various **banks** in town; foreign Visa cards are accepted in the ATMs of the Seylan Bank, NDB Bank, Bank of Ceylon and Commercial Bank (the last also accepts foreign MasterCards). The well-organized **post office** is next to the bus station. You'll probably **eat** where you're staying; the only other possibility (apart from the usual local cafés) is the drab *Rest House*, right in the middle of town.

Moving on from Badulla

Badulla is a major regional transport hub and sits at the end of the rail line from Kandy; see p.224 for **train** timetables. The **bus** station has a useful (though unsigned) information office on its south side. There are regular departures to **Bandarawela** (every 10min; 1hr 30min), **Ella** (every 30min; 45min; or catch a Bandarawela bus to Kumbalwela Junction, 3km from Ella, where the Ella road branches off the main Bandarawela–Badulla road, and either wait for another bus or catch a tuktuk), **Haputale** (direct services hourly, or change at Bandarawela; 1hr 30min), **Wellawaya** (every 30min; 1hr 30min), **Colombo** (hourly; 8hr), **Kandy** (hourly; 6hr), **Nuwara Eliya** (every 30–45min; 3hr) and **Monaragala** (every 30min; 3hr). Heading south, there's a once-daily early-morning service to **Matara** (7hr) and **Galle** (8hr), and one service to **Kataragama** (4hr).

There are a few passable **places to stay**. The attractive mid-range *Onix Hotel*, at 69 Bandaranayake Mw (☎055-222 2426; ④) in a peaceful area just north of town, has bright, nicely furnished rooms with air-conditioning and cable TV (plus one cheaper fan room, ③), while the cheaper *Dunhinda Falls Inn*, a few doors down at 35/10 Bandaranayake Mw (☎055-222 3028; ③, a/c ④) has large and comfortable rooms (some with a/c) and friendly staff who can help arrange interesting local tours. In town, the *River Side Holiday Inn* (☎055-222 2090; ❶–❸, US$5 a/c supplement) has pleasant modern rooms and a passable rooftop restaurant, though the view of the massed pylons next door probably isn't what you came to Sri Lanka to see.

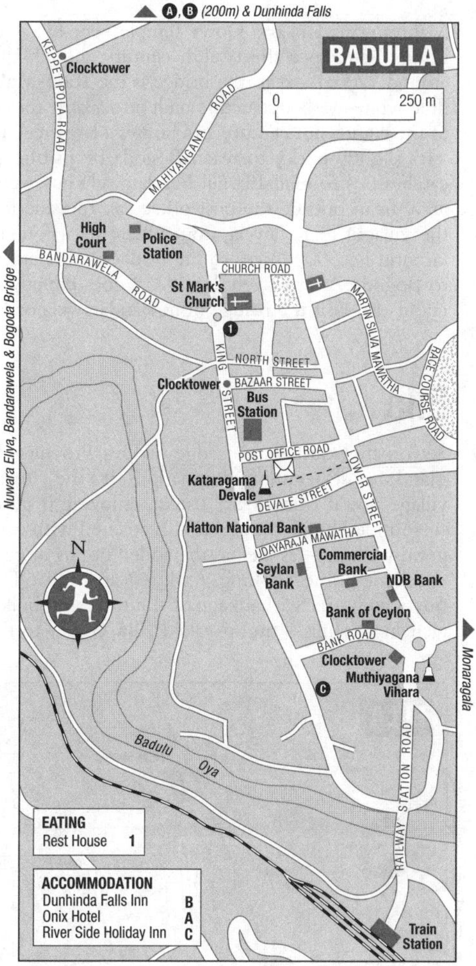

Around Badulla

Around 7km north of Badulla lie the majestic, 63-metre-high **Dunhinda Falls** (entrance Rs.50), reached via a beautiful drive from town, followed by a pleasant 1.5km scramble along a rocky little path during which you cross a wobbly, Indiana Jones-style suspension bridge. The falls themselves, fed by the Badulla Oya, are the island's seventh highest, but are most notable for their sheer volume, spewing out an impressive quantity of water which creates great clouds of spray as it crashes into the pool below. **Buses** running past the path to the falls leave town about every thirty minutes; alternatively, hire a tuktuk. Avoid weekends and public holidays, when the falls are thronged with locals. Whenever you visit, there should be a few stalls serving drinks and snacks.

Some 15km west of Badulla lies the remote village of **BOGODA**, squirrelled away in a deeply rural setting on the banks of the small Galanda Oya amidst the undulating fringes of the hill country. Steep steps lead from the village down to an unusual **roofed bridge**, a quaint little toy-like structure, with delicately balustraded sides and tiled roof elegantly balanced on a single wooden pier plunged into the rocky rapids below. The bridge lies on a pilgrimage route that connects with

Mahiyangana and the Dowa Temple near Ella – there's thought to have been a bridge here since the twelfth century, though the present structure dates from around 1700. Next to the bridge is the **Raja Maha Vihara** temple, an attractive little white-washed structure built into a large rock outcrop. The temple dates back to the eighteenth century and houses a large reclining Buddha, but not much else.

It's slightly tricky to reach Bogoda by **public transport** from Badulla. First, catch a bus to Hali-Ela (all Bandarawela buses pass through). In Hali-Ela, buses leave from outside the post office (on the side road on your right as you enter the village) to Katawela, from where it's a four-kilometre walk or tuktuk ride (around Rs.300 return) to the bridge. A few buses go all the way from Hali-Ela to Bogoda. Alternatively, bus #312 goes directly to Katawela from Badulla. You could also visit the bridge from Bandarawela or Ella.

Ella

Set on the southeastern edge of Uva Province, beautiful **ELLA** is one of the island's most beguiling destinations. It's the closest thing to an English country village you'll find in Sri Lanka, enjoying a pleasantly temperate climate and surrounded by idyllic green hills covered with tea plantations and offering some good walking – as well as the added bonus of good cheap accommodation and excellent home-cooking. And, to cap it all off, the village enjoys one of the finest views in Sri Lanka, past the towering bulk of **Ella Rock** and through a cleft in the hills – the so-called **Ella Gap** – to the plains far below.

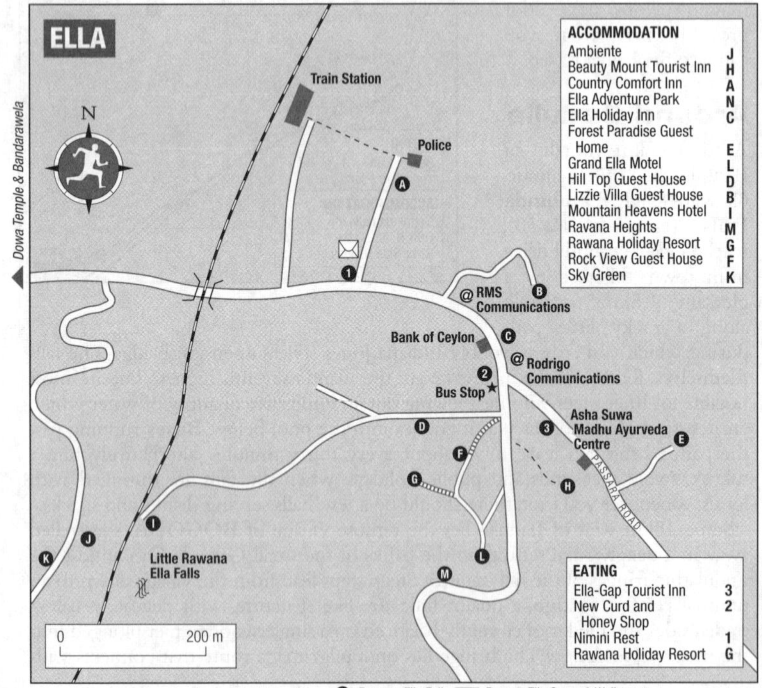

Ella is famous in Sri Lankan folklore for its *Ramayana* connections: according to one tradition, the demon king Rawana brought the captive Sita here and hid her away in a cave a couple of kilometres outside the present-day village. Rawana's name is now memorialized in the names of various guesthouses, as well as in the **Rawana Ella Falls**, which plunge magnificently down a series of rock faces 6km from Ella.

Arrival

Buses drop off passengers at the road junction outside the *Curd Shop* in the centre of the village, close to most of the guesthouses. The **train station** is on the north side of the village, a five- to ten-minute walk from most accommodation. Rodrigo Communications and RMS Communications, close to one another on the main street, have **internet** access (both roughly daily 7am–8pm; Rs.5 per min) and IDD **phone** facilities. There's a small Bank of Ceylon opposite the *Ella Holiday Inn* to **change money**, but no ATM. **Taxis** hang out around the centre of the village. Alternatively, most of the village's guesthouses can arrange taxis and tours. **Suresh Rodrigo** (who can usually to be found at the *Ella Holiday Inn*) is a good source of general info about the area, and runs a range of tours including day-walks (around US$32 for two people), camping trips to Yala and a useful day-trip combining the Diyaluma and Rawana Ella waterfalls along with Buduruwagala (US$55 for up to four people). He can also set up hiking, camping and nature tours in an area of lush jungle on the Kirinda Oya river nearby. They also have **motorbikes** for hire (250cc for Rs.2000 per day, plus a couple of scooters for Rs.1200per day) and organize **cooking lessons** (Rs.3000 for half a day). The well-run Asha Suwa Madhu **Ayurveda** centre, close to the village centre on Passara Road, offers reasonably priced massages, herbal and steam baths and a sauna.

Accommodation

Ella has one of the island's best selections of budget **guesthouses**, but only a few more upmarket options. In general, places with a view are significantly more expensive than those without. All of the following have hot water, although heating isn't provided – Ella doesn't generally get too cold.

Ambiente ⓣ057-222 8867, ⓦwww.ambiente.lk. One of Ella's most spectacularly located guesthouses, set high above the village and offering sublime views over Ella Gap. Modern, tiled rooms (though the cheaper ones are a bit small and bare), and there's good food, friendly service and a sociable atmosphere. The owner's two cute dogs take guests for walks in the surrounding hills. ❹

Beauty Mount Tourist Inn ⓣ057-222 8760. Set slightly away from the road in a pleasant garden (but no views), this place has a mix of old and cheap but OK rooms, and pricier modern "cottages" (sleeping two; extra beds available on request). Rooms ❶, cottages ❷–❸

Country Comfort Inn ⓣ057-222 8532. A good and slightly smarter alternative to Ella's standard family-run guesthouses, in a quiet (but viewless) spot on the north side of the village. The new block has sparklingly clean, modern tiled rooms with ugly wooden furniture; the more attractive old wing occupies a pretty little colonial villa with neat and very comfortable rooms. Rates may be susceptible to bargaining. Old wing ❸, new wing ❹

Ella Adventure Park ⓣ060-255 5038, ⓦwww.wildernesslanka.com. Some 10km south of Ella on the road to Wellawaya, this attractive eco-resort enjoys a tranquil forest setting and a rustic, environmentally sensitive design in a series of picturesque wooden structures (including one fun room in a tree house) – albeit stronger on jungle atmosphere than creature comforts. Mountain-biking, trekking and canoeing trips can be arranged, though the main appeal of the place is the chance to get very close to nature. Standard ❺, deluxe ❻

Ella Holiday Inn ⓣ057-222 8615, ⓦwww.ellaholiday.com. Biggish modern mid-range guesthouse bang in the middle of the village, with a wide range of attractively furnished tiled rooms (some with internet and satelite TV) of various standards and prices. Rates may be susceptible to bargaining in slow periods, and Rough Guide readers are promised a ten percent discount year-round. There are also plans to establish a simple new eco-resort, *Galaxy Grove*, in an area of unspoilt jungle nearby. ❸–❺

Forest Paradise Guest Home ⓣ057-222 8797, Ⓔnelly-forestparadise@hotmail.com. Low-key, friendly guesthouse with just five nicely furnished but slightly small rooms set next to pine forest on the outskirts of the village – very peaceful, though it's a bit of an uphill hike out of town. The owner arranges interesting and unusual activities in the surrounding countryside, including catamaran trips at Handapandagala (see p.288) and mountain-top barbecues. ❶

Grand Ella Motel ⓣ057-222 8655, Ⓦwww.ceylonhotels.lk. This attractively upgraded old rest house is the largest place in the village, and boasts one of the best views of Ella Gap from its garden and almost all the rooms. The slightly more expensive rooms in the new wing are spacious and comfortable; those in the old wing are simpler, cheaper and more old-fashioned, but beginning to look a touch drab. Old wing ❹, new wing ❺

Hill Top Guest House ⓣ057-222 8780. Perched at the top of a very steep hill, with fine views of Ella Gap from the upper storey and veranda. The large upstairs rooms are some of the nicest in the village in this price range; those downstairs are a bit simpler and cheaper. ❶–❷

Lizzie Villa Guest House ⓣ057-222 8643. Peaceful modern bungalow, set in a pleasant garden full of spices and fruit trees (but without any views), with nine bright, comfortable and well-maintained rooms. ❷

Mountain Heavens Hotel ⓣ057-492 0336, Ⓔmountainheavens@gmail.com. Small modern hotel set out in the countryside a 15min walk from the village, with a jaw-dropping view right down the middle of Ella Gap – one of the best in the area. Rooms are spacious and tiled and have big French windows through which to enjoy the scenery, though the whole place feels rather lifeless and under-used at present. ❹

Ravana Heights ⓣ057-222 8888, Ⓦwww.ravanaheights.com. One of the nicest places to stay in Ella, occupying a modern one-storey house with just four bright and spacious rooms decorated with colourful Thai fabrics, three offering picture-perfect views of Ella Rock and the Gap. ❺

Rawana Holiday Resort ⓣ057-222 8794, Ⓔnalankumara@yahoo.com. Perched on a hill above the village, with a selection of clean, comfortable and inexpensive rooms, plus good home-cooking (see p.286) in the large restaurant, which has fine views of Ella Gap. ❶–❷

Rock View Guest House ⓣ057-222 8561. One of the longest-established places in town, with a pleasantly old-fashioned atmosphere, a marvellous view of Ella Rock from the balcony and good-value rooms – choose between the older ones in the main house and a couple of newer ones outside. ❶–❷

Sky Green ⓣ057-492 0385. Just along the road from the *Ambiente*, and sharing the same spectacular view, this large and rather ugly new hotel isn't as nice as its neighbour, but does have smart, spacious and surprisingly inexpensive rooms with big French windows, four-poster beds and writing desks. Good value, though the atmosphere is moribund. ❹

The village and around

There's not much to **Ella village** itself: an attractive scatter of pretty little cottages and bungalows enclosed in neat, flower-filled gardens, it preserves a pleasingly low-key atmosphere despite the number of foreign tourists passing through. The single street meanders gently downhill, past assorted guesthouses and a couple of cafés, before reaching the edge of the escarpment, just below the *Grand Ella Motel*, from where there's the classic view of **Ella Gap**. There's also a small Buddhist temple on the road here, where passing motorists stop and donate a coin for good luck before negotiating the treacherously twisting highway to Wellawaya, which descends into the sheer-sided valley below.

Head down this spectacular road for 6km to reach the area's most notable sight, the massive **Rawana Ella Falls** (also known as the Bambaragama Falls), which tumble for ninety-odd metres over the valley wall. It's an impressive (if touristy) sight, and you can clamber some way up the rocks to one side of the falls – locals will offer to show you the way for a consideration. Other hawkers here will try to flog you pretty, but worthless little coloured stones taken from the falls. To reach the falls, catch any bus heading down towards Wellawaya.

En route to the falls, a few kilometres out of Ella, lies the **Rawana Ella Cave**, in which Rawana is claimed to have held Sita captive, as related in the *Ramayana*

– although a similar claim is made for the Sita Amman Temple (see p.276) near Nuwara Eliya, and in any case there's remarkably little to see, given the site's alleged significance. To reach the cave, head down the road from the village into the gap for about 1.5km, from where a side road on the right makes a stiff one-kilometre uphill climb to a small and rather rustic **temple**, built underneath a rock outcrop. From here, it's a steep and slippery climb – it can become treacherous after rain – up to the uninteresting cave itself. Local kids offer themselves as guides, and will pester you mercilessly even if you've no interest in visiting the cave, but it's really not worth the effort.

Little Adam's Peak

One of the best ways to spend a morning in Ella is to tackle the beautiful short walk up to the top of **Little Adam's Peak**, a pyramid-shaped rock which stands opposite the far larger Ella Rock and offers marvellous views out over the hills. The walk makes a very pleasant morning's excursion, and is fairly gentle and largely flat, apart from a small amount of climbing near the end. Count on around two hours return, and go early before the clouds set in. To begin the walk, head down the **Passara Road** for 1km, passing pine woods to your left. Just past the 1km marker the road turns sharp left by a garden centre; take the path that goes off the right-hand side of the road, straight ahead through beautiful tea plantations. Follow this path for 500m, ignoring the branch on your right which descends to a ramshackle tea pickers' village below. Keep left, following the path, with increasingly fine

Walking up Ella Rock

The most rewarding, and most taxing, hike around Ella is the ascent of the majestic **Ella Rock**, which looms over the village. It's around a four-hour hike in total, with an interesting mix of rail track, tea plantation, and some steep stuff near the summit. Take food, water and good footwear, and take care in wet weather, when tracks can get slippery. Also be aware that mist and rain can descend quickly at top. There are several different possible **routes**; most begin by following the rail line south out of the village, then following one of the various paths which strike off up the rock. Different people recommend different routes, but the following is perhaps the most direct and easy to follow.

Follow the rail line south out of Ella village for about 1.5km until the tracks cross a rickety bridge near the top of **Little Rawana Ella Falls**. A couple of metres before the bridge, a tiny path heads steeply down to the left. Scramble down this, then veer right, under the bridge, and follow the small irrigation channel back under the bridge again until you reach a small metal footbridge across top of Little Rawana Ella Falls.

Cross the footbridge and continue straight ahead. After 100m the path forks; bear right and follow the path as it climbs steeply for 300m. At the top of the hill (just before a large boulder) a narrow path cuts back on the right. Follow this path uphill, into a tea plantation. Keep left at the fork 200m further on and continue 150m until you reach a T-junction. Turn left here, aiming for the house on a low hill more or less directly ahead of you, keeping left at the next two forks to reach the house.

Directly in front of the house, a well-defined path branches off on the left. Ignore this and instead follow the very faint path straight ahead (it runs along the left-hand side of the small tea garden in front of the house). This path is very overgrown for the first 50m, but then becomes clearer. Follow this path as it climbs steadily for about 45 minutes until it reaches the edge of the ridge, keeping left wherever there's a choice of tracks. From here the path continues, very steep and stony now, to the summit of the rock – another thirty minutes or so of hard hiking.

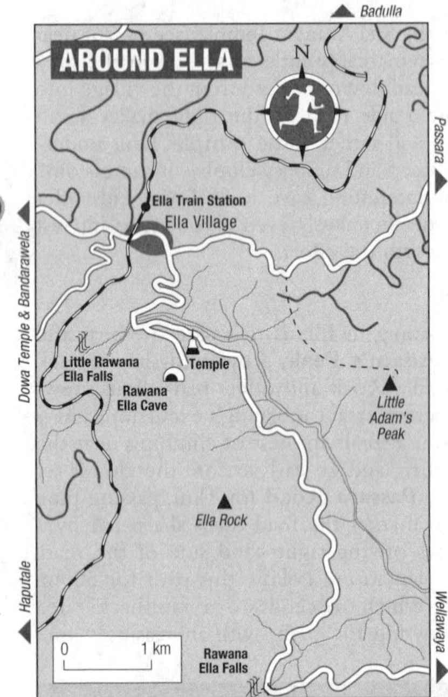

views to **Ella Rock** opposite and the **Newbourg Tea Factory** in the other direction. After another 500m you reach a point where two tracks go off on the right close to one another. Take the second track (past the green gate), and follow it for the final kilometre up to the top of Little Adam's Peak – the path weaves around the back of the peak and zigzags up to the summit, from where there are marvellous views of Ella Rock, Ella Gap and the very top of the Rawana Ella Falls.

Dowa Temple

About 10km from Ella and 6km from Bandarawela, the small **Dowa Temple** is set in a secluded and narrow wooded valley and boasts a striking low-relief Buddha, carved into the rock face which overlooks the temple. It's similar in style to the figures at Buduruwagala (see opposite), and may represent Maitreya, the future Buddha of the Mahayana pantheon who also appears at Buduruwagala. The temple itself is of some antiquity, though there's not much to show for it now apart from some fairly uninteresting paintings and a reclining Buddha. All buses from Ella to Bandarawela run past the temple.

Eating

Ella is perhaps the best place in the island to sample Sri Lankan **home-cooking** – this effectively means rice and curry, rice and curry and more rice and curry, although the quality of the food served up in many places here is miles removed from the fiery slop which so often passes for the national dish. Don't come to Ella if you want **nightlife**, however: even by somnolent Sri Lankan standards, everyone seems to go to bed incredibly early here.

Ella-Gap Tourist Inn Ella's prettiest dining room provides a pleasant setting for a wide range of Sri Lankan favourites, including above-average rice and curry (from Rs.350), *lamprais* (Rs.450), and a good range of local breakfasts, including *pittu*, *kiribath*, hoppers and string hoppers (all Rs.200).

New Curd and Honey Shop Long-established little local curry house-cum-backpacker café; handy for breakfast (both Western and Sri Lankan) and daytime snacks, though it's right next to where the buses stop, so can be a bit noisy and smelly.

Nilmini Rest The nicest of the impromptu little cafes strung out along the main road. Good for Western breakfasts (Rs.250) and light snacks, although no real meals to speak of.

Rawana Holiday Resort The main reason for coming here is to try the special garlic curry (Rs.400) – that's a plateful of curried whole garlic cloves, rather than garlic-flavoured curry (the cloves are first fried with onions and fenugreek, then boiled with coconut milk and tamarind to remove the after-smell) – it tastes great, and is good for you too. Pre-order by lunchtime. You can even come and watch it being prepared. Also a good place for traditional Sri Lankan breakfasts (order the day before).

Moving on from Ella

It's generally more comfortable and convenient to leave Ella by **train** where possible, especially if you're heading to Haputale or Nuwara Eliya, which are rather awkward to reach by bus – and railway buffs will also enjoy the famous loop which the train tracks make just east of Ella to gain height. For timetable details, see p.224.

No **buses** originate in Ella, so you might have a problem getting a seat, although Suresh Rodrigo at *Ella Holiday Inn* (see p.283) can reserve places on both government and private buses for a Rs.200 fee; he's also a good source of information on bus timetables. There are regular services to **Wellawaya** (every 15min; 45min), **Bandarawela** (every 10min; 30min), and **Badulla** (every 30min; 1hr). For **Haputale**, change at Bandarawela. There are also occasional buses to **Kandy** (2 daily; 7–8hr); and **Nuwara Eliya** (5 daily; 4hr). Ella is a convenient jumping-off point for the south coast, with around seven direct buses daily to **Matara** (7hr) via **Pamegamuwa Junction** (for Tissa), **Tangalla** and **Hambantota**. There are a couple of direct buses daily to **Kataragama** (2hr 30min) and **Tissa** (2hr 30min); alternatively, take a Matara bus to Pamegamuwa and change there, or go to Wellawaya and catch an onward connection from there.

Wellawaya and around

Standing in the dry-zone plains at the foot of the hills of Uva Province, the unexceptional little town of **WELLAWAYA** is, strictly speaking, not part of the hill country at all, though it's an important transport hub and provides regular connections to Ella, Haputale and beyond. The town itself is dusty and uninteresting, though there are a few worthwhile sights nearby – although it's also perfectly possible to visit these from Ella or Haputale. There are also a couple of excellent eco-lodges around the town of **Buttala**, about 15km east of Wellawaya – see p.393 for details.

The smart new **bus stand** is in the middle of town, along with a couple of banks (but no ATMs). The only reason **to stay** here is to spend a night at the family-run *Little Rose Inn* (ⓣ055-227 4410, ⓔlittlerose.inn@gmail.com; ❶), about 1km south of town on the Tissa road, which has clean, bright modern rooms, organic food, bike rental, internet access and a very hospitable atmosphere. They can also arrange local excursions.

Around Wellawaya

Just south of Wellawaya lie the magical rock carvings of **Buduruwagala**, located in a patch of beautifully unspoilt dry-zone forest populated by abundant birds and butterflies. The site is home to a series of seven figures carved in low relief into the face of a large rock outcrop (whose outline is sometimes fancifully compared to that of an elephant lying down). The figures are some of the largest in the island (the biggest is 16m tall), and are thought to date from the tenth century – they're unusual in displaying Mahayana Buddhist influence, which enjoyed a brief vogue in the island around this time. The large central standing **Buddha** in the *abhaya* ("have no fear") pose still bears traces of the stucco which would originally have covered his robes, as well as faint splashes of his original paint.

On the left-hand side of the rock stand a group of three figures. The central one, which retains its white paint and red halo, is generally thought to represent **Avalokitesvara**, one of the most important Mahayana divinities. To the left stands an unidentified attendant, while the female figure to his right in the "thrice-bent" pose is **Tara**, a Mahayana goddess. The three figures on the right-hand side of the

Moving on from Wellawaya

Wellawaya is the starting point for various **bus** routes, with frequent services to **Ella** (every 15min; 45min), **Haputale** (hourly; 1hr), **Bandarawela** (every 30min; 45min), **Badulla** (every 30–45min; 1hr 30min), **Monaragala** (every 15min; 1hr 15min) and **Colombo** (every 45min; 8hr), plus less frequent service to **Embilipitiya** (4 daily; 3hr), **Nuwara Eliya** (5 daily; 5hr) and **Kandy** (1 daily; 8hr), although for the last two you might prefer to take a bus to Ella and then catch the train from there (see p.224 for timetables). The town is also a major transit point for the **south coast**, with regular services south to Pannegamuwa Junction (every 30min; 1hr 45min), near Tissa, from where there are regular onward connections to Tissa, Kataragama, Tangalla and Matara. There are less frequent direct services to all these places as well.

rock are much more Hindu in style. The figure on the right is generally thought to represent the Tibetan Bodhisattva **Vajrapani**, holding a thunderbolt symbol (a *dorje* – a rare instance of Tantric influence in Sri Lankan Buddhist art); the central figure is **Maitreya**, the future Buddha, while the third figure is Vishnu. The presence of square-cut holes in the rock above some figures – particularly the central Buddha – suggests that they would originally have been canopied.

To reach the site, head 5km south of Wellawaya along the main road towards Tissa, then turn right onto a side road for another 5km. Entrance costs Rs.200. A tuktuk from Wellawaya will cost around Rs.400 return.

Handapanagala Tank

Just beyond Buduruwagala (continue 3km further south from Wellawaya, then 1.5km along a track to the left), lies the beautiful **Handapanagala Tank**. There are gorgeous views from here, especially if you scramble up the rock at the far end of the path that runs along the south side of the tank, with the great wall of Uva mountains spread out on one side and the arid dry-zone plains towards Tissa on the other. Although the tank is worth visiting just for the views, there's the possible added bonus of spotting wild **elephants**, who sometimes come to the tank to drink. Late afternoon is usually the best time. It might also be possible to arrange a **catamaran trip** on the lake with local boatmen; count on around Rs.1000.

Diyaluma Falls

Around 12km west of Wellawaya and 30km from Haputale are the **Diyaluma Falls**, the second-highest in Sri Lanka, tumbling for 220m over a sheer cliff-face in a single slender cascade. A circuitous walk (allow 1hr each way) to the top of the falls starts from the main road a few hundred metres east of the falls next to the km 207/5 marker. Follow the track here uphill for around twenty minutes until you reach a small rubber factory, where you'll need to stop and ask someone to point out the very faint and rough path up the steep and rocky hillside behind – if in doubt just keep on heading straight up. It's a steep and tiring hike, and there's not that much to look at (and you can't actually see the falls properly from the top), although you can cool off with a dip in one of the large natural rock pools at the top.

To reach the falls, take any bus heading west from Wellawaya. If you're coming from Haputale, take one of the hourly buses to Wellawaya or catch a bus to **Beragala** (from where there are stunning views over the plains to the south) and pick up a Wellawaya bus there. Buses back from the falls to Haputale stop running at around 3–4pm, so leave early to avoid getting stuck. The pleasant

Diyaluma Falls Inn, on the main road below the falls, has fine views of the cascades and is a pleasant spot for lunch or a drink.

Bandarawela

Midway between Ella and Haputale, the scruffy little town of **BANDARAWELA** lacks either the rural charm of the first or the dramatic setting of the latter. The only real reason to stay here is to spend a night at the time-warped *Bandarawela Hotel*, although you might well find yourself changing buses (or money) here en route to somewhere else.

Bandarawela is largely a locals' resort, and although there's plenty of **accommodation** around town, much of it is shabby and poor value for money compared to Haputale and Ella. Easily the best place to stay is the lovely old *Bandarawela Hotel*, 14 Welimada Rd (ⓣ057-222 2501, ⓦwww.aitkenspencehotels.com; ❺), set in a planters' clubhouse of 1893. The personable, rambling old wooden building is brimful of charm (albeit stronger on colonial atmosphere than modern creature comforts), with polished wooden floorboards, colonial fittings, bathtubs and quaint old metal bedsteads. An absolute bargain at current rates – although the lack of visitors can sometimes make the place feel a bit moribund. A fair number of package tours overnight at the *Orient Hotel*, 10 Dharmapala Mw (ⓣ057-222 2377, ⓦwww.orienthotelsl.com; ❹), a big, functional hotel, with bright, good-value rooms; staff here can also arrange tours around the hill country, including trekking and mountain-biking. For budget lodgings head either to the *Chinese Union Hotel*, 8 Mount Pleasant Rd (ⓣ057-222 2502; ❷), a characterful little establishment with old-fashioned but well-maintained rooms and a pleasant little (alcohol-free) dining room; or the *New Chinese Hotel*, Esplanade Road (ⓣ057-223 1767; ❷), which has characterless but spotless modern rooms and a decent range of Chinese food in the restaurant downstairs. **Food** is available at all the accommodation listed above; the *Bandarawela Hotel* is the nicest.

There are several **banks** scattered around town. The ATM at the Commercial Bank, near the Ella bus stand, accepts foreign Visa and MasterCards; that at People's Bank on Esplanade Road accepts Visa. About 3km east of Bandarawela

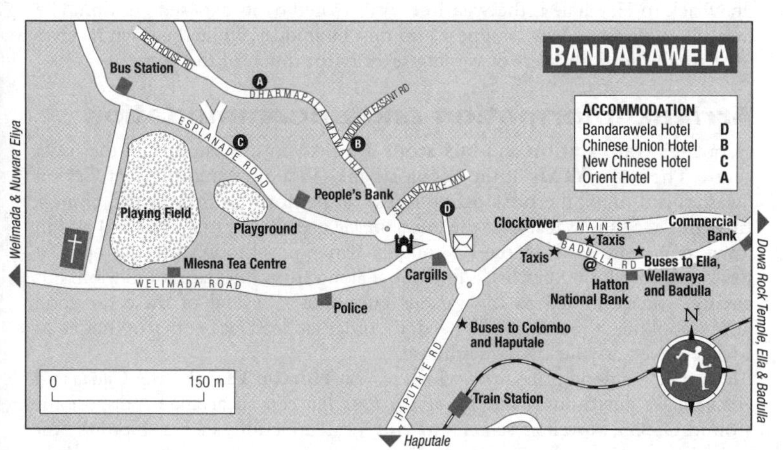

Moving on from Bandarawela

Bandarawela is on the main hill country **train** line. For timetables, see p.224.

Buses leave Bandarawela from a confusing variety of places. Buses leave roughly every thirty minutes from the stop near the main roundabout just south of Cargills for **Haputale** (30min), **Ratnapura** (3hr 30min) and **Colombo** (6hr). The stands opposite Hatton Bank on the east side of town are where you'll find buses to **Ella** (every 15min; 30min), **Wellawaya** (every 30min; 1hr) and **Badulla** (every 15min; 1hr). From the main bus station there are four daily services to **Nuwara Eliya** (1hr 30min) and **Kandy** (4–5hr); alternatively, take a bus to Welimada (every 30min; 45min), and pick up a Nuwara Eliya bus from there, although it's more enjoyable to take the train. There are a few services to **Matara** (3 daily; 7–8hr) and two morning departures to **Monaragala**, from where you can pick up a bus to **Arugam Bay**.

on the Badulla road, the popular Suwamadhu **Ayurveda** centre (T 057-222 2504, W www.ayurvedasuwamadhu.com) offers a standard selection of massages and herbal or steam baths at quite moderate prices.

Haputale and around

One of the most spectacularly situated of all Sri Lankan towns, **HAPUTALE** (pronounced "ha-*poo*-tah-lay") is perched dramatically on the crest of a ridge at the southern edge of the hill country with bird's-eye views in both directions – south to the plains and coast, and inland across the jagged lines of peaks receding away to the north. The town itself is a busy but fairly humdrum little commercial centre with a mainly Tamil population, though the mist that frequently blankets the place adds a pleasingly mysterious touch to the workaday markets and shops that fill the centre.

As with Ella, the principal pleasure of a stay in Haputale is the chance to get out and walk in the surrounding hills – most notably up to (or down from) the magnificent viewpoint at **Lipton's Seat**. Specific sights around town include the tea factory at **Dambatenne**, the evocative old country mansion of **Adisham** and the impressive **Diyaluma Falls** (covered on p.288). The major drawback to Haputale is the **weather**, exacerbated by its exposed position. The marvellous views usually disappear into mist by midday, while the town receives regular afternoon showers of varying severity for much of the year.

Arrival, information and accommodation

Haputale's **train station** and **bus stops** are close to one another in the town centre. There are **ATMs** at the People's Bank (Visa only) and Bank of Ceylon (MasterCard only); the **post office** is just to the north of St Andrew's church. **Internet** access is available at the *Amarasinghe* guesthouse (see opposite) and in town at Website Link (Mon–Fri roughly 8am–7pm, though may be open at weekends too; Rs.60 per hr), a few doors along from the Bank of Ceylon. For **eating**, you're limited to the various guesthouses; several of these do good home-cooking, though you'll need to order at least a couple of hours in advance, even at your own guesthouse.

Haputale is a good place from which to visit **Horton Plains** – the *Cuesta* and *Amarasinghe* guesthouses and *Royal Top Rest Inn* can all arrange transport for around US$35, as well as vehicles to visit local attractions such as Lipton's Seat

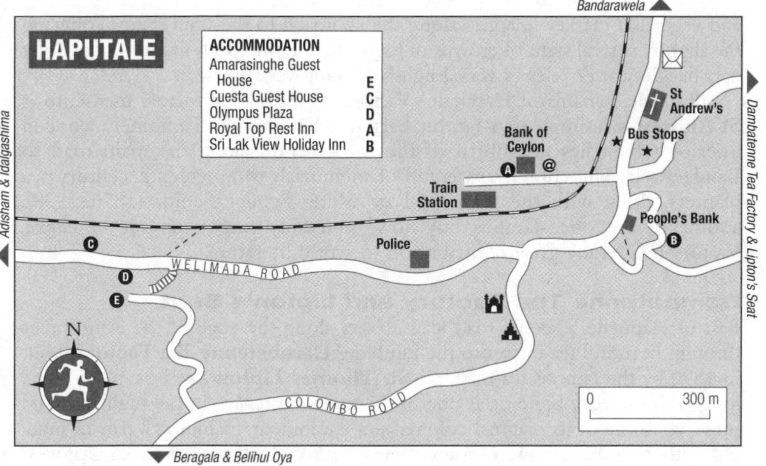

(around US$15 by car or US$10 by tuktuk one way). *Cuesta* also have four 250cc **motorbikes** for hire (Rs.1500 per day).

Accommodation

Accommodation in Haputale is extremely good value, with one of the best budget guesthouses in the hill country, plus several other options. Note that if you're staying at one of the guesthouses west of town, there's a useful little shortcut to the town centre, as follows: opposite where the path comes up onto the main road from the *Amarasinghe* guesthouse, follow the steps down to the rail line and then walk along the tracks into town (significantly quicker than following the slightly serpentine road). All the following places have hot water and serve food.

Amarasinghe Guest House ⓣ057-226 8175, ⓔagh777@sltnet.lk. The nicest place in town, this extremely well-run guesthouse has large, comfortable (if slightly bare) and very good-value rooms. Facilities include internet access (Rs.4 per min) and satelite TV in the lounge, plus excellent food, including good rice and curry. To reach the guesthouse, follow the tiny footpath (signed) from the road by the rail tracks, just east of the *Olympus Plaza* hotel. ❶

Cuesta Guest House ⓣ057-226 8110, ⓔkacp@sltnet.lk. Perched right on the edge of the ridge, the rooms here are small and a bit shabby, but are cheap and have dreamy views (and small private balconies to enjoy them from). There's also a cosy lounge and decent home-cooking. ❶

Olympus Plaza ⓣ057-226 8544, ⓦwww.olympusplazahotel.com. This ugly but comfortable new mid-range hotel is Haputale's only non-budget option. Rooms are spacious and nicely furnished, with fine views over the hills below, and there's also a so-so restaurant, a surprisingly chic little bar plus gym and kids' play areas. ❺

Royal Top Rest Inn ⓣ057-226 8178. Conveniently close to the train station, this place has well-maintained rooms, with or without views (a couple have shared bathrooms). Good value and comfortable, though not quite as nice as the nearby *Sri Lak*. ❶

Sri Lak View Holiday Inn ⓣ057-226 8125, ⓦwww.srilakviewholidayinn.com. The best option in the town centre, with spotless, modern, tiled rooms, some with marvellous views south, at bargain rates. ❶

The Town and around

Views excepted, **Haputale** has little to detain you. The town comprises a small but lively mishmash of functional concrete shops and cafés, while a small fruit and vegetable market straggles along the approach to the train station, offering the slightly surreal sight of crowds of loquacious Tamil locals in saris and woolly hats haggling over piles of very English-looking vegetables.

Sadly little remains of Haputale's Victorian past. The principal memento is **St Andrew's**, a simple neo-Gothic barn of a building with a homely wooden interior which lies just north of the town centre along the main road to Bandarawela. The churchyard is full of memorials to nineteenth-century tea planters, along with the grave of Rev Walter Stanley Senior (1876–1938), author of the once-famous but now mercifully forgotten *Ode to Lanka*, Victorian Ceylon's great contribution to world literature.

Dambatenne Tea Factory and Lipton's Seat

East of Haputale, a scenic road leads 10km along the edge of the escarpment through beautiful tea estates to the rambling **Dambatenne Tea Factory**, built in 1890 by the famous tea magnate **Sir Thomas Lipton** (see box, p.457). The long white factory building is one of the most impressive in the highlands and preserves some of its original colonial-era equipment, including a pair of huge old withering trays, demonstrating the extent to which the tea-making process (and often the actual machinery as well) has remained unchanged for a hundred years or more. Disappointingly, there's no tea for sale, either to take home or drink on the premises. An informative factory tour costs Rs.250 per person; visiting hours are 8am to 6pm, but you've got more chance of seeing the entire factory in operation if you come before noon.

Beyond Dambatenne, a marvellous walk leads up to **Lipton's Seat**, one of the finest viewpoints in the country – the equal of World's End, but without the hefty entrance fee. The road offers increasingly expansive views the higher you go, leading steeply up through a perfect landscape of immaculately manicured tea plantations with scarcely a leaf out of place, connected by flights of stone steps and enclosed in fine old drystone walls. It's quite a strenuous hike to the seat – about 7km by road, though you can avoid the lengthy hairpins made by the tarmac and so reduce the overall distance by taking short-cuts up the stone steps. Lipton's Seat itself – named after Sir Thomas Lipton, who often came here to admire the view – sits perched at the edge of a cliff, offering an almost 360-degree overview of the surrounding countryside; you can see all the way to the coast on a clear day. As with World's End, the viewpoint clouds over most days from about 10am, so it's best to arrive early. The walk from here down to Dambatenne takes around two hours.

Buses for the factory leave from the south side of the bus stops in the centre of town. Alternatively, a **taxi** will cost around US$10 return to Dambatenne, or US$15 one-way to Lipton's Seat. A good plan is to take a taxi all the way up to Lipton's Seat then walk back down, either to the tea factory or all the way back to Haputale – you should reach the viewpoint before it clouds over, after which you're walking downhill all the way.

Adisham and the walk to Idalgashina

Just east of Haputale, the grand colonial mansion of **Adisham** (Sat & Sun, poya days and school holidays 9.30am–12.30pm & 1.30–4pm; Rs.10) offers a misty-eyed moment of English nostalgia in the heart of the tropics. Adisham was built by **Sir Thomas Villiers**, who named it after the Kent village in which he was born. No expense was spared in the construction of the rather dour-looking building, with its rusticated granite walls and vaguely Tudor-style windows. The house was bought by the Benedictine monastic order in the 1960s and now functions as a monastery. Only the

Moving on from Haputale

Haputale is on the main hill-country **train** line, with direct connections to Ella, Bandarawela, Badulla, Nanu Oya (for Nuwara Eliya), Kandy and Colombo (see p.224 for timetable information), although services are very sporadic, and for short journeys it's often easier to take the **bus**. There are regular buses west to **Belihul Oya** (every 30–45min; 1hr 30min), **Ratnapura** (3hr) and **Colombo** (6hr), and south to **Wellawaya** (hourly; 1hr), as well two direct early-morning services to **Matara** (7hr). Heading east, there are regular services to **Bandarawela** (every 20–30min; 30min), plus less regular services to **Badulla** (hourly; 1hr 30min; or change at Bandarawela). For **Ella**, you'll need to change at Bandarawela. For **Nuwara Eliya**, you'll also need to change at Bandarawela, and probably at Welimada too – it's much easier to take the train. Note that hardly any bus services originate in Haputale, so it's pot luck whether or not you'll get a seat.

sitting room and library are open to visitors, complete with their musty and atmospheric original fittings; the monastery shop, selling home-made pickles, chutneys, sauces and cordials, is particularly popular with locals. Adisham is about 3km east of Haputale: take the main road west from the town centre and follow the signs.

Beyond Adisham, a fine walk leads west along the ridgetop towards the village of **Idalgashina** through the **Tangamalai** (or Tangmale) nature reserve (open access; free), home to plentiful birdlife, as well as other wildlife including lots of monkeys. The path starts just to the left of the Adisham gates and runs for 3km through alternating patches of dense subtropical jungle full of grey-barked, moss-covered *weera* trees and airy stands of eucalyptus. The track is reasonably easy to follow at first, though it becomes indistinct in places further on (the directions below should suffice, though). After about 1km, the path comes out to the edge of the ridge with panoramic hill views stretching from Pidurutalagala and Hakgala near Nuwara Eliya to the left, Bandarawela below, and right towards the distinctive triangular-shaped peak of Namunakula, south of Badulla. Below you can see Glenanore Tea Factory and (a little later) the rail tracks far below (they will gradually rise to meet you).

From here on, the path sometimes sticks to the edge of the ridge, sometimes turns away from it, undulating slightly but always keeping roughly to the same height. After a further 1.5km you'll see the rail tracks again, now much closer. Over the next 500m the path winds down the edge of the ridge to meet the ascending rail line, at which point there's a wonderful view south, with impressive sheer cliffs to the left framing views of the lines of hills descending to the south, and the flat, hot plains beyond. From here you can either continue along the tracks to Idalgashina (about 6km) and catch a train back, or return to Haputale along the tracks (about 4km).

Belihul Oya and around

Around 30km west of Haputale, the little town of **BELIHUL OYA** lies in prettily wooded scenery at the foot of the hill country. There's not much to the town itself, but there's a reasonable spread of **accommodation**, so you might find yourself overnighting here. Sadly, the challenging eleven-kilometre trek from Belihul Oya up to World's End is currently closed, although it is possible to walk up to World's End from nearby Bambarakanda – see below.

Belihul Oya is also the nearest jumping-off point for the **Bambarakanda Falls**, which tumble out of the dramatic hills below the towering escarpment of World's End. The long, slender cascade has a total drop of 241m, making it the highest in Sri Lanka – although it can be slightly underwhelming during periods of low rainfall. The falls are 5km north of the main A4 highway between Haputale and Belihul Oya at the village of **Kalupahana**; lots of buses pass through Kalupahana, from where you should be able to pick up a tuktuk to take you up the tiny, hairpinning road to the Bambarakanda. Bambarakanda is also the starting point for a seventeen-kilometre hike up to Horton Plains – a longer but less strenuous route than the old path up from Belihul Oya.

Accommodation

The places in **Belihul Oya** below are all situated close to one another along the main A4 highway, around 4km west of town (we listed them in the order you reach them heading west). The three places listed under **Bambarakanda Falls** are amongst the most remote and dramatically situated in Sri Lanka – though you'll have to brave steep, twisting and nerve-racking roads to reach them.

Belihul Oya

Pearl Tourist Inn ⓣ045-228 0157. The cheapest place in town, though relatively overpriced for what you get, with large, musty rooms and a flyblown restaurant. ❸

Rest House ⓣ045-228 0156, ⓦwww.ceylonhotels.lk. This attractively old-fashioned place is easily the nicest place to stay in Belihul Oya, with a breezy setting next to the foaming waters of the Kudu Oya, a picturesque terrace restaurant and comfortable, reasonably priced rooms (some with a/c). ❹

River Garden Resort ⓣ045-228 0222. A few nicely appointed "cottages" (sleeping two) in attractive wooded gardens running down to the river. Staff can arrange birdwatching, canoeing, camping, cycling and hiking trips. ❺

Water Garden ⓣ045-228 0254. Surprisingly swanky-looking place, with sparkingly modern rooms with a/c, hot water and lots of very minimalist pine furniture, plus a lovely garden terrace overlooking paddy fields. They also have mountain bikes (Rs.1000 per day). ❹

Around Bambarakanda Falls

Bambaranka Holiday Resort ⓣ057-567 0457. In an extremely remote and peaceful setting high up in the valley overlooking Bambarakanda Falls. Despite its name, this "resort" is actually nothing more than a small, old-fashioned cottage with a few simple but comfortable rooms, and a decidedly Shangri-La atmosphere. You can walk from here up to Horton Plains in around four hours. ❸

Hill Safari Eco-Lodge Off the road between Bambarakanda and Ohiya ⓣ0712 772 451 or 011-264 7582. Set in the middle of a tea estate in a dramatic location below the towering escarpment of World's End with simple but comfortable rooms. The access road is extremely steep and rather hair-raising. ❸ half-board

World's End Lodge ⓣ057-567 6977, ⓦwww.lankahotel.com. Perhaps the most spectacularly situated place to stay in Sri Lanka; look for the turn-off from the A4 highway between Haldumulla and Kalupahana, just east of the Bambarakanda Falls turning. From here, it's 4km up a very steep and rough hairpinning road – passable, but only just, in a normal car. Rooms are simple and slightly bare, with verandas from which to enjoy the wild and beautiful views, when they're not blanketed by mist, that is. You can walk from here up to Horton Plains in around four hours. ❸

Adam's Peak

Poking up from the southwestern edge of the hill country, the soaring summit of **ADAM'S PEAK** (**Sri Pada**) is simultaneously one of Sri Lanka's most striking natural features and one of its most celebrated places of pilgrimage – a miniature Matterhorn which stands head and shoulders above the

Saman

Saman is one of the four great protective divinities of Sri Lanka, and the one who boasts the most modest and purely Sri Lankan origins. He is believed originally to have been a pious Indian trader (or possibly a king) who, thanks to the merit he had acquired, was reborn as a god residing at Sumanakuta (as Adam's Peak was then called). According to the quasi-mythological chronicle of Sri Lankan history, the *Mahavamsa*, Saman was amongst the audience of gods to whom the Buddha preached during his visit to Mahiyangana, and upon hearing the Buddha, he immediately entered on the path of Enlightenment. When the Buddha returned to Sri Lanka on his final visit, Saman begged him to leave a footprint atop Sumanakuta to serve as a focus for worship; the Buddha duly obliged.

Saman is still believed to reside on the mountain, and to protect pilgrims who climb it. He is regarded as an entirely benevolent and rather well-behaved god, unlike the decidedly fierce Kataragama (see p.216), whose fighting prowess and amatory naughtiness appeal to a very different sort of pilgrim. Saman is usually shown with a white elephant, holding a red lotus, and Adam's Peak is often shown in the background. He is almost only ever shown in normal human form, unlike many other gods, such as Kataragama, who are often depicted with multiple arms and heads.

surrounding hills, giving a wonderful impression of sheer altitude (even though, at 2243m, it's actually only Sri Lanka's fifth-highest peak). The mountain has accumulated a mass of legends centred around the curious depression at its summit, the **Sri Pada** or Sacred Footprint. The original Buddhist story claims that this is the footprint of the Buddha himself, made at the request of the local god **Saman** (see box above); different faiths subsequently modified this to suit their own contrasting theologies. Sometime around the eighth century, Muslims began to claim the footprint as that of **Adam**, who is said to have first set foot on earth here after having been cast out of heaven, and who stood on the mountain's summit on one leg in penitence until his sins were forgiven. Hindu tradition, meanwhile, had claimed (though with no great conviction) that the footprint was created by **Shiva**. In the final and feeblest twist of the Sri Pada legend, the colonial Portuguese attempted to rescue the footprint for the Christian faith, claiming that it belonged to **St Thomas**, the founder of the religion in India, though this belief has never really taken popular root.

Despite all these rival claims, Adam's Peak remains an essentially Buddhist place of worship (unlike the genuinely multifaith pilgrimage town of Kataragama). The mountain has been an object of pilgrimage for over a thousand years, at least since the Polonnaruwan period, when Parakramabahu and Vijayabahu constructed shelters here for visiting pilgrims. In the twelfth century, Nissanka Malla became the first king to climb the mountain, while later foreign travellers including Fa-Hsien, Ibn Battuta, Marco Polo and Robert Knox all described the peak and its associated traditions with varying degrees of fanciful inaccuracy.

The climb

The ascent of Adam's Peak is traditionally made **by night**, allowing you to reach the top in time for dawn – this not only offers the best odds of seeing the extraordinary views free from cloud, but also the chance of witnessing one of Sri Lanka's strangest natural phenomena. As dawn breaks, the rising sun creates a **shadow** of the peak which seems to hang suspended in space in front of the mountain. The easiest ascent, described below, is from **Dalhousie**. An alternative, much longer route (15km; around 7hr), ascends from the **Ratnapura** side of the mountain via **Gilimale** – see p.299 for further details. An interesting walk, if you could arrange the logistics, would be to ascend from Dalhousie and then walk down to Gilimale. Another possibility is to take a tour from **Nuwara Eliya** (see p.275), climbing the peak from Dalhousie, although this makes for rather a long night.

Most visitors climb the mountain during the **pilgrimage season**, which starts on the Duruthu poya day in December or January and continues until the Vesak poya in May. During the season the weather on the mountain is at its best, and the chances of a clear dawn at the summit highest; the steps up the mountainside are also illuminated and little stalls and teashops open through the night to cater to the throngs of weary pilgrims dragging themselves up. It's perfectly possible, if less interesting, to climb the mountain **out of season**, though none of the teashops is open and the lights are turned off, so you'll need to bring a decent torch. Although most people climb by night, you can also go up the mountain **by day**, but the summit is often obscured by cloud and, even if it's clear, you won't see the famous shadow, or (assuming you're visiting during the pilgrimage season) be able to enjoy the spectacle of the night-time illuminations and all-night teashops on the way up. Finally, don't despair if you arrive in Dalhousie and it's **pouring with rain**. The daily deluge which usually descends on the village out of season often stops at around midnight, allowing you a clear run at the summit during the night, although the path will be wet and the leeches will be out in force.

Guides offer their services all round Dalhousie (Rs.1000–1500), though you'll only really need one if you're a solo woman or are attempting the climb out of season at night, when the mountain can be a very cold and lonely place. A (free) alternative is to borrow a dog – all the local mutts know the track well, and will be happy to accompany you – "Bonzo" at the *Green House* in Dalhousie is particularly companionable (although their famous three-legged dog known as "Tuktuk" is sadly no more).

However fit you are, the Adam's Peak climb is **exhausting** – a taxing 7km up a mainly stepped footpath (there are around 5500 steps) which can reduce even seasoned hill walkers to quivering wrecks. The best way to go up is slowly. Allow around four hours to get up the mountain, including time for tea stops (although at particularly busy times, such as poya days, the crowds can make the ascent slower still). Taking the climb at a gentle pace also gives you the chance to mingle with the crowds of pilgrims, which is at least half the fun. Dawn is at 6/6.30am, so a 2am start should get you to the top in time, and there are plenty of tea houses to stop at on the way if it looks like you're going to arrive early (there's not much point in sitting around at the summit in the darkness for any longer than you have to). It can get bitterly cold at the summit: take warm clothing.

The track up the mountain starts at the far end of Dalhousie village, passing a large standing Buddha, crossing a bridge and looping around the back of the large pilgrim's rest hostel (if you reach the *Green House* guesthouse you've gone wrong). For the first thirty minutes the path winds gently through tea estates, past Buddha shrines and through the big *makara torana* arch which marks the boundary of the sacred area (the fact that Adam's Peak remains an essentially Buddhist place of pilgrimage, despite the claims of rival religions, is borne out by the complete absence of Christian, Hindu and Muslim shrines). Beyond here the path continues to run gently uphill to the large **Peace Pagoda**, built with Japanese aid during the 1970s. In wet weather the cliff-face opposite is scored with myriad waterfalls.

Beyond the Peace Pagoda, the climb – and the steps – start in earnest; they're not too bad at first, but become increasingly short and steep. By the time you reach the leg-wrenchingly vertical section equipped with handrails you're within about 1500 steps of the summit, although by then it's a real physical struggle. The path is very secure and enclosed, however, so unless you suffer from unusually bad vertigo, this shouldn't be a problem (unlike at Sigiriya, for example). And, obviously, at night you won't be able to see anything on the way up in any case. The upper slopes of the mountain are swathed in dense and largely undisturbed stands of cloudforest which are home to various species of colourful montane birdlife such as the Sri Lanka white eye and Eurasian blackbird, the sight of which might offer some welcome distraction during the slog up or down.

The **summit** is covered in a huddle of buildings. The **footprint** itself is surprisingly unimpressive: a small, irregular depression, sheltered under a tiny pavilion and painted in gold, with a concrete surround – although tradition claims that this is actually only an impression of the true footprint, which lies underground. Upon reaching the summit, pilgrims ring one of the two bells (you are meant to ring once for every successful ascent of the mountain you have made, if you want to join in). The **shadow** itself lasts for around twenty minutes, given a clear sunrise. One of the mysteries of the peak is the shadow's perfectly triangular shape, which doesn't correspond to the actual – and far more irregular – outline of the summit. The Buddhist explanation is that this is not actually the shadow of the peak at all, but a miraculous physical representation of the "Triple Gem" (a kind of Buddhist equivalent to the Holy Trinity, comprising the Buddha, his teachings and the community of Buddhist monks). Locals reckon you've got an eighty percent chance to seeing the shadow during the pilgrimage season, falling to around forty percent (or less) at other times of year.

The **descent** is much quicker (count on around 2hr 30min) though no less painful, since by now your legs will have turned to jelly.

Adam's Peak practicalities: Dalhousie

The main *raison d'etre* for the extremely modest village of **DALHOUSIE** (pronounced "Del-house"; also increasingly known by its Tamil name of **Nallatanniya**) is as a base for the ascent of Adam's Peak. It's usually busy with visitors during the pilgrimage season, but can seem rather desolate at other times. The village is beautifully situated by a river and surrounded by hills and tea plantations; various tracks head into the plantations beyond *The Green House*, in the unlikely event that you still have the urge (or ability) to walk after tackling the peak.

Dalhousie lies just over 30km southwest of the busy town of **Hatton**, which is on the main rail line through the hill country. **During the pilgrimage season** there are once-daily buses to Dalhousie from Nuwara Eliya and Colombo. Alternatively, take a bus or train to Hatton (see p.224 for train timetables), from where there are regular buses (every 30min; 90min) to Dalhousie. **Outside the pilgrimage season** there are no buses from Nuwara Eliya or Colombo and you'll first have to reach Hatton, then take a bus from there to Maskeliya, and then pick up one of the battered old minibuses which ply between Maskeliya and Dalhousie (every 30min; 45min). The ride to Dalhousie is through beautiful tea country, with views of the Maskeliya reservoir. A **taxi** from Hatton to Dalhousie will cost around Rs.2000; a **tuktuk** will cost Rs.1500.

Accommodation

There's not much **accommodation** in Dalhousie; you might want to ring in advance, and you should definitely reserve if staying over a poya day. In addition to the places listed below, there are also the four superb Tea Trail bungalows (see p.268), dotted around the countryside nearby.

Dalhousie

The Green House Far end of the village, by the start of the track up Adam's Peak ⓣ060-251 9478. Friendly and long-established little place, occupying a small house surrounded by various rickety-looking wooden gazebo-type structures (and, yes, it *is* green). Rooms are basic but adequate, with shared bathrooms and hot water on request. Some smarter new en-suite rooms (❷) are currently under construction, and should be ready by the time you read this. Pickups from Hatton on request. ❶

Punsisi Rest Middle of village ⓣ051-492 0313, ⓔpunsisirest@yahoo.com. Modern hotel with comfortable and good-value rooms which get nicer (and more expensive) the higher up the building you go: those on the ground floor are dark and poky; those at the top are bright and spacious. Don't be put off by the unusually ugly exterior, or by the gloomy restaurant downstairs. ❶–❸

River View Wathsala Inn On the main road by the entrance to the village ⓣ060-251 9606, ⓦwww.adamspeaksrilanka.com. Simple, slightly musty but OK rooms (plus a couple of smarter ones upstairs), all with beautiful river views, plus the only bar in Dalhousie. Cheap pickups from Hatton on request, and they also arrange rafting trips to Kitulagala, canoeing and other excursions. Discounts out of season. ❸

Slightly Chilled Guest House (formerly the *Yellow House*). Just past *River View Wathsala Inn* ⓣ060-251 9430, ⓦwww.slightlychilled.tv. The smartest place in the village, with spacious and attractive modern rooms in an attractive riverside setting, plus internet, mountain bikes and information about local hikes. ❸–❹

White House Just past *Slightly Chilled Guest House* ⓣ0777 912 009, ⓦwww.whitehouse.lankabiz.lk. The cheapest place in the village, with simple but clean rooms and very basic log cabins, set in a pretty little garden. The friendly owner can arrange local walks and tours. ❶

Dickoya

Upper Glencairn Bungalow 4km from Dickoya (and 7km from Hatton) on the road to Dalhousie ⓣ051-222 2348. Fine old colonial-era tea planter's house set high above Castlereagh Reservoir in a working estate, with atmospheric, time-warped rooms (almost all have hot water and bathtubs to soothe aching post-peak limbs). Good value, though if you don't have your own transport you'll have to shell out for a taxi to Dalhousie. ❹

Kitulgala

The village of **KITULGALA** is set about halfway along the spectacular road that descends from Hatton down to the lowlands at Avissawella. The scenery is particularly dramatic hereabouts, with sheer-sided, forest-covered hills plunging down to the wild waters of the Kelani Ganga. The stretch of this river around Kitulgala provides the site for the best **whitewater rafting** in Sri Lanka, with grade two and three rapids some 5km upriver from the village. You can organize trips through the two hotels listed below (around US$25 per person for around 1hr 30min–2hr), or in advance through some of the companies listed on pp.30–32.

Kitulgala's other claim to fame is that it provided the location for David Lean's classic 1957 film *Bridge on the River Kwai*. If you know the film you'll probably recognize some of the locations down along the river. About 1.5km east of the *Plantation Hotel*, a very big sign ("Bridge of the River Kwai" [sic]) points to a very small track leading down to the river. Step onto the path and a guide or two will magically materialize to show you along the slightly confusing route to the river and point out a few locations associated with the film, including the slight remains of the bridge's concrete foundations.

There are a few **places to stay** in Kitulgala. The attractive *Kitulgala Rest House* (Ⓣ036-228 7528 or 011-534 5799, Ⓦwww.ceylonhotels.lk; fan ❹, a/c ❺) has a mix of comfortable, slightly chintzy fan rooms and more modern ones with air-conditioning, a scenic position facing the river and a gracious old restaurant. The considerably less appealing *Plantation Hotel* (Ⓣ036-228 7575, Ⓦwww.plantationgrouphotels.com; ❻), set in a restored colonial villa about 1.5km to the east, caters mainly to tour groups and has comfortable but very overpriced air-conditioned rooms and a pleasant riverside restaurant, though it gets absolutely overrun with passing coach parties at lunchtime, when it has all the charm of a motorway service station. A much more peaceful alternative is *Rafter's Retreat* (Ⓣ036-228 7598, Ⓦwww.raftersretreat.com; ❸), a peaceful eco-lodge with accommodation in simple little wooden huts in dense forest alongside the River Kelani. The owner runs adventure programmes featuring birdwatching, mountain-biking, whitewater rafting and rock climbing. He can also organize visits to the nearby **Beli Lena caves**, 8km from Kitulgala, famous in Sri Lankan prehistory as the place in which ten skeletons of the ancient "Balangoda People", Sri Lanka's oldest human inhabitants, were discovered, dating back some 32,000 years.

Ratnapura

Nestled amongst verdant hills at the southwestern corner of the hill country, **RATNAPURA** (literally "City of Gems") is famous for its **precious stones**, which have been mined here in extraordinary quantities since antiquity. Naturally, the town makes a big deal of this, with plenty of touts offering trips to gem mines and stones for sale, though unless you have a specialist interest, this alone isn't really a sufficient reason to visit the place. Ratnapura does have other attractions, however. The town makes a possible base for visits to **Sinharaja** and **Uda Walawe national parks**; trips to both involve a long (3–4hr) return drive, making for a big day, but this does avoid the considerable bother of getting to Deniyaya, Kudawa or Embilipitiya. Several guesthouses in town can arrange trips: the going rate for a jeep seating six to eight people is around US$50–60 to Sinharaja and US$60 to Uda Walawe – try *Travellers Halt* guesthouse or *Nilani Lodge* (see p.300). Ratnapura is also the starting point for an alternative ascent of **Adam's Peak**, though it's significantly longer and tougher than the route up from Dalhousie. The path starts from the village of **Palabaddale**, from where it's a climb of five to seven hours to the summit. Buses run to Palabaddale via Gilimale during the pilgrimage season.

Ratnapura also has the distinction of being one of the **wettest places** in Sri Lanka, with the annual rainfall sometimes exceeding four metres – and even when it's not raining, the climate is unusually humid and sticky.

Arrival and information

The **bus station** is on the north side of the town centre of Ratnapura on Inner Circular Road, within walking distance of several of the guesthouses. For **money**, there are various branches, mostly on or near Main Street, of the Bank of Ceylon, Commercial Bank, Hatton Bank and Sampath Bank. The ATMs at the first two accept foreign Visa and MasterCards; that at the Hatton Bank accepts MasterCard only. There's a Cargills **supermarket** (daily 8am–10pm) just south of the clocktower, with a pharmacy inside. The **post office** is near the clocktower on Main Street. There's currently no internet access in Ratnapura, although you could check out the various computer shops around the clocktower in case something opens.

Gems of Sri Lanka

Sri Lanka is one of the world's most important sources of precious stones, and its gems have long been famous – indeed one of the island's early names was **Ratnadipa**, "Island of Gems". According to legend, it was a Sri Lankan ruby which was given by King Solomon to the Queen of Sheba, while Marco Polo described a fabulous ruby – "about a palm in length and of the thickness of a man's arm" – set in the spire of the Ruvenveliseya dagoba at Anuradhapura. The island also provided the "Blue Belle" sapphire which now adorns the crown of the British queen, while in 2003 a 478-carat Sri Lankan sapphire – larger than a hen's egg – fetched US$1.5m at auction.

Gems are actually found in many parts of Sri Lanka, but the **Ratnapura** district is the island's richest source. The origin of these gems is the geological rubble eroded from the central highlands, which is washed down from the hills along the valleys which crisscross the area – a gravelly mixture of eroded rock, mineral deposits, precious stones and muddy alluvial deposits known as *illam*. Gem mining is still a low-tech, labour-intensive affair. Pits are dug down into riverbeds and amongst paddy fields, and piles of *illam* are fished out, which are then washed and sieved by experts who separate the precious stones from the mud. The mining and sorting is traditionally carried out by the Sinhalese, though the gem cutters and dealers tend to be Muslim. Your guesthouse or touts in town may be able to arrange a trip to a working mine, if you're interested in seeing the process first-hand.

Types of gem

The most valuable precious stones found in Sri Lanka are corundums, a mineral family which includes sapphires and rubies. **Sapphires** range in colour from blue to as clear as a diamond. Sri Lankan **rubies** are "pink rubies" (also known as pink sapphires); the better-known red rubies are not found in the island. **Garnets**, popularly known as the "poor man's ruby", and ranging in colour from red to brown, are also found. **Cat's eyes** (green to brown) and **alexandrite** (whose colour changes under different light) are the best known of the chrysoberyl group of stones. **Tourmalines** are sometimes passed off as the far more valuable cat's eyes. Other common stones, found in varying colours, are **quartz**, **spinel** and **zircon**. The greyish **moonstone** (a type of feldspar) is a particular Sri Lankan speciality, though these are not mined in the Ratnapura area. Diamonds and emeralds are not found in Sri Lanka, though **aquamarine** (like emerald, a member of the beryl family) is.

Accommodation and eating

All the following places do **food**; the restaurant at the *Rest House* is the town's best option, though the food (mains from Rs.350) is average.

Nilani Lodge Dharmapala Mw ⓣ045-222 2170, ⓔhashani@sltnet.lk. Functional building – it looks like an enormous a/c unit – in a quiet road close to the town centre. Rooms (some with a/c and hot water for Rs.500 extra) are comfy enough, although beginning to look a tad shabby, and are slightly pricey for what you get. ❸

Ratna Gems Halt 153/5 Outer Circular Rd ⓣ045-222 3745. Varied collection of well-maintained and good-value rooms, getting nicer (and more expensive) as you go up the building, from the rather poky and drab, but also very cheap, ground-floor offerings up to the bright, modern and spacious rooms on the top floor. ❶–❸

Ratnaloka Tour Inns Kosgala, 7km from Ratnapura ⓣ045-222 2455, ⓦwww.ratnaloka.com. Comfortable if unexceptional mid-range hotel in a pleasantly rural setting. Popular with tour groups. ❺–❻

Rest House Rest House Rd ⓣ045-222 2299. Imposing old colonial rest house in a wonderful position on a hilltop above town with fine views. Rooms (fan or a/c) are clean, comfortable and reasonable value, if a bit bare, and the in-house restaurant is the nicest in town. ❸

Travellers Halt 30 Outer Circular Rd ⓣ045-222 3092, ⓔno30_fernando@yahoo.com. Small selection of average, reasonable-value rooms (a few with a/c for Rs.1000 extra) in a quiet location just outside town. Also a good place to arrange trips to Sinharaja and Uda Walawe. ❷

The Town

A major regional commercial centre, Ratnapura is a busy and rather exhausting place, even before you've dealt with the attentions of touts trying to flog you gems or get you on visits to local mines. The heart of the town's gem trade is **Saviya Mawatha** (also spelt Zavier, Zaviya and Zavia), about 150m east of the clocktower, which presents an entertaining scene of crowds of locals haggling over handfuls of uncut stones; the shops of a few small dealers line the street (the town's traditional jewellers' shops are mainly located at the clocktower end of Main St). Trading takes place on weekdays until around 3pm. You're likely to be offered stones to buy – it should go without saying that unless you're an expert, steer well clear.

If you want a more detailed look at the area's mineral riches, head out to the **Ratnapura Gem Bureau**, usually simply referred to as the "Gem Museum" (daily 9.30am–3.30pm; free, although you might be asked for a small donation), a couple of kilometres west of town on Potgul Vihara Mawatha. The museum is the brainchild of local gemmologist Purandara Sri Bhadra Marapana, and is intended as an altruistic and educational venture (although they might make a gentle attempt to flog you a few stones). The centrepiece is a colourful display of minerals and precious stones from around the world, including interesting Sri Lankan gems in both cut and uncut states. There are also displays of other handicrafts – stone carvings, metalwork and so on – designed by the versatile Mr Marapana.

By contrast, there's surprisingly little coverage of the town's gem-mining heritage at the lacklustre **National Museum** (Tues–Sat 9am–5pm; Rs.300), off Main Street on the northwest side of the town centre. Exhibits here run through the predictable gamut of Sri Lankan arts and crafts, including the inevitable Kandyan fabrics, jewellery, ivory carvings, a few entertaining *kolam* masks and a handful of beautiful Buddha statuettes. You'll also find the usual depressing collection of pickled and stuffed wildlife, plus large and unquestionably dull quantities of assorted rocks, uncut minerals, fossilized bones, the fossilized shells of snails on which prehistoric Ratnapura man presumably feasted and a few lion and pig teeth (also fossilized).

The most interesting sight hereabouts is the **Maha Saman Devale**, 3km west of town, the most important temple in the island dedicated to Saman (see box, p.295), who is said to reside on nearby Adam's Peak. There has been a temple here since the thirteenth century. It was rebuilt by the kings of Kandy during the seventeenth century, destroyed by the Portuguese, then rebuilt again during the Dutch era (a carving to the right of the entrance steps, showing a Portuguese invader killing a Sinhalese soldier, recalls European attacks against the town and temple). The present-day structure is impressively large, and although the overall effect is not of any especial antiquity, the entire complex has a pleasantly harmonious appearance, with rising tiers of tiled roofs and white walls leading up from the entrance to the main shrine, the whole structure enclosed by a large white balustraded wall, scored with tiny triangular niches to hold oil lamps. The main shrine to Saman is flanked by subsidiary shrines to the Buddha and Pattini (see box, p.248) – the latter is very popular with local ladies, though her presence here is rather ironic: during the Kandyan era, the rise in her cult meant that she replaced Saman as one of the island's guardian deities. There's a

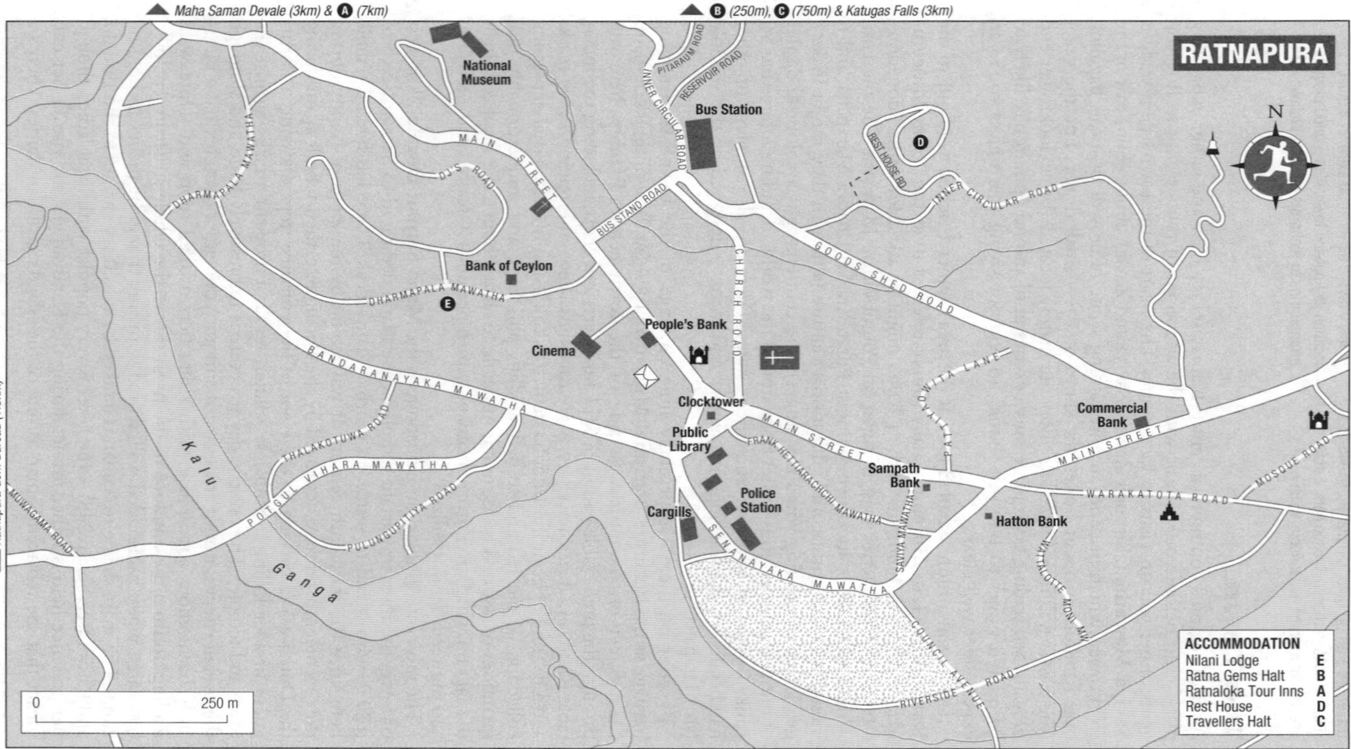
RATNAPURA
N
Maha Saman Devale (3km) & A (7km)
B (250m), C (750m) & Katugas Falls (3km)
Ratnapura Gem Bureau (1.5km)
ACCOMMODATION
Nilani Lodge E
Ratna Gems Halt B
Ratnaloka Tour Inns A
Rest House D
Travellers Halt C
National Museum
Bus Station
Bank of Ceylon
People's Bank
Cinema
Clocktower
Public Library
Police Station
Cargills
Sampath Bank
Commercial Bank
Hatton Bank
MAIN STREET
DJ'S ROAD
DHARMAPALA MAWATHA
BUS STAND ROAD
INNER CIRCULAR ROAD
PITARAUM ROAD
RESERVOIR ROAD
REST HOUSE RD
GOODS SHED ROAD
CHURCH ROAD
PATTIYAOWITA LANE
BANDARANAYAKA MAWATHA
THALAKOTUWA ROAD
POTGUL VIHARA MAWATHA
PULUNGUPITIYA ROAD
MUWAGAMA ROAD
FRANK HETTIARACHCHI MAWATHA
SENANAYAKA MAWATHA
SAVIYA MAWATHA
WARAKATOTA ROAD
MOSQUE ROAD
WATTALOTTE MONI MW
COUNCIL AVENUE
RIVERSIDE ROAD
Kalu Ganga
0 250 m

big **Esala Perahera** here during July or August. Numerous local **buses** run past the entrance to the temple, or catch a tuktuk.

Around 4km north of town, the **Katugas Falls** tumble down over boulders from a beautiful rainforested hillside – a little bit of Sinharaja on the edges of the modern town. It's possible to climb some way up the cascade into the trees. The falls are tricky to locate (ask for "Katugas Ela"); it's easiest to take a tuktuk at least one way. They're also best avoided at weekends, when they get totally overrun.

Uda Walawe National Park and around

Uda Walawe has developed into one of Sri Lanka's most popular national parks mainly thanks to its large (and easily spotted) population of elephants – it's the best place in the island to see pachyderms in the wild, although in other respects it doesn't have the range of fauna and habitats of Yala or Bundala. The park is beautifully situated just south of the hill country, whose grand escarpment provides a memorable backdrop, while at its centre lies the **Uda Walawe Reservoir**, whose catchment area it was originally established to protect. The actual landscape of the park is rather monotonous: most of Uda Walawe lies within the dry zone, and its terrain is flat and denuded, with extensive areas of grassland and low scrub (the result of earlier slash-and-burn farming) dotted with the skeletal outlines of dead trees, poked to death by the resident elephants. The overall effect, however, is not without a certain austere beauty, while the lack of forest cover makes wildlife spotting easier than in any other Sri Lankan park.

The principal attraction is, of course, **elephants**, of which there are usually around six hundred in the park; animals are free to migrate along an elephant corridor between here and Lunugamvehera National Park, though most stay here. There are also hundreds of **buffaloes**, plus macaque and langur monkeys, spotted and sambur deer and crocodiles. Rarely sighted residents include

▲ Elephant spotting in Uda Walawe National Park

Moving on from Ratnapura

The **bus station** is clearly laid out and signed; if you get stuck, ask the helpful chaps in the office signed "Sabaragamuwa Provincial Road Passenger Transport Authority" (on the left-hand side of the station towards the back). There are regular departures to **Colombo** (every 20min; 3hr; a/c express buses hourly); **Kandy** (every 30min; 3hr 30min); **Belihul Oya**, **Haputale, Bandarawela** and **Badulla** (every 30min; 2hr, 3hr, 3hr 30min & 5hr respectively); **Wellawaya** and **Monaragala** (every 30min; 4hr & 5hr 30min respectively); **Avissawella** (for Hatton and Nuwara Eliya; every 10min; 1hr); **Kalawana**, for Sinharaja (every 15min; 1hr); and **Embilipitiya** (every 15min; 2hr 30min). There are currently three buses daily to **Deniyaya** (2hr 30min) and on to **Matara** (5hr); you can also reach Matara via Embilipitiya. For **Galle**, take a Matara bus and change at Akuressa.

leopards, giant flying squirrels, jungle cats, sloth bears and porcupines. Uda Walawe is also good for **birds**, including a number of endemics and some birds of prey, while the reservoir also attracts a wide range of aquatic birds. If you're lucky you might also spot the lesser adjutant, Sri Lanka's largest – and ugliest – bird, standing at well over a metre tall.

About 5km west of the park entrance on the main road is the engaging **Elephant Transit Home** – usually referred to as the "Elephant Orphanage". Founded in 1995, the orphanage is home to around 25 baby elephants rescued from the wild after the loss of their parents. As at the better-known orphanage at Pinnewala, elephants here are bottlefed milk until the age of 3½, after which they're given a diet of grass. At the age of 5, most are released into the national park (around thirty so far); a few have been donated to important temples. There are daily **feeding sessions** at 9am, noon, 3pm, 6pm, though you can't get quite as close to the elephants as at Pinnewala, and outside feeding times the elephants are allowed to wander and, so there's usually nothing to see. The Transit Home is part of the national park, and entrance is free, although you might be asked for a donation.

Park practicalities

Uda Walawe's central location makes it accessible from a number of different places, and you can arrange tours here from as far afield as Ratnapura, Hambantota, Tissa and even Unawatuna (see the relevant town accounts for more details), although all these involve long drives to reach the park. The closest starting point is **Embilipitiya**, 20km distant (see opposite). It's possible to reach the park by **public transport** from Embilipitiya by catching one of the half-hourly buses to Tamanalwila, which go right past the entrance, where you can hire a jeep (seating 6–8) for around Rs.3000 for a few hours' drive.

The park **entrance** is at kilometre-post seven along the Embilipitiya to Tanamal road. **Admission** for foreigners currently costs Rs.1725 per person, plus the usual additional charges and taxes (see p.55). If you want **to stay** close to the park, there's the attractively rustic *Walawa Safari Village* (☎047-223 3201; ❸), 12km from the park entrance on Right Bank Canal Road (clearly signed off the Embilipitiya–Uda Walawe road), with neat and cosy little cabanas dotted around rambling gardens. You can arrange transport to and around the park from here for Rs.3000. Close by, back on the main road between Embilipitiya and Uda Walawe road, the much cheaper but rather shabby *Walawa Park View Hotel* (☎047-223 3312; ❷) has musty and rather gloomy rooms, some with very cheap air-conditioning.

Slightly further away, at Kitulkote, between Tanamalwila and Kuda Oya on the main road between Tissa and Wellawaya, is *Tasks Safari Camp* (ⓣ011-486 2225, ⓦwww.taskssafari.com; ❼ full board), vaguely reminiscent of an African bush camp, though the en-suite tents (no electricity) are fairly basic and rather overpriced. The camp is within striking distance of Uda Walawe, Yala and Bundala, and there's good birdwatching and walking in the surrounding jungle, plus occasional elephants, but it's not as good as similar eco-inspired hideouts around the island.

Embilipitiya

Halfway between Ratnapura and the coast, the medium-size town of **EMBILIPITIYA** is the closest base for visits to Uda Walawe, 20km distant. There's not much to the town itself. **Buses** arrive at the station about 100m south of the clocktower at the centre of town. There are several **banks** close to the clocktower: the ATMs at the Commercial and Sampath banks both accept foreign Visa and MasterCards; those at the Seylan and People's Bank take Visa only. There's not really anywhere **to eat** apart from the two hotels listed below, both of which can also arrange half-day trips to Uda Walawe for around Rs.2000. For **internet** access, try the Vanik IT Center next to *Sarathchandra Rest.*

Embilipitiya has two decent **places to stay**. The *Centauria Tourist Hotel* (ⓣ047-223 0514, ⓦwww.centauriatouristhotel.com; room ❺, villas ❻), about 1.5km south of the town, is a surprisingly well-appointed place for dusty little Embilipitiya. Accommodation is either in comfortable modern air-conditioned rooms (a bargain at current prices) or in more stylish and spacious two-person villas overlooking Chandrika Wewa, and there's also a decent restaurant, pool and Ayurveda centre. Alternatively, the well-run *Sarathchandra Rest* (ⓣ047-223 0044; ❸, a/c ❹), on the main road 100m south of the bus station, has very comfortable modern rooms, some with air-conditioning. Both these places can arrange jeeps for tours of Uda Walawe for around Rs.3500.

Sinharaja and around

The last extensive tract of undisturbed lowland rainforest in Sri Lanka, **Sinharaja** is one of the island's outstanding natural wonders and an ecological treasure box of international significance, as recognized by its listing as a UNESCO World Heritage Site in 1989. A staggering 830 of Sri Lanka's endemic species of flora and fauna are found here, including myriad birds,

Moving on from Embilipitiya

Leaving Embilipitiya, there are frequent **buses** to **Ratnapura** (every 15min; 2hr 30min), **Tangalla** (every 20min; 1hr 30min), **Matara** (every 20min; 2hr 30min), and **Hambantota** (every 15min; 1hr 30min). For **Tissa**, change at Hambantota. If you're heading towards the southeastern hill country, there are also buses east to **Tamanalwila** (every 30min; 1hr), from where you can pick up a bus to **Wellawaya**, which has frequent connections with Ella, Haputale, Bandarawela and Badulla. To reach **Deniyaya** (for Sinharaja) you'll need to catch one of the early-morning buses from Embilipitiya to **Suriyakanda** (a two-hour journey; check latest times the night before), from where you can wait around for one of the infrequent buses south or take a tuktuk (around Rs.1500).

reptiles and insects, while no fewer than sixty percent of the reserve's trees are endemic, too.

Sinharaja stretches for almost thirty kilometres across the wet zone at the southern edges of the hill country, enveloping a series of switchback hills and valleys ranging in altitude from just 300m up to 1170m. To the north and south, the reserve is bounded by two sizeable rivers, the Kalu Ganga and the Gin Ganga, which cut picturesque, waterfall-studded courses through the trees. The oldest parts of the rainforest comprise dense stands of towering trees enmeshed in fantastic tangles of ferns and lianas; the top of the canopy reaches heights of up to 45m. Sinharaja receives as much as five metres of rain annually – you'll be struck by the sudden overwhelming humidity (approaching ninety percent) as soon as you step into the forest, as well as by the incredible noise of cicadas.

According to tradition, Sinharaja was formerly a royal reserve (as suggested by its name, meaning "Lion King"). The first attempts to conserve it were made as far back as 1840, when it became property of the British Crown. Logging began in 1971, until being banned in the face of national protests in 1977, when the area was declared a national reserve. Sinharaja is now safely protected under UNESCO auspices, using a system whereby inhabitants of the twenty-odd villages which surround the reserve have the right to limited use of the forest's resources, including tapping kitul palms for jaggery and collecting rattan for building.

The reserve's most common **mammal** is the purple-faced langur monkey, while you might also encounter three species of squirrel – the dusky-striped jungle squirrel, flame-striped jungle squirrel and western giant squirrel – along with mongooses. Less common, and very rarely sighted, are leopards, rusty spotted cats, fishing-cats and civets. There's also a rich **reptile** population, including 21 of Sri Lanka's 45 endemic species, amongst them rare snakes and frogs. Many of the reserve's bountiful population of **insects** are yet to be classified, although you're likely to see various colourful spiders and enormous butterflies, while giant millipedes are also common.

Sinharaja has one of Sri Lanka's richest **bird** populations: 21 of the country's 26 endemic species have been recorded here (although some can only be seen in the reserve's difficult-to-reach eastern fringes). Unfortunately, the density of the forest and the fact that its birds largely inhabit the topmost part of the canopy means that actually seeing them is extremely difficult, and probably beyond the patience of all but committed birders – the tantalizing chirrupings of myriad invisible birds are an inevitable accompaniment to any visit to the reserve. It's much easier to spot birds around the edges of the forest, in the agricultural lands that bound the park. Less welcome inhabitants of the park are **leeches** (see p.69), abundant after rain.

Visiting the reserve

The closest starting points for visits to Sinharaja are **Deniyaya**, on the eastern side of the reserve, and **Kudawa**, on its northern edge (for full details of both these places, see below). It's also possible to arrange visits to the reserve from various guesthouses in Ratnapura or with a couple of tour operators in Unawatuna, though it will be a long day by the time you've driven to and from the reserve.

Sinharaja is open daily from 7am to 6pm and entrance costs Rs.660, plus Rs.400 per group for an obligatory guide (unless you bring your own), who will lead you on walking tours of up to three hours, depending on how taxing a hike you want (and how big a tip you want to produce). There are no driveable roads in the reserve, so you have to walk (which is, indeed, one of the pleasures of a visit, especially if you're fed up with rattling around national parks in smelly jeeps).

There are two **entrances** to the reserve. The most popular approach is via the northern entrance at **Kudawa**, which is closest to Ratnapura, and to the various hotels around Kalawana. The less frequently used eastern entrance to the reserve is at **Mederipitiya**, about 11km east of Deniyaya; the rainforest here is more dramatic than on the Kudawa side, though it makes bird-spotting correspondingly more difficult. The road from Deniyaya ends just short of the reserve, from where it's a pleasant one-end-a-half-kilometre walk through tea plantations, with Sinharaja sprawling impressively across the hills ahead. The path isn't signposted and can be slightly confusing (go right at the fork by the gravestones near the beginning).

Perhaps more than anywhere else in Sri Lanka, what you get out of a visit to Sinharaja relies on having a good **guide** – the rainforest is dense and difficult to decipher and, without skilful interpretation, can simply look to the uneducated like an awful lot of very big trees. Many of the reserve's guides speak very little English, although some may be able to turn up some interesting birdlife even so. A fail-safe option is to sign up for a tour with Bandula or Palitha Ratnayake, based at the *Sinharaja Rest* in Deniyaya (see p.308).

Kudawa

The village of **KUDAWA** is the most popular base for visiting Sinharaja. There's a better range of accommodation in the area on this side of the reserve, including a couple of tempting top-end options, but it's more difficult to reach by public transport, so is likely to be of interest mainly to those with their own vehicle. If you're using public transport, take one of the frequent **buses** from Ratnapura to **Kalawana** (15km north of Kudawa), from where there are infrequent (around four daily) buses to Kudawa itself.

Accommodation on this side of the reserve can be found in Kudawa itself and in the nearby villages of **Weddagala**, about 10km from the reserve entrance, and **Koswatta**, a further 10km back up the road back towards Kalawana.

Accommodation

Blue Magpie Lodge Kudawa ⓣ011-243 1872, ⓔbluemagpielodge@gmail.com. In a perfect location right next to the forest entrance in Kudawa, this functional place has rather plain and seriously overpriced rooms – though half- and full-board rates are much better value. ❺

Boulder Garden Koswatta ⓣ045-225 5812, ⓦwww.bouldergarden.com. Small and unusual (but also rather expensive, with rooms at around US$250) eco-resort with rustic rooms in a captivating natural setting, complete with the promised boulders and patches of rainforest. There's also fine dining in a striking open-air restaurant underneath a huge rock overhang, a (very shallow) swimming pool, and plenty of interesting walks in the surrounding jungle. ❾

Martin Wijesinghe's Guest House 3km from Kudawa ⓣ045-490 0863. Long-established guesthouse run by a knowledgeable former Sinharaja ranger, with a few simple but clean rooms and a convenient location just a few kilometres from the reserve entrance. ❸

Rainforest Edge Weddagala ⓣ045-225 5912, ⓦwww.rainforestedge.com. This striking eco-lodge offers a beautiful (if pricey) base for visits to Sinharaja. Perched atop a hill, with sweeping views, the thatched, orange-coloured buildings look vaguely like a dislocated African bush village. It's a completely mod-con-free area, with no TVs, a/c or phones, while rooms have a bright, ethnic look and lovely open-air bathrooms with solar-powered hot water. ❾

Singraj Rest Koswatta ⓣ045-225 5201. Moribund place, with adequate but slightly shabby and overpriced modern rooms. ❹

Deniyaya

The small town of **DENIYAYA** offers an alternative base for visiting Sinharaja if you haven't got your own vehicle; it can be reached either from Galle or Matara on the south coast or from Ratnapura to the north (although bus services are surprisingly skimpy). Buses arrive at the **bus station**, right in the middle of town; there are a couple of **banks** close by with ATMs, including the Commercial Bank (Visa and MasterCard) and People's Bank (Visa only). **Places to stay** are extremely limited. *Sinharaja Rest*, 500m north of the bus station (Ⓣ041-227 3368; ❷) has six simple but comfortable rooms and organic food. It's owned and managed by local guides Bandula and Palitha Ratnayake, who run day-trips to Sinharaja for Rs.2000 per person (including entrance fees), entering the reserve through Mederipitiya and walking 12–14km. Shorter trips can also be arranged, as can longer excursions, such as the seven-hour hike over to Kudawa or the two-day (27km) trek across the entire reserve to Lion Rock. Alternatively, the *Rest House*, 500m south of the bus station (Ⓣ041-227 3600; ❷) has large, bare and rather dimly lit rooms – all fairly shabby and basic, though fine views of hills from the veranda partly compensate. A more comfortable but expensive option is the modern *Sathmala Ella Rest* (Ⓣ041-227 3481; ❹), 4km from Deniyaya on the Mederitpitiya road. You can also arrange visits to the reserve from here.

Moving on from Deniyaya, there are a few direct buses to **Matara** and **Galle**. Otherwise change at **Akuressa** (every 30min; 1hr 30min), from where there are frequent onward connections to both these towns. Transport northwards is much more infrequent, with about four buses to **Pelmadulla** and **Ratnapura** daily.

4

The Cultural Triangle

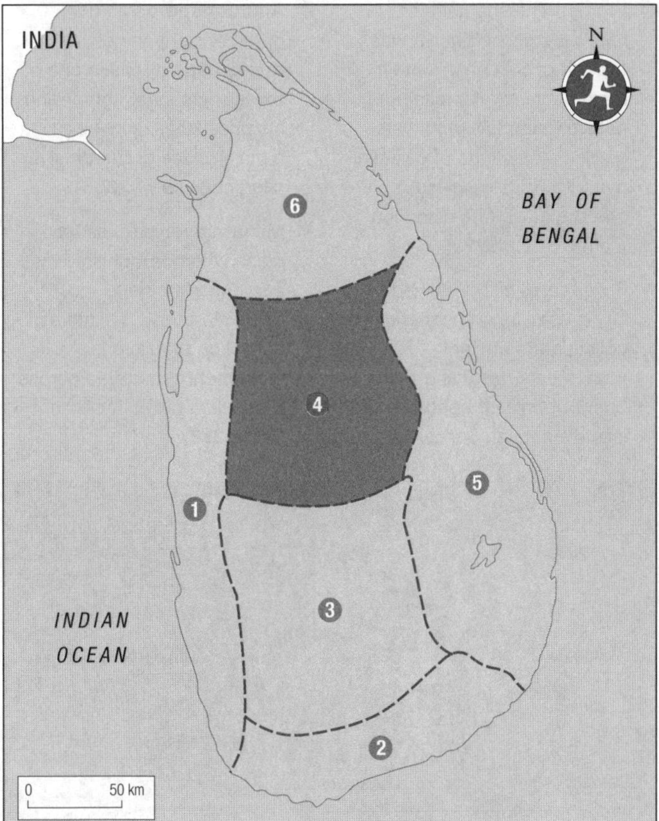
INDIA
N
BAY OF BENGAL
INDIAN OCEAN
6
4
5
1
3
2
0
50 km

CHAPTER 4

Highlights

* **Dambulla** The atmospheric rock temples of Dambulla are a veritable Aladdin's cave of Buddhist art, packed with hundreds of statues and decorated with the finest murals in the country. **See p.322**

* **Sigiriya** The spectacular rock outcrop of Sigiriya was the site of Sri Lanka's most remarkable royal capital and palace, complete with water gardens, paintings of celestial nymphs, 1300-year-old graffiti and the paws of a giant lion statue. **See p.329**

* **Polonnaruwa** This ruined city preserves an outstanding collection of ancient monuments, testifying to its brief but brilliant period as the island's capital. **See p.336**

* **"The Gathering", Minneriya National Park** Asia's largest gathering of wild elephants, as three hundred or more pachyderms congregate at the retreating waters of the Minneriya Tank during the northern dry season. **See p.352**

* **Anuradhapura** The ruins of the ancient city of Anuradhapura remain one of the island's most compelling historical sites, as well as a major place of Buddhist pilgrimage. **See p.356**

* **Mihintale** Revered as the place where Buddhism was introduced to the island, Mihintale boasts an interesting collection of religious monuments scattered across a beautiful hilltop location. **See p.373**

▲ Vatadage, Polonnaruwa

4

The Cultural Triangle

North of Kandy, the tangled green hills of the central highlands tumble down into the plains of the **dry zone**, a hot and denuded region covered in thorny scrub and jungle and punctuated by isolated mountainous outcrops which tower dramatically over the surrounding flatlands. The region's climate is a harsh contrast of famine and plenty, with brief monsoonal deluges separated by long periods of drought during which temperatures, untempered by the sea breezes which soften the climate on the coast, can rise to parching extremes.

Despite this unpromising natural environment, these northern plains served as the cradle of Sri Lankan civilization for almost two thousand years, from the establishment of the first Sinhalese capital in about 400 BC to the final abandonment of the city of Polonnaruwa in the thirteenth century. Much of this early civilization was centred around the great monastic city of Anuradhapura, one of the finest urban centres of its age, whose monumental **dagobas** were excelled in scale in the ancient world only by the Egyptian pyramids, and whose large-scale irrigation works – centred on the string of enormous man-made reservoirs, or "**tanks**", which still dot the region – succeeded in transforming the city's unpromisingly barren hinterland into an enormous rice bowl capable of supporting a burgeoning population.

Despite its glorious achievements, however, this early Sinhalese civilization lived under the constant threat of attack from southern India. Over the centuries countless Indian adventurers turned to their wealthy island neighbour for a spot of plunder, and although the Sinhalese periodically freed themselves from the Indian yoke, ultimately the pressure of interminable warfare destroyed the civilization of northern Sri Lanka, leading to the destruction of Anuradhapura in 993 and the abandonment of Polonnaruwa three centuries later, after which the great cities of the northern plains were abandoned and reclaimed by the jungle until being rediscovered by the British in the nineteenth century. Although the modern economic and cultural life of Sri Lanka has now largely bypassed the region, its great religious monuments still serve as potent reminders of the golden age of Sinhalese culture, providing a symbol of cultural identity which goes far beyond the merely archeological.

The island's northern plains are now often referred to as the **Cultural Triangle**, the three points of this imaginary triangle being placed at the great Sinhalese capitals of Kandy (see Chapter 3), Anuradhapura and Polonnaruwa. In fact, this tourist-oriented invention presents a rather warped sense of the region's past, given that the history of Kandy is quite different and separate – both chronologically and geographically – from that of the earlier capitals. The

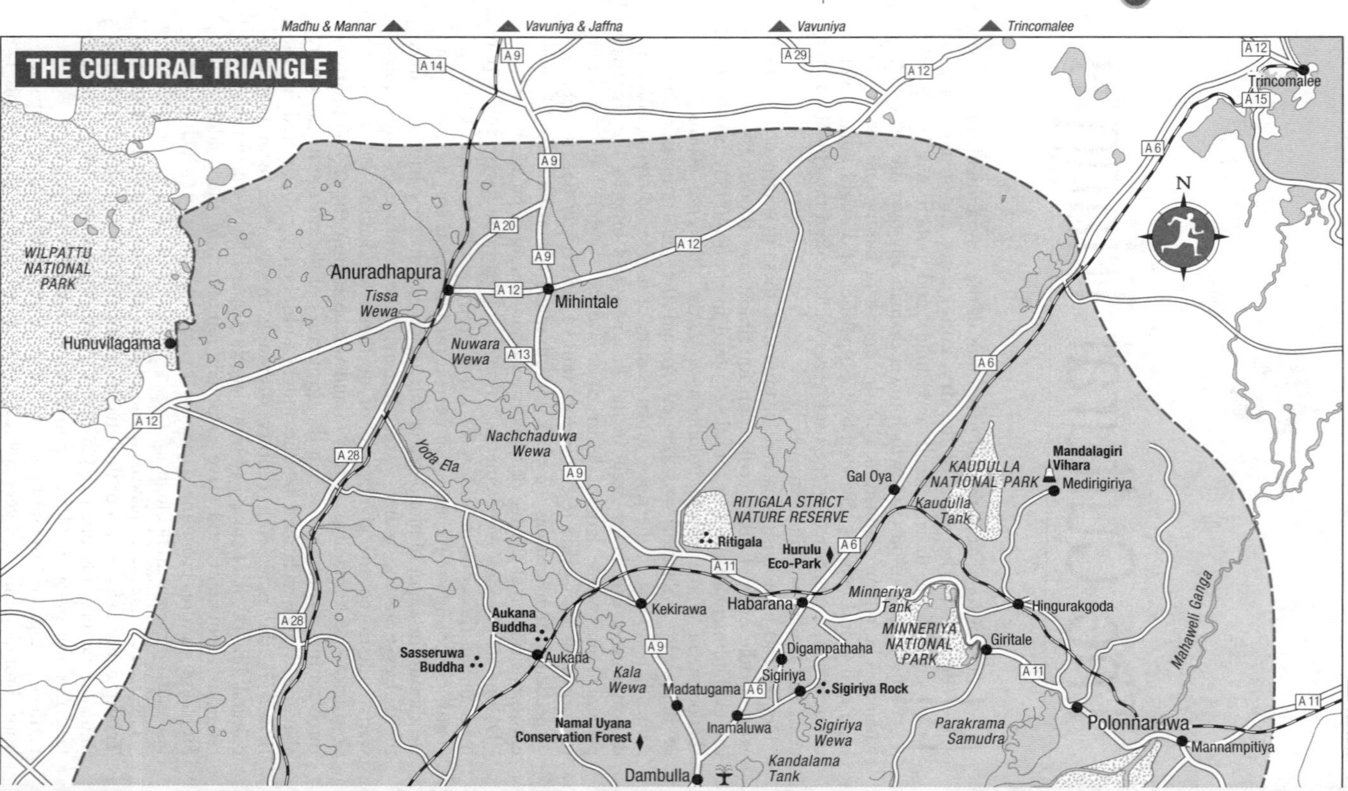
THE CULTURAL TRIANGLE
Madhu & Mannar
Vavuniya & Jaffna
Vavuniya
Trincomalee
Trincomalee
N
WILPATTU NATIONAL PARK
Hunuvilagama
Anuradhapura
Tissa Wewa
Mihintale
Nuwara Wewa
Nachchaduwa Wewa
Yoda Ela
RITIGALA STRICT NATURE RESERVE
Ritigala
Hurulu Eco-Park
Gal Oya
KAUDULLA NATIONAL PARK
Kaudulla Tank
Mandalagiri Vihara
Medirigiriya
Minneriya Tank
MINNERIYA NATIONAL PARK
Hingurakgoda
Giritale
Mahaweli Ganga
Habarana
Kekirawa
Aukana Buddha
Sasseruwa Buddha
Aukana
Kala Wewa
Madatugama
Digampathaha
Sigiriya
Sigiriya Rock
Sigiriya Wewa
Inamaluwa
Namal Uyana Conservation Forest
Dambulla
Kandalama Tank
Parakrama Samudra
Polonnaruwa
Mannampitiya
Puttalam
Batticaloa
A9
A14
A29
A12
A15
A6
A20
A13
A28
A11

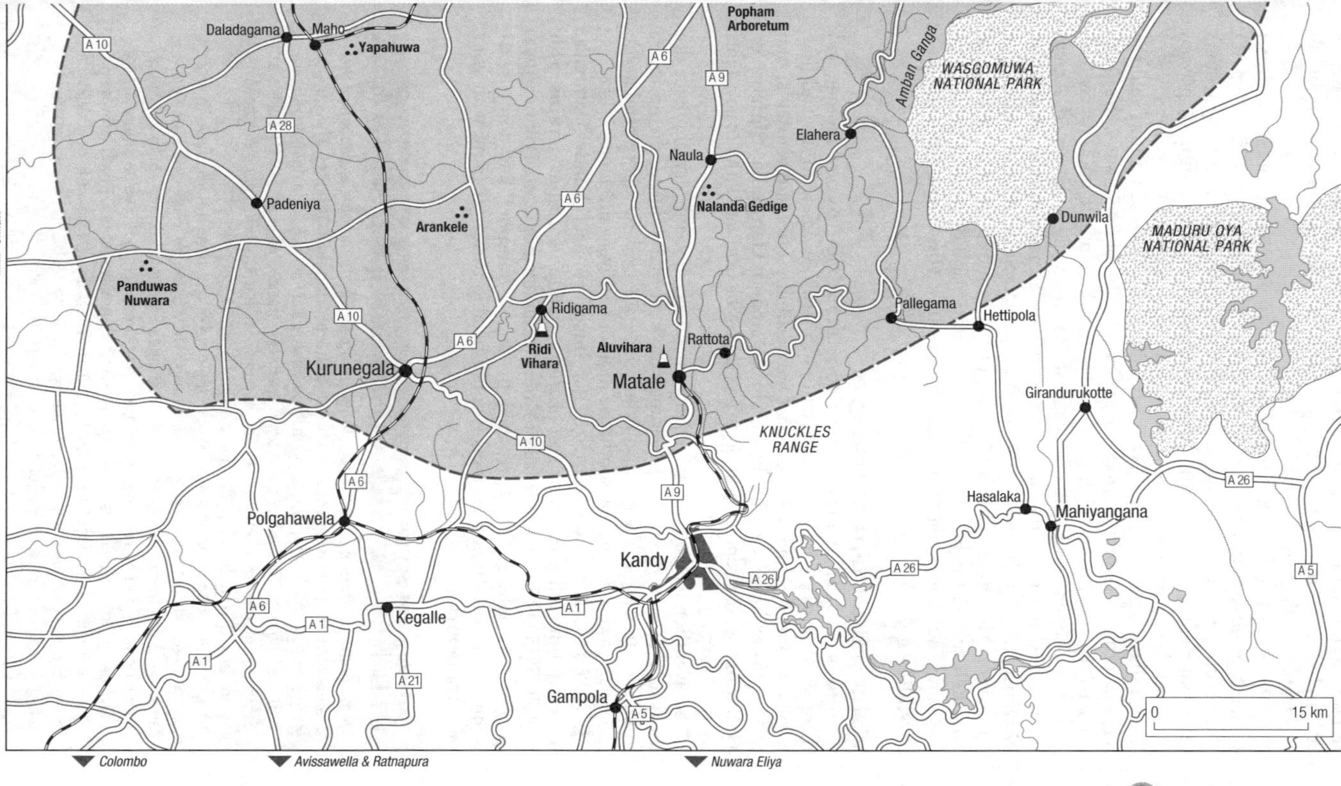
Daladagama
Maho
Yapahuwa
Popham Arboretum
Amban Ganga
WASGOMUWA NATIONAL PARK
Elahera
Naula
Nalanda Gedige
Padeniya
Arankele
Dunwila
MADURU OYA NATIONAL PARK
Chilaw
Panduwas Nuwara
Ridigama
Ridi Vihara
Aluvihara
Rattota
Pallegama
Hettipola
Kurunegala
Matale
Girandurukotte
KNUCKLES RANGE
Hasalaka
Mahiyangana
Polgahawela
Kandy
Kegalle
Gampola
A 10
A 28
A 6
A 9
A 1
A 21
A 5
A 26
0
15 km
Colombo
Avissawella & Ratnapura
Nuwara Eliya

real southern point of the Cultural Triangle lies some distance north of Kandy at Dambulla, and the region is better described by its traditional name of the **Rajarata**, or "The King's Land".

At the spiritual heart of the Triangle lie the two great ruined cities of early Sri Lanka: **Anuradhapura**, capital of the island from the third century BC to 993 AD, and its successor, **Polonnaruwa**, capital until the thirteenth century. The region's other outstanding attractions are the spectacular rock citadel of **Sigiriya**, perhaps Sri Lanka's single most extraordinary sight; the marvellous cave temples of **Dambulla**, a magical treasure box of Buddhist sculpture and painting; and the religious centre of **Mihintale**, scene of the introduction of Buddhism to the island.

There's far more to the Cultural Triangle than these highlights, however. The region is peppered with other intriguing but relatively little-visited ancient monuments, including the abandoned cities of **Yapahuwa** and **Panduwas Nuwara**; the great Buddha statues of **Aukana** and **Sasseruwa**; the absorbing temples of **Aluvihara** and **Ridi Vihara**; or the haunting forest monasteries of **Arankele** and **Ritigala**. And if you begin to tire of historic monuments, there are natural attractions aplenty at the national parks: **Minneriya**, **Kaudulla** and **Wasgomuwa**.

Visiting the Cultural Triangle

The major Cultural Triangle sites are all relatively close to one another, and there are all sorts of different permutations in terms of where to stay and how to plan an itinerary through the area. One possibility is to base yourself at one of the many hotels or guesthouses in or around **Dambulla**, **Sigiriya** or **Habarana**, whose central location makes it possible to visit all the major sights on day-trips.

The **weather** in the Cultural Triangle is usually hot and dry, although the usual state of semi-drought is interrupted by heavy rains during the northeast monsoon (usually at their worst from Nov–Jan), and by lighter and more sporadic showers during the southwest monsoon in May and June.

In terms of public transport, regular **buses** connect Kandy, Dambulla, Sigiriya, Anuradhapura and Polonnaruwa, while occasional **trains** run from Colombo, via Kurunegala, to both Anuradhapura and Polonnaruwa. Almost everywhere can be reached by public transport, but doing so is often a time-consuming business – you'll be able to see far more with your own **transport**.

Cultural Triangle tickets

Most of the principal sights in the Cultural Triangle (with the notable exception of the Dambulla rock temples) are covered by the **Cultural Triangle (CT) ticket**. This covers seven sites – Anuradhapura, Sigiriya, Polonnaruwa, Nalanda, Medirigiriya, Ritigala and the Dambulla Museum – plus various places in Kandy. You can buy CT tickets at Sigiriya, Polonnaruwa, Anuradhapura, and also at the Cultural Triangle offices in Kandy and Colombo (see p.234 and p.118).

Tickets are valid for fourteen days from the date of first use, and you have to start using them within three months of purchase. They currently **cost** US$50; children aged 5–12 pay half of this (and also get half-price admission on tickets to individual sites); under 5s get in free. Buying a combined ticket offers good value compared to purchasing individual tickets at each site (tickets to Anuradhapura, Polonnaruwa and Sigiriya, for instance, cost US$25 each). Unfortunately, the CT ticket is only valid for one day's entry at each site – a particularly frustrating restriction at Anuradhapura, which needs at least a couple of days to be explored fully.

Principal trains in the Cultural Triangle

Note that train timetables are subject to constant change, so if possible it's always best to check latest departure times before travelling. For details of trains **from Colombo to Anuradhapura and Polonnaruwa**, see p.120. All the following trains also call at **Kurunegala**.

Anuradhapura	05.00	06.37*	08.40	14.15	23.40
Colombo	10.05	10.20	14.00	19.00	04.45

*inter-city express

Polonnaruwa	08.15	20.15	22.15
Colombo	16.00	04.15	04.52

North of Kandy: Matale to Ridi Vihara

From Kandy, most visitors heading for the Cultural Triangle plough straight up the main road north to Dambulla, Sigiriya and beyond. If you have your own transport, however, there are several interesting sites en route. Two of these – the famous monastery of **Aluvihara** and the wonderful little temple at **Nalanda** – are right on the main highway, and easily visited, while the fascinating monastery of **Ridi Vihara** is just a short drive westwards towards Kurunegala.

The main road between Kandy and Dambulla is also littered with innumerable **spice gardens**. The temperate climate of the region – halfway in altitude between the coastal plains and the hill country – offers ideal horticultural conditions, and if you're interested in seeing where the ingredients of Sri Lankan cuisine come from, now is your chance. Entrance is generally free, but you'll be expected to buy some spices at inflated prices in return for a look at the various plants and shrubs.

Around 25km north from Kandy, the bustling town of **MATALE** and its surrounding area is an important centre for the production of traditional Sri Lankan arts and crafts (Matale itself is famous for its lacquerware). At the north end of town, 600m west of the main road (and 1km south of Aluvihara), the **Matale Heritage Centre** (Mon–Sat 9am–4.30pm) provides a showcase for local artisanal traditions. The centre was founded in 1960 by renowned designer Ena de Silva, who established a women's batik-making cooperative here; a carpentry shop and brass foundry came next, followed by a restaurant. The centre now provides work for 35 local villagers, turning out traditional crafts with a contemporary twist to designs by de Silva in a wide range of media. Its restaurant, **Aluvihara Kitchens** (ⓣ066-222 2404), serves up one of the area's most celebrated rice and curry spreads (Rs.1000 per head) featuring around 25 dishes, though unfortunately you'll need to pre-order a couple of days in advance and be in a party of ten or more people to experience this gastro-fest.

Aluvihara

The monastery of **Aluvihara** (Rs.200) lies about 2km north of Matale, right next to the main Kandy–Dambulla highway. Despite its modest size, Aluvihara is of great significance in the global history of Buddhism, since it was here that the most important set of Theravada Buddhist scriptures, the *Tripitakaya*, or "Three Baskets", were first committed to writing. During the first five centuries of the religion's existence, the vast corpus of the Buddha's teachings had simply been memorized and passed orally from generation to generation. Around 80 BC, however, fears that the *Tripitakaya* would be lost during the upheaval caused by repeated South Indian invasions prompted the industrious King Vattagamani Abhaya (who also created the Dambulla cave temples and founded the great Abhayagiri monastery in Anuradhapura) to establish Aluvihara, staffing it with five hundred monks who laboured for years to transcribe the Pali-language Buddhist scriptures onto ola-leaf manuscripts. Tragically, having survived almost two thousand years, this historic library was largely destroyed by British troops when they attacked the temple in 1848 to put down a local uprising.

The heart of the complex consists of a sequence of **cave temples**, tucked away in a picturesque jumble of huge rock outcrops and linked by flights of steps and narrow paths between the boulders. The caves are relatively modern in appearance and of limited artistic merit, but the setting is atmospheric. From the first temple (home to a ten-metre-long sleeping Buddha), steps lead up to the main level, where a second cave temple conceals another large sleeping Buddha and various pictures and sculptures demonstrating the lurid punishments awaiting wrongdoers in the Buddhist hell – a subject which seems to exert a ghoulish fascination on the ostensibly peace-loving Sinhalese.

To the left of the second temple, further steps lead up to another cave temple behind, devoted to the great Indian Buddhist scholar **Buddhaghosa**, who worked at Anuradhapura during the fifth century AD (though there's no evidence that he ever visited Aluvihara); a golden Buddhaghosa statue from Thailand stands outside. From here, a final flight of steps leads up past a bo tree to the very top of the complex, where a dagoba and terrace offer fine views across to the grand hills in the distance.

Just up the hill to the left of the temple complex is a building (signed "International Buddhist Library and Museum") where a resident caretaker will pounce on you and scribble your name messily on a piece of ola leaf in return for a donation – a rather sad come-down from the monastery's days as the world's greatest repository of Buddhist learning.

Aluvihara is easily reached by public transport: any **bus** heading north from Kandy to Dambulla goes right past the entrance; alternatively, take the train from Kandy to Matale and then a tuktuk.

Nalanda

Some 25km north of Matale, and a kilometre east of the main highway to Dambulla, stands the **Nalanda Gedige**, a little gem of a building and one of the most unusual monuments in the Cultural Triangle. The gedige (Buddhist image house) occupies a scenic location overlooking a tank, with fine views of the steep green surrounding hills – it originally stood nearby at a lower level amongst paddy fields, but was meticulously dismantled and reconstructed in its present location in 1980, when the Mahaweli Ganga hydro-electricity project led to its original site being flooded. The gedige is named after the great Buddhist university at Nalanda in northern India, though its origins remain mostly shrouded in mystery – different sources date it anywhere between the seventh and twelfth centuries. According to tradition, it's claimed that Nalanda is located at the exact centre of Sri Lanka, although a glance at any map shows that it's actually rather closer to the west coast than the east.

The gedige is pure South Indian in style, and looks quite unlike anything else in Sri Lanka. Constructed entirely of stone, it's laid out like a Hindu temple, with a pillared antechamber, or *mandapa* (originally roofed), leading to an inner shrine which is encircled by an ambulatory. There's no sign of Hindu gods, however, and it appears that the temple was only ever used as a Buddhist shrine.

The **main shrine** is entered through a fine square stone door flanked by beautifully carved (though eroded) columns with an architrave comprising two elephants and a line of miniature buildings. To the side, the southern tympanum of the unusual horseshoe-shaped roof features a carving of Kubera, the god of wealth, seated on a lotus pedestal, and the other walls are also richly carved, with many small faces in roundels. The carvings are now much eroded, although if you look carefully you may be able to find the erotic tantric carving which adorns the southern face of the base plinth on which the entire gedige stands – the only example in Sri Lanka of a typically Indian sculptural motif. The brick base of a ruined (but much more modern) dagoba stands close by.

Entrance is included as part of the Cultural Triangle ticket (see p.314); otherwise it costs a pricey US$5. The site is open-access, so if there's no one around checking tickets you can just walk in. Any **bus** from Kandy to Dambulla will drop you at the turn-off to the temple, from where it's a ten-minute walk.

Ridi Vihara

Tucked away in beautiful rolling countryside 15km west of the Kandy–Dambulla highway, roughly equidistant between Matale and Kurunegala, the cave temple of **Ridi Vihara** is well worth hunting out if you have your own transport. According to legend (though it may be no more than that), Ridi Vihara, or "Silver Temple", was built by the legendary King Dutugemunu (see p.362). Dutugemunu lacked the money to complete the great Ruvanvalisaya dagoba at Anuradhapura until the discovery of a rich vein of silver ore at Ridi Vihara allowed the illustrious king to finish his masterpiece – he expressed his gratitude by creating a temple at the location of the silver lode.

The vihara is hidden away behind a small monastery. Bear left as you enter the complex, past the bo tree and the messy modern temple buildings. The first building of interest, right up against a small rock outcrop on the left, is the **Varakha Valandu Vihara** ("Jackfruit Temple"), an exquisite little Hindu shrine that's strikingly South Indian in style. Dating from around the eleventh century, it was converted into a Buddhist sanctuary during the Kandyan period. The bases of the pillars are decorated with figures while inside the tiny shrine sits a small yellow Buddha,plus a few simple Kandyan-era paintings.

Beyond here, you pass through the wooden gate of the entrance pavilion and cross a simple courtyard to reach the main rock-cut temple, the **Pahala Vihara** (Lower Temple), entered from the right-hand side (the main doors to the shrine are usually locked). To the right as you enter is an exquisite ivory carving of five ladies, though sadly it's now barely visible behind a modern security grille. Inside, a huge sleeping Buddha lies to the left, in front of which is a platform inset with blue-and-white Dutch tiles, donated by a Dutch monk, showing pictures of Dutch village life along with a few biblical scenes – a sneaky bit of Christian proselytizing in the temple's most important Buddhist shrine. Amongst the weather-beaten statues at the far end of the temple, a delicate, sinuously reclining gold-clad Buddha from Burma stands out.

Behind the temple, steps lead up to the right to the eighteenth-century Upper Temple, or **Uda Vihara**, immediately behind – the work of another illustrious king, Kirti Sri Rajasinha (see p.231). The main chamber has an impressive seated Buddha set against a densely peopled background (the black figures are Vishnus), and a fine Kandyan-style moonstone, plus steps flanked by elephants. Next door is the small "**Cobra House**", above the entrance door to which is a painting of an elephant – a *trompe l'oeil* which on closer inspection is revealed to be composed of nine ladies in athletic positions. Inside are more Kandyan-era decorative murals of flowers and some fine wooden Buddhas, while outside (and to the right) sits a dagoba almost completely covered under another part of the overhanging rock.

Back at the entrance to the monastery, over a hundred steps, some cut into bare rock, lead up to a small restored **dagoba**, from which there are fine views across the surrounding countryside.

To reach the temple by public transport, take a **bus** from Kurunegala to **Ridigama** village (hourly; 45min), then either walk or take a tuktuk from the village for the two-kilometre trip to the temple.

Kurunegala

Busy and disorienting **KURUNEGALA** is the biggest town between Colombo and Anuradhapura, capital of the Northwest Province and an important commercial centre. The town also sits on a major junction on the roads between Colombo, Dambulla, Anuradhapura and Kandy, so you may well change buses here. There's no great incentive to visit Kurunegala in its own right, though it makes a convenient base for exploring the cluster of sights situated in the southwestern corner of the Cultural Triangle.

Kurunegala enjoyed a brief moment of eminence in Sri Lankan affairs during the late thirteenth and early fourteenth centuries, when it served as the capital of the Sinhalese kings under Bhuvanekabahu II (1293–1302) and Parakramabahu IV (1302–26), though hardly anything remains from this period. The present-day town is a tightly packed honeycomb of busy streets – a rude awakening if you're coming from the sleepy backwaters of the Cultural Triangle. Apart from a pretty stone **clocktower** and war memorial from 1922, which stands watch impassively over the hurly-burly of the

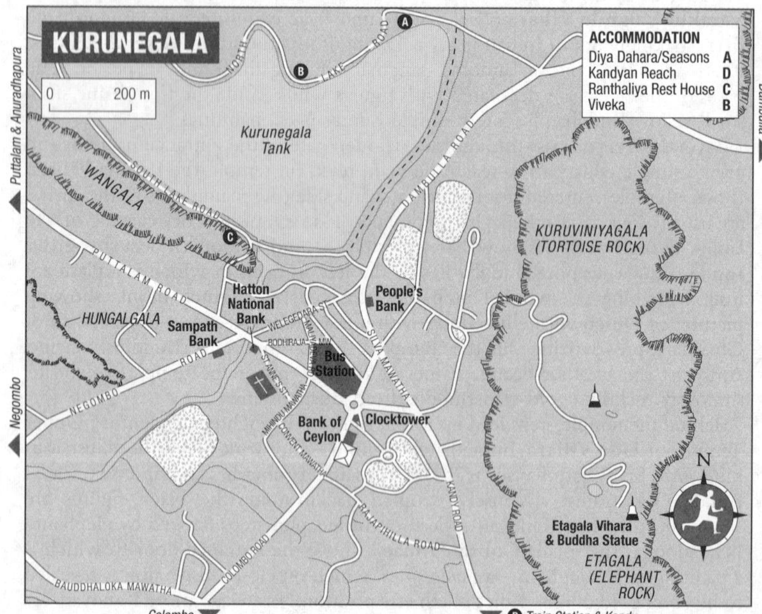

traffic-clogged centre, its main attractions are the breezy **Kurunegala Tank**, north of town, and the huge bare **rock outcrops** which surround the town, and lend the entire place a strangely lunar air. The inevitable legend professes that these are the petrified bodies of a strange menagerie of giant animals – including an eel, tortoise and elephant – who were threatening to drink the lake dry, only to be turned to stone by a demoness who inhabited the waters. If you've an hour or so to kill, it's worth walking or taking a tuktuk up to the enormous Buddha statue atop **Etagala** (Elephant Rock), immediately above town, from where there are fine views.

Practicalities

Buses arrive at the big new station bang in the town centre; the **train** station is just over a kilometre southeast of here (see p.120 & p.315 for timetables). **Leaving Kurunegala** there are regular buses to Anuradhapura (every 30min; 3hr), Colombo (every 20min; 2hr), Kandy (every 15min; 1hr 30min) and Negombo (every 20min; 2hr). There are numerous **banks** in town with ATMs accepting foreign cards and plenty of places around the bus station offering **internet** access.

Kurunegala's best place **to eat** is the shady garden restaurant at the *Diya Dahara*, which has a well-prepared selection of moderately priced standards. For more variety, make for the air-conditioned restaurant of the *Kandyan Reach*, whose broad-ranging menu stretches from burgers to burianis.

Accommodation

Most of Kurunegala's nicest places **to stay** are clustered around Kurunegala Tank, north of the town centre, but are more used to wedding parties than to foreign tourists.

Diya Dahara/Seasons 7 North Lake Rd ⓣ037-222 3452, ⓔdiyadahara@sltnet.lk. Straddling both sides of the road, with smarter, better-value rooms (with a/c and TV) above the huge, rather Italianate new *Seasons* wedding hall, plus rather pokier ones in the now-dwarfed *Diya Dahara* opposite – though some of the latter have lake views, and the garden restaurant is the nicest in town. *Diya Dihara* ❸, a/c ❹, *Seasons* ❹

Kandyan Reach Kandy Rd, 1km south of town ⓣ037-222 4218, ⓔkandyanreach@sltnet.lk. Though housed in a criminally ugly building on the main road, Kurunegala's biggest and poshest hotel has spacious, good-value rooms, all with a/c, TV and hot water, ranged around a pool (non-guests Rs.200). ❺

Ranthaliya Rest House South Lake Rd ⓣ037-222 2298. The closest place to the town centre with an attractive location, perched on the southern side of the lake with the terrace overlooking the water (a nice place for a sundowner). Rooms are comfortably furnished, if a bit old-fashioned, each with a private terrace and alarmingly pink bathrooms. ❸

Viveka 64 North Lake Rd ⓣ037-222 2897, ⓔvivekahotel64@sltnet.lk. Gracious old colonial house in a lovely dappled position close to the water, with lots of period furniture on the attractive veranda. Each of the four rooms is simple but homely, with TV and (optional) a/c. ❸, a/c ❹

North of Kurunegala

The little-visited area north of Kurunegala is home to an intriguing quartet of attractions: the abandoned cities of **Yapahuwa** and **Panduwas Nuwara**; the absorbing forest monastery of **Arankele**; and the beautiful Kandyan-era temple of **Padeniya**. Ridi Vihara (see p.317) is also easily accessible from the town. If you have your own transport, all of these sites could be visited in a leisurely day's excursion, either as a round-trip from Kurunegala, or en route to Anuradhapura. (If you don't want to pay for a car all the way to Anuradhapura, ask to be dropped at Daladagama, from where it's easy to pick up a bus.)

Panduwas Nuwara

Around 12km west of the main road from Kurunegala to Puttalam lie the ruins of **Panduwas Nuwara** (unrestricted access; free), the first capital of **Parakramabahu I** (see p.340), the royal adventurer who would later achieve lasting fame as perhaps the greatest ruler of Polonnaruwa. The city that Parakramabahu created at Panduwas Nuwara is often seen as a trial run for his spectacular achievements at Polonnaruwa, and although the individual remains are relatively underwhelming, the overall scale of the place is undeniably impressive, and exudes an Ozymandias-like aura of vanished splendour.

The ruined city sprawls over an area of several kilometres. At its centre lies the **citadel**, surrounded by wide walls protected by a (now dried-up) moat and pierced by just a single, east-facing entrance – the scale of the fortifications suggests that, at this stage in his career, Parakramabahu felt far from safe. Inside the citadel, facing the entrance, the main ruin is the two-tiered **royal palace**, reminiscent in layout of Parakramabahu's royal palace at Polonnaruwa, although far less of it survives. At the top of the steps on the left stands a table inscription recording a visit by the bumptious Nissankamalla (see box, p.345) to watch a dancing display. At the rear right-hand side of this terrace you can see the remains of an ingenious medieval latrine – a water channel leading into a well-like cesspit. The slight remains of a few further buildings around the palace have been neatly restored, but the rest of the citadel remains unexcavated, with the mounds of numerous of buildings still buried under established woodland.

South of the citadel, outside the walls, are the extensive remains of two **monasteries**. The first is some 200m south, with a ruined brick dagoba, bo tree enclosure (*bodhigara*) and the ruins of a pillared image house (only the Buddha's feet survive). Immediately south lies a second monastery, with a Tamil pillar inscription at its entrance, plus two more ruined dagobas and further monastic buildings. Further south still is a third, still-functioning monastery with an elegant Kandyan-style structure, with a walkway joined to a raised building. Driving to and from the site you'll pass the ruins of yet more dagobas and other buildings, pillars and walls, as well as a small **museum** (daily except Tues 9am–5pm; free) displaying finds from the site.

Buses run approximately every hour from Kurunegala to Chilaw, passing through Panduwas Nuwara village, from where it's a one-kilometre walk to the site – locals will point you in the right direction.

Padeniya Raja Mahavihara

Twenty-five kilometres northwest of Kurunegala, right in the centre of the village of **Padeniya**, the **Padeniya Raja Mahavihara** is one of Sri Lanka's most attractive Kandyan-era temples, and well worth a halt en route to Anuradhapura. The unusual main shrine is set on a small rock outcrop and enclosed by fine walls (topped by cute lion statues) which are covered by – but not connected to – the big wooden roof. The main **image house** is topped by a fine old wooden roof supported by around thirty beautifully carved wooden **pillars** – similar to those at the Embekke Devale near Kandy (see p.259). Panels on the pillars show various figures, including a double-headed swan, a lion, an elephant, a man smoking a pipe, a Kandyan drummer and (rather strangely for a Buddhist temple) a dancing girl. Further carved pillars support the roof of the ambulatory which, unusually for a Kandyan-style temple, completely encloses the principal **shrine**, which houses various Buddha images and a protective Vishnu.

Next to the shrine sits a beautiful pond and an imposing three-tiered bo tree platform – the roots of the bo tree have worked their way down through the bricks with marvellously photogenic results.

Arankele

Hidden away on a forested hillside at the end of a rough side road some 24km north of Kurunegala lie the remains of the sixth-century forest hermitage of **Arankele**. The jungle-shrouded ruins are hugely atmospheric and seldom visited by tourists, thanks to their remoteness and the difficulty of reaching them even with your own vehicle. A community of *pamsukulika* monks (see p.353) who have devoted themselves to a reclusive, meditative life still live at the monastery by the entrance to the site.

The **entrance** is deceptive: ignore the fine stone terrace and elaborate staircase to your left and instead go straight ahead, following the covered walkway which leads to the monks' quarters – a wooden bell-chime hung at the start of the walkway is used to mark the various stages of the monastic day. Continue straight ahead through the monks' quarters, shortly beyond which the path enters a stretch of beautifully unspoilt dry tropical forest (there are plenty of other paths branching off if you want to explore further). After about 500m you'll reach a small clearing, where an old stone monastic building nestles under a rock. Go round to the right of this to reach the beginning of the remarkable **meditation walkway**: a long, perfectly straight stone walkway, punctuated by small flights of steps, its geometrical neatness making a strange contrast with the wild forest through which it runs. This leads after 500m past the tumbled remains of a small hypostyle chamber, like a miniature Stonehenge, and then, after another 250m, to a large **clearing** with the extensive remains of various monastic buildings and a beautiful lily-filled tank. The remains are difficult to interpret (there are no guides at – or printed guides to – the site), but the magical remoteness and unspoilt forest setting are sufficient attractions in themselves.

Yapahuwa

Midway between Kurunegala and Anuradhapura lies the magnificent citadel of **Yapahuwa** (daily 8am–6pm; Rs.500), built around a huge granite rock rising almost a hundred metres above the surrounding lowlands. Yapahuwa was one of the short-lived capitals established during the collapse of Sinahalese power in the thirteenth century and served as the capital of **Bhuvanekabahu I** (ruled 1272–84), who transferred the capital here from the less easily defensible Polonnaruwa in the face of recurrent attacks from South India, bringing the Tooth Relic (see p.243) with him. The move proved to be of no avail, however. In 1284, Yapahuwa was captured by the army of the South Indian Pandyan dynasty, who carried off the Tooth Relic to Madurai in Tamil Nadu. Following its capture, Yapahuwa was largely abandoned and taken over by monks and hermits, and the capital was moved to Kurunegala.

The site's outstanding feature is the marvellous **stone stairway**, which climbs with Maya-like steepness up to the palace – its neck-cricking gradient was apparently designed to protect the Tooth Relic at the top from potential attackers. Its top flight is a positive riot of decoration. Statues of elephants, *makara toranas*, dwarfs, goddesses and a pair of goggle-eyed stone lions flank the stairs, which are topped by a finely carved doorway and windows. Panels around the base and sides of each window are embellished with reliefs of dancers and musicians, one playing a Kandyan drum – the oldest pictorial record of Sri Lanka's most famous musical instrument. The quality of the craftsmanship, carving and materials (solid stone, rather than plebeian brick) is strikingly high – this doesn't look like the statement of a largely powerless king, although the decidedly Indian style pays unintentional tribute to the invaders who had driven Bhuvanekabahu here in the first place.

At the top of the stairs, the so-called **Lion Terrace** is deeply anticlimactic after the grandiose approach. This was the site of the Temple of the Tooth itself, though there's not much to see now. At the rear left-hand side of the terrace, a rough path, criss-crossed with trailing tree roots, leads to the **summit** of the rock – a breathless ten-minute scramble offering panoramic views.

The **base of the rock** is dotted with the extremely modest remains of the city and of Bhuvanekabahu's palace. You can see the foundations of various buildings dotted round the base of the steps, bounded by a limestone wall and surrounded by a dried-up moat, though these cover a surprisingly small area.

Just to the right of the site is a gorgeous old Kandyan-style wooden barn with a quaint belltower attached; it formerly housed a museum, sadly shut at the time of writing. Behind is a **cave temple**, its entrance projecting out from the rock outcrop, inside which are some extremely faded Kandyan-era frescoes – you can't really make anything out apart from vague colours – plus old plaster, wood and bronze Buddha images. The temple is usually locked, though someone from the ticket office will probably offer to open it for you. A resident guide (tip) waits at the ticket office.

Practicalities

Yapahuwa is 5km from **Maho** train station, which is served by fairly regular local **trains** from Kurunegala and by fast trains running between Colombo and Anuradhapura. Alternatively, catch any **bus** travelling between Anuradhapura and Kurunegala and get off at **Daladagama**, 8km west of the site. A round-trip in a tuktuk from either village will cost around Rs.350, including waiting time. The cheery new *Yapahuwa Paradise Resort* (Ⓣ060-297 5055, Ⓦwww.hotelyapahuwaparadise.com; ❻), 1.5km west of the site – complete with obligatory stone lions – makes a more luxurious base than any of the guesthouses in Kurunegala for exploring the local area. Its brightly decorated, comfortable rooms, in attractive white cottages dotted around a palm garden, all have air-conditioning, satellite TV and minibar, and there's an inviting pool (non-guests Rs.300).

Dambulla and around

The dusty little town of **DAMBULLA** is famous for its remarkable **cave temples** – and given that they stand close to an important junction of the Colombo–Trincomalee and Kandy–Anuradhapura roads, you're almost certain to pass right by. The temples here are little masterpieces of Sinhalese Buddhist art: five magical, dimly lit grottoes which seem to glow with the rich reds and golds of the innumerable statues that fill every space and the paintings that cover every surface.

Dambulla's position close to the heart of the Cultural Triangle makes it a convenient base; there are a few passable guesthouses in town, and several tempting top-end hotels nearby. The **town** itself is one of the least attractive in the region, however, strung out along a single long, dusty and traffic-plagued main road. The centre is marked by the usual clocktower, north of which stretches the main run of shops, housed in a dispiriting string of ugly modern concrete buildings; to the south of the clocktower lies the town's bus stand, an anarchic wholesale **market** and, further south, most of its guesthouses.

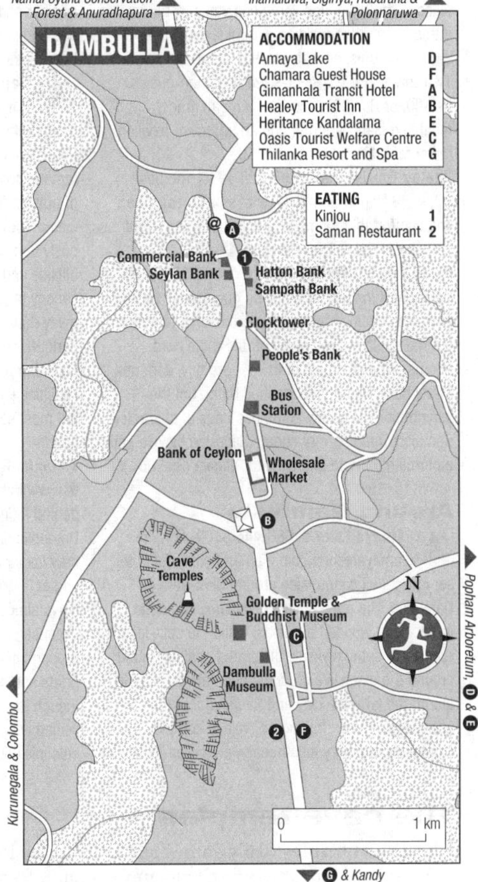

Arrival and information

Arriving in Dambulla by **bus**, you'll be deposited at the new bus terminal at the southern end of town, a Rs.70–100 tuktuk ride from the various guesthouses. The northern end of town has plenty of **banks** with ATMs accepting foreign cards; more easily accessible from the southern guesthouses is the Bank of Ceylon ATM in the wholesale market. There's speedy **internet** access (Rs.60 per hr) at Kopi Kade (daily 9am–8pm), at the northern end of town.

Accommodation and eating

There's no great choice of **accommodation** in Dambulla itself, and as all the town's options are strung out along the main road, traffic noise can be a problem – always try to get a room as far from the road as possible. The area immediately **around Dambulla** is home to a few enticing top-end places, while there are also accommodation options along the road to Sigiriya (see p.331) and Habarana (see p.351), none of which is much more than a half-hour drive from the cave temples.

All the guesthouses do meals, but the best **place to eat** in town is *Kinjou*, opposite the Commercial Bank, which serves up well-prepared Chinese dishes (mains around Rs.600), albeit in rather sterile surroundings. Closer to the guesthouses in the southern part of town, *Saman's Restaurant* offers a good-value rice and curry spread of up to twelve dishes (Rs.300), as well as a few Western mains.

Dambulla

Chamara Guest House ⓣ066-228 4488. Rooms here are clean and reasonably comfortable, if a bit small and relatively overpriced. It's worth paying an extra Rs.300 for one in the attractive main building, set back from the road. A/c is planned. ❷–❸

Gimanhala Transit Hotel ⓣ066-228 4864, ⓔgimanhala@sltnet.lk. The smartest place in the town, and very good value, set in an attractive modern building with pleasantly large and cool rooms, all with a/c, hot water and satellite TV. There's also a decent-sized pool (non-guests Rs.400, or Rs.200 if you take a meal), free mountain bikes, internet and an attractive pavilion restaurant. ❺

Healey Tourist Inn ⓣ066-228 4940. The best-value cheapie in Dambulla, with small, neat, clean and comfortable rooms, one with hot water – but get a room away from the road. ❶–❷

Oasis Tourist Welfare Centre ⓣ066-228 4388. Dambulla's longest-established guesthouse has an enviable position, right opposite the cave temples but mercifully tucked away off the main road. Rooms – the cheapest in town – are tiny, dark and pretty basic (none has attached bath), but the labyrinthine old family home has bags of character. Can also organize very cheap guide-led bicycle and motorbike tours to Sigiriya and Ritigala (Rs.500). ❶

Around Dambulla

Amaya Lake ⓣ066-446 8100, ⓦwww.amayaresorts.com. Fun and colourful hotel, set in tranquil countryside around 9km from Dambulla. The main building occupies two huge interlocking wooden pavilions, while the split-level rooms are set in stylishly decorated chalets dotted around the extensive grounds; alternatively, stay in one of the lakeside clay and *kadjan* (palm thatch) eco-lodges in the "traditional" village complex (complete with very inauthentic flat-screen TV, minibar and bathtub). Facilities include a huge pool and a luxuriantly thatched Ayurveda centre, plus boat trips on the lake. ❼

Heritance Kandalama ⓣ066-555 5000, ⓦwww.heritancehotels.com. Located around 9km from Dambulla on the beautiful Kandalama Lake, this is one of the country's most famous hotels, and ranks amongst the finest works of outstanding Sri Lankan architect Geoffrey Bawa (see p.146). The hotel manages to be simultaneously huge but almost invisible, being built into a hillside and concealed under a carefully nurtured canopy of jungle growth, so that nature is never far away (bats fly up and down the corridors after dark). Rooms are stylishly furnished, with all mod cons, big picture windows and marvellous views. Facilities include three excellent restaurants, one of the most spectacular swimming pools on the island and the gorgeous Six Senses spa. ❽–❾

Thilanka Resort and Spa ⓣ066-446 8001, ⓦwww.thilankaresortandspa.lk. Discreetly set behind a fine mango grove about 4km south of Dambulla on the Kandy road, this boldly simple new luxury hotel and spa – all clean lines and right angles – is dominated by its dazzling pool, which flows almost into reception, and magnificent expanse of paddy. Bright and stylish rooms, in well-proportioned villas, feature eye-catching oversized prints and mod cons including TV and DVD players, though the design is a bit muddled – the floor-to-ceiling windows and spacious terraces and balconies open out onto obscured views. ❼

The cave temples

The **cave temples** (daily 7am–7pm; US$10) are located about 2km south of the town centre, cut out of an enormous granite outcrop which rises over 160m above the surrounding countryside and offers majestic views across the plains of the dry zone as far as Sigiriya, over 20km distant. The temples' origins date back to the days of **Vattagamini Abhaya** (also known as Valagambahu or Valagamba; reigned 103 BC and 89–77 BC). Vattagamini lost his throne to a group of Tamil invaders and was forced into hiding for fourteen years, during which time he found refuge in these caves. Having reclaimed his throne at Anuradhapura, Vattagamini had temples constructed here in gratitude for the hiding place the rock had offered him – the individual caves which now house the temples were created by building partition walls into the space beneath what was originally a single huge rock overhang. The cave temples were further embellished by Nissankamalla (1187–96; see box, p.345), while comprehensive restorations and remodellings were carried out by the **Kandyan kings** Senerath (1604–35) and Kirti Sri Rajasinha (1747–82), who also created the magnificent Cave 3 and commissioned many of the vast number of **murals** which now decorate the interiors. Most of what you now see dates from the reigns of these last two kings, although precise dating of individual paintings is made difficult, since these are traditionally repainted on a regular basis once their paintwork fades, and further changes and embellishments were added right through to the twentieth century.

The **entrance** to the site is right on the main road, just to the left of the Golden Temple (see p.327); buy your ticket from the booth at the back of the Rangiri Dambulla Development Foundation building, straight ahead as you enter the complex. It's a steep ten-minute climb up to the caves, which are concealed by a quaint white colonnaded walkway. Photography is permitted but footwear must be removed and shoulders and knees covered. If you have them, binoculars give a better view of the frescoes, while a torch is also useful.

It's best to visit the caves in reverse order, starting at the end (cave 5) and working backwards – this way you get to see the caves in gradually increasing degrees of magnificence, culminating in the wonderful cave 2.

Caves 4 and 5

The small and atmospheric cave 5, the **Devana Alut Viharaya** ("Second New Temple"), is the most modern of the temples, and unlike most of the site's other statues, which are fashioned from solid rock, the images here are made of brick and plaster. The main figure is a ten-metre reclining Buddha. On the wall behind his feet are paintings of a dark Vishnu flanked by Kataragama with his peacock to the right and Bandara (a local deity) to the left. To the right of the door (as you exit) is a mural of a noble carrying lotus flowers, perhaps the man who endowed the temple.

Cave 4, the **Paccima Viharaya** ("Western Temple" – although cave 5, constructed later, is actually further west), is relatively small. Multiple identical figures of seated Buddhas in the meditation posture sit around the walls, along with a few larger seated figures, one (curtained) under an elaborate *makara torana* arch. There's a small dagoba in the middle, whose cracked appearance is the consequence of a raid by thieves who broke in, believing the dagoba to contain the jewellery of Vattagamini Abhaya's wife, Queen Somawathie. As in cave 5, the walls are covered with pictures of Buddhas and floral and chequered decorative patterns, most of which were heavily repainted in the early twentieth century.

▲ Cave temple 3, Dombulla

Cave 3

Cave 3, the **Maha Alut Viharaya** ("Great New Temple") was constructed by Kirti Sri Rajasinha, and is on a far grander scale – the sloping ceiling reaches a height of up to 10m and gives the cave the appearance of an enormous tent, lined with over fifty standing and seated Buddhas. To the right of the entrance stands a statue of **Kirti Sri Rajasinha**, with four attendants painted onto the wall behind him. The meditating Buddha, seated in the middle of the cave, and the sleeping Buddha by the left wall, are both carved out of solid rock – an extraordinary feat in an age when every piece of stone had to be hacked off with rudimentary chisels.

The cave has several interesting **murals**. Two ceiling paintings show the future Buddha, Maitreya, preaching in a Kandyan-looking pavilion. In the first (which can be seen looking up from the entrance), he preaches to a group of ascetic disciples; in the second (to the right of the entrance) he addresses a gathering of splendidly adorned gods in the Tusita heaven, where he is believed to currently reside pending his arrival on earth roughly five billion years from now. To the left of the door as you exit (behind a pair of seated Buddhas) is another interesting mural showing a picture of an idealized garden with square ponds, trees, elephants, cobras and Buddhas – a rather folksy, nineteenth-century addition to the original Kandyan-era murals.

Cave 2

Cave 2, the **Maharaja Vihara** ("Temple of the Great Kings"), is the biggest and most spectacular at Dambulla, an enormous, sepulchral space measuring over 50m long and reaching a height of 7m. Vattagamini Abhaya is credited with its creation, though it was altered several times subsequently and completely restored in the eighteenth century. The cave is named after the statues of two kings it contains. The first is a painted wooden image of **Vattagamini Abhaya** himself (just left of the door furthest away from the main entrance); the second is of **Nissankamalla** (see box, p.345), hidden away at the far right-hand end of the cave and almost completely concealed behind a large reclining Buddha – a rather obscure fate for this most vainglorious of Sinhalese kings.

The sides and back of the cave are lined with a huge array of Buddha statues. The main Buddha statue on the left of the cave, set under a *makara torana* in the *abhaya* ("Have No Fear") *mudra*, was formerly covered in gold leaf, traces of which can still be seen. To either side stand wooden statues of Maitreya (left) and Avalokitesvara or Natha (right), a rare touch of Mahayanist influence. Against the wall behind the main Buddha are statues of Saman and Vishnu, while images of Kataragama and Ganesh are painted onto the wall behind, an unusually varied contingent of gods within such a small space.

The ceiling and walls are covered in a fabulous display of **murals** – the finest in Sri Lanka. On the ceiling at the western end of the cave (to the left as you enter), Kandyan-style strip panels show pictures of dagobas at Sri Lanka's holy places and scenes from the Buddha's life (you can just make out the small white elephant which appeared in a dream to the Buddha's mother during her pregnancy, symbolizing the rare qualities of her future child). These murals pale in comparison, however, with the three adjacent ceiling panels showing the **Mara Parajaya** ("Defeat of Mara"), which depict the temptations meted out to the Buddha during his struggle for enlightenment at Bodhgaya. In the first he is shown seated under a beautifully stylized bo tree whilst crowds of hairy grey demons attack him with arrows (one technologically advanced devil even carries a musket), supervised by a magnificent Mara riding on an elephant. This attempt to break the Buddha's concentration having failed, the next panel, the **Daughters of Mara**, shows him being tempted by bevies of seductive maidens. The Buddha's triumph over these stupendous feminine wiles is celebrated in the next panel, the **Isipatana**, which shows him delivering his first sermon to a vast assembly of splendidly attired gods.

Across the cave, sitting in a wire-mesh enclosure in the right-hand corner, is a pot which is constantly fed by drips from the ceiling; it's said never to run dry, even in the worst drought.

Cave 1

Cave 1, the **Devaraja Viharaya** ("Temple of the Lord of the Gods") is named after Vishnu, who is credited with having created the caves; a Brahmi inscription outside the temple to the right commemorates the temples' foundation. Inside, the narrow space is almost completely filled by a fourteen-metre-long sleeping **Buddha**, carved out of solid rock, which preserves fine traces of beautiful gold gilding on his elbow (often covered). By the Buddha's head, images of Vishnu and other figures are hidden behind a brightly painted wooden screen (opened only during pujas), while a statue of the Buddha's most faithful disciple, Ananda, stands at his feet. The cave's unusual **murals** are quite badly eroded in places; some are said to be the oldest at the site, though constant repainting over the centuries has dulled any clear sense of their antiquity; the bright frescoes behind Ananda's head (including a weird tree sporting an Italian-style cherub) are clumsy twentieth-century additions.

Outside, next door, is a small, blue **chapel** dedicated to Kataragama; a bo tree stands opposite.

Golden Temple

At the bottom of the steps up to the cave temples stands the bizarre **Golden Temple**, a shamelessly kitsch building topped by a thirty-metre seated **golden Buddha**. The statue is extremely striking, if a little stern-looking (perhaps a mite perturbed at the money-grubbing circus of today's temple), and rather more artistic than the **Golden Temple Buddhist Museum** (daily 7am–9pm; entrance included in cave temples ticket) in the building below, entered through the golden mouth of an enormous lion-like beast. The museum itself is large but rather lacking in exhibits apart from some dull copies of the cave temple paintings, a few Buddhas donated from around the world and a sprinkling of other artefacts, none of them labelled.

Dambulla Museum

Some 100m south of the Golden Temple, the excellent **Dambulla Museum** (daily except Tues 7am–5pm; US$2, or free with CT ticket) offers a comprehensive and well-labelled chronological overview of the fascinating but little-known art of Sri Lankan painting, showing the development of the island's rock and wall paintings from the stick-figure scribbles of the Veddhas, through the frescoes of Sigiriya and on to the genre's golden era during the Kandyan period (from which most of Dambulla's murals date), ending with the European-influenced work of colonial-era artists such as George Keyt. The seven absorbing rooms consist of an expertly executed series of copies (on canvas) of paintings from cave temples, shrines and other locations around the island, gathering together under a single roof a compendium of Sri Lankan art from widely scattered and often remote and inaccessible locations; the copies manage to superbly mimic the cracked and flaking plaster effects of the older murals, and in many cases you get a much better view of the paintings here than in their original settings. With over

Moving on from Dambulla

Buses from Dambulla leave from the spacious bus station at the southern end of town. You can also flag down buses along the main road through Dambulla if you know where to stand and which bus to look out for (your guesthouse may be able to advise you), though it's probably easier just to head to the terminal. Few buses originate in Dambulla, however, so finding a seat can be a problem wherever you board. There are private minibuses plus a handful of CTB services to **Kandy** (every 20min; 2hr), **Colombo** (every 20min; 4hr), **Kurunegala** (every 20min; 2hr), **Habarana** (every 20min; 45min), **Anuradhapura** (every 30min; 1hr 45min) and **Polonnaruwa** (every 30min; 1hr 45min). There are also plenty of services to **Sigiriya** (every 30min; 30min); alternatively, take any northbound bus and get off at Inamaluwa Junction (every 15min; 15min), from where you can catch a tuktuk.

750 paintings in the collection, only a handful can be shown at any one time (which explains why artworks and explanation panels don't always match); the displays are refreshed every six months. A ground-floor gallery, with an exhibition on painting techniques and a display of archeological artefacts, is scheduled to open in 2010.

Around Dambulla

For a break from the ruins – and the tourists – there are a couple of little-visited areas of woodland in the countryside **around Dambulla** that provide for some tranquil sylvan walks. You'll need your own transport to reach them.

Popham Arboretum

Around 3km east of the cave temples, along the road to Kandalama Lake, the pleasantly cool **Popham Arboretum** (Rs.250) was the creation of British Old Etonian, former tea planter and keen dendrologist, Sam Popham. Dismayed by the destruction of Sri Lanka's dry-zone forests, Popham set up the arboretum in the 1960s as an experiment in reforesting an area of scrub jungle using minimal human interference. Popham's project was a success, and the arboretum now preserves over seventy species of tropical trees, including ebony, satinwood and *palu*, in a 36-acre woodland crisscrossed by a well-maintained network of paths. It's become popular with local wildlife too, with populations of mouse deer and the rare slender loris, as well as plenty of birdlife. You're welcome to explore the arboretum's colour-coded walking trails yourself, or book a daytime or evening **guided walk** (ⓣ072-406 2020; tip); these start from the arboretum's rustic **visitors' centre**, a modest bungalow originally designed as Popham's quarters by his friend Geoffrey Bawa – altogether a rather less grand affair than the architect's magnificent *Heritance Kandalama* hotel a few kilometres up the road (see p.324).

Namal Uyana Conservation Forest

Some 8km off the Dambulla to Anuradhapura road, around 15km from the cave temples, the Jathika Namal Uyana, or **Namal Uyana Conservation Forest** (daily 6am–6.30pm; Rs.500) is a remarkable natural phenomenon, preserving not just the largest extant forest of the indigenous **na tree**, or ironwood, in Sri Lanka but also a 550-million-year-old range of **rose quartz** hills, the biggest such deposit in South Asia, which rises lunar-like from the verdant woodland. The *na* is Sri Lanka's national tree, often planted close to Buddhist temples where its fragrant, four-petalled white flowers are a popular offering during puja. The forest, legend states, was planted by Devanampiya Tissa (see p.373), and later became a monastic retreat – various monastic remains are dotted around the site.

From the entrance, a path leads for about 1km though the forest, at its prettiest from April to June when the *na* trees are in bloom, to a ranger's hut, the ruins of a moss-covered **dagoba**, surrounded by a low wall decorated with pink-quartz stones, and a few other hard-to-decipher ruins. From here another trail climbs gently up the hillside (ask a ranger the way), the forest increasingly giving way to quartz outcrops; you'll pass a tiny waterfall, where the rock is stained almost black by the flowing water. It's about a ten-minute hike across the pinky-grey rockface above the tree canopy to the pleasantly breezy **summit** of the first low mountain, surmounted by a small pink fibreglass Buddha, from where there are magnificent views across to Dambulla.

Sigiriya

North of Dambulla, the spectacular citadel of **SIGIRIYA** rises sheer and impregnable out of the denuded plains of the dry zone, sitting atop a huge outcrop of gneiss rock towering 200m above the surrounding countryside. The shortest-lived but the most extraordinary of all Sri Lanka's medieval capitals, Sigiriya ("Lion Rock") was declared a World Heritage Site in 1982 and is the country's most memorable single attraction – a remarkable archeological site made unforgettable by its dramatic setting.

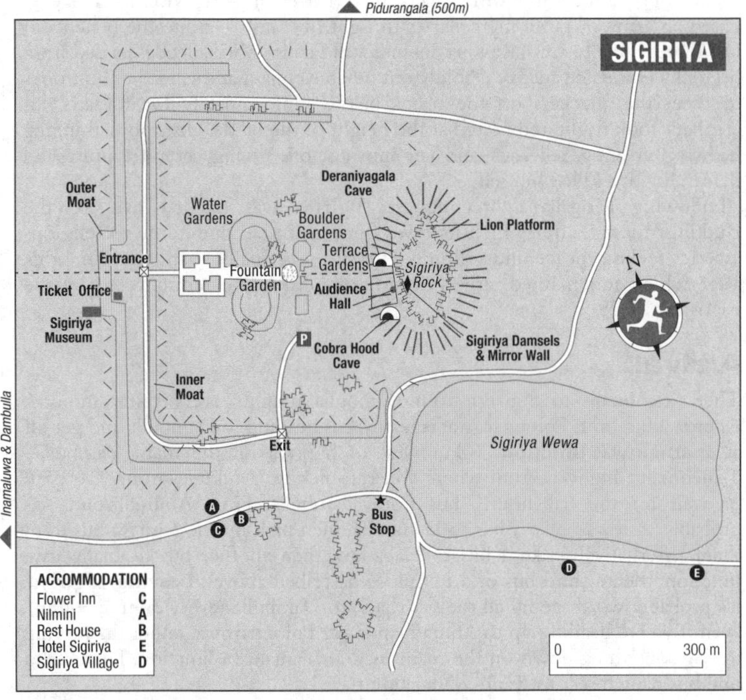

Some history

Inscriptions found in the caves that honeycomb the base of the rock indicate that Sigiriya served as a place of religious retreat as far back as the third century BC, when Buddhist monks established refuges here. It wasn't until the fifth century AD, however, that Sigiriya rose briefly to pre-eminence in Sri Lankan affairs, following the power struggle which succeeded the reign of **Dhatusena** (455–473) of Anuradhapura. Dhatusena had two sons, **Mogallana**, by the most pre-eminent of his various queens, and **Kassapa**, his son by a lesser consort. Upon hearing that Mogallana had been declared heir to the throne, Kassapa rebelled, driving Mogallana into exile in India and imprisoning his father. The legend of Dhatusena's subsequent demise offers an instructive illustration of the importance given to water in early Sinhalese civilization. Threatened with death if he refused to reveal the whereabouts of the state treasure, Dhatusena agreed to show his errant son its location if he was permitted to bathe one final time in the great Kalawewa Tank, whose creation he had overseen. Standing in the tank, Dhatusena poured its water through his hands and told Kassapa that this alone was his treasure. Kassapa, none too impressed, had his father walled up in a chamber and left him to die.

Mogallana, meanwhile, vowed to return from India and reclaim his inheritance. Kassapa, preparing for the expected invasion, constructed a new residence on top of the 200-metre-high Sigiriya Rock – a combination of pleasure palace and impregnable fortress, which he intended would emulate the legendary abode of Kubera, the god of wealth, while a new city was established around its base. According to tradition, the entire extraordinary structure was built in just seven years, from 477 to 485.

The long-awaited **invasion** finally materialized in 491, Mogallana having raised an army of Tamil mercenaries to fight his cause. Despite the benefits of his impregnable fortress, Kassapa, in an act of fatalistic bravado, descended from his rocky eminence and rode boldly out on an elephant at the head of his troops to meet the attackers on the plains below. Unfortunately for Kassapa, his elephant took fright and bolted at the height of the battle. His troops, thinking he was retreating, fell back and left him cut off. Facing certain capture and defeat, Kassapa killed himself.

Following Mogallana's reconquest, Sigiriya was handed over to the Buddhist monks, after which its caves once again became home to religious ascetics seeking peace and solitude. The site was finally abandoned in 1155, after which it remained largely forgotten until being rediscovered by the British in 1828.

Arrival

There are **buses** to Sigiriya from Dambulla roughly every thirty minutes. Approaching from Polonnaruwa, take any bus heading to Dambulla and get off at **Inamaluwa Junction**, 10km west of Sigiriya on the main Dambulla–Trincomalee highway, from where you can pick up a tuktuk (around Rs.350) or wait for the half-hourly bus from Dambulla. From Anuradhapura, it's probably easiest to take a bus to Dambulla, then pick up the Sigiriya bus from there (alternatively, take a bus to Habarana, then another bus to Inamaluwa Junction, then a third bus or a tuktuk as described above). **Leaving Sigiriya**, it's probably worth going all the way back to Dambulla (every 30min; 30min), even if you're heading up to Anuradhapura or Polonnaruwa, rather than trying to flag something down on the main road at Inamaluwa Junction. There's also one bus daily direct to Kandy (2hr 30min).

Accommodation and eating

There's only a small choice of **accommodation** in Sigiriya itself – government restrictions have kept development in the village mercifully in check. There's additional cheap accommodation, as well as a pair of top-end establishments (including one of Sri Lanka's most memorable places to stay), along the road to Inamaluwa Junction, plus a couple of good mid-range alternatives hidden away in the countryside north of Sigiriya en route to Habarana. It's likely that you'll **eat** where you're staying – if you do want to venture out, *Sigiriya Village* or the *Hotel Sigiriya* are the places to head for.

Sigiriya is also a convenient base for trips to **Minneriya** and **Kaudulla national parks**; most of the places below can arrange tours for around US$35 per half-day.

Sigiriya

Flower Inn ⓣ066-567 2197. Flowers are something of an obsession at this simple family guesthouse, with cosy and cheap little rooms set in the main house amidst a blossoming garden, plus bigger and more comfortable modern rooms out the back – all stuffed full of garish artificial flowers. Good home-cooking and very friendly owners, but not for anthrophobics. ❶–❷

Nilmini ⓣ066-567 0469, ⓔnilmini_lodge@yahoo.com. Neat little family-run guesthouse with friendly owners and a choice of accommodation ranging from cheap but clean fan rooms to one rather expensive a/c double with hot water. Reasonable home-cooking available, plus internet access (Rs.5 per min) and free bikes. ❶, a/c ❸

Rest House ⓣ066-223 1899, ⓦwww.ceylonhotels.lk. One of the better – and better-value – rest houses, this pleasantly old-fashioned place has the village's finest view of the rock, although service can be chaotic. Rooms have recently been upgraded, with TV and hot water, and a/c is available for a Rs.700 supplement. ❸

Hotel Sigiriya ⓣ066-223 1940, ⓦwww.serendibleisure.com. Appealing resort-style hotel, set in a rambling collection of attractive low-slung, Dutch-style buildings, with stylishly furnished and good-value a/c rooms (some with flat-screen TV and minibar), plus an Ayurveda centre and swimming pool (non-guests Rs.250). Strong and genuine emphasis is placed on environmental concerns, and there's a fascinating range of nature walks (with the resident naturalist), guided bike rides and local village tours. ❻

Sigiriya Village ⓣ066-492 7707, ⓔsigiriyavillage@sltnet.lk. Similar country-resort concept to the *Hotel Sigiriya*, but rather less characterful. Rooms (all a/c, some with TV and minibar) are large and comfortable, though expensive for what you get. There's also a pool (non-guests Rs.250) and Ayurveda centre. ❼

Around Sigiriya

Ancient Villas 2km east of Inamaluwa Junction ⓣ0773-971 921, ⓔancient@sltnet.lk. Very peaceful and rather rustic place – elephants occasionally cross the river at the end of the garden in the dry season – with accommodation in unusual but slightly shabby hexagonal cabanas. ❷

Elephant Corridor 4km east of Inamaluwa Junction, about 1.5km from the Sigiriya road ⓣ066-228 6950, ⓦwww.elephantcorridor.com. The proud owner of Sri Lanka's first US$1000-a-night suite may (just) have been superseded as the island's most expensive boutique hotel, but it still drips with a rare degree of (rather gimmicky) opulence – and boasts a mind-boggling roster of facilities. Its uniqueness lies in the dramatic wilderness of its setting – in 200 acres of dry-zone scrub with genuinely breathtaking views of Sigiriya. But for all their luxury and gadgetry, the suite-style rooms (each with private plunge pool) lack the finesse you might expect at rack rates starting at US$600. Ask about (regular) two-nights-for-the-price-of-one deals, which make it a more attractive proposition. ❾

Globetrotter Tourist Inn 1km east of Inamaluwa Junction ⓣ0777-801 813, ⓔrajaguna8@sltnet.lk. Pleasantly laid-back guesthouse in a rustic setting backing onto paddy fields, with immaculately clean, modern rooms (with hot water and optional a/c) and an open-air restaurant. Also offers cheap jeep tours. ❸

The Grand Tourist Holiday Resort 4km east of Inamaluwa Junction, at the beginning of the access road to *Elephant Corridor* ⓣ066-567 0136. A not at all grand but perfectly pleasant little guesthouse, with modern tiled rooms (all with hot water; some with a/c), a shady terrace restaurant, new Ayurveda centre and neat gardens. Not the best value, however. ❸, a/c ❹

Jetwing Vil Uyana 3km east of Inamaluwa Junction, 1km from the Sigiriya road ⓣ066-432 3583, ⓦwww.jetwing.com. The island's most audacious hotel project, born out of an ambitious scheme to create an artificial wetland out of abandoned agricultural land using ancient Sri Lankan irrigation techniques (combined with modern know-how). It's a fascinating (and very peaceful) environment, with its four habitats – marshland, paddy, patches of replanted forest, plus the central lake itself – attracting plenty of wildlife. Eco-credutials a ride, it's also a sumptuous place to stay: the luxuriantly thatched villas, modelled on traditional Sinhalese dwellings, house exquisite split-level suites, with teak floors and woven-rush walls, that combine state-of-the-art mod cons with the homeliness of an *über*-luxurious Japanese ryokan. Some have plunge pools, others are built on stilts over the lake, and all have private viewing decks. Other highlights include a magnificent infinity pool (non-guests Rs.1000), outstanding restaurant and a serene spa. ❾

Kassapa Lions Rock Digampathaha (8km from Sigiriya, 7km from Habarana) ⓣ066-567 7440, ⓦwww.kassapalionsrock.com. Very low-key new resort hotel with good-value, attractively kitted-out rooms (with TV, a/c and open-air showers) in concrete bungalows dotted across a well-manicured lawn. There's a pool, restaurant and bar but otherwise not much else to do except sit and admire the gorgeous views across the plains to Sigiriya and Pidurangala. ❺

Sigiri Holiday Inn 500m east of Inamaluwa Junction ⓣ060-266 0335. The best budget option in Inamaluwa, set in a lush little garden and with a mix of smart modern rooms with hot water and some older and cheaper ones without, plus a few family rooms – all very good value. ❷–❸

Teak Forest Audangawa (10km from Sigiriya and 8.5km from Habarana) ⓣ0777-742404, ⓦwww.theteakforest.com. Tranquil hideaway, well off the beaten track, in a sylvan setting overlooking wetlands teeming with birdlife. Accommodation is in stilted wooden chalets – rustic but comfortable – and the food is good. ❻

Sigiriya Rock

You'll need two to three hours to explore **Sigiriya Rock**; visit in the early morning or late afternoon, when the crowds are less dense and the temperature is cooler – late afternoon brings out the rock's extraordinary ochre colouration. The site is best avoided at weekends (especially Sun) and on public holidays, when its narrow staircases and walkways can become unbearably congested. The ascent of the rock is a stiff climb, but less gruelling than you might imagine when standing at the bottom of the towering cliff-face. Sufferers from vertigo might find some sections unpleasant.

The site divides into two sections: the **rock** itself, on whose summit Kassapa established his principal palace; and the area **around the base of the rock**, home to elaborate royal pleasure gardens, as well as various monastic remains pre-dating Kassapa's era. The entire site is a compelling combination of wild nature and high artifice – exemplified by the delicate paintings of the Sigiriya damsels which cling to the rock's rugged flanks. Interestingly, unlike Anuradhapura and Polonnaruwa, there's no sign here of large-scale monasteries or religious structures – Kassapa's Sigiriya appears to have been an almost entirely secular affair, perhaps a reflection of its unhallowed origins.

Buses stop in Sigiriya village near the south side of the rock, close to all the guesthouses and hotels, from which it's a ten-minute walk to the entrance. If you're coming **by car**, your driver will drop you by the entrance, and then park at the car park on the exit road south of the rock. **Tickets** can be purchased at the office diagonally opposite the main entrance gate. Entrance to Sigiriya is included in the CT ticket (see p.314); otherwise it costs the rupee-equivalent of US$25. The site is open from 7am to 6pm, though last entrance is at 5pm. Knowledgeable **guides** (or "tourist facilitators", as they have been rebranded) can usually be hired at the entrance, though there are still some pests around; it pays to ask a few questions before committing to anyone.

Although not yet open at the time of writing, the new **Sigiriya Museum**, close to the entrance, promises to be well worth visiting, with well-presented exhibits including a bird's-eye scale model of the rock, plus re-creations of the frescoes and a section of the Mirror Wall. Other items on show will include prehistoric skeletons and megalithic remains and artefacts discovered at the site. An **information centre** is also planned.

The Water Gardens

From the entrance, a wide and straight path arrows towards the rock, following the line of an imaginary east–west axis. This entire side of the city is protected by a pair of broad moats, though the Outer Moat is now largely dried out. Crossing the Inner Moat, enclosed within two-tiered walls, you enter the **Water Gardens**. The **first section** comprises four pools set in a square; when full, they create a small island at their centre, connected by pathways to the surrounding gardens. The remains of pavilions can be seen in the rectangular areas to the north and south of the pools.

Beyond here is the small but elaborate **Fountain Garden**. Features here include a serpentining miniature "river" and limestone-bottomed channels and ponds, two of which preserve their ancient fountain sprinklers – these work on a simple pressure and gravity principle and still spurt out modest plumes of water after heavy rain. The whole complex offers a good example of the hydraulic sophistication achieved by the ancient Sinhalese in the dry zone: after almost 1500 years of disuse, all that was needed to restore the fountains to working order was to clear the water channels which feed them.

The Boulder Gardens and Terrace Gardens

Beyond the Water Gardens the main path begins to climb up through the **Boulder Gardens**, constructed out of the huge boulders which lie tumbled around the foot of the rock. Many of the boulders are notched with lines of holes – they look rather like rock-cut steps, but in fact they were used as footings to support the brick walls or timber frames of the numerous buildings which were built against or on top of the boulders.

The gardens were also the centre of Sigiriya's monastic activity before and after Kassapa: there are around twenty rock shelters hereabouts which were used by monks, some containing inscriptions dating from between the third century BC and the first century AD. The caves would originally have been plastered and painted, and traces of this decoration can still be seen in a few places; you'll also notice the dripstone ledges which were carved around the entrances to many of the caves to prevent water from running into them. The **Deraniyagala Cave**, just to the left of the path shortly after it begins to climb up through the gardens (no sign), has a well-preserved dripstone ledge and traces of old paintings including the faded remains of various *apsara* figures very similar to the famous Sigiriya Damsels further up the rock. On the opposite side of the main path up the rock, a side path leads to the **Cobra Hood Cave**, named for its uncanny resemblance to that snake's head. The cave preserves traces of lime plaster, floral decoration and a very faint inscription on the ledge in archaic Brahmi script dating from the second century BC.

Follow the path up the hill behind the Cobra Hood Cave and up through "Boulder Arch no. 2" (as it's signed), then turn left to reach the so-called **Audience Hall**. The wooden walls and roof have long since disappeared, but the impressively smooth floor, created by chiselling the top off a single enormous boulder, remains, along with a five-metre-wide "throne", also cut out of the solid rock. The hall is popularly claimed to have been Kassapa's audience hall, though it's more likely to have served a purely religious function, with the empty throne representing the Buddha. The small **Asana Cave** on the path en route to the Audience Hall retains colourful splashes of various paintings on its ceiling (though now almost obliterated by idiotic contemporary graffiti) and is home to another throne, while a couple more thrones can be found carved into nearby rocks.

Carry on back to the main path, then head on up through "Boulder Arch no. 1". The path – now a sequence of walled-in steps – begins to climb steeply through the **Terrace Gardens**, a series of rubble-retaining brick and limestone terraces that stretch to the base of the rock itself, from where you get the first of an increasingly majestic sequence of views back down below.

The Sigiriya Damsels and the Mirror Wall

Shortly after reaching the base of the rock, two incongruous nineteenth-century metal spiral staircases lead to and from a sheltered cave in the sheer rock face that holds Sri Lanka's most famous sequence of frescoes, popularly referred to as the **Sigiriya Damsels** (no flash photography). These busty beauties were painted in the fifth century and are the only non-religious paintings to have survived from ancient Sri Lanka; they're now one of the island's most iconic – and most relentlessly reproduced – images. Once described as the largest picture gallery in the world, it's thought that these frescoes would originally have covered an area some 140 metres long by 40 metres high, though only 21 damsels now survive out of an original total of some five hundred (a number of paintings were destroyed by a vandal in 1967, while a few of the surviving pictures are roped off out of sight). The exact significance of the paintings is unclear: they were originally thought to depict Kassapa's consorts, though according to modern art historians the most convincing theory is that they are portraits of *apsaras* (celestial nymphs), which would explain why they are shown from the waist up only, rising out of a cocoon of clouds. The portrayal of the damsels is strikingly naturalistic, showing them scattering petals and offering flowers and trays of fruit – similar in a style to the famous murals at the Ajanta Caves in India, and a world away from the much later and more stylized murals at nearby Dambulla. An endearingly human touch is added by the slips of the brush visible here and there: one damsel has three hands, while another sports three nipples.

Just past the damsels, the pathway runs along the face of the rock, bounded on one side by the **Mirror Wall**. This was originally coated in highly polished plaster made from lime, egg white, beeswax and wild honey; sections of the original plaster survive and still retain a marvellously lustrous sheen. The wall is covered in **graffiti**, the oldest dating from the seventh century, in which early visitors recorded their impressions of Sigiriya and, especially, the nearby damsels – even after the city was abandoned, Sigiriya continued to draw a steady stream of tourists curious to see the remains of Kassapa's fabulous pleasure-dome. Taken together, the graffiti form a kind of early medieval visitors' book, and the 1500 or so decipherable comments give important insights into the development of the Sinhalese language and script.

Beyond the Mirror Wall, the path runs along a perilous-looking iron walkway bolted onto the sheer rock-face. From here you can see a huge **boulder** below, propped up on stone slabs. The rather far-fetched popular theory is that, in the event of attack, the slabs would have been knocked away, causing the boulder to fall onto the attackers below, though it's more likely that the slabs were designed to *stop* the boulder inadvertently falling down over the cliff.

The Lion Platform

Continuing up the rock, a flight of limestone steps climbs steeply up to the **Lion Platform**, a large spur projecting from the north side of the rock, just below the summit (vendors sell fizzy drinks here at inflated prices). From here, a final staircase, its base flanked by two enormous paws carved out of the rock, leads up across all that remains of a gigantic **lion statue** – the final path to the summit apparently led directly into its mouth. Visitors to Kassapa were, one imagines, suitably impressed by this gigantic conceit and by the symbolism – lions were the most important emblem of Sinhalese royalty, and the beast's size was presumably meant to reflect Kassapa's prestige and buttress his questionable legitimacy to the throne.

The wire-mesh cages on the Lion Platform were built as refuges in the (fortunately unlikely) event of bee attacks – you can see bees' nests clinging to the underside of the rock overhang above, to the left of the stairs. The whole section of rock-face above is scored with countless notches and grooves which once supported steps up to the summit: in a supreme irony, it appears that Kassapa was afraid of heights, and it's thought that these original steps would have been enclosed by a high wall – though this isn't much comfort for latter-day sufferers from vertigo, who have to make the final ascent to the summit up a narrow iron staircase attached to the bare rock-face.

The summit

After the tortuous path up, the **summit** seems huge. This was the site of Kassapa's palace, and almost the entire area was originally covered with buildings. Only the foundations now remain, though, and it's difficult to make much sense of it all – the main attraction is the fabulous views down to the Water Gardens and out over the surrounding countryside. The **Royal Palace** itself is now just a plain, square brick platform at the very highest point of the rock. The upper section is enclosed by steep terraced walls, below which is a large tank cut out of the solid rock; it's thought that water was channelled to the summit using an ingenious hydraulic system powered by windmills. Below here a series of four further terraces, perhaps originally gardens, tumble down to the lower edge of the summit above Sigiriya Wewa.

The path down takes you along a slightly different route – you should end up going right past the Cobra Hood Cave, if you missed it earlier, before exiting the site to the south.

Pidurangala Royal Cave Temple

A couple of kilometres north of Sigiriya, another large rock outcrop is home to the **Pidurangala Royal Cave Temple**. According to tradition, the monastery here dates from the arrival of Kassapa, when the monks who were then living at Sigiriya were relocated to make room for the king's city and palace; Kassapa constructed new caves and a temple here to recompense them. It's a pleasant short bike or tuktuk ride to the foot of Pidurangala rock: head down the road north of Sigiriya and continue for about 750m until you reach a modern white temple, the **Pidurangala Sigiri Rajamaha Viharaya** (about 100m further on along this road on the left you'll also find the interesting remains of some old monastic buildings, including the substantial ruins of a sizeable brick dagoba). Steps lead steeply up the hillside behind the Pidurangala Viharaya to a terrace just below the summit of the rock (a stiff 15-min climb), where you'll find the Royal Cave Temple itself, although despite the rather grand name there's not much to see apart from a long reclining Buddha under a large rock overhang, its upper half restored in brick. The statue is accompanied by figures of Vishnu and Saman and decorated with very faded murals.

From here you may be able to find the rough path up to the **summit** of the rock (a 5min scramble), but you'll need to be fit and agile, and take care not to lose your way when coming back down, which is surprisingly easy to do. The reward for your efforts will be the best view of Sigiriya you can get short of chartering a balloon, showing the far more irregular and interestingly shaped northern side of the rock which you don't get to see when climbing up it, with the ant-like figures of those making the final ascent to the summit (which you're almost level with) just visible against the huge slab of red rock.

Polonnaruwa and around

The great ruined capital of **POLONNARUWA** is one of the undisputed highlights of the Cultural Triangle – and indeed the whole island. The heyday of the city, in the twelfth century, represented one of the high watermarks of early Sri Lankan civilization. The Chola invaders from South India had been repulsed by Vijayabahu, and the Sinhalese kingdom he established at Polonnaruwa enjoyed a brief century of magnificence under his successors Parakramabahu and Nissankamalla, who planned the city as a grand statement of imperial pomp, transforming it briefly into one of the great urban centres of South Asia before their own hubris and excess virtually bankrupted the state. Within a century, their enfeebled successors had been driven south by new waves of invaders from southern India, and Polonnaruwa had been abandoned to the jungle, where it remained, unreclaimed and virtually unknown, for seven centuries.

Polonnaruwa's extensive and well-preserved remains offer a fascinating snapshot of medieval Sri Lanka, including some of the island's finest monuments, and is compact enough to be thoroughly explored in a single (albeit busy) day. Minneriya and Kaudulla national parks, though more quickly accessed from Habarana, are also not far away. Most of the guesthouses in town can arrange transport to any of these places.

Some history

The **history** of Polonnaruwa stretches far back into the Anuradhapuran period. The region first came to prominence in the third century AD, when the creation of the Minneriya Tank boosted the district's agricultural importance, while the development of the port of Gokana (modern Trincomalee) into the island's major conduit for overseas trade later helped Polonnaruwa develop into an important local commercial centre. As Anuradhapura fell victim to interminable invasions from India, Polonnaruwa's strategic advantages became increasingly apparent. Its greater distance from India made it less

Polonnaruwa or Anuradhapura?

Many visitors to Sri Lanka only have the time or the archeological enthusiasm to visit one of the island's two great ruined cities, but as the two are sufficiently different it's difficult to call decisively in favour of either. The ruins at **Polonnaruwa** cover a smaller area, are better preserved and offer a more digestible and satisfying bite of ancient Sinhalese culture – and there's nowhere at Anuradhapura to match the artistry of the Quadrangle and Gal Vihara. Having said that, **Anuradhapura** has its own distinct magic. The sheer scale of the site and the number of remains means that, although much harder to get to grips with, it preserves a mystery that much of Polonnaruwa has lost – and it's much easier to escape the coach parties. In addition, the city's status as a major pilgrimage centre also lends it a vibrancy lacking at Polonnaruwa.

vulnerable to attack and gave it easier access to the important southern provinces of Ruhunu, while it also controlled several crossings of the Mahaweli Ganga, Sri Lanka's longest and most important river. Such were the town's advantages that four rather obscure kings actually chose to reign from Polonnaruwa rather than Anuradhapura, starting with Aggabodhi IV (667–683).

Throughout the anarchic later Anuradhapuran era, Polonnaruwa held out against both Indian and rebel Sinhalese attacks until it was finally captured by **Rajahrajah**, king of the Tamil Cholas, following the final sack of Anuradhapura in 993. Rajahrajah made it the capital of his short-lived Hindu kingdom, but in 1056 the city was recaptured by the Sinhalese king **Vijayabahu** (1055–1110), who retained it as the new Sinhalese capital in preference to Anuradhapura, which had been largely destroyed in the earlier fighting. Vijayabahu's accession to the throne ushered in Polonnaruwa's golden age, although most of the buildings date from the reign of Vijayabahu's successor **Parakramabahu** (1153–86; see box, p.340). Parakramabahu developed the city on a lavish scale, importing architects and engineers from India whose influence can be seen in Polonnaruwa's many Hindu shrines. Indian influence continued with Parakramabahu's successor, **Nissankamalla** (1187–96; see box, p.345), a Tamil from the Kalinga dynasty and the last king of Polonnaruwa to enjoy any measure of islandwide power. Nissankamalla's death ushered in a period of chaos. Opposing Tamil and Sinhalese factions battled for control of the city – the next eighteen years saw twelve changes of ruler – while at least four invasions from India threatened the stability of the island at large. This era of anarchy culminated with the seizure of the increasingly enfeebled kingdom by the notorious Tamil mercenary **Magha** (1215–55). Under Magha the monasteries were pillaged and onerous taxes imposed, while his soldiers roamed the kingdom unchecked and the region's great irrigation works fell into disrepair, leading to a decline in agricultural produce and a rise in malaria. Although Magha was finally driven out of Polonnaruwa in 1255, the damage he had inflicted proved irreversible, and Polonnaruwa was finally abandoned in 1293, when Bhuvanekabahu II moved the capital to Kurunegala. The city was left to be swallowed up by the jungle, until restoration work began in the mid-twentieth century.

Arrival

The modern town of Polonnaruwa is a very modest little affair. The **train** and **bus stations** are actually in the larger town of **Kaduruwela**, 4km east along the road to Batticaloa; a tuktuk to Polonnaruwa costs around Rs.150. Arriving by bus, ask to be put off at Polonnaruwa "Old Town"; buses stop close to the Seylan Bank, within spitting distance of most of the guesthouses. The Seylan and People's banks both have **ATMs** accepting foreign cards. There's unreliable **internet** access at a couple of places along the main road; try Easy Seva (the second word is signed in Sinhala and Tamil only; 7am–9pm; Rs.100 per hr), or head into Kaduruwela.

Moving on from Polonnaruwa

Moving on from Polonnaruwa, there are regular services to **Anuradhapura** (hourly; 3hr 30min), **Batticaloa** (every 30min; 3hr), **Colombo** (every 30min; 6hr), **Dambulla** (every 30min; 1hr 45min), **Giritale** (every 15min; 30min), **Habarana** (every 20min; 1hr), and **Kandy** (every 30min; 3hr 45min). You could try to pick up a **bus** at the stop on the main road, but to be sure of a seat, it's easiest to take a tuktuk to the station at Kaduruwela and catch a bus there.

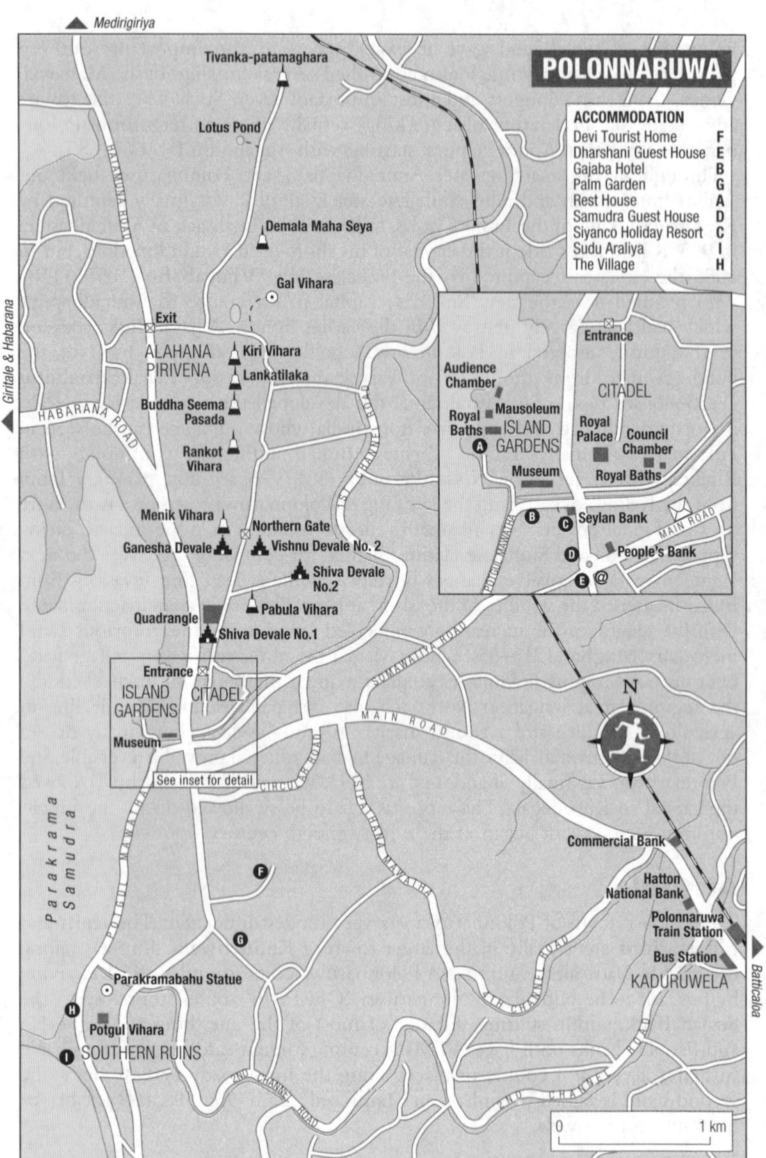

Accommodation and eating

Accommodation in Polonnaruwa is no great shakes, but is at least cheap. Given the paucity of mid- and top-end places, many people opt to stay at the village of **GIRITALE**, 15km down the road, which boasts three pleasant hotels, all perched on the edge of the beautiful Giritale lake. There are frequent buses to Polonnaruwa (every 15min) – or tuktuks for around Rs.400 – making Giritale a possible base even if you don't have your own transport.

As usual, all the hotels and guesthouses listed below do **meals**. The most atmospheric place is the lakeside dining room (or open-air terrace) at the *Rest House*, with a fine lunchtime rice and curry buffet (Rs.700) and good-value set dinners. Alternatively, the *Gajaba* has an attractive garden restaurant and a reasonable choice of inexpensive food, although service can be excruciatingly slow. As at Anuradhapura, the rather undernourished and bony fish caught in the lake are a local staple – they're best when fried.

Polonnaruwa

Devi Tourist Home ⓣ027-222 3181. Set in a peaceful location 1km south of town, this is the nicest and best-run guesthouse in Polonnaruwa, with five comfy rooms (two with a/c and hot water) and good home-cooking. ❶, a/c ❸

Dharshani Guest House ⓣ027-561 2902. Good-value cheapie, with clean, modern rooms in a kitsch pink building on two sides of a small courtyard. It's right on a roundabout, though, so can be noisy. ❶, a/c ❸

Gajaba Hotel ⓣ027-222 2394. This Polonnaruwa stalwart houses a panoply of well-maintained rooms in all shapes and sizes, both in the main house or (quieter) in the courtyard "cottage". The cheapest have little more than a fan and shower; pricier ones have a/c and TV. There are also reasonably priced jeeps, bikes to rent (Rs.200) and a nice garden restaurant. More luxurious rooms overlooking the tank and a new restaurant are under construction. ❶–❸, a/c ❸–❹

Palm Garden 2nd Canal Colony, 1km from town ⓣ027-222 2622. Well-run guesthouse with four modern, very clean and very bare rooms, plus good cooking, though the main attraction is the idyllic rural setting. There are free bikes for trips to town (or Rs.200 to visit the ancient city), and they can also arrange catamaran trips on the lake (Rs.700 per person). ❶, a/c ❸

Rest House ⓣ027-222 2299, ⓦwww.ceylonhotels.lk. In a peerless setting on a promontory jutting out into the lake, this venerable old place has a mix of well-furnished and spacious rooms (all with a/c and TV). Recent upgrading has, sadly, eroded some of the old colonial character (and pushed up prices), though it still retains plenty of period charm, and if you want to indulge a few royal fantasies you can stay in the room occupied by Queen Elizabeth II for a night during her visit here in 1954 (US$85), complete with photos of her visit. ❻

Samudra Guest House ⓣ027-222 2817. Simple but spacious and clean rooms (those inside the main house are larger but darker than those out the back), plus a pair of basic wooden cabanas, all at bargain rates. There's also a pretty little outdoor restaurant and lots of bikes to rent (Rs.200 per day). ❶, a/c ❷

Siyanco Holiday Resort ⓣ027-222 6867. Bright new place, with smallish but spotless tiled rooms, plus a restaurant in the snazzy glass building next door. Not much atmosphere, but the smartest option close to the central ruins. ❹

Sudu Araliya ⓣ027-222 5406, ⓦwww.hotelsuduaraliya.com. The smartest place in Polonnaruwa, with large, comfy a/c rooms equipped with chintzy neo-colonial furniture, minibar and TV. Facilities include a very large pool (non-guests Rs.300), a cute, cave-like Ayurveda centre and an entertainingly Tolkienesque garden bar, looking like a giant mushroom propped up on tree trunks. ❺

The Village ⓣ027-492 4824, ⓦwww.vilapol.com. Very low-key hotel arranged around attractive gardens, with comfortable, pleasantly old-fashioned and good-value rooms (all with a/c, hot water and satellite TV). There's also a decent-size pool (non-guests Rs.300, or free if you have a drink at the poolside bar), a small Ayurveda centre and bikes to rent (Rs.250 per day). ❹

Giritale

The Deer Park ⓣ027-224 6272, ⓦwww.angsana.com. Superior four-star establishment with accommodation in a mix of one- and two-storey cottages scattered around attractive wooded grounds. Rooms are large and comfortable, if a little old-fashioned; all have TV, a/c and nice open-air showers. Facilities include a good-sized pool and a swish if expensive Angsana spa. ❼

Giritale Hotel ⓣ027-224 6311, ⓔgiritaleh@carcumb.com. The oldest of the Giritale hotels could do with updating – its drab green, bare-brick walls give certain areas the architectural charm of a school gym – but it occupies an imperious position, perched high above the lake, and its grounds are a haven for wildlife. Rooms (with a/c) are comfy enough, and most have lake views, but pricey. Also has a pool, small gym and herbal massages. ❻

The Royal Lotus ⓣ027-224 6316, ⓔmanager@royallotus.com. This comfortable two-star, overlooking the tank, is Giritale's best-value option. Go for one of the plush and cheerily furnished rooms (with TV and a/c) in the main building, which all have lake-view balconies, over the older "cottages" behind. There's also a decent poolside restaurant and modest Ayurveda centre with bargain treatments. ❻

The ancient city

The ruins of Polonnaruwa are scattered over an extensive area of dry, gently undulating woodland. The entire site is about four kilometres from north to south, and rather too large to cover by foot. The best idea is to **rent a bicycle** (available from most of the town's guesthouses for Rs.200 per day). The site is open daily from 7am to 6pm and is covered by the CT ticket; otherwise **entrance** costs US$25. Tickets have to be bought at the museum

Parakramabahu the Great

Parakramabahu I (reigned 1153–86), or **Parakramabahu the Great**, as he is often styled, was the last in the sequence of famous Sinhalese warrior kings, stretching back to the legendary Dutugemunu (see p.362), who succeeded in uniting the entire island under the rule of a single native monarch. Like Dutugemunu, on whose example he seems consciously to have modelled himself, Parakramabahu grew up in the semi-autonomous southern kingdom and harboured dreams of islandwide domination.

Unlike his illustrious role model, however, Parakramabahu was not faced with an occupying foreign power, but with a series of rival Sinhalese claimants to the throne. The political situation at this time was deeply confused, with the island having split into a number of semi-independent kingdoms. Parakramabahu (a grandson of Vijayabahu) was born at **Dedigama** (see p.225), capital of the minor kingdom of Dakkinadesa, which was ruled by his father. Upon becoming ruler of Dakkinadesa, Parakramabahu established a new capital at **Panduwas Nuwara** (see p.320), before launching a campaign against the king of Polonnaruwa, his cousin **Gajabahu**. Parakramabahu succeeded in capturing Polonnaruwa, but the behaviour of his troops so incensed the people that they appealed for help to another prince from Ruhunu, **Manabharana**, who arrived at Polonnaruwa under the pretence of protecting Gajabahu. It soon became clear however, that Manabharana himself harboured designs on the throne, and the hapless Gajabahu was forced to jump sides and appeal to Parakramabahu for help, buying peace by declaring Parakramabahu his official heir. Upon Gajabahu's death, the inevitable fighting resumed. Despite initial reverses, during which Manabharana drove Parakramabahu all the way back to Dakkinadesa, Parakramabahu finally triumphed and was crowned king of Polonnaruwa in 1153, although it took a brutal and protracted series of military campaigns before the entire island was finally subdued.

Even while Parakramabahu was mopping up the last pockets of resistance in the south, he began to embark on the gargantuan programme of building which restored the economic fortunes of the island and transformed Polonnaruwa into one of the great cities of its age. According to the *Culavamsa*, the new king built or restored over six thousand tanks and canals, including the vast new **Parakrama Samudra** in Polonnaruwa, as well as restoring the three great dagobas at Anuradhapura and rebuilding the monastery at Mihintale. It was at his new capital, however, that Parakramabahu lavished his greatest efforts, supervising the construction of a spate of imposing new edifices. He also set about purifying the Buddhist clergy of disreputable elements and thoroughly overhauled the kingdom's administration, as well as launching a couple of rare military offensives overseas, first in Burma and then India.

For all his achievements, Parakramabahu seems a not entirely admirable figure. Unlike Dutugemunu's campaigns, the savage wars fought by Parakramabahu had no justification except to establish him on the throne at whatever human cost. Equally, his expansive programme of building works at home, combined with military campaigns overseas, laid a heavy burden of taxation and labour on his own subjects, and the resultant weakening of the kingdom's economy was perhaps ultimately one of the reasons for the rapid collapse in the fortunes of Polonnaruwa which followed Parakramabahu's own illustrious, but tarnished, reign.

(see opposite) in the village; they can't be bought at the entrance itself. You can see everything at Polonnaruwa in a single long day, but you'll have to start early to do the city justice.

Polonnaruwa was originally enclosed by three concentric walls and filled with parks and gardens. At its centre lay the royal residences of successive kings, comprising the **Citadel** (containing the palace of Parakramabahu), and the buildings of the **Island Gardens** (comprising the less well-preserved remains of Nissankamalla's palace complex). South of here are the scant remains of the **southern ruins**, while just to the north of the palaces lies the city's religious heart, known as the **Quadrangle**, which contains the densest and finest group of remains in the city – and, indeed, Sri Lanka. Polonnaruwa's largest monuments are found in the northern part of the city, comprising the buildings of the Menik, Rankot, Alahana Pirivena and Jetavana monasteries, including the famous Buddha statues of the **Gal Vihara** and the evocative **Lankatilaka** shrine.

To the west of the city lies the great artificial lake, the **Parakrama Samudra** ("Sea of Parakramabahu"), encircled by rugged hills and providing a beautiful backdrop to the town – an evening stroll along the waterside Potgul Mawatha makes a scenic way to end a day. The lake was created by the eponymous king, Parakramabahu, though sections of the irrigation system date right back to the third century AD. Covering some 26 square kilometres, the lake provided the medieval city with water, cooling breezes and an additional line of defence, and also irrigated over ninety square kilometres of paddy fields. After a breach in the walls in the late thirteenth century, the tank fell into disrepair, and was restored to its original size only in the 1950s.

The Polonnaruwa Museum

Close to the lakeshore on the northern edge of Polonnaruwa town (and a 5min walk from the main entrance to the ruined city) is the modern **Polonnaruwa Museum** (daily 9am–6pm; entrance with CT ticket only; no photography). Impressively laid out, the museum is well worth a visit before setting off around the site, or as a break from the heat (you have to buy your ticket here, in any case, if you don't have a Cultural Triangle ticket). Exhibits include some fascinating **scale models** showing how the city's buildings might have looked in their prime, notably a fine mock-up of the Vatadage and a rather more fanciful model of Parakramabahu's Royal Palace. There's also a fine collection of **bronzes** and **sculptures** recovered from the site – many are elaborately carved images of Hindu deities, testifying to the overwhelming Indian influence in the city's culture. Copious background descriptions (in English) of every part of ancient Polonnaruwa add interesting details and insights and help flesh out the exhibits.

The Citadel

At the heart of the ancient city lie the buildings of the **Citadel**, sometimes known as the Royal Palace Group, created by Parakramabahu and used by subsequent kings of Polonnaruwa until the snobbish Nissankamalla (see p.345) established a new palace further to the south. The entire area is surrounded by a (heavily restored) circuit of walls. At the centre of the complex lie the remains of Parakramabahu's **Royal Palace**. According to the *Culavamsa* (see p.415), the palace originally stood seven storeys high and boasted a thousand rooms, although this was probably an exaggeration (a model in the museum shows a speculative impression of how this seven-storey palace might have looked). The remains of three brick storeys have survived (any further levels would have been built of wood and have long since disappeared), although they don't give much idea of how the building would originally have appeared – the ruin now looks more like a Norman castle than a Sinhalese royal palace. The holes in the walls were for floor beams, while the vertical grooves up to the first floor would have held wooden pillars.

Just east of the Royal Palace stand the remains of Parakramabahu's **Council Chamber**, where the king would have granted audiences to his ministers and officials. The wooden roof has vanished, but the imposing base survives, banded with friezes of dwarfs, lions and galumphing elephants. The sumptuous steps are embellished with *makara* balustrades and topped with two of the rather Chinese-looking lions associated with Sinhalese royalty during this period; there are other fine examples at Nissankamalla's Audience Chamber (see p.349) and at Yapahuwa.

Just east of here are the **Royal Baths** (Kumara Pokuna), designed in an unusual geometric shape (a square superimposed on a cross) and fed by two spouts carved with eroded *makaras*. Next to here stands the impressive two-tiered base of what was presumably some kind of royal bathhouse; each tier is decorated with lions, and there's a good moonstone on the upper level.

Shiva Devale no. 1

About 300m north of the Citadel lies the **Shiva Devale no. 1**, one of many temples at Polonnaruwa dedicated to either Vishnu or Shiva. It dates from the Pandyan occupation of the early thirteenth century, following the collapse of Sinhalese power; the fact that the Indian invaders saw fit to construct an unabashedly Hindu shrine so close to the city's most sacred Buddhist precinct says much about their religious sympathies (or lack of). The temple is made of finely cut, slate-grey stone, fitted together without the use of mortar. The bottom halves of two rudely truncated guardian figures stand by the doorway, while inside there's a rather battered lingam – the extraordinary treasure trove of **bronze images** found here is now in the National Museum in Colombo. Around the back of the shrine stand cute and tiny statuettes of a couple of venerable and heavily bearded figures which possibly represent Agni, the pre-Aryan Indian god of fire.

The Quadrangle

Just north of the Shiva Devale no. 1 stands the **Quadrangle** – originally, and more properly, known as the Dalada Maluwa ("Terrace of the Tooth Relic"), since the famous relic (see p.243) was housed in various shrines here during its stay in the city. This rectangular walled enclosure, built on a raised terrace, was the religious heart of the city, conveniently close to the royal palace of Parakramabahu – the king would probably have come here to listen to readings from the Buddhist scriptures – and is now home to the finest and most varied collection of ancient buildings in Sri Lanka.

The Vatadage

The Quadrangle is dominated by the magnificent **Vatadage** (circular relic house), arguably the most beautiful building in Sri Lanka. Built by Parakramabahu, it was later embellished by the crafty Nissankamalla (see p.345), who placed the large inscription which can be seen around the upper level of the principal entrance claiming credit for the whole building. The entire outer structure is a fantastic riot of artistry, with almost every surface carved in a melee of decoration. The outer wall sports friezes of lions and dwarfs, and is topped by an unusually designed

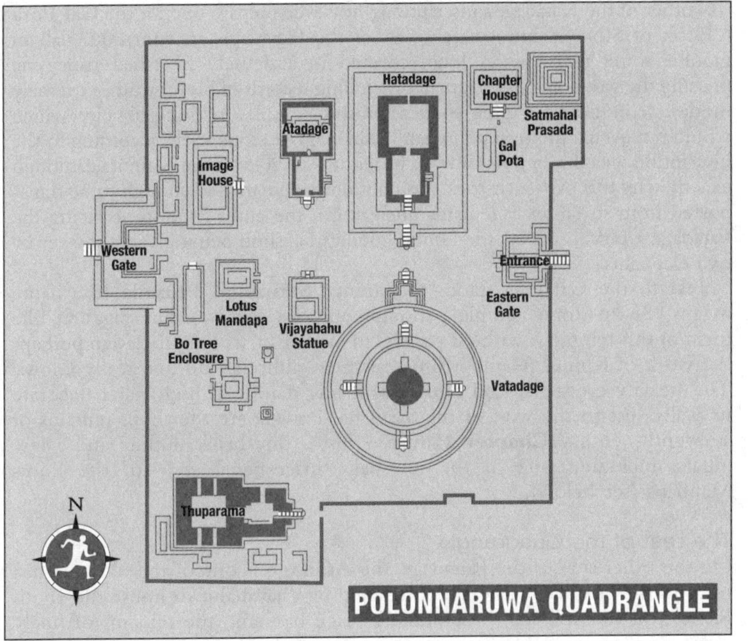

stone wall decorated with an abstract lotus design. Four sets of steps lead to the upper terrace, each one a little sculptural masterpiece, decorated with dwarfs, lions and *makaras*, as well as magnificently carved *nagaraja* guardstones and some of the finest moonstones in the city. The remains of further pillars and carved capitals which would once have supported the now vanished roof lie scattered about the upper terrace.

From the upper terrace, steps lead through four entrances, aligned to the cardinal points and each presided over by a seated Buddha, to the eroded remains of the central brick dagoba in which the **Tooth Relic** may have been enshrined – strangely enough, this inner sanctum is virtually unadorned, in striking contrast to the remainder of the building.

The Hatadage, Gal Pota and around

The remainder of the Quadrangle is packed with a dense assortment of buildings of enormous variety and interest (though none approaches the flamboyance of the Vatadage). Opposite the Vatadage stand the rather plain remains of the **Hatadage**, originally a two-storeyed building, though the upper storey, which was perhaps made of brick, has long since crumbled away. Thought to have been built by Nissankamalla (who placed two long inscriptions on the right of the outer and inner entrances claiming credit for the building), the Hatadage is also referred to as the Temple of the Tooth, since the relic may have been placed here for a time, probably on the upper floor. It now houses three Buddha statues, possibly intended to represent the Buddhas of the past, present and future; the central one is positioned to line up through the shrine's doorway with the Buddha directly opposite in the Vatadage.

Neither of the Hatadage's inscriptions, however, prepare one for the **Gal Pota** ("Book of Stone"), immediately east of the Hatadage, an enormous slab of granite, some nine metres long, covered in a densely inscribed panegyric praising the works of Nissankamalla, including records of his (in truth, extremely modest) conquests in India – an astonishing display of self-publicity which would put even a modern politician to shame. The stone itself, according to the inscription, weighs 25 tons and was brought over 90km from Mihintale, though exactly why this particular rock was considered remarkable enough to be transported from so far away remains unclear. On the end of the stone facing the Vatadage a carving shows the Hindu goddess Lakshmi being given a shower by two elephants.

Next to the Gal Pota stands the strange **Satmahal Prasada** (the name means "Seven-storey temple", though only six survive). The ziggurat-like form of this temple is without parallel in Sri Lanka, its unique design perhaps the work of Khmer (Cambodian) craftsmen, although no one really knows. The heavily eroded stucco figures of a few deities in high relief decorate its walls. Just to the west of the Satmahal Prasada are the slight remains of a seventh-century **Chapter House** – just a tiny brick outline and a few pillars, including one in the unusual "thrice-bent" style of the Lotus Mandapa (see below).

The rest of the Quadrangle

On the other side of the Hatadage, the **Atadage** is one of the oldest structures in the city, having been constructed by Vijayabahu to house the Tooth Relic; you can still see the building's brick base and the remains of finely carved pillars and door frames; a blackened Buddha statue stands in the centre. Next to the Atadage are the remains of an **image house** – the brick base inside would have supported a now-vanished reclining Buddha. Continuing anti-clockwise, the next building is the small but exquisite **Lotus Mandapa** (also known as the Latha Mandapaya or Nissankalata), built by Nissankamalla. It features an unusual latticed stone fence (faintly reminiscent of the Buddhist Railing at the Jetavana monastery in Anuradhapura) and a small platform surmounted by stone pillars shaped as thrice-bent lotus buds on stalks, a beautiful and very unusual design whose sinuous organic lines look positively Art Nouveau. In the centre of the platform are the remains of a tiny dagoba which was, according to different interpretations, either used to hold relics or which served as a seat for Nissankamalla during religious ceremonies (though not, presumably, both). In front of the Lotus Mandapa stands an armless **statue**, popularly thought to represent Vijayabahu, though it might be a bodhisattva.

Finally, in the southwest corner stands one of the oldest but also one of the most intact of the Quadrangle's structures, the **Thuparama**, an exceptionally large and well-preserved gedige (stone image house, misleadingly signposted as a "chapter house") thought to date back to the reign of Vijayabahu I. The building's original name is unknown; it was confusingly christened the Thuparama ("The Stupa") by the pioneering British archeologist H.C.P. Bell, though it isn't actually a stupa at all. The inner shrine preserves its sturdy vaulted brick roof, as well as exceptionally thick, plaster-covered brick walls whose massive dimensions keep the interior pleasantly cool – the walls are so thick that the architects were actually able to construct a staircase inside them (it's just through the door on the left), though it's usually locked. The shrine contains eight beautiful old standing and seated crystalline limestone Buddhas, which sparkle magically when illuminated. Beneath the scaffolding, the

Nissankamalla the vainglorious

Following Vijayabahu and Parakramabahu, **Nissankamalla** (reigned 1187–96) is the third of the famous trinity of Polonnaruwan kings. A Tamil prince, Nissankamalla originally hailed from South India, but married into the Sinhalese nobility by wedding a daughter of Parakramabahu, and then succeeded in attaining the throne after a brief political skirmish following the death of his father-in-law.

Nissankamalla was notable chiefly for being the last king of Polonnaruwa to exercise real power over the whole island; he even felt secure enough to launch military expeditions against the Pandyans of South India, one of which he accompanied in person. Perhaps conscious of his foreign birth, he seems to have endeavoured to become more Sinhalese than the Sinhalese, making a great show of his religious orthodoxy, purging the Sangha of disreputable monks and becoming the first king to make the pilgrimage to the summit of Adam's Peak. He is also known to have embarked on extensive tours of the island to discover the conditions under which his subjects were living, rather in the manner of a contemporary politician at election time – not that Nissankamalla would have worried much about public opinion, since he considered himself (as did many of the later Sinhalese kings) a living god.

For all his genuine achievements, however, Nissankamalla is best remembered for the long trail of **inscriptions** he left dotted around Polonnaruwa and other places in Sri Lanka, recording his valour, wisdom, religious merit and other outstanding qualities – he seems to have been the sort of monarch who wasn't able to sneeze without erecting a monument to commemorate the event. Prominent inscriptions can be found in Polonnaruwa at the Gal Pota, Hatadage and Vatadage in the Quadrangle, and at the Rankot and Kiri viharas (plus a couple more in the Polonnaruwa Museum), though some historians regard the claims made in them as somewhat dubious; Nissankamalla also stands accused of having stolen the credit for many of the building works carried out by Parakramabahu. Not content with leaving his scribbles all over Polonnaruwa, Nissankamalla also opted to construct a brand new royal palace rather than inhabit that of his predecessors, and even had the cheek to change the name of the great Parakrama Samudra tank (christened after its creator, Parakramabahu) to the Nissanka Sagara – subsequent generations, happily, chose to revert to the original name.

The only image of Nissankamalla stands in the Maharaja cave temple at Dambulla. Ironically for this great self-publicist, it's tucked away in a corner, and almost completely hidden from sight.

exterior walls are decorated with the South Indian-style niches, and the heavily recessed and elaborately decorated window frames which can be found on a number of buildings across the city.

North of the Quadrangle

The road north from the Quadrangle runs through attractive light woodland and past a scatter of minor monuments. The most interesting is the finely preserved **Shiva Devale no. 2**, the oldest surviving structure in Polonnaruwa. It dates back to the original Chola occupation during the early eleventh century; an inscription states that it was built as a memorial to the queen of the great Chola emperor Rajaraja, whose army destroyed Anuradhapura in 993. This pretty little domed building is pure Indian in style, boasting the same rounded capitals and niche windows which adorn the Shiva Devale no. 1; four headless Nandis (Shiva's bull) stand guard around the shrine.

Just to the southwest stands the **Pabula Vihara** ("Red Coral Shrine"), named by H.C.P. Bell for the red corals he discovered during excavations here. Said to have been built by a certain Rupavati, one of Parakramabahu's wives, the vihara's main structure is a large brick dagoba, the third largest in Polonnaruwa, though restorations have reduced it to strange two-tier stump which gives no clue as to its original form. The remains of various brick image houses and Buddha statues lie scattered around the base.

Continuing north along the main track brings you to the remains of the **Northern Gate**, which marked the northern end of the central walled city. The **Vishnu Devale no. 2** and **Ganesha Devale** stand on the main track opposite one another on the south side of the gate. The former has a fine Vishnu image and the remains of stone (rather than brick) walls, though little remains of the latter. Immediately south of the Ganesha Devale are the equally slight ruins of another **Shiva Devale**, comprising the base of a tiny one-room shrine enclosing a battered lingam.

The Menik and Rankot viharas

The northern districts of ancient Polonnaruwa were almost entirely given over to religious pursuits, home to a sequence of monastic foundations – the Menik Vihara, Rankot Vihara, Alahana Pirivena and Jetavana – whose magnificent statues, shrines, dagobas and other religious structures (many of which survive relatively intact) are amongst Polonnaruwa's most memorable attractions.

The city's monastic areas begin immediately north of the northern gate with the rather uninteresting scattered remains of the **Menik Vihara**. Little survives other than heavily restored foundations, a few armless (and sometimes also headless) Buddhas, and the lower portion of a small brick dagoba – you can (unusually) see the relic chamber exposed at the top of the dagoba. North of here is a further complex of monastic buildings.

North of the Menik Vihara stands Nissankamalla's monumental **Rankot Vihara**, an immense red-brick dagoba rising to a height of some 55m. The fourth largest such structure in Sri Lanka, it's surpassed in size only by the three great dagobas at Anuradhapura, in imitation of which it was built, although its unusually steep sides and flattened top (it looks as though someone very large has sat on it) are less graceful than its Anuradhapuran antecedents. An inscription to the left of the entrance pathway describes how Nissankamalla oversaw work on the building, testifying to his religious devotion and the spiritual merit he presumably expected to gain from the building's construction – whether the forced labourers who were obliged to raise this gargantuan edifice shared the king's sense of religious idealism is not recorded.

Alahana Pirivena

A few hundred metres beyond the Rankot Vihara stretch the extensive remains of the **Alahana Pirivena** ("Monastery of the Cremation Grounds"), named after the royal cremation grounds which were established in this part of the city by Parakramabahu – the many minor stupas scattered about the area would have contained the relics of royalty or prominent monks. The monastery was one of the most impressive in the ancient city, and the remains here are some of the finest at the site.

Lankatilaka

At the heart of the Alahana Pirivena, the **Lankatilaka** ("Ornament of Lanka") consists of a huge (though now sadly headless) standing Buddha, over 14m high, hemmed in between two narrow walls. Built by Parakramabahu, the shrine emphasizes the change in Buddhist architecture and thought from the abstract symbolic form of the dagoba to a much more personalized and devotional approach, in which attention is focused on the giant figure of the Buddha, which fills up the entire space within the shrine. The entrance is approached by two sets of steps; the outside face of the upper left-hand balustrade sports an unusually fine lion carving. More unusual are the intriguing **bas reliefs** on the exterior walls, showing a series of elaborate multistorey buildings, probably intended to represent the celestial dwellings (*vimanas*) of the gods.

Kiri Vihara and Buddha Seema Pasada

Next to the Lankatilaka is the so-called **Kiri Vihara**, the best preserved of Polonnaruwa's dagobas – *kiri* means "milk", referring to the white lime plaster that covers the building and which was almost perfectly preserved when the dagoba was rescued from the jungle after seven hundred years (though it's now faded to a dirty grey). Originally called the Rupavati Cetiya, it's believed to have been constructed at the behest of one of Parakramabahu's wives, Rupavati, who was also responsible for the Pabula Vihara. As at the Rankot Vihara, Kiri Vihara boasts four *vahalkadas* and an unusual number of brick shrines around its base, while to the left an inscription on a raised stone plinth records the location at which Nissankamalla worshipped.

South of the Lankatilaka, the **Buddha Seema Pasada** was the monastery's chapter house, a substantial building which might originally – judging by the thickness of its outer walls – have supported several upper storeys of brick or wood. At the centre of the building is a square pillared hall with a raised dais at its centre, surrounded by monks' cells and connected to the surrounding courtyard by four entrances, each with its own exquisite moonstone. Urns on pillars (symbolizing plenty) stand in the outer courtyard.

Gal Vihara

Just to the north, the **Gal Vihara** ("Stone Shrine"; also known as the Kalugal Vihara, or Black Stone Shrine) represents the pinnacle of Sri Lankan rock carving. The four Buddha statues here, all carved from the same massive granite outcrop, originally formed part of the monastery complex – each statue would

▲ Moonstone, Polonnaruwa

originally have been housed in its own enclosure – you still can see the sockets cut into the rock into which wooden beams would have been inserted behind the standing image (sadly, the modern answer to protecting the statues from the elements is a pair of huge and unsightly new metal shelters which detract massively from the atmosphere of the place and keeps the statues in a permanent twilight).

The massive **reclining Buddha**, 14m long, is the most famous of the four statues, a huge but supremely graceful figure which manages to combine the serenely transcendental with the touchingly human; the face, delicately flecked with traces of natural black sediment, is especially beautiful. The seven-metre-tall **standing Buddha** next to it is the most unusual of the set: its downcast eyes and the unusual position of its arms led some to consider it an image of Ananda, the Buddha's disciple, grieving for his departed master, though it's now thought to represent the Buddha himself in the weeks following his enlightenment – similar images are found in Kandyan-era murals.

Two splendid **seated Buddhas** complete the group, though they lack the iconic simplicity of the reclining figure, being posed against backdrops whose elaborate detail is rather unusual by the austere standards of Sri Lankan Buddhist art. The smaller seated Buddha, unfortunately now kept behind a metal grille and fibreglass shield, is placed in a slight cave-like recess (the other three would have been housed in brick shrines), seated in the *dhyani mudra* (meditation posture); other deities sit in the background, along with a distinctive arch modelled after the one at the great Buddhist shrine at Sanchi in India. The larger seated Buddha is also posed in *dhyani mudra* and entirely framed by another Sanchi-style arch, with tiny Buddhas looking down on him from their celestial dwellings – perhaps showing a touch of Mahayana Buddhist influence, with its belief in multiple buddhas and bodhisattvas.

North to the Tivanka-patamaghara

A kilometre north of the Gal Vihara, a rough side track leads to the **Demala Maha Seya** (or Damilathupa), an unfinished attempt by Parakramabahu to build the world's largest dagoba using labour supplied by Tamil (*damala*, hence the dagoba's name) prisoners of war captured during fighting against the Pandyans. The dagoba is actually constructed on top of a natural hill: a retaining wall was built around the hill and the gap between filled with rubble, though it seems the dagoba never reached its intended proportions. It's now almost completely reclaimed by the forest, and is barely detectable as a man-made object, though a short section of the massive three-tiered base has been excavated and restored next to the end of the approach path – not terribly interesting in itself, though it brings home the enormous scale of the restoration works carried out to rescue similarly jungle-covered stupas at both Polonnaruwa and Anuradhapura.

Another 500m north, and just to the west of the main track, is an unusual **lotus pond**, formed from five concentric rings of stone finely carved in the shape of stylized lotus petals. The pond may have been used as a ritual bath for those entering the **Tivanka-patamaghara** image house, an exceptionally large and sturdy gedige-style brick structure a further 400m on at the extreme northern end of the site. Along with the lotus pond, the Tivanka-patamaghara is one of the few surviving structures of the **Jetavana monastery**. *Tivanka* means "thrice-bent", referring to the graceful but headless Buddha image inside which is in a position (bent at the shoulder, waist and knee) usually employed only for female images. The interior is also home to a sequence of outstanding (but rather difficult to see) **frescoes**, depicting scenes from the Buddhist Jatakas and lines of very finely painted Hindu-looking deities in sumptuous tiaras. The **exterior** shows the influence of South Indian architecture more clearly than any other Buddhist building in Sri Lanka, with the usual friezes of lions and dwarfs plus densely pillared and niched walls with celestial beings squeezed between the pillars. The overall effect is richly exuberant, and a world away from the chaste Buddhist architecture of Anuradhapura. Restoration work continues inside and out.

The Island Gardens and southern ruins

Two further complexes of ruins lie outside the main site: the **Island Gardens**, on a promontory jutting out into the lake a little north of the museum, and **southern ruins**, 1.5km south along the lakeshore. Although of lesser interest, they're still worth a visit and, as entry to them is free, you don't have to try and cram seeing them and the rest of the site into a single day.

The Island Gardens

The modest ruins of the **Island Gardens**, also sometimes called the Rest House Group, comprise the remains of the palace of Nissankamalla, who built a brand new residence for himself here on the site of Parakramabahu's pleasure gardens. The most interesting structure here is the **Audience Chamber**, similar in form to that of Parakramabahu's. The roof has vanished, but the raised base survives, studded with four rows of sturdy columns, some inscribed with the titles of the dignitaries who would have sat next to them during meetings with the king. A marvellous stone **lion** stands at the end of the plinth, probably marking the position of Nissankamalla's throne.

Just south of the Audience Chamber are the remains of a small, square brick-built **mausoleum**, which may mark the site of Nissankamalla's cremation. The surviving walls reach heights of around five metres and retain traces of red and white paint on their exterior – surprisingly bright and well preserved in places, considering that it's over 800 years old. Nearby lie the remains of the extensive sunken **Royal Baths**.

The southern ruins

A scenic fifteen-minute walk along the raised bank of the lake lies one final group of minor remains, the **southern ruins**. The best-preserved building here is the **Potgul Vihara**, a circular image house surrounded by four small dagobas and the pillared ruins of monastic living quarters. The central room is thought to have housed a monastic library where the city's most sacred texts would have been stored, protected by massive walls which reach a thickness of around two metres at ground level. The principal attraction, however, lies about 100m to the north: an imposing 3.5-metre-high **statue** of a bearded figure, thought to date from the ninth century, which has become one of Polonnaruwa's most emblematic images. It's usually claimed that the statue is a likeness of Parakramabahu himself, holding an object thought to be either a palm-leaf manuscript, representing the "Book of Law", or a yoke, representing the burden of royalty (the less reverent claim it's a slice of papaya). Another theory holds that the statue could be the sage named Pulasti, a hypothesis lent credence by its position near the monastic library.

Around Polonnaruwa: Medirigiya

Some 33km north of Polonnaruwa, and 3km north of the town of **Medirigiriya**, are the remains of the **Mandalagiri Vihara**, which was built and flourished during the heyday of Polonnaruwa. It's an interesting site, but its remoteness and the difficulty (or expense, if you hire transport) of reaching it mean that unless you have an unusual interest in Sinhalese Buddhist architecture, you probably won't find it worth the effort. The main attraction here is the fine eighth-century **vatadage**, similar in size and design to the vatadage at Polonnaruwa, though the quality of the workmanship is of a far lower level. The vatadage sits atop an unusually high terrace and is approached by a long flight of stone steps, with *punkalas* (stone urns, signifying plenty) at the top. The remains of other **monastic buildings** lie around the vatadage, including the base of a sizeable brick dagoba, a couple of tanks and assorted shrines and Buddha statues, many of them now headless.

The site is covered by the Cultural Triangle ticket; otherwise, entrance costs US$5 – though there are no regular ticket checks and the site is unfenced, so you might be able to just walk in without paying. **Buses** run every fifteen minutes from Polonnaruwa to the bustling village of Hingurakgoda, 13km north, from which you can either change onto a second bus for the bumpy thirty-minute ride to Medirigiriya or take a tuktuk (around Rs.500, including waiting time). Alternatively, hiring a vehicle from Polonnaruwa should cost around US$20. Another possibility is to combine a trip to Medirigiya with a visit to Ritigala – count on around US$35 for the trip from Polonnaruwa.

Wasgomuwa National Park

Wasgomuwa National Park is one of the most unspoilt of all Sri Lanka's reserves, enjoying an isolated position and being largely enclosed – and offered a measure of protection – by two large rivers, the Amban Ganga and Mahaweli Ganga, which bound it to the east and west. The park straddles the northeastern edge of the hill country, and ranges in elevation from over 500m to just 76m along the Mahaweli Ganga; it comprises mainly dry-zone evergreen forest along the main rivers and on the hills, and open plains in the southeastern and eastern sections. The park features the usual cast of Sri Lankan fauna, including up to 150 **elephants**, best seen from November to May (and especially from Feb–April); at other times they tend to migrate to Minneriya and Kaudulla national parks. Other wildlife includes sambar and spotted deer, buffalo and rarely sighted leopards and sloth bears, plus around 150 species of bird, including a number of endemics.

Getting to Wasgomuwa is half the fun, with a range of scenic approach routes to the park providing views of pristine countryside and wildlife-spotting opportunities. The park's **entrance** is along its southern flank, about 20km north of the village of **Hettipola**, where all the roads in converge. Most people get to Hettipola via the Kandy to Dambulla road, turning off either at **Naula**, passing through Elahera (which can also be reached from Giritale to the north) and skirting the park's western side, or at **Matale**, from where the road climbs over the northern part of the Knuckles Range and through the villages of Rattota and Pallegama. An alternative approach to the park from Kandy is to take either of the two main highways that run east of the city to **Mahiyangana**. From Mahiyangana, head up north through Girandurukotte, and over the Japan Bridge to Hettipola. Alternatively, a more direct (though no quicker) alternative is to follow the northern road (the A26) from Kandy to Mahiyangana and turn off at **Hasalaka**, from which it's a beautifully rural 45-kilometre drive, via Hettipola, to the park entrance. Sumane Bandara Illangantilake and Ravi Desappriya (see p.254) in Kandy are both excellent **guides** to the park.

Practicalities

Tickets can be bought at the park's new **visitors' centre**; entrance costs US$10 per person, plus the usual additional fees and taxes (see p.54). There are a few **places to stay** overlooking Dunvila Lake, a popular spot with local elephants, about 5km from the main gate in the park's southeastern corner. The smartest option is *Willys Safari Hotel* (ⓣ011-280 6311, ⓦwww.willyssafari.com; half-board ❻), which has comfortable, modern rooms with air-conditioning and TV in an attractive low-slung white building, plus a pool. More rustic are the *Wasgamuwa Safari Village* (ⓣ011-259 1728, ⓦwww.dialogsl.net/kinjou; half-board ❺), with a dozen thatched cabanas overlooking the lake, and *Dunvila Cottage* (bookings via Red Dot Tours ⓦwww.reddottours.com; full-board ❻), a homely thatched and mud-walled cottage with just two rooms but plenty of charm, as well as vegetarian food and fine views towards the Knuckles Range across Dunvila Lake.

Habarana and the national parks

Sitting on a major road junction almost equidistant between Polonnaruwa, Anuradhapura and Dambulla (and close to Sigiriya and Ritigala), the large village of **HABARANA** is of little interest in itself, but has a couple of high-end resorts, plus a handful of cheaper places, that make it a convenient base from which to visit any of the Cultural Triangle's major sights. It's also the handiest point of departure for trips to **Minneriya and Kaudulla national parks**, which offer some of the island's best elephant-spotting. Several outfits along the main road south of Habarana Junction (and a couple more along the Anuradhapura road to the west) compete to arrange jeep tours; count on around US$25 for a three-hour trip to Minneriya, or US$30 to Kaudulla. Most of these places also organize pricey but fun **elephant rides** (US$20 for 1hr) along the main road and across to the nearby lake.

Practicalities

Buses stop at Habarana Junction, the crossroads at the centre of the village, where there's also a branch of the People's Bank with an **ATM** accepting foreign Visa cards. All of the hotels and guesthouses below offer **food** but it's also worth stopping by either the Acme Transit Hotel or Rukmali Restaurant, both on the road out of town towards Polonnaruwa, which compete with each other to serve gut-bustingly vast lunchtime rice and curry banquets (around Rs.750). **Leaving Habarana** there are regular buses to Anuradhapura (every 45min; 2hr 30min), Dambulla (every 20min; 45min), Giritale (every 20min; 30min), Kandy (every 30min; 2hr 45min) and Polonnaruwa (every 20min; 1hr).

Accommodation

Chaaya Village 100m south of Habarana Junction ⓣ066-227 0047, ⓦwww.chaayahotels.com. Traditional resort-style hotel close to the lake, with large, comfortable rooms (with a/c, TV and minibar) in chalets dotted around sylvan grounds; deluxe ones have bathtubs, DVD players and lake views. There's also an unusual four-tiered, fan-shaped pool, though overall it lacks the class of its sister establishment, *Cinnamon Lodge*, next door. ❼

Cinnamon Lodge 100m south of Habarana Junction ⓣ066-227 0012, ⓦwww.cinnamonhotels.com. One of the Cultural Triangle's nicest places to stay, this stylish five-star hotel has spacious and rather grand colonial-style rooms housed in pretty cottages scattered around extensive tree-filled grounds running down to the lake. There's also a large pool, attractive open-air pavilion restaurant and Ayurveda centre. ❼

Eagles Wings Guest House 2km west of Habarana Junction ☎0777-514 505. Friendly family guesthouse in a very rustic setting on the edge of the jungle, with two spotless rooms in the main house (including a two-level family room), plus a pair of simple stilted wooden cabanas in the fruit garden behind. Good home-cooking in the open-air thatched restaurant. ❸, a/c ❹

Habarana Inn Just south of *Cinnamon Lodge* ☎066-227 0010. The cheapest place in Habarana village, offering pleasingly old-fashioned rooms with modern bathrooms in an attractive building set a little back from the main road. ❸, a/c ❹

Rest House Habarana Junction ☎066-227 0003, ⓦwww.ceylonhotels.lk. Attractive rest house in the usual style, though a lick of paint can't disguise the lack of maintenance of its large but rather shabby rooms. ❷, a/c ❸

Minneriya National Park

Just a ten-minute drive east of Habarana, **Minneriya National Park** offers something of a change of scenery for those saturated on ruins. Its centrepiece is the large **Minneriya Tank**, created by the famous tank-builder and monk-baiter Mahasena (see p.366), and despite its relatively small size, the park also boasts an unusually wide range of habitat types, from dry tropical forest to wetlands, grasslands and terrain previously used for slash-and-burn (*chena*) agriculture. Much of the area around the entrance is covered in superb dry-zone evergreen forest dotted with beautiful satinwood, *palu* (rosewood), *halmilla* and *weera* trees – though the thickness of the forest cover means that it's relatively difficult to spot wildlife.

The principal attraction here is **elephants**. Minneriya forms part of the elephant corridor which joins up with Kaudulla and Wasgomuwa national parks, and large numbers of the beasts can be found here at certain times of year during their migrations between the various parks – local guides should know where the greatest concentrations of elephants are at any given time. They are most numerous from July to October, peaking in August and September when water elsewhere dries up and as many as three hundred or more come to the tank's ever-receding shores from as far away as Trincomalee to drink, bathe and feed on the fresh grass which grows up from the lake bed as the waters retreat – as well as to socialize and search for mates. This annual event has been popularly dubbed "**The Gathering**", the largest such meeting of Asian elephants anywhere in the world. At other times, you may spot only a few elephants, and in fact they're often more easily seen from the main Habarana–Polonnaruwa road which runs along the park's northern edge. Other **mammals** found in the park include sambar, spotted deer, sloth bears and around twenty leopards (although both these last two are very rarely sighted), and there's also a good chance of seeing macaque and purple-faced langur monkeys, plus an enormous number of **birds**.

The park **entrance** is 6km east of Habarana on the Polonnaruwa road, where there's a well-designed **visitors' centre**, a five hundred-metre walkway snaking through the forest canopy and some helpful staff on hand to answer questions. **Tickets** cost Rs.1500, plus the usual additional charges (see p.55). It can be marginally cheaper to pick up a jeep in Habarana to take you around the park, but most hotels and guesthouses in Polonnaruwa, Giritale, Sigiriya and Inamaluwa – all of which are relatively close to Minneriya – can arrange trips; count on US$30–35 per half-day.

Kaudulla National Park and Hurulu Eco-Park

Some 22km north of Habarana, **Kaudulla National Park** was established in 2002 to provide another link in the migratory corridor for elephants, connecting with Minneriya and Wasgomuwa national parks to the south, and Somawathiya National Park to the north and east. As at Minneriya, the centrepiece is a lake, the **Kaudulla Tank**, where elephants collect when water dries up elsewhere. The best time to visit is between August and December, with elephant numbers peaking in September/October (slightly later than Minneriya's "Gathering") when up to two hundred congregate at the tank. Outside the dry season much of the park is under water, and elephants can be more difficult to spot. Other wildlife inhabiting the park's mix of grasslands and scrubby forest includes sambar deer, monkeys and the inevitable (but very rarely seen) leopards and sloth bears, plus a characteristically wide array of bird life.

The **entrance** to Kaudulla is 6km off the main Habarana–Trincomalee road. **Tickets** cost US$10, plus the other standard charges and taxes (see p.55), payable at the informative new **visitors' centre**, where you can also hire paddle-boats for birdwatching on the tank (Rs.560 per hr). Jeep **tours** to Kaudulla usually cost US$30–35.

Outside the prime wildlife-spotting months at Minneriya and Kaudulla, jeep operators often run trips to **Hurulu Eco-Park** (daily 2–6.30pm; Rs.750), on the edge of the vast Huluru Biosphere Reserve which stretches west of the Habarana–Trincomalee road. There's no lake here, and the park's terrain is more reminiscent of Uda Walawe, dominated by long grass that makes elephant viewing easy: from January to March you stand a chance of spotting herds of thirty or more of the beasts, though you're unlikely to see much other wildlife. The park's entrance is around 3km north of Habarana along the road to Kaudulla and Trincomalee.

North from Dambulla: Ritigala to Aukana

The northern tip of the Cultural Triangle between Dambulla and Anuradhapura is home to a few relatively little-visited but interesting archeological sites, principally the two great Buddha statues at **Aukana** and **Sasseruwa** and the intriguing forest monastery at **Ritigala**. With your own transport, all three could be visited as a day-trip en route from Dambulla or Polonnaruwa to Anuradhapura.

Ritigala

Secreted away north of Habarana, on the slopes of a densely wooded mountainside protected by the Ritigala Strict Nature Reserve, lie the mysterious remains of the forest monastery of **Ritigala**. The mountainside on which the monastery sits is thought to be the *Ramayana*'s Aristha, the place from which Hanuman leapt from Lanka back to India, having discovered where Sita was being held captive. According to popular belief, Hanuman later passed by Ritigala again, carelessly dropping one of the chunks of Himalayan mountain which he was carrying back from India for its medicinal herbs (other fragments are found at Unawatuna and Hakgala); this is held to account for the unusually wide range of plants and herbs found at Ritigala, although the mundane explanation is that the area, being higher and wetter than the surrounding plains, supports a correspondingly wider range of plant species.

Ritigala's remoteness appealed to solitude-seeking **hermits**, who began to settle here as far back as the third century BC. In the ninth century, Ritigala became home to an order of reclusive and ascetic monks known as *pamsukulikas*, who devoted themselves to a life of extreme austerity – *pamsukulika*, meaning "rag robes", refers to the vow taken by these monks to wear only clothes made from rags either thrown away or recovered from corpses. The order (whose members also inhabited the forest monasteries at Arankele and the Western Monasteries at Anuradhapura) seems to have started as an attempt to return to traditional Buddhist values in reaction against the self-indulgent living conditions enjoyed by the island's clergy. So impressed was Sena I (831–851 AD) with the spirit of renunciation shown by the order that he built them a fine new monastery at Ritigala, endowing it with lands and servants – most of the remains you see today date from this era.

Ritigala is included in the Cultural Triangle **ticket**; otherwise, entry costs a hefty US$8. The site is located along a dirt track 8km north of the main Habarana–Anuradhapura highway, signposted 11km west of Habarana. A tuktuk from Habarana will cost around Rs.1000, including waiting time. There's a new **visitors' centre** at the site, from which you can pick up a guide.

The ruins

Ritigala is magical but enigmatic, while the setting deep in a totally undisturbed tract of thick forest (not to mention the lack of tourists) lends an additional sense of mystery. Parts of the complex have been carefully restored, while others remain buried in the forest, but despite the considerable archeological work which has been done here, the original purpose of virtually everything you now see remains largely unknown. One striking feature is the site's complete lack of residential quarters – the monks themselves may have lived entirely in caves scattered around the forest, with the complex itself serving a purely ceremonial function for visitors to the monastery.

Past the entrance, the path runs around the edge of the tumbled limestone bricks which once enclosed the **Banda Pokuna** tank – this possibly served a ritual purpose, with visitors bathing here before entering the monastery. At the far end of the tank, steep steps lead up to the beginning of a beautifully constructed **pavement** which runs through the forest and links all the major buildings of the monastery. After around 200m the pavement reaches the first of several sunken courtyards, bounded by a retaining wall and housing three raised terraces. The one nearest is one of the **double-platform** structures which are a characteristic feature of Ritigala. These generally consist of two raised terraces linked by a stone "bridge": one of the terraces usually bears the remains of pillars, while the other is bare; each double platform is oriented east–west. Various theories have been advanced as to the original functions of these buildings, but all are essentially glorified guesswork – one holds that the "moat" around the terraces would have been filled with water, providing a natural form of air-conditioning. These structures may have been used for meditation – communal meditation on the open terrace and individual meditation in the cells of the building on the other terrace. A few metres to the right-hand (east) end of this enclosure is a second sunken courtyard, usually described as the **hospital**, although it may have been an alms house or a bathhouse.

Beyond here, the pavement continues straight ahead to reach one of the "**roundabouts**" which punctuate its length – as with just about everything else at Ritigala, their original purpose remains unknown. About twenty metres before reaching the roundabout, a path heads off to the right, leading through enormous tree roots to the so-called "**Fort**", reached by a stone bridge high above a stream, and offering fine views over the forests below.

Continuing past the roundabout, a couple of **unexcavated platforms** can be seen off the path in the woods to the left, looking exactly as they must have appeared to British archeologist H.C.P. Bell when he first began exploring the site in 1893. After another 500m you reach two further sunken courtyards. The **first courtyard** contains a large double-platform structure, one of the largest buildings in the entire monastery; one of the platforms preserves the remains of the pillars which once supported a building. A smaller raised terrace stands next to it (the elaborate urinal stone which formerly lay next to this platform had apparently vanished at the time of writing). The left-hand side of the first courtyard is bounded by two **stele**; according to one theory, monks would have paced between these whilst practising walking meditation. A few metres beyond lies the **second courtyard** and another large double platform.

Aukana

Some 30km northwest of Dambulla, the village of **AUKANA** is home to a magnificent twelve-metre-high standing **Buddha** (Rs.500). The statue has become one of the defining symbols of Sri Lankan Buddhism, and full-scale copies can be found all over the country. The statue stands close to the vast **Kala Wewa** tank, created by the unfortunate King Dhatusena (see p.330) in the fifth century, though the Buddha itself is likely to date from some three or four centuries later, contemporaneous with Polonnaruwa's Gal Vihara and Lankatilaka, and the images at Buduruwagala and Maligawila. The brief craze for such monumental devotional statues may have been the result of Indian Mahayana influence, with its emphasis on the Buddha's superhuman, transcendental powers.

Aukana means "sun-eating", and dawn, when the low light brings out the fine detail of the east-facing statue, is the best time to visit (if you can organize a car and driver for such an early hour). The statue is in the unusual (for Sri Lanka) *asisa mudra*, the blessing position, with the right hand turned sideways to the viewer, as though on the point of delivering a swift karate chop. The figure is carved in the round, just connected at the back to the rock from which it's cut, though the lotus plinth it stands on is made from a separate piece of rock. The walls at the foot of the statue would originally have enclosed a vaulted image chamber.

Aukana is very difficult to reach by public transport. The best option is to catch a bus between Anuradhapura and Dambulla and get off at **Kekirawa**, then catch a local bus to Aukana or take a tuktuk.

Sasseruwa

Some 11km west of Aukana lies the remote and little-visited **Sasseruwa Buddha** (also known as the Reswehera Buddha), another standing Buddha of an almost equal height, though apparently uncompleted. Two legends connect it with the Aukana Buddha. The first, and more prosaic, says that cracks (which can be seen in the torso) started appearing during construction, and that it was therefore abandoned, with a new statue being created at Aukana. A second and more poetic legend relates that the two Buddhas were carved at the same time in competition between a master and his student. The master's Aukana Buddha was finished first and the frustrated student, realizing his own limitations, abandoned the Sasseruwa image in disappointment. A third, and perhaps more convincing, theory has it that the two statues were created at completely separate times, with the Sasseruwa image dating from the third century AD and reflecting the Greek-influenced Gandharan style of sculpture, which originated in present-day Afghanistan and provided a model for Buddha images across South Asia – certainly the Sasseruwa Buddha's ungainly square head and rather heavy features are in striking contrast to the chiselled elegance of the Aukana image. The figure is in the *abhaya mudra* ("Have No Fear" pose) and, as at Aukana, originally stood inside an image house, as shown by the holes for beams cut into the rock around it. The statue was once part of a **monastery** which tradition claims was established by Vattagamini Abhaya, who found refuge here during his period in hiding from Tamil invaders (see p.324). Remains of the monastic complex surround the statue, including a pair of cave temples, one with a large reclining Buddha and another with Kandyan-era paintings and further Buddha images.

Sasseruwa is difficult enough to find even with your own transport (follow the signs to Reswehera), and impossible by public transport.

Anuradhapura

For well over a thousand years, the history of Sri Lanka was essentially the history of **ANURADHAPURA**. Situated almost at the centre of the island's northern plains, the city rose to prominence very early in the development of Sri Lanka, and maintained its pre-eminent position for over a millennium until being finally laid waste by Indian invaders in 993. At its height, Anuradhapura was one of the greatest cities of its age, functioning as the island's centre of both temporal and spiritual power, dotted with dozens of monasteries populated by as many as ten thousand monks – one of the greatest monastic cities the world has ever seen. The kings of Anuradhapura oversaw the golden age of Sinhalese culture, and the temples and the enormous dagobas they erected were amongst the greatest architectural feats of their time, surpassed in scale only by the great pyramids at Giza. Anuradhapura also lay at the heart of the great Sinhalese hydraulic achievements (see p.361), with vast **reservoirs** (tanks) constructed around the city to store water through the long dry seasons and irrigate the surrounding paddy fields. The city's fame spread to Greece and Rome and, judging by the number of Roman coins found here, appears to have enjoyed a lively trade with the latter.

Anuradhapura remains a magical place. The sheer scale of the ruined ancient city – and the thousand-plus years of history buried here – is overwhelming, and you could spend days or even weeks ferreting around amongst the ruins, although sadly the hefty entrance charges levied on foreign tourists discourage visits of longer than a day.

Some history

From around 377 BC to 993 AD, the history of Anuradhapura was effectively the history of Sri Lanka – see pp.415–419 in Contexts for a full outline. Following the destruction of the city in 993 AD, the Cholas established themselves a new capital at **Polonnaruwa**, which thereafter took centre-stage in Sri Lankan history. Anuradhapura never recovered its previous glory, and in 1073 the city was finally abandoned, though as late as the 1260s, Parakramabahu II of Dambadeniya was restoring buildings at Anuradhapura – albeit more as a symbolic nod towards the illustrious past than as a practical attempt to restore the city to its former fortunes.

Following the collapse of the great northern Sinhalese civilization, Anuradhapura was reclaimed by the jungle, and largely forgotten by the outside world, except by the communities of reclusive monks and guardians of the sacred bo tree who continued to live here. The British "rediscovered" the city in the nineteenth century, making it a provincial capital in 1833, after which Anuradhapura slowly began to rise from the ashes. Since the 1950s, the considerable **Anuradhapura New Town** has sprung up to the east of the Sacred Precinct, while in 1980 a huge UNESCO programme began with the goal of effecting a complete **restoration** of the ancient city. The programme continues to this day, and has assumed enormous national significance for the Buddhist Sinhalese, who see the reclamation of Anuradhapura's great dagobas and other monuments from the jungle after

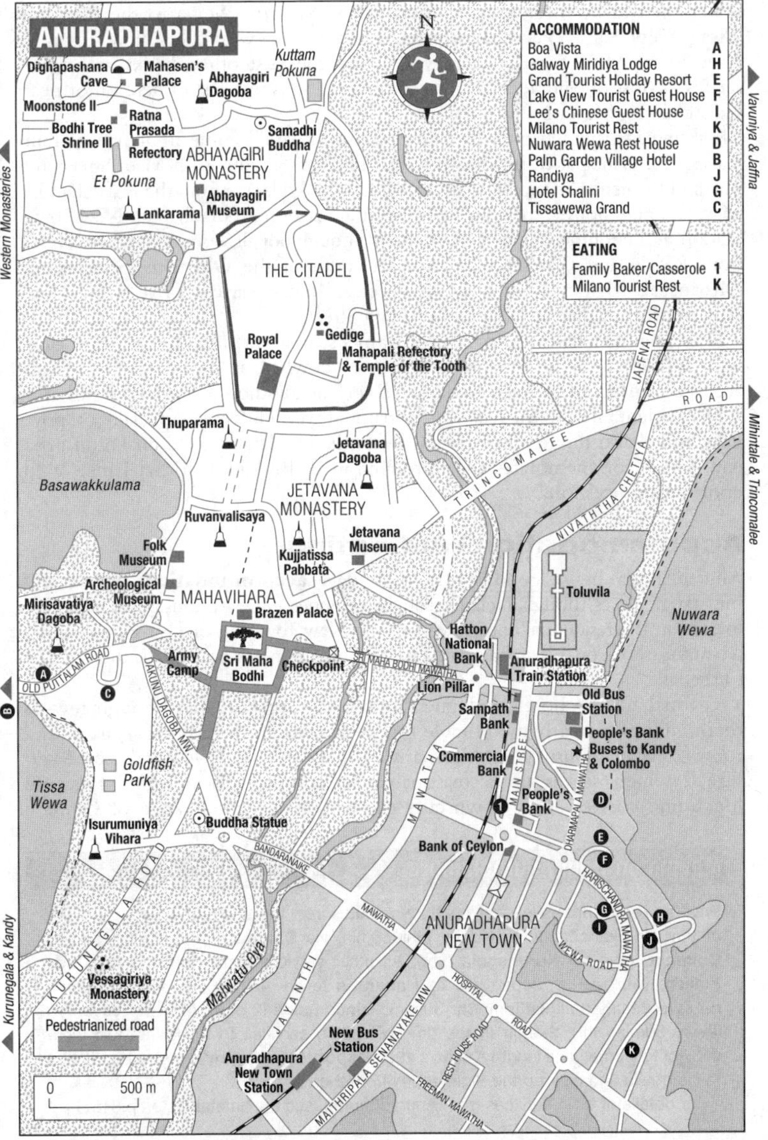

over a millennium as a powerful symbol of national identity and resurgence. As a consequence, the city has periodically been a target for separatist **bomb attacks**, and the army retains a highly visible presence.

Arrival

Anuradhapura divides into two distinct areas: **Anuradhapura New Town**, which is home to almost all the town's accommodation and practical services, and the **Sacred Precinct** to the west, site of the ancient city. The entire town is hemmed in by three great artificial lakes, **Nuwara Wewa** to the east, and **Tissa Wewa** and **Basawakkulama Tank** to the west. The New Town is bisected by Main Street, where you'll find the post office, banks and other services. Most of Anuradhapura's accommodation is just east of here on or near Harischandra Mawatha.

Arriving in Anuradhapura by public transport, you'll come in at one of four places. The principal **train station**, Anuradhapura Station, is on Main Street just north of the centre of the New Town, a Rs.100 tuktuk ride from the Harischandra Mawatha guesthouses; there's a subsidiary train station, Anuradhapura New Town Station, at the southern end of Main Street, though not all services stop here. Buses from Kandy and Colombo pull in just south of the **Old Bus Station** on Dharmapala Mawatha, east of Main Street. All other services arrive at the **New Bus Station**, at the southern end of Main Street.

There are branches of all the major **banks** strung out along Main Street, each with **ATMs** accepting foreign cards. There's nowhere in the centre of town to access the **internet**; *Milano*, *Shalini* or *Boa Vista* guesthouses are your best bet.

The ancient city is crowded with pilgrims at weekends and, especially, on poya days, and is also the focus of several **festivals**. The largest, held on Poson poya day (June), commemorates the introduction of Buddhism to Sri Lanka with enormous processions.

Accommodation and eating

Anuradhapura has a good spread of budget **accommodation**, plus a few mid-range places, though a relative paucity of upper-range options. Most places are located in the residential enclave east of the New Town on or near Harischandra Mawatha; those on Harischandra Mawatha itself aren't as peaceful as those closer to the lake.

As usual, all the hotels and guesthouses have **restaurants**, though few of them offer particularly memorable food – the best of them is the smart dining room at *Milano Tourist Rest*. Alternatively, make for the *Family Baker* on Main Street, which serves up a reasonable selection of cheap short eats and lunchtime curries at its downstairs canteen, and a good range of Chinese

Moving on from Anuradhapura

Private express **buses** leave every thirty minutes from the side of the road just south of the Old Bus Station to **Kandy** (3hr 30min) via **Dambulla** (1hr 45min), and to **Colombo** (5hr) via **Kurunegala** (3hr). All other services leave from the New Bus Station, with regular departures to **Habarana** (every 45min; 2hr 30min), **Polonnaruwa** (hourly until 3.45pm; 3hr 30min), **Trincomalee** (2 daily; 5hr) and **Vavuniya** (every 30min; 3hr), though at the time of writing services to these last two were subject to (sometimes lengthy) delays at checkpoints. For **Sigiriya**, take a Kandy bus to Dambulla and pick up the Sigiriya bus from there.

For details of **train** services from Anuradhapura, see the timetables on p.315.

dishes in the air-conditioned *Casserole* restaurant upstairs – though the latter is completely devoid of atmosphere. One speciality is **lake fish** from the local tanks – these rather undernourished creatures are fresh but decidedly bony, and are best when fried.

Budget

Boa Vista 142 Old Puttalam Rd ⓣ025-223 5052, ⓔshanidacunha@live.com. Excellent guesthouse in a superb position in the heart of the Sacred Precinct. Rooms are spacious, modern and spotlessly clean; the more expensive ones have a/c, hot water and balconies with lake views. Internet Rs.200 per hr. ❸, a/c ❺

Grand Tourist Holiday Resort Lake Rd ⓣ025-223 5173. Well-run guesthouse attractively located overlooking Nuwara Wewa, with views of Mihintale in the distance. The huge, high-ceilinged rooms in the main house (with a/c and hot water) are the ones to go for – those in the separate building are rather stuffy. There's also a pretty restaurant (especially attractive at night), though the food is disappointing and the whole place is a tad overpriced. Bikes Rs.300 per day. ❸, a/c ❹

Lake View Tourist Guest House Lake Rd ⓣ025-222 1593. Modern house in a peaceful location near Nuwara Wewa with a range of fan and a/c rooms; some are a bit old and worn, others are bright and new, while a few have hot water. Good value, if slightly uninspiring. Bikes Rs.250 per day. ❶–❷, a/c ❸

Lee's Chinese Guest House Off Harischandra Mw ⓣ025-223 5476. Three large, very bare but acceptable rooms – amongst the cheapest in town, and with excellent single rates (Rs.500). There's also a passable Chinese restaurant (bring your own booze) attached. ❷

Milano Tourist Rest J.R. Jaya Mw ⓣ025-222 2364, ⓔmilanotrest@yahoo.com. One of the friendliest and most popular places in town, with a big selection of well-maintained rooms spread across three separate buildings: all are bright and modern and smarter ones have a/c, hot water and satellite TV. There's also a good (if pricey) attached restaurant, a nice little beer garden and free pick up from the station. Bikes Rs.200 per day; internet Rs.50 per hr. ❷, a/c ❹

Hotel Shalini 41/388 Harischandra Mw ⓣ025-222 2425, ⓔhotelshalini@gmail.com. Well-run, slightly upmarket guesthouse with a big selection of comfortable a/c (Rs.500 supplement) rooms, all with hot water and satellite TV (but get one away from the road). The whimsical blue main building has an attractive restaurant under a big wooden roof, though the food is variable. There's also internet access (Rs.60 per hr), bikes (Rs.250 per day) and free pick up/drop off from bus or train stations on arrival/departure. ❸, a/c ❹

Mid-range and expensive

Galway Miridiya Lodge Wasaladantha Mw ⓣ025-222 2112, ⓦwww.galway.lk. The poshest New Town option, this resort-style hotel has bright, cheery rooms (all with a/c; some with TV for a supplement), a good-sized pool (non-guests Rs.350) and gardens running down to Nuwara Wewa. ❻

Nuwara Wewa Rest House Off Dharmapala Mw ⓣ025-222 1414, ⓦwww.quickshaws.com. Tranquil place in attractive gardens, with a small swimming pool (non-guests Rs.500) and a terrace restaurant. Rooms (all with a/c) are a bit drab, with painted brick walls and worn furniture, and poor value at quoted rates, though prices are highly negotiable. ❺

Palm Garden Village Hotel Puttalam Rd, Pandulagama, 6km west of town ⓣ025-222 3961, ⓦwww.palmgardenvillage.com. Anuradhapura's only upmarket option has a beautiful sylvan setting, with accommodation in two- to four-room colonial-style villas dotted around an orchard of mango and *margosa* trees. Furnished in whole forests of teak and mahogany, rooms are classic and elegant, with fine four-posters and plenty of mod cons; verandas bedecked with planters' chairs add to the appealingly indolent atmosphere. There's also good food and a lovely period-pastiche bar, and facilities include a large pool, Ayurveda centre and bullock-cart rides in the surrounding countryside. ❻

Randiya Muditha Mw, off Harischandra Mw ⓣ025-222 2868, ⓦwww.hotelrandiya.com. Small, well-run hotel with plush, modern (if rather bland) rooms; all have a/c and satellite TV, while smarter ones have bath tubs. Bikes Rs.200 per day; internet Rs.150 per hr. ❹–❺

Tissawewa Grand Sacred Precinct, near the Mirisavatiya dagoba ⓣ025-222 2299, ⓦwww.quickshaws.com. Anuradhapura's most memorable place to stay, this famous old rest house is set in a rambling and gorgeously atmospheric nineteenth-century villa (built for a former British governor) in the heart of the Sacred Precinct. Recent refurbishment work on the (a/c) ground-floor rooms has, in the main, enhanced the period charm (though prices have doubled); simpler and cheaper – but still full of character – are the creaky, old-fashioned rooms upstairs. No alcohol served, though you can bring your own. ❺, a/c ❼

The Sacred Precinct

Anuradhapura's scatter of monuments and remains is vast and potentially confusing. The easiest way to get a mental handle on the **Sacred Precinct** is to think of it in terms of its three great monasteries: the Mahavihara, Jetavana and Abhayagiri – about two-thirds of the main sites belong to one of these complexes. The most obvious place to start is the **Mahavihara**, at the physical and historical centre of the ancient city, beginning at the Ruvanvalisaya dagoba and walking south to Sri Maha Bodhi, before doubling back towards the Thuparama. From here you can either head east to the **Jetavana Monastery** or north to the **Abhayagiri** complex. There are further important clusters of sights at the **Citadel**, between the Mahavihara and Abhayagiri monasteries; and **south of the Mahavihara**, between the Mirisavetiya dagoba and Issurumuniya Temple. The major dagobas provide useful landmarks if you get disoriented.

Visiting the ancient city: practicalities

The whole site is much too big to cover on foot, and it's far easier to explore by **bicycle**; these can be hired from virtually all the town's guesthouses for Rs.200–300 per day, though bear in mind that bikes (or indeed any other type of vehicle) aren't allowed anywhere near the Sri Maha Bodhi. **Guides** around town are likely to offer their services; if not, you should be able to pick one up either at the Jetavana Museum (see p.367) or at the crossroads next to the Ruvanvalisaya. If you go with a guide, you might like to check their accreditation (they should be in possession of a Sri Lanka Tourism site guide's licence for Anuradhapura) to make sure you're getting someone genuine. Expect to pay around US$15 for half a day, though you may be able to bargain.

Most (but not all) the sites at Anuradhapura are covered by the **Cultural Triangle ticket** (see p.314), which can be bought at the Jetavana, Abhayagiri and Archeological museums, plus at the ticket office at the northern entrance to the Jetavana dagoba. Tickets are only valid for one day at each site, so if you want to explore properly you are obliged to shell out around US$25 on a fresh ticket each day, though the site is open access and in practice ticket checks are rare except at the three museums. Most visitors in any case tend to cram it all into a day, which really isn't long enough to get the full flavour of the place. A couple of sites – the Isurumuniya and Folk Museum – aren't covered by the CT ticket, while access to others, such as the Sri Maha Bodhi and the Western Monasteries, is free. The logical thing to do would be to visit these on a second day; you're allowed to go through the Sacred Precinct to reach these places even if you don't have a CT ticket. Visitors are increasingly being asked for **additional donations** at some sites, but given how much foreigners already pay to visit the place there's no reason why you should hand over even a single rupee more.

The tanks

Anuradhapura lies nestled between a trio of **tanks** (see box opposite) which provided the lifeblood of the ancient city – although from the fifth century onwards their waters were supplemented by those from larger and most distant tanks such as the Kalawewa. West of the Sri Maha Bodhi is the city's oldest tank, the **Basawakkulama**, created by Pandukabhaya around the fourth century BC. South of the city is the **Tissa Wewa**, built by Devanampiya Tissa, while on the east side of the city lies the largest of the city's tanks, the **Nuwara Wewa**, completed in around 20 BC and significantly expanded by later kings to reach its present imposing dimensions. The raised bunds (lakeside embankments) on the west and south sides of Nuwara Wewa are close to many of the town's guesthouses and perfect for an evening stroll and some birdwatching, while there are wonderful views of the city's dagobas from the north shore of the Basawakkulama.

The Mahavihara

The centre of ancient Anuradhapura was the **Mahavihara**, the oldest of the city's monasteries and for many centuries its most important. It was founded around the **Sri Maha Bodhi** by Devanampiya Tissa, who also built Sri Lanka's

Water world: irrigation in early Sri Lanka

The map of Sri Lanka is studded with literally thousands of man-made lakes, commonly known as **tanks**, or *wewas* (pronounced, and occasionally spelt, "vavas"). The civilization of early Sri Lanka was essentially agricultural, and the need to ensure a regular supply of water for rice cultivation posed a crucial problem, given the location of the island's early capitals in the dry plains of the north. The climate in these parts – long periods of drought alternating with brief monsoonal deluges – made the use of irrigation, based on the storage of water for the regular cultivation of wet fields, a vital element in early Sinhalese civilization.

The first, modest examples of hydraulic engineering date back to the earliest days of Sinhalese settlement in the third century BC, when the first farmers dammed rivers and stored water in small village reservoirs. With the later increase in royal power, Sri Lanka's kings began to take an active role in the construction of irrigation schemes, leading to the creation of the three tanks which now surround Anuradhapura. The first major irrigation works were undertaken in the reign of **Vasabha** (65–110), who is said to have created twelve irrigation canals and eleven tanks, the largest with a circumference of three kilometres. Soon afterwards, Sinhalese engineers mastered the technology which allowed water in tanks to be stored until needed, then released through sluice gates and channelled through canals to distant fields.

The first giant reservoirs were constructed in the reign of **Mahasena** (274–301), who oversaw the construction of some sixteen major tanks, including the vast Minneriya tank, and **Dhatusena** (455–473), who constructed the remarkable Jaya Ganga canal, almost 90km long and maintaining a subtle gradient of six inches to the mile, which delivered water to Anuradhapura from the huge Kalawewa (whose waters ultimately hastened that unfortunate king's demise – see p.330). Further tanks and canals were built during to the reigns of **Mogallana II** (531–551), whose Padaviya tank, in the northern Vavuniya district, was the largest ever constructed in ancient Sri Lanka, and **Aggabodhi II** (604–614), who was responsible for the tank at Giritale, amongst other works. Large new irrigation projects in the Anuradhapura region virtually ceased after the seventh century, and although the simple maintenance of the tanks and canals already built must have been a huge task, the entire system appears to have worked smoothly for the next three centuries until the final collapse of Anuradhapura in 993.

The construction of large-scale irrigation works became a defining feature of these Sinhalese civilizations: the maintenance of such massive hydraulic feats required skilled engineering and a highly evolved bureaucracy, and also encouraged the development of centralized control and hierarchical social structures. The captured waters allowed a second rice crop to be grown each year, as well as additional vegetables and pulses, all of which supported much higher population densities than would otherwise have been possible. The surplus agricultural produce created by large-scale irrigation and the taxes raised from the system were major sources of royal revenue, allowing expansive building works at home and military campaigns overseas – culminating in the reign of the Polonnaruwan king, **Parakramabahu I**, who famously declared that "not one drop of water must flow into the ocean without serving the purposes of man", and who oversaw the creation of the vast Parakrama Samudra at Polonnaruwa, one of the last but finest monuments of ancient Sinhalese irrigation.

first dagoba, the **Thuparama**, here, although this is now dwarfed by the great **Ruvanvalisaya**. The Mahavihara is still a living and vibrant place of pilgrimage rather than an archeological site, with pilgrims flocking to the Sri Maha Bodhi and Ruvanvalisaya – the former is still considered one of the world's most important Buddhist relics, rivalled in popularity in Sri Lanka only by the Tooth Relic in Kandy. Security is tight around the Sri Maha Bodhi, and you will have to go through at least one frisk and electronic check to gain access.

Sri Maha Bodhi

At the spiritual and physical heart of Anuradhapura stands the **Sri Maha Bodhi**, or Sacred Bo Tree (not included in the Cultural Triangle ticket; you may be asked for a donation). According to popular belief, this immensely venerable tree was grown from a cutting, brought to Sri Lanka by Princess Sangamitta, the sister of Mahinda (see p.373), which was taken from the original bo tree in Bodhgaya, India, under which the Buddha attained enlightenment. The original bo tree in India was destroyed not long afterwards, but the Sri Maha Bodhi survived. Cuttings from it have been grown all over the island (and indeed throughout the Buddhist countries of Southeast Asia).

The Sri Maha Bodhi sits at the centre of a large and elaborate enclosure, dotted with numerous younger bo trees and festooned with prayer flags. It grows out of the top of a series of terraces decorated with gold railings: you're

Dutugemunu the disobedient

Of all the two hundred or so kings who have ruled Sri Lanka over the past millennia, none is as revered as the semi-legendary **Dutugemunu**, the great warrior prince turned Buddhist king whose personality – a compelling mixture of religious piety and anti-Tamil nationalism – continues to provide inspiration for many Sinhalese today. Dutugemunu grew up during the reign of the Tamil general Elara, who seized control of Anuradhapura in around 205 BC and reigned there for 44 years. Much of the island remained outside the control of Anuradhapura, however, being ruled by various minor kings and chiefs who enjoyed virtual autonomy, although they may have professed some kind of token loyalty to Elara.

The most important of these subsidiary kings was **Kavan Tissa**, husband of the legendary Queen Viharamahadevi. From his base in the city of Mahagama (modern Tissamaharana), Kavan Tissa had gradually established control over the whole of the south, using a cunning mixture of marriage alliances and statecraft rather than outright military force. Despite his own growing power, the naturally cautious Kavan Tissa, anxious to protect his family and kingdom, demanded that his eldest son and heir, **Gemunu** (or Gamini, as it's often spelt), swear lasting allegiance to Elara. According to the *Mahavamsa*, on being asked to make this oath, the 12-year-old Gemunu threw his rice bowl from the table in a fury, saying he would prefer to starve rather than declare loyalty to a foreign overlord. Having made this declaration, the rebellious young prince henceforth refused to sleep with outstretched limbs, declaring that he felt unable to rest comfortably so long as he remained the subject of a foreign king, whilst demonstrating his contempt for his father by sending him items of women's clothing – all of which unfilial behaviour earned him the name of **Dutugemunu**, or "Gemunu the Disobedient".

On the death of his father, Dutugemunu acceded to the throne and set about raising an army; having assembled his forces, he set off to do battle mounted on his famous elephant, Kandula. He also took with him a spear with a Buddhist relic set into its shaft and a large contingent of Buddhist monks, thus casting himself not only as a political leader, but as the religious liberator of his island – the leader of a not able to reach the tree itself, however, and what you can see of it is curiously unimpressive, appearing neither particularly large nor old (despite one trailing branch propped up on iron supports). Far more interesting is the general scene in the enclosure, which is usually full of rapt pilgrims (the ladies dressed neatly in white saris) contemplating the tree and praying. During poya days, huge crowds of devotees flock here to make offerings.

The Brazen Palace

Just north of the Sacred Bo Tree stand the remains of the **Brazen Palace** ("Loha Pasada"), named on account of the copper roof which once covered it. The "palace" was built by Dutugemunu, though despite its name it only ever served as a monastic, rather than a royal, residence – the *Mahavamsa* describes a nine-storeyed structure with a thousand rooms (though the second part of this claim is doubtless hyperbole). Unfortunately, since most of the palace was made of wood, it burnt down just fifteen years after its construction and on a number of occasions thereafter, and had to be repeatedly rebuilt, most recently by Parakramabahu of Polonnaruwa in the twelfth century.

Little remains of the palace now apart from a dense forest of plain, closely spaced columns – some 1600 in total – each about 4m high, which would have supported the first floor. Many of these, however, did not belong to the original structure but were salvaged from other buildings at Anuradhapura. The only

kind of Buddhist jihad. Dutugemunu's campaign was a laborious affair. For some fifteen years he fought his way north, conquering the succession of minor kingdoms which lay between Mahagama and Anuradhapura, until he was finally able to engage Elara himself at Anuradhapura. After various preliminary skirmishes, Elara and Dutugemunu faced one another in single combat, each mounted on their elephants. As the *Mahavamsa* describes it:

King Duttahagamani proclaimed with beat of drum: "None but myself shall slay Elara." When he himself, armed, had mounted the armed elephant Kandula, he pursued Elara and came to the south gate of Anuradhapura.

Near the south gate of the city the two kings fought. Elara hurled his dart, Gamani evaded it; he made his own elephant pierce Elara's elephant with his tusks and he hurled his dart at Elara; and the latter fell there, with his elephant.

Dutugemunu buried Elara with full honours, decreeing that anyone passing the defeated general's tomb should dismount as a sign of respect – this decree was still apparently being obeyed in the early eighteenth century, some two thousand years later, though curiously enough, no one now knows where Elara's tomb is located. His conquest complete, the new king began an orgy of building works, including the Brazen Palace and Mirisavatiya dagoba. His most famous monument, however, was the mighty **Ruvanvalisaya** dagoba at Anuradhapura, which Dutugemunu himself did not live to see finished. He is supposed to have looked on the unfinished structure from his deathbed and said, "In times past…I engaged in battles; now, singlehanded, I commence my last conflict – with death, and it is not permitted to me to overcome my enemy."

As the leader who evicted the Tamils and united the island under Sinhalese rule for the first time, Dutugemunu is regarded as one of Sri Lanka's great heroes (at least by the Sinhalese). Despite his exploits, however, the fragile unity he left at his death quickly collapsed under subsequent, less able rulers, and within 35 years, northern Sri Lanka had once again fallen to invaders from South India.

hint of decoration is on the fallen capitals, carved with dwarfs, which lie scattered around the ground in the southeast corner of the palace. The entire palace is closed to visitors, although the modern brick pavilion surrounded by slender wooden pillars at the centre is popular with grey langur monkeys.

Ruvanvalisaya dagoba and around

North of the Brazen Palace stands the huge white **Ruvanvalisaya** (also known as the Maha Thupa, or "Great Stupa", though it's actually only the third largest in the city). Unlike the massive stupas at the Jetavana and Abhayagiri monasteries, the Ruvanvalisaya dagoba is fully restored, painted white and busy with pilgrims throughout the day. The dagoba was the crowning achievement of **Dutugemunu** (see p.362), built to commemorate his victory over Elara; it is popularly believed to enshrine various remains of the Buddha, and is thus the most revered in the city. Dutugemunu lavished enormous sums of money on the project, helped (according to legend) by the fortuitous discovery of a rich vein of silver at Ridi Vihara (see p.317), though sadly he died before his masterwork could be finished.

The dagoba now stands 55m high, rather less than its original height, its entire base encircled by a strip of orange ribbon almost 300m long. According to tradition, its original shape was inspired by the form of a bubble – a perfect hemisphere – though the effects of subsequent renovations have flattened its outline slightly. It stands on a terrace whose outer face is decorated with life-sized elephant heads (most are modern replacements). Symbolically, the elephants support the platform on which the dagoba is built, just as, in Buddhist cosmology, they hold up the earth itself (at a more prosaic level, elephants also helped in the construction of the stupa, being used to stamp down the dagoba's foundations). Four subsidiary dagobas stand in each corner of the terrace – considerable structures in their own right, but completely dwarfed by the main dagoba.

Entering the terrace on which the dagoba stands, you pass through a security check, then up a stairway flanked by fine *nagaraja* guardstones. Four **vahalkadas** mark the cardinal points around the base of the dagoba: tall, rectangular structures decorated with bands of elephant heads and, above, friezes of lions, bulls and elephants carved in low relief – the one on the western side is the oldest and not yet fully restored. Walking clockwise around the dagoba you reach a modern **shrine** holding five standing Buddha statues. The four identical limestone figures date back to the eighth century and are thought to represent three previous Buddhas and the historical Buddha; the fifth (modern) statue is of the future Buddha, Maitreya, wearing a tiara and holding a lotus – an unexpected Mahayanist touch in the heart of Anuradhapura's most conservative Theravada monastery. Continuing clockwise brings you to an ancient limestone **statue**, facing the dagoba's south side and popularly believed to represent Dutugemunu contemplating his masterpiece. A little further round stands a **model** of the dagoba, showing the original shape, with its slightly steeper sides and less flattened outline.

A couple of hundred metres east of the Ruvanvalisaya is the **Kujjatissa Pabbata**, the remains of a small dagoba on a stone base with well-preserved guardstones. The structure dates from around the eighth century, but probably occupies the site of an earlier building – it's been suggested that this was the place, just outside what was once the south gate into the city, where Dutugemunu buried Elara and raised a memorial in his honour.

Thuparama and around

Heading north from the Ruvanvalisaya, a broad walkway leads 300m to the **Thuparama**. This was the first dagoba to be built in Sri Lanka (its name means simply "The Stupa"), though by later Anuradhapuran standards it's a modest structure, standing less than 20m high. It was constructed by Devanampiya Tissa shortly after his conversion to Buddhism at the behest of Mahinda (see p.373), who suggested that the new Sinhalese faith be provided with a suitable focus for its worship. A monk was despatched to Ashoka, the Buddhist emperor of India, who obligingly provided Devanampiya Tissa with two of his religion's most sacred relics: the Buddha's right collarbone and alms bowl. The bowl was sent to Mihintale (and subsequently disappeared), whilst the bone was enshrined in the Thuparama, which remains a popular pilgrimage site to this day.

By the seventh century, the original structure had fallen into ruins; Aggabodhi II had it restored and converted into a **vatadage** (circular relic house), a uniquely Sri Lankan form of Buddhist architecture, with the original dagoba being enclosed in a new roof, supported by four concentric circles of pillars of diminishing height – an excellent model in the Archeological Museum shows how it would all have looked. The roof has long since disappeared and the surviving pillars now topple unsteadily in all directions, though you can still make out the very eroded carvings of geese (*hamsas*, a protective bird) which adorn their capitals. The dagoba itself is actually a reconstruction of 1862, when it was restored in a conventional bell shape – the original structure was built in the slightly slope-shouldered "heap of paddy" form.

The area just south of the Thuparama is littered with the remains of buildings from the Mahavihara monastery, including numerous living units arranged in the quincunx pattern (like the five dots on the face of a dice) which is characteristic of so many of the city's monastic dwellings. About 100m south of the Thuparama is a pillared shrine set on an imposing brick platform, with one of the most magnificent **moonstones** at Anuradhapura, though sadly it's protected – as are most of the city's best moonstones – by an ugly metal railing. The outer faces of the **balustrades** flanking the entrance steps are decorated with unusual carvings showing canopied panels filled with deer, hermits, monkeys, delicately sculpted trees and a pair of large lions. Their meaning remains unclear, though they may be intended to depict an ideal Buddhist realm in which creatures of all persuasions live harmoniously together.

The Archeological Museum and Folk Museum

West of the Ruvanvalisaya dagoba lie a pair of museums, although they can't be reached directly from the dagoba; you'll have to follow the road which runs north of Ruvanvalisaya and west to Basawakkulama, and then turn south along the lakeside road. The **Archeological Museum** (daily 8am–5pm; entrance only with CT ticket) has numerous sculptures from Anuradhapura displayed in the rooms and garden of a creaking old colonial British administrative building, though it's looking increasingly denuded as exhibits are carted away to fill newer museums around the Cultural Triangle. Items on show include a number of simple standing and seated Buddhas, various carvings, coins and bronzes, plus an interesting cut away model of the Thuparama vatadage (see opposite). The garden is full of an entertaining troupe of dwarfs and *nagarajas*, a selection of finely carved urinal stones and "squatting plates" and lots of pillar inscriptions recording grants of land and other administrative details.

The **Folk Museum** (Tues–Sat 9am–5pm; not included in the CT ticket, entrance Rs.300), a little further down the same road, explores rural life in the north central province, with forgettable displays of cooking vessels, handicrafts and the like. Save your money.

Jetavana monastery

The last of the three great monasteries built in Anuradhapura, the **Jetavana monastery** was raised on the site of the Nandana Grove – or *Jotivana* – where Mahinda (see p.373) once preached, and where his body was later cremated. The monastery was founded during the reign of the great tank-building king, **Mahasena** (274–301), following one of the religious controversies which periodically convulsed the ancient city. Relations between Mahasena and the Mahavihara monastery had been strained ever since the king had disciplined some of its monks. They retaliated by refusing to accept alms from the king, who responded by pulling down some of the Mahavihara's buildings and then establishing the new Jetavana monastery on land owned by the Mahavihara. The king gave the monastery to a monk called Tissa – who was then promptly expelled from the Sangha for breaking the rule that individual monks should not own any private property. Despite this, the new monastery continued under a new leader, becoming an important rival source of Theravada doctrine within the city.

The Jetavana dagoba

The centrepiece of Jetavana is its monumental red-brick **dagoba**. Descriptions of this massive edifice tend to attract a string of statistical superlatives: in its original form the dagoba stood 120m high, and was at the time of its construction the third-tallest structure in the world, surpassed only by the two great pyramids at Giza. It was also the world's biggest stupa and is still the tallest and largest structure made entirely of brick anywhere on earth: it took a quarter of a century to build and contains over ninety million bricks – enough, as the excitable Victorian archeologist Emerson Tennant calculated, to build a three-metre-high wall from London to Edinburgh (though why anyone would wish to erect such a pointless construction at this exact height and between these two particular cities has never been satisfactorily explained). The dagoba has now lost its topmost portion, but still reaches a neck-wrenching height of 70m – similar to the Abhayagiri dagoba. UNESCO-sponsored restoration began in 1981 and is slowly grinding towards completion, though there's plenty of rubble lying around, and sections on the north side remain to be excavated. All of the dagoba's four **vahalkadas** have now been restored, however, with gaps in the masonry filled by brick; the one facing the entrance on the southern side is particularly fine, studded with eroded elephant heads, with *naga* stones to either side and two figures to the right – the top is a *nagaraja*, the lower one an unidentified goddess.

The rest of the monastery

The area south of the dagoba is littered with the extensive remains of the Jetavana monastery, all carefully excavated and landscaped. The monastery would once have housed some three thousand monks, and the scale of the remains is impressive, although except in a few places only the bases of the various structures survive. The first monastery buildings were constructed during the third century in the area north of the dagoba (which remains largely unexcavated) and gradually spread south and east as the monastery expanded over the next six centuries – most of what you see today dates from the ninth and tenth centuries. Immediately behind the Jetavana Museum (see opposite) lies a deep and beautifully preserved **bathing pool** and the unusual latticed **Buddhist Railing**, which formerly enclosed either a bo tree shrine or an image house; the three tiers of the fence are claimed to represent Buddhism's "three jewels" (see p.442). Slightly east of here stands the **Uposathagara** (chapter house), with dozens of roughly hewn and very closely spaced pillars;

these probably supported upper storeys, since a room with this many pillars crowded into it would have been of little practical use.

To the west of the dagoba stands the **Patimaghara** (image house), the largest surviving building at Jetavana: a tall, slender door leads between eight-metre-high surviving sections of wall into a narrow image chamber, at the end of which is a lotus base which once supported a standing Buddha image. Below this is a latticed stone **reliquary** consisting of 25 holes in which relics or statues of various deities would have been placed; further examples are on show in the Jetavana Museum. Around the image house are more extensive remains of monastic residences – many are laid out in the characteristic quincunx (five-of-dice) pattern, with a large central building, in which the more senior monks would have lived, surrounded by four smaller structures, the whole enclosed by a square brick wall.

Jetavana Museum

The interesting **Jetavana Museum** (daily 8am–5pm; entrance with CT ticket only) holds a striking collection of objects recovered during excavations around the monastery. The first of the three rooms contains fine fragments of decorative friezes and carvings from the site, including Buddhas and a particularly magnificent guardstone. The second room is the most absorbing, filled with an assortment of finely crafted personal items which give a rare glimpse into the secular life of Anuradhapura, with displays of necklaces, beads, bangles, ear ornaments and gold jewellery, as well as precious stones such as amethysts and garnets. Next door is a less engaging collection of pottery, though look out for the skilfully engineered three-tiered urinal pot. A pavilion outside has more stone sculptures: friezes, elephants and guardstones.

The Citadel

The area north of the Thuparama, between the Mahavihara and Abhayagiri monasteries, is occupied by the **Citadel**, or Royal Palace area. This was the secular heart of the city, enclosed by a moat and thick walls, which perhaps reached a height of 5m. Although most of the visible remains here date from much later in Anuradhapura's history, various recent deep-level excavations have revealed ironware, beads and black- and red-ware pottery, confirming that the site was inhabited at least as far back as the tenth century BC. Impossible to miss from the main road, though sealed off behind barbed wire, is one of the largest – and most mysterious – areas of current excavation in Anuradhapura, where archeologists have dug down to the city's original level, around 8m deep. There's clear evidence of a complex hydraulic system, though the site's purpose remains unknown.

A couple of hundred metres south of here, the present **Royal Palace** is, in contrast, one of the newest buildings at Anuradhapura, having been built by Vijayabahu I after his victory over the Cholas in 1070. By this time power had shifted to Polonnaruwa; the palace here was no more than a secondary residence, and little remains of it apart from the terrace on which it stood and a few bits of wall. The main steps up to the terrace are flanked by two fine **guardstones** featuring a couple of unusually obese dwarfs (a similar pair guard the steps on the far side). A wall on the terrace, protected by a corrugated-iron shelter, bears a few splashes of paint, all that remains of the frescoes which once decorated the palace.

About 100m east of the palace, on the opposite side of the road, are the remains of the Mahapali Refectory, or **Royal Alms Hall**. The huge stone trough here (it looks like something a horse would eat from) would have been filled with rice for the monks by the city's lay followers and could have fed as many as five thousand – any monk could find food here, even during periods of famine. Next to the refectory is an impressively deep stepped **well**.

Immediately north of the refectory are the remains of a building studded with a cluster of columns reaching up to 4m high; this is thought to be the very first **Temple of the Tooth**, constructed to house the Tooth Relic (see p.243) when it was originally brought to the island in 313. The columns may have supported a second storey, and it's been suggested that the Tooth Relic was kept on the upper floor, thus setting the pattern for all the shrines which subsequently housed it. The Tooth Relic was taken annually in procession from here to the Abhayagiri in a ceremony which was the ancestor of today's great Esala Perahera at Kandy. Just east of here are the partially reconstructed remains, reaching up to eight metres high, of a brick **gedige**, with several original stone doorways and some of its window frames intact.

▲ Guardstone, Anuradhapura

Abhayagiri monastery

The third of Anuradhapura's great monasteries, **Abhayagiri** lies on the northern side of the city, and was founded by King Vattagamini Abhaya (also known as Valagamba or Valagambahu) in 88 BC. According to the *Mahavamsa*, Vattagamini had earlier lost his throne to a group of invading Tamils. While escaping from the city, the deposed king was jeered at by a Jain priest named Giri, who shouted, "The great black lion is fleeing." The exiled king retorted that, "If my wish [of regaining my kingdom] is fulfilled, I will build a temple here." Fourteen years later, Vattagamini returned with an army and drove the Tamils out of Sri Lanka. Upon returning to Anuradhapura he quickly established a new Buddhist monastery in the place of the existing one, naming it after the second part of his own name (meaning "fearless" – as in the *abhaya*, or "Have No Fear" Buddhist *mudra*), combined with the name of the priest who had taunted him.

Abhayagiri rapidly surpassed the older Mahavihara as the largest and most influential monastery in the country. By the fifth century it was home to five thousand monks and had become an important source of new Buddhist doctrine, and a flourishing centre of artistic activity and philosophical speculation. Although it remained within the Theravada tradition, elements of Mahayana and Tantric Buddhism were taught here (much to the disgust of the ultra-conservative clergy of the Mahavihara, who labelled the monks of Abhayagiri heretics), and the monastery established wide-ranging contacts with India, China, Burma and even Java.

Abhayagiri is the focus of much of the excavation work that continues at Anuradhapura, and in many ways is the most interesting and atmospheric quarter of the city. One of the great pleasures here is simply in throwing away the guidebook and wandering off at random amongst the innumerable ruins which litter the area – indeed getting lost is half the fun. The sheer scale of the monastic remains is prodigious, while their setting, scattered amidst beautiful light woodland, is magical – particularly memorable early in the morning or at dusk, when with only a little imagination you could fancy yourself an intrepid Victorian explorer stumbling upon the remains of a lost city.

Abhayagiri Museum and around

The logical place to start is at the impressive **Abhayagiri Museum** (daily 8am–5pm; entrance with CT ticket only), which gives a detailed account of the monastery's history backed by a small but interesting selection of well-preserved artefacts recovered here. A particular highlight are the fine ornamental altar stone slabs, retrieved from the dagoba site, which retain their original painting work, while other exhibits range from Buddha images through to more unusual fancy goods including tiny crystal dagobas, colourful beads and a few delicate gold objects. Larger stone sculptures are displayed on the veranda outside, including a beautiful pair of guardstones.

Just south of here on the main road (you probably passed it on the way in) is the **Lankarama**, a first-century BC *vatadage*; the rows of pillars which surround the ruins, some retaining finely carved capitals, would originally have supported a roof. The present dagoba is modern, white and unusually square in shape.

Abhayagiri dagoba

As at Mahavihara and Jetavana, Abhayagiri's most striking feature is its great **dagoba**, originally built by Vattagamini Abhaya (89–77 BC), enlarged during the reign of Gajabahu I (114–136) and later restored by Parakramabahu I in the twelfth century. It formerly stood around 115m tall, only slightly smaller than the Jetavana dagoba, making it the second tallest in the ancient world – the loss of its pinnacle has now reduced its height to around 70m. The dagoba is popularly believed to be built over a footprint of the Buddha, who is said to have stood with one foot here and the other one on top of Adam's Peak. It's still largely unrestored, and much of the structure remains covered in earth and vegetation – a great fuzzy mound which makes a rather mysterious sight when seen rising out of the forest from a distance – though close up, cloaked in scaffolding, it looks like an enormous building site.

Flanking the main entrance stand two guardian statues of **Padmanidhi** and **Samkanidhi**, two fat and dwarfish attendants of Kubera, the god of wealth. These statues have become objects of devotion in their own right, and are enclosed in ugly little concrete sheds with grilles to which pilgrims tie prayer ribbons. At the top of the steps stand a pair of the incongruously Grecian-looking urns, symbolizing prosperity, which can be found at several points around the monastery, while just beyond there's a modern temple with a large reclining Buddha.

The dagoba's four **vahalkadas** are similar in design to those at the Ruvanvalisaya, and are in various stages of decay. The eastern *vahalkada* is flanked by unusual low-relief carving showing Classical-looking elephants, bulls and lions, all jumping up on their hind legs, plus two winged figures looking like a pair of angels who've flown straight out of the Italian Renaissance. The western *vahalkada* is flanked by delicate floral patterns.

The Samadhi Buddha and Kuttam Pokuna

Around 250m east of the dagoba lies a famous early example of Sinhalese sculpture, the so-called **Samadhi Buddha**, carved from limestone in the fourth century AD and showing the Buddha in the meditation (*samadhi*) posture – a classic and serene example of early Buddhist art, now ignominiously enclosed in a concrete shelter modelled on the Buddhist Railing at the Jetavana monastery. The image is particularly revered, which means you should take your shoes off when you approach it. The Buddha was originally one of a group of four statues (the base and seated legs of another figure can be seen opposite it); it's thought that all four were originally painted and had gems for eyes.

Northeast of the Buddha lie the magnificent **Kuttam Pokuna** ("Twin Baths"), constructed in the eighth century for monks' ritual ablutions, with stepped sides leading down into the baths. These survive in marvellously good condition (despite being full of fetid green water, an unwholesome domain for the resident gunk-covered turtles) and are one of few places where you can get an obvious sense of the ancient city's original splendour. One of the two is significantly bigger than the other. Standing at the far end of the smaller pond and looking to your right you can see a small stone pool at ground level. Water would have been fed into this and the sediment left to settle, after which the cleaned water would have been released into the smaller bath through the conduit with the eroded lion's head on one side. The superb *naga* (snake) stone next to this conduit was a symbol of good fortune, while the urns at the top of the stairs down into the bath symbolize plenty. Water passed from the smaller to the larger bath through small holes which connect the two.

The rest of the monastery

About 200m west of the Abhayagiri dagoba lies **Mahasen's Palace** (also known as the Queen's Pavilion), though it's not actually a royal residence at all, but an image house dating from the eighth or ninth century. It's famous principally for its delicately carved **moonstone**, sadly enclosed within a metal railing. Behind this rises a flight of finely carved steps supported by the inevitable dwarfs, squatting like tiny sumo wrestlers.

Continuing west, just across the road, are the pillars of the **Ratna Prasada** ("Gem Palace"), originally a five-storey mansion that functioned as the main chapter house of the Abhayagiri monastery, built in the eighth century by Mahinda II. This boasts a magnificent **guardstone** dating from the eighth century and showing the usual *nagaraja* standing on a dwarf, shaded by a seven-headed cobra and carrying various symbols of prosperity: lotus flowers, a flowering branch and an urn. The **arch** which frames this figure shows an extraordinary chain of joined images, with four *makaras* swallowing two tiny human couples and two equally microscopic elephants, separated by four flying dwarfs; an unimpressed elephant stands to one side. Not surprisingly, the symbolism of this strange piece of sculpture remains obscure. About 100m west of here is another magnificent (and unfenced) **moonstone** ("Moonstone II"), almost the equal of the one at Mahasen's Palace, with more portly dwarf on the carved steps behind. North of here, you may be able to gain access to one of Abhayaghiri's most recently excavated sites, the partly reconstructed **Dighapashana Cave**, which stands in the lee of a giant boulder. On the right-hand side of the cave, steps lead up to a long Pali inscription, carved into the rock, while the base of the brick wall to the left is faced in plasterwork over two millennia old.

A couple of hundred of metres southeast of here are the remains of the so-called **Bodhi Tree Shrine III**, dating from the third century BC and boasting two plain *sri padas*, a sandstone Buddha statue minus one arm and a couple of pillar inscriptions, while the floor is studded with lotus-shaped pillar bases (the actual pillars are long gone). Further south of here is the colossal **Et Pokuna** ("Elephant Pool"). Dug out of the bedrock, this is the largest bathing pool in the ancient city and quite big enough to hold a whole herd of elephants. Spreading away south and east from here lie the remains of the **monastic residences**, with innumerable terraces, hypostyle rooms, stairways and baths, many set atop steep-sided plinths; the highlight is the **refectory**, with a huge, fifteen-metre-long rice trough, about a hundred metres east, across the road from the Et Pokuna.

The western monasteries

The countryside west of the Abhayagiri monastery, beyond the Bulankulam tank, was formerly home to Anuradhapura's **western monasteries**. These fourteen monasteries were home to the most extreme of the city's Buddhist sects – the *pamsukulika*, or "tattered-robe", monks, who decamped here during the seventh century in reaction to the relatively luxurious lifestyles enjoyed by monks in the city's great royal monasteries, devoting themselves to a life of privation and meditation. The best preserved of the monasteries lies about 2km southwest of Abhayagiri. Remains here include a double-platform structure (see p.354), similar to those found at Ritigala and Arankele, a meditation walk, the remains of monks' cells and baths, plus a sumptuously decorated urinal stone – the symbolism of monks urinating on the symbols of wealth depicted in these carvings (gems; the residence of Kubera, guardian of wealth) is obvious.

The southern city

If you have the energy for more, there's a further cluster of interesting remains west and south of the Sri Maha Bodhi along the banks of the Tissa Wewa. Around a kilometre west of the Sri Maha Bodhi lies the **Mirisavatiya dagoba**, a huge structure which was the first thing to be built by Dutugemunu after he captured the city; it looks very similar to – and only slightly smaller than – the

Ruvanvalisaya dagoba, which Dutugemunu subsequently had constructed. The obligatory legend recounts how the new king went to bathe in the nearby Tissa Wewa, leaving his famous spear (in which was enshrined a Buddhist relic) stuck in the ground by the side of the tank. Having finished bathing, he discovered that he was unable to pull his spear out of the ground – an unmistakeable message from the heavens. At the dagoba's consecration, Dutugemunu dedicated the monument to the Sangha, offering it in compensation, the great king declared, for his once having eaten a bowl of chillies without offering any to the city's monks, a small incident which says much about both the island's culinary and religious traditions.

The dagoba was completely rebuilt by Kassapa V in the tenth century and is surrounded by various largely unexcavated monastic ruins. Northeast of the dagoba you may be able to find the remains of a monks' **refectory**, furnished with the usual enormous stone rice troughs.

South of the dagoba, on the banks of the Tissa Wewa, lie the royal pleasure gardens, known as the **Goldfish Park** after the fish that were kept in the two **pools** here. The pools were created in the sixth century and used water channelled from the adjacent Tissa Wewa; the northern one has low-relief carvings of bathing elephants very similar to those at the nearby Isurumuniya temple, cleverly squeezed into the space between the pool and the adjacent rock outcrop – the contrast between the geometrical precision of the two pools and the untamed surroundings, littered with huge boulders and rock outcrops, is extremely picturesque.

Isurumuniya Vihara

Continuing south for 500m brings you to the **Isurumuniya Vihara** (daily 6am–8pm; museum daily 8am–6pm; not included in the CT ticket, Rs.200 entrance). This venerable old rock temple dates right back to the reign of Devanampiya Tissa, and though it's a bit of a hotch-potch architecturally, it's worth a visit for its interesting stone **carvings**. The steps leading up to the main shrine are embellished with the usual fine, though eroded, guardstones and moonstone, while to the right, just above the water line of the adjacent pool, are low-relief carvings of elephants in the rock, designed so that they appear to be bathing in the waters. To the right of the shrine door is an unusual carving showing a man with a horse looking over his shoulder, while inside the shrine a gold Buddha sits in a niche carved directly into the rock, framed by a finely carved and brightly painted *makara* arch.

To the left of the main shrine is a modern shrine with an ugly reclining Buddha and a small **cave** inhabited by an extraordinary number of bats. Beyond these is the temple's **museum**, now home to a number of its most famous carvings, all rather Indian in style. Perhaps the most famous is the fifth-century sculpture known as **The Lovers**, probably representing either a bodhisattva and his consort or a pair of Hindu deities, though the figures are popularly thought to represent Prince Saliya, the son of Dutugemunu, and Asokamala, the low-caste girl he fell in love with and married, thereby giving up his right to the throne. Another carving (labelled "King's Family") depicts a palace scene showing five figures, said to include Saliya, Asokamala and Dutugemunu.

Next to here steps lead up to the rock above the temple, passing two beautiful *sri padas* on the way up; very steep rock-cut steps go up to one of two platforms at the top. Climb the steps up to the top of the temple for a sweeping **view** east over the forest to the Jetavana dagoba, and west over Tissa Wewa, best at sunset.

Vessagiriya Monastery

South of Isurumuniya Vihara lie the large, scattered rock outcrops that formed the core of the **Vessagiriya Monastery**, once home to five hundred monks. The monastery was first established in the third century BC by King Tissa, but it was the infamous Kassapa of Sigiriya (see p.330) who rebuilt and expanded it, constructing an extensive monastery here, though most of the stone was later carted off for use elsewhere. It's a picturesque spot, with huge boulders and rock outcrops offering views out over the Sacred Precinct from the top, though there's not much to see apart from a few rock-cut steps, the stumps of pillars and occasional fragments of carved stone. An intriguing archeological footnote is provided (if you can find them) by the extremely ancient **inscriptions** written in a proto-Brahmi script similar to that found at the Kantaka Chetiya in Mihintale (it looks rather like cuneiform) – they're on the road-facing side of a few of the rocks – while further recent excavations have unearthed tools that suggest the caves were occupied in prehistoric times.

Mihintale

MIHINTALE, 12km east of Anuradhapura, is famous as the place where Buddhism was introduced to Sri Lanka. In 247 BC (the story goes) the Sinhalese king of Anuradhapura, **Devanampiya Tissa** (reigned 250–210 BC), was hunting in the hills of Mihintale. Pursuing a stag to the top of a hill, he found himself confronted by **Mahinda**, the son (or possibly brother) of the great Buddhist emperor of India, Ashoka, who had been despatched to convert the people of Sri Lanka to his chosen faith. Wishing first to test the king's intelligence to judge his fitness to receive the Buddha's teaching, Mahinda proposed his celebrated **riddle of the mangoes**:

"What name does this tree bear, O king?"
"This tree is called a mango."
"Is there yet another mango besides this?"
"There are many mango-trees."
"And are there yet other trees besides this mango and the other mangoes?"
"There are many trees, sir; but those are trees that are not mangoes."
"And are there, beside the other mangoes and those trees which are not mangoes, yet other trees?"
"There is this mango-tree, sir."

Having established the king's shrewdness by means of this laborious display of arboreal logic, Mahinda proceeded to expound the Buddha's teachings, promptly converting the king and his entire entourage of forty thousand attendants. The grateful king gave Mahinda and his followers a royal park in Anuradhapura, which became the core of the Mahavihara (see p.361), while Mihintale (the name is a contraction of *Mahinda tale*, or "Mahinda's hill") also developed into an important Buddhist centre. Although modern Mihintale is little more than a large village, it remains an important pilgrimage site, especially during **Poson Poya** (June), which commemorates the introduction of Buddhism to Sri Lanka by Mahinda, during which thousands of white-robed pilgrims descend on the place.

The ruins and dagobas at Mihintale are relatively ordinary compared to those at Anuradhapura, but the setting – with rocky hills linked by beautiful old flights of stone steps shaded by frangipani trees – is gorgeous. Mihintale can be tiring, however: there are 1850 steps, and if you want to see all the sights you'll have

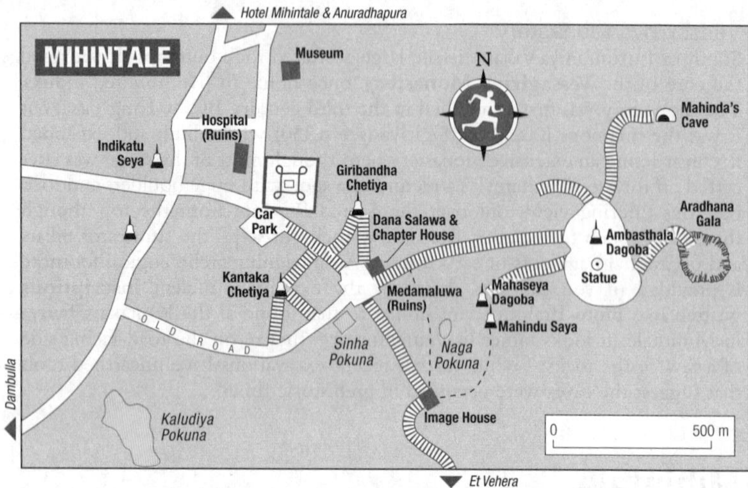

to climb almost every single one of them (although you can avoid the first flight by driving up the Old Road to the Dana Salawa level). It's a good idea to visit in the early morning or late afternoon to avoid having to tackle the steps in the heat of the day.

A **tuktuk** to Mihintale from Anuradhapura costs around Rs.800 return including waiting time. Alternatively, **buses** leave for Mihintale from Anuradhapura's New Bus Station roughly every fifteen minutes. You could also **cycle** here from Anuradhapura, but the road is quite busy and it's not a particularly relaxing ride. The best **accommodation** option is the pleasantly rambling *Hotel Mihintale* (ⓣ025-226 6599, ⓦwww.ceylonhotels.lk; ❻), one of the island's smarter rest houses.

The site

At the bottom of the site, near the car park, lie the remains of a **hospital**, including fragments of treatment rooms and a large stone bath in which patients would have been washed in healing oils and herbs. Most of the island's larger religious complexes had similar infirmaries, where doctors used a highly developed system of Ayurvedic medicines and treatments that were perhaps not so far from those used in today's hotels and clinics. On the other side of the road stand the remains of a monastic structure, its buildings arranged in a characteristically Anuradhapuran quincunx pattern.

Just north of the hospital is the site **museum**, closed at the time of writing, though it should have reopened by the time you read this. Its most interesting exhibit is the model of a relic chamber from a dagoba – a rare opportunity to see what goes on inside one of these structures.

The Kantaka Chetiya

The broad first flight of steps heads up directly from the car park. At the first small terrace, steps lead off on the right to the remains of the **Kantaka Chetiya** dagoba. Not much remains of the body of this dagoba, which originally stood over 30m high, but the four Anuradhapura-style *vahalkadas*, decorated with elephants, peacocks and *nagas*, are extremely well preserved. Just south of the dagoba, on a huge boulder perched precariously on its side, is an unusual inscription in a very early, proto-Brahmi script, similar to that found in inscriptions at the Vessagiriya monastery in Anuradhapura.

The Medamaluwa monastery

Returning to the main steps and continuing up brings you to a large terrace and the remains of the **Medamaluwa** monastery, the most important at Mihintale. The first building on your left is the **Dana Salawa** ("Refectory"), whose two big stone troughs would have been filled with food for the monks by lay followers. On the terrace immediately above are two large stone **tablets** in Sinhala, flanking the door into what was the monastery's image house. Erected by Mahinda during the tenth century, these stele lay down the rules and responsibilities pertaining to the various monks and lay staff at the monastery – a kind of medieval Sinhalese job description. The brick bases of vanished dagobas lie all around, along with the remains of further monastic buildings, including the **Conversation Hall**, which preserves a few of its original 64 pillars.

Slightly lower down the same terrace, near the top of Old Road, is the small **Sinha Pokuna** ("Lion Pool"), named after the unusual, though very eroded, sculpture of a lion rampant, through whose mouth water was fed into the pool. There are much better carvings on the small frieze above – they're small but relatively well preserved, showing lions and dancers in a rather Indian style.

The upper terrace

To the right of the Conversation Hall, another long flight of steps leads up to the heart of Mihintale, located (it's claimed) at the very spot at which Devanampiya Tissa met Mahinda. You have to buy a **ticket** (Rs.250) at the top of the stairs before entering the terrace, and hand over your shoes to an attendant (who will expect a tip). At the centre of the terrace is the **Ambasthala dagoba**, a surprisingly small and simple structure for such an important site – the name means "Mango Tree Dagoba", referring to the conundrum proposed by Mahinda to test Devanampiya Tissa's intelligence. The dagoba was subsequently roofed over, *vatadage*-style, as testified by the two rows of pillars around it. Immediately next to it is a single simple **sri pada** surrounded by two sets of railings covered with prayer flags; people throw coins in here for luck. Nearby is an extremely ancient **statue**, claimed to be of Devanampiya Tissa, though it might just be of a bodhisattva. Its arms have long since vanished, while its head has fallen off and now sits Yorick-like on a brick plinth in front. According to tradition, the Ambasthala dagoba covers the spot where Mahinda stood during the famous meeting, while the statue marks the position of Devanampiya Tissa, though given how far apart they are, this seems unlikely, unless their conversation – and the mango conundrum – was conducted as a kind of shouting match; the rather well-executed bearded **modern statue**, in a supplicating posture closer to the dagoba is in a more likely position.

Various pathways lead from here to a number of further sights. Close to the ancient statue, irregular rock-cut steps lead very steeply up the bare rock outcrop of **Aradhana Gala** ("Invitation Rock"), from which Mahinda preached his first sermon. On the other side, a shorter flight of steps lead up to a large, modern white **seated Buddha**, posed in an unusual composite posture: the left hand is in the meditation posture, while the right is in the "explanation" (*vitarka*) pose. A longer path leads to **Mahinda's Cave**, a bit of a hike down a rough woodland path. The "cave" is actually an opening beneath a huge boulder poised precariously on the edge of the hillside at the edge of a large drop. On the floor is a simple rectangular outline cut out of rock, popularly believed to be Mahinda's bed.

Mahaseya dagoba and Et Vehara

Once you've seen all the sights around the upper terrace, collect your shoes (but don't put them on) and head up one final set of steps to the white **Mahaseya dagoba**, claimed to enshrine some ashes and a single hair of the Buddha. The dagoba (which can be seen quite clearly all the way from Anuradhapura) is the largest and the second highest at Mihintale, in a breezy hilltop location and with wonderful 360-degree views over the surrounding countryside – you can usually just make out the great dagobas of Anuradhapura in the distance. Immediately next to it are the substantial remains of the lower portion of a large brick dagoba, the **Mahindu Saya**, which is thought to enshrine relics associated with Mahinda.

Carry on past the Mahindu Saya (you can put your shoes on now) down a path cut into the rock to the ruins of an **image house** atop the usual stone base with flights of stairs and remains of pillars. From here, a tough ten-minute slog up steep steps (and lots of them) leads to **Et Vehera**, located at what is easily the highest point at Mihintale. There's nothing much to see apart from the remains of a small brick dagoba – despite the great sense of altitude, the views aren't really any better than those from the Mahaseya dagoba.

Retrace your steps to the image house, then head back downhill via the **Naga Pokuna**, or "Snake Pool", a rock-cut pool guarded by a carving of a five-headed cobra (though it's sometimes submerged by water). Romantic legends associate this with the queen of Devanampiya Tissa, though the prosaic truth is that it was simply part of the monastery's water-supply system.

Outlying remains

Back on the main road by the turn-off to the site are the remains of another monastery and two dagobas – the larger is known as **Indikatu Seya**. South of here lies the hill of **Rajagiri Lena**. Brahmi inscriptions found here suggest that the caves on the hillside might have been home to Sri Lanka's first-ever Buddhist monks. Some 500m south of here along the Kandy road, the tranquil **Kaludiya Pokuna** pool looks natural but is actually man-made. Beside it are the remains of a small tenth-century monastery, including a well-preserved cave-building with windows and a door – either a bathhouse or a monk's dwelling.

The east

INDIA
N
BAY OF BENGAL
6
4
5
1
3
INDIAN OCEAN
2
0 50 km

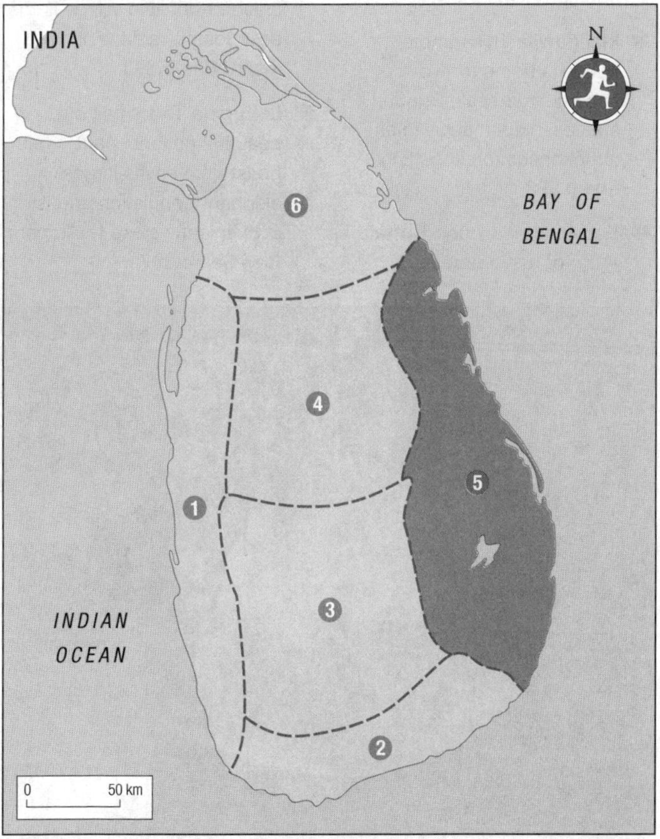

CHAPTER 5 Highlights

* **Trincomalee** Founded around one of the world's finest deep-water harbours, this characterful town has an attractive coastal setting, a fine colonial fort and an absorbing mixture of Hindu, Buddhist and Muslim traditions. See p.381

* **Maligawila** This remote village is home to two superb large-scale Buddha statues, hidden away in an atmospheric forest setting. See p.392

* **Eco-lodges around Buttala** A trio of rustic retreats close to the fringes of Yala National Park provide some memorably close encounters with nature. See p.393

* **Arugam Bay** With some charmingly ramshackle accommodation and the island's best surfing, this crashed-out little village is the east coast's most winsome resort. See p.393

* **Lahugala** This small but beautiful national park boasts the east's largest elephant population and is conveniently close to Arugam Bay. See p.397

▲ Surfing, Arugam Bay

5

The east

Sri Lanka's **east coast** is a mirror image of its west. When it's monsoon season in the west, the sun is shining in the east; where the west coast in predominantly Sinhalese, the east is largely Tamil and Muslim; and where parts of the west coast are crowded with tourists and almost buried under a surfeit of hotels, the east remains largely untouched and tourist-free, thanks to its distance from the international airport and to the effects of the ongoing political troubles which have dampened the region's appeal to visitors (and sometimes placed it off-limits entirely) for much of the last quarter of a century, and which continue to cloud its future. With some of the Sri Lanka's finest beaches, a string of beautiful lagoons and large expanses of uninhabited wilderness, the east has massive tourist potential, but developers remain reluctant to commit their cash to major tourist projects given the continued political uncertainties, while the region's recovery from the 2004 tsunami has been slower than elsewhere on the island.

The east's troubles are rooted in its complex **ethnic make-up**, with significant Sinhalese, Tamil and Muslim communities living alongside one another. Clashes between the latter two groups (and LTTE attacks against unprotected Sinhalese villagers) were a repeated feature of the war years, while the situation was further complicated in 2003–04 by a split between the northern and eastern factions of the LTTE, with cadres from both sides launching a series of bloody attacks against one another which engulfed significant parts of the region. Following the expulsion of the northern LTTE by the Sri Lankan Army in 2007 (see p.434), peace has finally returned, and the entire region is now generally considered safe to visit, and will hopefully remain so, given the induction of the eastern wing of the LTTE, under the controversial Colonel Karuna (see p.432), into the Sri Lankan parliamentary process.

Trains in the east

Note that train timetables are subject to constant change, so it's always best to check latest departure times before travelling at the nearest station (or online at Ⓦwww.bluehaventours.com).

Trincomalee	07.00	15.50	
Colombo	19.00	04.15	
Batticaloa	05.20	17.20	20.00*
Polonnaruwa	08.15	20.15	22.15
Colombo	16.00	04.15	04.52

*inter-city express

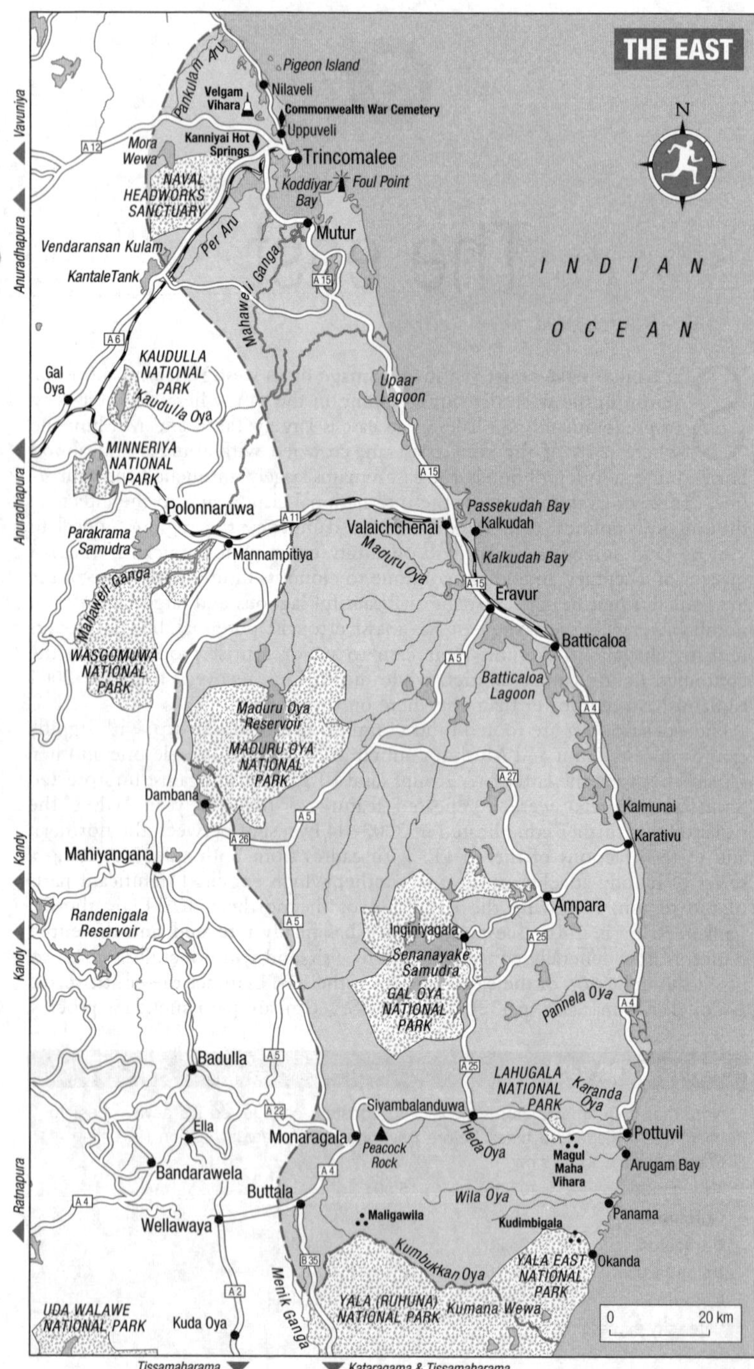
THE EAST
N
INDIAN OCEAN
Pigeon Island
Nilaveli
Velgam Vihara
Commonwealth War Cemetery
Uppuveli
Kanniyai Hot Springs
Trincomalee
Koddiyar Bay
Foul Point
Mutur
Pankulam Aru
Mora Wewa
NAVAL HEADWORKS SANCTUARY
Vendaransan Kulam
KantaleTank
Per Aru
Mahaweli Ganga
Vavuniya
Anuradhapura
A 12
A 15
A 6
Gal Oya
KAUDULLA NATIONAL PARK
Kaudulla Oya
MINNERIYA NATIONAL PARK
Upaar Lagoon
Polonnaruwa
Parakrama Samudra
Mannampitiya
A 11
Valaichchenai
Passekudah Bay
Kalkudah
Kalkudah Bay
Maduru Oya
Eravur
Batticaloa
Batticaloa Lagoon
WASGOMUWA NATIONAL PARK
Maduru Oya Reservoir
MADURU OYA NATIONAL PARK
Dambana
A 5
A 4
A 27
A 26
Kalmunai
Karativu
Mahiyangana
Kandy
Ampara
Randenigala Reservoir
Inginiyagala
Senanayake Samudra
GAL OYA NATIONAL PARK
A 25
Pannela Oya
Badulla
LAHUGALA NATIONAL PARK
Karanda Oya
Siyambalanduwa
A 22
Ella
Monaragala
Peacock Rock
Heda Oya
Pottuvil
Magul Maha Vihara
Arugam Bay
Bandarawela
Ratnapura
Buttala
Wila Oya
Panama
Wellawaya
Maligawila
Kudimbigala
Kumbukkan Oya
Okanda
B 35
A 2
YALA EAST NATIONAL PARK
Menik Ganga
YALA (RUHUNA) NATIONAL PARK
Kumana Wewa
UDA WALAWE NATIONAL PARK
Kuda Oya
0
20 km
Tissamaharama
Kataragama & Tissamaharama

However, it still pays to check latest information about security in the area as the situation may change.

At present, the east's main attraction is the laid-back surfing hotspot of **Arugam Bay**, which is also the starting point for trips to the national parks of **Lahugala** and **Yala East**, though both were officially closed to visitors at the time of writing. The only other beaches with any form of recognizable tourist infrastructure are the low-key resorts of **Uppuveli** and **Nilaveli**, adjacent to one another just north of the uniquely multiethnic town of **Trincomalee**, a major draw in itself with its appealing admixture of faded colonial charm and beautiful natural setting.

Getting to the east remains a bit of a slog, at least until flights from Colombo resume, and although the road infrastructure is improving, **getting around** is also less straightforward than in other parts of the country, with regular security checkpoints making bus travel a tediously drawn-out affair – if you want to explore the region in depth, you're best to come with your own transport. Broadly, the **best time** to go is from April to September, as the arrival of the northeast monsoon brings significant rainfall from around October/November to February/March, though in recent years there has been a trend towards drier weather, and clear skies are a possibility at any time of the year.

Some history

Although now something of a backwater, the east was for many centuries the most outward-looking and cosmopolitan part of the island, a fact borne out by the mixture of Tamils, Muslims and Sinhalese who make the region the most ethnically diverse in Sri Lanka. Much of the area's early history revolved around **Trincomalee**, the island's principal trading port during the Anuradhapuran and Polonnaruwan eras, and the harbours of the east continued to serve as an important conduit for foreign influences in subsequent centuries. Islam spread widely along the coast thanks to visiting Arab, Malay and Indian traders, while the European powers also took a healthy interest in the region. The Dutch first established a secure presence on the island at the town of Batticaloa, while it was the lure of Trincomalee harbour more than anything else which drew the British to the island.

With the rise of the new ports at Galle and later Colombo, the east gradually fell into decline, and its fortunes nosedived during the **civil war**, whose front line bisected the region and turned Tamils, Muslims and Sinhalese against one another in a frenzy of communal violence. A brief period of optimism followed the 2002 ceasefire, though this was rapidly shattered by further communal infighting and repeated clashes between the northern LTTE and its breakaway eastern wing. The possibility of a lasting peace finally arrived in 2007, when the Sri Lankan Army succeeded in driving the LTTE out of the area, although much of the coast remains heavily militarized, while the vast swathes of country inland (whose arid climate has always discouraged settled agriculture) remain sparsely populated and economically backward.

Trincomalee and around

Eastern Sri Lanka's major town, **TRINCOMALEE** (or "Trinco") has been celebrated since antiquity for its superlative deep-water **harbour**, one of the finest in Asia – the legendary Panduvasudeva (see p.417) is said to have sailed into Trincomalee (or Gokana, as it was originally known) with his followers, while the town served as the major conduit for the island's seaborne trade during the Anuradhapuran and Polonnaruwan periods. The harbour was later fought over repeatedly during the colonial period and even attracted the hostile attentions of the Japanese air force during World War II.

Trincomalee suffered with the onset of the **civil war** in 1983, becoming a flashpoint for ethnic tensions, thanks to a population which is almost evenly divided between Tamil, Muslim and Sinhalese communities. In addition, although Trincomalee avoided the massive bomb damage inflicted on Jaffna, its position close to the front line made it the island's major collecting point for war-displaced **refugees**, whose presence stretched resources and infrastructure to breaking point and beyond, while parts of the town were burnt to the ground during communal rioting. The town's fortune's have yo-yoed constantly since the 2002 ceasefire, though following the expulsion of the LTTE from the east in 2007, Trinco is now once again considered safe for visitors, and is looking to the future with renewed if cautious optimism.

Although most visitors are drawn to this part of the island by the beaches at Nilaveli and Uppuveli, a day in Trincomalee makes an interesting break from the beach, though the continued high military presence can be off-putting. The town has an understated but distinct charm, with a beautiful setting, a fine colonial fort and, in places, a certain old-fashioned elegance, while its mix of communities lends a multiethnic flavour whose subtle mingling of religions and traditions is unique in Sri Lanka.

Arrival

Buses arrive at the brand-new bus station, right in Trinco's centre at the bottom of Main Street. The **train** station is at the northwest end of town. The airport is at China Bay, a few kilometres out of town, though there were no flights at the time of writing.

There are plenty of **banks** with ATMs accepting foreign cards scattered across town. **Internet** access is available from several places at the junction of Post Office and Power House roads; try I.D.Com Net Café (daily 7.30am–8.30pm; Rs.50 per hr).

Accommodation

There's not a great deal of choice of accommodation in Trinco, though there's somewhere to stay in most price brackets and a couple of places have recently smartened up their acts.

Green Park Beach Hotel 312 Dyke St ⓣ026-222 2369, ⓔlathu@sltnet.lk. Newly refurbished mid-range place occupying a picturesque setting right on Dutch Bay. The comfortable rooms come with a/c, hot water, mini-fridges and Sony TVs, and there's a lovely terrace for soaking up the views over both town and ocean, plus a popular Indian restaurant (see p.386). ❹

Medway Hotel 250 Inner Harbour Rd ⓣ026-222 7655. Set in a nice location facing the Inner Harbour, this motel-style establishment has huge and rather bare rooms, with (optional) a/c, hot water, satellite TV and great expanses of tiled floor. ❸, a/c ❹

New Silver Star 27 College St ⓣ026-222 2348. Competently run, trim-looking place with a range of rooms spread over three floors: best are those on the first floor, with views over the cemetery to the sea (good value if you ask them to switch off the a/c); top-floor rooms are basic but very cheap, while those downstairs are the most modern, but noisy. ❶–❷, a/c ❹

Sunflower Guest House 154 Post Office Rd ⓣ0779 798 223. Clean, modern and cheap rooms above the *Sunflower Bake House*. ❷

Villa Hotel 22A Lower Rd, Orr's Hill ⓣ026-222 2284, ⓔnjeya3@yahoo.com. Formerly the *Harbour View Guest House*, this once insalubrious joint has had a refurb: gleamingly tiled rooms upstairs now boast a/c, TV, faux-leather armchairs and snazzy balconies overlooking the bay, but don't bother with the grim ones below. Also has a reasonable restaurant and pleasant bar (see p.386). ❹, a/c ❺

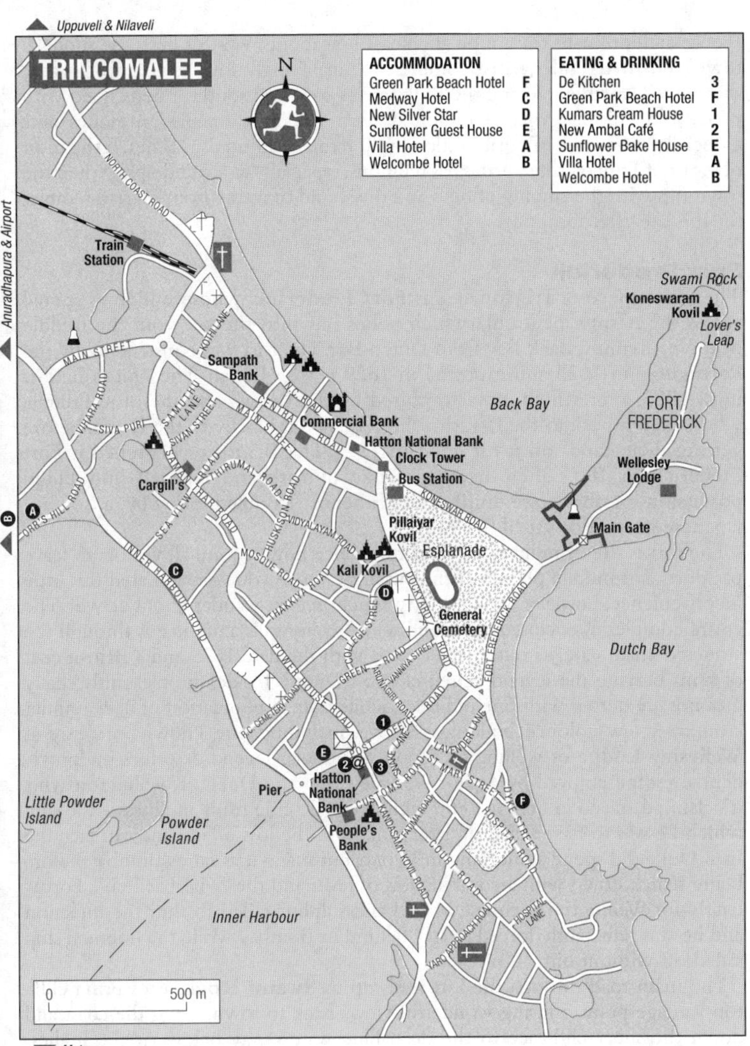

Welcombe Hotel 66 Lower Rd, Orr's Hill ⓣ026-222 2373, ⓔwelcombe@sltnet.lk. Set atop a headland above the Inner Harbour a couple of kilometres west of town, Trinco's only upmarket option occupies a gaudily painted, (vaguely) boat-shaped modern building. The cheerfully colourful if slightly bland rooms, including four in the period cottage at the front, all come with TV and minibar, and most with a/c; more luxurious ones have king-size beds, bath tubs and colonial-style furnishings. There's also a large, kidney-shaped pool (non-guests Rs.250), atmospheric bar and a variable restaurant. 5–6

The Town

Trincomalee occupies a splendid natural setting athwart a narrow peninsula between the Indian Ocean and the deep and sheltered waters of the Inner Harbour. The town itself is a bit of a mishmash. Much of the centre is occupied by the old colonial **Fort Frederick**, which climbs up to the cliff-top Swami

Rock, the dominant feature on the coast hereabouts. West of here, the modern town's **commercial centre** comprises a surprisingly low-key grid of streets, though it's worth exploring the back streets west and south of here, lined with pretty old colonial villas and dotted with Buddhist temples, mosques and, especially, dozens of colourful little Hindu temples. Hinduism is much the most obvious of Trinco's three principal religions, especially at around 4pm, when the town fills with the ringing of bells and the sound of music from myriad temples for the late-afternoon puja.

Fort Frederick

The centrepiece of Trincomalee is **Fort Frederick**, whose buildings sprawl across the narrow peninsula which pokes out into the sea from the middle of town, dividing Back Bay from Dutch Bay. The fort was constructed by the Portuguese in 1623 and captured in 1639 by the Dutch. The Dutch held it until 1782, after which it was captured by the British and then the French, who ceded it back to the British, who returned it briefly to the Dutch before getting their hands on it for good in 1795. The British rechristened it Fort Frederick in 1803 after the then Duke of York and enjoyed undisputed possession of the place until Independence, troubled only by a solitary Japanese air raid on April 9, 1942.

The fort is still in military use, and the police now require all visitors to leave passports and mobile phones at the entrance. Once you've negotiated this little inconvenience, however, you're pretty much free to wander about at will. The entire complex is enclosed by a solid set of stone walls; entrance is through the attractive main gate, its outer face carved with the date 1675 and a British coat of arms bearing the legend "Dieu et Mon Droit". Inside, the pleasantly shady grounds are dotted with fine old trees, while a small population of deer wander around. A few colonial buildings survive, including one known variously as **Wellesley Lodge** or Wellington House. A popular legend describes the providential escape enjoyed by Arthur Wellesley, later the Duke of Wellington who, it's claimed, stayed in here in 1800 whilst convalescing from an illness – the ship which he was to have sailed on later sank with the loss of all hands. In fact, the Iron Duke did spend some time in Trinco, but made it as far as Bombay before being struck down with a combination of fever and the "Malabar Itch". Fortunately for Wellington, a course of lard and sulphur failed to shift the infection and he was reluctantly forced to stay behind in Bombay while the doomed ship sailed off without him.

The main road through the fort leads up to **Swami Rock**, a towering clifftop vantage point offering wonderful views back to town, along the coast and down the sheer cliff-face to the deep-blue waters way below. At the highest point of the rock sits a Hindu shrine, the **Koneswaram** (or Tirukoneswaram) **Kovil**, one of the five most holy Shaivite temples on the island. The original structure was destroyed by the Portuguese in the early seventeenth century – they simply shoved it over the edge of the cliff into the waters below. Divers subsequently rescued a Shiva lingam from the water, which is now enshrined in the rather unexciting modern temple.

Just outside the temple close to the highest point of Swami Rock, a tree clings precariously to the edge of the rock, its branches adorned with prayer flags which supplicants have somehow managed to attach. This spot is popularly known as **Lover's Leap** in commemoration of a certain young Dutch lady, Francina van Rhede. The details are confused: some say that the heartbroken van Rhede, who had been abandoned by her lover, leapt but survived the fall; others claim that she didn't even jump. Whatever the truth, government archives record her subsequent marriage eight years later, after which she (presumably) lived happily ever after.

The rest of the town

West of the fort, modern Trincomalee's **commercial centre** comprises an undistinguished and low-key trio of parallel streets lined by tiny one-storey shops and dotted with the occasional small mosque. Turn right off N.C. Road, officially Ehamparam Road, down Pattana Road (there's a very faded road sign) to reach a magical little stretch of **beach**, with small pastel-painted Hindu temples on one side, colourful fishing boats drawn up at the water's edge on the other, and rabbit warrens of tiny shacks behind, their neat, brightly painted facades giving the beachfront a prettiness which belies the considerable poverty in which most of the people here live. Late afternoon is a particularly atmospheric time to come, when the tiny streets are crammed with families chatting and playing marbles, and there's usually an impromptu game or two of cricket on the beach.

At the southeastern end of the commercial centre lies the wide and grassy though unkempt expanse of the **esplanade**. A couple of pretty Hindu temples enliven the western side of the green, the large **Kali** and the much smaller (though equally gaudy) **Pillaiyar kovils**. Both burst into life with drumming, music and lines of supplicants during the late-afternoon puja (around 4–5pm). Immediately south of these – and in stark, moribund contrast – lies the decaying and utterly neglected old **General Cemetery**, the final resting place of Trinco's Christian population, with a few picturesquely dilapidated colonial tombs dating back to the 1820s alongside more modern graves. Jane Austen's brother, Charles, is supposed to be buried here – if you can find him. The cemetery is often locked, but it's easy enough to hop over the low wall (although slightly more difficult to climb out again).

A number of roads run southwest from the centre down towards the Inner Harbour – much of this quarter of town retains a pleasantly old-fashioned feel, with numerous colonial villas, some of them embellished with quirky, slightly

▲ Kali Kovil, Trincomalee

Art Deco-looking decorative motifs. The expansive **Inner Harbour** itself is an attractively breezy spot, its choppy waters dotted with container ships and various port facilities, framed against a circle of rugged green hills which ring the bay – it's particularly lovely at night, when a thousand lights twinkle around the vast bay.

Elsewhere in town, the ocean front Fort Frederick Road along **Dutch Bay** offers fine sea views, while the beach which edges the road is a popular spot around dusk, when half the town seems to congregate here to promenade along the seafront and loll around on the sands. Beyond here lie further low-key but charming rows of colonial villas, most particularly along **Dyke Street**, lined with quaint pastel facades.

On the far side of the enormous Koddiyar Bay lies the town of **MUTUR**. Ferries run four times a day from the pier at the western end of Post Office Road. It's an attractively breezy one-hour journey across the bay, though there's nothing specific to do in Mutur itself.

Eating and drinking

There are few culinary treats in Trincomalee but the town centre boasts a handful of reasonable **places to eat**, plus a well-stocked branch of Cargill's and a couple of decent **bakeries** along Post Office Road selling breakfast, ice cream and snacks; try *Kumars Cream House* or the *Sunflower Bake House*. The most atmospheric places for a **drink** are the *Villa Hotel*'s timber-clad open-air bar, overlooking the twinkling lights of the Inner Harbour, and the cute wood-panelled period piece at the *Welcombe Hotel*.

Restaurants

De Kitchen 360B Court Rd. Luridly painted new a/c restaurant, right in the centre, serving passable rice and curry, *kottu rotty* and a few seafood dishes to a steady soundtrack of Tamil pop.

Green Park Beach Hotel Popular with NGOs, this pleasant hotel restaurant offers a wide range of Indian food, encompassing tandooris, *shorba* and a good selection of paneer dishes. Evening meals are sometimes served up on the attractive bayside first-floor terrace.

New Ambal Café Post Office Rd. Central and dirt-cheap locals' place dishing up decent *kottu rotty*, *dosas* and few other staples.

Welcombe Hotel Trinco's smartest place to eat, with its widest array of international dishes, though both food and service are variable. Dine in the glassed-in restaurant, or alfresco on the terrace.

North of Trincomalee

The main attractions north of Trincomalee are the fine beaches at **Uppuveli** and **Nilaveli**, which have been saved from development by their position in the disputed region between LTTE- and SLA-controlled territories. Following the 2002 ceasefire, there was much optimism that the area would benefit from a

Moving on from Trincomalee

There are regular private and CTB **buses** from Trinco to **Colombo** (every 30min; 8hr), **Kandy** (hourly; 6hr) and **Habarana** (every 15min; 3hr), and rather less frequent services to **Batticaloa** via Habarana (3 daily; 8hr), **Anuradhapura** (2 daily; 4hr) and **Polonnaruwa** (3 daily; 4hr). As many of these leave early in the morning – around 6am – you might have to make an early start, and regular checkpoints currently slow down journeys in all directions.

Train services from Trinco are listed on p.379. There are currently no **flights** operating from Trinco.

revival in east-coast tourism, and a brief flurry of development ensued. With the twin blows of the 2004 tsunami and renewed local hostilities in 2006–07, however, the beaches once again slipped off the tourist radar, and business has been very slow to recover. In the circumstances it's a wonder that there's any tourist infrastructure here at all, but a handful of courageous local entrepreneurs continue to plug away against the odds, sustained by a steady stream of NGOs on weekend jollies.

Though swimming is safe year-round off both Nilaveli and Uppuveli, the resorts are best visited between May and September when the beaches are subject to a clean-up. Both remain exceptionally low-key, however, and out of season you may find the only signs of life at the area's pair of appealing resort hotels.

Uppuveli and around

Some 4km north of Trincomalee, the wide stretch of golden-sand beach at the village of **Uppuveli** managed to attract a trickle of visitors throughout the civil war years, and was lucky enough to escape the widespread destruction wrought by the tsunami on nearby Nilaveli thanks to its sheltered position behind Trincomalee's Swami Rock. More compact than its northern neighbour, with a few fishing boats, safe swimming and good views down the coast to Trinco, it has a little more life than Nilaveli, though the atmosphere remains deeply somnolent.

Practicalities

There are **buses** from Trinco to Uppuveli every twenty to thirty minutes; alternatively a **tuktuk** will cost Rs.250–300. Accommodation is clustered in the half-kilometre stretch between the *Club Oceanic* hotel and *French Garden Pragash*; all places serve **food**, though you won't find much beyond a few tourist basics except at the *Club Oceanic*'s nightly buffet or at the Italian restaurant at the *Palm Beach Resort*.

Accommodation

Beach Bangal ⓣ026-222 7599. Clean, comfortable and spacious rooms with (optional) a/c in a single sea-facing block, set in a sandy palm garden. Good value. ❷, a/c ❸

Club Oceanic ⓣ026-222 1611, ⓦwww.johnkeellshotels.com. Stretching along Uppuveli's best-maintained stretch of beach, this pleasantly breezy resort hotel is the village's fanciest option. The smartest rooms, in ice-cool blue shades, occupy two-storey chalets right on the beach; standard rooms, in a sea-facing block, are a little more worn but come in warmer tones. All are spacious and comfortable and have a/c, satellite TV and balconies or terraces. There's also a small Ayurveda centre and a decent-sized pool, which non-guests can use if they buy a drink at the bar. ❺–❻

French Garden Anton Guest House ⓣ060-226 3640. Set just back from the beach next to *French Garden Pragash*. Rooms are small and dark but tiled and spotlessly clean – and very cheap. ❶

French Garden Pragash Guest House ⓣ060-220 0397. The longest-established cheapie in Uppuveli, in an attractive beachfront location and with basic but clean rooms, though rather grubby bathrooms. ❶

Palm Beach Resort ⓣ026-222 1250. Cheerful Italian-run guesthouse set in lush gardens, with a sociable atmosphere, authentic Italian cooking and spotless, comfortable and well-maintained rooms. Closed Nov & Dec. ❸, a/c ❹

Around Uppuveli

There are a few low-key sights **around Uppuveli** if you want a break from lying on the beach. On the main road 200m north of the *Club Oceanic*, the **Commonwealth War Cemetery** holds 362 graves, mainly of Allied and other servicemen who died in Sri Lanka during World War II. Military personnel of many nationalities are buried together here, including Indians, Italians, Australians, Canadians, Dutch, Burmese and, of course, numerous British fighters, including the aircrews killed during the Japanese air raid of April 1942 and seamen who perished aboard various Royal Navy vessels sunk by the Japanese. In striking contrast to the General Cemetery in Trinco, the War Cemetery is beautifully looked after, though the long lines of graves and the ages recorded on the headstones (few of those interred here were older than 25) makes a visit a rather sombre experience.

For something a bit more cheerful, head to the **Kanniyai Hot Wells**, around 8km inland from Uppuveli and 1km south of the road to Anuradhapura. According to tradition, the springs were created by Vishnu himself, and these days are a popular bathing spot for local Tamils. You can't actually submerge yourself in the waters here – the springs are collected in small tiled tubs, and you use a bucket to pour the water over yourself – but they're fun for a quick splash and for mingling with good-humoured locals. A quick stop at the springs can be combined with a visit to the remains of the **Velgam Vihara** (donation), a few kilometres further on towards Anuradhapura and 4km north of the main road. The temple is thought to date back to the era of King Devanampiya Tissa, who is said to have planted a bo tree here, and although subsequently abandoned to the jungle following the collapse of Polonnaruwa, extensive remains survive, including a stupa, image house and a well-preserved standing Buddha.

Nilaveli and around

Ten kilometres north of Uppuveli, **Nilaveli** is the second of the Trincomalee area's pair of fabled beaches, though sadly these days the celebrated sugar-white strand of yesteryear, stained a dusty yellow by the depredations of the tsunami, is mostly neglected and the whole place feels rather desolate. Nilaveli's fortunes looked set to soar following the 2002 ceasefire, but the tsunami dealt a bitter blow, causing more destruction even than twenty years of civil war. Following a further round of east-coast hostilities, much of what was then rebuilt has again been forced to close, and the area, still heavily militarized, carries a rather moribund air – unless you want complete peace and solitude, you'll probably find the whole place unnervingly quiet. That said, if you hole yourself up in the ever-hopeful *Nilaveli Beach Hotel*, the plushest place to stay (for the moment at least) on the whole eastern seaboard, you can just about imagine yourself somewhere less forlorn, and future prospects for peace may yet bring some much-needed cheer to this forgotten little corner of the island.

Practicalities

There are **buses** from Trinco to Nilaveli every twenty to thirty minutes, but the journey can take a tedious hour or so once you've negotiated the three checkpoints en route. It's quicker to take a **tuktuk**, especially as the beach is a kilometre or more away from the main road; the journey from Trinco costs around Rs.600. There's not much **accommodation** left at Nilaveli, and what there is doesn't offer great value for money. Guesthouses lie dotted at wide intervals along the coast for 4km or so south of the *Nilaveli Beach Hotel* (popularly abbreviated to the *NBH*), the area's major – or indeed only – landmark. All the following do **food**, although only at the *NBH* will you find anything more than simple tourist staples.

Accommodation

Coral Bay 4km south of the *NBH* ☎026-226 6199. Small and very low-key hotel in a single sea-facing block, with bright if rather expensive modern rooms in a coconut-palm garden. There's also a pool right on the beach, though it might not have any water in it. ❹, a/c ❺

Mauro Beach Hotel 500m north of the *NBH* ⓣ 026-492 0633. Optimistically large but unpretentious hotel in a cheery blue-and-white building with spacious, modern, tiled rooms in varying states of repair, plus a pool and gardens running down to the sea. Rather worn but better value than the competition. ❹

Nilaveli Beach Hotel ⓣ 026-223 2295, ⓦ www.tangerinehotels.com. Completely rebuilt and modernized following the tsunami, this long-established landmark, set in shady, tree-studded gardens, is the east coast's most attractive resort hotel. It's worth paying an extra US$10 for the more spacious deluxe rooms, which have big balconies and rather more style than the uninspiring standard offerings, though all rooms have a/c and most have sea views. There's also a lovely big L-shaped pool (which shoots jacuzzi bubbles) and a smart new restaurant. Rates are highly negotiable. ❻

Sea View Hotel 2km south of the *NBH* ⓣ 026-223 2200. Rather striking, vaguely Islamic-looking building in a breezy position right on the beach, with clean, tiled (though pricey) fan rooms and sweeping views up and down the coast. Sandwiched between two navy camps, it's also one for the more security-conscious. ❹

Pigeon Island

About a kilometre offshore from Nilaveli, the coral reef off tiny **Pigeon Island** was formerly one of the east coast's primary natural attractions. Having been one of the few reefs in Sri Lanka to survive the mass bleaching that followed El Niño in 1998, however, it has been forced to endure a welter of depredations over the past decade: indiscriminate blast fishing, along with damage caused by careless day-trippers, who visited the island in droves following the ceasefire, plus the destructive effects of the tsunami have conspired to leave a legacy of broken coral washed up on Pigeon Island's white-sand beach. Despite the devastation, however, small patches of live coral survive on the island's ocean-facing side, and there are also lots of colourful fish here, making for good and sheltered **snorkelling**. Furthermore, Pigeon Island itself is looking in better condition than it has for years, an unwitting beneficiary of the Sri Lankan Navy's strict control of sea traffic off Trinco's coastline, which currently prevents private boats docking at the island. Having been trashed a few years ago by locals, Pigeon Island's beach is now seldom visited and, subject to periodic clean-ups organized by Nilaveli's hotels, is beginning to recapture its former desert-island appeal.

Boat trips to Pigeon Island are currently only run by the navy, and cost Rs.2500 per boat (seating up to eight people). The easiest way to organize a trip is via the *Club Oceanic* or *Nilaveli Beach* hotels (book a day in advance), which can also hire out snorkelling equipment (Rs.500). The best months for snorkelling are from May to September, when visibility is at its clearest; between November and March, seas are liable to be choppy and the navy may be reluctant to make the trip.

A bit further out to sea, tiny **Coral Island** once boasted the finest coral and snorkelling on the east coast, though it's currently inaccessible, and reports suggest that most of the coral has now been destroyed.

South from Trincomalee

The swathe of coastline between Trincomalee and Batticaloa remains one of the poorest and least-developed areas in Sri Lanka – until 2007 much of this area was controlled by the LTTE, and the twin scourges of civil war and tsunami have left indelible marks on the landscape. The A15 highway runs the length of the coast, though it's in poor condition (especially between Trinco and Mutur) and is punctuated by numerous river crossings where vehicles are carried over by ferry – buses from Trincomalee to Batticaloa make the long detour inland via Habarana.

Batticaloa and around

The principal east-coast town south of Trincomalee, **BATTICALOA** (often shortened to "Batti") sits on a narrow sliver of land backed by the serpentine **Batticaloa Lagoon**. The town is surrounded by water on three sides, and the constantly shifting views of land, lagoon and ocean lend Batticaloa an interesting – if disorienting – character. It's a pleasant enough place, although there's not much reason to come here apart from sheer curiosity or, if you've got your own vehicle, to explore the attractive and totally undeveloped coastline hereabouts.

Throughout the civil war years, Batticaloa was one of the east coast's major flashpoints, with innumerable clashes between different local ethnic groups and rival factions of the LTTE. Despite its troubled recent history, however, the town retains a solidly commercial feel, especially along Main Street, a neat collection of small lock-up shops with colourful signs in Tamil and huge wooden doors. It's also worth a stroll through the back streets which meander up the hill behind Main Street, dotted with colourful churches, a few old colonial villas and the grandiose **St Michael's College**.

Batticaloa was the first Sri Lankan stronghold of the Dutch, who constructed the town's solid-looking **Fort**, which stands some 200m behind the large public library at the west end of the town centre. The hulking and rather dour exterior walls are well preserved, while inside, an old colonial warehouse and various modern buildings are crammed together cheek by jowl. There's a grand view of the lagoon from the far side of the fort.

Practicalities

Batticaloa's **bus station** is right in the middle of town, a couple of minutes' walk from the *Subaraj Inn*. To reach either the *Avonlea*, *Riviera Resort* or *Bridge View* guesthouses you'll have to find one of the town's scarce and overpriced tuktuks. The **ATMs** at the Commercial (Visa and MasterCard) and Seylan (Visa only) banks on Bar Road both accept foreign cards. To reach Bar Road, head straight across the river from the clocktower in the centre of town, and continue straight ahead for 400m until you reach a roundabout; Bar Road is on your right.

Few tourists make it this far, but there are lots of NGO workers around, which pushes **accommodation** prices up and can make it difficult to find somewhere to stay. In the town centre the best option is the *Subaraj Inn* (Ⓣ065-222 5983; ❸), close to the bus station and next to the large (and horrible) *Lake View Inn*. This has a pleasant bar and restaurant and a varied selection of simple, slightly cell-like,

The singing fish of Batticaloa

Batti is famous in Sri Lankan folklore for its **singing fish**. According to tradition, between April and September a strange noise – described variously as resembling a plucked guitar or violin string, or the sound produced by rubbing a wet finger around the rim of a glass – can be heard issuing from the depths of the lagoon. The "singing" is allegedly strongest on full moon nights, though no one knows exactly what causes it. The most popular explanation is that it's produced by some form of marine life – anything from catfish to mussels – while another theory states that it's made by water flowing between boulders on the lagoon floor. The best way to listen to the singing is apparently to dip one end of an oar in the water and hold the other end to your ear. Kallady Bridge, a couple of kilometres outside town, is traditionally held to be a good place to tune in.

and rather overpriced rooms (some with shared bathroom). Don't even think about staying at the *Lake View Inn* next door – it looks plausible from the outside, but the rooms are disgusting fleapits. There are a couple of other options in the suburb of **Kallady**, about 2km from the town centre. The *Riviera Resort* (☎065-222 2165; ❸) is set in a peaceful riverside spot, with slightly rustic rooms in chalets in the garden, and good food. The *Bridge View*, about 200m further along the same road (☎065-222 3723; ❷, a/c ❸) is more modern but less characterful, with a range of fan and a/c doubles and triples.

Moving on from Batticaloa, there are reasonably frequent **bus** services to Polonnaruwa (every 1–2hr), and occasional services to Colombo (2 daily; 8hr) and Trincomalee (via Habarana; 3 daily; 8hr); services down the badly maintained coastal road to Pottuvil (for Arugam Bay) may also have resumed by the time you read this. There are no direct services to Kandy. **Trains** leave twice daily for Polonnaruwa and Colombo.

Maduru Oya National Park

Flanking the road inland from Batticaloa to Mahiyangana, the huge and remote **Maduru Oya National Park** was established in 1983 to protect the catchment area of the enormous **Maduru Oya Reservoir** and four other smaller reservoirs (over fifteen percent of the park area is made up of water). Much of Maduru Oya's predominantly low-lying terrain was previously used for slash-and-burn agriculture, and is now mostly covered by open grasslands and secondary vegetation, although there are a few rocky mountains in the southwest corner reaching elevations of 685m. The usual range of fauna can be seen here: elephants, various species of monkeys and deer, abundant birdlife, rare sloth bears and even rarer leopards. The park attracts very few visitors, and in truth it's probably the least interesting national park in the country.

The road to the park goes via the village of **Mannampitiya**, 14km east of Polonnaruwa on the main road to Batticaloa. From here, a road leads 25km south to the entrance. **Entrance** costs US$10 per person, plus the usual additional charges (see p.55). If you're approaching the park from the south, you might enter via the settlement of **Dambana** (see p.265).

Gal Oya National Park

The enormous **Gal Oya National Park** lies some 50km inland from the coast, in a little-visited corner of the island west of the regional capital of Ampara. Like the nearby Maduru Oya, it was closed for much of the civil war and remains poorly set up for visitors at present. The centrepiece of the park is the vast **Senanayake Samudra**, one of the largest lakes in Sri Lanka, and the tours of the park are usually made – uniquely in Sri Lanka – by boat. As usual, elephants are the main draw, with herds of up to 150 visiting during their annual peregrinations. Elephant-spotting is best from March to July.

The park entrance is at **INGINIYAGALA**, 20km west from Ampara, where you can hire a boat for a trip around the Senanayake Samudra (around 2hr; US$10). **Entry** costs US$10 per person, plus the usual additional charges and taxes (see p.55).

Monaragala and Maligawila

Just beyond the easternmost fringes of the hill country east of Wellawaya, the obscure little town of **MONARAGALA** (pronounced "monah*rah*gahlah") is principally of interest as the gateway to Arugam Bay and as a base for visiting the remote and magical Buddhist statues of Maligawila. Monaragala itself is

Moving on from Monaragala

Buses currently leave Monaragala for the three-hour journey to Arugam Bay at 9.30am, 11.20am and 12.30pm, though all schedules are liable to change, however, so check in advance if possible. There are additional services to the town of Pottuvil, a five-kilometre tuktuk ride from Arugam Bay, with the last one at 2.30pm – if you miss the last bus you'll need to catch a minibus **taxi** from Monaragala (around US$50); tuktuks are much cheaper, though the ride's not much fun. Heading west, regular buses depart for Ampara (hourly; 3hr), Buttala (every 30min; 45min), Wellawaya (every 10min; 1hr 15min) and Badulla (every 30min; 3hr), from where there are plentiful onward connections.

dominated by the huge sheer sides of **Peacock Rock**, though there's nothing much to see or do in town once you've explored its two streets.

The **bus station** is bang in the centre of town; there's also a **taxi** (minibus) rank where you can pick up transport to Maligawila or Arugam Bay. ATMs accepting foreign cards can be found at the branches of the Commercial, People's and Hatton National **banks** and the Bank of Ceylon, spread out along the main road. The best-value **accommodation** in town is provided by the *Wellassa Inn Rest House* (ⓣ055-227 6815; ❶), on the main Wellawaya road about 200m west of the clocktower and occupying a comfortable old rest house with a large terrace restaurant and pleasant gardens; rooms are a mite basic but very cheap. Nicer, but overpriced, is the *Victory Inn* (ⓣ055-227 6100; ❹), almost opposite, which has spotless modern rooms with optional air-conditioning (Rs.500 supplement). Both places do passable food. There are also three beautifully rustic eco-lodges in the surrounding countryside (see box opposite).

Maligawila

Around 17km south of Monaragala, the remote village of **MALIGAWILA** is home to two giant standing Buddhist **statues**, fashioned out of crystalline limestone, which are thought to have once formed part of an extensive monastic complex. The statues, which had collapsed and fallen to bits, were restored in 1991, when the various pieces were rescued from the jungle floor and painstakingly reassembled – though the Maitreya statue still looks rather patched up, and is missing parts of various fingers. The statues are impressive in themselves, but are made additionally mysterious by their setting, hidden away in a stretch of pristine lowland jungle.

Maligawila village itself is little more than a sandy clearing surrounded by a few makeshift shacks. From the car park, a path leads into the woods, reaching a T-junction after about 300m. Turn left to reach the first of the two statues, an eleven-metre-high standing **Buddha** in the *abhaya mudra* ("Have No Fear") pose, freestanding apart from a discreet supporting brick arch at the back. Return to the T-junction and follow the other path for 200m to reach the second statue, dating from the seventh century AD and thought to represent either the bodhisattvas **Maitreya** or **Avalokitesvara**. This is a more elaborate structure, with the remains of ornate entrance steps, a moonstone and two flanking guardstones, plus a pillar inscription in medieval Sinhala erected during the reign of Mahinda IV (956–972), recording acts performed by the king in support of the Buddhist order. The statue itself is set on a sequence of five raised plinths, like a ziggurat, and clothed in a richly ornamented dress; unfortunately, it's currently protected by an ugly concrete pavilion.

Buses from Monaragala to Maligawila leave roughly every 45 minutes and take around an hour. Alternatively a **taxi** will cost around Rs.2000. Taking

Eco-lodges around Buttala

Well off the beaten track, the remote countryside around the village of **Buttala**, close to the northern fringes of Yala National Park, is an unlikely home to three of the island's most memorable – and idiosyncratic – eco-retreats. It's an area of truly unspoilt wilderness, with few people but plenty of wildlife, and peppered with various mysterious Buddhist remains – this was the northern extent of the historic Ruhunu kingdom. Buttala and its environs were the target of **separatist attacks** in late 2007 and early 2008 and the main Kataragama–Buttala highway is notched with dozens of guard posts; you should check the security situation with one of the eco-lodges in advance before making the trip.

Galapita roughly halfway between Buttala and Kataragama ⓣ011-250 8755, ⓦwww.galapita.com. Accessed by a rickety rope bridge spanning a natural rock pool and waterfall, this magical place occupies a superb setting on the banks of the Menik ("Gem") River. Open-sided and with alfresco bathrooms, the four pavilion-rooms, treehouse and two-storey mud-brick and clay villa (sleeping six) are the last word in rustic chic, beautifully designed but very simple. You're awfully close to nature here (there's only a mosquito net between you and the elements) – you might feel like a very style-conscious forest hermit. Activities include prospecting for gems, elephant-spotting, night-time canoe trips, hiking with the resident naturalist, plus guided bike rides to Buduruwagala and excursions further afield. There's also tasty vegetarian food (meat on request), using mainly local organic produce, and a new Ayurveda pavilion may be ready by the time you read this. ❻ full board

KumbukRiver 9km from Buttala ⓣ0773 632 182, ⓦwww.kumbukriver.com. Voted the world's leading eco-lodge at the 2008 World Travel Awards, this unique riverside retreat offers you probably the only chance you'll ever get to sleep *in* an elephant – an extraordinary twelve-metre-long, thatch-roofed beast constructed from local *kumbuk* wood which comes complete with its own plunge pool. There's also a second, and equally comfortable and spacious, non-pachyderm eco-chalet; both sleep up to ten and are rented out exclusively. No alcohol served but you can bring your own. Elephant Villa from US$175, Kumbuk Chalet from US$125 full board.

Tree Tops Jungle Lodge 9km south of Buttala ⓣ0777 036 554, ⓦwww.treetopsjunglelodge.com. With impeccable eco-tourism credentials, this award-winning jungle lodge really is out in the wilds – visitors are advised to arrive no earlier than 9am and no later than 3pm to avoid wandering elephants – with accommodation in rustic clay and wood huts in an unspoilt forest setting. There are no mod cons here (and no electricity) but it manages to be very comfortable even so, and the excellent and highly informative jungle walks, accompanied by a four-man local tracker team, are second to none. Book at least three days in advance. ❻ full board

a tuktuk is much cheaper – around Rs.700 – though it's a long journey, and you won't be able to appreciate the attractive countryside en route to the site.

Arugam Bay and around

Some 70km due east from Monaragala, and 5km south of the dusty town of Pottuvil, easygoing **ARUGAM BAY** is by far the most engaging of the east coast's resorts. A-Bay, as it's sometimes known, has long been popular with the long-term **surfing** fraternity, who come here to ride what are generally acknowledged to be the best waves in Sri Lanka, but it also has plenty to offer non-surfers, with an appealingly crashed-out ambience, some charmingly

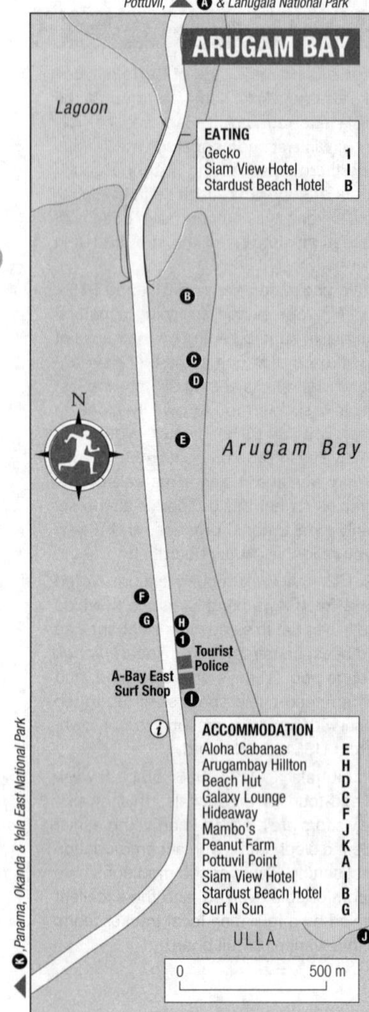

tumbledown places to stay and a host of attractions in the gorgeous surrounding countryside, from the elephant-rich **Lahugala National Park** to the atmospheric ruins at **Magul Maha Vihara**. The village is a long way from anywhere else, and there are more attractive – and far more easily accessible – beaches in the south, but if the idea of exploring a friendly and neglected corner of the east, a world away from the commercialism of the west coast, appeals, then it's a great place to head for.

There's not much to Arugam Bay village: just a single, wide main road running parallel to a broad though not especially attractive expanse of beach, with a cluster of palm-thatch huts at its southern end signalling the tiny Muslim hamlet of **Ulla**. (In fact the village's most talked-about feature is the absurdly high-spec new road bridge spanning the lagoon that separates it from Pottuvil, to the north; constructed at a cost of over US$10 million to the US taxpayer following tsunami damage to the previous crossing, it's a source of much local bemusement.) Yet you may still find yourself tempted to linger, won over not just by the surf or the nearby countryside but by the warmth of this well-integrated community. Predominantly Muslim, with significant minorities of Tamils and Sinhalese – plus a few ageing Western hippies thrown in – Arugam Bay's local population is a harmonious ethnic mix, fiercely proud of the bay and resistant to all attempts to change its character. This resolve was sorely tested in the wake of the tsunami, which laid waste to much of the village. A government plan for a series of luxury tourist developments intended to fast-track its recovery was fiercely rebuffed by the local Arugam Bay Tourism Association, which preferred to maintain its own brand of homespun enterprise. As the east coast's principal draw, development may yet change the bay from a surfers' hangout to a mainstream beach destination, but at least it looks set to be on the local community's terms.

Practicalities

Buses stop along the main road. The best sources of **information** are the eco-tours hut at the *Arugambay Hillton,* and the *Stardust* and *Siam View* hotels; there's also an information hut run by the Arugam Bay Tourism Association

Surfing at Arugam Bay

With waves fresh from Antarctica crashing up onto the beach, Arugam Bay is sometimes claimed to be one of the top ten surf points in the world, and periodically plays host to international tournaments. The best surfing is between April/May and October/November. There are four main point breaks reasonably close to Arugam Bay, plus several others further afield. The biggest and most popular waves are at **The Point**, a long right-hand break close to Arugam Bay, which has (on a good day) 2m waves and a 400m ride. About 9km north of Arugam Bay (Rs.800 in a tuktuk), just beyond Pottuvil, **Pottuvil Point** breaks off a long and deserted sandy beach and is less crowded than The Point; the ride can be as long as 800m, though the waves are a bit smaller. About 3km south of Arugam Bay (30min in a tuktuk, then a 20min walk), the break near **Crocodile Rock** is an excellent spot for beginner and intermediate surfers if there's sufficient swell, while another 5km on, **Peanut Farm** has two surf points: a perfect tube for expert surfers and a smaller ride ideal for beginners. In Arugam Bay itself, there's a beach break in front of the *Stardust Beach Hotel* which can be fun for body surfing or for beginners, while there are several other well-known breaks further down the coast towards Yala East National Park.

The best places for general **surfing** info and equipment hire are the A-Bay East Surf shop, just north of the *Siam View Hotel*, and the surf shop at the *Surf N Sun* guesthouse. These places and some of the village's guesthouses rent surfboards (from Rs.500 per day) and bodyboards (from Rs.400 per day), as well as offering **surfing safaris** to various hotspots along the idyllic coastline south of Arugam Bay (prices vary depending on the length of the trip and the amount of driving involved), including to Peanut Farm and the break at **Okanda** – ask at A-Bay East Surf or *Surf N Sun*, or look for signs around the village advertising trips.

(8.30am–noon & 2–5pm) opposite the *Siam View*, with English-speaking staff on hand in season and a few leaflets about the local community tourism programmes on offer. The *Stardust* and *Siam View* hotels have useful **websites**, Ⓦwww.arugambay.com and www.arugam.info respectively; the latter in particular is a mine of local gossip.

There's nowhere to **change money** in the village, though there are branches of the People's Bank and Bank of Ceylon in Pottuvil; neither has an ATM or gives advances on credit cards, however, so unless you have traveller's cheques or foreign currency to change, make sure you bring enough money with you for the duration of your stay. The most reliable places for **internet** access are currently the *Arugambay Hillton* and *Siam View Hotel*, though more places are likely to open up in the future. The **tourist police** hut is just north of the *Siam View Hotel*.

Accommodation

Arugam Bay's **guesthouses** have a distinctive style all of their own, with a number of places offering rustic and rather quirky accommodation in quaint palm-thatch cabanas, huts on stilts, treehouses and the like – fun, if fairly basic. There are a handful of more conventional places to stay too, though avoid the bay's twin low-grade resort-style hotels, the cheerless and badly maintained *Tri-Star* and *New Tri-Star*. In addition, the local tourism association can organize **homestays**; ask at the *Arugam Bay Hillton* or the information hut opposite the *Siam View*. Arugam Bay is very quiet out of season, during which time you may find some of the places listed below (and many others which aren't) are closed for repairs.

Tours from Arugam Bay

In addition to surfing tours (see box, p.395) and visits to Lahugala and Yala East national parks, there are several more unusual excursions organized by the Arugam Bay Tourism Assocation, all of which can be arranged through the *Arugambay Hillton* (book the day before). The **Pottuvil Lagoon Tour** (Rs.3000 per two-person boat) consists of a gentle two-hour canoe trip during which a local fisherman will paddle you out into Pottuvil lagoon, 8km north of town, and through the beautiful mangrove swamps which fringe its shores, offering the chance to spot birds, monitor lizards and perhaps the occasional crocodile or elephant. They also arrange **sea safaris** (1hr 30min; Rs.6000 for up to four people) in engine-powered boats, giving you a good chance of seeing dolphins, flying fish and other marine life. You can also **dive** from the boat if you have your own equipment.

They also offer various guided **cycling tours** (Rs.1000 per bike, plus Rs.500 guide fee) to nearby farming villages, giving you the opportunity to learn about local rice, fruit and vegetable cultivation, and visit a dairy farm; at the latter you can stop for lunch and try your hand at milking a buffalo.

Arugam Bay

Aloha Cabanas ⓣ063-224 8379, ⓦwww.aloha-arugambay.com. Decent-value surfers' hangout, with a mix of bright and roomy two-storey concrete cabanas (with attractive little first-floor open-air areas for lounging) and smaller, rather rickety but very sweet palm-thatch ones, set in a rambling garden leading down to the beach. Long and short surfboards are available to rent. ❸–❹

Arugambay Hillton ⓣ063-224 8189, ⓦwww.arugambayhillton.com. Long-established and good-value guesthouse, with a mix of neat and comfortable if compact rooms and simpler, cheaper cabanas (occupying Arugam Bay's cutest wooden building) set around a pleasant courtyard garden. There's also a clay pizza oven, internet (Rs.100 per hr), and motorbikes (Rs.1000–1500 per day) and bikes (Rs.600 per day) to rent, and the very clued-up owner can arrange all sorts of local tours (see box above). ❷–❸

Beach Hut ⓣ0773 179 594, ⓔrangabeachhut@gmail.com. Friendly place with a selection of quaint wooden cabanas (including several on stilts, two of which miraculously survived the tsunami). It's rustic and fairly basic, but excellent value, and has bags of laid-back charm and character. Also a sociable choice for evening meals, with good, inexpensive Sri Lankan food served at a communal table (book in advance), and occasional beach barbecues. ❶–❷

Galaxy Lounge ⓣ063-224 8415, ⓦwww.galaxysrilanka.com. Nice beachfront location with accommodation in a mix of large and attractive two-storey palm-thatch cabanas, plus a breezy open-air restaurant, strewn with comfy outdoor sofas and hammocks. ❸–❹

Hideaway ⓣ063-224 8259, ⓔtisseragv@sltnet.lk. One of the nicest places to stay in Arugam Bay, set on the land side of the main road in a characterful two-storey house swathed in tropical greenery. The rooms in the main house are good value and attractively furnished, with open latticework brick walls and slatted wooden fronts – pleasantly cool, if not especially private. There's also a mix of spacious and stylishly minimalist whitewashed brick cabanas, a cut above those in the rest of the village; the bright new a/c family ones at the front offer some of Arugam Bay's most comfortable accommodation, though lack the cosy charm of the older ones behind. Rooms ❸, cabanas ❹, a/c cabanas ❺

Mambo's ⓣ0777 822 524, ⓦwww.mambo.nu. Mainly aimed at surfers, this crashed-out place has the closest accommodation to the Arugam Bay surf point, right over the breaking waves with a fetching view of the bay and village opposite. Accommodation is in spacious modern cabanas with cool, tiled interiors, or cheaper but more basic thatched wooden cabanas, plus an oceanfront bungalow (US$40). There's also a funky restaurant, bar and chill-out zone, plus Saturday night beach barbecues in season. ❸–❹

Siam View Hotel ⓣ063-224 8195, ⓦwww.arugam.com. Set around an attractive Thai-style wooden restaurant, this A-Bay landmark is the liveliest place along the main beach strip, with an excellent restaurant (see opposite) and occasional full-moon parties. Rooms are spacious and modern and most come with a/c; the family room, with cable TV and a rock bathroom is the nicest. The red English phone box outside provides another distinctive local landmark. ❸, a/c ❹

Stardust Beach Hotel ⓣ063-224 8191, ⓦwww.arugambay.com. Arugam Bay's smartest hotel has bright and stylish rooms; those upstairs have great ocean views from the sea-facing balconies. There's also a selection of good-value high-ceilinged wood and palm-thatch cabanas, both in the attractive main garden and tucked away in the peaceful "Rainbow Village" next door, plus a new yoga pavilion and Arugam's most civilized restaurant (see below). Rooms ⑤, cabanas ④

Surf N Sun ⓣ0776 065 099, ⓦthesurfnsun.com. The village's main surfers' hangout, with comfortable and reasonable-value cabanas, some of them almost buried under luxuriant thatched roofs. There's a lively restaurant and reggae bar (open till 3/4am in season) attached, and it's also a good place to organize tours. Often closed in the off-season. ④

Around Arugam Bay

Peanut Farm 8km south of Arugam Bay ⓣ0777 822 524, ⓔsurfmambo50@hotmail.com. In a dramatic position on a vast and utterly deserted stretch of virgin beach occasionally visited by elephants, this remote and windswept place opens out onto a celebrated local surfing spot. Accommodation is in stilted wooden huts, full of rustic chic, which resemble giant thatched birdhouses, and it hosts increasingly legendary full-moon parties. Getting there, on a series of confusing trails through wild countryside, is at least half the fun. Best is a 4X4; a tuktuk can (just about) make the journey if there hasn't been much rain, though it's liable to get stuck – come in a group and be prepared to dig. April–Oct only. ④

Pottuvil Point 9km north of Arugam Bay ⓣ0773 507 088, ⓦwww.pottuvilpoint.com. Situated on a wide and breezy sweep of beach, strewn with giant boulders, above another of the area's prime surfing breaks, this simple but stylish surfer's hangout comprises *kadjan*-thatched cabanas, including some right on the rocks, plus a funky restaurant. April–Oct only. ④

Eating and drinking

There's a surprisingly good range of **places to eat** in Arugam Bay. For a fun evening, head to the *Siam View Hotel*, whose upstairs terrace restaurant is one of the nicest and most sociable places in the village, with authentic Thai and other international cuisine, plus a pizza oven. The real-ale-enthusiast German owner, Fred, also usually has an excellent range of home-brewed beers on tap (all conforming to German purity laws), a blessed relief from yet more Lion Lager. For more sophistication, there's an appetizing selection of expertly prepared meals and snacks at the *Stardust Beach Hotel*'s smart pavilion restaurant, with mains ranging from paella to steak tartare, plus home-made ice cream, cakes and cookies. Similar fare, with a particularly good range of salads and sandwiches (made with home-baked bread), is on offer at the attractive open-air *kadjan*-thatched restaurant at *Gecko*; it's also the only place on the east coast for a full English breakfast (Rs.650). All these places also serve accomplished Sri Lankan food.

Around Arugam Bay

Half the pleasure of visiting Arugam Bay is getting out into the beautiful surrounding **countryside**, which boasts superb scenery, a pair of national parks and a smattering of historical attractions – although you'll need your own transport to see the best of it.

Lahugala National Park

About 15km inland from Arugam Bay, the main road passes through the small but beautiful **Lahugala National Park**. The park encloses the extensive

Moving on from Arugam Bay

Moving on from Arugam Bay, there are three early-morning buses to Monaragala and destinations beyond (currently 6.15am, 7.15am and 8.30am); alternatively, catch a tuktuk to Pottuvil, from where there are services west roughly every hour. There are also two daily services from Pottuvil to Batticaloa (5hr).

Lahugala Tank and its surrounding dry mixed evergreen forest, an unusually fine stretch of woodland including numerous lofty rosewoods and satinwoods – particularly magical in the low light and long shadows of early morning or late afternoon. The park is best known for its **elephants**: up to 150 congregate around the tanks during July and August, when the rest of Lahugala's waters dry up, to drink and feed on the *beru* grass which grows prolifically around the water. The tanks are also good for spotting a wide range of aquatic **birds**, including innumerable snowy white egrets which can often be seen hitching a ride on the backs of obliging elephants. When the rains come the elephants disperse, and large sections of the park turn a brilliant, post-monsoonal green.

Lahugala isn't currently open to vehicles, but this also means that there are no **entrance charges**, so you can walk into the park from the main road between Arugam Bay and Monaragala, which runs right through it. Be aware, however, that walking through jungle with a large elephant population carries a degree of risk, so it's best to stick to one of the recognized viewpoints close to the road. The easiest (and safest) option is to head to Lahugala Hospital (at the 306km post). Just west of here along the main road, several small paths run off to the right to the raised bund at the edge of Lahugala Tank, about 100m away, which offers a secure vantage point and good chances of spotting elephants and lots of water birds.

A number of guesthouses in Arugam Bay can arrange **jeeps** to the park for around US$40 (try the *Surf N Sun* or *Hideaway*), although given that you can't actually drive these into the park, you might as well catch the bus or take a tuktuk – the latter can be arranged through the *Arugambay Hillton* for Rs.1200.

Magul Maha Vihara

Just east of Lahugala (and signposted from the main road just west of the 309km post) lie the evocative remains of the **Magul Maha Vihara** (no set hours; donation). According to tradition, the temple was originally a garden in which Kavan Tissa and Viharamahadevi, his bride, were united – the resident monk will point out the *poruwa*, a special wedding platform decorated with a lion frieze, which was erected for the event. Following the ceremony, the gardens were walled and presented to the Sangha, who established a monastery here. The unexcavated remains of Kavan Tissa's palace lie in jungle to south; it was here that the couple's son, the legendary Dutugemunu (see p.362), was born and lived until his teens, when he and his parents moved to Tissa.

Stone inscriptions found at the site record that the current temple buildings were erected by King Dhatusena during the mid-fifth century, and later restored in the mid-fourteenth century. The extensive remains include a Buddha shrine, image house, dagoba, *poyage* and well-preserved moonstones, as well as the finely carved *poruwa*, all lent an additional layer of mystery by the thick jungle which surrounds them on every side.

South to Okanda and beyond

The countryside and coastline **south of Arugam Bay** is beautifully unspoilt. Buses run three times daily along the narrow, paved but bone-shakingly potholed road, which runs a short way inland through rice paddies and scrub jungle as far as the lively, dusty little village of **PANAMA**, 12km south of Arugam Bay. There are miles of superb deserted beach along this stretch, and a pair of huge rock outcrops popularly known as **Elephant Rock** and **Crocodile Rock** for their alleged resemblance to these creatures, though you'll need a tuktuk (or 4X4) to reach them. Elephants are sometimes seen wandering in the

▲ Panama

vicinity. Panama itself has a fine, dune-backed beach, 1km south of town; to reach it, pass through the village and follow the road round to the left.

Unmetalled but graded, the main road improves **south of Panama**, though access is sometimes prevented by the military at the checkpoint on the way into the village. The countryside here is almost completely uninhabited, and very similar in appearance to that of Yala (West) National Park, with extensive lagoons, scrub jungle and huge populations of aquatic birds, as well as occasional elephants and crocodiles.

Some 30km south of Arugam Bay lies the village of **OKANDA**. There's another popular surfing spot here, and the village also boasts a major **Hindu temple**, which marks the spot where Kataragama is said to have landed on the island and is now an important staging point on the overland pilgrimage to Kataragama. A few kilometres inland from Okanda lies the extensive forest hermitage of **Kudimbigala**, whose hundreds of caves are thought to have been occupied by Buddhist monks as far back as the first century BC.

Okanda is also the entrance point for **Yala East National Park**, where the Kumana Wewa tank and surrounding mangroves support an outstanding array of aquatic birds. Believed to be an LTTE holdout, the park was officially closed at the time of writing, though some guesthouses offer (expensive) trips: a day-trip by jeep (seating four to six people), encompassing Okanda, Kudimbigala and Yala East, costs around US$80–85.

6

Jaffna and the north

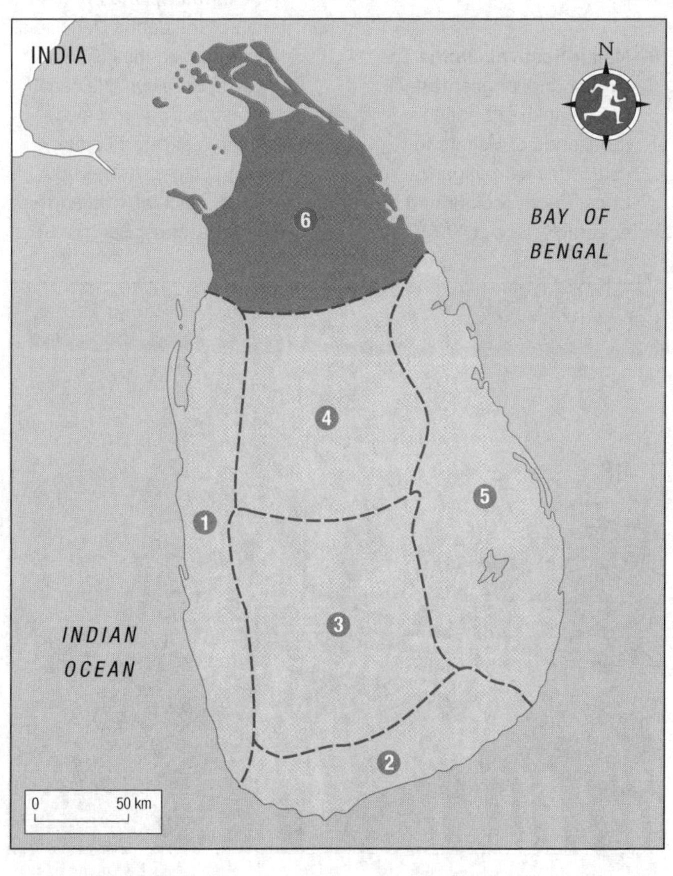

CHAPTER 6

Highlights

* **Jaffna** Quite unlike anywhere else in Sri Lanka, the vibrant city of Jaffna offers a fascinating insight into the island's distinctive Tamil culture, as well as many intriguing reminders of its colonial and civil war past. See p.407

* **Nallur Festival, Jaffna** The largest and longest festival in Sri Lanka, attracting thousands of visitors to its 25-day extravaganza of ceremony, colour and spectacle. See p.409

* **Jaffna Peninsula** This densely populated peninsula is home to myriad contrasting sights, from sand dunes and hot springs to abandoned villages and war-torn temples. See p.409

* **The islands** Splintering off the tip of the Jaffna Peninsula, the starkly beautiful islands of Keyts, Karaitivu, Nainativu and Delft are a world away from the rest of Sri Lanka, home to little-visited Hindu temples, colonial forts and remote beaches. See p.410

▲ Nallur Kandaswamy Temple, Jaffna

6

Jaffna and the north

The **north** is a world away from the rest of Sri Lanka. Closer to southern India than to Colombo, the region was settled early on by **Tamil** migrants from southern India and has retained a unique character and culture, one which owes more to Hindu India than Buddhist Sri Lanka. The tensions and recurring conflicts between Tamils and Sinhalese lie at the very heart of Sri Lankan history. Throughout much of the island's earlier history, Tamil adventurers and mercenaries – either from the north of the island or from South India – interfered, usually with disastrous consequences, in Sinhalese affairs, creating a deep-seated suspicion which continues to cloud Sinhalese attitudes towards Tamils to this day. Since 1983, excepting a brief spell of peace between 2002 and 2006, the entire region has been engulfed in the **civil war** between the rebel guerrillas of the **LTTE** (Liberation Tigers of Tamil Eelam, or Tamil Tigers), and the Sri Lankan Army (SLA), and the decades of fighting have further reinforced the two-thousand-year history of difference that separates the Tamil north from the Sinhalese south.

For much of the past two decades, large areas of the north have been controlled by the LTTE, who established their own de facto independent state stretching from just north of Vavuniya through to Elephant Pass (while for a period they also controlled the Jaffna peninsula until it was recaptured by the SLA in 1995). All this has now dramatically changed. Starting in early 2008, the SLA mounted its largest-ever sustained offensive against the Tamil Tigers, gradually pushing north into LTTE-controlled territory, and capturing the Tigers' erstwhile "capital" at Kilinochchi, and their east-coast stronghold of Mullaitivu in early 2009 before finally capturing the last fragment of LTTE-controlled territory (and allegedly killing their legendary commander, Prabhakaran, in the process) in May 2009.

At the time of writing, large parts of the north were a war zone, and completely out-of-bounds to all foreigners. It has therefore been impossible to check information for this latest edition of the guide; the following text is based on research conducted in 2006, though naturally many things will have changed. Following the cessation of hostilities in May 2009, it's likely that travel to the north will once again become possible in the reasonably near future. **Domestic flights** from Colombo to Jaffna continue to operate, but are not currently accepting casual foreign passengers, although this is likely to change soon. In addition, it's likely that the **A9 highway** to Jaffna will reopen to civilian traffic during 2010 (or perhaps even by late 2009). Check with the tourist office in Colombo (see p.89) for the latest information on both land and air routes.

The Liberation Tigers of Tamil Eelam

Terrorists in the eyes of some, freedom fighters to others, the **Liberation Tigers of Tamil Eelam** (LTTE), popularly known as the **Tamil Tigers**, were until recently one of the world's most committed, effective and ruthless militant organizations. The LTTE was founded in the early 1970s, one of a string of paramilitary groups established by young Tamils in response to the decades of official discrimination meted out by the Sinhalese governments of Colombo to the Tamils of the north and east. The failure of the older Tamil politicians to secure justice for Tamils within the island's flawed parliamentary democracy drove many young Tamils to espouse violence, while the heavy-handed behaviour of the Sinhalese-dominated Sri Lankan Army and police in Tamil areas added to the discontent.

All these groups of young militants called for the establishment of an independent Tamil state in the north and east of the island, to be called **Eelam** ("Precious Land"), and a number received training from special Indian government forces who were initially sympathetic to their cause. The LTTE gradually rose to pre-eminence thanks to its ruthless suppression of all competing political groups and the assassination of rival politicians, and by the beginning of the civil war in 1983, the LTTE had become the leading player in Tamil affairs.

At the heart of the LTTE's mystique lay their founder and leader, the enigmatic **Velupillai Prabhakaran** (born 1954). Legends about this reclusive figure abound. According to some, he was a shy and bookish student with a fascination for Napoleon and Alexander the Great, who turned militant when he saw an uncle burnt alive by Sinhalese mobs, and who later trained himself to endure pain by lying in sacks of chillies. Known as *Thambi*, or "Little Brother", Prabhakaran was held in quasi-religious veneration by his recruits, and proved a consummate political survivor who evaded capture for two decades until finally being ambushed and killed by the SLA in May 2009 – at least according to the Sri Lankan authorities, although doubts about the authenticity of the body produced, and rumours that the real Prabhakaran is still alive and well and somewhere completely different, will possibly continue to circulate for years to come. He has also proved a gifted military strategist, although reports suggest that much of the LTTE's earlier engagements were based on the study of *Rambo* and Arnold Schwarzenegger videos – a classic example of life imitating (bad) art.

The LTTE began life as a classic guerrilla operation, harrying the (to begin with) far better-equipped and numerically superior forces of the Sri Lankan Army and later the Indian Peacekeeping Force (IPKF; see p.429) with hit-and-run attacks, before retreating back into the countryside and mixing with local populations. These guerrilla

The Vanni

The huge area of northern Sri Lanka between **Vavuniya** and the Jaffna Peninsula – **the Vanni** – has been devastated by the civil war, and large areas now lie ruined, abandoned and heavily mined – the task of bringing life back to the region following the most recent round of fighting is likely to be a long and difficult one. This entire region was controlled by the LTTE until 2008–09 from their "capital" at **Kilinochchi**, on the northern edge of the Vanni.

Gateway to the Vanni is the town of **VAVUNIYA** (pronounced "Vowvneeya"), the largest between Anuradhapura and Jaffna. Vavuniya sits roughly at the borderline between Sinhalese and Tamil Sri Lanka, and has frequently found itself on or close to the front line of the fighting, serving as an important staging post for the SLA from which to mount military operations to the north.

Some 45km from Vavuniya, north of the A14, lies the remote village of **MADHU**, the most important place of Christian pilgrimage in Sri Lanka. The tactics have been combined with bloody and attention-grabbing attacks such as that at Anuradhapura in 1985, when dozens of civilians and pilgrims were gunned down by LTTE soldiers in the symbolic centre of Sinhalese culture. The LTTE also pioneered the gruesome practice of **suicide bombing** (whose technology they are believed to have exported to militant Palestinian organizations such as Hamas), with notable attacks against Colombo, the international airport and the Temple of the Tooth in Kandy, amongst many others. Suicide bombers have also been used in a string of high-profile **political assassinations** – victims have included former Indian Prime Minister Rajiv Gandhi in 1991, and Sri Lankan Prime Minister Ranasinghe Premadasa in 1993. As the war progressed and the LTTE Acquired better armaments and military know-how, they gradually began to function more as a conventional army – exemplified by their seizure of Elephant Pass, at the southern end of the Jaffna Peninsula, from the heavily entrenched forces of the SLA in 2000.

The LTTE's ability to take on and defeat the huge forces of the Indian and Sri Lankan armies reflects its legendary discipline and commitment to the cause, fostered by relentless **political indoctrination** and quasi-monastic **discipline**. In addition, hardly any LTTE fighters were ever captured alive, thanks to the phials of cyanide which all cadres wore around their necks. They also – by Asian standards at least – had impeccable **feminist** credentials. The shortage of men of fighting age led to many women – the so-called "Freedom Birds", memorably described by British writer William Dalrymple as "paramilitary feminist death squads" – being absorbed into the LTTE military apparatus and often pitched into its toughest fighting engagements.

Attitudes towards the LTTE remain divided. In the early years of the civil war they were widely regarded as heroes who were prepared to lay down their lives in the fight against the shamelessly self-interested anti-Tamil policies of successive Sinhalese governments in Colombo. As the conflict dragged on, however, opinions changed. The LTTE's systematic assassination of rival Tamil politicians, their massacres of innocent Sinhalese civilians, Muslims and suspected "collaboraters", their use of child soldiers and abduction of young Tamils to fight for the LTTE, their habit of extorting money under duress from Tamils at home and abroad, their ethnic cleansing of areas under their control and their indiscriminate use of suicide bombers have all earned them censure in the eyes of the world, and led to them being widely classified as a terrorist organization. As of May 2009, the LTTE had finally lost its last remaining fragment of territory, while its fighters had been decimated and its leader, Prabhakaran, allegedly killed by the SLA, bringing one of the world's most fearsome rebel organizations to a predictably bloody end.

large, nineteenth-century Portuguese-style **church** here is home to the allegedly miraculous statue of **Our Lady of Madhu**. The image was brought to Madhu in 1670 by Catholics fleeing Dutch persecution in the Mannar area, and subsequently became revered for its magical qualities, particularly its supposed ability to protect devotees against snakebites.

Beyond Madhu, **Mannar Island** pokes a finger westwards towards India. The island is virtually part of the mainland, to which it's joined by a bridge; it's also the closest part of Sri Lanka to India, and was formerly the starting point for the ferry to that country, suspended since 1983. Mannar was long famous for its **pearl banks**, which were exploited from antiquity until the colonial period: as late as 1905 some five thousand divers recovered a staggering eighty million oysters here in a single season – they also provided the inspiration for Bizet's *The Pearl Fishers*, the only opera ever to be set in Sri Lanka. Arab traders also flocked to Mannar, introducing donkeys (an animal virtually unknown elsewhere in Sri Lanka) and planting the baobab trees which remain another

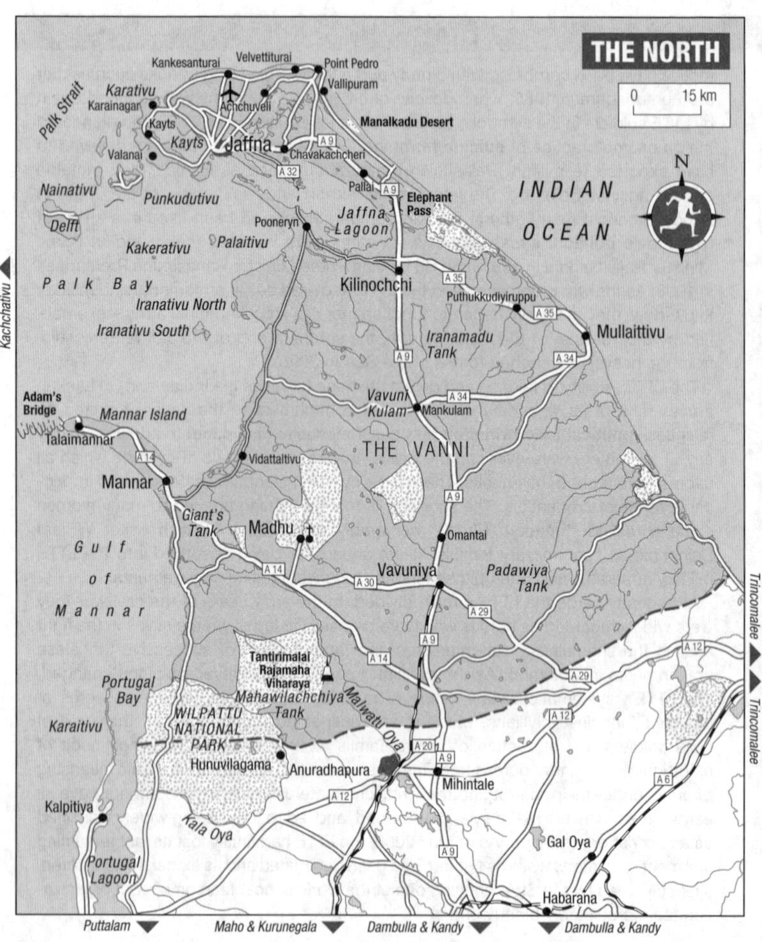

of the island's distinctive features. Mannar suffered greatly during the civil war, when its position close to India made it a major conduit for refugees fleeing the country. The island's large Muslim population, a legacy of its years of Arab trade, was driven out by the LTTE in 1990, though the local population still includes many Catholics – some forty percent, the highest proportion of anywhere in Sri Lanka.

The principal settlement is the woebegone town of **Mannar**, at the island's eastern end, whose main sight is the imposing **Portuguese fort** (later strengthened by the Dutch), near the entrance to town. West of Mannar Island, a chain of islets and sandbanks known as **Adam's Bridge** stretches all the way to India, 30km distant. According to the *Ramayana*, these were the stepping stones used by the monkey god Hanuman to travel from India to Lanka, and they also served as the causeway by which the earliest human settlers reached the island some 250,000 to 300,000 years ago. These sandbanks lie less than two metres under water in many places, and may only have been submerged as recently as 1480, according to temple records from Rameswaram in India.

About 80km **north of Vavuniya**, the small town of **KILINOCHCHI** served as the headquarters of the LTTE administration in the north until being recaptured by the SLA in January 2009 after a long and bloody three-month siege. Some 15km further north along the A9 lies **Elephant Pass**, where a causeway connects the Jaffna Peninsula with the rest of the island. The pass was named for the elephants that were once driven across to the peninsula here, though it's now best known as the location of two of the civil war's most bitter battles, fought here in 1991 and 2000.

Jaffna and the peninsula

Poised close to the northernmost tip of the island, the war-torn town of **JAFFNA** lay at the heart of many of the civil war's fiercest struggles, and symbolizes more than anywhere else in Sri Lanka the terrors, absurdities and pointless destructiveness of the war years – such was Jaffna's symbolic importance that when government forces captured it in 1995, the LTTE marched the entire population out into the surrounding countryside, leaving the advancing army to occupy a ghost town.

Inaccessible for two decades, Jaffna briefly opened to casual visitors during the period of peace from 2002 to 2006, but is now once again off-limits, following the severing of all road and air links with the rest of the island during the most recent round of fighting (unless you hire your own helicopter to fly in). The good news is that, having has remained under government control throughout recent years, Jaffna and the peninsula have avoided being caught up in the devastating military confrontations which have enveloped the rest of northern Sri Lanka during 2008–09, leading to the possibility that the area may perhaps reopen to visitors in the not too distant future.

Jaffna is closer to India than to Colombo, and in many ways looks across the Palk Strait to the Indian state of Tamil Nadu rather than to Sinhalese Sri Lanka for much of its cultural and political inspiration. Arriving in Jaffna can come as something of a culture shock if you've spent time in the rest of the island, and even the most casual visitor will notice the profound **Indian influence** here, exemplified by the replacement of the Buddhist dagoba with the Hindu *gopuram*, and by the switch from the singsong cadences of Sinhala to the quickfire intonations of Tamil – not to mention myriad other details like the sultry Indian pop music which blares out of shops and cafés, and the quasi-subcontinental hordes of kamikaze cyclists who rattle around the congested streets. Yet although there's a fair bit of India in Jaffna, the town has its own unique and complex identity shaped, in true Sri Lankan fashion, by a wide cross-section of influences, including Muslim, Portuguese, Dutch, British – and

Getting to Jaffna

Following the end of the civil war, regular transport connections between Jaffna and the rest of the island will hopefully be re-established by sometime in 2010 (or perhaps even earlier). **Flights** to Jaffna from Colombo's Ratmalana airport have previously been operated by Expo Aviation (466 Galle Rd, Kollupitiya, Colombo) and Serendib Express (500 Galle Rd, Wellawatta, Colombo), while various companies have operated comfortable inter-city **buses** from Colombo to Jaffna, with the journey taking around 10–12 hours (try Thampi Travels, at 296 Galle Rd in Wellawatta). The tourist office in Colombo (see p.89) should be able to provide you with all the latest details.

even Sinhalese. Although Hinduism remains the dominant religion, Christianity is also strong, and the town presents an intriguing mixture of Tamil and European elements, with colourful temples set next to huge churches, and streets of a beguiling, faded colonial charm dotted with old Dutch and British residences. Perhaps most striking of all, however, is the sense of cultural sophistication here, embodied by the remarkably cosmopolitan and highly educated populace who, despite battling for almost half a century against institutionalized racism and devastating civil war, retain a charm, curiosity and intelligence which is one of Jaffna's most unexpected but memorable attractions.

Arrival, accommodation and eating

Buses arrive right in the middle of Jaffna at the bus station on Hospital Road, the main road in the modern town centre. Jaffna was formerly served by **flights** from Colombo, which arrived at Palali Airport, around 15km north of Jaffna. There are several **banks** along Hospital Road.

Most accommodation in Jaffna is clustered in the suburb of **Chundukuli**, mainly along Kandy Road. Reliable options have previously included *Bastian's Hotel* at 37 Kandy Rd (ⓣ021-222 2605; ❸–❹), *Green Inn*, 60 Kandy Rd (ⓣ021-222 3898; ❸), and the excellent *Old Park Chinese Restaurant*, 40 Kandy Rd (ⓣ021-222 3790; ❹). A couple of nearby options included the *New Rest House* (ⓣ021-222 7839; ❸), just north of Kandy Rd, the US Guest House, 874 Hospital Rd (ⓣ021-222 7029; ❸) and *Serendib Inn*, 86 Point Pedro Rd (ⓣ021-222 3984; ❸). Further out, the good GTZ Guest House, 114A Temple Rd (ⓣ021-222 2203; ❹), has traditionally been popular with visiting aid workers, as has the (unsigned) *Morgan's Guest House* (ⓣ021-222 3666; ❹), more or less opposite at 103 Temple Rd. Whether any of these places manage to survive the latest round of fighting remains to be seen. The best places to eat were previously the *Cosy Restaurant* on Sirambiyadi Lane, the *Old Park Chinese Restaurant* (see above) and the *Hotel Rolex*, in the centre of town on Hospital Road.

The Town

Immediately south of the modern centre lies the town's immense **fort**. The largest Dutch fort in Asia, this huge structure was built on the site of the former Portuguese stronghold in the characteristic star shape favoured by the Dutch (the pointed bastions offered greater protection against cannon fire). The inner defences were completed in 1680 and the outer ring of bastions in 1792, though just three years after it was completed the fort was surrendered to the British without a shot being fired. Sadly, having survived two hundred years without seeing action, the fort was finally pressed into military service during the civil war, when the outer defences were repeatedly bombarded by both sides and the old Dutch buildings inside, including the beautiful **Groote Kerk** ("Great Church"), destroyed. The fort is still in military use, and currently off-limits. A walk around the outside gives some idea of the strength of the massive exterior walls, although war damage, tangles of barbed wire and the luxuriant spread of unchecked vegetation make it difficult to see anything very clearly.

The south side of the fort is bounded by the calm, shallow waters of the **Jaffna lagoon**, the ocean inlet that divides the Jaffna Peninsula from the rest of Sri Lanka (and from the islands of Kayts and Karaitivu). This is one of the few places in town where you can actually reach the lagoon, since most of the shoreline has been fenced off by the SLA; the low-lying bridge-cum-causeway which connects Jaffna to Kayts can be seen disappearing into the waters close to the fort.

Ceylon tea

In the minds of many outsiders, Sri Lanka remains synonymous with one thing: tea (still usually referred to as "Ceylon" tea). Tea cultivation underpinned much of the island's prosperity during the British colonial period, and also had important cultural and environmental side-effects, leading to the clearance of almost all the highland jungles and to the arrival of large numbers of Tamil labourers, drafted in to work the plantations. The industry remains crucial to Sri Lanka's economy, and tea estates still dominate the hill country, with endless miles of neatly trimmed bushes carpeting the rolling terrain.

Tea fields near Lipton's Seat ▲

Tea estate sign ▼

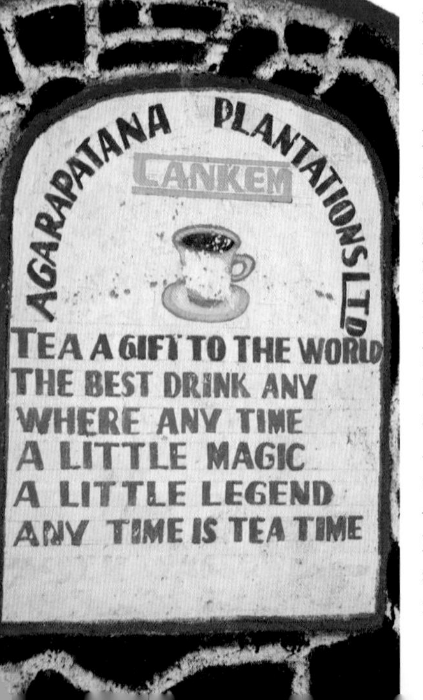

Sri Lanka's green gold

The first tea seeds were planted in Sri Lanka in Peradeniya Botanical Gardens in 1824, but it wasn't until the sudden collapse of the island's coffee industry during the 1860s that tea's commercial possibilities were seriously investigated. The island's first commercial tea plantation – covering a modest nineteen acres – was established at Loolecondera near Kandy in 1867 by enterprising Scotsman **James Taylor**. Taylor's fledgling tea garden thrived, and hundreds of other planters soon followed, buying up abandoned coffee estates and clearing the hill country's jungles in order to establish new plantations. Within a few years the upland environment of Sri Lanka was changed forever, while rapid fortunes were made from what soon became known as Sri Lanka's "green gold" – most notably by the entrepreneurial **Thomas Lipton** (see p.457), who bought up a chain of estates and factories and did more than anyone else to put Ceylon tea on the global map, and to develop a market for it back home in Britain.

Although tea is no longer Sri Lanka's leading export, it's still crucial to the national economy, and the island remains one of the world's top exporters. Locally grown tea is widely available here at a few specialist outlets – principally the islandwide Mlesna chain. Dilmah and Lipton's are the most common brands, but for a real taste of Sri Lanka, look for high-grown, unblended, single-estate teas, and check which grade you're getting. As a general rule of thumb, the higher the plantation, the more prized the tea – among connoisseurs, the premium **high-grown Ceylon teas** are rated as second only to the finest Indian Darjeelings in terms of delicacy and subtlety of flavour.

The making of a perfect cuppa

Tea production remains a labour-intensive, resolutely low-tech industry, and the manufacturing process – indeed sometimes the machinery itself – has remained pretty much unchanged since Victorian times. It's well worth visiting a working **tea factory**, both to learn something about the way in which tea is made, and to enjoy the old-fashioned industrial scene, with bustling factory workers stuffing piles of leaves into strange-looking machines and the earthy smells of heaped-up mounds of tea permeating the air. Three of the **best factories to visit** are the Pedro Tea Estate, just outside Nuwara Eliya (see p.274); the Labookelie Tea Estate, between Kandy and Nuwara Eliya (see p.275); and the Dambatenne Tea Estate near Haputale (see p.292).

Tea goes from bush to beverage in just 24 hours. The first stage is **plucking** – only the top two leaves and the bud are taken, to guarantee flavour and freshness. At the factory, the first stage in the production process is **withering**, during which the plucked leaves are dried in huge trays. Next, the withered leaves are **crushed**, releasing enzymes which trigger **fermentation**. Leaves are allowed to ferment for a short period, then placed in an oven and **fired**, which removes all remaining moisture, arrests fermentation and turns the tea black. All that is then left is for the tea to be **graded** into different sizes. Following production, tea is **sampled** by tea tasters – a highly specialist profession, as esteemed in Sri Lanka as wine tasting is in France – before being packed up and sent off for auction in Colombo.

▲ The bud and top two leaves ready for plucking

▼ Tasting cups, Dambatenne Tea Factory

Types of tea

Like wine, tea comes in an endless variety of forms and flavours, and a complex and colourful vocabulary has grown up over the centuries to describe it. Tea is first categorized by its place of **origin** (Assam, Darjeeling, Ceylon and so on) and by its basic type, either fermented (**black**), unfermented (**green**) or semi-fermented (**oolong**). Most Sri Lankan tea is black, though a few estates have recently diversified into producing greens and oolong, the staple form of the drink in China and Japan.

The basic grades of Sri Lankan tea (usually clearly marked on packets) are **Orange Pekoe** (OP), signifying a tea made with young, whole leaves, and **Broken Orange Pekoe** (BOP), which uses broken pieces of the same leaves. "**Flowery**", "**Golden**" and "**Tippy**" varieties of OP and BOP include varying quantities and types of young buds mixed in with the leaves to give the tea a distinctively delicate flavour, such as the prized FTGFOP, or (to give it its full name) **Finest Tippy Golden Flowery Orange Pekoe** – also known amongst aficionados as Far Too Good For Ordinary People. At the lower end of the leaf hierarchy are smaller particles known as "**fannings**" (BOPF), and even finer residue, unappetizingly described as "**dust**" (D). Despite the names, however, these grades are two of the most important, since their tiny particles produce a rich, strong, instant brew which is perfect for the tea bags favoured in many parts of the world. Ceylon tea, blended with leaves from other countries, is used in many major international tea brands, including Lipton's and Tetley's, while the larger OP and BOP grades, which yield a much paler and more delicate liquor, are traditionally favoured in the Middle East.

Plucked tea leaves ▲

Sign showing correct tea-picking technique ▼

Hospital Road forms the spine of the **modern town centre**, dotted with imposing Hindu temples such as the **Vaitheeswara Temple**, on Kankesanthurai (KKS) Road, and the **Varatharaja Perumal Kovil**, just off Stanley Road. A short way east of the Vaitheeswara Temple and north of the bus station is **Kasturiya Road**, the heart of Jaffna's **jewellery industry**, and the town's equivalent to the colourful Sea Street in Colombo. It's home to a long sequence of jewellers, mainly trading in gold, each announced by a lurid Tamil sign set up on the pavement outside.

East of the centre, Jaffna assumes a more residential and colonial character, with quiet, tree-shaded streets lined by sedate Dutch villas and a string of imposing churches strung out around **Main Street**, which runs through the middle of Jaffna's best-preserved colonial district, notable for a sequence of remarkably large – if otherwise unexceptionable – churches, as well as other engaging colonial-era structures such as the old Dutch **Rosarian Convent** and the equally atmospheric **St Martin's Seminary**, an attractive Victorian neo-Gothic period piece dating from the 1880s (both on Main Street). Just south of St Martin's Seminary stands the largest of Jaffna's outsize churches, the gigantic **St Mary's Cathedral** – quasi-Portuguese in style, although actually dating from the Dutch era.

Nallur Kandaswamy Temple

Jaffna's most notable sight is the large **Nallur Kandaswamy Temple**, about 2km northeast of the town centre, or 1km from Chundukuli. Dedicated to Murugam (known to the Buddhist Sinhalese as Kataragama – see p.216), this is the most impressive Hindu temple in Sri Lanka, and the only one on the island to rival the great shrines of India. The original temple is thought to date back to the mid-fifteenth century, though it was destroyed in 1620 by the Portuguese. The present structure was begun in 1807 and has now developed into an enormous religious complex, surrounded by red-and-white striped walls. There are numerous shrines inside, richly decorated corridors framed in rows of golden arches and a beautiful courtyard with a large tank. Men must remove their shirts before entering. There are no fewer than six **pujas** daily, with three between 4pm and 5pm, the best time to visit. The temple is also the centrepiece of the hugely popular **Nallur Festival**, which runs for 25 days, finishing on the poya day in August.

The Jaffna Peninsula

The agricultural hinterland of Jaffna town – and the source of much of its former prosperity – is the **Jaffna Peninsula**, a narrow but fertile arc of land which adds a delicate flourish to the northern tip of Sri Lanka. The peninsula is virtually an island, physically and culturally almost completely detached from the rest of the country, and has always been far more densely populated than the more arid lands of the Vanni further south.

About 10km north of Jaffna, and 2km west of the village of Chunnakam on the main road to Kankesanturai, lies the curious archeological site of **Kantharodai** – an unusual huddle of around twenty miniature dagobas, ranging in height from one to three metres, crammed together in a small plot along with the unexcavated bases of many other dagobas. The site is quite unlike anything else in Sri Lanka, and is of great antiquity, dating back at least two thousand years, though no one can quite agree on its exact purpose – a popular theory is that the dagobas enshrine the remains of Buddhist monks; others claim that they are "votive" dagobas erected in fulfilment of answered prayers.

A couple of large temples – the **Naguleswaram** and **Maviddapuram** – survive in proud isolation towards the northern edge of the peninsula, although both have suffered significant bomb damage. Just past the Naguleswaram temple on the peninsula's northern shore are the **Keerimalai hot springs**, whose therapeutic powers have been recognized since the time of the *Mahabharata*: a princess whose face had been transformed to resemble a horse and an Indian holy man who resembled a mongoose both found cures here, and a steady string of bathers now follow in their footsteps.

Northeast to Point Pedro

The road northeast from Jaffna to Point Pedro passes several points of interest. About 5km along near the main road, the village of **Kopai** is home to an enormous **LTTE cemetery**, containing the neatly ordered graves of around two thousand cadres killed in the civil war, a sobering sight, especially when you realize that this is just a small portion of the 17,000 or so LTTE fighters who have so far died in the conflict – pessimistic locals like to point out, with very black humour, that there is still plenty of room left in the cemetery for new arrivals. A couple of kilometres further along, right next to the road, is the **Nilavarai well**, traditionally believed to have been the work of Rama himself, who created it by sticking an arrow into the ground to assuage his thirst. Its waters are said to be bottomless and appear to be somehow connected directly to the sea: the water is fresh near the top, but becomes increasingly salty the deeper you go.

On the north shore of the peninsula, 30km from Jaffna, the fishing village of **VELVETTITURAI** (widely abbreviated to "VVT") is famous nowadays principally as the birthplace of the leader of the LTTE, **Velupillai Prabhakaran**. Some 500km west of the town centre on the road to Kankesanturai, his childhood **home** now attracts a steady stream of visitors, many of whom have recorded their flattering views of the great leader in graffiti on the walls of the now wrecked and roofless house; one prominent message, left by visiting LTTE cadres, is written in blood. Just east of Prabhakaran's house lies a large **Amman Temple**. Immediately behind this lies a second large temple, dedicated to Shiva, which was formerly owned by Prabhakaran's family and which the guerilla leader often visited as a child for religious festivals or to swim in the tank.

East of VVT, the breezy seafront road runs due east, past the ruined shells of numerous houses destroyed in the tsunami, to the modest little town of **POINT PEDRO** ("PPD"), at the extreme northeastern tip of the peninsula. Just west of here, **Point Pedro Lighthouse** marks the most northerly point in Sri Lanka. South of the lighthouse lies the strange **Manalkadu Desert**, a small range of coastal sand dunes. At the northern end of the desert, 5km from Point Pedro, is the village of **VALLIPURAM**. This was formerly one of the peninsula's principal towns, and the tiny settlement is still home to its second-largest temple, and one of the very few in Sri Lanka dedicated to Vishnu; it's a sprawling, rustic complex which is thought to date back to the first century AD.

About 2km south of here lie the remains of **St Anthony's Church**, built around 1900 and now picturesquely half-buried in the sand. From the church there's a clear view of the strange and melancholy seafront cemetery nearby, with dozens of crosses stuck into the top of the dunes marking the graves of locals, most of whom perished in the tsunami, with the fateful date 2004.12.26 written on cross after cross.

The islands

West of Jaffna, a string of **islands** straggles out into the waters of the Palk Strait towards India. Two of them – **Kayts** and **Karaitivu** – virtually join up with the mainland, to which they are connected by causeways, as is **Punkudutivu** further west. Punkudutivu is the starting point for ferries to **Nainativu**, home to two important religious shrines, and to the remote island of **Delft**.

Kayts and Karaitivu

KAYTS (pronounced "Kites") is the largest of the islands and the closest to Jaffna – its eastern tip lies just over the lagoon from Jaffna town and is reached via a causeway through very shallow water. Like the other islands, Kayts is only lightly inhabited and largely devoid of either people or buildings – a pancake-flat expanse studded with innumerable Palmyra palms and a succession of imposing Hindu temples standing in proud isolation in the middle of empty countryside.

At the far (western) end of the island is **Kayts town** (actually little more than a sleepy village), just beyond which lie the scant remains of **Urundi Fort**, also known as Fort Eyrie, now no more than a couple of picturesquely decaying coral-stone walls which are being gradually swallowed up by vegetation. Urundi and Hammenhiel (see below) forts were originally built by the Portuguese to control this entrance to the Jaffna lagoon, though the Dutch neglected Urundi, concentrating their defences in Hammenhiel – of which there's a beautiful view from here. Kayts town is also home to the beautiful shell of the nineteenth-century **St James** church (the facade bears the date 1716, but the building actually dates from 1815); the facade and exterior walls survive, but the roof has gone and there's nothing inside but wooden scaffolding, giving the entire structure the appearance of an elaborate film prop.

The most northerly of the islands, **KARAITIVU**, is reached by road some 12km north of Jaffna. En route to the island, 10km from Jaffna at the village of Vaddukoddai, you'll pass the barn-like **Portuguese Church**, in whose churchyard lie 27 tombstones which were recently moved here for safekeeping from the Groote Kerk in Jaffna fort. Most are Dutch colonial; the oldest dates back to 1666. A kilometre further down the road is the **Punnalai Varatharaja Perumal Kovil**, dedicated to Vishnu and one of the peninsula's two oldest temples. The shrine holds an ancient stone tortoise which was apparently fished ashore here.

On the north coast of Karaitivu itself is **Casuarina Beach**, formerly the peninsula's most popular stretch of sand. Just off the southern tip of the island, in the waters between Karaitivu and Kayts, is the old Dutch fort of **Hammenhiel** – its name, literally "Heel of Ham", refers to the prosaic old Dutch belief that Sri Lanka resembled a leg of ham. The fort is a fine sight, seemingly floating on the waters of the lagoon, though it's still in operational use so you can't visit.

The outer islands

The island of **PUNKUDUTIVU** lies southeast of Kayts, to which it's connected by a four-kilometre causeway through the very shallow waters of the Palk Strait – looking out of the windows of your vehicle while crossing the causeway will give you the bizarre illusion that you're driving across the top of the sea. The road across the island reveals constantly shifting vistas of sea and land, passing tiny country hamlets, bombed-out buildings and a succession of large Hindu temples, often the only buildings to be seen in this very rural landscape – as throughout the Jaffna region, the number and size of these shrines seems completely out of proportion with the island's very modest number of inhabitants. At the end of the road, a tiny jetty on the island's western side is the departure point for boats to Nainativu and Delft.

A couple of kilometres east of Punkudutivu lies the small island of **NAINATIVU**. Immediately in front of the ferry jetty is the ornate **Naga Pooshani Ambal Kovil**, a Hindu temple sacred to the goddess Ambal – newborn babies are brought here to receive the goddess's blessings. A ten-minute walk south of here lies the **Nagadipa Vihara**, a rare place of Buddhist worship in the Hindu north, commemorating the second of the Buddha's three legendary visits to Sri Lanka. A rather modest little temple marks the spot; the building next to it houses a superb golden Buddha from Thailand.

By the time you reach the island of **DELFT**, named after the famous Dutch town, you'll begin to feel you're a long way from anywhere – although, despite its remoteness, the island was occupied by all three colonial powers. It's a place of bleak, minimalist beauty, crisscrossed with coral-rock walls and boasting an unusual population of **wild ponies**, the descendants of those first introduced by the Portuguese – they're found mainly in the southern centre of the island, as well as a stumpy **baobab tree**, thought to have been planted by Arab seamen.

A further 30km southwest of Delft lies the tiny island of **KACHCHATIVU**, used as a base by passing Sri Lankan and Indian fishermen, but otherwise uninhabited, inaccessible and boasting just a single man-made structure, the church of **St Anthony** – Sri Lanka's most isolated building and almost as close to India as to Jaffna.

Contexts

Contexts

History

Sri Lanka's past is sunk in an inextricable mixture of the historical and the mythological, exemplified by the curious story of Prince Vijaya (see box, p.416), from whom the Sinhalese people claim descent. Despite the colourful legends which surround Sri Lanka's prehistory, however, actual archeological evidence of early settlement here is relatively slight, despite the fact that the island is thought to have been inhabited since around 125,000 BC. The only modern survivors of these prehistoric peoples are the Veddhas (see p.266), probably related to the aborigines of Australia, the Nicobar Islands and Malaysia, who had arrived in Sri Lanka by around 16,000 BC, or perhaps much earlier. The Veddhas initially lived by hunting and gathering, and later developed knowledge of iron and agriculture, while quartz tools have been discovered at Bandarawela and simple pottery at Balangoda. There is also evidence of early trading contacts between the island and South India.

The arrival of the Sinhalese

From around the fifth century BC, waves of Indo-Aryan immigrants began to arrive in Sri Lanka from northern India (perhaps following in the wake of Indian mariners who may already have been sailing down the coast in search of trade). Their exact origins remain obscure, though it's now thought that the first settlers came from present-day Gujarat, and were followed by subsequent waves of migrants from Orissa and Bengal. These people, the ancestors of the present-day **Sinhalese**, first arrived on the western coast of the island. At first they were limited to river valleys, these being the only areas in which they were able to cultivate rice, but as their expertise in irrigation increased, they were able to strike inland towards the island's dry northern plains – during which expansion the indigenous Veddhas were either absorbed by intermarriage with the new arrivals or driven east and south.

The Anuradhapura period

The first major Sinhalese kingdom developed around the city of **Anuradhapura**, in the island's dry northern plains. The city's origins are shrouded in the semi-legendary depths of early Sinhalese history, though archeological evidence suggests that the city has been occupied for at least three thousand years. The first documented history comes from the *Mahavamsa*, which states that Anuradhapura was founded in 377 BC by the third king of the Vijaya dynasty, Pandukabhaya (reigned 380–367 BC), a rebellious noble of the Vijaya clan, who built a new

The Mahavamsa and Culavamsa

Much of our knowledge of early Sri Lankan history is owed to the **Mahavamsa** ("Great Chronicle") and its continuation, the **Culavamsa** ("Little Chronicle"). The *Mahavamsa* was compiled by Buddhist monks during the sixth century (the *Culavamsa* dates from the thirteenth century) and was intended to commemorate and legitimize the Sinhalese royal lineage and the island's impeccable Buddhist credentials. Their narration of actual historical events is therefore at best questionably biased, and at worst totally imaginary – a fact illustrated by the *Mahavamsa*'s meticulous descriptions of the three visits which the Buddha himself is claimed to have made to the island.

capital on the site of the palace of his great-uncle, a certain Anuradha, after whom the new city was named.

The fledgling city initially enjoyed only limited power over the surrounding region, though its status rose significantly during the reign of **Devanampiya Tissa** (c.300–260 BC), who oversaw the arrival of Buddhism in the island and established the city as a major centre of Buddhist pilgrimage and learning. According to the *Mahavamsa*, **Mahinda**, son of the great Indian Buddhist emperor Ashoka, arrived in Sri Lanka in 246 BC with a retinue of monks to proselytize on behalf of Buddhism, quickly converting the king of Anuradhapura, Devanampiya Tissa. Mahinda was soon followed by his sister, **Sangamitta**, who arrived with a valuable collection of relics including the Buddha's begging bowl, collarbone and a cutting from the sacred bo tree under which the Buddha attained enlightenment in Bodhgaya – the tree subsequently grown from this cutting still flourishes today.

Buddhism found a ready audience in Sri Lanka, and within half a century the island's Sinhalese had all converted to the new faith. Buddhism gave the Sinhalese a new-found sense of national identity and inspired the development of a distinctively Sri Lankan culture, exemplified by the religious architecture of Anuradhapura, whose enormous stupas were amongst early Asia's greatest monuments. Sri Lanka's proximity to South India made it a constant target of invasions, however, while the reliance of the Sinhalese on Tamil mercenaries (given the traditional Buddhist regard for the sanctity of life, the Sinhalese have always had difficulties raising an effective army) left them at the mercy of their

Prince Vijaya

According to Sinhalese tradition, recorded in the *Mahavamsa*, the Sinhalese people trace their origins back to the union between a lion ("sinha", hence Sinhalese) and a rather disreputable North Indian princess ("Very fair she was and very amorous, and for shame the king and queen could not suffer her"). The princess is said to have been travelling in a caravan when the lion attacked. The princess's companions fled, but, as the *Mahavamsa* touchingly relates:

When the lion had taken his prey...he beheld her [the princess] from afar. Love laid hold on him, and he came towards her with waving tail and ears laid back. Seeing him...without fear she caressed him, stroking his limbs.

The lion, roused to fiercest passion by her touch, took her upon his back and bore her with all speed to his cave, and there he was united with her.

In due course the princess gave birth to twins, a boy and a girl, who subsequently married one another. The fruit of this incestuous union was sixteen sons, the eldest of whom was **Prince Vijaya**. Growing to manhood, Vijaya made such a nuisance of himself that there were calls for him and seven hundred of his male companions to be put to death. Instead, the king packed them all into a boat and sent them off into exile. Vijaya and his friends arrived on Sri Lanka sometime in the sixth century BC (although the writers of the *Mahavamsa* – ever on the lookout for an opportunity to boost Sri Lanka's Buddhist credentials – later changed this date to 483 BC, the year in which the Buddha is traditionally said to have died, claiming that the master himself had declared a blessing on Vijaya's enterprise as he lay on his deathbed, announcing that Sri Lanka would henceforth be one of the faith's principal heartlands). Landing on the island's west coast, they were confronted by a *yaksa*, or devil, who appeared to them in the form of a dog. Following the dog, they found another *yaksa*, this one in the shape of a woman hermit named **Kuveni**, who proceeded to magically ensnare all Vijaya's friends until the prince, protected by a magic thread own fighting forces. Tamils had already begun migrating to the island from the third century BC, and shortly after Devanampiya's death, two Tamil captains in the Anuradhapuran army – Sena and Guttika – staged a coup and ruled over the city for two decades. Following their murder, another Tamil soldier, **Elara**, seized power around 205 BC and ruled the city for a further 44 years.

Elara's reign was finally ended in 161 BC by **Dutugemunu** (161–137 BC; see box, p.362), who eventually defeated the old Tamil general after a protracted period of war. Dutugemunu succeeded in uniting Sri Lanka under Sinhalese rule for the first time, and celebrated his achievement by launching into a huge spree of building work – including the construction of two of Anuradhapura's greatest stupas: the Ruvanvalisaya and the Mirisavatiya – which did much to establish the city's magnificently theocratic character.

Dutugemunu's heady combination of military heroics and unimpeachable Buddhist piety proved an inspiration for all who followed him, even if none of the other 113 kings (and two queens) of Anuradhapura was able to emulate his achievements. Of the kings who followed, fifteen ruled for under a year, 22 were murdered, four committed suicide, thirteen were killed in battle and eleven were dethroned.

Soon after Dutugemunu's death, Anuradhapura was once again the target of South Indian attacks, and this constant external pressure, combined with incessant internal feuding, regularly succeeded in reducing the city to chaos. Tamil invaders seized Anuradhapura again in 103 BC, and despite being swiftly evicted by Vattagamini Abhaya (89–77 BC), founder of the Abhayagiri

conferred by the god Vishnu himself, seized her and threatened to cut off her head. Kuveni released the men, agreed to hand over the kingdom to Vijaya and, transforming herself into a young and desirable woman, retired with Vijaya to a splendidly appointed bed. They subsequently married and had two children, though Vijaya eventually came to feel the need for a more reputable consort, and drove Kuveni back into the forest. Their children escaped and married one another; it was their descendants who became, according to tradition, the **Veddhas**.

The lack of women on the island was finally relieved when Vijaya sent to the Pandyan court in India for wives for himself and his followers. Vijaya himself married a Pandyan princess, but failed to produce an heir, and towards the end of his reign sent for his younger brother to come and take his place as ruler. The brother, unwilling to leave his native land, instead sent his youngest son, **Panduvasudeva**. Having landed with 32 followers on the east coast at Gokanna (present-day Trincomalee), Panduvasudeva was duly enthroned and continued the Vijaya dynasty.

To what extent these mythological events reflect actual history is a matter of considerable speculation. Vijaya himself was perhaps a symbolic rather than an actual historical figure – his name means "victory", perhaps representing the triumph of the North Indian immigrants over the native Veddhas. Equally, Vijaya's union with Kuveni would seem to commemorate the intermingling of the Sinhalese immigrants with the Veddhas, while his subsequent marriage to a Pandyan princess again probably has its roots in actual historic links between the early Sinhalese and the Tamils of South India – even Panduvasudeva may simply be another symbolic figure representing the second wave of settlement. The essentially symbolic nature of the tale is supported by fact that the Sinhalese themselves – and indeed the staunchly Buddhist writers of the *Mahavamsa* – feel no compunction in tracing their ancestry to a violent outcast whose immediate ancestry included both bestial and incestuous relations.

monastery and the cave temples at Dambulla, the kingdom soon descended once again into a period of chaos, exemplified by the reign of the notorious queen Anula (48–44 BC) who in five years is said to have married and then murdered 32 husbands.

The great tank builders

In 67 AD, the accession to the throne of Vasabha (67–111), the first of the **Lambakanna** dynasty, inaugurated Anuradhapura's greatest era of peace and prosperity. Vasabha initiated the first of the massive irrigation works which transformed the arid plains of the northern island into fecund agricultural land capable of supporting a dense population and a highly developed civilization. Despite further struggles with invading Tamil forces – encapsulated in the legendary exploits of Gajabahu (114–136; see p.232) – the following four centuries of Lambakanna rule were largely peaceful. Later kings contributed further to the city's magnificent Buddhist heritage and the Rajarata's irrigation system, most notably Mahasena (274–301), who is said to have constructed no fewer than sixteen major reservoirs, including the Minneriya and Kaudulla tanks, as well as the Jetavana, the last of the city's three great monasteries.

A new period of uncertainty began in 429 with yet another invasion from South India and the rule of seven Tamil generals who reigned in succession until being evicted by **Dhatusena** (455–473), who celebrated in the by now customary fashion by constructing (according to the *Mahavamsa*) no fewer than eighteen new temples and the enormous Kalawewa reservoir, near Aukana. Dhatusena met an unholy end at the hands of his own son, **Kassapa** (see p.330), who temporarily removed the capital to Sigiriya, before another of Dhatusena's sons, Mogallana, succeeded in wresting back control, albeit again with South Indian assistance.

This event signalled a renewal of Tamil influence: the island's kings again sought Tamil support in their own disputes, and South Indian mercenaries became both an important and unpredictable faction in the Sinhalese state and a powerful influence at court. **Tamil** influence in Sri Lankan affairs continued to grow during the fifth century AD, following the resurgence of Hinduism in southern India and the rise of three powerful new Tamil kingdoms there: the Cholas (based in Thanjavur), the Pandyas (Madurai) and the Pallavas (Kanchipuram), all of whom would at various times become entangled in Sri Lankan affairs.

Decline and fall

A final interlude of peace was enjoyed during the reigns of Aggabodhi I (571–604) and Aggabodhi II (604–14), who between them restored many of Anuradhapura's religious edifices and carried out further irrigation projects. The latter's death ushered in the most chaotic period in the history of the Anuradhapura kingdom, with incessant civil wars and the growing influence of South Indian mercenaries, who were recruited by disaffected Sinhalese nobles or rival claimants to the throne and frequently paid for by wealth plundered from Buddhist monasteries.

By the end of the seventh century, power had effectively passed to these Tamil mercenaries, who acted as kingmakers until the last of the great Anuradhapuran kings, **Manavamma** (684–718), was placed on the throne with the support of the Pallavas, establishing a second Lambakanna dynasty. Manavamma's reign ushered in a final century of relative peace before Anuradhapura's destruction. In 853, an invading Pandyan army sacked Anuradhapura, before being bought off at great cost. Despite the best efforts of Sri Lankan diplomacy, the ever-present threat of South Indian invasion continued to hang over the kingdom, fuelled by the religious animosity which the Hindu kingdoms of South India bore towards their Buddhist neighbour. In 946–947, the Cholas sacked Anuradhapura, and the city's soldiers were obliged to flee to Ruhunu until the Cholas had returned home. By 992, the last king of Anuradhapura, Mahinda V (983–993), found he had no funds to pay the wages of his mercenaries and was forced to flee to Ruhunu. Anuradhapura and the northern areas of the island fell into chaos, with bands of soldiers pillaging at will. Attracted by the disorder, the Chola king **Rajaraja** despatched an army which sacked Anuradhapura for the very last time in the fateful year of **993**, reducing the once great city to ruins – the single greatest watershed in Sri Lankan history.

The Polonnaruwa period

Having destroyed Anuradhapura, the Cholas established themselves in the city of **Polonnaruwa**, from where they ruled for the next 75 years until **Vijayabahu I** ejected them from the island in 1070 AD. Although Vijayabahu had himself crowned for symbolic reasons amidst the ruins of Anuradhapura, he decided to move the capital to Polonnaruwa, which was further removed from India and situated in more easily defensible territory.

The relocation ushered in the beginning of a final Sinhalese golden age. Vijayabahu's successor **Parakramabahu I** (1153–86; see box, p.340), one of the most flamboyant of all Sri Lankan monarchs, reformed the island's economy, transformed Polonnaruwa into one of the great cities of South Asia and even launched raids against the Pandyas and a naval expedition against Burma. After Parakramabahu, the throne passed to his Tamil brother-in-law, **Nissankamalla** (1186–96; see p.345), and the influence of South India increased once again. Nissankamalla was the last effective ruler of Polonnaruwa, though his zeal for lavish new building projects came close to bankrupting the state, which had already been labouring under the expense of Parakramabahu's wars overseas. Nissankamalla's death without a designated heir resulted in the usual disorder. A series of weaker rulers followed until, in 1212, a new wave of Tamil invaders, the Pandyans, arrived in the island and seized power, only to be displaced three years later by another South Indian adventurer, the despotic **Magha** (1215–55), who instituted a chaotic reign of terror during which the kingdom's complex irrigation systems gradually fell into disrepair, and the population began to abandon Polonnaruwa and move steadily southwards.

The Sinhalese move south

The following period of Sri Lankan history presents a complex and disordered picture, as various Sinhalese and South Indian factions jockeyed for position amidst an increasingly politically fragmented island. As Polonnaruwa fell into chaos under Magha, so the Sinhalese aristocracy began to establish rival centres of power located in inaccessible terrain beyond his reach. Initially, the Sinhalese established a new capital at **Dambadeniya**, about seventy miles southwest of Polonnaruwa, under Vijayabahu III (1232–36). Vijayabahu III's successor, **Parakramabahu II** (1236–70), succeeded in expelling Magha with Pandyan help, though further political instability soon followed. Under Bhuvanaikabahu I (1272–84) the Sinhalese capital was moved briefly northwards to the isolated rock fortress of **Yapahuwa**. After further skirmishes, Bhuvanekabahu II (1293–1302) moved the capital south again, to **Kurunegala**, though the increasing fragmentation of power meant that none of these kings enjoyed much real control. By around 1340, the monarchy itself had split, and rival Sinhalese kings had established themselves at **Gampola** and **Dedigama**.

The southwards drift of Sinhalese power had dramatic social and economic consequences. As the island's population moved quickly from one town to another, so the complex **irrigation systems** which had supported the advanced civilization of the dry zone fell into further disrepair. The carefully oiled machinery of Sinhalese society wound down: the great tanks and canals of the northern plains dried up, reducing the area of cultivable land (with a consequent decline in population and revenue), while a losing battle was fought against the encroaching jungle, which began to reclaim the abandoned cities and villages. The Sinhalese increasingly found themselves driven south into the central highlands. Capital cities were now selected mainly for their defensibility, and became military strongholds rather than economic centres, situated in difficult terrain and away from populous areas. As irrigation systems and large-scale agriculture broke down, so fewer taxes were paid to the state, further weakening centralized control. The southwards migration increasingly forced the population to adapt to the different climate and topography of their new surroundings, obliging them to develop new agricultural techniques. Rice cultivation remained important, but was now supplemented by other highland grains. The lack of major irrigation works also meant that farming diminished to subsistence character, with shifting cultivation practised amongst the hills, aided by the region's copious rainfall. Coconuts, easily grown in the highlands and coastal wetlands, became an important crop.

These economic changes also had implications for the island's cherished Buddhist faith. As revenues – literally – dried up, so the funds available to the Buddhist establishment declined. Kings continued as patrons of Buddhism, but their own reduced circumstances meant that Buddhist institutions no longer enjoyed the wealth they once had. The great monasteries of Anuradhapura and Polonnaruwa were disbanded, and though new institutions were established around the various subsequent capitals, they lacked the scale and magnificence of their predecessors. In addition, the absence of strong royal authority affected the unity of the **Buddhist Sangha** (clergy), and indiscipline and theological schisms spread, so that kings were frequently obliged to purge the Sangha of disreputable elements. Along with this weakening of Buddhist cohesion came a new influence of Hinduism on Buddhist institutions. The increasing contact between the Sinhalese ruling classes and the Tamil nobility was followed by an influx of South Indian Brahmins, and Hindu gods began to assume important roles both in popular Buddhism and in elaborate festivals.

The Jaffna kingdom

The erosion of Sinhalese authority left a power vacuum in the north of the island. At the beginning of the fourteenth century a South Indian general, **Arya Chakaravarti**, seized power in the north, founding a Tamil kingdom, **Jaffnapatnam**, with its capital at Nallur in the Jaffna Peninsula. This kingdom soon expanded southwards, coming into conflict with the centres of Sinhalese power, until by the mid-fourteenth century the Tamil kingdom even attacked and defeated the rulers of Gampola, establishing its own tax collectors in the kingdom. One consequence of the Sinhalese movement southwards and the establishment of the Tamil kingdom to the north was the division of the island into two ethno-linguistic zones. Previously, Tamil settlements had been interspersed among the Sinhalese. Now, for the first time, the island's northern and eastern areas became predominantly Tamil, and fresh migrations from

South India following the collapse of the Pandyan kingdom in the fourteenth century served to compound this. Jaffna became the heart of Tamil Hindu culture, with its society organized along similar lines to the Tamil regions of South India, overseen by the landowning cultivators, or Vellala. Hindu institutions were supported by the kings and were strengthened by the influx of Brahmins, while the Tamil language became entrenched in the island, developing a literary culture which was nurtured by the kings of Jaffna and enriched by contact with South India.

The rise of Kotte

The Jaffna kingdom's mid-fourteenth-century attack against Gampola marked its high-water point. In the second half of the fourteenth century a new Sinhalese dynasty, the **Alagakkonaras** (or Alakesvaras) rose to power in Gampola. Establishing a fort at **Kotte**, near Colombo, they expelled the Tamil tax collectors and re-established their independence, though internal feuding fatally weakened them. In 1405, a Ming Chinese fleet under the legendary general **Cheng Ho** arrived in Sri Lanka on a mission to gain possession of the **Tooth Relic**. The Alagakkonaras, not surprisingly, refused to hand it over. A few years later, Cheng Ho returned and carried off the last of the Alagakkonara rulers, Vira Alekesvara, to China for five years in retaliation.

Vira Alekesvara was eventually returned unharmed to Sri Lanka, only to find that during his absence a minor member of the Gampola nobility had seized power and had himself crowned as **Parakramabahu VI** of Kotte (1412–67). The last of the great Sinhalese unifiers, Parakramabahu first subdued the independent kingdom of the highlands, then saw off an invasion of the Vijayanagarans, who had become the dominant power in southern India, until in 1450 he succeeded in taking possession of the Jaffna kingdom and uniting the entire island, for the final time, under Sinhalese rule. As on so many previous occasions, however, the unity achieved by one strong ruler failed to survive his death, and within a few years of Parakramabahu's demise, the kingdoms of Jaffna, Rajarata and the central highlands had once more asserted their independence, so that the subsequent rulers of Kotte, although they continued to claim sovereignty over the whole of Sri Lanka, increasingly found themselves hemmed into a small area in the island's southwestern corner.

The Portuguese

As agricultural revenues declined following the collapse of irrigation systems and the loss of territory, so **trade** became an increasingly significant Sinhalese concern. Spices were the most important exports: cinnamon, found in the southwestern forests, was first exported in the fourteenth century, and was soon followed by pepper and other spices – all of them subject to royal monopolies. Colombo, Galle and other coastal settlements in the island's southwest developed into important **ports**, becoming centres of coastal and Indian trade and attracting foreign merchants, who came both to trade and to settle permanently. The extent of this trade can be seen by the fact that King Bhuvanaikabahu I sent a mission to the Mamluk sultan of Egypt in 1283. The most important of these traders were the **Arabs**, who began trading with Sri Lanka from around the tenth century, and who established settlements around the coast – including the small town of Kolamba, which would later develop into the nation's capital, Colombo. They also brought Islam to the island, and exported cinnamon and other spices which had begun to fetch good prices in Western markets.

The island's trading possibilities soon began to attract attention from even further afield. In 1497, the **Portuguese** navigator Vasco da Gama pioneered the sea route to India around the southern tip of Africa, opening the Indian Ocean to European mariners. In 1505, a Portuguese fleet, prospecting for spices, was blown off course into the mouth of the Kelani Ganga, near Colombo. The Portuguese received a friendly audience from the king of Kotte, Vira Parakramabahu, who was understandably fascinated by these exotic, armour-clad foreigners, described by one of the king's scouts as "a race of men, exceeding white and beautiful. They wear boots and hats of iron, and they are always in motion. They eat white stones [bread] and they drink blood [wine]."

The Portuguese had noted the island's commercial and strategic value – in particular its vast supply of cinnamon – and soon returned, being granted trading concessions and permission to build a fort at Colombo. They found themselves rapidly overtaken by the imbroglio of Sri Lankan politics, however, and spent much of the next seventy years embroiled in intermittent fighting with various local rulers, including **Mayadunne**, the indomitable king of Sitawake (part of the kingdom of Kotte), and later his son **Rajasinha**, both of whom were able to harry the Portuguese successfully on land, though they had no way of combating the Europeans' naval power. Rajasinha's death in 1593, however, left the Sitawake kingdom in want of a strong ruler, and the Portuguese were able to take control of much of the kingdom of Kotte. Meanwhile, a series of Portuguese expeditions against Jaffna had begun, culminating in the successful annexation of the kingdom of Jaffna in 1619. The Portuguese continued to expand their control, taking in the lower reaches of the central highlands and, taking in the east-coast ports of Trincomalee and Batticaloa and eventually gaining ascendancy over the entire island except for the kingdom of Kandy in the central highlands.

Portuguese rule largely retained the traditional Sinhalese systems of caste and tribute, using local officials from the Sinhalese nobility who were loyal to the incomers; however, all tribute that had been due to the Sinhalese kings was now taken by the Portuguese, including a monopoly in elephants and cinnamon, and control of the lucrative trade in pepper and betel nuts. Even so, the burdens they placed upon the island's inhabitants led to hardship and popular hostility. In addition, Portuguese rule was also marked by intense Roman Catholic **missionary activity**. The Franciscans arrived in Sri Lanka in 1543, followed by Jesuits, Dominicans and Augustinians. Missionary orders were lavishly endowed, often using funds from Buddhist and Hindu temples, while members of the landed aristocracy embraced Christianity and took Portuguese surnames – the origins of the thousands of de Silvas, de Zoysas, Fernandos and

Taking the Portuguese to Kotte

Following the arrival of the first Portuguese on the coast of Sri Lanka, they were invited to present themselves to the king of Kotte, who was understandably intrigued by these strange foreigners. A delegation was prepared and dispatched to meet the king. However, before they could meet the king, the king's messengers, in order to disguise the smallness of their kingdom and the fact that the royal capital lay a mere thirteen kilometres inland from the coast, led the Portuguese on a convoluted three-day march around the coastal regions in a vain attempt to delude them into believing the kingdom of Kotte a much grander affair than it actually was. Sadly, the Portuguese saw straight through this attempted subterfuge, but despite the failure of the attempt, the expression "**Taking the Portuguese to Kotte**" remains to this day a Sri Lankan euphemism for all kinds of double-dealing.

Pereiras who still fill the telephone directories of modern Sri Lanka. Many coastal communities underwent mass conversion, particularly around Jaffna and Mannar, and in the fishing communities north of Colombo. Surnames and religion apart, hardly any physical evidence remains of Portuguese rule – virtually all their modest houses, churches and forts were subsequently rebuilt or knocked down by the Dutch or the British.

The Kandyan kingdom and the arrival of the Dutch

The origins of the Kingdom of **Kandy**, situated in the remote and rugged hill country at the heart of the island, date back to the early thirteenth century, during the southwards drift of the Sinhalese. By the time the Portuguese arrived, it had developed into one of the island's three main kingdoms, along with Kotte and Jaffna. The Portuguese first turned their attention to Kandy in 1591, though their attempt to place a puppet ruler on the throne was thwarted by an ambitious Sinhalese nobleman sent to accompany the Portuguese nominee, who enthroned himself instead, proclaiming independence from the Portuguese and taking the name of **Vimala Dharma Suriya**. Using guerrilla tactics, Vimala Dharma Suriya routed a Portuguese attack in 1594, as well as subsequent attacks in 1611, 1629 and 1638.

Realizing he couldn't drive the Portuguese out of Sri Lanka without sea power, Dharma Suriya saw the arrival of the **Dutch**, who had had their eyes on the island for a number of years, as an opportunity to gain naval support against his adversaries. Dutch envoys met Dharma Suriya in 1602 and determined upon a joint attack against the Portuguese. At least that was the plan. The Dutch leader, Admiral Sebald de Weert, invited the king to come back to the coast and inspect his ships. Dharma Suriya demurred, replying that he was reluctant to leave his queen, Dona Caterina, alone. De Weert, who appears to have been somewhat the worse for drink, replied that from what he had heard the queen was unlikely to be alone for long, whereupon he and his companions were, perhaps not surprisingly, hacked to death. Despite this unfortunate turn of events, Dharma Suriya's successor, **Senarat**, continued to seek Dutch support. The Dutch again promised military help, though in the event they were unable to provide it and the king turned instead to the Danes, who dispatched an expedition, though by the time it arrived Senarat had concluded a peace agreement with the Portuguese (the tardy Danes instead founded a colony on the Coromandel coast of India). The truce was short-lived, however, and in 1630 the Kandyans invaded Portuguese territory, laying siege to Colombo and Galle, though again their lack of sea power prevented them from dislodging the Portuguese permanently.

In 1635, Senarat was succeeded by his son **Rajasinha II**. The new king once again sent emissaries to the Dutch, who arrived in Sri Lanka with a fleet of ships and began attacking Portuguese positions. Between 1638 and 1640 they drove the Portuguese out of a number of important coastal towns, but refused to hand over their conquests to Rajasinha, saying they had not been paid their expenses. The king of Kandy was still waiting when, in 1640, the offensive against the Portuguese was temporarily halted by a truce declared in Europe between the United Provinces of the Netherlands and Spain, which at that time ruled Portugal and its overseas possessions. Fighting didn't resume until 1652. The Kandyans launched attacks on Portuguese positions in the interior provinces, pushing them back to their coastal strongholds despite fierce Portuguese resistance. The Dutch, meanwhile, laid siege to Colombo by sea and land, and in May 1656 the Portuguese surrendered the city to the Dutch, who promptly shut the

Kandyans out of its gates. Faced with this duplicity, Rajasinha torched the lands around Colombo and then withdrew back to the hills. Despite this loss of local support, the Dutch continued to drive the Portuguese from the island, attacking Portuguese strongholds in northern Sri Lanka until, with the conquest of Jaffna in 1658, they had replaced the Portuguese as masters of coastal Sri Lanka. Following their expulsion of the Portuguese, the Dutch gradually pushed on around the island, until by 1665 they had reached the east coast, controlling most of Sri Lanka's cinnamon-growing lands as well as its ports.

Compared with the Portuguese, the Dutch were less interested in saving souls than in making money – as an early governor, Van Goens, wrote: "It can easily be seen what a mischievous and horrible thing war is…All our efforts should be directed in future to reduce our expenses by a well-regulated establishment and to increase our profits by faithful economy." Even so, the early years of **Dutch rule** did see an enthusiastic effort to spread the Reformed Calvinist faith in Sri Lanka. Roman Catholicism was declared illegal, and its priests banned from the country; Catholic churches were given to the Reformed faith, and many Sinhalese and Tamil Catholics nominally embraced Protestantism. Meanwhile, the Dutch tried to promote trade with neighbouring countries, though these efforts were stifled by the strict monopolies which they maintained in the lucrative export markets of cinnamon, elephants, pearls and betel nuts.

Their most lasting contributions to Sri Lanka, however, can be seen in the nation's cuisine, culture and architecture. The Dutch are credited with the invention of the popular dish of *lamprais* (see p.43), while the classic Sri Lankan rice and curry spread may also have been inspired by the *rijstaffel* (literally "rice table"), an elaborate type of meal created by the Dutch in Indonesia and comprising numerous contrasting dishes accompanied by rice. They also brought several classic Southeast Asian fruits such as durian, mangosteen and rambutan from their colonies in the Dutch East Indies (modern-day Indonesia), from where they also imported the stitched sarong and the art of batik-making. In architecture they established the style of colonial villa – with shady interior courtyards and huge, pillared verandas – which is still widely employed to this day, and which can be seen at its finest in the magnificent old fort at **Galle**, the Sri Lankan Dutch colonial town par excellence. Dutch settlers stayed in Sri Lanka even after they had lost control of the island to the British (see below), and their descendants – the so-called **Burghers** (see box, p.172) – remain a small but significant element in the nation's life right up to the present day.

The arrival of the British

The French Revolution initiated a major shake-up in relations between the leading European powers. When the Netherlands fell to the French in 1794, the **British East India Company**'s forces occupied Sri Lanka, having already for some time coveted the magnificent natural harbour at Trincomalee. In theory, the British were meant to be protecting Dutch territory against the French, though the forgivably suspicious Dutch mounted a halfhearted resistance before surrendering the island to their British "protectors" in 1796. Despite the avowedly temporary nature of the British administration, the new colonists soon began to appreciate Sri Lanka's strategic and commercial value, and quickly moved to make their hold on the island permanent, and, in 1802, Sri Lanka was ceded to Britain under the Treaty of Amiens with France.

One of the priorities of the new colonizers was to subdue the Kandyan kingdom and finally unify the island under a single rule. The British launched a disastrous expedition against the kingdom in 1803, but it wasn't until 1815 that they finally achieved their end, when the Kandyans, enraged by the megalomaniac behaviour of their king, Sri Wickrama Rajasinghe, simply stood to one side and allowed British soldiers to march in and occupy the city. After two centuries of spirited resistance, the last bastion of Sri Lankan independence had finally been extinguished.

Though reluctant to upset traditional Sinhalese institutions, the British abolished slavery, relieved native officials of judicial authority, paid salaries in cash and relaxed the system of compulsory-service tenure. Agriculture was encouraged, and production of cinnamon, pepper, sugar cane, cotton and coffee flourished. Internal communications were extended, Christian missions dispatched and restrictions on European ownership of land lifted. English became the official language of government, and the medium of instruction in schools. In addition, the British quickly opened up the island's economy, abolishing all state monopolies. Crown land was sold off cheaply to encourage the establishment of new plantations, and capital flowed in. The most notable result of these changes was the spectacular growth in the island's **coffee** production, from around 1830 to 1870. As the area under cultivation for coffee expanded, so new roads, rail lines and port facilities were constructed to service the industry, while indentured labourers from southern India begin arriving in large numbers to make good the island's labour shortage – almost a million arrived between 1843 and 1859. In the 1870s, however, the island's coffee production was destroyed by a leaf disease. The void, however, was soon filled by the introduction of **tea**, with plantations quickly spreading around the slopes of the central highlands, while rubber and coconuts also acquired increasing importance.

The rise of nationalism

Sri Lanka's traumatic encounters with European colonial powers led to a major re-evaluation of its own traditional culture. In the nineteenth century, revivalist Buddhist and Hindu movements sprang up, with the aim both of modernizing native institutions in the face of the Western onslaught, and of defending the island's traditional culture against missionary Christianity. The major figure in this movement was the charismatic David Hewavitharane (1864–1933), who subsequently adopted the name **Anagarika Dharmapala** ("Protector of the Dharma") upon committing himself to a life of Buddhist activism – almost every town in Sri Lanka now has a road named after him. Dharmapala campaigned tirelessly for Buddhist rights and recognition, receiving unexpected support from the maverick American theosophist **Henry Steel Olcott** (see p.100). Gradually, this burgeoning **nationalist consciousness** acquired a political dimension. Grassroots organizations began to demand greater Sri Lankan participation in government, though the uncoordinated nature of these protests meant they were easily ignored by the government – even so, **constitutional reforms** passed in 1910 made the small concession of allowing a limited number of "educated" Sri Lankans to elect one member to the government's Legislative Council.

During World War I, the forces of nationalism gathered momentum. British arrests of prominent Sinhalese leaders after minor civil disturbances in 1915 provoked widespread opposition, leading in 1919 to the foundation of the **Ceylon National Congress**, which united both Sinhalese and Tamil organizations and drafted proposals for constitutional reforms. Gradual reforms slowly followed, and in 1931 a new constitution gave the island's leaders the chance to exercise political power and gain legislative experience, with a view towards eventual self-government. In addition, the new constitution granted universal franchise, bringing all Sri Lankans into the political process for the first time (and making the country the first Asian colony to achieve universal suffrage).

During **World War II**, Sri Lankan nationalist leaders supported the British war effort while continuing to lobby for full independence. When Singapore, Indonesia and Burma fell to the Japanese, Sri Lanka suddenly found itself close to the front line of the war in the east, a fact brought home by Japanese bombing raids against Colombo and Trincomalee (during which a number of British warships were sunk). By the end of 1942, Sri Lanka had become the major base of British operations in Asia. Lord Mountbatten established his South East Asia Command headquarters at Kandy, while Trincomalee hosted a wing of the Special Operations Executive, which launched saboteurs and resistance coordinators behind Japanese lines.

Independence

Sri Lanka's long-awaited **independence** finally came on February 4, 1948, with power passing from the British to the **United National Party** (**UNP**), under the leadership of **Don Stephen Senanayake**. The essentially conservative UNP was dominated by the English-educated leaders of the colonial era, though it did include people from all the country's ethno-linguistic groups. Its members were bound by the common ideals of Sri Lankan nationalism, parliamentary democracy and gradual economic progress through free enterprise.

The first years of independence were kind to Sri Lanka: exports were doing well in world markets, there was a sizeable sterling balance earned during the war, and the coalition government had a substantial majority in parliament – the island even came close to eradicating malaria. There were, however, some basic weaknesses. The ruling parties largely represented the views of the island's English-educated, Westernized elite – an ideology which most of the population found incomprehensible or irrelevant. In addition, **economic difficulties** began to emerge. Falling rubber and tea prices on the world markets, rises in the cost of imported food and a rapidly increasing population ate quickly into the country's foreign exchange, while the expanded school system produced large numbers of educated persons unable to find suitable employment. Meanwhile, Tamil plantation workers found themselves suddenly disenfranchised by the UNP (conveniently so, given that they largely voted for their own, sectarian, Tamil parties). The Senanayake government insisted on classifying the **Plantation Tamils** as "foreigners", even if they had been living on the island for generations, and attempted to repatriate them to India, an episode which tarnished relations between the two countries for years.

In 1952, D.S. Senanayake died after being thrown from his horse on Galle Face Green in Colombo and was briefly succeeded by his son, Dudley Senanayake, though he was forced to resign following disastrous attempts to cut rice subsidies, an act which provoked widespread strikes and rioting. In 1953, he was succeeded by his uncle, **John Kotelawala**, a bout of nepotism which earned the UNP the name of the "Uncle Nephew Party".

The Bandaranaikes

As the 1950s progressed, the UNP's Westernized and elitist political leaders proved increasingly out of touch with the views and aspirations of the majority of the island's population. In the elections of 1956, the UNP lost to the socialist-nationalist **Sri Lanka Freedom Party** (**SLFP**) under the leadership of the charismatic **S.W.R.D. Bandaranaike**, ushering in an extraordinary dynastic sequence in which power alternated between various members of the Senanayake clan (through the guise of the UNP), and assorted Bandaranaikes (through various incarnations of the SLFP). The new government immediately set about changing the country's political landscape, instigating a huge programme of nationalization, making Sinhala the sole official language and instigating state support for the Buddhist faith and Sinhalese culture, largely in reaction to the Anglo-Christian culture left by the British. Bandaranaike's new policies had the unfortunate side effect of stoking the fires of ethnic and religious tension. His language policy alienated the Tamils, his educational policies outraged the small but influential Christian community, while even factions amongst the Sinhalese communities were disturbed by his cultural and religious reforms. As passions grew, the island experienced its first major **ethnic riots**. Tamils were driven from Colombo and other places where they had traditionally lived alongside the Sinhalese, while Sinhalese in turn fled from Tamil areas in the north and east. In September 1959, Bandaranaike opened **talks with the Tamils** in an attempt to calm the situation, and was promptly assassinated by a militant Buddhist monk – not the first or last time the island's Buddhist clergy would play a role in stoking up religious intolerance on the island.

Bandaranaike was succeeded by his widow, Sirimavo – or **Mrs Bandaranaike**, as she is usually known – who thus became the world's first-ever female prime minister. Mrs Bandaranaike's government continued to implement the policies of Sinhalese nationalism: all private schools were nationalized in an attempt to neutralize the influence of Christian missions in the educational system, while important national industries were also taken over by the state; in addition, she had half a million Plantation Tamils deported to India. Despite her symbolic importance for women worldwide, Mrs Bandaranaike was less appreciated at home, and had to survive an attempted coup before being finally trounced at the polls in 1965 by the UNP, who returned to power under **Dudley Senanayake**, with the emphasis once again put on private enterprise and economic stability.

The JVP and the road to civil war

The Sri Lankan electorate's habit of kicking out whichever party happened to be in power repeated itself in the **1970 elections**, when the UNP were defeated and the irrepressible Mrs Bandaranaike once again became prime minister at the head of a new SLFP-led coalition, the **United Front**. The interminable yo-yoing between parties and policies thus continued, with Mrs Bandaranaike reversing the policies of the UNP and resuming her old aims of restricting private enterprise and increasing nationalization of key industries, while introducing policies aimed at reducing social inequality via an ambitious programme of land reform. Her government also ditched a further element of the island's colonial past by changing its **name** from Ceylon to Sri Lanka (see box, p.428).

Though these measures appeased the island's underprivileged, they did nothing to address basic economic problems such as the mounting trade deficit. The country's youth, impatient for radical change, expressed their discontent through the extreme left-wing and anti-Tamil **JVP** (Janatha Vimukthi Peramuna, or People's Liberation Front). In 1971, the JVP launched an armed rebellion with the aim of overthrowing the government, but despite brief successes, the insurrection was easily and ruthlessly suppressed by the army, with thousands of the poorly organized rebels (mainly students) losing their lives.

Sri Lanka or Ceylon?

The origins of Sri Lanka's colonial name, **Ceylon**, stretch back to the island's ancient Sanskrit name of Sinhaladvipa, meaning the land (*dvipa*) of the Sinhala tribe. In the classical Buddhist language of Pali, Sinhala is Sihalam, pronounced "Silam", which mutated over the centuries into the Portuguese Ceilão, and thence into the Dutch Zeylan and the British Ceylon. Arab traders, meanwhile, transformed Sihalam into Serendib (or Serendip), the root of the English word "serendipity" (or the making of fortuitous discoveries by accident), which was invented in the eighteenth century by the English man of letters Horace Walpole, inspired by a Persian fairy tale, "The Three Princes of Serendip".

Not that this was the only name by which the island was known overseas. The Greeks and Romans had previously called the island **Taprobane**, derived from another ancient Sanskrit name for the island, Tambapanni, after the copper-coloured beach on which Prince Vijaya and his followers (see p.416) are claimed to have first landed. The island's own inhabitants, however, have always known the island by a different name entirely: in Sinhalese, **Lanka**, and in Tamil as **Ilankai**. The reversion from the British colonial Ceylon to the indigenous **Sri Lanka** (or, to be precise, the Democratic Socialist Republic of Sri Lanka) was finally made in 1972 – the additional Sri is Sinhalese for "auspicious" or "resplendent".

Meanwhile, Sri Lanka's **economic decline** continued, and the immense power held by the state provided the party in power with the opportunity for patronage, nepotism and corruption. Mrs Bandaranaike continued her nationalization programme, seizing hold of tea estates and private agricultural lands, two of the few areas of the economy which were still functioning successfully. By 1977, unemployment had risen to about fifteen percent.

The LTTE and civil war

In June 1977, the United Front was defeated by a reinvigorated UNP under the leadership of **J.R. Jayawardene**, who became the first non-Senanayake to control the UNP. Jayawardene began to tamper with the democratic process, writing yet another new constitution in 1978 which gave the country's president (previously an essentially ceremonial role) new powers. In the same year, Jayawardene resigned as prime minister and was promptly elected the country's first president (and re-elected in 1982, after further tinkering with the constitution).

The Jayawardene government again tried to revitalize the private sector and attract back some of the foreign capital driven away by Mrs Bandaranaike. These policies enjoyed some success: by 1983, unemployment had been halved, while the island became self-sufficient in rice by 1985. Meanwhile tourism and expatriate Sri Lankans working in the Middle East brought in valuable foreign currency, though these gains were undercut by rampant inflation, unstable tea and rubber prices and, most seriously, by the country's descent into **civil war**.

The origins of this latest Sinhalese–Tamil conflict had first been sparked in the early 1970s via new legislation designed to cut the number of Tamil places at the country's universities, while the new constitution of 1972 further aggravated Tamil sensibilities by declaring Buddhism to hold the "foremost place" amongst the island's religions. These measures provoked growing unrest amongst Sri Lanka's Tamils, culminating in a **state of emergency** which was imposed on northern areas of the island for several years from 1971. Since the police and army who enforced this state of emergency included few Tamils (one result of the constitution's insistence that only Sinhala speakers be allowed to occupy official posts), and were often undisciplined and heavy-handed, they were increasingly seen by the Tamils as an occupying force.

By the mid-1970s, some young Tamils had begun to resort to violence, calling for an independent Tamil state, **Eelam** ("Precious Land"). Tamil bases were established in jungle areas of northern and eastern Sri Lanka, as well as in the southern districts of the Indian state of Tamil Nadu, where Tamil groups received considerable support. The Liberation Tigers of Tamil Eelam (LTTE), usually known as the **Tamil Tigers**, were the strongest of these, but there were other competing groups which were sometimes hostile to each other.

Despite limited **reforms** – such as the promotion of Tamil to the status of a "national language" to be used in official business in Tamil areas – violence continued to escalate in the north. The point of no return arrived in 1983, following the ambush and massacre of an army patrol by a group of Tamil Tiger guerrillas in the Jaffna region. For several weeks afterwards, Sinhalese mobs indulged in an orgy of killing and looting against Tamils all over the country, a period, subsequently christened "**Black July**", which saw the slaughter of perhaps as many as two thousand people, and virtually levelled areas with a large Tamil population, such as Colombo's Pettah district.

The government, police and army showed themselves unable – or unwilling – to stop this violence. Tens of thousands of Tamils fled to the north of the island, while many others left the country altogether. Equally, Sinhalese started to move out of Jaffna and other Tamil areas. In the following years, violence continued to escalate, with several massacres, including a notorious attack at Anuradhapura in May 1985, when 150 mainly Sinhalese victims were gunned down at one of the symbolic centres of the island's Sinhalese and Buddhist culture. Both sides were accused of torture, intimidation and disappearances.

The government's offer, in the mid-1980s, of **limited Tamil self-government**, proved to be too little and too late. By the end of 1985, fighting between Sri Lankan government forces and the LTTE had spread across the north and down the east coast, while there were also conflicts between Tamils and the east coast's significant Muslim population. War had a devastating effect on the economy. Tourism slumped, military spending rose and aid donors threatened to cut money over human rights abuses. And, to add to the country's woes, tea prices collapsed.

The Indian Peace Keeping Force

In 1987, government forces pushed the LTTE back to Jaffna city, prompting a further exodus of Tamil refugees to India. The Indian government (for whom the fate of the Sri Lankan Tamils has always been a sensitive issue, given the massive number of Tamils in its own country) began supplying food by air and sea to the beleaguered Tamils, leading to clashes between the Indian and Sri Lankan navies. In the same year, President Jayawardene came to an arrangement with India whereby the government pledged that the Sri Lankan Army would hand its positions over to an **Indian Peace Keeping Force**, or **IPKF**, whose aim would be to disarm the Tamil rebels and maintain peace in the north and east.

The deal attracted opposition from all quarters, including Muslims and the LTTE, and provoked riots in Colombo amongst Sinhalese, who saw the Indian presence in the north as a threat to national sovereignty and a latter-day re-enactment of previous Indian invasions. In the event, the Indian army's hopes of simply keeping the peace proved to be purest fantasy. No sooner had they arrived than they became embroiled in clashes with the LTTE, which soon escalated into full-scale war, culminating in the bloody siege and capture of Jaffna.

Then, in 1987–88, a second **JVP rebellion** broke out in the south and centre of the island, launching a series of strikes and political assassinations which terrorized the inhabitants of the highlands and crippled the economy. At the end of 1988, President Jayawardene retired, and the new UNP leader, **Ranasinghe Premadasa**, defeated the indefatigable Mrs Bandaranaike in new presidential elections. Premadasa was a new thing in Sri Lankan politics: a low-caste boy made good, who had grown up in a shack in Colombo and who introduced a blast of fresh air into the insular world of island politics. Premadasa promised to end the fighting against both the JVP and the LTTE and succeeded at least in the first pledge. When the JVP refused to lay down its arms, Premadasa sent out paramilitary death squads, which went about the country assassinating suspected JVP activists. By the end of 1989, most JVP leaders were dead or in prison, while thousands of their sympathizers disappeared amidst an international human rights outcry. Some estimates put the number of those killed in the insurrection as high as 17,000.

The IPKF, meanwhile, remained in an impossible position. Despite having managed to contain the LTTE, Sinhalese nationalists were vociferous in demanding that the IPKF leave the country. The LTTE themselves, who had suffered so greatly at their hands, agreed a ceasefire in the hope of seeing the back of them, and the IPKF finally pulled out in March 1990. At their height they had numbered some eighty thousand soldiers, a thousand of whom had died in the fighting.

The 1990s

The fact that a home-grown guerilla organization like the LTTE had been able to survive a massive offensive by the world's second-largest army enormously enhanced its own sense of power and self-confidence, and no sooner had the IPKF withdrawn than it resumed hostilities against the Sri Lankan government. By the end of 1990, the LTTE had recaptured much of the north, though the east was back under government control. This new war reached a peak in mid-1991 with a series of battles around Jaffna, while the LTTE's influence also reached into India itself, where they assassinated India's former prime minister, Rajiv Gandhi, using a new and deadly weapon – the **suicide bomber**. In mid-1992, a major new assault against the LTTE was launched by the Sri Lankan Army, coupled with a long-overdue attempt to rebuild relations with terrorized Tamil civilians. By this time, tens of thousands had died in the conflict, while 700,000 people had been displaced, including 200,000 Sri Lankan Tamils who had fled to Tamil Nadu in India, about half of whom were living in refugee camps.

In 1993, President Premadasa became the first Sri Lankan head of state to be **assassinated**, blown up by another suicide bomber – the LTTE, though suspected, never claimed responsibility. At around the same time, **Chandrika Bandaranaike Kumaratunga**, the daughter of none other than S.W.R.D. and Sirimavo Bandaranaike, gained leadership of the SLFP (it was around this time that people began referring to the SLFP as the "Sri Lanka Family Party"). Following her election victory in 1994 at the head of the SLFP-dominated **People's Alliance (PA)** coalition, Kumaratunga became Sri Lanka's first female president. One of her first acts was to appoint her mother prime minister, thus continuing the clannishness which had marked the country's politics since the early days of independence.

The new PA was largely unrecognizable as the old SLFP, having abandoned Sinhalese nationalism and pseudo-socialism in favour of national reconciliation and free-market economics. The PA's principal pledge was to end the civil war, but Kumaratunga's attempts to negotiate with the LTTE in 1995 soon broke down, leading to yet another round of attacks against LTTE positions and to retaliatory LTTE **bomb attacks**, most notably the devastating strikes against the Central Bank in Colombo in 1996 and the Temple of the Tooth in Kandy in 1998. By the end of 1995 thousands of troops had been dispatched to the Jaffna peninsula, and Jaffna itself was taken by the Sri Lankan Army in December 1995; further major offensives against the LTTE followed in 1997 and 1998. In December 1999, shortly before new presidential elections, Kumaratunga survived an assassination attempt, though she was blinded in one eye. A few days later, she was re-elected president for a second term.

Despite her electoral success, Kumaratunga was unable to make any steps towards a lasting peace. In addition, her policy of trying to negotiate from a position of military strength received a huge blow in April 2000 when the LTTE captured the strategic **Elephant Pass** (see p.406) – perhaps their greatest military success of the entire conflict. In addition, in July, LTTE suicide bombers led a daring raid against the **international airport**, destroying half of SriLankan Airlines' fleet. The pictures of bombed-out planes and eyewitness accounts by hapless holidaymakers caught in the crossfire made headline news around the globe, and had a predictably disastrous effect on the country's already fragile tourist industry.

The ceasefire

In October 2001, Kumaratunga dissolved parliament just before a no-confidence vote which her PA coalition looked likely to lose. In the ensuing **elections of December 2001**, the UNP won a narrow victory under the leadership of **Ranil Wickramasinghe.** Despite her party's defeat, Kumaratunga remained president, the first time Sri Lanka's prime minister and president had come from different parties, a situation which would have disastrous political consequences. Wickramasinghe had made an end to the civil war central to his candidacy, and he quickly moved to open **negotiations with the LTTE**, mediated by diplomats from Norway – who had previously played a key role in securing the famous peace deal between Israel and the Palestinians in 1993. The timing for talks seemed propitious. Both the Tamil and Sinhalese people had become intensely war-weary, whilst the LTTE appeared to have increasingly lost the support of its own people. Wickramasinghe's conciliatory approach was also an important factor, while the events of September 11 and the subsequent US-led "War on Terror" threatened to cut off international funding for the LTTE, who were proscribed as a terrorist organization by many countries, including the US and UK.

In December 2001, the LTTE declared a temporary **ceasefire**, which was made permanent in February 2002. Events thereafter moved with unexpected swiftness: decommissioning of weapons began; the road connecting Jaffna to the rest of the island was reopened; and in September 2002 the government lifted its ban on the LTTE. The initial stages of the peace process proved hugely positive, but despite early successes, the inevitable **problems** began to emerge during the latter part of 2002 and 2003. President Kumaratunga became an increasingly vociferous critic of the peace process, claiming that the government was making too many concessions to the Tamils, who were to have enjoyed a large degree of autonomy, with their own parliament, prime minister and even army, and accusing the Norwegian mediators of bias – including one famous outburst during which she labelled them "salmon-eating busy-bodies". Sporadic clashes between the LTTE and Sri Lankan Army, as well as serious civilian conflicts between Tamils and Muslims in the east of the country, were seen by Kumaratunga and her allies as evidence that the LTTE was simply using the peace process as a cover under which to regroup and rearm. In April 2003, against a background of increasing political uncertainty and arguments over the implementation of the peace process, the LTTE pulled out of talks.

Even with talks stalled, the ceasefire held, and attention increasingly turned to the growing **tension between Kumaratunga and Wickramasinghe**. Events came to a head in November 2003, when Kumaratunga invoked her presidential powers, sacking three of Wickramasinghe's ministers and taking personal charge of the key Defence Ministry. At the same time, the LTTE themselves faced a unprecedented crisis, as their commander in the east, **Colonel Karuna**, broke away from the rest of the movement, taking several thousand troops with him and raising the spectre of a further battle for power amidst the protagonists in the increasingly precarious peace process.

With the peace process paralysed and the government rendered virtually powerless, fresh **elections** were called for April 2004. Kumaratunga's new coalition, the so-called **Freedom Alliance** (FA), won a narrow victory. After frantic political horse-trading, the FA managed to create an unlikely **coalition government**, their principal partners being the newly respectable JVP (Kumaratunga thus found herself sharing power with the people who had killed her husband, the popular actor-turned-politician Vijaya Kumaratunga, in 1988). The populist southern politician **Mahinda Rajapakse** was appointed prime minister, whilst reassuring noises were made about the coalition's commitment to the peace process. The LTTE leadership, meanwhile, regained control of its eastern wing after brief fighting, forcing Colonel Karuna to flee.

Not surprisingly, the peace process, which had already stumbled under Wickramasinghe, became completely stalled under Rajapakse. Although both sides paid lip service to the agreement, growing violence in the east between the Sri Lankan military, the LTTE and the remains of Colonel Karuna's forces increasingly undermined all real confidence in it.

The tsunami

The country's deteriorating political situation, however, was suddenly and dramatically overshadowed by a far more immediate and tragic natural disaster. Early on the morning of December 26, 2004, a sub-oceanic earthquake off the coast of Indonesia generated a massive **tsunami** which, radiating outwards in all directions, caused havoc along the coastlines of countries around the Indian Ocean as far apart as Malaysia and Tanzania, and which wrought particular devastation in Sri Lanka, with three-quarters of the island's coastline reduced to a rubble of collapsed houses, smashed boats and wrecked vehicles. Over forty thousand people were killed here and a million displaced from their homes, while thousands of buildings were destroyed, along with at least half the island's fishing boats and significant sections of road and rail line – the total damage was estimated at well over a billion dollars. The only good news was that, mercifully, Colombo itself was largely untouched.

The scale of the devastation was astonishing, although the massive **international response** to the event was heartening. Huge quantities of aid and money poured into the country, and numerous agencies sponsored by international governments began work around the coast, alongside the more modest, but equally valuable, efforts of innumerable foreigners who established their own fund-raising efforts and worked with local communities in helping to rebuild the island.

Sadly, the Sri Lankan government itself appeared to contribute very little to this frantic relief effort. Few Sri Lankans received anything more than token insurance payouts, while even fewer received direct government aid, despite the millions of dollars pouring into the country. The government's main contribution to the disaster relief was the enactment, in January 2006, of the infamous **100-metre rule**, which forbade those living within 100m of the coast from rebuilding their houses on their previous sites. Officially this was designed to protect those living around the coast from the possibility of a second tsunami, although many saw the ruling as a cynical attempt to steal valuable coastal land from impoverished villagers in order to hand it over to hotel developers at a later date. Whatever the government's motives, the practical consequence was that those with money – mainly meaning those involved in the tourist trade – were able to get around the ruling and rebuild their properties. Meanwhile, the hundreds of thousands of villagers without access to funds who had lived close to the sea now found themselves deprived not only of their destroyed homes, but also of the land on which they had previously stood, leaving them no alternative but to live in the temporary tents or wooden shelters provided by international aid agencies, while their own government debated their case with infinite slowness. In addition, aid, when it was offered, was often seen as hopelessly inappropriate, with fishermen being moved to new homes miles inland, or entire villages being relocated to new and often unsuitable sites.

Post-tsunami reconstruction efforts were also considerably hindered by **worsening violence** in the east and north of the country. Periodic clashes between the Sri Lankan military, the LTTE and the Karuna faction continued throughout 2005, although the seriousness of the situation was brought home by a pair of events in Colombo itself. In July, the capital saw its first **suicide bomb attack** since the ceasefire, when a female bomber attempted to gain access to the offices of the well-known anti-LTTE Tamil politician Douglas Devananda. This event was overshadowed, however, by the assassination in August of one of the country's most respected politicians, Foreign Minister **Lakshman Kadirgamar**, another Tamil who had consistently fought against the LTTE.

The presidency of **Chandrika Kumaratunga**, the woman who had dominated Sri Lankan politics for a decade, thus stumbled towards a messy and unsatisfactory conclusion. In July 2005, incumbent prime minister Mahinda Rajapakse was chosen as the SLFP's presidential candidate and successor to Kumaratunga in the forthcoming elections.

The Rajapakse era begins

The **presidential elections of November 2005** were widely seen as one of the most important in Sri Lankan history: effectively a head-to-head between the former prime minister **Ranil Wickramasinghe**, the business-minded and peace-oriented UNP leader who had brokered the original ceasefire in 2002 and the populist, nationalist SLFP prime minister **Mahinda Rajapakse**. The choice appeared clear: between a Westernized, liberal candidate committed to the ongoing peace process, and a populist Sinhalese demagogue who was likely to tip the island back into civil war. Shortly before the election, Rajapakse signed a controversial agreement with the JVP. In return for their backing, Rajapakse agreed to refuse the LTTE the right to share aid and promised to remove the

Norwegians from their role as mediators in the peace process. He also committed himself to reviewing (and potentially revoking) the ceasefire agreement and, perhaps most importantly, to denying the possibility of self-rule under a federal system for the north and east – a stridently confrontational, anti-Tamil agenda which drew howls of protest even from members of his own party, including outgoing president Chandrika Kumaratunga.

In the event, Rajapakse triumphed over Wickramasinghe by the narrowest of margins, although the results were tainted by an **LTTE-imposed boycott** which ensured that none of the Tamils living in LTTE-controlled areas or the Jaffna peninsula was able to vote (the only person who did had his hand cut off). The loss of these votes – which would traditionally have gone to Wickramasinghe – almost certainly cost him the presidency, although the reasons for the LTTE boycott remain unclear. One theory is that they wished completely to diassociate themselves from the Sinhalese electoral process; another, and more sinister, explanation is that in helping Rajapakse to power, they increased the possibility of an early return to hostilities, which many people believe was their objective all along.

Rajapakse's election was followed, unsurprisingly, by a massive **upsurge in violence** in the north and east, with a spate of landmine and bomb attacks, mainly aimed at SLA personnel. By early 2006, the general consensus was that although the ceasefire might still exist on paper, in reality, the north and east of the country had returned to a state of undeclared civil war. Violence continued apace against both military and civilian targets, with massacres of non-combatants on both sides of the ethnic divide and repeated bomb attacks against buses, markets and other unprotected targets claiming hundreds of lives. In May, an LTTE suicide bomber narrowly failed to assassinate SLA supremo General Sarath Fonseka in Colombo, shortly after which the European Union joined the UK and US in proscribing the LTTE as a terrorist organization.

Fighting in the east...

The two sides were finally tipped back into full-scale war in July 2006, when the Tigers closed the sluice gates of the **Mavil Oya reservoir**, in LTTE territory south of Trincomalee, cutting off the water supply to thousands of villages further down the river in government-held areas. Heavy fighting ensued, as government forces first captured the reservoir itself, and then beat off large-scale LTTE assaults around Trincomalee, Mutur and the Jaffna peninsula.

These sudden attacks heightened SLA fears about the vulnerability of Trincomalee harbour to attack from nearby LTTE posts, SLA forces set about driving the Tigers from the town of **Sampur**, near Mutur, and nearby camps – the Tigers' first significant loss of territory since the ceasefire was implemented. The LTTE launched inevitable retaliatory attacks, including the massacre of around a hundred off-duty sailors returning home on leave, followed by an attack on Galle harbour, the furthest point south the Tigers had ever ventured. They also staged a notable coup in March 2007 when they launched their first-ever **air attack**, targeting the military airport adjoining the international airport at Katunayake, apparently using small Czech-made light aircraft which had being smuggled into the country piece by piece and then reassembled and fitted with home-made bomb racks.

Following the capture of Sampur, the government began to talk openly about its plan to drive the LTTE from the few remaining pockets of territory which they still held in the east. The SLA's next target was the town of **Vakarai**, about halfway between Batticaloa and Trincomalee – and an important LTTE supply line, being the Tigers' last piece of eastern territory with direct access to the sea. Heavy fighting and the displacement of thousands of civilians, many of whom died in the clashes, ensued, before the town was finally captured in January 2007. The SLA followed this up with successful attacks against LTTE-held areas first in Ampara district and finally in Thoppigala region, northwest of Batticaloa. By July 2007, the whole of eastern Sri Lanka was under government control for the first time in twenty years.

...and the north

Back **in the north**, clashes between the SLA and LTTE along the front lines dividing their respective territories had become an almost daily fact of life, with the SLA making some territorial gains during the later part of 2007. At the same time, attempts were made to take out the top of the LTTE hierarchy. In November, the Tigers' political supremo **S.P. Thamilselvan** was killed in an airstrike, while the government claimed that Prabhakaran himself was seriously injured in a subsequent airstrike later in the same month. The assassination of LTTE military intelligence chief Colonel Charles soon afterwards was another notable success.

The year **2008** began in ominous fashion: on January 2, the government officially pulled out of the by-now derisory official ceasefire as if symbolically to clear the decks for a final assault on the LTTE. The SLA was now larger, more disciplined and better equipped and financed than perhaps at any time in its previous history, as well as being backed by the implacable political will of Rajapakse and his hard-line allies in Colombo. At the same time, the LTTE's international reputation was becoming increasingly tarnished, while its sources of foreign funding and supply lines through India and eastern Sri Lanka were being increasingly squeezed, or cut off entirely.

Despite setbacks, during the first half of 2008 the SLA began to advance slowly but steadily northwards into LTTE territory. By the middle of the year the army had recaptured the whole of the Mannar area and the town of Vidattaltivu, the biggest settlement on the northwest coast and a major LTTE naval base. By October they had fought their way to within two kilometres of the hugely symbolic town of Kilinochchi, the de facto capital of the Tigers' independent northern regime. By November, a further wing of the SLA had succeeded in pushing up to Pooneryn, clearing the entire western coast of LTTE fighters and reopening a land route between the Jaffna peninsula and the rest of government-controlled Sri Lanka for the first time in decades.

The long-awaited **fall of Kilinochchi**, after months of intense fighting, finally occurred on January 2, 2009. Within a week the SLA had captured the strategically and symbolically important Elephant Pass, and by the end of the month had taken the east coast town of Mullaitivu, the last significant LTTE stronghold. Following the fall of Mullaitivu, the surviving LTTE fighters found themselves pinned by the SLA into a tiny strip of territory, just few kilometres long, to the north of Mullaitivu, along with thousands of trapped **civilians** who were unable to flee the conflict zone. The SLA alleged that the LTTE was using these trapped civilians as a human shield, while the LTTE countered that they were too afraid to leave, and that thousands were being killed by heavy artillery shells being fired by the SLA at civilian targets, including hospitals. As usual, the absence of any independent observers made all such claims impossible to verify, though the horrific scale of the ensuing casualties was abundantly clear, with an estimated seven thousand civilians (or more) being massacred during the final months of fighting. The scale of the casualties aroused global concern and condemnation, with worldwide Tamil protests and UN suggestions that both sides may have committed war crimes.

This last enclave of LTTE territory finally fell in late May 2009, at which point President Rajapakse triumphantly announced victory for the SLA and an end to all hostilities. Most dramatic, though, was the claim that rebel leader **Prabhakaran** had finally been killed. A body was produced and DNA tests allegedly carried out, although conflicting reports about the precise nature, time and location of his death inevitably led many to believe that the entire thing had been stage-managed by the government.

Prospects for peace?

The cost of the latest round of fighting has, predictably, been felt in virtually every aspect of Sri Lankan life. Thousands more soldiers and civilians have died, while hundreds of thousands of Tamils have been forced to leave their homes in the north. Increasing military and government heavy-handedness has been accompanied by brazen intimidation of the island's few independent journalists (culminating in the January 2009 murder of the hugely respected *Sunday Leader* editor Lasantha Wickramatunga), as well as reports of widespread human rights violations against innocent Tamils. The parlous state of communal relations was symbolized by the **expulsion of hundreds of Tamil civilians** from Colombo in June 2007 for no proven reason apart from Sinhalese paranoia. The massive increase in military spending has also created major financial problems. The country, already struggling to recover from the effects of the tsunami, remains economically moribund, and tourist arrivals have slumped, thanks to the fighting, depriving the country of much-needed income. Meanwhile, the prices of essentials ranging from rice to petrol have skyrocketed, leaving many ordinary Sri Lankans mired in poverty, even while the vast entourage of Rajapakse's government ministers and family members continue to live in considerable style at the island's expense.

Despite the apparent annihilation of the LTTE, the death of Prabhakaran and the conclusion of hostilities in the north, Sri Lanka's future remains clouded in uncertainty. The vital question is exactly how Rajapakse's government intends to rebuild the north and help relieve the interminable suffering of ordinary Tamil civilians – not to mention how (or if) it intends to meet Tamil political aspirations and calls for some form of regional autonomy and self-determination. The example of eastern Sri Lanka gives some grounds for optimism; newly revitalized since the end of fighting in 2007, it is now enjoying a long-overdue period of peace and political stability. For the moment at least, the door to peace appears to be opening slightly. Whether or not Sri Lanka will manage to get through it before it slams shut again remains to be seen.

Sri Lankan Buddhism

Sri Lanka has always been considered one of the heartlands of **Buddhism**, thanks to the fact that it was one of the first countries to be converted to the faith as well as its vital role in preserving the religion and its most important scriptures. Although Buddhism had more or less died out in neighbouring India by the eighth century, it has remained the dominant religion in Sri Lanka in the face of considerable adversity, including repeated invasions by Hindu Tamils, the arrival of proselytizing Muslim traders and the onslaught of colonialism and missionary Christianity. Despite these challenges, Sri Lanka has preserved the Theravada tradition (indeed it was in Sri Lanka that the principal Theravada Buddhist scriptures were first written down) and subsequently exported it to Southeast Asia, via Burma and on to Thailand – Buddhists in Southeast Asia still regard Sri Lanka as the guardian of the original Theravada tradition. But while it's true that Buddhism in Sri Lanka hasn't experienced the byzantine transformations it experienced in, say, China or Japan, the religion in Sri Lanka has acquired its own particular flavour and local characteristics.

The life of the Buddha

Siddhartha Gautama, the Buddha-to-be, was (according to tradition) born the son of the king in the small kingdom of Lumbini in what is now southern Nepal during the fourth or fifth century BC – 563 BC is often suggested as a possible date, though modern scholars have suggested that it might have been as much as a century later. Auspicious symbols accompanied the prince's conception and birth: his mother dreamt that a white elephant had entered her womb, and according to legend Siddhartha emerged from beneath his mother's right arm and immediately talked and walked, a lotus flower blossoming beneath his foot after each of his first seven steps.

Astrologers predicted that the young prince would become either a great king or a great ascetic. His father, keen to prevent the latter, determined to cater to his son's every desire, and to protect him from all knowledge of worldly suffering. Thus as Siddhartha grew up he knew only the pampered life of a closeted prince. Not until the age of 29 did he venture out of his palace to ride through the city. Despite his father's attempts to clear all elderly, ugly and sick people from the streets, a frail elderly man wandered into the path of Siddhartha's chariot. The young prince, who had never seen an old person before, was, not surprisingly, deeply troubled by the sight, having previously been spared all knowledge of the inevitability of human mortality and physical decay.

On subsequent occasions the prince travelled from his palace three more times, seeing first a sick person, then a corpse, and finally an ascetic sitting meditating beneath a tree – an emblematic representation of the inevitability of age, sickness and death, and of the possibility of searching for a state which transcended such suffering. Determined to discover the path which led to this state, Siddhartha slipped away from the palace during the night, leaving his wife and young son asleep, exchanging his royal robes for the clothes of his servant, and set out to follow the life of an ascetic.

For six years Siddhartha wandered the countryside, studying with sages who taught him to achieve deep meditative trances. Siddhartha quickly equalled the attainments of his teachers, but soon realized that these accomplishments failed to release him from the root causes of human suffering. He then met up with five other ascetics who had dedicated themselves to the most extreme austerities. Siddhartha joined them and followed their lifestyle, living on a single grain of rice and a drop of water each day until he had wasted away virtually to nothing. At this point, Siddhartha realized that practising pointless austerities was equally unhelpful in his spiritual quest. He therefore determined to follow the so-called **middle way**, a route which involved neither extreme austerities nor excessive self-indulgence.

His five companions having contemptuously abandoned him on account of his apparent lack of willpower, Siddhartha sat down beneath a bo tree and vowed to remain there until he had found an answer to the riddle of existence and suffering. Siddhartha plunged himself into profound meditation. Mara, the god of desire, seeing that the prince was attempting to free himself from craving, and therefore from Mara's control, attempted to distract him with storms of rocks, coals, mud and darkness. When this failed, he sent his three beautiful daughters to tempt Siddhartha, but this attempt to distract the prince also proved fruitless. Finally, Mara attempted to dislodge the prince from the ground he was sitting on, shaking the very earth beneath him. Siddhartha extended his right hand and touched the earth, calling it to witness his unshakeable concentration, after which Mara withdrew.

Having conquered temptation, Siddhartha continued to meditate. As the night progressed he had a vision of all his millions of previous lives and gained an understanding of the workings of karma and of the way in which good and bad actions and desires bear fruit in subsequent lives, creating a potentially infinite and inescapable sequence of rebirths. During the final phase of his great meditation, Siddhartha realized that it was possible to pass beyond this cycle of karma and to reach a spiritual state – which he called **nirvana** – where desire, suffering and causality finally end. At this point he attained **enlightenment** and ceased being Prince Siddhartha Gautama, instead becoming **the Buddha**, "the Enlightened One".

Following his enlightenment, the Buddha at first felt reluctant to talk to others of his experience, doubting that it would be understood. According to tradition, it was only at the intervention of the god Brahma himself that the Buddha agreed to attempt to communicate his unique revelation and help others towards enlightenment. He preached his **first sermon** to his former ascetic companions, whom he found in the Deer Park in Sarnath, near present-day Varanasi in north India. In this sermon he outlined the **Four Noble Truths** (see p.440). The five companions quickly understood the Buddha's message and themselves became enlightened. After this, the Buddha's teaching spread with remarkable rapidity. An order of monks, the **Sangha**, was established (a less successful order of nuns was also subsequently created) and the Buddha appears to have travelled tirelessly around northeast India preaching. He continued to travel and teach right up until his death – or, to be precise, his passing into nirvana – at the age of around 80 at the town of Kusinagara.

The history of Buddhism in Sri Lanka

Over the centuries following the Buddha's death, Buddhism rapidly established itself across much of India, becoming the state religion under the great Indian emperor **Ashoka**. Ashoka sent out various Buddhist missions to neighbouring countries, one of which, under the leadership of his son, Mahinda, arrived in Sri Lanka in 247 BC (see p.373). Mahinda's mission was spectacularly successful and Buddhism quickly became the dominant faith on the island, the religion giving the Sinhalese people a new-found sense of identity. Buddhism and Sinhalese nationalism have remained closely connected ever since, linked to a view of Sri Lanka as the chosen land of the faith – a kind of Buddhist Israel.

Buddhism gradually withered away in India over the following centuries, but continued to flourish in Sri Lanka despite repeated Tamil invasions and the attendant influx of Hindu ideas. It was the chaos caused by these invasions, and the fear that the main Buddhist teachings (which had hitherto been passed orally from generation to generation) would be lost that prompted King Vattagamini Abhaya to have them transcribed in the first century BC – the first time that the key Buddhist texts were committed to writing.

Although Buddhism in India had fallen into terminal decline by the fourth century AD, it continued to spread to new countries. From India it travelled north into Nepal, Tibet and China, developing in the process into a new type of Buddhism, **Mahayana** (see p.440). Sri Lanka, by contrast, preserved the **Theravada** tradition (see p.440), which it subsequently exported to Burma and Thailand, from where it spread to the rest of Southeast Asia. Buddhism continued to flourish throughout the Anuradhapuran and Polonnaruwan periods – indeed for much of these epochs Sri Lanka was virtually a theocracy. Huge monasteries were established and much of the island's agricultural surplus went to supporting a vast population of monks – the resources devoted to maintaining the clergy meant that the practice of begging for alms largely disappeared in Sri Lanka from an early date, while the Buddha's traditional requirement that monks lead a wandering life in order to spread the religion was similarly ignored.

Not until the abandonment of Polonnaruwa in the face of further Tamil assaults in the thirteenth century did Sri Lankan Buddhism begin to face serious difficulties. As Sinhalese power and civilization fragmented over the following centuries, so Buddhism lost its central role in the state. Monasteries were abandoned and the population of monks declined. Hinduism became entrenched in the north, where a new Tamil kingdom had been established in the Jaffna Peninsula, while further religious competition was provided by the traders who began to arrive from Arabia from around the eighth century, and who established sizeable Muslim enclaves around parts of the coast.

Buddhism reached its lowest point in Sri Lanka during the seventeenth and eighteenth centuries, as the coast fell to Portuguese (and later Dutch) colonists. Portuguese missionaries set about winning over the natives for the Roman Catholic faith with a will, ordering the destruction of innumerable temples and converting considerable sections of the population. Meanwhile, the throne of the Kingdom of Kandy, the island's last independent region, passed into Tamil hands, and Hindu influence gradually spread.

By 1753, the situation had become so bad that there were not enough monks left to ordain any further Buddhist clergy. The king of Kandy, Kirti Sri Rajasinha, sent out for monks from Thailand, who performed the required ordination services, thus re-establishing the Sangha in the island and founding the so-called **Siyam Nikaya**, or "Siam Order". The revived order flourished, although it became increasingly exclusive, so that only members of the upper-caste Goyigamas were allowed to be ordained (a very un-Buddhist practice). A second sect, the **Amarapura Nikaya**, was established, again with Thai monks providing the initial ordinations. Further disputes over points of doctrine led to the foundation of the **Ramanna Nikaya** in the late nineteenth century. These three *nikayas* remain the principal orders right up to the present day, with each sect preserving its own ordination tradition.

The Buddhist belief system

The Buddha's teachings, collectively known as the **dharma**, were codified after his death and passed on orally for several centuries until finally being written down at Alu Vihara in Sri Lanka in the first century BC. The essence of Buddhist belief is encapsulated in the **Four Noble Truths**. Simply put, these are (1) life is suffering; (2) suffering is the result of craving; (3) there can be an end to suffering; (4) there is a path which leads to the end of suffering, the so-called **Noble Eightfold Path**, which consists of a set of simple rules to encourage good behaviour and morals.

All beings, Buddhism asserts, will experience a potentially infinite sequence of rebirths in various different forms: as a human, an animal, ghost or god, either on earth on in one of various heavens or hells. The engine which drives this permanent sequence of reincarnations is **karma**. Meritorious actions produce good karma, which enables creatures to be reborn higher up the spiritual food chain; bad actions have the opposite result. In this classically elegant system, good deeds really are their own reward. No amount of good karma, however, will allow one to escape the sequence of infinite rebirths – good behaviour and the acquiring of merit is simply a stage on the route to enlightenment and the achievement of nirvana. Every desire and action plants seeds of karma which create the impetus for further lives, and further actions and desires – and so on. Some schools of ancient Indian philosophy took this idea to its logical conclusion – the Jains, for example, decided that the best thing to do in life was nothing at all, and more extreme proponents of that religion were known to sit down and starve themselves to death in order to avoid involvement in worldly actions, for good or bad.

The exact route to enlightenment and nirvana is long and difficult – at least according to the older schools of Buddhism – requiring millions of lifetimes. Exactly what **nirvana** is meant to be remains famously vague. The Buddha himself was notoriously elusive on the subject. He compared a person entering nirvana to a flame being extinguished – the flame doesn't go anywhere, but the process of combustion ceases.

Theravada and Mahayana

Theravada Buddhism (the "Law of the Elders") is the dominant form of the religion in Sri Lanka, as well as in Southeast Asia. It is the older of the two main schools of Buddhism and claims to embody the Buddha's teachings in their original form. These teachings emphasize that all individuals are responsible for their own spiritual welfare, and that any person who wishes to achieve enlightenment must pursue the same path trodden by the Buddha himself, giving up worldly concerns and developing spiritual attainments through meditation and self-sacrifice. This path of renunciation is, of course, impossible for most members of the Theravada community to follow, which explains the importance of **monks** in Sri Lanka (and in other Theravada countries), since only members of the Sangha are considered fully committed to the Theravada path, and thus capable of achieving enlightenment – and even then only in rare instances. Lay worshippers do have a (limited) role in the Theravada tradition, though this is mainly to earn merit by offering material support to monks. Otherwise they can hope for little except to lead a moral life and hope to be reborn as a monk themselves at some point in the future.

The rather elitist aspect of Theravada doctrine led to it being dubbed **Hinayana Buddhism**, or "Lesser Vehicle", a slightly pejorative term which compares it unfavourably with the **Mahayana**, or "Greater Vehicle", sect. Mahayana Buddhism developed as an offshoot of Theravada Buddhism, eventually becoming the dominant form in China, Tibet and Japan, although it has had only a slight influence on Sri Lankan Buddhism. As Theravada Buddhism developed, it came to be believed that the Buddha himself was only the latest of a series of Buddhas – Sri Lankan tradition claims that there have been either sixteen or 24 previous Buddhas, and holds that another Buddha, Maitreya, will appear at some point in the remote future when all the last Buddha's teachings have been forgotten. The Mahayana tradition expanded this aspect of Buddhist cosmology to create a grand array of additional deities, including various additional Buddhas and **bodhisattvas** – a Buddha-to-be who has chosen to defer entering nirvana in order to remain on earth (or in one of the various Buddhist heavens) to help others towards enlightenment. Instead of trying to emulate the Buddha, devotees simply worship one or more of the Mahayana deities and reap the spiritual rewards. Not surprisingly, this much more populist – and much less demanding – form of the religion became widely established in place of the Theravada tradition. Compared with the countless lifetimes of spiritual self-improvement which Theravada Buddhism requires its followers to endure, some schools of Mahayana claim that even a single prayer to the relevant bodhisattva can cause one to be reborn in one of the Buddhist heavens – hence its description of itself as the "Greater Vehicle", a form of the religion capable of carrying far greater numbers of devotees to enlightenment.

The Buddhist pantheon in Sri Lanka

The odd Mahayana bodhisattva occasionally crops up in temples around the island, but almost all the additional gods and goddesses associated with Buddhism in Sri Lanka are the result of its proximity to Hindu India and to the influence of successive waves of Tamil invaders. Buddhism evolved from the same roots as **Hinduism** and makes many of the same assumptions about the universe, so the inclusion of many Hindu deities within the pantheon of Sri Lankan Buddhist gods is not as inconsistent as it might initially appear. (The Buddha himself never denied the existence or powers of the myriad gods of ancient Indian cosmology, simply arguing that they were subject to the same laws of karma and rebirth as any other creature – indeed according to tradition the Buddha ascended to the various heavens to preach to the gods on several occasions.) Thus, although other gods may be unable to assist in helping one towards the ultimate goal of attaining nirvana, they can still have power to assist in less exulted aims – the success of a new business, the birth of a child, the abundance of a harvest – and they can therefore be worshipped alongside the Buddha.

Various Hindu gods have been appropriated by Sri Lankan Buddhism over the centuries – and have gone in and out of fashion according to the prevailing religious or political climate. There are countless shrines across the island dedicated to these subsidiary gods, either as lesser shrines within Buddhist temples or as separate, self-contained temples – these shrines or temples are known as **devales** to differentiate them from purely Buddhist temples (viharas) and Hindu temples (kovils). Thus, the supreme Hindu deity, **Vishnu** (often known locally as **Upulvan**), is regarded in Sri Lanka as a protector of Buddhism and is worshipped by Buddhists, as is the god **Kataragama** (see p.216), also of mixed Hindu–Buddhist origins. Other popular gods in the Buddhist pantheon are **Saman** (see p.295) and **Pattini** (see p.248), while the elephant-headed Hindu god **Ganesh** is also widely worshipped. Recent decades have also seen a dramatic increase in the popularity of the fearsome goddesses **Durga** and **Kali**.

Daily Buddhist ritual and belief

Despite the Buddha's emphasis on the search for enlightenment and nirvana, for most Sri Lankans, daily religious life is focused on more modest goals. Theravada Buddhism traditionally states that only monks can achieve enlightenment, and even then only on very rare occasions: Sri Lanka's last arhat (enlightened monk) is supposed to have died in the first century BC. Thus, rather than trying to emulate the Buddha's own spiritual odyssey and attempt the near-impossible task of achieving enlightenment, the average Sri Lankan Buddhist will concentrate on leading a moral life and on acquiring religious merit in the hope of ensuring rebirth higher up the spiritual ladder.

To become a Buddhist, one simply announces the fact that one is "taking refuge" in the **Three Jewels**: the Buddha, the Dharma and the Sangha. There is no form of organized or congregational worship in Buddhism, as there is in Christianity or Islam – instead, devotees visit their local temple as and when they please, saying prayers at the dagoba or Buddha shrine (or that of another god), perhaps offering flowers, lighting a candle or reciting (or having monks recite) Buddhist scriptures, an act known as **pirith**. Although Theravada holds that the Buddha himself should not be worshipped, many Sinhalese effectively do so. Buddhist **relics** are also objects of devotion, and many Sinhalese still visit Kandy to pay homage to the Buddha's Tooth.

Full-moon – or **poya** – days are considered particularly important, since the Buddha himself is said to have been born, achieved enlightenment and passed into nirvana on a poya day. Buddhist devotees traditionally visit their local temple on poya days to spend time in prayer or meditation; they might also practise certain abstinences, such as fasting or refraining from alcohol and sex.

The Sangha

Sri Lanka's twenty thousand-odd **Buddhist monks** form a distinctive element of national life, instantly recognizable in their brightly coloured robes. The monastic tradition is deeply embedded in the national culture, and the importance of the Buddhist clergy can been seen in myriad ways, from the monks who sit in the nation's parliament to the seats in every bus which are reserved for their use. The Sinhala language, meanwhile, features special forms of address only used when talking to a monk, even including a different word for "yes".

Young boys are chosen to be monks if they show a particular religious inclination or if their horoscope suggests that they would be suitable candidates – material factors can also play a part for children of poor families, since entering the Sangha offers access to education and a reasonable standard of living. Boy monks are first initiated as novices around their tenth birthday (there is no minimum age at which boys can be ordained – according to tradition, a boy can become a novice when he is old enough to chase away crows). Higher ordination occurs at the age of 20. At this point the monk becomes a full member of the **Sangha**. Monks are supposed to enter for life – the custom, popular in Thailand and Burma, of laymen becoming monks for a short period then returning to normal life is not considered acceptable in Sri Lanka – although in practice significant numbers of monks do leave the Sangha, often once they've secured an education.

On entering the Sangha the new monk shaves his head and dons the characteristic robes of a Buddhist cleric (usually saffron, less commonly red or yellow – the precise colour has no significance, and monks wear whatever is given to them, apart from forest-dwelling monks, who tend to wear brown robes). He also takes a new name: the honorific *thero* or *thera* is often added after it, along with the name of the town or village in which the monk was born, while "The Venerable" (or "Ven.") is frequently added as a prefix. Monks commit themselves to a code of conduct which entails various prohibitions. These traditionally include: not to kill; not to steal; not to have sex; not to lie about spiritual attainments; not to drink alcohol; not to handle money; not to eat after midday; and not to own more than a bare minimum of personal possessions.

The great monastic foundations of ancient Sri Lanka have largely vanished, and most monks now live in small groups attached to their local village temple, and as such are often intimately connected to the life of the village, which usually provides their only source of material support via offerings to the temple. The actual functions required of a Buddhist monk are few. The only ceremonies they preside at are funerals, although they are sometimes asked to recite Buddhist scriptures (*pirith*). Monks traditionally act as spiritual advisers; some monks also gain reputations as healers or astrologers, and many teach.

A less savoury aspect of the Sri Lankan Buddhist clergy has been their involvement in **ultra-nationalistic politics** – the view which many monks hold of Sri Lanka as the "chosen land" of Buddhism has disturbing parallels with hard-line Jewish attitudes towards Israel. In 1959, Prime Minister S.W.R.D Bandaranaike, was shot dead by a Buddhist monk, and the clergy have constantly involved themselves in politics ever since; some of the more right-wing monks reputedly formed a clandestine ultra-nationalist group called the Circle of Sinhalese Force, whose members used Nazi salutes and spouted wild propaganda about the perceived threat to their land, race and religion – a mixture of *Mahavamsa* and *Mein Kampf*. In earlier decades, monks had contented themselves with influencing politicians, though in recent years they have started entering politics on their own account – a Buddhist monk was first elected to parliament in 2001, while in the elections of 2004 a total of seven were voted into office, forming a significant political grouping in a delicately balanced minority government. Leading monks have consistently denounced any attempts by the government to cede autonomy to the Tamils of the north and have campaigned vigorously for a military rather than a negotiated solution to the civil war, apparently seeing no contradiction between the Buddhism in which they profess to believe and their aggressively warmongering and anti-Tamil rhetoric – all the more unfortunate, given that they continue to command widespread popular support and respect.

Sri Lankan Buddhist art and architecture

Sri Lanka's **art** and **architecture** – ranging from Dravidian temples to Portuguese Baroque churches – offer a fascinating visual legacy of the varied influences which have shaped the island's eclectic culture. Despite the number of races and religions that have contributed to the artistic melting pot, however, the influence of Buddhism remains unchallenged at the centre of the nation's cultural fabric, and it is in Buddhist art and architecture that Sri Lanka's greatest cultural achievements can been found.

Sri Lanka's early Buddhist art exhibits a restrained classicism, exemplified by the monumental simplicity of the great dagobas of **Anuradhapura**. Although the **Mahayana** doctrines (see p.440) which transformed Buddhist art in many other parts of Asia largely bypassed Sri Lanka, the island's religious art was significantly enriched from around the tenth century by the influence of **Hinduism**, introduced by the numerous Tamil dynasties which periodically overran parts of the north. This influence first showed itself in the art of **Polonnaruwa**, and later blended with Sinhalese traditions to create the uniquely syncretized style of **Kandyan** temple architecture, which reached its apogee during the fifteenth to eighteenth centuries.

Buddha images

Early Buddhist art was symbolic rather than figurative. The Buddha himself (according to some traditions) asked that no images be made of him after his death, and for the first few centuries he was represented symbolically by objects such as dagobas, bo trees, thrones, wheels, pillars, trees, animals or footprints.

Exactly why the first **Buddha images** were made remains unclear, though they seem initially to have appeared in India in around the first century BC. Buddha images are traditionally highly stylized: the intention of Buddhist art has always been to represent the Buddha's transcendental, superhuman nature rather than to describe a personality (unlike, say, Western representations of Jesus). The vast majority of Buddha figures are shown in one of the canonical poses, or **mudras** (see box opposite).

Many sculptural details of Buddha figures are enshrined in tradition and preserved in the *Sariputra*, a Sinhalese treatise in verse for the makers of Buddha images. Some of the most important features of traditional Buddha images include the **ushnisha**, the small protuberance on the top of the head, denoting superior mental powers; the **siraspata**, or flame of wisdom (the Buddhist equivalent of the Christian halo), growing out of the *ushnisha*; the elongated **earlobes**, denoting renunciation (the holes in the lobes would have contained jewels which the Buddha gave up when he abandoned his royal position); the shape of the **eyes**, modelled after the form of lotus petals; the **eyebrows**, whose curves are meant to resemble two bows; the **mouth**, usually closed and wearing the hint of a smile; and the **feet**, which traditionally bear 32 different auspicious markings.

The one area in which Mahayana Buddhism has had a lasting impact on Sri Lankan religious art is in the **gigantic Buddha statues**, some standing up to 30m high, which can be found all over the island, dating from both ancient (Aukana, Sasseruwa, Maligawila, Polonnaruwa) and modern (Dambulla, Weherehena, Wewurukannala) times. Such larger-than-life depictions reflect the change from Theravada's emphasis on the historical, human Buddha to

Buddhist mudras and their meanings

The following are the *mudras* most commonly encountered in Sri Lankan art, though others are occasionally encountered, such as the *varada mudra* ("Gesture of Gift Giving), and the *asisa mudra* ("Gesture of Blessing", a variant form of the *abhaya mudra*), employed in the famous Aukana Buddha.

Abhaya mudra The "Have No Fear" pose shows the Buddha standing with his right hand raised with the palm facing the viewer.

Dhyani or **samadhi mudra** Shows the Buddha in meditation, seated in the lotus or half-lotus position, with his hands placed together in his lap.

Bhumisparsha mudra The "Earth-Witness" pose shows the Buddha touching the ground with the tips of the fingers of his left hand, commemorating the moment in his enlightenment when the demon Mara, in attempting to break his concentration, caused the Earth to shake beneath him, and the Buddha stilled the ground by touching it.

Vitarka mudra ("Gesture of Explanation") and **dharmachakra mudra** ("Gesture of the Turning of the Wheel of the Law") In both positions the Buddha forms a circle with his thumb and one finger, representing the wheel of dharma. Used in both standing and sitting poses.

Reclining poses In Asian Buddhist art, the reclining pose is traditionally considered to represent the Buddha at the moment of his death and entrance into nirvana – the so-called **Parinirvana** pose. Sri Lankan art makes a subtle distinction between two types of reclining pose: the **sleeping** pose, and the true *parinirvana* pose. Sleeping and *parinirvana* Buddhas are distinguished by six marks (although the distinctions between the two are often quite subtle). In the sleeping pose: the eyes are open; the right hand is at least partially beneath the head; the stomach is a normal size; the robe is smooth beneath the left hand; the bottom of the hem of the robe is level; and the toes of the two feet are in a straight line. In the *parinirvana* pose, the hand is away from the head; the eyes are partially closed; the stomach is shrunken; the robe is bunched up under his left hand (the clenched hand and crumpled robe indicating the pain of the Buddha's final illness); the hem at the bottom of the robe is uneven; and the left knee is slightly flexed, so that the toes of the two feet are not in a straight line. Reclining poses are particularly common in Sri Lanka.

Mahayana's view of the Buddha as a cosmic being who could only be truly represented in figures of superhuman dimensions.

Dagobas (stupas)

The stupa, or **dagoba**, as the structures are known in Sri Lanka, is the world's most universal Buddhist architectural symbol, ranging from the classically simple hemispherical forms found in Sri Lanka and Nepal to the spire-like stupas of Thailand and Burma and the pagodas of China and Japan (the Sinhalese term "dagoba" has even been mooted as one possible source for the word pagoda). Dagobas originally developed from the Indian burial mounds which were raised to mark the graves of important personages, although popular legend traces their distinctive form back to the Buddha himself. Upon being asked by his followers what shape a memorial to him should take, the Buddha is said to have folded his robe into a square and placed his upturned begging bowl and umbrella on top of it, thus outlining the dagoba's basic form. As Buddhist theology developed, so the elements of the dagoba acquired more elaborate symbolic meanings. At its simplest level, the dagoba's role as an enormous burial mound serves to recall the memory of the Buddha's passing away and entering into nirvana. A more elaborate explanation describes the dagoba in cosmological terms: the main dome (*anda*), built in the shape of a hill, is said to represent Mount Meru, the sacred peak which lies at the centre of the Buddhist universe, while the spire (*chattravali*) symbolizes the axis mundi, or cosmic pillar, connecting earth and heaven and leading upwards out of the world towards nirvana.

The earliest dagobas were built to enshrine important **relics** of the Buddha himself or of other revered religious figures (the Buddha's own ashes were, according to tradition, divided into forty thousand parts, providing the impetus for a huge spate of dagoba building, while many notable monks were also interred in dagobas). These relics were traditionally placed in or just below the harmika, the square relic chamber at the top of the dome. As Buddhism spread, the building of dagobas became seen as an act of religious merit, resulting in the construction of innumerable smaller, or "votive", dagobas, some no larger than a few feet high.

It was in the great dagobas of Anuradhapura and Polonnaruwa, however, that early Sri Lankan architecture reached its highest point. These massive construction feats were Asia's nearest equivalent to the Egyptian pyramids. The foundations were trampled down by elephants, then the main body of the dagobas filled with rubble and vast numbers of bricks (it's been estimated that the Jetavana dagoba at Anuradhapura uses almost one hundred million), after which the entire structures were plastered and painted with a coat of lime-wash. Constant repairs, and the fact that new outer shells were often constructed around old stupas, means that it's often difficult to determine the exact origins or original shape of some of the island's most famous dagobas.

Sri Lankan dagobas preserve the classic older form of the stupa, following the pattern of the great stupa at Sanchi in central India erected in the third century BC by the emperor Ashoka, who was also responsible for introducing Buddhism to the island. Despite the superficial similarities shared by all Sri Lankan dagobas, there are subtle variations, with six different basic shapes being recognized (ranging from the perfectly hemispherical "bubble-shape" to the narrower and more elongated "bell-shape"), as well as innumerable other small nuances in design. Dagobas consist of four principal sections. The entire structure usually sits on a square terrace whose four sides are oriented towards the cardinal points. Many larger stupas have four small shrines, or **vahalkadas** (a uniquely Sri Lankan architectural element), arranged around the base of the dagoba at the cardinal points. The main hemispherical body of the stupa is known as the **anda**, surmounted by a cube-like structure, the **harmika**, from which rises the **chattravali**. In the earliest Indian stupas this was originally a pillar on which a series of umbrella-like structures were threaded, though in Sri Lankan-style dagobas the umbrellas have fused into a kind of spire. Dagobas are solid structures (apart from a single hollow example at Kalutara).

Dagobas still serve as important objects of pilgrimage and religious devotion: as in other Buddhist countries, devotees typically make clockwise circumambulations of the dagoba – an act known as *pradakshina* – which is meant to focus the mind in meditation, although this practice is less widespread in Sri Lanka than in other countries such as Nepal (similarly, the prohibition against walking around dagobas in an anticlockwise direction, which is frowned upon in some other countries, isn't much observed).

Buddhist temples

Sri Lankan **Buddhist temples** (viharas or viharayas) come in a bewildering range of shapes and sizes, ranging from the intimate cave temples of Dambulla and Mulkirigala to the enormous monastic foundations of Anuradhapura and Polonnaruwa. Despite their variety, however, most of the island's Buddhist places of worship comprise three basic elements: an image house, a dagoba (see above),

A Buddhist bestiary

Animals, both real and imaginary, form an important element in Buddhist iconography. The following are some of the most common.

Makaras The *makara* is a mythical beast of Indian origin, formed from parts of various different animals: the body of a fish; the foot of a lion; the eye of a monkey; the trunk and tusk of an elephant; the tail of a peacock; the ear of a pig; and the mouth of a crocodile. One of the most ubiquitous features of Sri Lankan Buddhist architecture is the **makara torana**, or "dragon arch", made up of two *makaras* connected to a dragon's mouth, which is designed to ward off evil spirits and used to frame entrances and Buddha images in virtually every temple in the island.

Nagarajas *Nagarajas* (snake kings) are represented as human figures canopied by cobra hoods. They apparently derive from pre-Hindu Indian beliefs and are regarded as symbols of fertility and masters of the underground world. Despite their apparently pagan origins, they derive some Buddhist legitimacy from the fact that the *nagaraja* Muchalinda is said to have sheltered the meditating Buddha as he achieved enlightenment – as a result of which cobras are held sacred. *Nagarajas* (plus attendant dwarfs) are often pictured on the **guardstones** which flank the entrances to many buildings of ancient Sri Lanka, and were intended, like *makara toranas*, to prevent evil influences from entering the building.

Dwarfs *Nagarajas* are often shown with dwarfs (*gana*), who can also often be seen supporting the base of steps or temple walls – these jolly-looking pot-bellied creatures are associated with Kubera, the god of wealth, though their exact significance and origins remain obscure.

Elephants Carved in low relief, elephants commonly adorn the walls enclosing religious complexes, their massive presence symbolically supporting the temple buildings.

Lions Though they possess no definite religious significance except to suggest the Buddha's royal origins, lions are also common features of Buddhist architecture. The lion is also an emblem of the Sinhalese people, who trace their ancestry back to – and indeed owe their name to – a lion.

Geese (*hamsa*) Considered a symbol of royal spiritual knowledge, geese are often found on moonstones, and used decoratively elsewhere in temples.

and a bo tree enclosure. The **image house** (*pilimage* or *patimaghara*) houses the temple's Buddha image (or images) along with statues and/or paintings of other gods and attendants; it may be preceded by an antechamber or surrounded by an ambulatory, although there are countless variations in the exact form these shrines take and in the particular gods found inside them. During the late Polonnaruwan and early Kandyan period, image houses developed into the **gedige**, a type of Buddha shrine strongly influenced by South Indian Hindu temple architecture, being constructed entirely out of stone on a rectangular plan, with enormously thick walls and corbelled roofs. Important examples can be found at Polonnaruwa, Nalanda and at the Natha Devale in Kandy.

The **bo tree enclosure** (*bodhighara*) is a uniquely Sri Lankan feature. The Buddha achieved enlightenment while meditating beneath a bo (or bodhi) tree, and these trees serve as symbols of, and a living link with, that moment – many of the island's specimens have been grown from cuttings taken from the great tree at Anuradhapura, which is itself believed to have been grown from a cutting taken from the very tree under which the Buddha meditated in India. More important bo trees are often surrounded by gold railings, with tables set around them on which devotees place flower offerings; the trees themselves (or the surrounding railings) are often draped in colourful strings of prayer flags. Older and larger bo trees are sometimes enclosed by retaining brick terraces with

Moonstones

Originally from India, the **moonstone** developed in Sri Lanka from a plain slab to the elaborate semicircular stones, carved in polished granite, which are found at Anuradhapura, Polonnaruwa and many other places across the island. Moonstones are placed at the entrances to shrines to concentrate the mind of the worshipper upon entering. Carved in concentric half-circles, they represent the spiritual journey from samsara, the endless succession of deaths and rebirth, to nirvana and the escape from endless reincarnations.

The exact design of moonstones varies; not all contain every one of the following elements, and the different animals are sometimes combined in the same ring.

Flames (often in the outermost ring), representing the flames of desire – though they also purify those who step across them.

The four **Buddhist animals**, representing the inevitability of birth, death and suffering, are the **elephant** (symbolizing birth), the **horse** (old age), the **lion** (illness) and the **bull** (death and decay) – the way in which the images in each ring chase one another around the moonstone symbolizes samsara's endless cycle of deaths and rebirths. The animals are sometimes shown in separate rings, but more usually combined into a single one.

Vines (or, according to the interpretations of some art historians, snakes), representing desire and attachment to life.

Geese, representing purity (the goose is a Hindu symbol: as Hamsa it is the vehicle of Brahma, and a sign of wisdom).

A **lotus** at the centre of the design is the symbol of the Buddha and nirvana, and of escape from the cycle of reincarnation.

The classic moonstone pattern described above experienced two important modifications during the **Polonnaruwa period**. To begin with, the bull was omitted: as an important Hindu image (the bull Nandi is the vehicle, or chariot, of Shiva), this particular animal had become too sacred to be trodden on in the increasingly Hinduized city. In addition, the lion was also usually absent (although one can be seen in the moonstone at the Hatadage) due to its significance as a royal and national symbol of the Sinhalese.

Moonstone design continued to evolve right up until the **Kandyan period**, by which time the moonstone had evolved into the almost triangular designs found at the Temple of the Tooth and many other shrines in the central highlands. During this evolution, the moonstone also lost virtually all its symbolic meaning; the floral designs found on Kandyan-era moonstones are of purely decorative import, although the lotus survives at the heart.

conduits at each corner into which devotees pour water to feed the tree's hidden roots; these are gradually up built around the trunk as it grows, and can sometimes reach a surprising size and height, as at the massive Wel-Bodhiya at the Pattini Devale in Kandy.

Larger temples often have two or even three bo tree enclosures and perhaps one or two subsidiary **shrines** devoted to different deities from the Sinhalese Buddhist pantheon, such as Vishnu or Kataragama. Temples attached to monasteries also have dormitories and refectories for the monks, as well as a **poyage** ("House of the Full Moon") in which monks assemble to recite Buddhist scriptures on poya (full-moon) days. Kandyan-era temples sometimes have a **digge**, or drummer's hall, usually an open-sided columned pavilion, where drummers would have performed during temple ceremonies – there's a good example at the Vishnu Devale in Kandy.

Even more unusual is the **vatadage**, or a circular image house, of which only a few examples remain. These have a small dagoba at their centre, flanked by four Buddha images at the cardinal points, and then surrounded by concentric rows of pillars which would originally have supported a wooden roof. There are notable examples at Medirigiya, at the Thuparama in Anuradhapura and in the Quadrangle at Polonnaruwa.

Buddhist temple iconography

Sri Lankan temples typically sport a wealth of symbolic decorative detail. The bases of stairways and other entrances into temples are often flanked by **guardstones** (*doratupalas* or *dvarapalas*), showing low-relief carvings of protective **nagarajas** (snake kings; see box, p.447), who are believed to ward off malign influences. Another notable feature of Sri Lankan art found at the entrances to temples is the **moonstone** (see box opposite), carved either in the classic semicircular shape found at Anuradhapura, Polonnaruwa and elsewhere, or in the more asymmetric examples typical of Kandy.

Many details of Buddhist iconography depict real or imaginary animals; the most common are described in the box on p.447. Another standard decorative element is the **lotus**, the sacred flower of Buddhism; the fact that these pure white flowers blossom directly out of muddy waters is considered symbolic of the potential for Buddhahood which everyone is believed to carry within them. Lotuses are found everywhere in Buddhist design, often painted decoratively on ceilings and walls; Buddha figures are usually shown seated on lotus thrones. Other common symbolic devices include the **chakra**, or Buddhist wheel, symbolizing the Buddha's teaching – the eight spokes represent the Eightfold Path (see p.440). A common detail in the doors of Kandyan temples is the **sun and moon** motif, originally a symbol of the Buddha during the Anuradhapura period, though later appropriated by the kings of Kandy as a royal symbol.

Temples are often decorated with **murals** of varying degrees of sophistication, ranging from primitive daubs to the great narrative sequences found in the cave temples at Dambulla. Perhaps the most popular subject for murals, especially in the south of the island, is tales from the **Jatakas**, the moral fables describing the Buddha's 547 previous lives, while pictures of **pilgrimage sites** around the island are another common theme.

Sri Lankan wildlife

Sri Lanka boasts a variety of **wildlife** quite out of proportion to its modest physical dimensions, including one of the world's largest populations of both wild and captive elephants plus an array of other fauna ranging from leopards, sloth bears and giant squirrels through to huge monitor lizards and crocodiles – not to mention a fascinating collection of endemic birdlife. This richness is partly a result of Sri Lanka's complex climate and topography, ranging from the denuded savannahs of the dry zone to the lush montane forests of the hill country, and partly due to its geographical position, which makes it a favoured wintering spot for numerous birds, as well as a nesting site for five of the world's species of marine turtles.

Elephants

No animal is as intimately connected with the history and culture of Sri Lanka as the **elephant**, an animal which has fulfilled many different social, religious and economic roles in the island over the centuries (some of the most important are described on p.10). The Sri Lankan elephant (*elephas maximus maximus*) is a subspecies of the Asian elephant (*elephas maximus*), which is lighter and has smaller ears than the African elephant (*loxodonta africana*), and also differs from its African cousins in that only around one in ten males – so-called **tuskers** – have tusks. This at least had the benefit of discouraging ivory poachers, although it failed to deter British colonial hunters, who saw the elephant as the ultimate big-game target – the notorious Major Rogers is said to have dispatched well over a thousand of the unfortunate creatures during a twelve-year stint around Badulla, before his murderous career was terminated by a well-aimed blast of lightning. By the beginning of the twentieth century there were only around twelve thousand elephants left in Sri Lanka, and this figure has now fallen to 2000–2500; although this is still a remarkably large population for such a small island, there are fears that these numbers will continue to decrease. Many elephants were injured or killed in the civil war, though the principal pressure on them nowadays is **habitat loss**, as more and more of the island's undeveloped areas are cleared for agriculture. This has led to numerous conflicts between villagers and roaming elephants, with tragic consequences – it has been estimated that around a hundred elephants and fifty people are killed in elephant–human clashes every year. Elephant herds still migrate across the island for considerable distances, sometimes gathering in large herds during the dry season around the shores of receding lakes and other water sources, most spectacularly at Minneriya National Park. Large sections of these well-established migratory routes – popularly known as "**elephant corridors**" – now fall within areas protected by various national parks, but despite this, there are still frequent conflicts between farmers and wandering herds, which trample crops and raid sugar plantations (elephants have a pronounced sweet tooth). Herds are periodically rounded up and chased back to the national parks, though these so-called "elephant drives" have frequently become a source of conflict between locals and conservationists.

Wild elephants usually live in close-knit family groupings of around fifteen under the leadership of an elderly female; each herd needs a large area to survive – around five square kilometres per adult – not surprising, given that a grown elephant drinks 150 litres of water and eats up to 200kg of vegetation daily. Elephants' gestation period averages 22 months and they can live up to 70 years.

Trained elephants are still a major feature of Sri Lankan life, and can often be seen shambling along roads around the island. Captive elephants work under the guidance of skilled **mahouts**, who manipulate their charges using a system of 72 pressure points, plus various verbal commands – a measure of the animals' intelligence is given by the fact that elephants trained to recognize instructions in one language have been successfully re-educated to follow commands in a different one. The life of a trained elephant can be demanding, and it's likely that not all are treated as well as they should be – mahouts are occasionally injured or even killed by their disgruntled charges, proving the truth of the old adage about elephants never forgetting (one particular elephant who had killed two of his mahouts was even put on trial in a court of law – and subsequently acquitted after evidence was presented that he had been mistreated by his handlers). Having said that, elephants can also become objects of remarkable veneration, most famously in the case of the venerable Maligawa Tusker Raja (see p.246), whose death in 1998 prompted the government to declare a day of national mourning.

Leopards

The Sri Lankan **leopard** (*Panthera pardus*) is the island's most striking – and one of its most elusive – residents. These magnificent animals, which can grow to over two metres in length, are now highly endangered in Sri Lanka due to habitat destruction, although the island still has more of the creatures than almost anywhere else in the world. It's thought that there are around five hundred in the whole of the island, with some two hundred concentrated in **Yala National Park**. Each hunts within a set territory, preying on smaller or less mobile mammals, most commonly deer; most hunting is done at dawn or dusk, which is generally the best time to spot them. Leopards have a diverse diet and will eat anything from insects to deer, although some leopards develop a taste for certain types of meat – the notorious man-eating leopard of Punanai (whose story is recounted in Christopher Ondjaate's *The Man-Eater of Punanai*; see p.460) is said to have acquired a particular fondness for human flesh. They are also expert climbers, and can sometimes be seen sitting in trees, where they often store the remains of their kills; they are also commonly spotted basking in the sun on rocky outcrops.

Leopards can be found in various parts of the island, including many national parks. Easily the best place to spot one is Yala National Park; you'll have to be amazingly lucky to come across one anywhere else. Block 1 of Yala (the area which is open to the public) is thought to have a leopard density of as high as one animal per kilometre, probably the highest in the world. Leopards here, particularly young males, have become remarkably habituated to human visitors, and often stroll fearlessly along the tracks through the park.

Monkeys and other mammals

Three species of **monkey** are native to Sri Lanka. The most distinctive and widely encountered is the graceful **grey langur** (*Semnopithecus priam* (*thersites*); also known as the common or Hanuman langur), a beautiful and delicate long-limbed creature with silver-grey hair, a small black face and an enormous tail. Grey langurs can be seen all over the island and are particularly numerous around the southeast, both in national parks and in areas of human habitation, ranging from Bundala National Park to the sacred precinct at Kataragama. They are naturally shy, though some troupes in places frequented by humans have become slightly less reclusive, albeit still engagingly skittish.

Also relatively common, though rather less attractive, is the endemic **toque macaque** (*Macaca sinica*; also known as the red-faced macaque), a medium-sized, reddish-brown creature with a rather baboon-like narrow pink face topped by a distinctive circular tuft of hair. Macaques are much bolder (and noisier) than langurs, and sometimes behave aggressively towards humans when searching for food; they also frequently raid gardens with destructive results. They can be found in most rural parts of the island, usually in troupes of twenty to thirty.

The third native species, also endemic to Sri Lanka, is the **purple-faced leaf monkey** (*Trachypithecus vitulus*; also known as the purple-faced langur). This is similar in build to the grey langur, with long, slender limbs, but with a blackish coat and a white rump and tail. They're found along the west coast, while a more shaggy-coated subspecies, known as the **bear monkey**, is found in the hill country, particularly in the area around Horton Plains.

Sri Lanka's most endearing mammal is the rare **sloth bear** (*Melursus ursinus*), an engagingly shaggy, shambling creature, about a metre in length, which is occasionally spotted in Yala and other national parks. You're far more likely to see the island's various types of **deer** – species include the spotted, sambar and muntjac (or "barking") deer. Wild **buffalo** are also common. Sri Lanka boasts several species of **squirrel**, ranging from the beautifully delicate little palm squirrels, instantly recognizable by their striped bodies and found everywhere (even on the beach), to the rare giant squirrels which can occasionally be seen in montane forests. **Flying foxes** – large, fruit-eating bats which can reach up to a metre in length – are a common sight islandwide, while **mongooses** are also often encountered in the island's national parks, as are rabbits. Less common is the **wild boar**, similar to the wild boars of Europe, and equally ugly. A number of local mammals are largely nocturnal, including the **porcupine** and **pangolin**, as well as the rare **fishing cat**, a large, greyish-brown creature which can grow up to almost a metre in length. They usually live near water, scooping prey out with their paws – hence the name.

Birds

Sri Lanka is a rewarding and well-established destination for dedicated birders: the island's range of habitats – from coastal wetlands to tropical rainforest and high-altitude cloudforest – supports a huge variety of birdlife, which is further enriched by migrants from the Indian Subcontinent and further afield. The island boasts 233 **resident species**, including 33 **endemics**, while another two hundred **migratory** species have been recorded here. Most of the latter visit the island during the northern hemisphere's winter, holidaying in Sri Lanka from around August through to April. In addition, some pelagic birds visit Sri Lanka during the southern hemisphere's winter.

Some species are confined to particular **habitats**, and most of the island's endemics are found in the wet zone that covers the southwestern quarter of the country. For casual bird-spotters, any of Sri Lanka's national parks should yield a large range of species – Bundala, Yala and Uda Walawe are all excellent destinations, and a day's birdwatching in any of these could easily turn up as many as a hundred species. Dedicated birders generally head to more specialist sites, such as Sinharaja, which is home to no fewer than seventeen endemics (although they can be difficult to see), and Horton's Plains and Hakgala in the hill country, both excellent for spotting montane species. With careful planning, dedicated birders might succeed in seeing all the island's endemics in a week or two.

Sri Lanka's 33 **endemic birds** range from the spectacular, multicoloured Sri Lanka blue magpie to relatively dowdy and elusive species such as the tiny

Legge's flowerpecker, the Sri Lanka whistling thrush and the ashy-headed laughing thrush. Other attractive endemics include the dusky-blue flycatcher, yellow-eared bulbul, black-crested bulbul, yellow-fronted and crimson-fronted barbets, Layard's parakeet, Sri Lanka hanging parrot and the Sri Lanka white-eye, as well as the national bird, the Sri Lanka jungle fowl, which can often be seen rootling around the ground in the island's forests. Even for nonspecialists, catching a glimpse of one of these rare and beautiful birds is a memorable moment.

Even if you don't manage to catch any of the endemics, there are plenty of other eye-catching birds to watch out for. **Common species** include bee-eaters, scarlet minivets, orioles, parakeets, Indian rollers, Indian pittas, hoopoes, sunbirds and the various species of dazzling kingfisher – the latter is a frequent sight around water (or perched on cables) throughout the island. Other ubiquitous – albeit less colourful – species include the common myna, bulbul, spotted dove and the yellow-billed babbler, the last instantly recognizable thanks to its distinctive hopping gait. Another frequently encountered resident of the national parks is the peacock (or, more precisely, the Indian peafowl), a common but always memorable sight when perched in the trees of the dry-zone jungle. Other spectacular Sri Lankan birds include the Malabar pied hornbill, with its strange double beak, and the Asian paradise flycatcher, with its sweeping brown tail feathers.

The rich population of resident and migrant **water birds** includes various species of grebe, cormorant, pelican, bittern, heron, egret, stork, ibis, plover, lapwing, sandpiper, tern and stilt. Look out particularly for the colourful painted stork, the magnificent Indian darter and the huge (and impressively ugly) lesser adjutant, while Bundala National Park attracts huge flocks of migrant flamingoes. **Birds of prey** include the common Brahminy kite (frequently spotted even in the middle of Colombo), the majestic sea eagle and the huge black eagle and grey-headed fish eagle. The island's fine range of **owls** includes the extraordinary-looking spot-bellied eagle owl, oriental scops owl and the difficult-to-spot frogmouth.

Finally, one bird you can't avoid in Sri Lanka is the **crow** – indeed the rasping and cawing of flocks of the creatures is one of the distinctive sounds of the island. Burgeoning numbers of these avian pests can be found wherever there are heaps of rubbish, and infestations are now common not only in towns but also in formerly unspoilt areas as diverse as Pigeon Island near Nilaveli and Horton Plains National Park, where they have been responsible for eating many of the beautiful lizards which formerly lived here.

Reptiles

Sri Lanka boasts two species of **crocodile**: **mugger** (also known as marsh or swamp) crocodile (*Crocodilus palustrus*), and the **saltwater** (or estuarine) crocodile (*Crocodilus porosus*); both species live in burrows and feed on fish, birds and small mammals, killing their prey by drowning. Muggers can grow up to 4m in length and tend to frequent shallow freshwater areas around rivers, lakes and marshes; the larger and more aggressive saltwater crocs can reach lengths of up to 7m and prefer the brackish waters of river estuaries and lagoons near the sea. Crocodiles are commonly seen in Bundala and Yala – despite their fearsome appearance they aren't usually considered dangerous unless provoked, although attacks are not unknown.

Sri Lankan crocodiles are occasionally confused with **water monitors**, or *kabaragoya* (*Varanus bengalensis*), though these grow up to only 2m in length and have a quite different – and much more lizard-like – appearance, with a narrower, blue-black head and yellow markings on their back. Water monitors are just one of numerous impressive monitor species found here, including the similar land monitor, or *talagoya* (*Varanus salvator*). The island also boasts a wide and colourful range of smaller lizards, which can be seen islandwide, from coastal beaches to the high-altitude moorlands of Horton Plains National Park.

Sri Lanka is home to eighty-odd species of **snake**, including five poisonous varieties, all relatively common (especially in northern dry zones) and including the cobra and the extremely dangerous Russell's viper. The island has the dubious distinction of having the highest number of **snakebite** fatalities, per capita, of any country in the world.

Turtles

Five of the world's seven species of **marine turtle** visit Sri Lanka's beaches to nest, a rare ecological blessing which could potentially make the island one of the world's leading turtle-watching destinations; however official support for conservation efforts remains lukewarm, despite the number of privately run turtle hatcheries which have sprung up along the west coast.

Turtles are amongst the oldest reptiles on earth, and offer a living link with the dinosaur age, having first evolved around two hundred million years ago; they also have a longer lifespan than most creatures, reaching ages of over 100 years. Tragically, despite having survived for so long, the world's population is now on the point of being wiped out. All five of the species which visit the island are now highly endangered, thanks to marine hazards such fishing nets and rubbish thrown into the sea, as well as widespread poaching of eggs, hunting for meat and shells, and the disturbance or destruction of nesting sites.

Sea turtles occupy an unusual evolutionary niche. Originally land-dwelling reptiles like tortoises, their limbs evolved into flippers, transforming them into marathon swimmers, and they now generally only leave the water during the breeding season, when females emerge onto land to lay eggs in a hole scooped out of the sand (male turtles, by contrast, rarely leave the ocean). The eggs take six to eight weeks to hatch – if they escape the attentions of human poachers or avoid being dug up by dogs or other creatures. When the newborn turtles hatch, they head instinctively towards the sea – the first journey across the beach to the water is the most dangerous, since they're at the mercy of birds, crabs and other predators. Most females go back to lay their own eggs on the very same stretch of sand on which they were born – their so-called **natal beach** – proof of an extraordinary natural homing instinct, although the disturbance or destruction of such beaches is one of the crucial factors in declining turtle populations. This homing instinct is particularly remarkable given the immense distances sea turtles sometimes travel to return from their feeding grounds to their natal beaches: green turtles can travel up to 5000km, while tagged leatherbacks have swum across the Atlantic, though exactly how they navigate over such vast distances is imperfectly understood.

The most widespread marine turtle – and the one most commonly sighted in Sri Lanka – is the **green turtle** (*Chelonia mydas*), named for its greenish fat; green turtles are actually brown in colour, albeit with a greenish tinge. They grow to up to 1m in length and 140kg in weight and are found in warm coastal waters worldwide, feeding mainly on marine grasses. Female green turtles are the most prolific egg-producers of any sea turtle, laying six or seven hundred eggs every two weeks. The largest and more remarkable sea turtle is the **leatherback** (*Dermochelys coriacea*), which commonly grows to over 2m in length (indeed unconfirmed sightings of three-metre-long specimens have been reported) and weighs up to 800kg. One of the planet's greatest swimmers, the leatherback can be found in oceans worldwide, ranging from tropical waters almost to the Arctic Circle; they can also dive to depths of up to a kilometre and hold their breath for half an hour. The leatherback's name derives from its unique carapace – the "shell" is actually made up of separate bones buried in blackish skin; another unique evolutionary adaptation is their spiny throats, designed to help them swallow their favourite food, jellyfish.

The reddish-brown **loggerhead** (*Caretta caretta*) is another immense creature, reaching lengths of up to 2m; it's similar in appearance to the green turtle, but with a relatively larger head. The **hawksbill** (*Eretmochelys imbricata*) is one of the smaller sea turtles, reaching a length of around 0.5m and a weight of 40kg – it's named for its unusually hooked jaws, which give its head a rather birdlike appearance. Both the hawksbill and loggerhead are found in warm waters worldwide and feed on both plants and animals. The **olive ridley** (*Lepidochelys olivacea*) – one of the ridley turtles, named for its greenish colour – has a wide, rounded shell and reaches sizes of up to 1m. It inhabits the warm waters of the Indo-Pacific region and feeds on both animal and vegetable material.

Whales and dolphins

The recent discovery of whale migratory routes around southern Sri Lanka (see box, p.192) means that Sri Lanka may turn out to be one of the top two or three places in the world for seeing blue whales, and perhaps the best place in the world for seeing them alongside sperm whales (although whale-watching in Sri Lanka is still in its relative infancy, and long-term data are not yet available). The **best time** for whale-watching is presently thought to be from November through to April, with particularly large numbers visiting in December/January and again in April. All current whale-watching trips leave from Mirissa, strategically situated near the narrowest part of the Sri Lankan continental shelf, and therefore closest to the deep waters in which whales can be found.

Blue whales are the most commonly seen cetacean off the Mirissa coast. Believed to be the largest animal ever to have lived on the planet, the blue whale reaches over 30m in length and weighing almost two hundred tons. The blue whale is a "baleen whale", feeding mainly on huge quantities of small crustaceans, or krill, which they catch by sieving water through the three hundred or so metre-long baleen plates in their mouths (ingesting 40–60 tonnes of water in a single "mouthful", and consuming around 40 million krill per day). If you're lucky, you may also catch sight of a **sperm whale** (named for the milky-white "spermaceti" oil found in tubes in the front of their heads), slightly smaller than the blue whale, though with the largest brain of any creature on the planet. The sperm whale is a "toothed whale" and hunts for fish, squid and other deep-water creatures; they can dive up to 3km and hold their breath for more than an hour. The easiest way to distinguish between the two while at sea is usually by comparing their "blows": that of the blue whale is tall (typically around 10m) and upright, while that of the sperm whale is smaller and more "bushy", and also typically slanted forwards and to the left. **Humpback** and **Bryde's whales** are also occasionally spotted.

In addition to whales, numerous pods of **spinner dolphins** can be found around the island, an extrovert creature well known for (and named after) its acrobatic spins out of the water. In parts of the island, as many as two thousand spinner dolphins have been sighted at one time, not just in whale-watching areas such as Mirissa but in other places around the coast, most notably Kalpitiya. **Risso's and bottlenose dolphins** are other species known to inhabit Sri Lanka's waters.

Ceylon tea

The first use of the leaves of the **tea** plant as a beverage is generally credited to the Chinese emperor Sheng-Nung, who – in truly serendipitous manner – discovered the plant's potable qualities around 2700 BC when a few leaves chanced to fall off a wild tea bush into a pot of boiling water. Tea developed into a staple drink of the Chinese, and later the Japanese, though it wasn't until the nineteenth century that it began to find a market outside Asia. The British began commercial production in India in the 1830s, establishing tea plantations in Assam and, later, Darjeeling, where it continues to flourish today.

The success of Ceylon tea was built on the failure of the island's coffee trade. Throughout the early British colonial period, coffee was the principal plantation crop in the highlands, until the insidious leaf virus *hemileia vastratrix* – popularly know as "Devastating Emily" – laid waste to the industry during the 1870s. Sri Lanka's first commercial tea plantation was established in 1867 at Loolecondera estate, southeast of Kandy, by the Scottish planter **James Taylor**, though it was only following the collapse of the coffee industry that interest in tea really took off. Bankrupt estates were snapped up for a song and converted to tea production by entrepreneurs such as **Sir Thomas Lipton** (see box opposite), who did much to establish a market for Ceylon tea worldwide. Once it had become obvious how much money there was to be made, hundreds of colonial planters and speculators descended on the island to clear new land and establish estates of their own.

The introduction of tea also had a significant social byproduct. The coffee estates had already employed large numbers of migrant Tamil labourers, brought to Sri Lanka from South India due to a chronic shortage of local manpower in the hills. Work on the coffee plantations was seasonal, meaning that these labourers returned to South India for six months of the year. By contrast, tea production continued year-round, which led to the permanent settlement of thousands of these labourers, Sri Lanka's so-called **"Plantation" Tamils**, whose descendants still work the island's tea gardens today, although they remain one of the island's poorest and most marginalized communities.

Tea remains vital to the **economy** of modern Sri Lanka – so much so that the entire industry was nationalized, with disastrous consequences, in 1975. The government's inept management of the estates over the following decade led to plummeting standards which came close to crippling the entire industry in Sri Lanka; the situation was arrested only when the estates were gradually restored to private ownership, where they remain to this day. Sri Lanka is currently one of the world's top three exporters, along with India and Kenya, and tea still makes up around a quarter of the country's export earnings. Almost half these exports now go to Middle Eastern countries, however, which has made the industry vulnerable to the effects of warfare and sanctions in that region, although significant quantities of low-grade tea particles find their way into the tea-bags of major international brands such as Tetley's and Lipton's.

Tea production

The tea "bush" is actually an evergreen tree, *Camellia sinensis*, which grows to around ten metres in height in the wild. Cultivated tea bushes are constantly pruned, producing a repeated growth of fresh young buds and leaves throughout the year. "Ceylon" tea (as it's still known) is divided into three types, depending on the altitude at which it is grown. The best-quality tea, so-called **high-grown**, only flourishes above 1200m in a warm climate and on sloping terrain – hence the suitability of the island's central highlands. Bushes at higher altitude grow more slowly but produce a more delicate flavour. **Low-grown tea** (cultivated below 600m) is stronger and less subtle in taste; **mid-grown tea** is somewhere between the two – in practice, blends of the various types are usually mixed to produce the required flavour and colour. The island's finest teas are grown in Uva province and around Nuwara Eliya, Dimbula and Dickoya; the flavours from these different regions are quite distinct, showing (at least to trained palates) how sensitive tea is to soil

Sir Thomas Lipton and the rise of Ceylon tea

For all the pioneering efforts of Sir James Taylor, the father of Sri Lanka's tea industry, it was another Scot, **Sir Thomas Lipton**, who almost single-handedly put Ceylon tea on the global map. Born in 1850 in Glasgow, Lipton displayed his appetite for adventure young, stowing away at the age of 14 on a ship to the US, where he worked for five years as a farm labourer and grocery clerk. Returning to Glasgow, Lipton opened his first grocery store in 1871, using the sort of eye-catching **publicity stunts** he had seen employed to tremendous effect in America, including leading a parade of well-fed pigs through the streets of Glasgow, their backs hung with placards declaring "I'm going to Lipton's, the best shop in town for Irish bacon!" By 1880 he had twenty shops; by 1890, three hundred.

In 1889, Lipton moved into **tea** retailing, announcing his new wares with a parade of brass bands and bagpipers; by undercutting the then going price by two-thirds, he succeeded in selling ten million pounds of tea in just two years. The real birth of the Lipton's tea dynasty, however, began in 1890. En route to Australia, Lipton stopped off in Ceylon and – true to his "cut out the middleman" motto – bought up five bankrupt tea estates, including what would become his favourite, at Dambatenne. Trumpeting his new acquisitions with relentless advertising and a new slogan ("Direct from the Tea Gardens to the Teapot"), Lipton put Ceylon tea firmly on the world map and massively stimulated demand for it back in Britain. His was also the first company to sell tea in pre-packaged cartons, thus guaranteeing quantity and quality to hard-pressed housewives – while ensuring that the Lipton's brand received the widest possible exposure.

As a commercial expression of the might of the British Empire, Lipton's tea was unparalleled. Lipton succeeded not only in establishing his brand as the number one tea at home and throughout the colonies, but also largely killed off demand for the traditional and more delicate but unpredictable China teas which had previously formed the mainstay of the trade, fostering a taste for the black, full-bodied and reliably strong blends which remain the norm in the UK right up to the present day. The Lipton's tea phenomenon in turn paved the way for the commercial success of other brands established in the late nineteenth century, such as Typhoo (despite the compellingly oriental-sounding name, the tea itself was, again, sourced entirely from Sri Lanka) and Brooke Bond's PG Tips.

The fortunes of Lipton's own brand were mixed, however. It continued to be a major player in British markets well into the twentieth century, but gradually lost out to Brooke Bond, Typhoo and others, largely due to the fact that it was sold only through Lipton's own shops. With the rise of supermarkets such as Tesco (which itself had its roots in the tea trade – the name is an amalgam of the name of another entrepreneurial grocer, Jack Cohen, with that of his tea dealer, T.E. Stockwell), sales slowly decreased and the Lipton's brand disappeared from Britain, leading to the final irony whereby Lipton's, which is still synonymous with tea throughout Asia and in many other parts of the world, is now virtually unknown in the land of its founder's birth.

and climate. Low-grown teas are mainly produced in the Galle, Matara and Ratnapura regions of the south.

The entire tea production process, from plucking to packing, takes around 24 hours. The first stage – **plucking** the leaves – is still extremely labour-intensive, providing work for some 300,000 estate workers across the island (mainly but not exclusively women). Tea pickers select the youngest two leaves and bud from the end of every branch – bushes are plucked every seven days in the dry season, twice as often in the wet. Following plucking, leaves are **dried** by being spread out in huge troughs while air is blown through them to remove the moisture, after which they are **crushed** for around thirty minutes, an action which releases juices and triggers fermentation – the conditions and length of time under which the leaves ferment is one of the crucial elements in determining the quality of the tea. Once sufficient fermentation has taken place, the tea is **fired** in a heated chamber, preventing further fermentation and producing the black tea which is the staple form of the drink consumed worldwide (except in China and Japan, where unfermented green teas still hold sway).

The resultant "bulk" tea is then filtered into different-sized particles and **graded**. The finest teas – often described as "leaf" teas, since they consist of relatively large pieces of unbroken leaf – are known as "orange pekoes", "pekoes" or "souchongs" (almost all Ceylon tea is orange pekoe; the pekoe and souchong varieties are relatively uncommon), sometimes with the addition of the word "flowery", "golden" or "tippy" to indicate that they use only the finest tips of the tea plant. Lower grades are indicated by the addition of the word "broken", while at the bottom of the scale come "fannings" and "dust", which form the basis of most cheap commercial tea – although scorned by the connoisseur, these tiny particles produce a quick, strong brew, and so are perfect for tea-bags. Sri Lankan tea-growers have also starting producing fine green (unfermented) and oolong (partially fermented) varieties.

Following production, tea is **sampled** by tea tasters – a highly specialist profession, as esteemed in Sri Lanka as wine tasting is in France – before being sent for auction. Unfortunately, 94 percent of all the island's tea is exported, meaning that it's difficult actually to sample the end product in situ. Most tea is sold at auction in Colombo, though it's also possible to buy pure, unblended teas at shops around the island (see the colour insert on tea for more details) and sometimes on the estates themselves. When buying tea, look out for the Ceylon Tea Board lion logo, which guarantees that the stuff you're buying comprises only pure Ceylon tea.

Books

Contemporary Sri Lanka has a rich literary tradition, and the island has produced a string of fine **novelists** in recent years, including Booker Prize-winner Michael Ondaatje. Although virtually all of them now live abroad, the island, its culture and twentieth-century history continue to loom large in their work – all the novels of Shyam Selvadurai and Romesh Gunesekera, for instance, deal with Sri Lankan themes, even though Gunesekera now lives in London and Selvadurai in Canada.

In the selection of books below, publishers are detailed in the form of British/American/Sri Lankan; where a book is published in one country, or by the same publisher in more than one country, we've just given the name of the publisher. The ★ symbol marks books that are particularly recommended.

Fiction

★ **Romesh Gunesekera** *Reef* (Granta, UK/New Press, US/Penguin India, Sri Lanka). This deceptively simple but haunting story about a house boy, his master and their twin obsessions – cooking and marine science – beautifully captures the flavour of the island, as well as plumbing some surprising depths. Gunesekera's other three books, *Monkfish Moon*, *The Sandglass* and *Heaven's Edge*, are also partly or wholly set in Sri Lanka, though none is a patch on *Reef*.

★ **Michelle de Kretser** *The Hamilton Case* (Chatto & Windus). Set in the years just before and after independence, this beautifully written and cunningly plotted novel – part period piece, part elegant whodunnit – chronicles the career of lawyer Sam Obeysekere, a loyal subject of the Empire, whose life and loyalties are blighted by his chance involvement in the mysterious murder of a British tea planter.

Carl Muller The prolific novelist and journalist Carl Muller is something of a cultural institution in Sri Lanka. His most famous work, *The Jam Fruit Tree* trilogy (*The Jam Fruit Tree*, *Yakada Yaka* and *Once Upon a Tender Time*), is an intermittently entertaining account of the lives, loves and interminable misadventures of the von Bloss clan, a family of ruffianly, party-loving and permanently inebriated Burghers. Other books include the comic short stories of *A Funny Thing Happened on the Way to the Cemetery*; the chunky historical epics *The Children of the Lion* (based on the mythological history of early Sri Lanka) and *Colombo*; and a collection of essays, *Firing At Random*. All of the above are published by Penguin India.

★ **Michael Ondaatje** *Running in the Family* (Picador, UK/Vintage, US). Perhaps the best book ever written about the island, this marvellous memoir of Ondaatje's Burgher family and his variously dipsomaniac and wildly eccentric relations is at once magically atmospheric and wonderfully comic. Ondaatje's other Sri Lankan book, the altogether more sombre *Anil's Ghost* (same publishers), offers a very lightly fictionalized account of the civil war and JVP insurrection seen through the eyes of a young forensic pathologist attempting to expose government-sponsored killings.

Shyam Selvadurai *Funny Boy* (Vintage) and *Cinnamon Gardens* (Harvest Books). *Funny Boy* presents a moving and disquieting picture of Sri Lanka seen through the eyes of a gay Tamil boy growing up in

Colombo in the years leading up to the civil war. *Cinnamon Gardens* offers a similarly simple but eloquent account of those trapped by virtue of their sex or sexuality in the stiflingly conservative society of 1930s Colombo.

A. Sivanandan *When Memory Dies* (Arcadia). Weighty historical epic describing the travails of three generations of a Sri Lankan family living through the end of the colonial period and the island's descent into civil war. The same author's *Where The Dance Is* (same publisher) comprises a sequence of inventive and acutely observed short stories set in Sri Lanka, India and England.

Leonard Woolf *The Village in the Jungle* (Eland). Future luminary of the Bloombury set, Leonard Woolf served for several years as a colonial administrator in the backwaters of Hambantota. First published in 1913, this gloomy little masterpiece tells a starkly depressing tale of love and murder in an isolated Sri Lankan village, stifled by the encroaching jungle and by its own poverty and backwardness.

History, religion and travelogues

Juliet Coombe and Daisy Perry *Around the Fort in 80 Lives* (Sri Serendipity Publishing). Warm, evocative and beautifully illustrated portrait of today's Galle Fort, told in a series of affectionate sketches of its diverse cast of idiosyncratic characters, from street peddlers to millionaire expats.

Richard Gombrich *Theravada Buddhism: A Social History from Ancient Benares to Modern Colombo* (Routledge). This academic but accessible guide to Theravada Buddhism gives an absorbing account of the religion from a social and cultural, rather than theological, angle, with extensive coverage of the faith's development in Sri Lanka. The same author's difficult-to-find *Precept and Practice: Traditional Buddhism in the Rural Highlands of Ceylon* (Oxford UP) offers a revealing insight into the idiosyncrasies of local Buddhist practice.

Yasmine & Brendan Gooneratne *This Inscrutable Englishman: Sir John D'Oyly (1774–1824)* (Cassell). Detailed biography of the brilliant English diplomat who brokered the surrender of the Kandyan kingdom to the British in 1815 – the sheer drama of the events described makes it an interesting read, despite the authors' laboriously academic tone.

H.A.J. Hulugalle *Ceylon of the Early Travellers* (Arjuna Hulugalle). This tiny book offers a series of entertaining snapshots of Sri Lankan history seen through the eyes of foreign travellers, traders and soldiers, including accounts of some of the more bizarre incidents in the island's past, such as the British plan to capture Colombo using a giant cheese.

Robert Knox *An Historical Relation of Ceylon* (Tisara Prakasakayo). Knox's account of his twenty-year captivity in the Kandyan kingdom (see p.251). An interesting read, especially the autobiographical section, dealing with Knox's own Job-like trials and tribulations and culminating in the nail-biting story of his carefully planned escape.

Roy Moxham *Tea: Addiction, Exploitation and Empire* (Constable). This detailed and very readable account of the development of the tea industry in the British colonies paints a compelling portrait of Victorian enterprise and greed – and of the terrible human price paid by Indian plantation workers. Includes extensive coverage of Sri Lanka.

Christopher Ondaatje *The Man-Eater of Punanai* (Rare Books & Berry, UK/Long Rider's Guild Press,

US). Famous Sri Lankan expatriate and entrepreneur Christopher Ondaatje (brother of Michael) returns to the island of his birth to go searching for leopards in the war-torn east, and for memories of his own youth – including the spectre of his maverick father (who also appears as one of the stars of *Running in the Family*; see p.459). Ondaatje's more recent *Woolf in Ceylon: An Imperial Journey in the Shadow of Leonard Woolf 1904–11* (HarperCollins) offers an interesting and beautifully illustrated account of Leonard Woolf's seven years in Ceylon (see opposite & p.207), mixed up with further bits and pieces of Sri Lankan history and personal reminiscence.

K.M. de Silva *A History of Sri Lanka* (Vikas, India). The definitive history of the island, offering a considered and intelligent overview of events from prehistory to the present day, although somewhat spoilt by gaps and some baffling inconsistencies. Available in full-length and abridged versions.

Rory Spowers *A Year in Green Tea and Tuk-Tuks* (Harper Element). Insightful account of British environmental activist's attempts to create an ecologically sustainable farm in the hills near Galle, while dealing with natural hazards, disgruntled workers and the occasional death threat en route.

Nath Yogasundram *A Comprehensive History of Sri Lanka: From Prehistory to Tsunami* (Vijitha Yapa Publications). Less scholarly than de Silva's *History* (see above), though intelligently written, and also much more up to date, with coverage right up to 2006.

The civil war

William McGowan *Only Man Is Vile* (Picador, UK/Farrar Straus & Giroux, US). Written in the late 1980s, this classic account of the civil war and JVP insurrection combines war reportage, travelogue and social commentary to produce a stark, compelling and extremely depressing insight into the darker aspects of the Sinhalese psyche.

M.R. Narayan Swamy *Inside An Elusive Mind: Prabhakaran* (Vijitha Yapa). Detailed account of the career of the LTTE supremo, covering events up until the turn of the millennium, although many of the LTTE's less savoury activities – such as their numerous massacres of civilians, political assassinations, the use of child soldiers and the widespread terrorizing of their own people – are conveniently ignored or white-washed. The same author's *Tigers of Lanka* covers very similar ground, although again only up to the turn of the millennium.

Anita Pratap *Island of Blood: Frontline Reports from Sri Lanka, Afghanistan and other South Asian Flashpoints* (Vijitha Yapa). Vivid, if sometime irritatingly self-congratulatory, eyewitness accounts of various Asian flashpoints by a well-known Indian journalist, including extended coverage of the Sri Lankan civil war.

K.M. de Silva *Reaping the Whirlwind: Ethnic Conflict, Ethnic Politics in Sri Lanka* (Penguin India). Definitive exploration of the social and political roots of the island's Tamil–Sinhalese conflict. Excellent on the decades preceding the war, although with relatively little coverage of the war itself.

Nirupama Subramanian *Sri Lanka: Voices from a War Zone* (Vijitha Yapa). Published in 2005, this eloquent collection of essays by an Indian Tamil journalist gives a powerful account of the later stages of the civil war, combining military and political analysis of the conflict with the personal stories of those affected by the fighting on both sides of the ethnic divide.

Art, architecture and culture

Emma Boyle *Culture Smart! Sri Lanka: A Quick Guide to Customs and Culture* (Kuperard). Insightful look at Sri Lankan society, customs and cultural quirks by a seasoned UK expat.

Robert E. Fisher *Buddhist Art and Architecture* (Thames & Hudson). Concise, well-illustrated overview of Buddhist architecture, sculpture and painting. There's little specific coverage of Sri Lanka, although the discussions of different national styles provide illuminating context.

Ronald Lewcock, Barbara Sansoni & Laki Senanayake *The Architecture of an Island: the Living Heritage of Sri Lanka* (Barefoot). This gorgeous book is a work of art in itself, and offers revealing insights into the jumble of influences that have gone into creating Sri Lanka's distinctive architectural style. The text discusses 95 examples of traditional island architecture – from palm shacks and hen coops to Kandyan temples and colonial cathedrals, all beautifully illustrated with line drawings by Barbara Sansoni. Sadly, it's only available in Sri Lanka itself.

Meher McArthur *Reading Buddhist Art* (Thames & Hudson). Absorbing, richly illustrated introduction to the myriad signs and symbols of Buddhist iconography, with clear explanations of everything from sacred footprints to mythical animals, as well as introductions to the main deities of Mahayana Buddhism.

David Robson *Geoffrey Bawa: The Complete Works* (Thames & Hudson). Written by a long-term Bawa associate, this comprehensive volume offers the definitive overview of the work of Sri Lanka's outstanding modern architect, with copious beautiful photographs and fascinating text on Bawa's life and creations, plus many revealing insights into Sri Lankan culture and art.

Flora and fauna

Indraneil Das & Anslem de Silva *Snakes and Other Reptiles of Sri Lanka* (New Holland). Excellent photographic pocket guide to Sri Lanka's fascinating but little-known population of lizards, snakes and other slithery creatures.

John Harrison and Tim Worfolk *A Field Guide to the Birds of Sri Lanka* (Oxford UP). The definitive guide to Sri Lanka's avifauna.

Sriyanie Miththapala and P.A. Miththapala *What Tree is That?* (Ruk Rakaganno) Well-presented basic guide to the most common tree species of Sri Lanka, with good line drawings.

Gehan de Silva Wijeyeratne *Sri Lankan Wildlife: A Visitor's Guide* (Bradt). Excellent introductory primer covering the full range of island wildlife, from elephants, leopards and birds through to dragonflies, lizards and whales.

Gehan de Silva Wijeyeratne, Deepal Warakagoda and **T.S.U. de Zylva** *A Photographic Guide to Birds of Sri Lanka* (New Holland). Invaluable pocket-sized tome, with excellent photos of all listed species and clear descriptions.

Language

Language

Language

Sri Lanka is a trilingual nation. The main language, **Sinhala**, is spoken by around 75 percent of the population; **Tamil** is spoken by around 25 percent (including not only the Tamils themselves, but most of the island's Muslims). **English** is also widely used by Westernized and urban sections of the population, and is the first language of most Sri Lankan Burghers – many people speak it more or less fluently, and even native Sinhala speakers (especially in Colombo) often employ English in conversation alongside their native tongue, switching between languages as the mood takes them. English sometimes serves as a link language between the island's communities, too – relatively few Tamils speak Sinhala, and even fewer Sinhalese speak Tamil.

Language is an emotive issue in Sri Lanka – the notorious "Sinhala Only" legislation of 1956, which downgraded Tamil from the status of an official language and effectively barred Tamils from most forms of government employment, was one of the most significant root causes behind the subsequent civil war, and although Tamil was restored to the status of an official language in 1988, the subject is still politically sensitive. All official signs, banknotes, government publications and the like are printed in all three languages, and (except in the north, where Sinhala is rarely seen or heard) many businesses and shops follow suit.

Sinhala

Sinhala (or Singhala; also frequently referred to as "Sinhalese/Singhalese", although properly speaking this is the name of the people themselves, rather than their language) is an Indo-Aryan language, related to other North Indian languages such as Hindi and Bengali, as well as to Sanskrit, the classic ancient language of the Indian Subcontinent, and Pali, the sacred language of Buddhism. The language was first brought to Sri Lanka by the original Sinhalese settlers from North India around the fifth century BC, though it has developed since then in complete geographical isolation from other North Indian Indo-Aryan languages, being heavily influenced by Tamil, as well as acquiring numerous words from Dutch, Portuguese, Malay and English. Sinhala is found only in Sri Lanka; its closest relative is Divehi, spoken in the Maldives.

Sinhala **pronunciation** is relatively straightforward – most Sinhala words, despite their sometimes fearsome length, are generally built up out of chains of simple vowel sounds, typically a vowel plus a consonant, as in the expression for "please", *karuna karala*. There are a few awkward consonant clusters, but these are relatively uncommon.

Written Sinhala uses a beautifully elegant and highly distinctive system of 47 curvilinear characters. Most characters represent a consonant plus a vowel sound which is indicated by a subtle addition to the basic character (see the box on p.466 for more details).

There's little printed material available on Sinhala. The best resource is Lonely Planet's *Sinhala Phrasebook* by Swarna Pragnaratne. *Say it in Sinhala* by J.B. Dissanayake and the *Sri Lanka Words and Phrases* phrasebook published by Arjuna Hulugalle are both useful, though only usually available in Sri Lanka itself.

Tamil

Tamil is one the most important of the various Dravidian languages of South India, spoken by almost sixty million people in the southern Indian state of Tamil Nadu, as well as by Tamils in Sri Lanka, Singapore, Malaysia and elsewhere around the world. The language in Sri Lanka has developed in isolation from the Tamil spoken in South India, acquiring its own accent and vocabulary – the relationship between Indian and Sri Lankan Tamil is roughly similar to that between British and North American English. Tamil has a long and distinguished history, and a literary tradition stretching back to the third century BC – surpassed amongst Indian languages only by Sanskrit. It's also a famously difficult language to master, thanks to its complex grammar, extended alphabet and repertoire of distinctive sounds (the so-called "reflexive consonants", common to all Dravidian languages, pronounced with the tongue curled back against the roof of the mouth) – these also make the language virtually impossible to transliterate into Roman script. The language is written in the beautiful **Vattelluttu** ("round script"), a combination of rectangular shapes and elegant curvilinear flourishes.

Sri Lankan English

As with Indian English, the version of the language spoken in Sri Lanka (sometimes referred to as "Sringlish" – but not to be confused with "Singlish", or Singaporean English) is not without its own charming idiosyncrasies of grammar, spelling and punctuation, along with a few colourful local expressions. A "bake house" is of course a bakery, though you might not realize that a "cool spot" is a small café, or that a "colour house" is a paint shop. Remember too that "taxis" are most often just everyday tuktuks, while a "hotel" is frequently a cheap eating establishment rather than a place to stay. And if someone at your

The Sinhala alphabet

අ	ah	ආ	aah	ඇ	a	ඈ	aa
අං	ahng	ඉ	i	ඊ	ee	උ	u
ඌ	oo	එ	e	ඒ	eh	ඔ	o
ඕ	oh	ඖ	au	ක	kah	ඛ	khah
ග	gah	ඝ	ghah	ච	cha	ඡ	chah
ජ	jah	ට	tah	ඨ	tah	ඩ	dah
ණ	nah	ත	tah	ථ	thah	ද	dhah
ධ	dhah	න	nah	ප	pah	ඵ	phah
බ	bah	භ	bhah	ම	mah	ය	yah
ර	rah	ල	lah	ව	vah	ශ	shah
ෂ	shah	ස	sah	හ	hah	ළ	lah

Some vowel sounds are represented using the characters shown above. Others are shown by modifying a basic consonant character, either by adding small additional strokes to it or by placing vowel symbols on one or both sides of the basic character. Most characters follow the same basic pattern:

ප	pah (basic character)	පු	pu
ප්	p (consonant only)	පූ	poo
පා	paah	පෙ	pe
පි	pi	පො	po
පී	pee		

(real) hotel starts talking about their "backside", don't worry – they're referring to the rear of the building, not a part of their anatomy. You might also come across classic old-time Sri Lankan idioms such as "men" (which can be used to refer to anyone listening, men and women); the monosyllabic "Is it?" (meaning anything from "I'm sorry, I don't quite understand" to "Go jump off a cliff"); or the quintessentially Sri Lankan "What to do?" – a kind of verbal shrug of the shoulders, which can mean virtually anything from "What shall we do?" to "The situation's completely hopeless" or "Shall we have another beer?"

For more on the idiosyncracies of Sringlish, get hold of a copy of Michael Meyler's comprehensive and entertaining *A Dictionary of Sri Lankan English*.

Useful Sinhala and Tamil words and expressions

Basics

	Sinhala	Tamil
hello/welcome	hello/ayubowan	vanakkam
goodbye	ayubowan	varavaanga
yes	oh-ooh	aam
no	nay	illai
please	karuna karala	thayavu seithu
thank you	es-toothee	nandri
OK	hari (or hari-hari)	sari (or sari-sari)
excuse me	sama venna	enga
sorry	kana gartui	mannikkavum
do you speak English?	Oh-ya Inghirisee kata karenavada?	ningal angilam paysu virhala?
I don't understand	matah obahvah thehrum gahna baha	enakku puriyavillaiye
what is your name?	nama mokada?	ungaludaya peyr enna?
my name is...	mahgay nama...	ennudaya peyr...
how are you?	kohomada?	ningal eppadi irukkirigal?
well, thanks	hondeen innava	romba nallayirukkudhu
not very well	vadiya honda nay	paruvayillai
this	mayka	ithu
that	ahraka	athu
when?	kawathatha?	eppa?
where?	kohedah?	enge?
when does it open/close?	ehika kiyatada ahrinnay/ vahhannee	e thirakkiruthu/ moodukiradu
I want	mata onay	enakku venam
is there any...?	...-da?	vere ethavathu irikkirutha
how much?	ahhekka keeyada	ahdu evvalah-vur?

	Sinhala	Tamil
can you give me a discount?	karuna karala gana	ithil ethavathu salugai adukaranna irikkirutha?
big	loku	pareya (perisu)
small	podi	sarreya
excellent	hari hondai	miga nallathu
hot (weather)	rasnai	ushnamana
open	erala	thira
closed	vahala	moodu
shop	kaday	kadi (kadai)
post office	teppa kantorua	anja lagam
bank	bankua	vangi
toilet	vesikili	kahlippadem
police	polisiya	kavalar
pharmacy	farmisiya/bayhet sapua	marunthu kadai
doctor	dostara	maruthuvar (vaidyar)
hospital	rohala	aspathri
ill	asaneepai	viyathi

Getting around

boat	bohtua	padadur
bus	bus ekka	bas
bus station	bus stand	baas nilayem
train	kohchiya	rayil
train station	dumriya pala	rayil nilayem
car	car	car
bicycle	bicycle	saikal
road	para	pathai
left	vama	idathu
right	dakuna	valathu
straight on	kelin yanna	naerakapogavum
near	langa	arukkil
far	athah	turam
station	is-stashama	nilayam
ticket	tiket ekkah	anumati situ

Accommodation

hotel	hotelaya	hotel
guesthouse	guesthouse ekka	virun-dhinnar vidhudheh
bathroom	nahnah kamarayak	kulikkum arai
clean	suda	suththam
cold	seethai	kulir
dirty	apirisidui	alukku (azhukku)
room	kamaraya	arai
do you have a room?	kamara teeyenavada	arekil kidehkkumah?

	Sinhala	Tamil
may I see the room?	kamaraya karuna karala	koncham kanpikkireengala penvanna
is there an a/c room?	a/c kamaraya teeyenavada?	kulir seithu arayai park mudiyama?
is there hot water?	unuvatura teeyenavada?	sudu thanir irukkuma?
please give me the bill	karuna karala bila ganna	bill tharavum

Time and numbers

1	ekka	ontru
2	dekka	erantru
3	toona	moontru
4	hatara	nangu
5	paha	ainthu
6	hiya	aru
7	hata	aelu
8	ahta	ettu
9	navighya	onpathu
10	dahhighya	pattu
20	vissai	erpathu
30	teehai	mupathu
40	hatalihai	natpathu
50	panahai	ompathu
100	seeya	nooru
200	dayseeya	irunooru
1000	daha	aiyuram
2000	daidaha	iranda iuram
100,000	lakshaya	latcham
today	ada	indru
tomorrow	heta	naalay
yesterday	eeyai	neh-truh
morning	udai	kaalai
afternoon	havasa	matiyam
day	davasa	pakal
night	reh	eravu
last/next week	giya/ilanga sahtiya	pona/adutha vaaram

Food and drink

Basics

Sinhala	Tamil	
kanda	unavu	food
kamata	unavu aalayam	restaurant
menu eka penvanna	thayavu seithu thinpandangal patti tharavum	the menu, please
mama elavalu vitaray	naan oru saivam kannay	I'm vegetarian
karuna karala bila ganna	bill tharavum	please give me the bill
paan	rotti/paan	bread
bittaraya	muttai	egg
ay-is	ice	ice
baht	arisi	rice (cooked)
vaturah	thannir	water
drink botalayak genna	oru pottal soda panam	mineral water (bottle)
tay	teyneer	tea
kopi	kapi	coffee
kiri	paal	milk
seeni	seeni	sugar
bahta	butter/vennai	butter
hakuru	seeni/vellam	jaggery

Fruit and vegetables

palaturu	palam	fruit
keselkan	valaipalam	banana
pol	thengali	coconut
amba	mangai	mango
papol	pappa palam	papaya
annasi	annasi	pineapple
elavelu	kai kari vagaigal	vegetables
luunu	venkayam	onion
ala	uruka kilangu	potato
thakkali	thakkali	tomato

Meat and fish

harak mas	mamism	meat
kukulmas	koli (kozhi)	chicken
uroomas	pantri	pork
harak mas	maattu mamism	beef

batalu mas	aattu mamism	lamb
kakuluvo	nandu	crab
isso	iraal	prawns
pokirissa	periya iraal	lobster
malu	min	fish

Sinhala place-names

Aluthgama	අලුත්ගම
Ambalangoda	අම්බලන්ගොඩ
Anuradhapura	අනුරාධපුර
Arugam Bay	ආරුගම්බේ
Badulla	බදුල්ල
Bandarawela	බන්ඩාරවෙල
Batticaloa	මඩකලපුව
Bentota	බෙන්තොට
Beruwala	බේරුවල
Colombo	කොළඹ
Dambulla	දඹුල්ල
Ella	ඇල්ල
Galle	ගාල්ල
Giritale	ගිරිතලේ
Habarana	හබරණ
Hambantota	හම්බන්තොට
Haputale	හපුතලේ
Hikkadduwa	හික්කඩුව
Jaffna	යාපනය
Kalutara	කළුතර
Kandy	මහනුවර
Kataragama	කතරගම
Kitulgala	කිතුල්ගල
Kurunegala	කුරුණෑගල
Matara	මාතර
Mihintale	මිහින්තලේ
Mirissa	මිරිස්ස
Monaragala	මොණරාගල
Negombo	මීගමුව
Nilvaveli	නිලාවේලි
Nuwara Eliya	නුවර එළිය
Polonnaruwa	පොළොන්නරුව
Ratnapura	රත්නපුර
Sigiriya	සීගිරිය
Tangalla	තංගල්ල
Tissamaharama	තිස්සමහාරාමය
Trincomalee	ත්‍රිකුණාමලය
Unawatuna	උණවටුන
Uppaveli	උප්පුවේලි
Weligama	වැලිගම
Wellawaya	වැල්ලවාය

Glossary

abhaya mudra "Have No Fear" pose; see p.445

anda the main, hemispherical section of a dagoba

apsara heavenly nymph

arhat enlightened monk

Avalokiteshvara Mahayana bodhisattva who is worshipped as the lord of infinite compassion, able to save all beings from suffering

Ayurveda Ancient Indian system of holistic healthcare; see p.138

-arama or **-rama** park, garden or monastic residence

betel popular and mildly narcotic snack, combining leaves from the betel tree with flakes of areca nut, a pinch of lime and sometimes a piece of tobacco; produces the characteristic red spittle whose stains can be seen on pavements throughout the country

bhikku Buddhist monk

bo tree (*ficus religiosa*; also known as the bodhi tree) Species of tree held sacred by Buddhism, since the Buddha is believed to have achieved enlightenment while meditating under one

bodhigara bo tree enclosure

bodhisattva a Buddha-to-be who, rather than passing into nirvana, has chosen to stay in the world to improve the spiritual welfare of other, unenlightened beings; see p.441

bund bank of a reservoir or tank

Burghers Sri Lankans of European (usually Dutch) descent; see p.172

cetiya/chaitya stupa; see p.445

chattravali spire-like pinnacle at the top of a stupa

chena slash-and-burn farming

Cholas (or **Colas**) the dominant power in South India from the tenth to the twelfth centuries, with their capital at Thanjavur in Tamil Nadu; overran Sri Lanka in the late tenth century, sacking Anuradhapura in 993, after which they established a new capital at Polonnaruwa

coir fibre made out of coconut husks

Culavamsa the "Lesser Chronicle" and continuation of the *Mahavamsa*; see p.415

dagoba stupa; see p.445

devale shrine or temple to a deity, either freestanding or part of a Buddhist temple; nominally Buddhist, but often showing strong Hindu influence

dhyani mudra meditation pose; see p.445

digge drummers' hall; often a pillared hall or pavilion in a temple where drummers and dancers rehearse

Durga the most terrifying of female Hindu deities, the demon-slaying Durga is considered an aspect of Shiva's consort, Parvati

duwa small island

dwarfs attendants of Kubera, the god of wealth, and thus symbols of prosperity

-ela stream

-gaha tree

-gala rock

-gama village

Ganesh popular elephant-headed Hindu god, the son of Shiva, remover of obstacles and bringer of success and prosperity

ganga river

-ge hall or house

gedige shrine built in South Indian style, with thick, richly decorated stone walls and vaulting

-giri rock

gopuram tower of a Hindu temple, usually richly decorated with multicoloured statues

guardstone carved figure placed at the entrance to a temple to protect against malign influences; often shows a figure of a nagaraja (see p.447)

Hanuman monkey god who assisted Rama in recovering Sita from the demon Rawana, as related in the *Ramayana*

harmika the box-shaped section of a dagoba which sits on top of the dome (*anda*) and supports the *chattravali*

Hinayana alternative and pejorative name for Theravada Buddhism

hypostyle building constructed using many columns

image house (pilimage) building in a Buddhist temple housing a statue of the Buddha

Jatakas stories describing the 547 previous lives of the Buddha

JHU the Jathika Hela Urumaya, or National Heritage Party, led by Buddhist monks promotes a broadly right-wing, nationalist and anti-Tamil agenda

JVP (Janatha Vimukthi Peramuna, or People's Liberation Front). Marxist party with an extreme nationalist, anti-Tamil agenda. Originally made up largely of rural poor and students, the JVP launched armed insurrections against the government in 1971 and 1987–89, both put down with considerable loss of life. Since the second insurrection has transformed itself into an important mainstream political party with a strong parliamentary presence

-kanda or -kande hill/mountain

Kataragama one of the principal Sri Lankan deities, believed to reside in the town of Kataragama; see p.216

kavadi the "peacock dance" performed by devotees of the god Kataragama; see p.218

kolam masked dance-drama; see p.151

kovil Hindu temple

-kulam tank, lake

Lakshmi Hindu goddess of wealth, Vishnu's consort

lingam phallic symbol representing Shiva; often placed within a yoni, representing female sexuality

LTTE Liberation Tigers of Tamil Eelam, popularly known as the Tamil Tigers; see p.404

maha great

Mahavamsa the "Great Chronicle"; see p.415

Mahayana Buddhism one of the two major schools of Buddhism, and the dominant form of the religion in China, Japan and Tibet, though it has had only superficial influence on Sri Lankan Buddhism; see p.440

mahout elephant handler

Maitreya the next Buddha. Mahayana Buddhists believe Maitreya will reintroduce Buddhism to the world when all knowledge of the religion has been lost

makara imaginary composite animal derived from Indian bestiary; see p.447

makara torana arch formed from two linked *makaras*

mawatha (abbreviated to "Mw") street

moonstone carved semicircular stone placed in front of entrance to shrine; see p.448. Also a type of gemstone mined in the island

Moors Sri Lankans of Arab or Indian-Arab descent

mudra traditional pose in Buddhist iconography; see p.445

naga stone stone decorated with the image of a hooded cobra

nagaraja serpent king

nuwara town

ola/ola leaf parchment made from the talipot palm (see box, p.255) used as a writing material in Sri Lanka up to the nineteenth century

oya stream, small river

Pali the sacred language of Theravada Buddhism; this early Indo-European language, related to Sanskrit, is close to the language spoken by the Buddha himself. The scriptures of Theravada Buddhism were originally written in Pali and are still recited in this language in Buddhist ceremonies

Pallavas South Indian Tamil dynasty (fifth–ninth centuries), based in Kanchipuram, who, along with the Pandyans and Cholas, periodically interfered in Sri Lankan affairs

Pandyans major Tamil dynasty (sixth–fourteenth centuries), based in Madurai, who vied for control of South India with the Cholas and Pallavas from the ninth to thirteenth centuries and periodically involved themselves in Sri Lankan affairs. Sacked Anuradhapura in the ninth century

parinirvana mudra reclining pose showing the Buddha on the point of entering into nirvana. One of the most common *mudras* (see p.445) in Sri Lankan art

pasada palace

Pattini Hindu goddess worshipped as paragon of marital fidelity; see p.248

perahera procession

pirith ceremonial chanting of Buddhist scriptures

-pitiya field or park

poya full-moon day

poyage building in a monastery used for ceremonial gatherings of monks on poya days (hence the name); sometimes translated as "chapter house"

puja Hindu or Buddhist religious offering or ceremony

-pura/-puram town

Rajarata literally "The King's Land" – the traditional name for the area now more generally known as the Cultural Triangle

Rama the seventh incarnation of Vishnu and hero of the *Ramayana*

Rawana (or **Ravana**) Demon-king and arch villain of the *Ramayana*; responsible for kidnapping Rama's wife Sita and holding her captive in Sri Lanka

Ruhunu (or **Rohana**) traditional name for southern Sri Lanka

samadhi (dhyani) mudra pose showing Buddha in state of meditation, seated in the lotus or half-lotus position; see p.445

Saman the god of Adam's Peak; see p.295

samudra large tank

Sangha the worldwide community of Buddhist monks

Shiva one of the two principal Hindu gods, worshipped in many forms, both creative and destructive

Shiva Nataraj classic subject of Hindu sculpture, showing a four-armed dancing Shiva enclosed by a circle of fire

sinha lion

Skanda son of Shiva (also known as Murugam and Subramanian). His identity in Sri Lanka has merged with that of Kataragama

SLA Sri Lankan Army

SLFP one of the two main Sri Lankan political parties, led successively by S.W.R.D. Bandaranaike, his wife and his daughter. Policies have tended to be the opposite of the pro-Western, free-market UNP, leaning instead towards a brand of populist nationalism (often with an anti-Tamil bias) featuring extensive state control of the economy

sri pada holy footprint

tank large man-made lake constructed for irrigation – almost always much larger than the English word suggests; see p.361

-tara/-tota port

Theravada Buddhism the older of the two main schools of Buddhism, and the dominant form of the religion in Sri Lanka; see p.440

tuktuk motorized rickshaw; also known as a three-wheeler, trishaw or taxi

UNP United National Party; one of Sri Lanka's two main political parties and the first ruling party of independent Sri Lanka. Policies have traditionally tended to be pro-Western and free market

Upulvan Sri Lankan name for Vishnu

vahalkadas shrines placed at the four cardinal points of a stupa

vatadage characteristic Sri Lankan style of building formed by adding a roof and ambulatory to a dagobas

Veddha Sri Lanka's original aboriginal inhabitants; see p.266

ves dancer style of traditional costume and dancing employed by Kandyan dancers

Vibhishana the youngest brother of Rawana. Despite his demonic nature, Vibhishana is revered in Sri Lanka, since he pleaded the captive Sita's cause with Ravana and later fought with Rama against his brother, suggesting the potential for right action in even the lowest creature

vidiya street (in Kandy)

vihara (sometimes spelt vehera or wehera) Buddhist temple or monastery

Vishnu one of the two principal Hindu gods, considered a protector of Buddhism in Sri Lanka

VOC Vereenigde Oost Indische Compagnie (Dutch East India Company)

-watte garden

-wewa (pronounced "-vava") man-made reservoir (tank)

-wila pond

Travel store

NOTES

NOTES

NOTES

NOTES

Small print and

Index

A Rough Guide to Rough Guides

Published in 1982, the first Rough Guide – to Greece – was a student scheme that became a publishing phenomenon. Mark Ellingham, a recent graduate in English from Bristol University, had been travelling in Greece the previous summer and couldn't find the right guidebook. With a small group of friends he wrote his own guide, combining a highly contemporary, journalistic style with a thoroughly practical approach to travellers' needs.

The immediate success of the book spawned a series that rapidly covered dozens of destinations. And, in addition to impecunious backpackers, Rough Guides soon acquired a much broader and older readership that relished the guides' wit and inquisitiveness as much as their enthusiastic, critical approach and value-for-money ethos.

These days, Rough Guides include recommendations from shoestring to luxury and cover more than 200 destinations around the globe, including almost every country in the Americas and Europe, more than half of Africa and most of Asia and Australasia. Our ever-growing team of authors and photographers is spread all over the world, particularly in Europe, the US and Australia.

In the early 1990s, Rough Guides branched out of travel, with the publication of Rough Guides to World Music, Classical Music and the Internet. All three have become benchmark titles in their fields, spearheading the publication of a wide range of books under the Rough Guide name.

Including the travel series, Rough Guides now number more than 350 titles, covering: phrasebooks, waterproof maps, music guides from Opera to Heavy Metal, reference works as diverse as Conspiracy Theories and Shakespeare, and popular culture books from iPods to Poker. Rough Guides also produce a series of more than 120 World Music CDs in partnership with World Music Network.

Visit www.roughguides.com to see our latest publications.

Rough Guide travel images are available for commercial licensing at www.roughguidespictures.com

Rough Guide credits

Text editor: Emma Gibbs
Layout: Pradeep Thapliyal
Cartography: Ashutosh Bharti
Picture editor: Sarah Cummins
Production: Rebecca Short
Proofreader: Jennifer Speake
Cover design: Chloë Roberts
Photographer: Gavin Thomas
Editorial: Ruth Blackmore, Andy Turner, Keith Drew, Edward Aves, Alice Park, Lucy White, Jo Kirby, James Smart, Natasha Foges, Róisín Cameron, Emma Traynor, Kathryn Lane, Christina Valhouli, Monica Woods, Mani Ramaswamy, Harry Wilson, Lucy Cowie, Helen Ochyra, Amanda Howard, Lara Kavanagh, Alison Roberts, Joe Staines, Peter Buckley, Matthew Milton, Tracy Hopkins, Ruth Tidball; **Delhi** Madhavi Singh, Karen D'Souza, Lubna Shaheen
Design & Pictures: **London** Scott Stickland, Dan May, Diana Jarvis, Mark Thomas, Nicole Newman, Emily Taylor; **Delhi** Umesh Aggarwal, Ajay Verma, Jessica Subramanian, Ankur Guha, Sachin Tanwar, Anita Singh, Nikhil Agarwal, Sachin Gupta
Production: Vicky Baldwin
Cartography: **London** Maxine Repath, Ed Wright, Katie Lloyd-Jones; **Delhi** Rajesh Chhibber, Rajesh Mishra, Animesh Pathak, Jasbir Sandhu, Karobi Gogoi, Alakananda Bhattacharya, Swati Handoo, Deshpal Dabas
Online: **London** George Atwell, Faye Hellon, Jeanette Angell, Fergus Day, Justine Bright, Clare Bryson, Aine Fearon, Adrian Low, Ezgi Celebi, Amber Bloomfield; **Delhi** Amit Verma, Rahul Kumar, Narender Kumar, Ravi Yadav, Debojit Borah, Rakesh Kumar, Ganesh Sharma, Shisir Basumatari
Marketing & Publicity: **London** Liz Statham, Niki Hanmer, Louise Maher, Jess Carter, Vanessa Godden, Vivienne Watton, Anna Paynton, Rachel Sprackett, Libby Jellie, Laura Vipond, Vanessa McDonald; **New York** Katy Ball, Judi Powers, Nancy Lambert; **Delhi** Ragini Govind
Manager India: Punita Singh
Reference Director: Andrew Lockett
Operations Manager: Helen Phillips
PA to Publishing Director: Nicola Henderson
Publishing Director: Martin Dunford
Commercial Manager: Gino Magnotta
Managing Director: John Duhigg

Publishing information

This third edition published October 2009 by
Rough Guides Ltd,
80 Strand, London WC2R 0RL
14 Local Shopping Centre, Panchsheel Park, New Delhi 110017, India
Distributed by the Penguin Group
Penguin Books Ltd,
80 Strand, London WC2R 0RL
Penguin Group (USA)
375 Hudson Street, NY 10014, USA
Penguin Group (Australia)
250 Camberwell Road, Camberwell, Victoria 3124, Australia
Penguin Group (Canada)
195 Harry Walker Parkway N, Newmarket, ON, L3Y 7B3 Canada
Penguin Group (NZ)
67 Apollo Drive, Mairangi Bay, Auckland 1310, New Zealand
Cover concept by Peter Dyer.
Typeset in Bembo and Helvetica to an original design by Henry Iles.
Printed in Singapore

496pp includes index
A catalogue record for this book is available from the British Library
ISBN: 978-1-84836-069-3

1 3 5 7 9 8 6 4 2

Help us update

We've gone to a lot of effort to ensure that the third edition of **The Rough Guide to Sri Lanka** is accurate and up-to-date. However, things change – places get "discovered", opening hours are notoriously fickle, restaurants and rooms raise prices or lower standards. If you feel we've got it wrong or left something out, we'd like to know, and if you can remember the address, the price, the hours, the phone number, so much the better.

Please send your comments with the subject line "**Rough Guide Sri Lanka Update**" to Ⓔmail@roughguides.com. We'll credit all contributions and send a copy of the next edition (or any other Rough Guide if you prefer) for the very best emails.

Have your questions answered and tell others about your trip at Ⓦcommunity.roughguides.com

Acknowledgements

Gavin Thomas: In Sri Lanka, thanks to Sue & Faeiz Samad (*Sharon Inn*, Kandy); Nalini & Sarath (*Freedom Lodge*, Kandy); Sumane & Kanthi (*Expeditor*, Kandy); Tania Brassey (*The Kandy House*, Kandy); Mark Thamel (*Ocean View*, Negombo); Milindu Mallawaratchie and Leslie Gunawardana (Malkey); Neil "Raja" Rajanayake; and Dominic Sansoni. Thanks also to Linton Wanniarachchi (Rail Tours/*Blue Haven Guest House*), for once again updating the train timetables; Emma Boyle, for providing a regular supply of priceless updates (and for keeping stray travel writers entertained in Unawatuna); and the indefatigable Gehan de Silva Wijeyeratne (Jetwing Eco) for information on all things wild, winged and whale-like.

In the UK and elsewhere, thanks to John Kupiec for further updates, and to historian Robert Egeter van Kuyk for numerous corrections and suggestions. At Rough Guides, a big bouquet for Emma Gibbs for an exceptionally smooth editorial ride, and a large helping of rice and curry for Ed Aves, who updated the sections on the Cultural Triangle and much of the coast with his customary aplomb, superb eye for detail and uncanny ability to sniff out a bottle of arrack at fifty paces. And, finally, a huge hug for Allison, with whom I first discovered Sri Lanka, and to Laura and Jamie, who I hope will one day discover it for themselves. This book is dedicated to the three of them, with all my love.

Edward Aves: First and foremost, huge thanks to Gavin for encouraging me to dust down my sarongs and make the long overdue trip back to Sri Lanka, and for having written such a superb book in the first place. In Colombo, thanks to Annouchka and Mihiri (John Keells), and Angie and Trevor (Jetwing); particular thanks too to Gehan for taking me on my first (false) whale-watching trip – I'm sure the real ones are in there somewhere. In Galle, warm thanks to Henri, Geoffrey, Jack, Jo, Karl and all who looked after me over a memorable Christmas; and to Juliet Coombe, a fount of knowledge on all things Galle. Special thanks to Emma Boyle for her invaluable advice on Unawatuna (and elsewhere) and some nifty last-minute map work; and to Azmi Thassim for telling me everything I needed to know about Hambantota. Thanks also to Merete and Fred in Arugam Bay for entertaining me over New Year, and to Sarath for getting me there. As ever, I'm greatly indebted to my Sri Lankan guardian angel, Gamage – I'm sorry about the dents in the Nissan. And in London, thanks to Jean-Marc Flambert for his help in the preparation of my trip, and to Emma Gibbs for her calmness and encouragement during the editing process. And finally, a huge thank you to Sparky for her support, morale-boosting and unflagging optimism.

Readers' letters

Many thanks to all the readers who took time to write in with their comments, updates and suggestions (and apologies to anyone whose name we've omitted or mispelled):

Trevor Alexander; Emanuele Arnoldi; Georgina Ash; Jeremy Askew; Karsten Bachem; Helen Barnett; Helen Batten; K. Behr; Frank Bellamy; Garth Booth; Emma Boyle; Neil Brading; Djoeke Brons; Peter Bruckmann; Paul Chard; Andrew Craig; Steve Dellow; Faye; Shehan Fernando; Gillian Fielding; Rosa Freitas; Dorothy Frost; Terry & Jenny Gale; Billie Goodman; Jonathan Gorvett; Felix Grey; Chris Hall; Judith Harrison; Jason Hogg; Caroline Howson; David and Carole James; Bernadette Jenkins; Kate Kelly; Becca Kenneison; John Kupiec; RHJ Egeter van Kuyk; Roger Lavis; Colin Leckey; Elizabeth and Fred Lipsett; Gillian Merron; Ambreen Nawaz; Gavin Northover; Roy O'Brien; Tim Pare; Lukas Probst; Egbert-Jan and Carin Rots; Brian Sandford; Chantal Sucaud; Frances Thompson; Peter Turner; Jane Willis; Dan Windross.

Photo credits

All photos © Rough Guides except the following:

Things not to miss

01 Yala National Park © Sebastian Posingis/Three Blind Men
03 Adam's Peak © Dominic Sansoni/Three Blind Men
10 Little Green Bee Eater © David Hosking/Alamy
12 Dancers in the great Kandy Esala Perahera festival © dbimages/Alamy
14 Kataragama Annual Festival © Dominic Sansoni/Three Blind Men
18 Blue Whale © Gehan de Silva Wijeyeratne/www.jetwingeco.com

Ceylon Tea colour section

Picked tea leaves near the village of Nuwara Eliya © Mediacolor's/Alamy

Sri Lankan Buddhism colour section

Buddhist nun at prayer, Anuradhapura © Dominic Sansoni/Three Blind Men
Anuradhapura, the Sri Maha Bodhi sacred Bo tree © Neil McAllister/Alamy

Black and whites

p.208 Flamingos, Bundala National Park © Anuruddha Lokuhapuarachchi/Reuters/Corbis
p.303 Uda Walawe National Park © Frederic Soreau/Photolibrary
p.378 Surfing in Arugam Bay © Anuruddha Lokuhapuarachchi/Reuters/Corbis

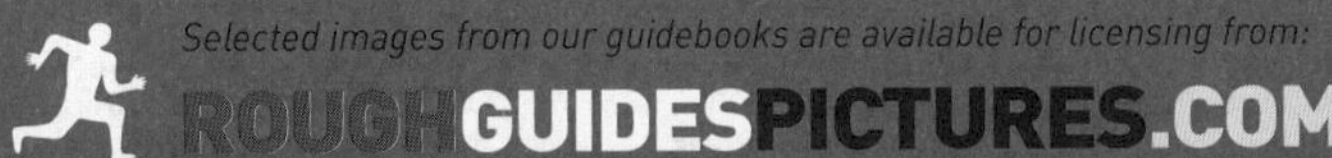

Index

Map entries are in colour.

C

D

E

F

G

H

I

K

L

M

N

O

P

INDEX

Q

R

S

T

U

V

W

Y

Map symbols

maps are listed in the full index using coloured text

- Chapter boundary
- Major road
- Minor road
- Pedestrianized street
- Steps
- Unpaved road
- Railway line
- Path
- Ferry route
- River
- Wall
- Rocks
- Reef
- Hill
- Earthworks
- Peak
- Viewpoint
- Cave
- Waterfall
- Swamp
- Tree
- Banyan tree
- Place of interest
- Statue
- Ruin
- Lighthouse
- Fortress
- Golf course
- Internet access
- Tourist office
- Post office
- Accommodation
- Restaurant
- Airport
- Bus stop
- Parking
- Bridge
- Hospital
- Gate
- Gardens
- Stupa/Buddhist temple
- Hindu temple
- Mosque
- Church (regional maps)
- Church (town maps)
- Building
- Market
- Stadium
- Christian cemetery
- Muslim cemetery
- Park/jungle/forest
- Beach